Seventh Edition

INTERNATIONAL ACCOUNTING

Frederick D. S. Choi
New York University

Gary K. Meek
Oklahoma State University

Prentice Hall
Boston   Columbus   Indianapolis   New York   San Francisco   Upper Saddle River
Amsterdam   Cape Town   Dubai   London   Madrid   Milan   Munich   Paris
Montreal   Toronto   Delhi   Mexico City   Sao Paulo   Sydney   Hong Kong
Seoul   Singapore   Taipei   Tokyo

Editorial Director: Sally Yagan	**Cover Designer:** Bruce Kenselaar
Editor in Chief: Donna Battista	**Manager, Visual Research:** Beth Brenzel
Acquisitions Editor: Julie Broich	**Manager, Cover Visual Research & Permissions:**
Director Editorial Services: Ashley Santora	Karen Sanatar
Editorial Project Manager: Karen Kirincich	**Cover Art:** Fotolia
Editorial Assistant: Brian Reilly	**Full-Service Project Management:** Hemalatha /
Director of Marketing: Patrice Lumumba Jones	Integra
Senior Managing Editor: Cynthia Zonneveld	**Printer/Binder:** Courier/Westford
Project Manager: Lynne Breitfeller	**Cover Printer:** Lehigh-Phoenix Color/Hagerstown
Operations Specialist: Clara Bartunek	**Text Font:** 10/12 Palatino
Creative Art Director: Jayne Conte	

Credits and acknowledgments borrowed from other sources and reproduced, with permission, in this textbook appear on appropriate page within text.

Many of the designations by manufacturers and seller to distinguish their products are claimed as trademarks. Where those designations appear in this book, and the publisher was aware of a trademark claim, the designations have been printed in initial caps or all caps.

Library of Congress Cataloging-in-Publication Data

Choi, Frederick D. S.,
　International accounting / Frederick D.S. Choi, Gary K. Meek.—7th ed.
　　p. cm.
　Includes index.
　ISBN-13: 978-0-13-611147-4 (alk. paper)
　ISBN-10: 0-13-611147-5 (alk. paper)
　1. International business enterprises—Accounting.　I. Meek, Gary K.,　II. Title.
　HF5686.I56C53 2011
　657'.96—dc22

　　　　　　　　　　　　　　　　　　　　　　　　　　　2010014971

10 9 8 7 6 5 4 3 2 1

Prentice Hall
is an imprint of

www.pearsonhighered.com

ISBN 10:　　　0-13-611147-5
ISBN 13:　978-0-13-611147-4

To our families

CONTENTS

PREFACE

This book is written with the express purpose of introducing students to the international dimensions of accounting, financial reporting and financial control. The world in which they will pursue their professional careers is a world dominated by global business and cross-border investing. As these activities require decisions premised on financial data, a knowledge of international accounting is crucial for achieving proper understanding in external and internal financial communications. While ideal for upper division undergraduate students and masters students, we are pleased that the contents of this award-winning effort have also benefited practicing accountants, financial executives, investment managers, university educators and professional administrators around the world.

This revision of a work that has spanned four decades features a number of enhancements. These include:

- Updated coverage of corporate governance and related legislation. See Chapters 4, 5, 8 and 9.
- Examination of international auditing, both external and internal. See Chapters 8 and 9.
- Current discussion of comparative accounting emphasizing developments in Europe, the Americas and Asia in Chapters 3 and 4.
- Capital market, managerial, taxation and institutional updates reflective of current trends and issues throughout most chapters.
- Discussion of international accounting convergence and the major players in this important effort. See Chapters 3, 5 and 8.
- Examination of reporting and disclosure practices spanning both developed and emerging market countries. See Chapters 4, 5 and 7.
- Expanded listings of relevant international Web site addresses and data sources.
- Updated discussion questions, exercises and cases.

We have benefited from the professional literature and from many of our students and faculty colleagues whose thoughtful comments have triggered new ideas for us to consider. We are in their debt. In addition, many individuals furnished able assistance in producing the manuscript. We especially thank Julie Broich, Karen Kirincich and Christina Rumbaugh at Prentice Hall for their encouragement and editorial support.

However hard one tries to avoid them, errors are bound to occur in a work of this type. As authors, we accept full responsibility for all errors and omissions in the manuscript. As always we welcome constructive comments from all who use this book as students are the ultimate beneficiaries of your thoughtfulness.

F. D. S. Choi
New York, N.Y.

G. K. Meek
Stillwater, OK

CHAPTER 1

Introduction

Accounting plays a vital role in society. As a branch of economics, it provides information about a firm and its transactions to facilitate resource allocation decisions by users of that information. If the information reported is reliable and useful, scarce resources are allocated in an optimal fashion, and conversely, resource allocations are less than optimal when information is less reliable and useful.

International accounting, the subject of this text, is no different in its intended role. What makes its study distinctive is that the entity being reported on is either a multinational company (MNC) with operations and transactions that cross national boundaries, or an entity with reporting obligations to users who are located in a country other than that of the reporting entity.

Recall that accounting entails several broad processes: measurement, disclosure, and auditing. Measurement is the process of identifying, categorizing, and quantifying economic activities or transactions. These measurements provide insights into the profitability of a firm's operations and the strength of its financial position. Disclosure is the process by which accounting measurements are communicated to their intended users. This area focuses on issues such as what is to be reported, when, by what means, and to whom. Auditing is the process by which specialized accounting professionals (auditors) attest to the reliability of the measurement and communication process. Whereas internal auditors are company employees who answer to management, external auditors are nonemployees who are responsible for attesting that the company's financial statements are prepared in accordance with generally accepted standards.

An understanding of the international dimensions of the accounting processes that were just described is important to those engaged in importing or exporting activities, as well as those seeking to manage a business, or obtain or supply financing across national borders. Even a company operating solely within the confines of a single country is no longer insulated from the international aspects of accounting as reliance on international vendors to contain production costs and remain globally competitive is a common feature of contemporary business. Accounting amounts may vary significantly according to the principles that govern them. Differences in culture, business practices, political and regulatory structures, legal systems, currency values, local inflation rates, business risks, and tax codes all affect how the MNC conducts its operations and financial reporting around the world. Financial statements and other disclosures are impossible to understand without an awareness of the underlying accounting principles and business culture.

The importance of studying international accounting has grown over the years. We begin with a brief history of this subject.

HISTORICAL PERSPECTIVE

The history of accounting is an international history. The following chronology demonstrates that accounting has been remarkably successful in its ability to be transplanted from one national setting to another while allowing for continued development in theory and practice worldwide.

To begin, double-entry bookkeeping, generally thought of as the genesis of accounting as we know it today, emanated from the Italian city states of the 14th and 15th centuries. Its development was spurred by the growth of international commerce in northern Italy during the late Middle Ages and the desire of government to find ways to tax commercial transactions. "Bookkeeping in the Italian fashion" then migrated to Germany to assist the merchants of the Fugger era and the Hanseatic league. At about the same time, business philosophers in the Netherlands sharpened ways of calculating periodic income, and government officials in France found it advantageous to apply the whole system to governmental planning and accountability.

In due course, double-entry accounting ideas reached the British Isles. The development of the British Empire created unprecedented needs for British commercial interests to manage and control enterprises in the colonies, and for the records of their colonial enterprises to be reviewed and verified. These needs led to the emergence of accounting societies in the 1850s and an organized public accounting profession in Scotland and England during the 1870s. British accounting practices spread not only throughout North America but also throughout the British Commonwealth as it then existed.

Parallel developments occurred elsewhere. The Dutch accounting model was exported to Indonesia, among other places. The French accounting system found a home in Polynesia and French-administered territories in Africa while the reporting framework of the Germans proved influential in Japan, Sweden, and czarist Russia.

As the economic might of the United States grew during the first half of the 20th century, its sophistication in matters of accounting grew in tandem. Business schools assisted in this development by conceptualizing the subject matter and eventually having it recognized as an academic discipline in its own right on college and university campuses. After World War II, U.S. accounting influence made itself felt throughout the Western world, particularly in Germany and Japan. To a lesser extent, similar factors are directly observable in countries like Brazil, Israel, Mexico, the Philippines, Sweden, and Taiwan.

Despite this international heritage, in most countries accounting remained a nationalistic affair, with national standards and practices deeply anchored into national laws and professional regulations. (Examples of comparative accounting practices are provided in Chapters 3 and 4.) There was little understanding of parallel requirements in other countries. Yet, accounting increasingly serveed people and organizations whose decisions were increasingly international in scope.

Resolving the historical paradox of accounting has long been a concern of both users and preparers of accounting information. In recent years, institutional efforts to narrow differences in measurement, disclosure, and auditing processes around the world have intensified. A description of this effort and the major players with an important stake in attaining convergence of global accounting systems is the focus of Chapter 8.

CONTEMPORARY PERSPECTIVE

While the effort to reduce international accounting diversity is important in its own right, there are today a number of additional factors that are contributing to the growing importance of studying international accounting. These factors stem from significant and continuing reductions in national trade barriers and capital controls together with advances in information technology.

National controls on capital flows, foreign exchange, foreign direct investment, and related transactions have been dramatically liberalized in recent years, reducing the barriers to international business. Changes in financial sector policy in both developed and developing countries reflect the growing realization that information and financial technolgy render capital controls ineffective. National governments also realize that financial market liberaliztion affords them access to international funds with which to finance national debts. As accounting is the language of business, cross-border economic interactions mean that accounting reports prepared in one country must increasingly be used and understood by users in another.

Advances in information technology are also causing a radical change in the economics of production and distribution. Vertically integrated production is no longer proving an efficient mode of operation. Real-time global information linkages mean that production, including accounting services, is increasingly being outsourced, or *offshored*, to whomever in the world can do the job, or portions of the job, best.[1] Leading locations for offshore services today include Argentina, Brazil, Canada, Chile, Costs Rica, Mexico, and Panama in the Americas; Australia, China, India, Malaysia, New Zealand, Pakistan, the Philippines, Singapore, Thailand, and Vietnam in Asia Pacific; and the Czech Republic, Egypt, Hungary, Ireland, Israel, Morocco, Poland, Romania, Russia, Slovakia, South Africa, Spain and the Ukraine in Europe, the Middle East, and Africa.[2] Adversarial, arm's-length relationships that have characterized companies' relations with their suppliers, middle persons, and customers are being replaced by cooperative global linkages with suppliers, suppliers' suppliers, middle persons, customers, and customers' customers.

Exhibit 1-1 provides an illustration of the outsourcing phenomenon. In producing the ProLiant ML150, a small box that helps companies manage customer databases and run e-mail systems, among other things, Hewlett-Packard (H-P) turned to the usual sources of low-cost labor: China and India. However, it also decided to make some ML150s in higher-cost locations such as Singapore and Australia, which were closer to targeted customers. Initial design for the ML150 was done in Singapore and then handed off to an outside contractor in Taiwan. Although China possesses the lowest wage rates, it is but one part of a highly specialized manufacturing system.

---

[1] For example, see Arie Lewin, Silvia Massini, and Carine Peters, "Why Are Companies Offshoring Innovation? The Emerging Global Race for Talent," *Journal of International Business Studies* 40 (2009): 901–925.
[2] Robert Kennedy, "The Tough Game You Have to Play," *Financial Executive*, May 2009, pp. 23–25.

EXHIBIT 1-1	Outsourcing Process for Hewlett-Packard's ProLiant 150

India   ←

5

China   ←   Taiwan

5   4

Australia   ←   ↓↑

5   Singapore   →   Houston

               5 3 1   ←   2

H-P's Path to Market
1. Idea for ML150 spawned in Singapore
2. Concept approved in Houston
3. Concept design performed in Singapore
4. Engineering design and initial manufacture in Taiwan
5. Final assembly in Australia, China, India, and Singapore. Machines produced in Australia, China, and India sold in local markets; machines assembled in Singapore marketed to Southeast Asia.

Considerations ranging from logistics to tariff policies reportedly kept H-P from putting all of its production lines in China. It would take too long for machines manufactured in China to reach customers in other Asian markets. Moreover, shipping goods to India triggered steep tariffs, so it made sense to produce some ML150s in India with imported parts for the local market. All of the links in this outsourcing example are associated with accounting issues discussed in the following pages of this chapter.

Spurred by the twin developments we have just described, there are several factors that are contributing to the growing importance of the subject matter of this text. We describe each in turn.

GROWTH AND SPREAD OF MULTINATIONAL OPERATIONS

International business has traditionally been associated with foreign trade. This activity, rooted in antiquity, continues unabated. While trade in services has traditionally paled in comparison to trade in merchandise, the former is gaining in significance and growing at a faster rate than the latter. Current trends in exports and imports of both goods and services by region and selected economy are depicted in Exhibit 1-2.

What is not shown in Exhibit 1-2 is the composition of each region's exports and imports. To obtain a better picture of the pattern of global trade at the micro level, one could examine the foreign operations disclosures of any major MNC. Exhibit 1-3 contains the geographic distribution of sales of AKZO Nobel, a multinational company headquartered in the Netherlands and concentrating on healthcare products, coatings, and chemicals. As can be seen, the company's sales literally blanket every continent in the world. Unisys, the U.S.-based information technology services company, provides its expertise to clients in over 100 countries, while

EXHIBIT 1-2   World Trade by Region

Total Merchandise Trade — Unit: U.S. dollar at current prices (millions)

Region	Activity	Partner	Stet	1990	1995	2000	2005	2007
Africa	Exports	World		106,000	112,000	147,800	297,700	424,100
Africa	Imports	World		99,600	126,700	129,400	249,300	358,900
Asia	Exports	World		792,400	1,446,800	1,836,200	3,050,900	4,131,000
Asia	Imports	World		761,500	1,403,300	1,677,100	2,871,000	3,804,300
Europe	Exports	World		1,684,940	2,335,635	2,633,930	4,371,915	5,722,205
Europe	Imports	World		1,750,925	2,334,760	2,774,755	4,542,675	6,060,845
Mid. East	Exports	World		138,400	151,000	268,000	538,000	759,900
Mid. East	Imports	World		101,300	132,500	167,400	322,100	479,300
N. America	Exports	World		562,035	856,550	1,224,975	1,477,530	1,853,500
N. America	Imports	World		684,460	1,015,760	1,687,580	2,284,735	2,707,460
S./C. America	Exports	World		106,000	148,900	195,800	354,900	499,200
S./C. America	Imports	World		85,900	176,900	206,300	297,600	456,000
World	Exports	World		3,449,000	5,164,000	6,452,000	10,431,000	13,950,000
World	Imports	World		3,550,000	5,284,000	6,724,000	10,783,000	14,244,000

Total Trade in Commercial Services — Unit: U.S. dollar at current prices (millions)

Region	Activity	Partner	1985	1990	1995	2000	2005	2007
Africa	Exports	World		18,600	25,700	31,300	56,900	78,400
Africa	Imports	World		26,500	34,400	37,400	69,300	102,100
Asia	Exports	World		131,500	257,800	309,500	525,300	739,600
Asia	Imports	World		178,800	328,100	367,900	573,500	760,000
Europe	Exports	World			597,100	721,900	1,244,800	1,703,200
Europe	Imports	World			560,200	674,100	1,120,100	1,461,300
Mid. East	Exports	World				33,100	54,900	76,900
Mid. East	Imports	World				48,800	85,400	132,900
N. America	Exports	World		135,500	171,200	268,200	366,300	535,600
N. America	Imports	World		135,500	171,200	268,200	366,300	440,100
S./C. America	Exports	World		22,400	34,600	47,100	68,200	92,200
S./C. America	Imports	World		24,900	45,300	54,600	70,500	98,600
World	Exports	World		780,500	1,185,100	1,491,000	2,414,300	3,291,500
World	Imports	World		820,500	1,200,700	1,474,600	2,347,400	3,085,900

Source: World Trade Organization, International Trade Statistics, 2008.

Japan's Cannon Inc. sells cameras and other professional and consumer imaging equipment in virtually every country of the world. An aggregation of such disclosures for all MNCs in all countries would confirm that trade today is neither bilateral nor regional, but truly global.

EXHIBIT 1-3	Selected 2008 Foreign Operations Data for AKZO Nobel (Euro millions)			
	Net Sales By Destination	Capital Expenditures	Invested Capital	Number of Employees
The Netherlands	867	86	2,007	5,000
Germany	1,141	25	1,006	3,600
Sweden	478	50	557	3,800
U.K.	1,093	31	1,324	4,200
Other Europe	3,666	81	2,359	3,666
U.S./Canada	3,330	94	3,250	12,000
Latin America	1,306	49	776	4,800
China	1,054	67	861	6,300
Other Asia	1,866	43	1,030	7,800
Other regions	614	8	174	2,400

A major accounting issue associated with export and import activities relates to accounting for foreign currency transactions. Assume, for example, that Heineken exports a certain quantity of beer to a Brazilian importer and invoices the sale in Brazilian reals. Should the real devalue relative to the euro prior to collection, Heineken will experience a foreign exchange loss as reals will yield less euros upon conversion after the devaluation than before. The measurement of this transaction loss is not straightforward and is a subject that is dealt with in Chapter 6.

Today, international business transcends foreign trade and is increasingly associated with foreign direct investments, which involve operating production or distribution systems abroad by way of a wholly or majority-owned affiliate, a joint venture, or a strategic alliance.

While there is clearly a developed country bias of foreign direct investors, the boom of foreign direct investment flows to developing countries since the early 1990s indicates that MNCs are increasingly finding these host countries to be attractive investment locations.[3]

At the level of the firm, foreign direct investment activities are captured by a company's segmental disclosures and its roster of shareholdings in affiliated companies. Exhibit 1-3 also provides operating statistics by region for AKZO Nobel.

Exhibit 1-4 illustrates the extensive holdings in operating group companies of Nestle, one of the world's largest food and beverage companies headquartered in Vevy, Switzerland. While both AKZO and Nestle's foreign operations are extensive, the numbers relating to capital expenditures, invested capital, production sold locally, and number of foreign employees understate the extent of their foreign operations. They do not reflect the extent of either company's joint venture, strategic alliance, or other cooperative arrangements.

---

[3] World Bank Chief Economist, Francois Bourguignon, predicts that over the next 25 years, developing countries will move to the center stage in the global economy, "Global Economic Prospects 2007: Managing the Next Wave of Globalization," World Bank Panel Discussion sponsored by the Global Business Institute, NYU Stern School of Business, December 12, 2006.

EXHIBIT 1-4	Countries in Which Nestle Owns One or More Majority-Owned Companies	

Europe		Egypt	2	Dom Rep.	1
Germany	14	Gabon	1	Trinidad	2
Austria	4	Ghana	1	Uruguay	1
Belgium	8	Guinea	1	Venezuela	3
Bulgaria	1	Kenya	1	**Asia**	
Crotia	1	Mauritius	2	Saudi Arabia	3
Denmark	3	Morocco	1	Bangladesh	1
Spain	10	Mozambique	1	Cambodia	1
Finland	3	Niger	1	UAE	1
France	18	Nigeria	1	India	2
Greece	2	Senegal	1	Indonesia	1
Hungary	5	Tunisia	1	Israel	1
Italy	8	Zimbabwe	1	Japan	9
Lithuania	1	**Americas**		Jordan	1
Malta	1	Argentina	3	Kuwait	1
Norway	3	Bolivia	1	Lebanon	3
The Netherlands	6	Brazil	5	Malaysia	7
Poland	5	Canada	2	Pakistan	1
Portugal	7	Chile	2	Philippines	4
Ireland	1	Colombia	5	S. Korea	4
Czech R.	3	Costa Rica	1	China	21
Romania	1	Cuba	2	Singapore	1
U.K.	9	Salvador	2	Sri Lanka	1
Russia	12	Ecuador	2	Syria	2
Serbia	1	U.S.	9	Thailand	9
Slovakia	1	Guatemala	1	Vietnam	2
Sweden	7	Honduras	1	**Oceana**	
Switzerland	8	Jamaica	1	Australia	3
Turkey	3	Mexico	8	Fiji	1
Ukraine	3	Nicaragua	2	N. Zealand	1
Africa		Panama	2	New Guinea	1
S. Africa	4	Paraguay	1	F. Polynesia	1
Cameroon	1	Peru	1	New Caledonia 1	1
Cote d'Ivoire	1	Puerto Rico	2		

Note: This list is conservative as it does not include affiliated companies for which proportionate consolidation is employed, associated companies for which the equity method is used, subholding financial and property companies, and technical assistance, research and development companies.

Operations conducted in foreign countries expose both financial managers and accountants alike to an additional set of problems that they do not encounter when solely engaged in international trade. As one example, how should an MNC like Nestle report the results of its operations, both domestic and international, to its South Korean investors? Each affiliate listed in Exhibit 1-4 must prepare its accounts according to the generally accepted accounting principles of the country in which it is domiciled for statutory and tax purposes. As Chapters 3 and 4 will attest, national financial reporting principles can vary significantly from country to country as they are shaped by different socio-economic environments. Environmental influences that impinge on accounting development are examined in Chapter 2. Nestle's domestic shareholders are used to seeing reports on the basis of Swiss reporting conventions. Examination of Nestle's accounting policies on consolidation suggests that the company first restates all of its foreign accounts to the reporting framework of the parent company prior to consolidation. The report of Nestle's auditors state that the consolidated financial statements comply with Swiss Law and are in accordance with International Financial Reporting Standards (IFRS) issued by the International Accounting Standards Board (IASB) and with the Interpretations issued by the International Financial Reporting Interpretations Committee (IFRIC). But in restating from one set of principles to another, does something get lost in the translation? To illustrate, Mexican companies adjust their financial statements for changing prices (a subject that we cover in Chapter 7), owing to serious bouts of inflation in the past. Their adjustment for changing prices utilizes a methodology that incorporates changes in specific prices or replacement costs. Nestle, on the other hand, restates assets located in hyperinflationary countries for changes in the general purchasing power of the local currency prior to consolidation. Since general price changes seldom move in tandom with specific price changes, does Nestle's methodology reduce the information content of the Mexican subsidiary's inflation-adjusted accounts? Yamaha, producer of world-renowned musical instruments and other lifestyle products, expresses this concern in the first footnote to its consolidated financial accounts:

> Yamaha Corporation (the Company) and its domestic subsidiaries maintain their accounting records and prepare their financial statements in accordance with accounting principles and practices generally accepted in Japan, and its foreign subsidiaries maintain their books of account in conformity with those of their countries of domicile. The Company and all consolidated subsidiaries are referred to as the "Group." The accompanying consolidated financial statements have been prepared from the financial statements filed with the Ministry of Finance as required by the Securities and Exchange Law of Japan. Accordingly, the accompanying consolidated financial statements may differ in certain significant respects from accounting principles and practices generally accepted in countries and jurisdictions other than Japan.

> Then there is the choice of exchange rate to use in converting foreign accounts to a single reporting currency. As Chapter 6 explains, there are a variety of rates that an MNC can use. As foreign exchange rates are seldom constant, restating accounts using exchange rates that gyrate almost daily produces gains and losses that can have a significant effect on the reported profitability and perceived riskiness of multinational operations. As you might suspect, accounting treatments for these gains and losses are far from uniform internationally.

Domestic readers are not the only audience that reporting entities must address. What about statement readers that are domiciled abroad? Their information needs must be considered when a firm seeks access to foreign sources of capital and at reasonable costs. Market access and cost of capital considerations are, in turn, related to the nature and quality of a firm's external financial communications. Should a company send the same set of accounts that it prepares for its domestic readers to its foreign readers? Or, should the reporting entity restate its reports according to the language, currency and/or accounting principles of the reader's country? This is not a trivial consideration as foreign readers are generally unaccustomed to providing money capital on the basis of an unfamiliar currency, language, and measurement framework. Evidence suggests that some institutional investors tend to exhibit a home country bias in their portfolio choices and tend to invest in nondomestic firms whose accounting and reporting methods conform to the GAAP framework that they are accustomed to.[4] Would you be interested in investing in the shares of a Chinese company if the numbers in the annual report you received were expressed in Renmenbi, the text written in Mandarin, and the accounting measurements based on Chinese GAAP?

Both AKZO and Nestle, mentioned earlier, have chosen to accommodate their foreign readers by restating their financial statements to International Financial Reporting Standards (IFRS). AKZO's initiative is in compliance with a European Union (EU) directive that mandates all EU listed companies to follow IASB standards. Nestle's decision is voluntary as its decision to conform to IFRS predates the EU requirement. Issues associated with management's use of special disclosures for nondomestic financial statement readers are covered in Chapter 5.

In addition to external reporting, a firm's internal users of accounting information, that is, financial managers and accountants, must also understand the effects of environmental complexities of an MNE's accounting measurements. Discussion of these topics begins in Chapter 10. For example, understanding the effects of changes in foreign exchange and inflation rates is critical in areas such as the preparation of short- and long-term budgets for parent companies and their subsidiaries (or branches), measuring and evaluating the performance of local business units and managers, and making corporate-wide decisions on the allocation of investment capital and retained earnings, among others. To make matters more complex, foreign exchange and inflation rates do not work in tandem. The effect on accounting measurements of changes in foreign exchange rates and foreign inflation is so pervasive that domestic financial control systems cannot serve managers well in the absence of appropriate environmental adaptation. Then there are issues of management control. While companies often expand operations abroad to take advantage of low-cost labor or untapped markets, productivity and decision-making styles can be so different that company expectations are often met with disappointment. Imposing culturally inappropriate control systems on foreign managers only magnifies such disappointments.[5] Managerial accounting from an international perspective includes possibly the most complex and detailed material in this book.

---

[4] See Mark T. Bradshaw, Brian J. Bushee, and Gregory S. Miller, "Accounting Choice, Home Bias and U.S. Investments in Non-U.S. Firms," *Journal of Accounting Research*, 42, No. 5 (December 2004): 795–841.
[5] Stephen B. Salter, Philip A. Lewis, and Luis Felipe Juarez Valdes, "Aqui No Se Habla Agencia. An Examination of the Impact of Adverse Selection and Framing in Decision-Making: a US/Mexico Comparison," *Journal of International Financial Management and Accounting*, 15, No. 2 (June 2004): 93–117.

Chapter 12 addresses the important issues of international taxation and transfer pricing. Businesses that operate in more than one country need to carefully examine and manage their tax exposure.[6] Knowledge of tax codes and currency values is only the beginning. It is very possible that steps taken by management to lower taxes in one place will raise taxes elsewhere, possibly by an amount greater than the original reduction. The effects of tax strategies on corporate budgeting and control procedures must be considered carefully. For example, a good strategy to reduce taxes might have unintended effects on the performance evaluation system. Transfer prices—the prices charged to business units for internal transactions that cross national borders—frequently are set with tax minimization in mind. The basic idea is to concentrate expenses (as far as possible) in high-tax countries and to concentrate revenues in low-tax countries, thus maximizing overall profit. Governments are well aware of this strategy and have adopted complex rules to prevent abusive use of this strategy. While the notion of the "arm's-length" price is widespread, its definition and the methods for calculating it have many variations. On top of all this, unexpected changes in exchange rates or inflation rates can wreak havoc on tax planning strategy. Managerial accountants must often devise complex computer models to calculate the overall expected impact of a company's tax strategy.

FINANCIAL INNOVATION

Risk management has become a hot buzzword in corporate and financial circles. The reason is not hard to find. With continued deregulation of financial markets and capital controls volatility in the price of commodities, foreign exchange, credit, and equities has become the order of the day. These price gyrations not only impact internal reporting processes but also expose the firm to the risk of economic losses. This has spurred a host of managerial activities aimed at identifying a firm's exposure to this volatility, deciding which risks to hedge against, and evaluating the results of a given risk management strategy. The rapid growth of risk management services suggests that management can enhance firm value by managing market risks. Investors and other corporate stakeholders expect financial managers to identify and actively manage such exposures. At the same time, advances in financial technology have made it possible to shift market risks to someone else's shoulders. However, the burden of assessing counterparty risk, that is, the risk that this someone else will not default on their obligation, cannot be transferred and is now placed on the shoulders of a larger pool of market participants, many of whom may be located thousands of miles apart. The dependence this creates on international reporting practices and the resulting confusion caused by diversity in accounting for financial risk products is onerous. Those with risk management skills are highly valued by the market. Hence we devote an entire chapter, Chapter 11, to the topic of financial risk management.

---

[6] A good example in this regard is the international tax effects surrounding the contemporary use of fair values. See Edward Abahoonie and Yosef Barbut, "Fair Value Accounting: Tax Considerations," *Financial Executive*, (March 2009): 49–51.

GLOBAL COMPETITION

Another factor contributing to the growing importance of international accounting is the phenomenon of global competition. Benchmarking, the act of comparing one's performance against an appropriate standard, is not new. What is new is that standards of comparison now transcend national boundaries. The relevant question today is not "How am I doing relative to my competitor who may be right across the street?", but "Am I adding more value to my customer base than my counterpart who may be located in another country?"

In benchmarking against international competitors, one must be careful to ensure that comparisons are indeed comparable. For example, one frequently used perform-ance metric is return on equity (ROE). In comparing the ROE of an American telecom company with India's Infosys, are you really comparing apples to apples or are you comparing apples to oranges?

Exhibit 1-5 suggests that differences in accounting measurements between coun-tries could complicate meaningful comparisons. Exhibit 1-5 begins with the net income of Infosys as reported in its recent consolidated financial statements. For the convenience of U.S. investors, Infosys has translated its financial statements from Indian GAAP to U.S. GAAP. Net income and shareholders' equity figures are first reported based on Indian GAAP. These metrics are then modified by a series of adjustments that restate them to a basis consistent with U.S. GAAP. A comparison of the unadjusted ROE with the adjusted ROE yields return statistics of 33.8% versus 29.5%. While adjustments from

EXHIBIT 1-5	**Adjusting Infosys' Consolidated Earnings and Equity from Indian to U.S. GAAP (Dollars in millions)**	
	U.S. GAAP	**Indian GAAP**
Revenues (Fiscal 08)	$4,176	$4,176
Cost of revenues	2,453	2,452
Gross profit	1,723	1,724
Selling and marketing expenses	230	229
General and administrative expenses	334	333
Amortization of intangible assets	8	—
Total operating expenses	572	562
Operating income	1,151	1,162
Other income, net	175	175
Income before income taxes	1,326	1,337
Provision for income taxes	171	171
Net income	$1,155	$1,166
ASSETS		
Cash and cash equivalents	$2,058	$2,058
Investments in liquid mutual fund units	18	18
Trade accounts receivable, net	824	824
Unbilled revenue	120	120
Prepaid expenses	107	107
Property, plant and equipment, net	1,022	1,022

(continued)

		U.S. GAAP	Indian GAAP
EXHIBIT 1-5	Adjusting Infosys' Consolidated Earnings and Equity from Indian to U.S. GAAP (Dollars in millions) (Continued)		
Goodwill		150	172
Intangible assets, net		25	—
Deferred tax assets		68	74
Advance income taxes		55	55
Other assets		45	45
Total assets		$4,492	$4,495
LIABILITIES AND STOCKHOLDERS' EQUITY			
Accounts payable		$ 12	$ 12
Income taxes payable		101	101
Client deposits		1	1
Unearned revenue		71	71
Other current and noncurrent liabilities		397	862
Common stock		64	64
Additional paid in capital		718	652
Retained earnings		2,817	2,432
Accumulated other comprehensive income		311	300
Total stockholders' equity		3,910	3,448
Total liabilities and stockholders' equity		$4,492	$4,495

Indian GAAP to U.S. GAAP did not have a significant effect on earnings, it did have a 13.4% effect on equity. Statement readers who are not aware of national measurement differences and required accounting adjustment algorithms are obviously at a disadvantage. These and related statement analysis considerations are the subject of Chapter 9.

CROSS-BORDER MERGERS AND ACQUISITIONS

As the global trend toward industrial consolidation continues, news about international mergers and acquisitions is practically a daily occurrence. While mergers are normally rationalized in terms of operating synergies or economies of scale, accounting plays a crucial role in these mega-consolidations as accounting numbers are fundamental in corporate valuation. Differences in national measurement rules can complicate the corporate valuation process (see Chapter 9).

For example, corporate valuations are often based on price multiples, such as the price-to-earnings (P/E) ratio. The approach here is to derive an average P/E multiple for comparable firms in the industry and apply this multiple to the reported earnings of the firm being valued to arrive at a reasonable offering price. A major concern of the acquiring firm when bidding for a foreign acquisition target is to what extent the E in the P/E metric is a true reflection of the attribute being measured, as opposed to the result of an accounting measurement difference!

Differences in accounting measurement rules could also create an unlevel playing field in the market for corporate control. Thus, if Company A in Country A is allowed to take purchased goodwill directly to reserves, while Company B in Country B must amortize purchased goodwill to earnings, Company A may very well enjoy a bidding advantage over B when seeking to acquire a common target company. Company A could offer a higher purchase price knowing that its earnings will not be penalized by the hit to earnings of any excessive premiums paid.

INTERNATIONALIZATION OF CAPITAL MARKETS

The factor that has perhaps contributed most to the growing interest in international accounting among corporate executives, investors, market regulators, accounting standard setters, and business educators alike is the internationalization of the world's capital markets. Statistics indicate that the dollar volume of cross-border equity flows increased by more than twenty-fold since 1990 while the value of international securities offerings more than quadrupuled during the same time period exceeding $1.5 trillion today. International offerings in bonds, syndicated loans, and other debt instruments have also grown dramatically since the 1990s. Investment banks Russel, Greenwich Associates, Morgan Stanley, Merrill Lynch, and Grail Partners estimate that global retail hedge fund investments will grow to $2.5 trillion by 2010, representing a 14.3% compounded annual growth rate since 2005.

As financial markets are becoming more integrated, we are witnessing an increase in the number of companies listed on the world's stock exchanges. Exhibit 1-6 discloses the number of domestic and foreign companies listed on the world's major exchanges. Over the last ten years, global market capitalization more than doubled to well over $40 trillion. The World Federation of Exchanges reports that while the number of domestic companies with shares listed increased in some markets and decreased in others during the early part of this decade, the average sizes and and annual trading volumes of listed companies have grown substantially, in part due to mergers and acquisitions, which also result in delistings of some of the entities involved.

In recent years, world financial markets have experienced tumultuous declines owing to the recent credit crisis and its effects on economic performance. On a relative basis, however, some emerging markets have experienced lower relative declines. Exhibit 1-7 discloses the percentage change in stock market capitalization, not to be confused with market returns, for the year ended 2008 in both U.S. dollars and local currency by international time zones. The countries listed exhibited the smallest declines in market capitalization in U.S. dollars from the prior year. It is notable that most of the exchanges identified were located in emerging markets. It should also be evident that foreign exchange rate changes must be taken into account by nondomestice investors when gauging market performance. It is not surprising that the traditional preference of investing in one's back yard is beginning to give way to investors exploiting the most attractive investment opportunities whereever they may be located.

The three largest equity market regions are the Americas, Asia-Pacific, and Europe, including Africa and the Middle East.[7] Since the tragic events of 9/11, markets in all three regions have grown significantly.

---

[7] Each equity market region is comprised of equity markets in multiple countries, and some of these national equity markets are comprised of several stock exchanges (as well as off-exchange trading systems). (For example, four stock exchanges operate in Spain and eight stock exchanges operate in the United States.) A stock exchange is an entity that plays a central role in the regulation of trading markets and develops, operates, and manages those markets.

EXHIBIT 1-6	Number of Listed Companies (Equity)

| | 2008 | | | 2007 | | |
Exchange	Total	Domestic Companies	Foreign Companies	Total	Domestic Companies	Foreign Companies
Americas						
American SE	**486**	391	95	**599**	495	104
Bermuda SE	**52**	16	36	**53**	16	37
BM&FBOVESPA	**392**	383	9	**404**	395	9
Buenos Aires SE	**112**	107	5	**111**	106	5
Colombia SE	**89**	89	0	**90**	90	0
Lima SE	**244**	201	43	**226**	188	38
Mexican Exchange	**373**	125	248	**367**	125	242
NASDAQ OMX	**2,952**	2,616	336	**3,069**	2,762	307
NYSE Euronext (U.S.)	**3,011**	2,596	415	**2,297**	1,876	421
Santiago SE	**238**	235	3	**241**	238	3
TSX Group	**3,841**	3,755	86	**3,951**	3,881	70
Total region	***11,790***			***11,408***		
Asia-Pacific						
Australian SE	**2,009**	1,924	85	**1,998**	1,913	85
Bombay SE	**4,921**	4,921	0	**4,887**	4,887	0
Bursa Malaysia	**976**	972	4	**986**	983	3
Colombo SE	**235**	235	0	**235**	235	0
Hong Kong Exchanges	**1,261**	1,251	10	**1,241**	1,232	9
Indonesia SE	**396**	396	0	**383**	383	0
Jasdaq	**926**	926	0	**979**	979	0
Korea Exchange	**1,793**	1,789	4	**1,757**	1,755	2
National Stock Exchange India	**1,406**	1,406	0	**1,330**	1,330	0
New Zealand Exchange	**172**	147	25	**178**	152	26
Osaka SE	**470**	469	1	**477**	476	1
Philippine SE	**246**	244	2	**244**	242	2
Shanghai SE	**864**	864	0	**860**	860	0
Shenzhen SE	**740**	740	0	**670**	670	0
Singapore Exchange	**767**	455	312	**762**	472	290
Taiwan SE Corp.	**722**	718	4	**703**	698	5
Thailand SE	**525**	525	0	**523**	523	0
Tokyo SE Group	**2,390**	2,374	16	**2,414**	2,389	25
Total region	***20,819***			***20,627***		
Europe-Africa-Middle East						
Amman SE	**262**	262	0	**245**	245	0
Athens Exchange	**285**	282	3	**283**	280	3

(continued)

EXHIBIT 1-6	Number of Listed Companies (Equity) (Continued)

| | | 2008 | | | 2007 | |
| | | Domestic | Foreign | | Domestic | Foreign |
Exchange	Total	Companies	Companies	Total	Companies	Companies
BME Spanish Exchanges	**3,576**	3536	40	**3,537**	3498	39
Borsa Italiana	**300**	294	6	**307**	301	6
Budapest SE	**43**	40	3	**41**	39	2
Cyprus SE	**119**	119	0	**124**	124	0
Deutsche Börse	**832**	742	90	**866**	761	105
Egyptian Exchange	**373**	372	1	**435**	435	0
Irish SE	**68**	58	10	**73**	60	13
Istanbul SE	**317**	317	0	**319**	319	0
Johannesburg SE	**411**	367	44	**411**	374	37
Ljubljana SE	**84**	84	0	**87**	87	0
London SE	**3,096**	2,415	681	**3,307**	2,588	719
Luxembourg SE	**262**	34	228	**261**	34	227
Malta SE	**19**	19	0	**16**	16	0
Mauritius SE	**68**	65	3	**70**	67	3
NASDAQ OMX Nordic Exchange	**824**	801	23	**851**	825	26
NYSE Euronext (Europe)	**1,002**	1,002	0	**1,155**	930	225
Oslo Børs	**259**	209	50	**248**	208	40
SIX Swiss Exchange	**323**	253	70	**341**	257	84
Tehran SE	**356**	356	0	**329**	329	0
Tel Aviv SE	**642**	630	12	**657**	643	14
Warsaw SE	**458**	432	26	**375**	352	23
Wiener Börse	**118**	101	17	**119**	102	17
Total region	**14,097**			**14,457**		
WFE Total	**46,706**			**46,492**		

Americas

The U.S. economy and its stock market had unprecedented growth during the 1990s through 2008. Today both the NYSE and NASDAQ dominate other stock exchanges worldwide in terms of market capitalization, value of trading in domestic shares, value of trading in foreign shares (except for the London Stock Exchange [LSE]), numbers of domestic listed companies, and numbers of foreign listed companies. The relative importance of the Americas in the global equity market has also increased. Market capitalization in the Americas as a percentage of the global total stood at 43% at the start of 2008. But even here, the forces of global competition are making themselves felt. The Committee on Capital Market Regulation, whose members are appointed by the SEC in consultation with the Federal Reserve Board of Govenors and the U.S. Treasury, has concluded that the United States could lose its dominance in the global capital markets

EXHIBIT 1-7	Ten Exchanges Exhibiting the Smallest Relative Declines in Market Capitalization in 2008	
Americas	**% Change 2008/2007 (in USD)**	**% Change 2008/2007 (in local currency)**
1. Bermuda	−30.0%	−30.0%
2. Buenos Aires SE	−30.2%	−23.3%
3. Colombia SE	−14.0%	−4.8%
4. Santiago SE	−38.1%	−20.4%
Region Total	−42.9%	
Asia-Pacific		
Jasdaq	−22.8%	−37.1%
Osaka SE	−30.5%	−43.4%
Tokyo SE	−28.1%	−41.4%
Region Total	−48.6%	
Europe-Africa-Middle East		
Amman SE	−12.9%	−13.0%
Malta SE	−36.5%	−33.4%
Tehran SE	11.0%	17.6%
Region Total	−49.3%	

unless it streamlines its regulatory provisions, which the market feels is onerous. This issue is discussed further in Chapter 8 in conjunction with the topic of corporate governance and the U.S. Sarbanes-Oxley Act.

Western Europe

Europe is the second largest equity market region in the world in terms of market capitalization and trading volume. Economic expansion significantly contributed to the rapid growth in European equity markets. A related factor in Continental Europe has been a gradual shift to an equity orientation that long has characterized the London and North American equity markets.[8] Privatizations of large government entities have made European equity markets more prominent and have attracted noninstitutional investors, who until recently were not active in Continental Europe. Finally, confidence in European markets has grown with the success of the European Monetary Union (EMU).

---

[8] Developed countries around the world can be divided roughly into those having a common law (English) orientation and those having a code law (Continental Europe) orientation (see Chapter 2). Common law countries include the United Kingdom, Canada, the United States, and Australia. In these countries, equity investors are widely dispersed and are the most important suppliers of capital. As a result, capital markets in many common law countries have evolved credible and open disclosure and accounting systems, and relatively stringent market regulation. In code law countries such as France, Germany, and Japan, banks provide most of the financing, and ownership tends to be concentrated among small groups of insiders. Demand for detailed public disclosure is generally lower in these countries than in common law countries, but is increasing.

European equity markets will continue to grow. Pension reforms, for one, are creating new demand for investment opportunities.[9] Also, more and more foreign investors are entering European equity markets. Cross-border equity flows are increasing as a percentage of cross-border bond flows, in part because equity has proved to be a profitable investment. In addition, the advent of the euro has prompted a rush of cross-border mergers, which are expected to continue.

Intense rivalry among European stock exchanges has contributed to the development of an equity culture. Continental European markets have become more investor oriented to increase their credibility and attract new listings. External investors, in particular foreign investors and institutional investors, are demanding expanded disclosure and improved corporate governance. In addition, equity market development has become increasingly important to national governments and regulators, who also compete for recognition and prestige. Many European securities regulators and stock exchanges have implemented more stringent market rules and are strengthening their enforcement efforts.

Asia

Many experts are predicting that Asia will become the second most important equity market region. The People's Republic of China (China) has emerged as a major global economy, and the "Asian Tiger" nations continue to experience phenomenal growth and development.

Critics argue that Asian accounting measurement, disclosure, and auditing standards and the monitoring and enforcement of those standards are weak.[10] Some Asian governments periodically announce that they will intervene in equity markets to boost share prices, and market manipulation is not uncommon.[11]

However, the prospects for continued growth in Asian equity markets are strong. Market capitalization as a percentage of gross domestic product (GDP) in Asia is lower than that in the United States and several major European markets. This suggests, however, that equity markets can play a much larger role in many Asian economies. Also, Asian governments and stock exchanges appear eager to improve market quality and credibility to attract investors.[12] As mentioned earlier, Asian-Pacific markets (e.g., China, India, Korea, Taiwan, and Hong Kong) have grown rapidly, and are experiencing heavy trading volume relative to market capitalization.

---

[9] With aging populations causing the numbers of pensioners to increase, a major initiative across much of Europe has been to move toward the private funding of pensions. The goal is to relieve the strain on "pay-as-you-go" state pension schemes. The growing numbers of private pension funds are allocating more of their assets to equities to increase returns. Also, some countries are liberalizing restrictions on pension fund investment.

[10] These attributes are neither good nor bad. Each market develops in response to economic conditions, the nature of its investors, sources of financing, and other factors. In Japan, for example, banks have long been the primary sources of finance. These banks have had full access to inside information about Japanese companies, and so there has been less demand in Japan for credible external financial reporting.

[11] For example, Taiwan announced in November 2000 that it would institute emergency action to support share prices after a recent, dramatic fall.

[12] The Singapore Exchange has moved aggressively to position itself as the premier financial exchange in Asia outside of Japan. The exchange recently implemented new listing rules and more stringent disclosure requirements to attract new domestic and foreign listings.

Cross-Border Equity Listing and Issuance

The current wave of interest in cross-border listings on major world exchanges is not a chance phenomenon. Evidence suggests that issuers seek cross-border listings to broaden their shareholder base, promote awareness of their products, and/or build public awareness of the company, particularly in countries where the company has significant operations and/or major customers.

National regulators and stock exchanges compete fiercely for foreign listings and trade volume, considered necessary for any stock exchange that seeks to become or remain a global leader. In response, organized exchanges and market regulators have worked to make access faster and less costly for foreign issuers and at the same time increase their markets' credibility. As capital markets become more specialized, each can offer unique benefits to foreign issuers.

Many companies have difficulty deciding where to raise capital or list their shares. Knowledge of many equity markets with different laws, regulations, and institutional features is now required. Also required is an understanding of how issuer and stock exchange characteristics interact. The issuer's home country, industry, and offering size are just some of the factors that need to be considered.[13] In addition, the costs and benefits of different market combinations need to be understood. One entrepreneur planning to raise capital said, "I spoke to three investment banks about it, and I had three different answers about which would be the right market for me." Exhibit 1-8 presents a detailed list of factors companies consider in choosing a foreign capital market.[14]

The pace of change in the world's capital markets show no signs of slowing. One example is the growing importance of stock exchange alliances and consolidation. In a strategic move, the New York Stock Exchange acquired Euronext, the pan-European stock exchange created by a merger of the Amsterdam, Brussels, Lisbon, and Paris exchanges. This business combination creates the world's first trans-Atlantic stock market. Some are even predicting that financial markets and trading will be dominated by two or three global exchange groups operating across continents within the not too distant future.[15] This will increase significantly the exposure of international investors to international companies. Similarly, the emergence of newer markets, such as London's Alternative Investment Market (AIM), France's Alternext and Germany's Entry Standard, expands the pool of companies that can now break the bonds of local debt financing. All of these developments present a highly complex setting for financial reporting regulation.

---

[13] Home country is relevant because companies can raise capital more easily in foreign countries that have legal and regulatory environments similar to their own. For example, an Australian company can probably access the U.K. equity market more easily than the French equity market. Industry is important because, other things equal, issuers seek to raise capital in markets where other companies in the same industry are listed in order to improve the chances for adequate attention by financial analysts. For example, the SWX Swiss Exchange's New Market is attractive to biotechnology companies in part because Novartis and Roche (two of the world's largest pharmaceutical companies) are listed on the SWX Swiss Exchange and have attracted many pharmaceutical/biotech analysts to Zurich. Offering size is important because only relatively large offerings attract sufficient attention in the United States. Much smaller IPOs are common in Europe's new markets.

[14] Appendix 1-1 presents Web site addresses for stock exchanges in more than 50 countries. Many stock exchange Web sites include information on unique stock exchange features that may attract foreign companies considering listing or raising capital in those markets.

[15] Alistair McDonald, "Euronext Head Sees Markets Dominated by Global Exchanges," *WSJ Online*, Jannuary 22, 2007.

EXHIBIT 1-8	Factors Relevant in Choosing an Overseas Market

1. What is the extent of interest in a company shown by financial analysts and investors who normally participate in a market?
2. What is the level of trading activity on the exchange? Higher trading volume means more potential buyers of a company's securities.
3. How easy is it to raise capital? Some jurisdictions have complex listing or ongoing reporting requirements that may be difficult or impossible for a smaller company to meet.
4. What is the availability of capital in a market?
5. What is the reputation of the exchange? A growing international company may want the increased credibility and recognition that come with listing on a preeminent market such as the New York Stock Exchange.
6. To what extent does the company desire to raise its profile and establish its brand identity in a particular market? A stock exchange listing can benefit companies that operate or plan to operate in an overseas country.
7. To what extent are the market's regulatory environment and language similar to those in the company's home market? For example, a company from an English-speaking country with a common law (British-American) legal and regulatory system, such as Australia, might find it easier to list in the United Kingdom than in Continental Europe.
8. To what extent do institutional investors face statutory or self-imposed restrictions on the proportion of their investment portfolio that they can hold in securities of foreign companies? Sometimes these restrictions force a large international company to list on many stock exchanges to have access to sufficient institutional capital. These restrictions are difficult to overcome in some jurisdictions.
9. What are the nature and activities of investors in the market? For example, large pension funds in the Netherlands, Switzerland, and the United Kingdom invest heavily in equities of both domestic and foreign companies.
10. What is the likelihood that the company will be required to have locally listed shares to carry out a merger or acquisition in a particular country?
11. Will there be a need for locally listed shares to be used in employee stock option plans?

WHERE ARE WE?

The rapid growth in global capital markets and cross-border investment activity means that the international dimensions of accounting are more important than ever for professionals who have to deal in one way or another with these areas. Accounting plays a critical role in the efficient functioning of capital markets. Lenders, investors, financial analysts, regulators, and stock exchanges require information about the financial performance, position, and the future prospects of companies seeking financing. In turn, the needs of capital market participants have strongly shaped the development of accounting practice, as discussed in Chapter 2. Demands of market participants strongly influence companies' accounting and disclosure choices and national and international efforts to harmonize accounting measurement, disclosure, and auditing practices around the world.

How does, for example, a British or American investor make sense of Japanese accounts or Brazilian accounts where measurement and transparency rules are very different from what they are typically accustomed to? Until Japan and Brazil formally implement international financial reporting standards, should investors attempt to restate Japanese or Brazilian accounts to a more familiar set of reporting norms such as U.S. or IASB measurement rules prior to analysis? Or should they put themselves in the shoes of a Japanese or Brazilian shareholder and conduct their analysis from a local perspective? These and other related issues are covered in Chapter 9.

On the other side of the coin, a major factor motivating many corporations to raise monies abroad is to increase their access to funds and lower their capital costs. The challenge here is trying to ensure that the foreign reader receives the same intended message as the domestic reader. This challenge is significant in a world where firms compete for funds, an issue explored in Chapter 5.

LEARNING OBJECTIVES

Having set the stage for your study of international accounting, we identify below the essential ideas that you should get out of each chapter. We invite you to revisit this section before you begin reading each chapter and upon completion of each chapter to be sure that you understand the essential ideas that are being conveyed. This text is intended to sensitize you to the important concepts and issues in the field of international accounting and reporting, and in so doing, enable you to ask the "right questions" as a reader of international financial statements, whether you opt for a career in the corporate, legal, financial services, or not-for-profit world.

After studying Chapter 1, you should be able to:

1. Explain how international accounting is distinct from domestic accounting.
2. Describe what the term *accounting diversity* entails.
3. Identify the factors that are contributing to the internationalization of the subject of accounting.
4. Understand how foreign direct investment activities differ from international trade and the implications of this difference for accounting.
5. Appreciate, in general terms, the historic development of international accounting.
6. Comprehend the reasons why the study of international accounting is so important.
7. Identify several internal and external reporting issues that arise when business and investments transcend national borders.
8. Explain what is meant by *global capital markets* and what this development means for capital market participants.

After studying Chapter 2, you should be able to:

1. Identify and understand the importance of the eight factors that have a significant influence on accounting development.
2. Understand the four approaches to accounting development found in market-oriented Western economies and identify countries in which each one in prevalent.
3. Have a basic working knowledge of accounting classifications and how they compare with one another.
4. Explain the difference between the "fair presentation" and "legal compliance" orientations of accounting and identify nations in which each is prevalent.
5. Explain why distinctions of accounting at the national level are becoming blurred.

After studying Chapter 3, you should be able to:

1. Understand how financial reporting is regulated and enforced in five European countries: France, Germany, the Czech Republic, the Netherlands, and the United Kingdom.
2. Describe the key similarities and differences among the accounting systems of these five countries.
3. Identify the use of International Financial Reporting Standards at the individual company and consolidated financial statement levels in these five countries.
4. Describe the audit oversight mechanisms in these five countries.

After studying Chapter 4, you should be able to:

1. Understand how financial reporting is regulated and enforced in five countries of the Americas and Asia: the United States, Mexico, Japan, China, and India.
2. Describe the key similarities and differences among the accounting systems of these five countries.
3. Describe the auditor oversight mechanisms in these five countries.
4. Explain the difference between principle-based and rules-based accounting standards.

After studying Chapter 5, you should be able to:

1. Distinguish voluntary and mandatory disclosure and its regulation.
2. Identify the broad objectives for accounting disclosure systems in investor-oriented equity markets.
3. Discuss "triple bottom line" reporting and why it is a growing tendency among large multinational corporations.
4. Gain a basic understanding of the following selected corporate financial disclosure practices: (a) disclosures of forward-looking information, (b) segment disclosures, (c) social responsibility reporting, (d) special disclosures for nondomestic financial statement users, and (e) corporate governance disclosures.

After studying Chapter 6, you should be able to:

1. Describe the nature of foreign currency transactions done in the spot, forward, and swap markets.
2. Understand the foreign currency translation terms set forth in Exhibit 6-1.
3. Explain the difference between a translation gain or loss and a transaction gain or loss.
4. Comprehend alternative foreign currency translation methods that exist and their rationale.
5. Evaluate which of the available foreign currency translation methods are best under which specific business and currency market conditions.
6. Compare and contrast the financial statement effects of the temporal versus the current rate method of foreign currency translation.
7. Understand the relationship between foreign currency translation and inflation.
8. Appreciate how foreign currency translation is handled outside the United States.

After studying Chapter 7, you should be able to:

1. Understand why financial statements potentially are misleading during periods of changing prices.
2. Define the inflation accounting terms listed in Exhibit 7-1.
3. Comprehend the effect of general price-level adjustments on financial statement amounts.
4. Describe in what ways the current cost accounting framework differs from conventional accounting.
5. Appreciate how and why adjustments for changing prices may vary from country to country.
6. Have a basic understanding of the IASB's pronouncement on changing prices in "hyperinflationary economies."
7. Discuss whether constant dollars or current costs better measure the effects of changing prices.
8. Understand how changing prices and foreign exchange rates are related and their financial statement effects.

After studying Chapter 8, you should be able to:

1. Define and understand the distinction between "harmonization" and "convergence" as they apply to accounting standards.
2. State the pros and cons of adopting international accounting standards.
3. Understand what is meant by "reconciliation" and "mutual recognition" of different sets of accounting standards.
4. Identify the six organizations that have leading roles in setting international accounting standards and in promoting international accounting convergence.
5. Describe the structure of the International Accounting Standards Board and how it sets International Financial Reporting Standards.
6. Understand what the major provisions of the U.S. Sarbanes-Oxley Act are and why similar legislation is being enacted in other countries.

After studying Chapter 9, you should be able to:

1. Understand the special difficulties involved in undertaking international business strategy analysis.
2. Identify basic approaches to information gathering.
3. Describe the steps involved in conducting an accounting analysis.
4. Appreciate the impact on accounting analysis of (a) cross-country variation in accounting measurement, disclosure, and auditing quality and (b) the difficulty in obtaining necessary information.
5. Comprehend several coping mechanisms available to deal with cross-country accounting measurement differences.
6. Expose the particular difficulties and pitfalls involved in doing an international prospective analysis.
7. Undertake a more intelligent approach to international financial ratio analysis.
8. Appreciate national variations associated with the audit or attest function.

After studying Chapter 10, you should be able to:

1. Identify four critical dimensions of business modeling.
2. Understand the distinction between standard and Kaizen costing concepts.
3. Measure expected returns of a foreign investment.
4. Calculate (in general fashion) a firm's cost of capital in a multinational framework.
5. Comprehend the basic issues and complexities involved in designing multi-national information and financial control systems.
6. Perform an exchange rate variance analysis.
7. State the unique difficulties involved in designing and implementing perform-ance evaluation systems in multinational companies.
8. Deal with the effects of inflation and exchange rate fluctuation on performance measurement of multinational companies.

After studying Chapter 11, you should be able to:

1. Describe what Enterprise Risk Management (ERM) entails.
2. Define market risk and provide an example of this risk with a foreign exchange example.
3. State four tasks involved in managing foreign exchange risk.
4. Define and calculate translation exposure.
5. Define and calculate transaction exposure.
6. Understand the distinction between accounting exposure and economic exposure.
7. Explain what a financial derivative is and the accounting issues associated with it.
8. Comprehend the types of foreign currency hedges recognized by IAS 39 and FAS 133 and their accounting treatments.

After studying Chapter 12, you should be able to:

1. Identify the major types of tax systems that exist around the world.
2. Understand what determines a multinational entity's effective tax burden.
3. Understand concepts relating to the taxation of foreign source income and the rationale behind the foreign tax credit.
4. Identify the major variables that complicate international transfer pricing.
5. Explain the meaning of *arm's-length price* and the transfer pricing methods designed to achieve it.
6. Explain what an advance pricing arrangement is.

Appendix 1-1

Stock Exchange Web Sites

Country	Stock Exchange	Web Site
Argentina	Buenos Aires	www.bcba.sba.com.ar
Australia	Australia	www.asx.com.au
Austria	Vienna	www.wbag.at
Azerbaijan	Baku	www.az/bicex
Belgium	Euronext—Belgium	www.euronext.com
		www.stockexchange.be/enindex.htm
Bermuda	Bermuda	www.bsx.com
Brazil	Rio de Janeiro	www.bvrj.com.br (Portuguese only)
Brazil	Sao Paulo	www.bovespa.com.br (Portuguese only)
Canada	Montréal	www.me.org
Canada	Toronto	www.tse.com
Canada	Canadian Venture	www.cdnx.ca
Chile	Santiago	www.bolsadesantiago.com
China	Schenzhen	222.sse.org.cn
Colombia	Bogotá	www.bolsabogata.com.co/ (Spanish only)
Colombia	Medellín	www.bolsamed.com.co (Spanish only)
Croatia	Zagreb	www.zse.hr
Czech Republic	Prague	www.pse.cz
Denmark	Copenhagen	www.xcse.dk
Finland	Helsinki	www.hex.fi
France	Paris	www.euronext.com
		www.bourse-de-paris.fr/defaultgb.htm
Germany	Deutsche Börse	deutsche-boerse.com/
Greece	Athens	www.ase.gr
Hong Kong	Hong Kong	www.hkex.com.hk
India	National Stock Exchange	www.nseindia.com
India	Surabaya	www.bes.co.id
Indonesia	Jakarta	www.jsx.co.id
Iran	Tehran	www.tse.or.ir
Israel	Tel-Aviv	hebrew.tase.co.il/www/intro.asp
Italy	Italy	www.borsaitalia.it
Japan	Osaka	www.ose.or.jp
Japan	Tokyo	www.tse.or.jp
Jordan	Amman	www.access2arabia.com/AFM/
Luxembourg	Luxembourg	www.bourse.lu
Macedonia	Macedonian	www.mse.org.mk

(continued)

Country	Stock Exchange	Web Site
Malaysia	Kuala Lumpur	www.klse.com.my
Mexico	Mexico	www.bmv.com.mx
Netherlands	Euronext—Netherlands	www.euronext.com
		www.aex.nl/aex.asp?taal=en
New Zealand	New Zealand	www.nzse.co.nz
Norway	Oslo	www.ose.no
Pakistan	Lahore	www.lse.brain.net.pk
Peru	Lima	www.bvl.com.pe
Philippines	Philippines	www.pse.org.ph
Poland	Warsaw	www.gpw.com.pl
Portugal	Lisbon	www.bvl.pt
Russia	Siberian	www.sse.nsk.su (Russian only)
Singapore	Singapore	www.ses.com.sg
Slovakia	Bratislava	www.bsse.sk
Slovenia	Ljubljana	www.ljse.si
South Africa	Johannesburg	www.jse.co.za
South Korea	Korea	www.kse.or.kr
Spain	Barcelona	www.borsabcn.es
Spain	Bilbao	www.bolsabilbao.es
Spain	Madrid	www.bolsamadrid.es
Sweden	Stockholm	www.xsse.se
Switzerland	Swiss	www.swx.ch
Taiwan	Taiwan	www.tse.com.tw
Thailand	Thailand	www.set.or.th
Turkey	Istanbul	www.ise.org
United Kingdom	London	www.londonstockexchange.com
United States	American (Amex)	www.amex.com
United States	Chicago	www.chicagostockex.com
United States	Nasdaq	www.nasdaq.com
		www.nasdaqnews.com
		www.nasdr.com
		www.nasdaqtrader.com
United States	New York	www.nyse.com

Note: All Web site addresses here begin with the prefix http://

Appendix 1-2

Financial Statements and Selected Notes from the Annual Report of INFOSYS.

Please refer to pages 85-148 of the 2009 annual report of Infosys. Its web address is www.infosys.com.

Discussion Questions

1. Explain how international accounting differs from purely domestic accounting.
2. Accounting may be viewed as having three components: measurement, disclosure, and auditing. What are the advantages and disadvantages of this classification? Can you suggest alternative classifications that might be useful?
3. What contemporary factors are contributing to the internationalization of the subject of accounting?
4. Describe in two short paragraphs how foreign direct investment activities differ from international trade and the implications of this difference for accounting.
5. Given the international heritage of accounting, do you feel that efforts to harmonize global accounting standards are a good thing? Why or why not?
6. Why have international accounting issues grown in importance and complexity in recent years?
7. Identify several internal and external reporting issues that arise when business and investments transcend national borders.
8. Explain the term global capital markets. This chapter primarily discusses global equity markets. What other types of financial instruments are traded in these markets? How important are global capital markets in the world economy?
9. Over time, national governments in many countries have sold shares in state-owned financial institutions to nongovernmental entities. Discuss how these privatizations might affect the capital markets as well as the accounting systems of these companies.
10. Outsourcing, especially from vendors located abroad, has become a politically sensitive issue, especially in the United States. Do you think this argument has merit? What are the consequences of this debate for international accounting?

Exercises

1. Re-examine Exhibit 1-1 which describes the outsourcing process for HP's production of the Proliant ML150. For each leg of the production chain, identify the various accounting and related issues that might arise.
2. Examine Exhibit 1-2 and compute the compounded annual growth rate of merchandise trade versus the global trade in services for the 20 year period beginning 1985 and ending 2005. What implication does your finding have for accounting as a service activity?
3. Examine the Web sites of five exchanges listed in Appendix 1-1 that you feel would be most attractive to foreign listers. Which exchange in your chosen set proved most popular during the last two years? Provide possible explanations for your observation.
4. Does the geographic pattern of merchandise exports contained in Exhibit 1-2 correlate well with the pattern of AKZO Nobel's geographic distribution of sales shown in Exhibit 1-3? What might explain any differences you observe?
5. What international reporting issues are triggered by AKZO NOBEL's foreign operations disclosures appearing in Exhibit 1-3 for investors? For managerial accountants?
6. Exhibit 1-4 lists the number of majority-owned foreign affiliates in each country that Nestle includes in its consolidated results. What international accounting issues are triggered by this Exhibit?
7. Revisit Exhibit 1-5 and show how the ROE statistics of 33.8 percent and 29.5 percent were derived. Which of the two ROE statistics is the better performance measure to use when comparing the financial performance of Infosys with that of Verizon, a leading U.S. telecom company?
8. Stock exchange Web sites vary considerably in the information they provide and their ease of use.

   Required: Select any two of the stock exchanges presented in Appendix 1-1. Explore the Web sites of each of these stock exchanges. Prepare a table that compares and contrasts the sites for types and quality of information presented and the ease of using the Web site. Are English-language press releases of listed companies available? Links to listed companies' Web sites? Listing requirements? Price and volume data for listed securities? Helpful information for investors?

9. Referring to Exhibit 1-6, which geographic region of the world, the Americas, Asia-Pacific, or Europe-Africa-Middle East is experiencing the most activity in foreign listings? Do you expect this pattern to persist in the future? Please explain.

10. If you had a nontrivial sum of money to invest and decided to invest it in a country index fund, in which country or countries identified in Exhibit 1-7 would you invest your money? What accounting issues would play a role in your decision?

CASES

Case 1-1

E-centives, Inc.—Raising Capital in Switzerland

On October 3, 2000, E-centives, incorporated in the United States, made an initial public offering on the Swiss Stock Exchange's New Market. The company raised approximately US$40 million. E-centive's offering circular stated that no offers or sales of the company's common stock would be made in the United States, and that there would be no public market for the common stock in the United States after the offering.

The Swiss Exchange's

New Market

The Swiss Exchange launched the New Market in 1999. The New Market is designed to meet the financing needs of rapidly growing companies from Switzerland and abroad. It provides firms with a simplified means of entry to the Swiss capital markets. Listing requirements for the New Market are simple. For example, companies must have an operating track record of 12 months, the initial public listing must involve a capital increase, and to ensure market liquidity, a bank must agree to make a market in the securities.

E-centives

E-centives, Inc. is a leading online direct marketing infrastructure company. The company offers systems and technologies that enable businesses to build large, rich databases of consumer profiles and interests. In return, consumers receive a free personalized service that provides them with promotional offers based on their interests. At the time of the public offering, E-centives maintained over 4.4 million e-centives online accounts for members. The company does not charge members a fee for its service. Instead, the company generates revenue primarily from marketers whose marketing matter is delivered to targeted groups of E-centives members. E-centives currently employs more than 100 people in its Bethesda, Maryland headquarters, and its offices in Redwood City, New York, and Los Angeles.

As of the offering date, the company had little revenue and had not been profitable. Revenue for the year-ended December 31, 1999, was US$740,000, with a net loss of about US$16 million. As of June 30, 2000, the company had an accumulated deficit of about US$39 million. E-centives' growth strategy is to expand internationally. To date, the company has focused on pursuing opportunities in the United States. E-centives intends to expand into Europe and other countries. The company is currently considering expanding into Switzerland, the United Kingdom, and Germany.[19]

Required

1. Refer to Exhibit 1-8, which lists factors relevant for choosing an overseas market for listing or raising capital. Which factors might have been relevant in E-centives' decision to raise capital and list on the Swiss Exchange's New Market?

---

[19] From E-centives' offering circular dated October 2, 2000.

2. Why do you believe E-centives chose not to raise public equity in the United States? What are the potential drawbacks related to E-centives' decision not to raise capital in the U.S. public markets?

3. What are the advantages and disadvantages to E-centives of using U.S. GAAP?

4. Should the SWX Swiss Exchange require E-centives to prepare its financial statements using Swiss accounting standards?

5. Learn more about the New Market at the SWX Swiss Exchange's Web site (http://www.swx.com). What are the listing requirements for the New Market? What are the financial reporting requirements? Does E-centives appear to fit the profile of the typical New Market company?

Case 1-2

Global Benchmarks: Infosys Technologies Limited

Investors, individual, corporate and institutional, are increasingly investing beyond national borders. The reason is not hard to find. Returns abroad, even after allowing for foreign currency exchange risk, have often exceeded those offered by domestic investments. Information provided in a firm's annual report is often the major source of information available to those seeking to sample foreign equities. In attempting to assess the risk and return attributes of a given company, readers must answer questions such as the following: What accounting principles were employed? Should the financial statements be restated according to a different set of accounting principles to be more useful? What types of information are not provided that one would expect to find in financial statements of companies from the investor's home country? How would one compensate for limited disclosure? What does the audit report reveal about the level of audit quality? What auditing standards were used? Are they acceptable? Does the audit report mean the same thing as it does in the reader's home country?

Appendix 1-2 (refers you to) the financial statements (including selected notes) and auditor's report for Infosys Technologies Limited. Infosys was incorporated in 1981 as Infosys Consultants Private Limited, as a private company under the Indian Companies Act. Its name eventually evolved into Infosys Technologies Limited in 1992, when the company went public. Its mission is to provide high quality and cost competitive technology solutions for companies around the world. It has grown into a $5 billion company with a market capitalization in excess of $15 billion.

In examining the information (referred to) in Appendix 1-2, comment on how the statements of Infosys stack up to other companies in the industry in meeting the information needs of a nondomestic investor such as yourself. Specifically, what reporting practices raise issues for you? What reporting practices do you find particularly helpful? In preparing your critique, compare the reporting practices of Infosys to a service provider in your country, most of whom maintain corporate Web sites on the Internet.

CHAPTER 2

Development and Classification

Accounting must respond to society's ever-changing informational needs and reflect the cultural, economic, legal, social, and political conditions within which it operates. The history of accounting and accountants reveals continuing change. At first, accounting was little more than a recording system for certain banking services and tax-collection schemes. Double-entry bookkeeping systems were later developed to meet the needs of trading ventures. Industrialization and division of labor made cost-behavior analysis and managerial accounting possible. The rise of the modern corporation stimulated periodic financial reporting and auditing. In keeping with society's increased concerns about the environment and about corporate integrity, accountants have found ways to measure and report environmental remediation liabilities and to uncover money laundering and other white-collar crimes. Accounting provides decision information for huge domestic and international public securities markets. It extends into management consulting and incorporates ever-increasing information technology within its systems and procedures.

Why should we want to know how and why accounting develops? The answer is the same as for developmental studies in other fields. We can better understand a nation's accounting by knowing the underlying factors that have influenced its development. Accounting differs around the world, and knowledge of the developmental factors helps us see why. In other words, they can explain the observable differences as well as the similarities. Because accounting responds to its environment, different cultural, economic, legal, and political environments produce different accounting systems, and similar environments produce similar systems.

This leads us to classification. Why should we classify (compare) national or regional financial accounting systems? Classification is fundamental to understanding and analyzing why and how national accounting systems differ. We can also analyze whether these systems are converging or diverging. The goal of classification is to group financial accounting systems according to their distinctive characteristics. Classifications reveal fundamental structures that group members have in common and that distinguish the various groups from each other. By identifying similarities and differences, our understanding of accounting systems is improved. Classifications are a way of viewing the world.

DEVELOPMENT

Every nation's accounting standards and practices result from a complex interaction of economic, historical, institutional, and cultural factors. Diversity among nations is to be expected. The factors that influence national accounting development also help explain the accounting diversity among nations.

The following eight factors have a significant influence on accounting development. The first seven are economic, sociohistorical, and/or institutional in nature, and they have occupied most of the attention of accounting writers. The relationship between culture (the eighth item) and accounting development ends the discussion in this section.

1. *Sources of Finance.* In countries with strong equity markets, such as the United States and the United Kingdom, accounting profits measure how well management is running the company. Accounting is designed to help investors assess future cash flows and the associated risks, and to value the firm. Disclosures are extensive to meet the requirements of widespread public share ownership. By contrast, in credit-based systems, where banks are the dominant source of finance, accounting focuses on creditor protection through conservative earnings measures to minimize dividend payouts and retain sufficient funds for the protection of lenders. Because financial institutions have direct access to any information they want, extensive public disclosures are not considered necessary. Japan and Switzerland are examples.[1]

2. *Legal System.* The legal system determines how individuals and institutions interact. The Western world has two basic orientations: code (or civil) law and common (or case) law. Code law derives mainly from Roman law and the Code Napoléon.[2] In code law countries, laws are an all-embracing set of requirements and procedures. Codification of accounting standards and procedures is natural and appropriate. Thus, in code law countries, accounting rules are incorporated into national laws and tend to be highly prescriptive and procedural.[3] By contrast, common law develops on a case-by-case basis with no attempt to cover all cases in an all-encompassing code. Statute law exists, of course, but it tends to be less detailed and more flexible than in a code law system. This encourages experimentation and permits the exercise of judgment.[4] Common law derives from English case law. In most common law countries, accounting rules are established by private sector professional organizations. This allows them to be more adaptive and innovative. Except for broad statutory requirements, most accounting rules are

---

[1] For further discussion of this point, see C. Nobes, "Towards a General Model of the Reasons for International Differences in Financial Reporting," *Abacus* (September 1998): 162–187. He points out that outsiders (e.g., individual and institutional shareholders) normally dominate ownership in strong equity countries, causing a demand for high levels of disclosure. Insiders (families, other companies, government, and banks) usually dominate ownership in credit-based countries, which is why low levels of disclosure are usually found there. Germany is an exception. Although Germany is a credit-based country, German-listed companies have high disclosures because of Germany's unusually large market in listed debt (p. 169).

[2] There are three major families in the code law tradition: French, German, and Scandinavian. French and German code law, like the common law, spread around the world through conquest, imperialism, or borrowing.

[3] There are exceptions to this generalization; for example, the Netherlands (Chapter 3) and Mexico (Chapter 4), where accounting is like that in common law countries.

[4] Irving Fantl, "The Case Against International Uniformity," *Management Accounting* (May 1971): 13–16.

not incorporated directly into statute law.[5] Code law accounting tends to focus on legal form, whereas common law accounting tends to focus on economic substance. For example, leases are normally not capitalized under code law. In contrast, under common law leases are capitalized when they are, in substance, the purchase of property. Exhibit 2-1 lists code and common law countries.

3. *Taxation*   In many countries, tax legislation effectively determines accounting standards because companies must record revenues and expenses in their accounts to claim them for tax purposes. In other words, financial and tax accounting are the same. This is the case, for example, in Germany and Sweden.

EXHIBIT 2-1	Code and Common Law Countries

Code law—French origin	The Netherlands	Common law
Africa	Portugal	*Africa*
Egypt	Spain	Kenya
Americas	**Code law—German origin**	Nigeria
Argentina		South Africa
Brazil	*Asia*	Zimbabwe
Chile	Japan	*Americas*
Colombia	South Korea	Canada
Ecuador	Taiwan	United States
Mexico	*Europe*	*Asia*
Peru	Austria	Hong Kong
Uruguay	Czech Republic	India
Venezuela	Germany	Israel
Asia	Hungary	Malaysia
Indonesia	Slovak Republic	Pakistan
Jordan	Switzerland	Singapore
Philippines		Sri Lanka
Turkey	**Code law—Scandinavian origin**	Thailand
Europe		*Australasia*
Belgium	*Europe*	Australia
France	Denmark	New Zealand
Greece	Finland	*Europe*
Italy	Iceland	Ireland
Luxembourg	Norway	United Kingdom
	Sweden	

Source: Adapted from Rafael La Porta, Florencio Lopez-de-Silanes, Andrei Shleifer, and Robert W. Vishny, "Law and Finance," *Journal of Political Economy* 106, No. 6 (1998): 1142–1143; and David Alexander and Simon Archer, *European Accounting Guide*, 5th ed., New York: Aspen, 2003.

---

[5] Under martial law or other national emergency situations, all aspects of the accounting function may be regulated by a central governmental court or agency. This was the case, for instance, in Nazi Germany, where intensive war preparations and World War II itself required a highly uniform national accounting system for total control of all national economic activities.

In other countries, such as the Netherlands, financial and tax accounting are separate: Taxable profits are essentially financial accounting profits adjusted for differences with the tax laws. Of course, even where financial and tax accounting are separate, tax legislation may occasionally require the application of certain accounting principles. Last in, first out (LIFO) inventory valuation in the United States is an example.

4. *Political and Economic Ties*   Accounting ideas and technologies are transferred through conquest, commerce, and similar forces. Double-entry bookkeeping, which originated in Italy in the 1400s, gradually spread across Europe along with other ideas of the Renaissance. British colonialism exported accountants and accounting concepts throughout the empire. German occupation during World War II led France to adopt its Plan Comptable (see Chapter 3). The United States imposed U.S.-style accounting regulatory regimes on Japan after World War II. Many developing economies use an accounting system that was developed elsewhere, either because it was imposed on them (e.g., India) or by their own choice (e.g., countries of Eastern Europe that modeled their accounting systems after European Union [EU] regulations). As discussed more generally in Chapter 8, economic integration through the growth of international trade and capital flows is a powerful motivator for the convergence of accounting standards in countries around the world.

5. *Inflation*   Inflation distorts historical cost accounting by understating asset values and related expenses, and overstating income. Countries with high inflation often require that companies incorporate price changes into the accounts. For example, Mexico applies general price-level accounting when its cumulative three-year inflation rate equals or exceeds 28 percent (an annual average compounded rate of 8 percent).[6] In the late 1970s, in response to unusually high rates of inflation, both the United States and the United Kingdom experimented with reporting the effects of changing prices. Accounting responses to inflation are explored in Chapter 7.

6. *Level of Economic Development*   This factor affects the types of business transactions conducted in an economy and determines which ones are most prevalent. The type of transactions, in turn, determines the accounting issues that are faced. For example, stock-based executive compensation or asset securitization makes little sense in economies with underdeveloped capital markets. Today, many industrial economies are becoming service economies. Accounting issues relevant in manufacturing, such as valuing fixed assets and recording depreciation, are becoming less important. New accounting challenges, such as valuing intangibles and human resources, are emerging.

7. *Educational Level*   Highly sophisticated accounting standards and practices are useless if they are misunderstood and misused. For example, a complex technical report on cost behavior variances is meaningless unless the reader understands cost accounting. Disclosures about the risks of derivative securities are not informative unless they can be read competently. Professional accounting education is difficult to achieve where general educational levels are low. Mexico is a country

---

[6] Israel discontinued inflation-adjusted accounting in 2004 after drastic reductions in inflation.

where this difficulty has been overcome. In other situations, a country must import accounting training or send its citizens elsewhere to get it, something that China is now doing. (Mexico and China are discussed in Chapter 4.)

Several of these first seven variables are closely associated. For example, the common law legal systoem originated in Britain and was exported to such countries as Australia, Canada, and the United States. These four countries all have highly developed capital markets that dominate the orientation of their financial reporting. Financial and tax accounting are separate. By contrast, most of continental Europe and Japan have code law legal systems and rely on banks or the government for most of their finance. Thus, their accounting rules generally conform to tax laws. Establishing cause and effect is difficult. The type of legal system may predispose a country toward its system of finance. A common law legal system emphasizes shareholder rights and offers stronger investor protection than a code law system. The outcome is that strong equity markets develop in common law countries and weak ones develop in code law countries.[7] Taxation is an important function of accounting in any country with a corporate income tax. Whether it dominates the orientation of accounting may depend on whether accounting has a major competing purpose, namely, informing outside shareholders. (Tax accounting is not suitable for this purpose.) If common law results in strong equity markets, taxation will not dominate. There will be two sets of accounting rules: one for taxation and another for financial reporting. Tax rules will dominate in code law/credit-based countries, and accounting for taxation and financial reporting will be the same.[8] Two basic orientations of accounting have evolved out of these circumstances. One is oriented toward a fair presentation of financial position and results of operations; the other is designed to comply with legal requirements and tax law. The *fair presentation* versus *legal compliance* distinction is further discussed at the end of the chapter.

8. **Culture**   Culture encompasses the values and attitudes shared by a society. Cultural variables underlie nations' legal systems and other institutional arrangements. Hofstede identified four national cultural dimensions (or societal values): (1) individualism, (2) uncertainty avoidance, (3) power distance, and (4) masculinity. His analysis is based on data from employees of a large U.S. multinational corporation operating in 40 different countries.[9]

Briefly, *individualism* (versus *collectivism*) is a preference for a loosely knit social fabric over an interdependent, tightly knit fabric (*I* versus *we*). *Uncertainty avoidance* is the degree to which society is uncomfortable with ambiguity and an uncertain future. *Power distance* is the extent to which hierarchy and an unequal distribution of power in institutions and organizations are accepted. *Masculinity* (versus *femininity*) is the extent to which gender roles are differentiated and performance and visible achievement (traditional masculine values)

---

[7] R. La Porta, F. Lopez-de-Silanes, A. Shleifer, and R.W. Vishny, "Legal Determinants of External Finance," *Journal of Finance* (July 1997): 1131–1150.
[8] C. Nobes, "Towards a General Model of the Reasons for International Differences in Financial Reporting," *Abacus* (September 1998): 162–187.
[9] G. Hofstede, *Culture's Consequences: International Differences in Work-Related Values* (Beverly Hills, CA: Sage Publications, 1980).

are emphasized over relationships and caring (traditional feminine values). Some scholars now call this *achievement orientation*.[10]

Drawing on Hofstede's analysis, Gray proposed a framework linking culture and accounting.[11] He suggests that four *accounting value dimensions* affect a nation's financial reporting practices. They are:

1. Professionalism vs. statutory control: a preference for the exercise of individual professional judgment and professional self-regulation, as opposed to compliance with prescriptive legal requirements.

   > A preference for independent professional judgment is consistent with a preference for a loosely knit social framework where there is more emphasis on independence, a belief in fair play and as few rules as possible, and where a variety of professional judgments will tend to be more easily tolerated. . . . [P]rofessionalism is more likely to be accepted in a small power-distance society where there is more concern for equal rights, where people at various power levels feel less threatened and more prepared to trust people, and where there is a belief in the need to justify the imposition of laws and codes.[12]

2. Uniformity vs. flexibility: a preference for uniformity and consistency over flexibility in reacting to circumstances.

   > A preference for uniformity is consistent with a preference for strong uncertainty avoidance leading to a concern for law and order and rigid codes of behaviour, a need for written rules and regulations, a respect for conformity and the search for ultimate, absolute truths and values. [Uniformity] is also consistent with a preference for collectivism . . . with its tightly knit social framework, a belief in organization and order, and respect for group norms. . . . [U]niformity is more easily facilitated in a large power-distance society in that the imposition of laws and codes of a uniform character are [*sic*] more likely to be accepted.[13]

---

[10] Later work documents a fifth cultural dimension, *Confucian dynamism* (also called *long-term orientation*). This later work contends that only individualism, power distance, and masculinity are universal across all cultures. Uncertainty avoidance is a unique characteristic of Western societies, whereas Confucian dynamism is unique to Eastern societies. See G. Hofstede and M.H. Bond, "The Confucian Connection: From Cultural Roots to Economic Growth," *Organizational Dynamics* 16, No. 1 (1988): 4–21; G. Hofstede, *Cultures and Organizations: Softwares of the Mind* (London: McGraw-Hill, 1991). The existence of this fifth dimension has been contested. See R. Yeh and J.J. Lawrence, "Individualism and Confucian Dynamism: A Note on Hofstede's Cultural Root to Economic Growth," *Journal of International Business Studies* (third quarter 1995): 655–669. These authors note a data problem in Hofstede's subsequent work. Once an outlier is removed, Confucian dynamism no longer emerges as an independent construct; it reflects the same cultural dimension as individualism. It should also be pointed out that there are other cultural dimensions that are not considered by Hofstede. For example, religion, which extends beyond national boundaries, underlies business practices, institutional arrangements, and, by extension, accounting. Language is another cultural input. For a critique of Hofstede, see B. McSweeney, "Hofstede's Model of National Cultural Differences and Their Consequences," *Human Relations* (January 2002): 89–118.
[11] S. J. Gray, "Towards a Theory of Cultural Influence on the Development of Accounting Systems Internationally," *Abacus* (March 1988): 1–15.
[12] Ibid., 9.
[13] Ibid., 9–10.

3. Conservatism vs. optimism: a preference for a cautious approach to measurement to cope with the uncertainty of future events instead of a more optimistic, risk-taking approach.

> A preference for more conservative measures of profits is consistent with strong uncertainty avoidance following from a concern with security and a perceived need to adopt a cautious approach to cope with uncertainty of future events. . . . [A]n emphasis on individual achievement and performance is likely to foster a less conservative approach to measurement.[14]

4. Secrecy vs. transparency: a preference for confidentiality and the restriction of business information on a need-to-know basis versus a willingness to disclose information to the public.

> A preference for secrecy is consistent with strong uncertainty avoidance following from a need to restrict information disclosures so as to avoid conflict and competition and to preserve security. . . . [H]igh power-distance societies are likely to be characterized by the restriction of information to preserve power inequalities. Secrecy is also consistent with a preference for collectivism . . . with its concern for those closely involved with the firm rather than external parties. . . . [S]ocieties where more emphasis is given to the quality of life, people, and the environment, will tend to be more open especially as regards socially related information.[15]

Exhibit 2-2 shows how Gray's accounting values relate to Hofstede's cultural dimensions.[16]

EXHIBIT 2-2   **Relationships Between Accounting Values and Cultural Dimensions**

	Accounting Values			
Cultural Dimensions	Professionalism	Uniformity	Conservatism	Secrecy
Individualism	+	−	−	−
Uncertainty Avoidance	−	+	+	+
Power Distance	−	+	•	+
Masculinity	•	•	−	−

Note: + indicates a direct relationship between the variables; − indicates an inverse relationship; • indicates no relationship. Gray hypothesizes that individualism and uncertainty avoidance will influence accounting the most, followed by power distance, then masculinity.

---

[14] Ibid., 10.
[15] Ibid., 11.
[16] The empirical work testing Gray's framework is reviewed in T.S. Doupnik and G. T. Tsakumin, "A Critical Review of Gray's Theory of Cultural Relevance and Suggestions for Future Research," *Journal of Accounting Literature* 23 (2004): 1–48.

CLASSIFICATION

International accounting classifications fall into two categories: judgmental and empirical. Judgmental classifications rely on knowledge, intuition, and experience.[17] Empirically derived classifications apply statistical methods to databases of accounting principles and practices around the world.[18]

Four Approaches to Accounting Development[19]

The pioneering classification is the one proposed by Mueller in the mid-1960s. He identified four approaches to accounting development in Western nations with market-oriented economic systems. (1) Under the *macroeconomic* approach, accounting practices are derived from and designed to enhance national macroeconomic goals. Firm goals normally follow rather than lead national economic policies as business firms coordinate their activities with national policies. Thus, for example, a national policy to maintain stable employment by avoiding big swings in business cycles would result in accounting practices that smooth income. As another example, a nation that wished to promote the development of certain industries could permit them to rapidly write off capital expenditures. Accounting in Sweden developed from the macroeconomic approach. (2) Under the *microeconomic* approach, accounting develops from the principles of microeconomics. The focus is on individual firms whose main goal is to survive. To accomplish this goal, firms must maintain their physical capital. It is also critical that they clearly separate capital from income to evaluate and control their business activities. Accounting measurements based on replacement cost best fit this approach. Accounting developed from microeconomics in the Netherlands. (3) Under the *independent discipline* approach, accounting derives from business practices and develops on an ad hoc, piecemeal basis from judgment and trial-and-error. Accounting is viewed as a service function that derives its concepts and principles from the business process it serves, not from a discipline such as economics. Businesses cope with real-world complexities and ever-present uncertainties through experience, practice, and intuition. Accounting develops the same way. For example, income is simply what seems to be the most useful in practice, and disclosures respond pragmatically to user needs. Accounting developed as an independent discipline in the United Kingdom and the United States. (4) Under the *uniform* approach, accounting is standardized by the central government and employed as a tool for administrative control. Uniformity in measurement, disclosure, and presentation makes it easier for government planners, tax authorities, and even managers to use accounting information to control all types of businesses. In general, the uniform approach is used in

---

[17] Examples are C. W. Nobes, "A Judgmental International Classification of Financial Reporting Practices," *Journal of Business Finance & Accounting* (spring 1983): 1–19; idem, "Towards a General Model of the Reasons for International Differences in Financial Reporting," *Abacus* (September 1998): 162–187.

[18] Examples are R. D. Nair and W. G. Frank, "The Impact of Disclosure and Measurement Practices on International Accounting Classifications," *Accounting Review* (July 1980): 426–450; T. S. Doupnik and S. B. Salter, "External Environment, Culture, and Accounting Practice: A Preliminary Test of a General Model of International Accounting Development," *International Journal of Accounting* 30, No. 3 (1995): 189–207.

[19] The concepts underlying these developmental patterns were first proposed in G. Mueller, *International Accounting* (New York: Macmillan, 1967). This work is the basis for most of the classifications of accounting systems worldwide.

countries with strong governmental involvement in economic planning where accounting is used to measure performance, allocate resources, collect taxes, and control prices, among other things. France, with its national uniform chart of accounts, is the leading exponent of the uniform approach.[20]

Legal Systems: Common Law vs. Code Law Accounting

Accounting can also be classified by a nation's legal system.[21] This view has dominated accounting thinking for the last 25 years or so. (1) Accounting in *common law* countries is characterized as oriented toward "fair presentation," transparency and full disclosure, and a separation between financial and tax accounting. Stock markets dominate as a source of finance, and financial reporting is aimed at the information needs of outside investors. Setting accounting standards tends to be a private sector activity, and the accounting profession plays an important role. Common law accounting is often called "Anglo-Saxon," "British-American," or "micro-based." Common law accounting originated in Britain and was exported to such countries as Australia, Canada, Hong Kong, India, Malaysia, Pakistan, and the United States. (2) Accounting in *code law* countries is characterized as legalistic in orientation, opaque with low disclosure, and an alignment between financial and tax accounting. Banks or governments ("insiders") dominate as a source of finance, and financial reporting is aimed at creditor protection. Setting accounting standards tends to be a public sector activity, with relatively less influence by the accounting profession. Code law accounting is often called "continental," "legalistic," or "macro-uniform." It is found in most of the countries of continental Europe and their former colonies in Africa, Asia, and the Americas.

This characterization of accounting parallels the so-called stockholder and stakeholder models of corporate governance in common and code law countries, respectively. As noted earlier in this chapter, a nation's legal system and its system of finance may be linked in a cause-and-effect way.[22] A common law legal system emphasizes shareholder rights and offers stronger investor protection than a code law system. Laws protect outside investors and are generally well enforced. The outcome is that strong capital markets develop in common law countries and weak ones develop in code law countries. Relative to code law countries, firms in common law countries raise substantial amounts of capital through public offerings to numerous outside

---

[20] European academics like K. Käfer (Switzerland), L. L. Illetschko (Austria), E. Schmalenbach (Germany), and A. ter Vehn (Sweden) are largely identified with generalizing accounting processes from comprehensive charts of accounts.

[21] See, for example, C. W. Nobes, "A Judgmental International Classification of Financial Reporting Practices," *Journal of Business Finance & Accounting* (spring 1983): 1–19; I. Berry, "The Need to Classify Worldwide Accountancy Practices," *Accountancy* (October 1987): 90–91; T. S. Doupnik and S. B. Salter, "An Empirical Test of a Judgmental International Classification of Financial Reporting Practices," *Journal of International Business Studies* 24, No. 1 (1993): 41–60.; R. Ball, S. P. Kothari, and A. Robin, "The Effect of International Institutional Factors on Properties of Accounting Earnings," *Journal of Accounting and Economics* 29, No. 1 (2000): 1–51.

[22] R. La Porta, F. Lopez-de-Silanes, A. Shleifer, and R.W. Vishny, "Legal Determinants of External Finance," *Journal of Finance* (July 1997): 1131–1150; R. La Porta, F. Lopez-de-Silanes, A. Shleifer, and R.W. Vishny, "Law and Finance," *Journal of Political Economy* 106, No. 6 (December 1998): 1113–1155; R. La Porta, F. Lopez-de-Silanes, A. Shleifer, and R. W. Vishny, "Investor Protection and Corporate Governance," *Journal of Financial Economics* 58, Nos. 1–2 (2000): 3–27.

investors. Because investors are at arm's length to the firm, there is a demand for accounting information that accurately reflects the firm's operating performance and financial position. Public disclosure resolves the information asymmetry between the firm and investors.

By contrast, ownership of firms in code law countries tends to be concentrated in the hands of families, other corporations, and large commercial banks. Firms satisfy substantial fractions of their capital needs from the government or through bank borrowing. Debt as a source of finance is relatively more important in code law countries than in common law countries. Conservative accounting measurements provide a cushion to lenders in the event of default. Major lenders and significant equity investors may occupy seats on boards of directors, along with other stakeholders, such as labor and important suppliers and customers. Because information demands are satisfied by private communication, there is less demand for public disclosure. Accounting income is the basis for income taxes owed and often, as well, for dividends and employee bonuses, resulting in pressures for smooth income amounts from year to year.

Practice Systems: Fair Presentation vs. Legal Compliance Accounting

Many accounting distinctions at the national level are becoming blurred. There are several reasons for this. (1) The importance of stock markets as a source of finance is growing around the world. Capital is increasingly global, creating pressure for a world standard of corporate reporting. For many companies, global convergence of financial reporting standards will reduce the costs of complying with different accounting rules and may also reduce their costs of capital. The integration of the world's capital markets is arguably the most important reason why the International Accounting Standards Board has emerged as the focal point for accounting standard setting in Australia, Japan, Europe, Singapore, South Africa, the United States, and elsewhere (see Chapter 8). Stock market development is also a top priority in many countries, especially those emerging from centrally planned to market-oriented economies. Two such countries are the Czech Republic and China, discussed in Chapters 3 and 4, respectively. (2) Dual financial reporting is becoming more common. One set of financial statements complies with local, domestic financial reporting requirements, while the other set uses accounting principles and contains disclosures aimed at international investors. Starting in 2005, all European listed companies were required to adopt International Financial Reporting Standards in their consolidated financial statements.[23] However, some EU code law countries, such as France and Germany, sanctioned a duality whereby individual company financial statements comply with national legal standards and consolidated financial statements comply with IFRS. In other words, it is necessary to distinguish accounting practice at the *national* level from that at the *transnational* level. (3) Some code law countries, in particular Germany and Japan (Chapters 3 and 4, respectively), are shifting responsibility for setting accounting standards from the government to independent professional, private-sector groups. This change makes the standard-setting process more like that in common law countries such as Australia, Canada, the United Kingdom, and the United States, and is

---

[23] Approximately 8,000 companies are affected by this requirement.

seen as a way to more actively influence the agenda of the IASB. These points indicate that another framework besides legal systems is needed to classify accounting worldwide.[24]

We believe that a classification based on *fair presentation* versus *legal compliance* describes accounting in the world today.[25] The distinction between fair presentation and legal compliance has pervasive effects on many accounting issues, such as (1) depreciation, where the expense is determined based on the decline in an asset's usefulness over its economic useful life (fair presentation) or the amount allowed for tax purposes (legal compliance); (2) leases that are in substance a purchase of property are treated as such (fair presentation) or are treated like regular operating leases (legal compliance); and (3) pensions with costs accrued as earned by employees (fair presentation) or expensed on a pay-as-you-go basis (legal compliance). In addition, the issue of deferred income taxes never arises when tax and financial accounting are the same.

Another issue is the use of discretionary reserves to smooth income from one period to the next. Generally, these reserves work the following way. In good years extra expenses are provided for, with the corresponding credit going to a reserve account in shareholders' equity. In lean years reserves are dissolved to boost income. This process irons out year-to-year fluctuations in income. Because this practice jeopardizes a fair presentation, it is less common under fair presentation and more common under legal compliance. Of course, if such manipulations are fully disclosed, investors can undo the effects on income. This may not be the case; reserves often are secret.

Fair presentation and *substance over form* characterize common law accounting described above. It is oriented toward the decision needs of external investors. Financial statements are designed to help investors judge managerial performance and predict future cash flows and profitability. Extensive disclosures provide additional information relevant for these purposes. IFRS are also aimed at fair presentation. IFRS are particularly relevant for companies relying on international capital markets for finance. Fair presentation accounting is found in the United Kingdom, the United States, the Netherlands, and other countries influenced by political and economic ties to them (such as British influence throughout the former British Empire and U.S. influence on

---

[24] The common law vs. code law distinction can be criticized on other grounds. First, there are exceptions. The Netherlands (Chapter 3) and Mexico (Chapter 4) are code law countries with fair presentation accounting. Some observers doubt that legal systems are the sole cause of differences in accounting systems worldwide, but one of several contributing factors, including sources of finance and colonial or cultural influence. They say that there are too many exceptions for causality to run from legal system to accounting system. See, in particular, C. Nobes and A. Roberts, "Towards a Unifying Model of Systems of Law, Corporate Financing, Accounting and Corporate Governance," *Australian Accounting Review* 10, No. 1 (2000): 26–34. Enforcement is another significant point. If laws and accounting standards are not enforced, they exist on paper only. Distinctions based on legal systems are less clear in countries where standards are not enforced. See C. Leuz, D. Nanda, and P. Wysocki, "Investor Protection and Earnings Management: An International Comparison," *Journal of Financial Economics* (September 2003): 505–527.

[25] For completeness, *inflation-adjusted* accounting should also be considered. Accounting in Mexico is fair presentation with general price level accounting added on when inflation is high. (Chapter 4 discusses accounting in Mexico.) Countries also abandon inflation adjustments once inflation is tamed, as happened in Brazil and Israel. Islamic accounting, which has a theological base, is also omitted from this framework. It prohibits recognizing interest on money, and current market values are favored as measures of assets and liabilities. Islamic accounting has not yet evolved to the point where it represents a comprehensive pattern of accounting.

Canada, Mexico, and the Philippines). All listed European companies follow fair presentation accounting in their consolidated statements since they now use IFRS. Further, IFRS are the benchmark for standards now being developed in China and Japan (Chapter 4).

Legal compliance accounting is designed to satisfy government-imposed requirements, such as calculating taxable income or complying with the national government's macroeconomic plan. The income amount may also be the basis for dividends paid to shareholders and bonuses paid to managers and employees. Conservative measurements ensure that prudent amounts are distributed. Smooth patterns in income from year to year mean that tax, dividend, and bonus payouts are more stable. Legal compliance accounting will probably continue to be used in individual-company financial statements in those code law countries where consolidated statements adopt fair presentation reporting. In this way, consolidated statements can inform investors while individual-company accounts satisfy legal requirements.

We believe that the integration of the world's capital markets will be the most significant influence shaping accounting development in the future. This development is the reason behind the trend toward fair presentation accounting, at least for consolidated financial statements. It is also the key driver behind the activities of the International Accounting Standards Board and the European Union's "IFRS 2005" decision, and it is why financial statement analysis is increasingly global in nature.

Discussion Questions

1. The chapter identifies seven economic, socio-historical, and institutional factors believed to influence accounting development. Explain how each one affects accounting practice.

2. How do cultural values influence accounting? Are there parallel influences between the factors identified in Question 1 and the cultural factors identified here?

3. Are national differences in accounting practice better explained by culture or by economic and legal factors? Why?

4. The four approaches to accounting development discussed in the chapter were originally outlined in 1967. Do you think these patterns will persist in the future? Why or why not?

5. Countries that have relatively conservative measurement practices also tend to be secretive in disclosure, while countries that have less conservative measurement practices tend to be transparent in disclosure. Why is this so?

6. What is the purpose of classifying systems of accounting? What is the difference between a judgmental and an empirical classification of accounting?

7. What are the major accounting classifications in the world? What are the distinguishing features of each model?

8. Why does the chapter contend that many accounting distinctions at the national level are becoming blurred? Do you agree? Why or why not?

9. The authors contend that a classification based on fair presentation vs. legal compliance describes accounting in the world today better than one based on common law and code law legal systems. Do you agree? Why or why not?

10. What are the prospects of a convergence or harmonization of national systems of accounting and financial reporting? What factors might be influential in promoting or inhibiting change?

Exercises

1. The chapter identifies seven economic, historical, and/or institutional variables that influence accounting development: sources of finance, legal system, taxation, political and economic ties, inflation, level of economic development, and education level.

   Required:
   a. Consider the case of Taiwan. Describe it on the basis of these seven dimensions. Web sites include the *Encyclopaedia Britannica Online* (www.eb.com) and *The World Factbook* (www.cia.gov/library/publications/the-world-factbook).
   b. Using this description, predict a general profile of financial accounting in Taiwan.
   c. Go to the library and find a reference that describes accounting in Taiwan. Is your prediction accurate? Why or why not?

2. Consider the following countries: (1) Belgium, (2) China, (3) the Czech Republic, (4) Gambia, (5) India, (6) Mexico, (7) Senegal, and (8) Taiwan.

   Required: Where would they be classified based on legal system? Where would they be classified based on accounting practice systems? Justify your answers. (*Hint:* Web sites with information on countries of the world include the *Encyclopaedia Britannica Online* (www.eb.com) and *The World Factbook* (www.cia.gov/ library/publications/the-world-factbook).)

3. Go to the World Federation of Exchanges Web site (www.world-exchanges.org) and obtain the latest annual report. The market statistics section on equity markets has information on the numbers of domestic and foreign companies listed on member stock exchanges.

   Required: Which five stock exchanges have the most foreign listed companies? Which five stock exchanges have the highest proportion of foreign to total listed companies? Discuss possible reasons for this.

4. The European Union (EU)—formerly known as the European Community and, at its start, as the European Common Market—was founded in 1957 and had 15 members at the end of 2003: Austria, Belgium, Denmark, Finland, France, Germany, Greece, Ireland, Italy, Luxembourg, the Netherlands, Portugal, Spain, Sweden, and the United Kingdom. To encourage capital movement and capital formation, the EU has issued various *Directives* designed to harmonize the generally accepted accounting principles of its member countries.

   Required: Which of the factors affecting accounting development are likely to be the most serious obstacles to the EU harmonization effort? What factors indicate that the EU harmonization effort can succeed?

5. Refer to Exercise 4. In May 2004, the EU expanded to incorporate 10 Central and East European nations: Cyprus, the Czech Republic, Estonia, Hungary, Latvia, Lithuania, Malta, Poland, Slovakia, and Slovenia. Bulgaria and Romania joined in January 2007.

   Required: Which factors affecting accounting development are likely to be the most serious obstacles to achieving accounting harmonization with the other 15 member nations?

6. Gray proposed a framework linking culture and accounting. He predicts four accounting values (professionalism, uniformity, conservatism, and secrecy) based on Hofstede's four cultural dimensions (individualism, uncertainty avoidance, power distance, and masculinity). Exhibit 2-2 has Gray's predictions and also notes that individualism and uncertainty avoidance are expected to have the most significant influence on accounting values.

   Required:
   a. Go to Hofstede's Web site (www.geert-hofstede.com/hofstede_dimensions.php) and find the individualism scores for the following 10 countries: China, the Czech Republic, France, Germany, India, Japan, Mexico, the Netherlands, the United Kingdom, and the United States.
   b. Characterize the individualism scores as high, medium, or low.
   c. Based on your characterizations in the preceding item, predict Gray's four accounting values for the 10 countries.

7. Refer to Exercise 6.

    Required:
    a. Go to Hofstede's Web site (www.geert-hofstede.com/hofstede_dimensions. php) and find the uncertainty avoidance scores for the same 10 countries.
    b. Characterize the uncertainty avoidance scores as high, medium, or low.
    c. Based on your characterizations in the preceding items, predict Gray's four accounting values for the 10 countries.
    d. Are these predictions consistent with those in Exercise 6?

8. Many countries permit or require their domestic listed companies to use International Financial Reporting Standards (IFRS) in their consolidated financial statements for investor reporting.

    Required: Consider the following 10 countries: China, the Czech Republic, France, Germany, India, Japan, Mexico, the Netherlands, the United Kingdom, and the United States. For which countries are IFRS (a) not permitted, (b) permitted, (c) required for some, or (d) required for all domestic listed companies? Discuss the possible reasons for the observed patterns. (*Hint:* Refer to the IAS Plus Web site, www.iasplus.com.)

9. Consider the development factors in the following five countries: France, India, Japan, the United States, and the United Kingdom:

Development Factor	France	India	Japan	United Kingdom	United States
Main source of finance	Banks; government	Government; Stock market	Banks	Stock market	Stock market
Legal system	Code law	Common law	Code law	Common law	Common law
Taxation (link to accounting)	Linked	Separate	Linked	Separate	Separate
Political and economic ties	Europe	U.K., U.S., China	U.S., China	U.S., Europe	Canada, Mexico
Inflation	Low	Low	Low	Low	Low
Level of economic development	High	Low	High	High	High
Educational level	High	Low	High	High	High

Required: Based on the information provided in this chapter, prepare a profile of accounting in each of the countries.

10. Think ahead 10 years from now. Prepare a classification of accounting systems that you think will exist then. What factors motivate your classification?

CASES

Case 2-1

Are Classifications of Accounting Outmoded?

Consider the following statements by David Cairns, former secretary-general of the International Accounting Standards Committee.[26]

> When we look at the way that countries or companies account for particular transactions and events, it is increasingly difficult to distinguish in a systematic way so-called Anglo-American accounting from Continental European accounting or American accounting from, say, German accounting.[27]
>
> I am increasingly persuaded ... that the distinction between Anglo-American accounting and Continental European accounting is becoming less and less relevant and more and more confused. In reaching this conclusion, I do not dispute that different economic, social and legal considerations have influenced the development of accounting in different countries. I also do not dispute the fact that there have been, and still are, differences in the means by which different countries determine accounting requirements and the form of the resulting requirements. I do believe, however, that those who continue to favour these classifications are ignoring what is happening in the world and how

companies actually account for transactions and events.

> It is increasingly apparent that the different economic, social and legal considerations which have influenced national accounting do not necessarily result in different accounting and that countries are reaching the same answers irrespective of their different cultural backgrounds (or reaching different answers in spite of the similar cultural backgrounds). In fact, there are now probably far more similarities between American and German accounting than there are between American and British accounting. There are many reasons for this not least the increasing practice of standard setting bodies and other regulators to share ideas and learn from one another. They do this in the IASC, the UN, the OECD, the EU, and such groupings as G4. This cross-fertilization of ideas is not surprising because standard setting bodies in all countries are having to address the same accounting problems.[28]

Required

1. Do you agree with Cairns's assertion that classifications of accounting are simplistic and of little

---

[26] D. Cairns, "The Future Shape of Harmonization: A Reply," *European Accounting Review* 6, No. 2 (1997): 305–348.

[27] Ibid., 306.

[28] Ibid., 316.

relevance in today's world? Are attempts to classify accounting futile and outmoded? Why or why not?

2. Some observers contend that financial reporting is becoming more and more alike among "world-class" companies—the world's largest multinational corporations—and especially those listed on the major stock exchanges, such as London, New York, and Tokyo. What is the relevance of this contention for classifications of accounting, and what are the factors that would cause this to happen?

Case 2-2

Volkswagen Group

The Volkswagen Group adopted International Accounting Standards (IAS, now International Financial Reporting, or IFRS) for its 2001 fiscal year. The following is taken from Volkswagen's 2001 annual report. It discusses major differences between the German Commercial Code (HGB) and IAS as they apply to Volkswagen.

General

In 2001 VOLKSWAGEN AG has for the first time published its consolidated financial statements in accordance with International Accounting Standards (IAS) and the interpretations of the Standing Interpretations Committee (SIC). All mandatory International Accounting Standards applicable to the financial year 2001 were complied with. The previous year's figures are also based on those standards. IAS 12 (revised 2000) and IAS 39, in particular, were already complied with in the year 2000 consolidated financial statements. The financial statements thus give a true and fair view of the net assets, financial position and earning performance of the Volkswagen Group.

The consolidated financial statements were drawn up in Euros. Unless otherwise stated, all amounts are quoted in millions of Euros (million €).

The income statement was produced in accordance with the internationally accepted cost of sales method.

Preparation of the consolidated financial statements in accordance with IAS requires assumptions regarding a number of line items that affect the amounts entered in the consolidated balance sheet and income statement as well as the disclosure of contingent assets and liabilities.

The conditions laid down in Section 292a of the German Commercial Code (HGB) for exemption from the obligation to draw up consolidated financial statements in accordance with German commercial law are met. Assessment of the said conditions is based on German Accounting Standard No. 1 (DSR 1) published by the German Accounting Standards Committee.

In order to ensure equivalence with consolidated financial statements produced in accordance with German commercial law, all disclosures and explanatory notes required by German commercial law beyond the scope of those required by IAS are published.

Transition to International Accounting Standards

The accounting valuation and consolidation methods previously applied in the financial statements of VOLKSWAGEN AG as produced in accordance with the German Commercial Code have been amended in certain cases by the application of IAS.

Amended accounting, valuation and consolidation methods in accordance with the German Commercial Code

- Tangible assets leased under finance leases are capitalized, and the corresponding liability is recognized under liabilities in the balance sheet, provided the risks and rewards of ownership are substantially attributable to the companies of the Volkswagen Group in accordance with IAS 17.
- As a finance lease lessor, leased assets are not capitalized, but the discounted leasing installments are shown as receivables.
- Movable tangible assets are depreciated using the straight-line method instead of the declining balance method; no half-year or multi-shift depreciation is used. Furthermore, useful lives are now based on commercial substance and no longer on tax law. Special depreciation for tax reasons is not permitted with IAS.

- Goodwill from capital consolidation resulting from acquisition of companies since 1995 is capitalized in accordance with IAS 22 and amortized over its respective useful life.
- In accordance with IAS 2, inventories must be valued at full cost. They were formerly capitalized only at direct cost within the Volkswagen Group.
- Provisions are only created where obligations to third parties exist.
- Differences from the translation of financial statements produced in foreign currencies are not recorded in the income statement.
- Medium- and long-term liabilities are entered in the balance sheet including capital take-up costs, applying the effective interest method.

Amended accounting, valuation and consolidation methods that differ from the German Commercial Code

- In accordance with IAS 38, development costs are capitalized as intangible assets provided it is likely that the manufacture of the developed products will be of future economic benefit to the Volkswagen Group.
- Pension provisions are determined according to the Projected Unit Credit Method as set out in IAS 19, taking account of future salary and pension increases.
- Provisions for deferred maintenance may not be created.
- Medium- and long-term provisions are shown at their present value.
- Securities are recorded at their fair value, even if this exceeds cost, with the corresponding effect in the income statement.
- Deferred taxes are determined according to the balance sheet

liability method. For losses carried forward deferred tax assets are recognized, provided it is likely that they will be usable.
- Derivative financial instruments are recognized at their fair value, even if it exceeds cost. Gains and losses arising from the valuation of financial instruments serving to hedge future cash flows are recognized by way of a special reserve in equity. The profit or loss from such contracts is not recorded in the income statement until the corresponding due date. In contrast, gains and losses arising from the valuation of derivative financial instruments used to hedge balance sheet items are recorded in the income statement immediately.
- Treasury shares are offset against capital and reserves.

- Receivables and payables denominated in foreign currencies are valued at the middle rate on the balance sheet date, and not according to the imparity principle.
- Minority interests of shareholders from outside the Group are shown separately from capital and reserves.

The adjustment of the accounting and valuation policies to International Accounting Standards with effect from January 1, 2000 was undertaken in accordance with SIC 8, with no entry in the income statement, as an allocation to or withdrawal from revenue reserves, as if the accounts had always been produced in accordance with IAS.

The reconciliation of the capital and reserves to IAS in shown in the following table:

	million €
Capital and reserves according to the German Commercial Code as at January 1, 2000	**9,811**
Capitalization of development costs	3,982
Amended useful lives and depreciation methods in respect of tangible and intangible assets	3,483
Capitalization of overheads in inventories	653
Different treatments of leasing contracts as lessor	1,962
Differing valuation of financial instruments	897
Effect of deferred taxes	−1,345
Elimination of special items	262
Amended valuation of pension and similar obligations	−633
Amended accounting treatment of provisions	2,022
Classification of minority interests not as part of equity	−197
Other changes	21
Capital and reserves according to IAS as at January 1, 2000	**20,918**

Source: Volkswagen AG Annual Report 2001, pp. 84–86.

Required

1. Based on the information provided in the chapter, describe the basic features of German accounting at the time Volkswagen adopted IAS. What developmental factors cause these features?

2. What differences between the accounting requirements in the HGB and IAS are highlighted in Volkswagen's disclosure? Are the German requirements consistent with your characterizations in requirement 1?

3. What is the relevance of Volkswagen's adoption of IAS to the classifications studied in this chapter?

Comparative Accounting: Europe

In Chapter 2 we learned about the factors that affect the development of a nation's accounting system, including its sources of finance, legal system, taxation, political and economic ties, and inflation. Chapter 2 went on to classify accounting systems according to their common elements and distinctive features.

Chapters 3 and 4 more closely examine accounting in a few selected countries. Specific knowledge of accounting in a country is needed to analyze financial statements from that country. Chapter 3 deals with five European countries. Chapter 4 deals with five countries from the Americas and Asia. Background information for each country is provided in both chapters, along with a discussion of each country's institutional framework for regulating and enforcing accounting. Financial reporting based on local generally accepted accounting principles (GAAP) is also discussed. The global convergence toward International Financial Reporting Standards (IFRS) (Chapter 8), notwithstanding, we believe that analysts need to have knowledge about local GAAP and institutional arrangements. That's because many companies are simply unaffected by the convergence movement. For example, some 8,000 listed European companies must now prepare their consolidated financial statements according to IFRS. But the estimated 3 million nonlisted European companies are not directly affected by the IFRS requirement. Research also shows that the application of IFRS by European companies reflects national norms and conventions.[1] As another example, U.S., Japanese, and Chinese companies must follow their respective national GAAP, not IFRS. Even though financial reporting standards and practices are converging for many companies around the world, differences remain for many others.

Chapter 3 focuses on five members of the European Union (EU): the Czech Republic, France, Germany, the Netherlands, and the United Kingdom. France, Germany, and the Netherlands were original members of the European Economic Community when it was established in 1957. The United Kingdom joined in 1973.

---

[1] Isabel von Keltz and KPMG, *The Application of IFRSs: Choices in Practice* (December 2006), www.kpmg.com.

All four of these countries have highly developed economies and are home to many of the world's largest multinational corporations. They were among the founders of the International Accounting Standards Committee (now the International Accounting Standards Board, or IASB), and they have a major role in directing its agenda. The Czech Republic is an "emerging" economy.[2] Until 1989 a member of the now defunct Soviet bloc, it is converting from a planned to a market economy. Accounting developments there are representative of those in other former Soviet bloc countries. The Czech Republic joined the EU in 2004.

Exhibit 3-1 contains some comparative economic data about the five countries discussed in this chapter. The contrast between the Czech Republic and the other four countries is apparent. Its gross domestic product (both in absolute terms and per capita), imports and exports, and stock market capitalization are significantly smaller than those of the other four countries. It also has more of an industrial and less of a service economy than the other countries.

EXHIBIT 3-1	**Economic Data for Selected Countries**				
	France	Germany	Czech Republic	The Netherlands	United Kingdom
Area: sq. km.(in thousands)	544	358	79	42	243
Population (in millions)	60.7	82.7	10.2	16.4	59.8
Gross Domestic Product (in billions)	$2,248	$2,897	$143	$662	$2,377
GDP per Capita	$37,040	$35,030	$14,020	$40,380	$39,750
GDP by Sector					
Agriculture	2%	1%	3%	2%	1%
Industry	20%	30%	38%	24%	23%
Services	78%	69%	59%	74%	76%
Imports (in billions)	$535	$922	$93	$359	$591
Exports (in billions)	$483	$1,122	$95	$401	$448
Market Capitalization (in billions), end 2007	$2,771	$2,106	$73	$956	$3,859
Major Trading Partners	Germany, Spain, Italy	France, U.S.A., U.K.	Germany, Slovakia, Russia	Germany, Belgium, U.K.	U.S.A., Germany, France

Source: Compiled from *Pocket World in Figures, 2009 Edition* (London: The Economist, 2008) and *The World Factbook,* www.cia.gov/library/publications/the-world-factbook/, May 2009.

---

[2] The term emerging economy refers loosely to newly industrialized countries (NICs) and countries in transition from planned to free-market economies. NICs have experienced rapid industrial growth, but their economies are not yet rich in terms of per capita gross domestic product. India, discussed in Chapter 4, is a NIC. The Czech Republic has an economy in transition.

SOME OBSERVATIONS ABOUT ACCOUNTING STANDARDS AND PRACTICE

Accounting standards are the regulations or rules (often including laws and statutes) that govern the preparation of financial statements. *Standard setting* is the process by which accounting standards are formulated. Thus, accounting standards are the outcome of standard setting. However, actual practice may deviate from what the standards require. There are at least three reasons for this. First, in many countries the penalties for noncompliance with official accounting pronouncements are weak or ineffective. Companies don't always follow standards when they are not enforced. Second, companies may voluntarily report more information than required. Third, some countries allow companies to depart from accounting standards if doing so will better represent a company's results of operations and financial position. To gain a complete picture of how accounting works in a country, we must pay attention to the accounting standard-setting process, the resulting accounting standards, and actual practice. *Auditing* adds credibility to financial reports. Thus, we also discuss the role and purpose of auditing in the countries we examine.

Accounting standard setting normally involves a combination of private- and public-sector groups. The private sector includes the accounting profession and other groups affected by the financial reporting process, such as users and preparers of financial statements and employees. The public sector includes such agencies as tax authorities, government agencies responsible for commercial law, and securities commissions. Stock exchanges may influence the process and may be in either the private or public sector, depending on the country. The roles and influence of these groups in setting accounting standards differ from country to country. These differences help explain why standards vary around the world.

The relationship between accounting standards and accounting practice is complex, and does not always move in a one-way direction. In some cases, practice derives from standards; in others, standards are derived from practice. Practice can be influenced by market forces, such as those related to the competition for funds in capital markets. Companies competing for funds may voluntarily provide information beyond what is required in response to the demand for information by investors and others. If the demand for such information is strong enough, standards may be changed to mandate disclosures that formerly were voluntary.

Chapter 2 distinguished the fair presentation and legal compliance orientations of accounting. Fair presentation accounting is usually associated with common law countries, whereas legal compliance accounting is typically found in code law countries. This distinction applies in standard setting, in that the private sector is relatively more influential in fair presentation, common law countries, while the public sector is relatively more influential in legal compliance, code law countries. Auditing parallels the type of legal system and the role and purpose of financial reporting. The auditing profession tends to be more self-regulated in fair presentation countries, especially those influenced by the United Kingdom. Auditors also exercise more judgment when the purpose of an audit is to attest to the fair presentation of financial reports. By contrast, in code law countries the accounting profession tends to be more state regulated. In such countries, the main purpose of an audit is to ensure that the company's records and financial statements conform to legal requirements.

IFRS IN THE EUROPEAN UNION

The trend in financial reporting is toward fair presentation, at least for consolidated financial statements. This trend is particularly true in the European Union. In 2002, the EU approved an accounting regulation requiring all EU companies listed on a regulated market to follow IFRS in their consolidated financial statements, starting in 2005. Member states are free to extend this requirement to all companies, not just listed ones, including individual company financial statements. Exhibit 3-2 summarizes the EU requirements for using IFRS in the five countries surveyed in this chapter. Convergence in financial reporting can be expected where IFRS are required, but differences remain where they are not.

To understand accounting in Europe, one must understand both IFRS and local accounting requirements. Many companies will choose to follow local requirements in instances where IFRS are permitted. For example, they may view IFRS as not relevant for their needs or too complicated. Thus, we provide an overview of IFRS in this section. The rest of the chapter looks at accounting in the five countries surveyed.

FINANCIAL REPORTING   IFRS financial statements consist of the consolidated statement of financial position, statement of comprehensive income, cash flow statement, a statement of changes in equity, and explanatory notes. Note disclosures must include:

- Accounting policies followed
- Judgments made by management in applying critical accounting policies
- Key assumptions about the future and other important sources of estimation uncertainty

EXHIBIT 3-2	**IFRS Requirements**				
	Czech Republic	**France**	**Germany**	**The Netherlands**	**United Kingdom**
Listed companies—consolidated financial statements	Required	Required	Required	Required	Required
Listed companies—individual company financial statements	Required	Prohibited[a]	Permitted, but for informational purposes only[a]	Permitted	Permitted
Nonlisted companies—consolidated financial statements	Permitted	Permitted	Permitted	Permitted	Permitted
Nonlisted companies—individual company financial statements	Prohibited[b]	Prohibited[a]	Permitted, but for informational purposes only[a]	Permitted	Permitted

[a]*French and German individual company financial statements must be prepared using local accounting requirements because these statements are the basis for taxes and dividends.*

[b]*IFRS are not allowed in individual company financial statements of Czech nonlisted companies because it is thought that IFRS would be too complex and costly for these small, privately owned firms.*

Comparative information is only required for the preceding period. There is no IFRS requirement to present the parent entity's financial statements in addition to the consolidated financial statements. There are also no IFRS requirements to produce interim financial statements. Consolidation is based on control, which is the power to govern the financial and operating activities of another entity.[3] Generally, all subsidiaries must be consolidated even if control is temporary or the subsidiary operates under severe long-term funds-transfer restrictions. Fair presentation is required. IFRS may be overridden in extremely rare circumstances to achieve a fair presentation. When they are, the nature, reason, and financial impact of the departure from IFRS must be disclosed.

ACCOUNTING MEASUREMENTS   Under IFRS, all business combinations are treated as purchases. Goodwill is the difference between the fair value of the consideration given and the fair value of the subsidiary's assets, liabilities, and contingent liabilities. Goodwill is tested annually for impairment. Negative goodwill should be immediately recognized in income. Jointly controlled entities may be accounted for either by proportional consolidation (preferred) or the equity method. Investments in associates are accounted for by the equity method. An associate is an entity in which the investor has significant influence, but which is neither a subsidiary nor a joint venture. Significant influence is the power to participate in the financial and operating policy decisions of the investee but not to control those policies. It is presumed to exist when the investor holds at least 20 percent of the investee's voting power and not to exist when less than 20 percent is held; these presumptions may be rebutted if there is clear evidence to the contrary.

Translation of the financial statements of foreign operations is based on the functional currency concept. The functional currency is the currency of the primary economic environment in which the foreign entity operates. It can be either the same currency that the parent uses to present its financial statements or a different, foreign currency. (a) If the foreign entity has a functional currency different from the reporting currency of the parent, the financial statements are translated using the current rate method with the resulting translation adjustment included in stockholders' equity. (Under the current rate method, assets and liabilities are translated at the year-end, or current, exchange rate; revenues and expenses are translated at the transaction rates [or, in practice, the average rate].) (b) If the foreign entity has the same functional currency as the reporting currency of the parent, financial statements are translated as follows:

- Year-end rate for monetary items
- Transaction-date exchange rates for nonmonetary items carried at historical cost
- Valuation-date exchange rates for nonmonetary items carried at fair value

Translation adjustments are included in current period income. (c) If a foreign entity has the functional currency of a hyperinflationary economy, its financial statements are first restated for the effects of inflation, then translated using the current rate method described above.

Assets are valued at either historical cost or fair value. If the fair value method is used, revaluations must be carried out regularly and all items of a given class must be

---

[3] The IASB is proposing a new definition of control: when the reporting entity has the power to direct the activities of another entity to generate returns for the reporting entity.

revalued. Revaluation increases are credited to equity. Depreciation is charged system-atically over the asset's useful life, reflecting the pattern of benefit consumption. Research costs are charged to expense when incurred. Development costs are capital-ized after the technical and commercial feasibility of the resulting product or service has been established. Inventories are valued at the lower of cost or net realizable value. FIFO and weighted average are acceptable cost bases under IFRS, but LIFO is not.

Finance leases are capitalized and amortized, while operating leases are expensed on a systematic basis, usually expensing the lease payments on a straight-line basis.[4] The cost of providing employee benefits is recognized in the period in which the bene-fit is earned by the employee rather than when it is paid or payable. Provisions are liabilities of uncertain timing or amount. They are recognized when a past event has created a legal or constructive obligation, an outflow of resources is probable, and the amount of the obligation can be estimated reliably. Contingent liabilities are a possible obligation, an obligation that will probably not require an outflow of resources, or an obligation that cannot be reliably estimated. They are not recognized as liabilities, but are instead disclosed in the notes.[5] Contingent assets are also not recognized. Deferred taxes are provided in full, using the liability method, for temporary differences between the carrying amount of an asset or liability and its tax base. Deferred tax assets and liabilities should be measured at the tax rates that are expected to apply when the asset is realized or the liability is settled. They are not discounted.

FIVE NATIONAL FINANCIAL ACCOUNTING SYSTEMS[6]

France

France is the world's leading advocate of national uniform accounting. The Ministry of National Economy approved the first formal Plan Comptable Général (national accounting code) in September 1947. A revised plan came into effect in 1957. A further revision of the plan was enacted in 1982 under the influence of the Fourth Directive of the European Union (EU). In 1986 the plan was extended to implement the require-ments of the EU's Seventh Directive on consolidated financial statements, and it was further revised in 1999.

The Plan Comptable Général provides:

- objectives and principles of financial accounting and reporting
- definitions of assets, liabilities, shareholders' equity, revenues, and expenses
- recognition and valuation rules

---

[4] The IASB is proposing that all material leases be capitalized, discontinuing the distinction between financing and operating leases.

[5] The IASB is currently deliberating the definitions of the elements of the financial statements in its joint Conceptual Framework project with the U.S. Financial Accounting Standards Board (see Chapter 8). The term "contingent liability" will probably no longer be used. Instead, liabilities will be assessed in terms of whether they are "conditional or unconditional obligations." See *Conceptual Framework – Phase B: Elements and Recognition* at the IASB Web site, www.iasb.org.

[6] The discussion in this section draws on the references cited in this chapter and on references cited in earlier editions of this book. The Big Four accounting firms and the IAS Plus Web site (www.iasplus.com) periodically update details of accounting in individual countries. For example, the discussion of accounting in the Netherlands later in this chapter is based in part on Deloitte, *IFRSs and NL GAAP: A Pocket Comparison* (April 2008), www.iasplus.com/dttpubs/0805ifrsnlgaap.pdf.

- a standardized chart of accounts, requirements for its use, and other bookkeeping requirements
- model financial statements and rules for their presentation

The mandatory use of the national uniform chart of accounts does not burden French businesses because the plan is widely accepted in practice. Moreover, various schedules required for income tax returns are based on the standardized models of the income statement and balance sheet, and the state statistical office produces macroeconomic information by aggregating the financial statements of enterprises.

French accounting is so closely linked to the plan that it is possible to overlook the fact that commercial legislation (i.e., the Code de Commerce) and tax laws dictate many of France's actual financial accounting and reporting practices. Both of these predate the plan. The Code de Commerce has its roots in the 1673 and 1681 ordinances of Colbert (finance minister to Louis XIV) and was enacted by Napoleon in 1807 as a part of the legal system he created, based on written law. The first income tax law was passed in 1914, thereby linking taxation and the need to keep accounting records.

The main bases for accounting regulation in France are the 1983 Accounting Law and 1983 Accounting Decree, which made the Plan Comptable Général compulsory for all companies. Both texts are inserted in the Code de Commerce.[7] Commercial legislation in the Code de Commerce has extensive accounting and reporting provisions. Annual inventories of assets and liabilities are required. The true and fair view for financial reporting must be evidenced, and certain accounting records are granted a privileged role in specified judicial proceedings. Accounting records, which legally serve purposes of proof and verification, are increasingly considered sources of information for decision-making.

Each enterprise must establish an accounting manual if it believes that this is necessary to understand and control the accounting process. At a minimum, the manual includes a detailed flow chart and explanations of the entire accounting system, descriptions of all data-processing procedures and controls, a comprehensive statement of the accounting principles underlying annual financial statements, and the procedures used in the mandatory annual counting of inventory.

Tax laws also significantly influence accounting in France. Business expenses are deductible for tax purposes only if they are fully booked and reflected in annual financial statements.

ACCOUNTING REGULATION AND ENFORCEMENT   Five major organizations are involved in setting standards in France:[8]

1. Counseil National de la Comptabilité, or CNC (National Accounting Board)
2. Comité de la Réglementation Comptable, or CRC (Accounting Regulation Committee)

---

[7] The legal framework for accounting includes laws passed by Parliament, government decrees dealing with the application of these laws, and ministerial orders by the Ministry of Economy and Finance.
[8] The Web site addresses are CNC and CRC: www.minefi.gouv.fr/directions_services/CNCompta; AMF: www.amf-france.org; OEC: www.experts-comptables.com; and CNCC: www.cncc.fr.

3. Autorité des Marches Financiers, or AMF (Financial Markets Authority)[9]
4. Ordre des Experts-Comptables, or OEC (Institute of Public Accountants)
5. Compagnie Nationale des Commissaires aux Comptes, or CNCC (National Institute of Statutory Auditors)

The CNC consists of 58 members representing the accounting profession, civil servants, and employer, trade union, and other private-sector groups. Attached to the Ministry of Economy and Finance, the CNC issues rulings and recommendations on accounting issues and has major responsibility for keeping the plan current. It is consulted on accounting matters requiring regulation, but has no regulatory or enforcement powers. In 2007, a 16-member Collège was formed to debate accounting issues before the CNC and make recommendations on their resolution. The establishment of the Collège is an interim step to further reforms of the standard-setting process, as discussed later.

Due to a need for a flexible and expeditious means of providing regulatory authority for accounting standards, the CRC was established in 1998. The CRC converts CNC rulings and recommendations into binding regulations. Under the jurisdiction of the Ministry of Economy and Finance, it has 15 members, among them representatives of different ministries, the CNC, AMF, OEC, and CNCC, and judges from the two highest courts in France. CRC regulations are published in the *Official Journal of the French Republic* after ministerial approval. Thus, the CRC has real regulatory power.

The French standard-setting system is undergoing a reform that will eventually replace the CNC and CRC with a new standard-setting body, the Autorité des Normes Comptables, or ANC (National Accounting Authority). Like the CNC and CRC, the ANC will be a state agency. It will be charged with issuing national accounting rules required for individual-company accounts. (Unlisted companies may use them in their consolidated financial statements, but they will also have the option of using IFRS.)

French companies traditionally have relied less on capital markets than on other sources of finance.[10] The French equivalent of the U.S. Securities and Exchange Commission—the AMF—has important but limited influence on accounting standard setting. The AMF supervises the new-issues market and the operations of regional and national stock exchanges. It has authority to issue additional reporting and disclosure rules for listed companies. The president of France appoints the chair of the AMF, and the commission reports annually to the president. This arrangement provides independence from other government departments.[11] The AMF is responsible for enforcing compliance with reporting requirements by French listed firms. Two divisions verify compliance. The Division of Corporate Finance (SOIF) conducts a general review of the legal, economic, and financial aspects of documents filed with the AMF (including annual reports). The Accounting Division (SACF) verifies compliance with accounting

---

[9] The AMF was established in 2003 from the merger of the Commission des Operations de Bourse (COB), the Conseil des Marchés Financiers, and the Conseil de Discipline de la Gestion Financière. The COB was the previous organization with authority over the stock exchanges.

[10] France has a tradition of family businesses and nationalized industries, both of which rely on debt financing.

[11] A predecessor body to the AMF, the Commission des Opérations de Bourse (COB), was an early advocate of consolidation requirements for French companies and, in general, sought French acceptance of world-class accounting and reporting standards—at least for larger publicly listed French companies. The COB pressed for better accounting and disclosure, and successfully improved the quality of information in French consolidated financial statements.

standards. The AMF has broad powers to require companies to modify questionable items in their filings. If necessary, the AMF can take administrative action against a company to force compliance.[12]

In France the accounting and auditing professions have historically been separate. French accountants and auditors are represented by two bodies, the OEC and the CNCC, despite substantial overlap in their memberships. Indeed, 80 percent of France's qualified accountants hold both qualifications. The two professional bodies maintain close links and cooperate on issues of common interest. Both participate in the development of accounting standards through the CNC and CRC, and they represent France on the IASB.

The practice of public accounting and the right to the title *expert-comptable* is restricted to OEC members, who contract with clients to maintain and review accounting records and prepare financial statements. They may also provide tax, information systems, and management advisory services. The OEC is under the jurisdiction of the Ministry of Economy and Finance. Most of its effort is devoted to professional-practice issues, although before the CRC was established it issued interpretations and recommendations on the application of accounting legislation and regulations.

By contrast, the CNCC (professional association of statutory auditors, *commissaires aux comptes*) is under the jurisdiction of the Ministry of Justice. By law, only statutory auditors may audit and give an opinion on financial statements.[13] The CNCC publishes a member handbook that contains extensive professional standards. It also publishes information bulletins that provide technical assistance. Audits in France are generally similar to their counterparts elsewhere. However, French auditors must report to the state prosecutor any criminal acts that they become aware of during an audit. The Haut Conseil du Commissariat aux Comptes (High Council of External Auditors) was established in 2003 to monitor the audit profession, particularly in the areas of ethics and independence. Like the CNCC, it is under the Ministry of Justice. The 2003 law also requires an auditor's report on internal controls.[14]

The AMF is responsible for overseeing the audits of listed companies. However, the AMF relies on a committee of the CNCC (the Comité de l'Examen National des Activités, or CENA) to conduct audit-quality reviews on its behalf. By arrangement with the AMF, CENA examines the audit of each listed company at least once every six years.[15] Follow-up examinations are also done in cases where the auditor's work is found to be deficient.

FINANCIAL REPORTING   French companies must report the following:

1. Balance sheet
2. Income statement
3. Notes to financial statements
4. Directors' report
5. Auditor's report

---

[12] For further information, see T.H.P Dao, "Monitoring Compliance with IFRS: Some Insights from the French Regulatory System," *Accounting in Europe* 2 (2005): 107–135.

[13] The same person can practice both accounting and auditing. However, independence rules prohibit the statutory auditor from also providing accounting services to the same client firm.

[14] The heightened oversight of the auditing profession and the new report on internal controls are in part a response to the same accounting scandals that gave rise to the Sarbanes-Oxley Act in the United States (Chapter 4).

[15] The normal period for an audit contract of a listed company in France is six years.

The financial statements of all corporations and other limited liability companies above a certain size must be audited. Large companies must also prepare documents relating to the prevention of business bankruptcies and a social report, both of which are unique to France. There are no requirements for a statement of changes in financial position or a cash flow statement. However, the CNC recommends a cash flow statement, and nearly all large French companies publish one. Individual company and consolidated statements are both required, but small groups are exempt from the consolidation requirement. The Code de Commerce allows simplified financial statements for small and medium-sized companies.

To give a true and fair view (*image fidèle*), financial statements must be prepared in compliance with legislation (*régularité*) and in good faith (*sincérité*). A significant feature of French reporting is the requirement for extensive and detailed footnote disclosures, including the following items:

- Explanation of measurement rules employed (i.e., accounting policies)
- Accounting treatment of foreign currency items
- Statement of changes in fixed assets and depreciation
- Details of provisions
- Details of any revaluations
- Breakdown of receivables and liabilities by maturity
- List of subsidiaries and share holdings
- Amount of commitments for pensions and other retirement benefits
- Details of the impact of taxes on the financial statements
- Average number of employees listed by category
- Analysis of turnover by activity and geographically

The directors' report includes a review of the company's activities during the year, the company's future prospects, important post–balance sheet events, research and development activities, and a summary of the company's results for the past five years. The financial statements of commercial companies must be audited, except for small, limited liability companies and partnerships.

Listed companies must provide half-yearly interim reports and the results of their environmental activities. Among other items, information must be given on:

- Water, raw material, and energy consumption, and actions taken to improve energy efficiency
- Activities to reduce pollution in the air, water, or ground, including noise pollution, and their costs
- Amount of provisions for environmental risks

French law also contains provisions aimed at preventing bankruptcies (or mitigating their consequences). The idea is that companies that have a good understanding of their internal financial affairs and prepare sound projections can better avoid financial difficulties. Accordingly, larger companies prepare four documents: a statement of cash position, a statement of changes in financial position or cash flow statement, a forecast income statement, and a business plan. These documents are not audited, but are given a limited examination by the auditors. They are submitted only to the board of directors and employee representatives; they are not made available to the shareholders or the general public unless provided voluntarily (such as the cash flow statement). Thus, this information is designed as an internal early-warning signal for management and workers.

A social report also is required for all companies with 300 or more employees. This report describes, analyzes, and reports on matters of training, industrial relations, health and safety conditions, wage levels and other employment benefits, and many additional relevant work-environment conditions. The report is required for individual companies, not consolidated groups.

ACCOUNTING MEASUREMENTS   Listed French companies follow IFRS in their consolidated financial statements, and nonlisted companies also have this option. However, all French companies must follow the fixed regulations of the plan at the individual company level. Accounting for individual companies is the legal basis for distributing dividends and for calculating taxable income. Exhibit 3-3 provides an example of financial reporting by French listed firms. Saint-Gobain, a materials and construction products company listed in Paris and on other European stock exchanges, explains its accounting policies for its consolidated and nonconsolidated financial statements.

Tangible assets are normally valued at historical cost. Although revaluations are allowed, they are taxable and, therefore, are seldom found in practice. Fixed assets are depreciated according to tax provisions, normally on a straight-line or declining balance basis. Extra tax depreciation is sometimes available, in which case the additional amount taken is shown as an exceptional charge on the income statement and the corresponding credit as a tax-related provision in equity. Inventory must be valued at the lower of cost or realizable value using either First in, First Out (FIFO) or weighted-average methods.

Research and development costs are expensed as incurred, but may be capitalized in restricted circumstances. If capitalized, research and development costs must be amortized over no more than five years. Leased assets are not capitalized, and the rent paid is expensed. Pension and other retirement benefits are normally expensed when paid, and future commitments are seldom recognized as liabilities. Probable losses whose amounts can be determined with reasonable accuracy are accrued. Many other risks and uncertainties may be provided for, such as those relating to litigation, restructurings, and self-insurance; these allow income-smoothing opportunities. Given the link between book and tax income, companies do not account for deferred taxes in individual company financial statements. Legal reserves must be created by appropriating 5 percent of income each year until the reserve equals 10 percent of legal capital.

EXHIBIT 3-3   **Saint-Gobain Accounting Policies**

Note to consolidated financial statements
These consolidated financial statements of Compagnie de Saint-Gobain and its subsidiaries ("the Group") have been prepared in accordance with International Financial Reporting Standards (IFRS), as adopted by the European Union at December 31, 2008.

Note to parent company financial statements
The financial statements of Compagnie de Saint-Gobain have been drawn up in accordance with the accounting principles set out in the 1999 French Chart of Accounts.

Source: 2008 Saint-Gobain Annual Report, pp. 192 and 271.

With a few exceptions, French rules regarding consolidated financial statements follow the fair presentation approach of reporting substance over form. Two exceptions are that liabilities for post-employment benefits do not have to be recognized and finance leases do not have to be capitalized. (In both cases, the fair presentation treatment of accrual and capitalization is recommended, but still optional.) Deferred taxes are accounted for using the liability method, and are discounted when the reversal of timing differences can be reliably estimated. The purchase method is normally used to account for business combinations, but the pooling method is allowed in some circumstances. Goodwill normally is capitalized and amortized to income, but no maximum amortization period is specified. Goodwill is not required to be impairments tested. Proportional consolidation is used for joint ventures and the equity method is used to account for investments in nonconsolidated entities over which significant influence is exercised. Foreign currency translation practice is consistent with IFRS, as previously described.

Germany

The German accounting environment has changed continuously and remarkably since the end of World War II. At that time, business accounting emphasized national and sectional charts of account (as in France). The Commercial Code stipulated various principles of "orderly bookkeeping," and independent auditing barely survived the war.

In a major turn of events, the 1965 Corporation Law moved the German financial reporting system toward British-American ideas (but only for larger corporations). More disclosure, limited consolidation,[16] and a corporate management report were required. The management report and additional audit requirements became legal requirements through the 1969 Corporate Publicity Law.

In the early 1970s the European Union (EU) began issuing its harmonization directives, which member countries were required to incorporate into their national laws. The Fourth, Seventh, and Eighth EU Directives all entered German law through the Comprehensive Accounting Act of December 19, 1985. This legislation is remarkable because (1) it integrates all existing German accounting, financial reporting, disclosure, and auditing requirements into a single law; (2) this single law is specified as the *third book* of the German Commercial Code (HGB), thus becoming applicable to all business entities, from limited partnerships to private and publicly held corporations; and (3) the legislation is based predominantly on European concepts and practices. The 1985 act was significantly updated in 2009 with the passage of the German Accounting Law Modernization Act.

Two laws were passed in 1998. The first added a new paragraph in the third book of the German Commercial Code allowing companies that issue equity or debt on organized capital markets to use internationally accepted accounting principles in their consolidated financial statements. The second allowed the establishment of a private-sector organization to set accounting standards for consolidated financial statements.

Creditor protection is a fundamental concern of German accounting as embodied in the Commercial Code. Conservative balance sheet valuations are central to creditor protection. This creates a tendency to undervalue assets and overvalue liabilities. Reserves are seen as protection against unforeseen risks and possible insolvency. These practices also result in a conservative income amount that serves as the basis for

---

[16] For example, the law only required consolidation of German subsidiaries.

dividends to owners. Thus, German accounting is designed to compute a prudent income amount that leaves creditors unharmed after distributions are made to owners.

Tax law also influences commercial accounting. Available tax provisions can be used only if they are fully booked, meaning that there is no distinction between financial statements prepared for tax purposes and those published in financial reports. The concept of "tax determines financial accounting" once characterized German accounting. However, German accounting requirements in the HGB are gradually being aligned with international accounting standards.

The third fundamental characteristic of German accounting is its reliance on statutes and court decisions. Nothing else has any binding or authoritative status. To understand German accounting, one must look to both HGB and a considerable body of case law.

ACCOUNTING REGULATION AND ENFORCEMENT Before 1998, Germany had no financial accounting standard-setting function, as it is understood in English-speaking countries. The German Institute provided consultation in various processes of lawmaking that affected accounting and financial reporting, but legal requirements were absolutely supreme. Similar consultation was given by the Frankfurt Stock Exchange, German trade unions, and accounting academics. The 1998 law on control and transparency (abbreviated KonTraG) introduced the requirements for the Ministry of Justice to recognize a private national standard-setting body to serve the following objectives:

- Develop recommendations for the application of accounting standards for consolidated financial statements.
- Advise the Ministry of Justice on new accounting legislation.
- Represent Germany in international accounting organizations such as the IASB.

The German Accounting Standards Committee (GASC), or in German, the *Deutsches Rechnungslegungs* Standards Committee (DRSC), was founded shortly thereafter, and duly recognized by the Ministry of Justice as the German standard-setting authority.[17]

The GASC oversees the German Accounting Standards Board (GASB), which does the technical work and issues the accounting standards. The GASB is made up of seven independent experts with a background in auditing, financial analysis, academia, and industry. Working groups are established to examine and make recommendations on the issues before the board. As a rule, these working groups have representatives from trade and industry and the auditing profession, a university professor, and a financial analyst. GASB deliberations follow a due process and meetings are open. Once issued, the standards must be approved and published by the Ministry of Justice.

The new German accounting standard-setting system is broadly similar to the systems in the United Kingdom (as discussed in this chapter) and the United States (Chapter 4), and to the IASB (Chapter 8). It is important to emphasize, however, that GASB standards are authoritative recommendations that only apply to consolidated financial statements. They do not restrict or alter HGB requirements. The GASB was created to develop a set of German standards compatible with international accounting standards. Since its founding, the GASB has issued German Accounting Standards (GAS) on such issues as the cash flow statement, segment reporting, deferred taxes, and foreign currency translation. However, in 2003, the GASB adopted a new strategy that aligned its work

---

[17] The GASC Web site is www.drsc.de.

program with the IASB's efforts to achieve a convergence of global accounting standards. These changes recognized the EU requirement for IFRS for listed companies.

The Financial Accounting Control Act (abbreviated BilKoG) was enacted in 2004 to improve compliance with German financial reporting requirements and IFRS by listed companies. The law established a two-tiered enforcement system. A private-sector body, the Financial Reporting Enforcement Panel (FREP), reviews suspected irregular financial statements that come to its attention. It also conducts random reviews of financial statements. The FREP relies on companies to voluntarily correct any problems it finds. The FREP refers matters that are not resolved to the Federal Financial Supervisory Authority (German abbreviation BaFin), the public-sector regulatory body that oversees securities trading (stock exchanges) and the banking and insurance industries. BaFin will then take authoritative action to resolve the issue. BaFin refers questionable auditing to the *Wirtschaftsprüferkammer*, discussed next.

Certified public accountants in Germany are called *Wirtschaftsprüfer* (WPs), or enterprise examiners.[18] All WPs are legally required to join the official Chamber of Accountants (*Institut der Wirtschaftsprüferkammer*). The Auditor Oversight Commission, which reports to the Ministry of Economics and Labor, is responsible for overseeing the Chamber of Accountants. By international standards, the German auditing (accounting) profession is small. The 1985 Accounting Act extended the audit requirement to many more companies. As a result, a second-tier body of auditors was created in the late 1980s. These individuals, known as sworn book examiners (*Vereidigte Buchprüfer*), are only allowed to audit small and medium-sized companies, as defined in the act. Thus, two classes of auditors are legally sanctioned to conduct independent audit examinations of companies. German audit reports emphasize compliance with requirements over the "true and fair view." Exhibit 3-4, the opinion paragraph of KPMG on the 2008 financial statements of the BMW automobile company, is illustrative.

FINANCIAL REPORTING   German law specifies different accounting, auditing, and financial reporting requirements depending on company size rather than the form of business organization.[19] There are three size classes—small, medium, and large—defined in terms of balance sheet totals, annual sales totals, and numbers of employees. Companies with publicly traded securities are always classified as large. The law specifies the content and format of financial statements, which include the following:

1. Balance sheet
2. Income statement
3. Notes
4. Management report
5. Auditor's report

---

[18] The Institut der Wirtschaftsprüfer's Web site is www.wpk.de.

[19] The three major forms of business organizations in Germany are (1) *Aktiengesellschaft* (AG), (2) *Kommanditgesellschaft auf Aktien* (KGaA), and (3) *Gesellschaft mit beschränkter Haftung* (GmbH).

AGs are typically large corporations with two senior boards: a management board and a supervisory board. The supervisory board appoints and dismisses members of the management board, supervises the management board, and reviews and approves annual financial statements. The KGaA is a mixture of the limited partnership and the corporate form of business organization. It must have at least one shareholder who is personally liable for the company's indebtedness (the remaining shareholders are liable only to the extent of their investments in the company). KGaAs are unknown in English-speaking countries. GmbHs are privately held companies. Most medium and small businesses operate in this form.

EXHIBIT 3-4 **Audit Opinion on BMW Group Financial Statements**

In our opinion, based on the findings of our audit, the consolidated financial statements comply with IFRS, as adopted by the EU, the additional requirements of German Commercial Law pursuant to §315a (1) HGB and give a true and fair view of the net assets, financial position, and results of operations of the Group. The Group Management Report is consistent with the consolidated financial statements and as a whole provides a suitable view of the Group's position and suitably presents the opportunities and risks of future development.

Munich, 27 February 2009
KPMG AG

Source: 2008 BMW Annual Report, p. 133.

Small companies are exempt from the audit requirement and may prepare an abbreviated balance sheet. Small and medium-sized companies may prepare abbreviated income statements. These companies also have fewer disclosure requirements for their notes. A cash flow statement and a statement of changes in owners' equity are required for consolidated financial statements but not individual company statements.

The notes section of the financial statements is usually extensive, especially for large companies. Disclosures include the accounting principles used, the extent to which results are affected by claiming tax benefits, unaccrued pension obligations, sales by product line and geographic markets, unaccrued contingent liabilities, and average number of employees. The management report describes the financial position and business developments during the year, important post-balance sheet events, anticipated future developments, and research and development activities. Publicly traded companies are required to provide additional segment disclosures. They must also provide abbreviated half-yearly financial statements that are reviewed by an auditor and accompanied by an interim management report.

A feature of the German financial reporting system is a private report by the auditors to the company's managing board of directors and supervisory board. This report comments on the company's future prospects and, especially, factors that may threaten its survival. The auditor must describe and analyze items on the balance sheet that have a material impact on the company's financial position. The auditor also has to evaluate the consequences of and pass judgment on all significant accounting choices. This report can run several hundred pages for large German companies. As noted, it is private information, not available to shareholders.

Consolidated financial statements are required for enterprises under unified management and with a majority of voting rights, dominant influence by virtue of control contracts, or the right to appoint or remove a majority of the board of directors. For purposes of consolidation, all companies in the group must use identical accounting and valuation principles. However, they need not be the same as those used in individual company statements. In this way, tax-driven accounting methods in individual accounts can be eliminated in the group accounts. Consolidated accounts are not the basis for either taxation or profit distributions.

All companies, not just listed ones, may use IFRS in preparing their consolidated financial statements. However, individual company financial statements must follow

HGB requirements. Companies also have the option of publishing individual company financial statements according to IFRS for informational purposes.

ACCOUNTING MEASUREMENTS   Under the Commercial Code (HGB), the purchase (acquisition) method is used for business combinations. Until 2009, two forms of the purchase method were permitted: the book-value method and the revaluation method (they essentially differed in the treatment of minority interests).[20] Now, the revaluation method must be used whereby assets and liabilities of acquired enterprises are brought up to current value, and any amount left over is goodwill. Goodwill must be amortized over its useful life, normally five years or less. The equity method is used for associates that are owned 20 percent or more, but only in consolidated financial statements. Joint ventures may be accounted for using either proportional consolidation or the equity method. The modified closing rate method is used for foreign currency translation (see Chapter 8).

GAS are somewhat different than the HGB regarding consolidated financial statements. Under GAS 4, the revaluation method must be used, whereby assets and liabilities acquired in a business combination are revalued to fair value, and any excess allocated to goodwill. Goodwill is tested annually for impairment. GAS 14 adopts the functional currency approach to foreign currency translation, in line with IFRS, as previously described.

Historical cost is the basis for valuing tangible assets. (Germany is one of the world's staunchest adherents to the historical cost principle. Its strong anti-inflation attitudes are the result of the ravages of the two debilitating inflationary periods it went through in the 20th century.) Inventory is stated at the lower of cost or market; FIFO, LIFO, and average are acceptable methods of determining cost. Depreciable fixed assets are subject to tax depreciation rates.

Research and development costs are expensed when incurred. Finance leases typically are not capitalized, but pension obligations are accrued based on their actuarially determined present value consistent with tax laws. Deferred taxes do not normally arise in individual company accounts, because these are consistent with tax law. However, they may arise in consolidated statements if accounting methods used for consolidations are different from those used for the individual accounts. In this case, deferred taxes must be set up using the liability method.

Provisions as estimates of future expenses or losses are used heavily. Provisions must be set up for deferred maintenance expenses, product guarantees, potential losses from pending transactions, and other uncertain liabilities. Optional provisions, such as those for future major repairs, are also allowed. Most companies make provisions as large as possible because legally booked expenses directly affect the determination of taxable income. Provisions give German companies many opportunities to manage income. Portions of retained earnings often are allocated to specific reserves, including a mandated legal reserve and those resulting from the provisions just described.

As noted earlier, listed German companies must prepare their consolidated financial statements in accordance with IFRS. Other companies have a choice of using either

---

[20] Dieter Ordelheide, "Germany: Group Accounts," in *Transnational Accounting*, ed. Dieter Ordelheide (London: Macmillan Press, 1995): 1599–1602.

IFRS or German rules already described for consolidation purposes. Both choices are found in practice, and the reader of German financial statements should be careful to know which accounting standards are being followed.

Czech Republic

The Czech Republic (CR) is located in Central Europe with Germany to the west and northwest, Austria to the south, the Slovak Republic to the east, and Poland to the north. Its territory was a part of the Austro-Hungarian Empire for nearly 300 years (from 1620 to 1918), ruled by the Austrian monarchy, the Hapsburgs. The empire collapsed at the end of World War I, and the independent nation of Czechoslovakia was founded in 1918. Between the two world wars, Czechoslovakia was a prosperous parliamentary democracy with universal voting rights. This ended in 1938, when Britain and France allowed Nazi Germany to annex Czechoslovakia's ethnically German border territories. Within a year, Hitler controlled the rest of the nation and the Nazi occupation began. After the end of World War II, the 1946 elections and subsequent political maneuvering brought the Communist Party to power. This began the Soviet Union's domination over Czechoslovakia, which lasted until 1989. The internal disintegration of the Soviet regime and the collapse of the Czechoslovak Communist government in that year led to the so-called Velvet Revolution and the establishment of a new government. In 1993 Czechoslovakia peacefully split into two nations, the Czech Republic and the Republic of Slovakia.

Accounting in the Czech Republic has changed direction several times, reflecting the country's political history. Accounting practice and principles reflected those of the German-speaking countries of Europe until the end of World War II. Then, with the construction of a centrally planned economy, accounting practice was based on the Soviet model. The administrative needs of various central government institutions were satisfied through such features as a uniform chart of accounts, detailed accounting methods, and uniform financial statements, obligatory for all enterprises. A focus on production and costing, based on historical costs, was emphasized over external reporting. A unified system of financial and cost accounting used the same pricing and other principles.

Of course, prices did not reflect the market forces of supply and demand. They were centrally determined and controlled, primarily on a *cost plus* basis. Losses were normally subsidized. Accounting was of limited importance in managing an enterprise. Furthermore, accounting information was considered to be secret and financial statements were not published. While accounting information was inspected, it was not independently audited.[21]

After 1989 Czechoslovakia moved quickly toward a market-oriented economy. The government revamped its legal and administrative structure to stimulate the economy and attract foreign investments. Commercial laws and practices were adjusted to fit Western standards. Price controls were lifted. Accounting again turned westward, this time reflecting the principles embodied in the European Union Directives.

The division of Czechoslovakia did not appreciably affect this process. In 1993 the Prague Stock Exchange began regular operations. Considering the high level of

---

[21] Rudolf Schroll, "The New Accounting System in the Czech Republic," *European Accounting Review* 4, No. 4 (1995): 827–832; Jan Dolezal, "The Czech Republic," in *European Accounting Guide*, 2nd ed., ed. David Alexander and Simon Archer (San Diego: Harcourt Brace Jovanovich, 1995).

economic and political development achieved in pre-1938 Czechoslovakia, these events were more a matter of returning to previously held norms than discovering new ones.[22]

Privatization of the economy involved the return of property to former owners, small privatizations in which more than 20,000 shops, restaurants, and other small businesses were sold to Czech citizens at public auction, and a series of large privatizations. A key element of the latter was a coupon voucher system allowing adult Czech citizens to buy investment vouchers for a nominal price. These vouchers were used to acquire shares of newly privatized large industrial concerns. However, many Czechs, with no experience as shareholders, sold their shares to investment funds owned by state-controlled Czech banks. One result was a conflict of interest for the banks, which ended up owning the same companies to which they were lending money. A second round of privatizations involved auctions or direct sales, often to the companies' own managers. Many of these newly privatized businesses subsequently failed, leaving little or no collateral and overloading the court system with business cases. Both waves of privatization are now viewed as a mistake of trying to do too much at once.[23] A few remaining state-owned enterprises are still to be privatized. The economic reforms are ongoing. Among the more pressing issues are improving the openness and transparency of stock market operations through tighter regulations, and restructuring enterprises.[24]

In 1995 the Czech Republic became the first post-Communist member of the Organization for Economic Cooperation and Development (OECD). The Czech Republic joined NATO in 1999 and the European Union in 2004.[25]

ACCOUNTING REGULATION AND ENFORCEMENT   The new Commercial Code was enacted by the Czech parliament in 1991 and became effective on January 1, 1992.[26] Influenced by the Austrian roots of the old commercial code and modeled on German commercial law, it introduced a substantial amount of legislation relating to businesses. (Czech law is based on the civil code law system of continental Europe.) This legislation includes requirements for annual financial statements, income taxes, audits, and shareholders meetings.

---

[22] Willie Seal, Pat Sucher, and Ivan Zelenka, "The Changing Organization of Czech Accounting," *European Accounting Review* 4, No. 4 (1995): 667.

[23] The first wave of coupon privatization occurred in 1992 and involved 1,491 state-owned companies. The second round ended in 1994, privatizing a further 861 companies.

[24] U.S. Department of State, "Background Notes: Czech Republic" (July 2008); U.S. Central Intelligence Agency, "The World Factbook—Czech Republic" (May 2009); Daniel Michaels and John Reed, "Halfway There," *Wall Street Journal Interactive Edition* (September 18, 1997): 1–6; Mark Andress, "Czech, Please!," *Accountancy* (September 2000): 60–61; Zuzana Kawaciukova, "Privatization Theft," *Prague Post Online* (July 24, 2003).

Czech capital markets are largely illiquid. In 1995 and 1996, after the initial large privatizations, there were over 1,600 Czech companies listed on the Prague Stock Exchange. However, in 1997 the exchange started delisting securities that were rarely traded. By the end of 1999, the Prague Stock Exchange had approximately 200 listed companies and there were 29 at the end of 2008. The Czech stock market is not seen as a place to raise new capital. For example, there have only been five initial public offerings of shares since it began operations in 1993 through the end of 2008. Transparent reporting, tight regulations, investor protection, and judicial enforcement are still lacking. See Pat Sucher, Peter Moizer, and Marcela Zarova, "The Images of the Big Six Audit Firms in the Czech Republic," *European Accounting Review* 8, no. 3 (1999): 503, 519; "After the Chaos: A Survey of Finance in Central Europe," *Economist* (September 14, 2002): 5–7, 10–11.

[25] The Czech Republic is not expected to adopt the euro until after 2012. Some experts predict that euro adoption may even be as late as 2014 or 2015.

[26] In 1991 legislation was passed by the then Czechoslovak parliament. The Czech Republic carried forward its provisions after the division.

The Accountancy Act, which sets out the requirements for accounting, was passed in 1991 and became effective on January 1, 1993. Based on the EU's Fourth and Seventh Directives, the act specifies the use of a chart of accounts for record keeping and the preparation of financial statements.[27] It was significantly amended with effect from January 1, 2002 and 2004, primarily to bring Czech accounting closer to IFRS. The Ministry of Finance is responsible for accounting principles. Ministry of Finance decrees set out acceptable measurement and disclosure practices that companies must follow. Thus, accounting in the CR is influenced by the Commercial Code, the Accountancy Act, and Ministry of Finance decrees. The stock exchange has so far had little influence, and, despite the German origins of the Commercial Code, tax legislation is not directly influential. As discussed in the following section, the true and fair view embodied in the Accountancy Act and taken from EU Directives is interpreted to mean that tax and financial accounts are treated differently.[28] Nevertheless, legal form takes precedence over economic substance in some cases. The Ministry of Finance also oversees the Czech Securities Commission, responsible for supervising and monitoring the capital market and enforcing the Securities Act.

Auditing is regulated by the Act on Auditors, passed in 1992. This act established the Chamber of Auditors, a self-regulated professional body that oversees the registration, education, examination, and disciplining of auditors, the setting of auditing standards, and the regulation of audit practice, such as the format of the audit report. An audit of financial statements is required for all corporations (joint stock companies) and for large limited liability companies (those exceeding two of the following three criteria: turnover of CzK80 million, net assets of CzK40 million, 50 employees).[29] The audit is designed to assure that the accounts have been kept according to applicable legislation and decrees and that the financial statements present a true and fair view of the company's financial position and results. The Chamber of Auditors has adopted International Standards on Auditing (see Chapter 8). The chamber is overseen by the Audit Public Oversight Council, established in 2009.

FINANCIAL REPORTING   Financial statements must be comparative, consisting of:

1. Balance sheet
2. Profit and loss account (income statement)
3. Notes

Consistent with the requirements of the EU Directives, the notes include a description of the accounting policies and other relevant information for assessing the financial statements. Examples of the latter include employee information, revenues by segment, and contingencies. The notes must also include a cash flow statement. Consolidated financial statements are required for groups meeting at least two of the following criteria: (1) assets of CzK350 million, (2) revenues of CzK700 million, and (3) 250 employees. Controlling interest in a subsidiary is based on either owning a majority of shares or

---

[27] Charts of accounts are not new to the Czech Republic because their use was required under communism. The Czechs based their new system on the French Plan Comptable and received substantial help from the French Ministry of Finance and the French accounting profession in developing their new charts of account.
[28] Pat Sucher, Willie Seal, and Ivan Zelenka, "True and Fair View in the Czech Republic: A Note on Local Perceptions," *European Accounting Review* 5, No. 3 (1996): 551.
[29] Corporations issue shares, whereas limited liability companies do not. The latter are similar to limited partnerships.

having a direct or indirect dominant influence. Small and other companies not subject to audit have abbreviated disclosure requirements. Financial statements are approved at the annual meeting of shareholders. Listed Czech companies must use IFRS for both their consolidated and individual company financial statements. Nonlisted companies have the option of using IFRS or Czech accounting standards for their consolidated statements, but must use Czech standards in their individual company statements. Listed companies are also required to present quarterly income statements.

ACCOUNTING MEASUREMENTS   The acquisition (purchase) method is used to account for business combinations. Goodwill arising from a business combination is written off in the first year of consolidation or capitalized and amortized over no more than 20 years. The equity method is used for associated companies (those over which the company exercises significant influence but which are not consolidated), and proportional consolidation is used for joint ventures.[30] The year-end (closing) exchange rate is used to translate both the income statement and balance sheet of foreign subsidiaries. There are no guidelines for reporting foreign currency translation adjustments.

Tangible and intangible assets are valued at cost and written off over their expected economic lives. Inventory is valued at the lower of cost or net realizable value, and FIFO and weighted average are allowable cost-flow assumptions (LIFO is not). Research and development costs may be capitalized if they relate to projects completed successfully and capable of generating future income. Leased assets are typically not capitalized—an example of form over substance. Deferred income taxes are provided in full for all temporary differences. Contingent losses are recorded when they are probable and can be reliably measured. Companies may also take provisions for future repairs and maintenance expenditures. Legal reserves are required: Profits are appropriated annually until they reach 20 percent of equity for corporations and 10 percent for limited liability companies.

The Netherlands

Dutch accounting presents several interesting paradoxes. The Dutch have relatively permissive statutory accounting and financial reporting requirements but very high professional practice standards. The Netherlands is a code law country, yet accounting is oriented toward fair presentation. Financial reporting and tax accounting are two separate activities. Further, the fairness orientation developed without a strong stock market influence. The United Kingdom and the United States have influenced Dutch accounting as much (or more) than other continental European countries. Unlike the norm elsewhere in continental Europe, the accounting profession has had a significant influence on Dutch accounting standards and regulations.[31]

---

[30] In individual company statements, either the equity or cost method may be used to account for associated companies.

[31] The idea that the business community is capable of adequate financial reporting is well entrenched in Dutch thinking. The first limited liability companies were formed in the 17th century without a clear legal framework on the matter. The first commercial code, introduced in the 19th century, viewed shareholders as responsible for management, which prompted little need for extensive accounting requirements in the law. As in the United Kingdom, the Dutch accounting profession emerged in the 19th century and has had a substantial influence on accounting. By the time an income tax on corporations was introduced (in 1940), financial reporting was already too well developed to be dominated by tax accounting. See Kees Canfferman, "The History of Financial Reporting in the Netherlands," in *European Financial Reporting: A History*, ed. Peter Walton (London: Academic Press, 1995).

Accounting in the Netherlands is considered a branch of business economics.[32] As a result, much economic thought has been devoted to accounting topics and especially to accounting measurements. Highly respected professional accountants are often part-time professors. Thus, academic thought has a major influence upon ongoing practice.

Dutch accountants are also willing to consider foreign ideas. The Dutch were among the earliest proponents of international standards for financial accounting and reporting, and the statements of the IASB receive substantial attention in determining acceptable practice. The Netherlands is also home to several of the world's largest multinational enterprises, including Philips, Royal Dutch Shell, and Unilever.[33] These enterprises have been internationally listed since the 1950s and have been influenced by foreign (particularly U.K. and U.S.) accounting. Through example, these large multinationals have influenced the financial reporting of other Dutch companies. The influence of the Amsterdam Stock Exchange, however, has been minimal because it does not provide much new business capital.

ACCOUNTING REGULATION AND ENFORCEMENT   Accounting regulations in the Netherlands remained liberal until the passage of the Act on Annual Financial Statements in 1970. The act was a part of an extensive program of changes in company legislation and was introduced partly to reflect the coming harmonization of company law within the EU. Among the major provisions of the 1970 act are the following:

- Annual financial statements shall show a fair picture of the financial position and results of the year, and all items therein must be appropriately grouped and described.
- Financial statements must be drawn up in accordance with sound business practice (i.e., accounting principles acceptable to the business community).
- The bases of stating assets and liabilities and determining results of operations must be disclosed.
- Financial statements shall be prepared on a consistent basis, and the material effects of changes in accounting principles must be properly disclosed.
- Comparative financial information for the preceding period shall be disclosed in the financial statements and accompanying footnotes.

The 1970 act introduced the mandatory audit. It also set into motion the formation of the Tripartite Accounting Study Group[34] and gave birth to the Enterprise Chamber. The act, incorporated into the civil code in 1975, was amended by legislation in 1983 to incorporate the EU Fourth Directive, and further amended in 1988 to incorporate the EU Seventh Directive.

---

[32] Refer to the microeconomic approach to accounting development discussed in Chapter 2.
[33] Unilever is a binational (British and Dutch) concern. Royal Dutch Shell is headquartered in the Netherlands but incorporated in Britain.
[34] The Tripartite Accounting Study Group was replaced in 1981 by the Council on Annual Reporting (CAR). The CAR changed its name to the Dutch Accounting Standards Board in 2005.

The Dutch Accounting Standards Board (DASB) issues guidelines on generally acceptable (not accepted) accounting principles.[35] The board is composed of members from three different groups:

1. Preparers of financial statements (employers)
2. Users of financial statements (representatives of trade unions and financial analysts)
3. Auditors of financial statements[36]

The DASB is a private organization financed by grants from the business community and the auditing profession. Its activities are coordinated by the Foundation for Annual Reporting (FAR). FAR appoints the members of the DASB and ensures adequate funding. Even though the board's guidelines do not have the force of law, they have traditionally been followed by most companies and auditors.[37] The guidelines are comprehensive in scope and incorporate as far as possible the standards of the IASB. (As an aid in drafting new or revised guidelines, the DASB uses a conceptual framework that is a translation of the IASB framework.) Nevertheless, the only legally enforceable accounting rules are those specified in the accounting and financial reporting provisions of the Dutch civil code. Before 2005, the DASB had a strategy to implement changes in IFRS into its own standards. But this strategy changed as a result of the EU regulations requiring IFRS for listed companies. The current strategy of the DASB is to focus on reporting standards for nonlisted companies.

The Netherlands Authority for the Financial Markets (AMF) supervises the operations of the securities markets. Although it falls under the Ministry of Finance, the AMF is an autonomous administrative authority. Among the responsibilities given it in 2006 is the oversight of annual reporting and auditing of listed companies. Its Financial Reporting Supervision Division examines financial statements filed with the AMF to ensure that they comply with applicable standards and the law. Its Audit Firm Oversight Division ensures that applicable audit standards are followed. The 2006 Supervision of Auditors' Organizations Act also provides for AMF oversight of the audit profession.

The Enterprise Chamber, a specialist court connected with the High Court of Amsterdam, is a unique feature of the Dutch system of enforcing compliance with accounting requirements. Any interested party may complain to this chamber if it believes that a company's financial statements do not conform to applicable law. Shareholders, employees, trade unions, and even the public prosecutor (but not independent auditors) may bring proceedings to the chamber. The chamber is composed of three judges and two expert accountants, and there is no jury. Chamber decisions may lead to modifications of financial statements or various penalties. Even though the rulings apply only to defendant companies, they sometimes state general rules that may influence the reporting practices of other companies.

Auditing is a self-regulated profession in the Netherlands. Its governing body is the Netherlands Institute of Registeraccountants (NIvRA), which has approximately 14,000 members.[38] It is autonomous in setting auditing standards, and its strong professional code of conduct has statutory status.

---

[35] The DASB Web site is www.rjnet.nl.
[36] Neither the Amsterdam Stock Exchange nor shareholder representatives participate in the board.
[37] However, auditors can issue an unqualified opinion when there is noncompliance with a guideline, as long as the financial statements still convey a true and fair view.
[38] The NIvRA Web site is www.nivra.nl.

Until 1993, only members of NIvRA could certify financial statements, but changes were made that year to incorporate the EU Eighth Directive. In the Netherlands there are two kinds of auditors: registeraccountants (RAs, or chartered accountants) and administrative accountants (AAs).[39] The 1993 changes allowed AAs to also certify financial statements if they undergo additional training. Over time, educational and training qualifications for RAs and AAs will be standardized, and the code of conduct will be the same in relation to audit work, the auditor's responsibilities, and independence. One set of disciplinary rules will apply. However, NIvRA is likely to continue to dominate auditing and accounting in the Netherlands.

NIvRA is involved in everything that is accounting related in the Netherlands. It participates in the Dutch Accounting Standards Board and in commissions charged with revising the accounting statutes of the civil code. NIvRA members serve on the Enterprise Chamber, as accounting faculty at leading Dutch universities, on the IASB, and on committees of the EU, the OECD, the UN, and the International Federation of Accountants.

FINANCIAL REPORTING   The quality of Dutch financial reporting is uniformly high. Statutory financial statements should be filed in Dutch, but English, French, and German are also acceptable. The financial statements must include the following:

1. Balance sheet
2. Income statement
3. Notes
4. Directors' report
5. Other prescribed information

A cash flow statement is required for large and medium-sized companies. The notes must describe the accounting principles used in valuation and the determination of results, and the reasoning behind any accounting changes. The directors' report reviews the financial position at the balance sheet date, and performance during the financial year. It also provides information about the expected performance during the new financial year and comments on any significant post-balance sheet events. "Other prescribed information" must include the auditor's report and profit appropriations for the year.

Annual financial reports must be presented on both a parent-company-only and a consolidated basis. Group companies for the purpose of consolidation are companies that form an economic unit under common control. Consistent with EU Directives, reporting requirements vary by company size. Small companies are exempt from the requirements for an audit and for consolidated financial statements, and they may file an abbreviated income statement and balance sheet. Medium-sized companies must be audited, but may publish a condensed income statement. Small, medium-sized, and large companies are defined in the civil code. Listed Dutch companies must prepare IFRS consolidated statements. Their parent-company statements may also be prepared

---

[39] The Nederlandse Orde van Accountants-Administratieconsultenen (NovAA) Web site is www.novaa.nl.

using IFRS, Dutch accounting guidelines, or a mixture of the two. All Dutch companies are allowed to use IFRS instead of Dutch guidelines.

ACCOUNTING MEASUREMENTS Although the pooling-of-interests method of accounting for business combinations is allowed in limited circumstances, it is rarely used in the Netherlands. The purchase method is the normal practice. Goodwill is the difference between the acquisition cost and the fair value of the assets and liabilities acquired. It is normally capitalized and amortized over its estimated useful life, up to a maximum of 20 years. It may also be charged immediately to shareholders' equity or to income. The equity method is required when the investor exercises significant influence on business and financial policy. Joint ventures may be accounted for using either the equity method or proportional consolidation. Foreign currency translation is similar to IFRS. The balance sheet of a "foreign entity" is translated at the closing (year-end) rate, while the income statement is translated at the closing or average rate. Translation adjustments are charged to shareholders' equity. The temporal method is used for "direct foreign activities," with the translation adjustment charged to income.

The Dutch flexibility toward accounting measurements is most evident in permitting the use of current values for tangible assets such as inventory and depreciable assets. When current values are used for these assets, their corresponding income-statement amounts, cost of goods sold and depreciation, are also stated at current values. Current value can be replacement value, recoverable amount, or net realizable value. Current value accounting is expected to be consistently applied; piecemeal revaluations normally are not allowed. Revaluations are offset by a revaluation reserve in shareholders' equity. Companies using current values should provide additional historical cost information in the notes. Historical cost is also acceptable. While much has been made of current value accounting in the Netherlands, few companies actually use it. Philips, arguably the most conspicuous example, started using current value accounting in 1951, but abandoned it in 1992 in the interests of international comparability. Nevertheless, current values have a place in Dutch accounting because companies that use historical cost for the balance sheet and income statement are expected to disclose supplemental current cost information in their notes. Current cost accounting is discussed in detail in Chapter 7.

When historical cost is used for inventory, it is generally stated at the lower of cost or net realizable value, with cost determined by FIFO, LIFO, or average methods. All intangibles are assumed to have a finite life, normally no more than 20 years, and are amortized over that life. Intangibles with lives longer than 20 years must be impairments tested each year. Research and development costs are capitalized only when the amounts are recoverable and sufficiently certain. Leases, contingencies, and pension costs are generally measured as they are in the United Kingdom and United States, although the applicable rules are more general. Deferred income taxes are recognized on the basis of the comprehensive allocation concept (full provision) and measured according to the liability method. They may be valued at discounted present value. Current value accounting is not acceptable for tax purposes, so when current values are used for financial reporting, permanent rather than temporary differences arise.

Because Dutch companies have flexibility in applying measurement rules, one would suspect that there are opportunities for income smoothing. In addition, there is flexibility in providing for probable future obligations. For example, provisions for periodic maintenance and major overhauls are allowed.[40]

United Kingdom

Accounting in the United Kingdom developed as an independent discipline, pragmatically responding to the needs and practices of business.[41] Over time, successive companies laws added structure and other requirements, but still allowed accountants considerable flexibility in the application of professional judgment. Since the 1970s, the most important source of development in company law has been the EU Directives, most notably the Fourth and Seventh Directives. At the same time, accounting standards and the standard-setting process have become more authoritative.

The legacy of British accounting to the rest of the world is substantial. The United Kingdom was the first country in the world to develop an accountancy profession as we know it today.[42] The concept of a fair presentation of financial results and position (the true and fair view) is also of British origin. Professional accounting thinking and practice were exported to Australia, Canada, the United States, and other former British possessions including Hong Kong, India, Kenya, New Zealand, Nigeria, Singapore, and South Africa.

ACCOUNTING REGULATION AND ENFORCEMENT   The two major sources of financial accounting standards in the United Kingdom are companies law and the accounting profession. Activities of companies incorporated in the United Kingdom are broadly governed by statutes called companies acts. Companies acts have been updated, extended, and consolidated through the years. For example, in 1981 the EU Fourth Directive was implemented, adding statutory rules regarding formats, accounting principles, and basic accounting conventions. This introduced standardized formats for financial statements into Britain for the first time. Companies may choose from alternative balance sheet formats and four profit and loss account formats. The 1981 act also sets out five basic accounting principles:

1. Revenues and expenses are matched on an accrual basis.
2. Individual asset and liability items within each class of assets and liabilities are valued separately.
3. The principle of conservatism (prudence) is applied, especially in the recognition of realized income and all known liabilities and losses.
4. Consistent application of accounting policies from year to year is required.
5. The going concern principle is applicable to the entity being accounted for.

---

[40] For evidence that Dutch firms use provisions to smooth earnings, see Erik Peek, "The Use of Discretionary Provisions in Earnings Management," *Journal of International Accounting Research* 3, no. 2 (2004): 27–43.

[41] The United Kingdom of Great Britain and Northern Ireland is a union of England, Scotland, Wales, and Northern Ireland. Even though the United Kingdom has an integrated system of laws, monetary and fiscal policies, and social rules and regulations, important individual differences remain among these four countries. The term "Britain" is often used for the United Kingdom. "British," "Anglo," and "Anglo-Saxon" are often used interchangeably to describe accounting in the United Kingdom.

[42] The first recognized accounting society was the Society of Accountants in Edinburgh, which was granted a royal charter in 1854. Similar societies were officially recognized in Glasgow in 1855 and in Aberdeen in 1867. Professional accounting began with these early professional societies. The United Kingdom has less than 1 percent of the world's population, yet has more than 13 percent of its accountants. See Bob Parker, "Accountants Galore," *Accountancy* (November 2001): 130–131.

The act contains broad valuation rules in that the accounts may be based on either historical or current cost.

The Companies Act 1985 consolidated and extended earlier legislation and was amended in 1989 to recognize the EU Seventh Directive. This act requires the consolidation of financial statements, although consolidation was already standard practice.[43] The legal stipulations are general and allow considerable flexibility in case-by-case applications.

The following six accountancy bodies in the United Kingdom are linked through the Consultative Committee of Accountancy Bodies (CCAB), organized in 1970.[44]

1. The Institute of Chartered Accountants in England and Wales
2. The Institute of Chartered Accountants of Scotland
3. The Institute of Chartered Accountants in Ireland
4. The Association of Chartered Certified Accountants
5. The Chartered Institute of Management Accountants
6. The Chartered Institute of Public Finance and Accountancy

British standard setting evolved from recommendations on accounting principles (issued by the Institute of Chartered Accountants in England and Wales) to the 1970 formation of the Accounting Standards Steering Committee, later renamed the Accounting Standards Committee (ASC). The ASC promulgated Statements on Standard Accounting Practice (SSAPs). SSAPs were issued and enforced by the six accounting bodies, any one of which could effectively veto the standard. The veto power of these organizations often led to excessive delays and compromises in developing SSAPs. In addition, SSAPs were more in the nature of recommendations than compulsory requirements, and had little authority.

The Dearing Report, issued in 1988, expressed dissatisfaction with the existing standard-setting arrangement.[45] It recommended a new structure for setting accounting standards and more authoritative support for them. The Companies Act 1989 was important not only for incorporating the EU Seventh Directive but also for enacting the recommendations of the Dearing Report. The 1989 act created a new Financial Reporting Council (FRC) with the duty of overseeing its three offshoots: the Accounting Standards Board (ASB), which replaced the ASC in 1990, an Urgent Issues Task Force (UITF), and a Financial Reporting Review Panel.[46]

The FRC sets general policy. It is an independent body whose members are drawn from the accounting profession, industry, and financial institutions. The ASB has a full-time chair, a technical director, and up to eight paid part-time members, and is empowered to issue accounting standards. The ASB issues Financial Reporting Standards (FRSs) after considering comments on Discussion Papers and Financial Reporting Exposure Drafts (FREDs). The ASB is guided by a Statement of Principles for Financial Reporting, a conceptual framework for setting accounting standards.[47] The ASB also established the UITF to respond quickly to new problems and issue clarifications of the accounting

---

[43] The companies act is periodically updated, most recently in 2006.
[44] The Web site addresses are: CCAB: www.ccab.org.uk; ICAEW: www.icaew.com; ICAS: www.icas.org.uk; ICAI: www.icai.ie; ACCA: www.acca.co.uk; CIMA: www.cimaglobal.com; CIPFA: www.cipfa.org.uk.
[45] Sir Ron Dearing, (The Dearing Report) "The Making of Accounting Standards, Report of the Review Committee," presented to the Consultative Committee of Accountancy Bodies, 1988.
[46] Web sites are: Financial Reporting Council: www.frc.org.uk; Accounting Standards Board and Urgent Issues Task Force: www.frc.org.uk/asb/; Financial Reporting Review Panel: www.frc.org.uk/frrp.
[47] Work on the Statement of Principles began soon after the ASB was formed and was completed in 1999.

standards and other regulations (called UITF Abstracts). Because listed British (and other EU) companies must now use IFRS in their consolidated financial statements, the ASB has turned its attention away from developing U.K. GAAP to gradually converging U.K. accounting standards with IFRS. Another major role of the ASB is partnering with the IASB and other standard setters in the development of IFRS.

The 1989 act enacted legal sanctions for companies that do not comply with accounting standards. Both the Financial Reporting Review Panel and the Department of Trade and Industry can investigate complaints about departures from accounting standards. They can go to court to force a company to revise its financial statements. Companies must adopt the accounting policies most appropriate to their specific circumstances in order to give a true and fair view, and they must regularly review their policies to ensure that they remain appropriate.

All but small limited liability companies must be audited. Of the six accountancy bodies listed earlier, only members of the first four are allowed to sign audit reports. The audit report affirms that the financial statements present a true and fair view and comply with the Companies Act 1985. For example, the opinion paragraph of PricewaterhouseCoopers on the 2008 financial statements of BG Group, the British natural gas company, is reproduced in Exhibit 3-5.

Until 2000, auditing standards were the responsibility of a board of the CCAB. In that year the Accountancy Foundation was set up to regulate and oversee the auditing profession. Following a review of the accounting profession by the Department of Trade and Industry in 2003, the Accountancy Foundation was dissolved and its functions transferred to the FRC. A newly established Professional Oversight Board (POB) oversees the regulation of the auditing profession by monitoring the activities of the professional accounting bodies, including education and training, standards, professional conduct, and discipline. The POB also oversees an independent Audit Inspection

---

EXHIBIT 3-5   **Audit Opinion on BG Group Financial Statements**

In our opinion:

- The Group Financial Statements give a true and fair view, in accordance with IFRSs as adopted by the European Union, of the state of the Group's affairs as at 31 December 2008 and of its profit and cash flows for the year then ended;
- The parent company Financial Statements give a true and fair view, in accordance with IFRSs as adopted by the European Union as applied in accordance with the provisions of the Companies Act 1985, as of the state of the parent company's affairs as at 31 December 2008 and cash flows for the year then ended; and
- The Financial Statements and the part of the remuneration report to be audited have been properly prepared in accordance with the Companies Act 1985 and, as regards the Group Financial Statements, Article 4 of the IAS Regulation; and
- The information given in the Directors' Report is consistent with the Financial Statements.

PricewaterhouseCoopers LLP
11 March 2009

Source: 2008 BG Group Annual Report, p. 64.

Unit (AIU), which monitors the audits of listed companies and other public interest entities. The Auditing Practices Board (APB) was transferred from the Accountancy Foundation to the FRC. It prescribes the basic principles and practices that an auditor must follow when conducting an audit, and is responsible for ethical standards and standards on audit independence. British auditing standards follow International Standards on Auditing. Finally, the Accountancy Investigation and Discipline Board (now the Accountancy and Actuarial Discipline Board, or AADB) was established as a mechanism to investigate and discipline accountants or accounting firms for professional misconduct. All of these reforms were designed to strengthen the accounting and audit profession, and provide a more effective system of regulation of the profession. Thus, the Financial Reporting Council has responsibility for both accounting and auditing standards, and their enforcement.[48]

FINANCIAL REPORTING   British financial reporting is among the most comprehensive in the world. Financial statements generally include:

1. Directors' report
2. Profit and loss account and balance sheet
3. Cash flow statement
4. Statement of total recognized gains and losses
5. Statement of accounting policies
6. Notes referenced in the financial statements
7. Auditor's report

The directors' report addresses principal business activities, review of operations and likely developments, important post-balance sheet events, recommended dividends, names of the directors and their shareholdings, and political and charitable contributions. Listed companies must include a statement on corporate governance with disclosures on directors' remuneration, audit committees and internal controls, and a declaration that the company is a going concern. They must also report on social and environmental matters. Financial statements must present a true and fair view of a company's state of affairs and profits. To achieve this, additional information may be necessary, and in exceptional circumstances requirements may be overridden. The latter is known as the "true and fair override."[49]

Group (consolidated) financial statements are required in addition to a parent-only balance sheet. Control of subsidiary "undertakings" occurs when the parent has power to exercise dominant influence or control over the undertaking, or the parent and subsidiary are managed in a unified basis. The London Stock Exchange requires that listed companies provide half-year interim reports. Listed companies must also report basic and diluted earnings per share.

---

[48] The FRC was given the responsibility for setting actuarial standards and overseeing the actuarial profession in 2006.

[49] Research shows that the true and fair override has been used to mask poor performance and that its use has declined since the EU requirement for IFRS. See Gilad Livne and Maureen McNichols, "An Empirical Investigation of the True and Fair Override in the United Kingdom," *Journal of Business Finance and Accounting* (January/March 2009): 1–30.

Another feature of U.K. financial reporting is that small and medium-sized companies are exempt from many financial reporting obligations. The Companies Act sets out size criteria. In general, small and medium-sized companies are permitted to prepare abbreviated accounts with certain minimum prescribed information. Small and medium-sized groups are exempt from preparing consolidated statements.

ACCOUNTING MEASUREMENTS   The United Kingdom allows both the acquisition and merger methods of accounting for business combinations. However, the conditions for the use of the merger method (*pooling-of-interests* in the United States) are so narrow that it is almost never used. Under the acquisition method, goodwill is calculated as the difference between the fair value of the consideration paid and the fair value of the net assets acquired. FRS 7 specifies that fair values are assigned to identifiable assets and liabilities that exist at the date of acquisition, reflecting the conditions at that time. Future operating losses and reorganization costs cannot be considered in the calculation of goodwill, but must be reflected in post-acquisition income. Goodwill is capitalized and amortized over 20 years or less; however, a longer period or an indefinite period (resulting in no amortization) is possible if goodwill is subject to an annual impairment review. Proportional consolidation is only permitted for unincorporated joint ventures. The equity method is used for *associated* undertakings and for joint ventures that are companies. Foreign currency translation follows the requirements of IFRS, as discussed previously.

Assets may be valued at historical cost, current cost, or (as most companies do) using a mixture of the two. Thus, revaluations of land and buildings are permissible. Depreciation and amortization must correspond to the measurement basis used for the underlying asset. Research expenditures are written off in the year of the expenditure, and development costs may be deferred under specific circumstances. However, in practice, few British companies capitalize any development costs. Inventory (referred to as "stocks") is valued at the lower of cost or net realizable value on a FIFO or average cost basis; LIFO is not acceptable.

Leases that transfer the risks and rewards of ownership to the lessee are capitalized and the lease obligation is shown as a liability. The costs of providing pensions and other retirement benefits must be recognized systematically and rationally over the period during which the employees' services are performed. Contingent losses are accrued when they are probable and can be estimated with reasonable accuracy. Deferred taxes are calculated under the liability method on a full provision basis for most timing differences.[50] Long-term deferred tax balances may be valued at discounted present value. Income smoothing opportunities exist given the flexibility that exists in asset valuation and other measurement areas.

---

[50] Providing deferred taxes based on timing differences is not the same as the temporary-difference approach of IFRS and U.S. GAAP. The timing difference approach calculates deferred taxes when there are differences between accounting and taxable income, while the temporary difference approach calculates deferred taxes when there are differences between the accounting and tax carrying amounts of assets and liabilities. Thus, the former is an income statement approach and the latter is a balance sheet approach. All timing differences generate temporary differences, but the reverse isn't true. As a result, U.K. GAAP potentially provides for lower deferred taxes than would be calculated under IFRS and U.S. GAAP. The two main places causing such a divergence are (a) revaluations of assets and liabilities in a business acquisition without a corresponding change in their tax basis and (b) revaluations of nonmonetary assets credited to reserves (equity).

EXHIBIT 3-6 Summary of Significant Accounting Practices

	IFRS	France	Germany	Czech Republic	The Netherlands	United Kingdom
1. Business combinations: purchase or pooling	Purchase	Purchase[a]	Purchase	Purchase	Purchase[a]	Purchase[a]
2. Goodwill	Capitalize and impairments test	Capitalize and amortize	Capitalize and amortize[b]	Capitalize and amortize[b]	Capitalize and amortize[c]	Capitalize and amortize[d]
3. Associates	Equity method	Equity method	Equity method	Equity method	Equity method	Equity method
4. Asset valuation	Historical cost & fair value	Historical cost	Historical cost	Historical cost	Historical cost & fair value	Historical cost & fair value
5. Depreciation charges	Economic based	Tax based	Tax based	Economic based	Economic based	Economic based
6. LIFO inventory valuation	Not permitted	Not permitted	Permitted	Not permitted	Permitted	Not permitted
7. Probable losses	Accrued	Accrued	Accrued	Accrued	Accrued	Accrued
8. Finance leases	Capitalized	Not capitalized	Not capitalized	Not capitalized	Capitalized	Capitalized
9. Deferred taxes	Accrued	Not accrued	Not accrued	Accrued	Accrued	Accrued
10. Reserves for income smoothing	No	Used	Used	Some	Some	Some

[a]Pooling also allowed in narrow circumstances, but not widely used.
[b]May also be written off to reserves.
[c]May also be written off to shareholders' equity or to income.
[d]Nonamortization permitted if subject to annual impairment review.

All U.K. companies are permitted to use IFRS instead of U.K. GAAP just described. Thus, the EU 2005 initiative for listed companies is extended to nonlisted U.K. companies as well. In August 2009, the Accounting Standards Board issued a consultation paper setting out a roadmap for the replacement of U.K. GAAP with a new three-tiered reporting framework based on IFRS. Under the framework, all public companies will continue to apply full IFRS. Other companies, other than those classified as small, would use IFRS for SMEs (see Chapter 8) or full IFRS. Small companies would use U.K. Financial Reporting Standards for Smaller Entities.

Exhibit 3-6 summarizes the significant accounting practices in the countries surveyed in this chapter.

Discussion Questions

1. Compare and contrast the mechanisms for regulating and enforcing financial reporting in the five countries discussed in this chapter.
2. Compare and contrast the main features of financial reporting in the five countries discussed in this chapter.
3. Auditor oversight bodies have recently been established in several countries discussed in this chapter. Identify the auditor oversight bodies discussed in the chapter. What is the reason for this recent trend?
4. What is the difference between consolidated and individual company financial statements? Why do some EU countries prohibit IFRS in individual company financial statements while others permit or require IFRS at the individual company level?
5. Consider the following statement: "Experience shows that the needs of national and international markets, for international harmonization in particular, are better served by self-regulation and development than by government regulation." Do you agree? Why or why not?
6. In France, financial accounting standards and practices originate primarily from three authoritative sources: (a) companies legislation (Plan Comptable Général and Code de Commerce), (b) professional opinions and recommendations (CNC, CRC, OEC, and CNCC), and (c) stock exchange regulations (AMF). Which of these three has the greatest influence on day-to-day French accounting practice?
7. Consider the following statement: "The German Accounting Standards Committee is modeled on Anglo-American and international practice." Do you agree? Why or why not?
8. How have accounting requirements and practices in the Czech Republic been influenced by European Union requirements?
9. The most novel feature of the Dutch accounting scene is the Enterprise Chapter of the Court of Justice of Amsterdam. What is the mission of the Enterprise Chamber? How is this mission carried out?
10. A feature of British accounting is the "true and fair override." What is the meaning of this term? Why is the true and fair override found in the United Kingdom but almost nowhere else?

Exercises

1. This chapter provides synopses of national accounting practice systems in five European countries.

   Required: For each country, list:
   a. the name of the national financial accounting standard-setting board or agency.
   b. the name of the agency, institute, or other organization charged with supervising and enforcing financial accounting standards.

2. Refer to your answer to Exercise 1.

   Required: Which country discussed in this chapter appears to have the most effective accounting and financial reporting supervision mechanism for companies whose securities are traded in public financial markets? Should each country that has a stock exchange (and therefore a public financial market) also have a regulatory agency that enforces accounting and financial reporting rules? Write a concise paragraph to support your answer.

3. The International Federation of Accountants (IFAC) is a worldwide organization of professional accounting bodies. IFAC's Web site (www.ifac.org) has links to a number of accounting bodies around the world.

Required: Visit IFAC's Web site. List the accounting organizations discussed in this chapter that are linked to IFAC's Web site.

4. Reread Chapter 3 and its discussion questions.

Required:
a. As you go through this material, prepare a list of five expressions, terms, or short phrases that are unfamiliar or unusual in your home country.
b. Write a concise definition or explanation of each item.

5. Analyze the five national accounting practice systems summarized in this chapter.

Required:
a. For each of the five countries discussed in this chapter, select the most important financial accounting practice or principle at variance with international norms.
b. For each selection you make, state briefly your reasons for its inclusion on your list.
c. How does this variance affect reported earnings and the debt to asset ratio?
d. How likely is it that an analyst could adjust for this variance to achieve an "apples to apples" comparison with companies from other countries?

6. Refer to Exhibit 3-6.

Required: Which country's GAAP appears to be the most oriented toward equity investors? Which country's GAAP appears to be the least oriented toward equity investors? Why do you say so?

7. The role of government in developing accounting and auditing standards differs in the five countries discussed in this chapter.

Required: Compare the role of government in developing accounting and auditing standards in France, Germany, the Czech Republic, the Netherlands, and the United Kingdom.

8. Countries of the European Union are establishing oversight bodies to regulate the activities of statutory auditors. These national bodies are also coordinated at the EU level.

Required: Find information on the European Group of Auditors' Oversight Bodies (EGAOB) on the European Union Web site (ec.europa.eu/internal_market/auditing/egaob). Discuss the role of the EGAOB. Identify the European countries with a public oversight body for auditing and name the country's related body.

9. In most countries, accounting standard setting involves a combination of private- and public-sector groups. The private sector includes the accounting profession and other groups affected by the financial reporting process, such as users and preparers of financial statements, and organized labor. The public sector includes government agencies, such as tax authorities, ministries responsible for commercial law, and securities commissions. The stock market is another potential influence.

Required: Complete a matrix indicating whether each of the above groups significantly influences accounting standard setting in the five countries discussed in this chapter. List the groups across the top and the countries down the side; indicate the influence of each group with a yes or a no.

10. Listed below are certain financial ratios used by analysts:
   • *Liquidity:* current ratio; cash flow from operations to current liabilities
   • *Solvency:* debt to equity; debt to assets
   • *Profitability:* return on assets; return on equity

Required: Assume that you are comparing the financial ratios of companies from two countries discussed in this chapter. Discuss how the accounting practices identified in Exhibit 3-6 would affect your comparison for each of the six ratios in the list.

CASES

Case 3-1

Old Habits Die Hard

"The ethical climate in the Czech Republic has improved since the early days, but we still have a long way to go," said Josef Machinka, an economic adviser to the Ministry of Finance, while attending an investment seminar sponsored by the Prague Stock Exchange. "We really lack an established ethical framework."

Adds Charles University professor Jana Vychopeň, "Ethical problems still exist, but they stem from 40 years under a system that promoted corruption. Under the communists it was all political influence. There wasn't an economy—corruption sustained the system back then, but now chokes it. We were shocked into a market economy and our coupon privatization was racked with scandal. Even the word 'tunneling,' meaning asset stripping, was coined here."

"Ethics hangs over the market but so does a lack of transparency," states Pavel Kraus, analyst for Merta Investment Management. "Many of today's managers forged their attitudes in the 70s and 80s. Under communism, secrecy—not transparency—was the watchword. They just don't think it's important to keep investors informed, so how do you know they're not a bunch of shady managers trying to hide something?"

He goes on to give the example of Bednar, a large chemical company that was one of the first state-owned enterprises to be privatized. "Bednar is run by old dogs who can't—or won't—learn new tricks. Like a lot of Czech companies, Bednar didn't come to the stock market, but found itself on the stock exchange because of the privatization. The managers found themselves in a publicly traded company against their will.

"Still, it's better than the old days. Back in the 90s I asked to meet with them to discuss their business plan and was told, 'Sure—for CzK 400 an hour.' I kept phoning them for several weeks and finally wore them down. They ended up meeting me for free!"

Agreeing with Kraus is Jiri Michalik, a broker with Habova Securities. "Things are getting better. Czech companies are finally realizing that they have to let investors know what they're getting into if they are going to attract more investment. They looked around and realized that our Polish and Hungarian rivals were leaving us in the dust. Right after privatization most managers didn't have experience at quickly compiling and disseminating their financial information. Even if they had good intentions, it was hard for them to do. But now more and more of them have the experience."

The conversation comes back to Jana Vychopeň. "I put a lot of the blame on the Prague Stock Exchange. It's still not seen as a place to raise capital. Five IPOs between 1993 and 2008 is not a good track record. We have the rules in place and managers' attitudes are changing, if slowly. But poor enforcement means that investors don't always get what they need or they get it too late to be of any good. Of course, Czech citizens have never gotten used to being shareholders. They put most of their savings in banks, so banks have a lot of money to lend. It's easy for Czech companies to get credit, so they have little incentive for going public."

Required

1. Describe the problems characterized in this case.
2. What are the likely causes of these problems?

3. What are consequences of these problems for investors, Czech companies, and the Prague Stock Exchange?
4. Outline a program of changes needed to correct the problems identified.

Case 3-2a

What Difference Does It Really Make?

As an analyst for a securities firm, you are aware that accounting practices differ around the world. Yet you wonder whether these differences really have any material effect on companies' financial statements. You also know that the SEC in the United States requires non-U.S. registrants to reconcile key financial data from the GAAP used in their financial statements to U.S. GAAP. However, companies using IFRS were exempt from this reconciliation requirement starting in 2007. You obtain the last reconciliation from sanofi-aventis (a French pharmaceutical company) in its 2006 Form 20F SEC filing [en.sanofi-aventis.com/binaries/20-F_2006_EN_tcm28-1518.pdf, pages F107-F120].

Required:

1. Document the effects of the GAAP differences in the 20F by doing the following:
   a. For the current year, calculate the percentage change for net income and for total shareholders' equity indicated by the reconciliation and using the non-U.S. GAAP (i.e., IFRS) numbers as a base.
   b. Repeat the same calculations for the preceding year. Are the percentage changes approximately the same? What is significant about your findings?
   c. For the current year, identify the two income statement items and the two balance sheet items that exhibit the relatively largest differences. Would you expect other French multinational companies to be subject to similar item-by-item differences?

2. Should a U.S. reader of non-U.S. financial statements find this SEC-mandated reconciliation useful?

3. Based on your analysis of the sanofi-aventis 2006 limited restatement, do you support the SEC's decision to exempt companies using IFRS from the reconciliation requirement? Why or why not?

Case 3-2b

Do the Differences Really Matter?

As an analyst for a securities firm, you are aware that accounting practices differ around the world. Yet you wonder whether these differences really have any material effect on companies' financial statements. You also know that the SEC in the United States requires non-U.S. registrants to reconcile key financial data from the GAAP used in their financial statements to U.S. GAAP. However, companies using IFRS were exempt from this reconciliation requirement starting in 2007. You obtain the last reconciliation from Unilever (a Dutch consumer products company) in its 2006 Form 20F SEC filing [www.unilever.com/images/ir_06%20form-20F_tcm13-88525.pdf, pages 124–131].

Required

1. Document the effects of the GAAP differences in the 20F by doing the following:
   a. For the current year, calculate the percentage change for net income and for total shareholders' equity indicated by the reconciliation and using the non-U.S. GAAP (i.e., IFRS) numbers as a base.
   b. Repeat the same calculations for the preceding year. Are the percentage changes approximately the same? What is significant about your findings?
   c. For the current year, identify the two income statement items and the two balance sheet items that exhibit the relatively largest differences. Would you expect other Dutch multinational companies to be subject to similar item-by-item differences?

2. Should a U.S. reader of non-U.S. financial statements find this SEC-mandated reconciliation useful?

3. Based on your analysis of the Unilever 2006 limited restatement, do you support the SEC's decision to exempt companies using IFRS from the reconciliation requirement? Why or why not?

Comparative Accounting: The Americas and Asia

Chapter 4 looks at accounting in five countries, two in the Americas (Mexico and the United States) and three in Asia (China, India, and Japan). The United States and Japan have highly developed economies, whereas Mexico, China, and India are "emerging" economies.[1] The United States is the largest economy in the world and home to more large multinational corporations than any other nation. Japan has the second biggest economy in the world and is also home to many of the world's largest businesses. Both countries were founders of the International Accounting Standards Committee (now the International Accounting Standards Board, or IASB), and they have a major role in directing the IASB's agenda.

Why were the other countries chosen for this chapter? We picked Mexico because we wanted to include a Latin American country. Free-market reforms accelerated in the 1990s throughout much of Latin America. These reforms involved removing protectionist barriers to imports, welcoming foreign investment, and privatizing state-owned companies. The 1994 North American Free Trade Agreement (NAFTA) created much new interest in Mexican accounting in Canada, the United States, and elsewhere. Accounting in Mexico has many features in common with accounting in other Latin American countries. The choice of China may be obvious: It is the largest and most populous country in the world. Companies from all around the world are eager to do business there. Like the Czech Republic, discussed in Chapter 3, China is converting from a centrally planned economy to one that is more market oriented. However, the extent to which these two countries are embracing market reforms is different. The Czech Republic is moving toward a complete market economy, while China is taking a middle course in moving to

---

[1] As noted in Chapter 3, the term "emerging economy" refers loosely to newly industrialized countries (NICs) and to countries in transition from planned to free-market economies. NICs have experienced rapid industrial growth, but their economies are not yet rich in terms of per capita gross domestic product. Mexico and India are NICs; China has an economy in transition.

a *socialist market economy*, that is, a planned economy with market adaptations. Accounting developments are an important part of the structural changes in the Chinese economy. India, the second most populous country in the world, has been described as "the next big thing. . . . No big international company can do without an India strategy."[2] Reforms that began in 1991 have resulted in a remarkable transformation of its economy, and most observers feel that the next decade and half will see equally dramatic changes.

Mexico and India are capitalist countries but with traditionally heavy central-government intervention and government ownership of key industries. Historically, their economies have been somewhat closed to foreign investment and international competition. This relative isolation is now changing, because both governments are privatizing their industry holdings and opening up to the global economy. Their financial accounting systems are more developed than China's in terms of standard setting, requirements, and practices. Naturally, accounting is evolving in these two countries as well, but not as rapidly as in China.

Exhibit 4-1 contains some comparative economic data about the five countries that are the focus of this chapter. China's area dwarfs the others'. Another contrast is gross domestic product (GDP) per capita and by sector. Overall, China and India are significantly poorer than the other three nations, and their economies are much more agricultural. Both of these factors are indicators of significant development potential.

EXHIBIT 4-1	Economic Data for Selected Countries				
	United States	**Mexico**	**Japan**	**China**	**India**
Area: sq. km. (in thousands)	9,827	1,973	378	9,597	3,288
Population (in millions)	301	108	128	1,324	1,120
Gross Domestic Product (in billions)	$13,164	$839	$4,368	$2,645	$912
GDP Per Capita	$43,730	$7,750	$34,080	$2,000	$810
GDP by Sector					
Agriculture	1%	4%	1%	11%	17%
Industry	20%	34%	26%	49%	29%
Services	79%	62%	72%	40%	54%
Imports (in billions)	$1,953	$256	$579	$792	$191
Exports (in billions)	$1,163	$250	$646	$969	$126
Market Capitalization (in billions), end 2007	$19,947	$398	$4,453	$6.226	$1,819
Major Trading Partners	Canada, Mexico, China	U.S.A., China	U.S.A., China, S. Korea	U.S.A., Japan, Hong Kong	U.S.A., China

Source: Compiled from *Pocket World in Figures, 2009 Edition* (London: The Economist, 2008) and *The World Factbook*, www.cia.gov/library/publications/the-world-factbook/, May 2009.

---

[2] *Economist,* "Now for the Hard Part: A Survey of India" (June 3, 2006): 3.

The United States is at the other end of the economic spectrum. Its GDP (in absolute terms and per capita) and stock market capitalization exceed that of the other countries. Its economy is also more service oriented than that of the others. The United States is the largest trading partner of the other four countries.[3] Japan also has an advanced economy, as evidenced by its GDP (in absolute terms, per capita, and by sector) and stock market capitalization. Japan is also a major trading partner of China and Mexico, in addition to the United States.

Political and economic ties have been an important influence on accounting in these five countries. U.S. accounting was originally imported from Great Britain (along with the English language and the common law legal system). Most of the first accountants in the United States were British expatriates. However, as a result of the growth of U.S. economic and political power in the 20th century, U.S. ideas on accounting and financial reporting have had substantial influence on the rest of the world for some time now. Mexico's close economic ties with the United States are why it has fairness-oriented accounting despite being a code law country. India was once part of the British Empire. Like the United States, India imported its accounting from Great Britain. In China, the effect of political and economic ties is more anticipatory than historical. China is basing its new accounting standards on International Financial Reporting Standards (IFRS) because it hopes to better communicate with the foreign investors so vital to its economic development plans.

As discussed later, the accounting standard-setting bodies in the United States, Mexico, Japan, and China are committed to converging their national generally accepted accounting principles (GAAP) with IFRS. Thus, national financial reporting standards will remain in these countries, though closely aligned with IFRS. India, on the other hand, plans to adopt IFRS as its local reporting requirement, thus doing away with Indian GAAP.

FIVE NATIONAL FINANCIAL ACCOUNTING SYSTEMS[4]

United States

Accounting in the United States is regulated by a private-sector body (the Financial Accounting Standards Board, or FASB), but a governmental agency (the Securities and Exchange Commission, or SEC) underpins the authority of its standards. The key link allowing this shared-power system to work effectively is the 1973 SEC Accounting Series Release (ASR) No. 150. This release states:

> The Commission intends to continue its policy of looking to the private sector for leadership in establishing and improving accounting principles. For purposes of this policy, principles, standards, and practices promulgated by the FASB in its statements and interpretations, will be considered by the

---

[3] The United States accounts for more than two-thirds of Mexico's exports and imports.

[4] The discussion in this section draws on the references cited in this chapter and on references cited in earlier editions of this book. The Big Four accounting firms and the IAS Plus Web site (www.iasplus.com) periodically update details of accounting in individual countries. For example, the discussion of accounting in India later in this chapter is based in part on Deloitte, *IFRSs and Indian GAAP: A Comparison* (March 2008), www.iasplus.com/asia/2008ifrsindiangaap.pdf.

Commission as having substantial authoritative support, and those contrary to such FASB promulgations will be considered to have no such support.[5]

Until 2002, the American Institute of Certified Public Accountants (AICPA), another private-sector body, set auditing standards. In that year, the Public Company Accounting Oversight Board (PCAOB) was established, with broad powers to regulate audits and auditors of public companies. The PCAOB, discussed later, is a private organization overseen by the SEC.[6]

ACCOUNTING REGULATION AND ENFORCEMENT   The U.S. system has no general legal requirements for the publication of periodic audited financial statements. Corporations in the United States are formed under state law, not federal law. Each state has its own corporate statutes; in general, these contain minimal requirements for keeping accounting records and publishing periodic financial statements. Many of these statutes are not rigorously enforced, and reports rendered to local agencies are often unavailable to the public. Thus, annual audit and financial reporting requirements realistically exist only at the federal level as specified by the SEC. The SEC has jurisdiction over companies listed on U.S. stock exchanges and companies traded over-the-counter.[7] Other limited-liability companies have no such compulsory requirements for financial reporting, making the United States unusual by international norms.

The SEC has the legal authority to prescribe accounting and reporting standards for public companies but relies on the private sector to set the standards. It works with the FASB and exerts pressure when it believes the FASB is moving too slowly or in the wrong direction. At times, the SEC has delayed or overruled pronouncements or has imposed its own requirements.

Since the SEC is an independent regulatory agency, Congress and the president have no direct influence over its policies. However, the five full-time SEC commissioners are appointed by the president and confirmed by the Senate, and the SEC has only those powers that Congress has granted it by statute. As part of the regulatory process, the SEC issues Accounting Series Releases, Financial Reporting Releases, and Staff Accounting Bulletins. Regulations SX and SK contain the rules for preparing financial reports that must be filed with the SEC. Annual filings by U.S. and Canadian companies are on Form 10K, while those from non-Canadian foreign companies are on Form 20F.[8]

---

[5] Securities and Exchange Commission, *Statement of Policy on the Establishment and Improvement of Accounting Principles and Standards*, Accounting Series Release No. 150. Reprinted in *The Development of SEC Accounting*, G. J. Previts, ed., Reading, MA: Addison-Wesley, 1981, 228. The SEC reaffirmed the FASB as the designated accounting standard setting body in April 2003. This reaffirmation followed an SEC study of the U.S. accounting standards setting process, as mandated by the 2002 Sarbanes-Oxley Act (discussed later).

[6] The Web sites of these organizations are: Securities and Exchange Commission: www.sec.gov; Financial Accounting Standards Board: www.fasb.org; American Institute of Certified Public Accountants: www.aicpa.org; and Public Company Accounting Oversight Board: www.pcaobus.org.

[7] There are approximately 15,000 companies that must report to the SEC, including over 1,100 foreign companies. Companies traded on the "pink sheets" over-the-counter market are exempt from the SEC's periodic filing requirements if they meet a minimum-size test and certain other requirements.

[8] The SEC rigorously enforces its filing requirements. Over half of SEC filers had their disclosures reviewed by the SEC in 2005, twice the percentage from a few years earlier.

The FASB was established in 1973[9] and as of June 2009 issued 165 Statements of Financial Accounting Standards (SFASs). The objective of the SFASs is to provide information that is useful to present and potential investors, creditors, and others who make investment, credit, and similar decisions. The FASB has five full-time members, representing accounting firms, academia, corporations, and the investor community. Board members must sever all economic and organizational ties to prior employers or ownership in order to serve. The FASB's use of a conceptual framework is a significant feature of accounting standard setting in the United States. Statements of Financial Accounting Concepts set forth the fundamentals on which financial accounting and reporting standards are based.

The FASB goes through lengthy due-process procedures before issuing an SFAS. In developing its work agenda, it listens to individuals, professional firms, courts of law, companies, and government agencies. It also relies on an emerging-issues task force and an advisory council to help identify accounting issues that need attention. Once a topic is added to the agenda, the FASB's technical staff does research and analysis and an advisory task force is appointed. A Discussion Memorandum or other discussion document is disseminated for comment, and public hearings are held. The FASB considers oral and written comments in meetings open to the public. Next, an Exposure Draft is issued and further public comments are considered. The process ensures that standard setting in the United States is both political and technical. An SFAS must be approved by three of the five members.

Generally accepted accounting principles (GAAP) comprise all the financial accounting standards, rules, and regulations that must be observed in the preparation of financial reports. The SFASs are the major component of GAAP. The accounting and auditing regulations are probably more voluminous in the United States than in the rest of the world combined and substantially more detailed than in any other country. For this reason, the FASB and SEC are considering moving U.S. GAAP away from rules-based standards toward principles-based standards.

The FASB did not seriously engage itself internationally until the 1990s. In 1991, the FASB developed its first strategic plan for international activities. In 1994, the FASB added the promotion of international comparability to its mission statement. The FASB is now a major cooperative international player, committed to converging U.S. GAAP and IFRS. In 2002, the FASB and IASB formalized their commitment to convergence by signing the so-called Norwalk Agreement. Under this agreement, the two boards pledge to remove existing differences between their standards and coordinate future standard setting agendas so that major issues are worked on together.[10] The commitment to convergence was reaffirmed in 2005. Convergence is scheduled for completion in 2011.

The Sarbanes-Oxley Act was signed into law in 2002, significantly expanding U.S. requirements on corporate governance, disclosure and reporting, and the regulation of the audit profession. Among its more important provisions is the

---

[9] Two other private-sector bodies established U.S. generally accepted accounting principles (GAAP) before the FASB. These were the Committee on Accounting Procedure (1938 to 1959) and the Accounting Principles Board (1959 to 1973).
[10] For example, the FASB and IASB have issued a joint discussion paper on improving their conceptual frameworks. The intention is to develop a common conceptual framework.

creation of the PCAOB, a nonprofit organization overseen by the SEC. The PCAOB is responsible for:

- Setting auditing, quality control, ethics, independence, and other standards relating to the preparation of audit reports on companies issuing securities to the public
- Overseeing the audit of public companies subject to the securities laws
- Inspecting registered public accounting firms
- Conducting investigations and disciplinary proceedings
- Sanctioning registered public accounting firms, and referring cases to the SEC or other enforcement bodies for further investigation

Previously, the AICPA issued auditing standards, was responsible for the Code of Professional Ethics, and disciplined auditors. The PCAOB effectively assumed these responsibilities from the AICPA.[11]

The Sarbanes-Oxley Act was passed in the wake of numerous corporate and accounting scandals, such as Enron and WorldCom. The act limits the services that audit firms can offer clients and prohibits auditors from offering certain nonaudit services (including types of consulting services) to audit clients. It also requires that lead audit partners rotate off audits every five years. Section 302 of the act requires a company's chief executive officer and chief financial officer to certify each quarterly and annual report. Section 404 requires management's assessment of internal control over financial reporting, along with a related report by the independent auditor.[12]

Thus, the auditor's report covers both the financial statements and internal controls. For example, the auditor's report on the financial statements in Colgate-Palmolive's 2008 annual report says the following:

> In our opinion, the consolidated financial statements . . . present fairly, in all material respects, the financial position of Colgate-Palmolive Company and its subsidiaries . . . at December 31, 2008 and 2007, and the results of their operations and their cash flows for each of the three years in the period ended December 31, 2008 in conformity with accounting principles generally accepted in the United States of America.

The auditor's report on internal controls over financial reporting says the following:

> [I]n our opinion, the Company maintained, in all material respects, effective internal control over financial reporting as of December 31, 2008, based on criteria established in *Internal Control—Integrated Framework* issued by the Committee of Sponsoring Organizations of the Treadway Commission (COSO).

---

[11] The act is the most substantial piece of U.S. business legislation since the 1934 Securities Exchange Act established the SEC.

[12] Section 404 is viewed by many observers as the most burdensome (and costly) provision of the act. The PCAOB has five board members, two CPAs and three non-CPAs. Board members are appointed by the SEC after consultation with the Chairman of the Federal Reserve Board and the Secretary of the Treasury. They serve five-year terms. The PCAOB is funded by fees assessed against SEC-registered public companies and registered accounting firms.

Financial statements are supposed to "present fairly" the financial position of the company and the results of its operations "in conformity with generally accepted accounting principles." Compliance with GAAP is the test for fair presentation. There is no subjective override, such as the "true and fair" override in the United Kingdom. The SEC also expects compliance with GAAP and will not accept an auditor's report with an "adverse" opinion.

FINANCIAL REPORTING[13]   A typical annual financial report of a large U.S. corporation includes the following components:

1. Report of management
2. Report of independent auditors
3. Primary financial statements (income statement, balance sheet, statement of cash flows, statement of comprehensive income, and statement of changes in stockholders' equity, etc.)
4. Management discussion and analysis of results of operations and financial condition
5. Disclosure of accounting policies with the most critical impact on financial statements
6. Notes to financial statements
7. Five- or ten-year comparison of selected financial data
8. Selected quarterly data

Consolidated financial statements are required, and published U.S. financial reports typically do not contain parent-company-only statements. Consolidation rules require that all controlled subsidiaries (i.e., ownership of more than 50 percent of the voting shares) be fully consolidated, including those with nonhomogeneous operations.[14] Interim (quarterly) financial reports are required for companies listed on major stock exchanges. These reports typically contain only abbreviated, unaudited financial statements and a concise management commentary.

ACCOUNTING MEASUREMENTS   Accounting measurement rules in the United States assume that a business entity will continue as a going concern. Accrual basis measurements are pervasive, and transactions and events-recognition rules rely heavily on the matching concept. A consistency requirement insists on uniformity of accounting treatment of like items within each accounting period and from one period to the next. If changes in practices or procedures occur, the changes and their effects must be disclosed.

Business combinations must be accounted for as a purchase. Goodwill is capitalized as the difference between the fair value of the consideration given in the exchange and the fair value of the underlying net assets acquired (including other intangibles). It is reviewed for impairment annually and written off and expensed to earnings when its

---

[13] In 2008, the SEC issued a proposal that would permit the use of IFRS by certain U.S. issuers. The SEC also proposed a "roadmap" with a timetable and milestones that need to be achieved for the mandatory transition to IFRS for all U.S. issuers, starting in 2014.
[14] The FASB has proposed extending the consolidation requirement to other entities that a company controls based on its ability to direct the entity's policies and management.

book value exceeds its fair value.[15] Proportional consolidation is not practiced. Joint ventures are accounted for using the equity method, as are investments nonconsolidated, 20 percent– to 50 percent–owned affiliated companies. Foreign currency translation follows the requirements of SFAS No. 52, which relies on the foreign subsidiary's functional currency to determine translation methodology (Chapter 6).

The United States relies on historical cost to value tangible and intangible assets. Revaluations are permitted only after a business combination. Both accelerated and straight-line depreciation methods are permissible. Estimated economic usefulness determines depreciation and amortization periods. All research and development costs are typically expensed as incurred, though there are special capitalization rules for computer software costs.

LIFO, FIFO, and average cost methods are permissible and widely used for inventory pricing. LIFO is popular because it can be used for federal income tax purposes. However, if LIFO is used for tax purposes, it must also be used for financial reporting purposes. Marketable securities are valued at market unless they are classified as held-to-maturity and valued at historical cost.[16]

When financial leases are in substance the purchase of property, the value of the property is capitalized and a corresponding liability is booked.[17] The costs of pensions and other post-retirement benefits are accrued over the periods in which employees earn their benefits, and unfunded obligations are reported as a liability. Contingent losses/ liabilities are accrued when they are probable and the amount can be reasonably estimated.[18] Income-smoothing techniques are not allowed.

Finally, there is the issue of deferred taxes, because (except for LIFO) financial and tax reporting are distinct. Income taxes are accounted for using the liability method. Deferred taxes are accrued for the tax effects of temporary differences between financial and tax accounting methods, and are measured based on the future tax rates that will apply when these items reverse. Comprehensive income tax allocation is required.

Chapter 3 described IFRS. Some of the significant differences between U.S. GAAP and IFRS are summarized in Exhibit 4-2.

Mexico

Before the Spanish conquest in the 1500s, Mexico was home to several highly advanced cultures, including the Olmecs, Mayas, Toltecs, and Aztecs. Hernando

---

[15] Both the purchase and pooling-of-interests (merger) methods were previously used to account for business combinations. They were not alternatives: pooling-of-interests was used when the combination met specified criteria. Under the purchase method, goodwill was capitalized and amortized on a straight-line basis over a maximum of 40 years and the amortization amount was included in current period income. SFAS 141 and 142, issued in 2001, changed how business combinations were accounted for, as described above.

[16] Unrealized gains and losses from value changes on trading securities are recognized in current income while unrealized gains and losses on available-for-sale securities are taken to equity.

[17] The FASB is proposing that all material leases be capitalized, discontinuing the distinction between financing and operating leases.

[18] The FASB is deliberating the definitions of the elements of the financial statements in its joint Conceptual Framework project with the International Accounting Standards Board. The term "contingent liability" will probably no longer be used. Instead, liabilities will be assessed in terms of whether they are "conditional or unconditional obligations." See *Conceptual Framework – Phase B: Elements and Recognition* at the FASB Web site is www.fasb.org.

EXHIBIT 4-2	Significant Differences between U.S. GAAP and IFRS	
Accounting Issue	**U.S. GAAP**	**IFRS**
1. Nature of standards	Rules-based with significantly more implementation guidance	Principles-based
2. Revaluations of property, plant, and equipment	Prohibited: historical costs only	Allowed
3. Extraordinary items on income statement	Used	Prohibited
4. Consolidation of subsidiaries	Based on voting interest	Based on control
5. Joint ventures	Equity method	Proportional consolidation or equity method
6. Development costs	Expensed	Capitalized
7. LIFO	Permitted	Prohibited

1. U.S. GAAP is more rules-based with significantly more implementation guidance, while IFRS are more principles-based.
2. Revaluations of property, plant, and equipment are not allowed under U.S. GAAP. Only historical cost may be used. Revaluations are allowed under IFRS.
3. Extraordinary gains and losses are disclosed on the income statement under U.S. GAAP, but are prohibited under IFRS.
4. Under U.S. GAAP, consolidation is based on ownership: owning more than 50% of a subsidiary' voting power. Consolidation is based on control under IFRS. Control means the power to govern the subsidiary's financial and operating policies.
5. Only the equity method is used to account for joint ventures under U.S. GAAP. Joint ventures are accounted for by either proportional consolidation or the equity method under IFRS.
6. Development costs are expensed under U.S. GAAP. Development costs are capitalized when certain conditions are met under IFRS.
7. LIFO is permitted under U.S. GAAP, but it is not permitted under IFRS.

Note: Detailed differences between U.S. GAAP and IFRS are available from various online sources. A search of "U.S. GAAP versus IFRS" will reveal the most up-to-date ones.

Cortés conquered Mexico in 1521 and founded a Spanish colony that lasted for nearly 300 years. Mexico declared independence in 1810, and an 1821 treaty recognized its independence from Spain. Except for 30 years of internal peace under General Porfírio Díaz (1877 to 1880 and 1884 to 1911), Mexico experienced political and military strife until 1929, when what is now known as the Institutional Revolutionary Party (PRI) was formed. The PRI controlled Mexico's government continuously for 70 years. The 2000 presidential election was won by the National Action Party (PAN), a center-right opposition party, thus ending the supremacy of the PRI in Mexican politics.[19]

---

[19] For a history of the 2000 election, see J. Preston and S. Dillon, *The Making of Democracy* (New York: Farrar, Straus, & Giroux, 2004). The PAN also won the divisive, and contested, 2006 election.

Mexico is the most populous Spanish-speaking country in the world and the second most populous country in Latin America (after Portuguese-speaking Brazil).[20] Mexico has a largely free-market economy: Government-owned or controlled companies dominate petroleum and public utilities, but private enterprise dominates manufacturing, construction, mining, entertainment, and the service industries. In recent years, the government has been privatizing its holdings in nonstrategic industries. Free-market economic reforms during the 1990s helped reduce inflation, increase the rate of economic growth, and deliver healthier economic fundamentals. The reforms included dismantling protectionist trade barriers, opening up to foreign investment, and signing regional trade agreements. The most important agreement for Mexico is the North American Free Trade Agreement (NAFTA), signed with Canada and the United States in 1994. The United States accounts for nearly half of Mexico's imports and 85 percent of Mexico's exports. Mexico has the world's fourteenth-largest economy (in terms of gross domestic product).[21]

Family-controlled conglomerates dominate Mexico's private sector and, by world standards, are relatively small.[22] Although Mexico's stock market is the second largest in Latin America, it is still relatively small by international standards, because firms prefer to raise capital through debt rather than equity. Given the dominance of family-controlled enterprises, Mexican companies traditionally guarded their information and were secretive in their financial reporting. This is changing, however, and more and more Mexican firms are entering U.S. capital markets. Disclosure practices of Mexican companies are increasingly influenced by the expectations of the U.S. market.

The U.S. influence on Mexico's economy extends to accounting. "[M]any of the early leaders of the Mexican profession grew up on 'American accounting,'"[23] and U.S. textbooks and professional literature (either in the original English or translated into Spanish) are used extensively in the education of accountants and as guidance on accounting issues. NAFTA accelerated a trend toward closer cooperation between professional accounting organizations in Mexico, Canada, and the United States. As a founding member of the International Accounting Standards Committee (now the International Accounting Standards Board), Mexico is also committed to convergence with IFRS. Mexico now looks to the IASB for guidance on accounting issues, especially in cases where there is no corresponding Mexican standard.

ACCOUNTING REGULATION AND ENFORCEMENT   The Mexican Commercial Code and income tax laws contain requirements for keeping certain summary accounting records and preparing financial statements, but their influence on financial reporting is generally minimal. Accounting standards are issued by the Council for Research and Development of Financial Information Standards (Consejo Mexicano para

---

[20] The capital, Mexico City, is the second most populous city in the world.

[21] *Pocket World in Figures, 2009 Edition* (London: *The Economist*, 2008): 26 and 181.

[22] It is estimated that up to 95 percent of Mexican businesses are family owned. Over 40 percent of the value of the Mexican stock market is in firms controlled by one family. See "Still Keeping It in the Family," *Business Week* (March 20, 2004): 63–64.

[23] Stephen A. Zeff, *Forging Accounting Principles in Five Countries: A History and an Analysis of Trends* (Champaign, IL: Stipes Publishing, 1971): 96–97.

la Investigación y Desarrollo de Normas de Información Financiera, or CINIF). CINIF is an independent public/private-sector partnership patterned after the U.S. Financial Accounting Standards Board and the International Accounting Standards Board. Its specific aim is to converge Mexican GAAP with IFRS.[24] The Mexican Institute of Public Accountants (Instituto Mexicano de Contadores Públicos) issues auditing standards through its Auditing Standards and Procedures Commission. The institute, a federation of state and other local associations of registered public accountants, is an independent nongovernmental professional association representing the overwhelming majority of public accountants. The Mexican accounting profession is mature, well organized, and highly regarded by the business community.

Despite a legal system based on civil law, accounting standard setting in Mexico takes a British-American, or Anglo-Saxon, approach rather than a continental European one. The standard-setting process is well developed. Before standards are finalized, exposure drafts of proposed standards are issued for review and public comment. Accounting standards are recognized as authoritative by the government, and in particular by the National Banking and Securities Commission, which regulates the Mexican Stock Exchange. Mexican accounting principles do not distinguish between large and small companies, and so are applicable to all business entities. In some cases the National Banking and Securities Commission issues rules for listed companies that limit certain options in generally accepted accounting principles.

Requirements for preparing financial statements and having them audited vary by type and size of company. All companies incorporated under Mexican law (*sociedades anónimas*) must appoint at least one statutory auditor to report to the shareholders on the annual financial statements. Statutory auditors do not have to be public accountants, but when a firm uses independent auditors, a member of the auditing firm frequently acts as statutory auditor. Companies or consolidated groups that meet certain size criteria must file a tax-compliance audit report every year with the Federal Tax Audit Department of the Ministry of Finance. The report consists of audited financial statements, additional schedules, and a statement by the auditor that no irregularities were observed regarding compliance with tax laws. This audit must be done by a Mexican public accountant. Finally, companies listed on the Mexican Stock Exchange must submit annual consolidated financial statements audited by a Mexican public accountant both to the exchange and to the National Banking and Securities Commission.

Starting in 2012, all companies listed on the Mexican Stock Exchange will be required to use IFRS in their financial statements. Listed companies also have the option of using IFRS earlier (from 2008 on). Mexican GAAP, as developed by CINIF, will continue to be required for nonlisted companies.

---

[24] The Web site is www.cinif.org.mx. CINIF was established in 2004 and took over from the Mexican Institute of Public Accountants' Accounting Principles Commission, which had been responsible for developing accounting standards since 1968. CINIF was created by a mutual agreement of organizations representing financial executives, securities brokers, financial institutions, the stock exchange, and the accounting profession, among others. It is backed by government agencies such as the National Banking and Securities Commission, discussed later.

FINANCIAL REPORTING   The fiscal year of Mexican companies must coincide with the calendar year. Comparative consolidated financial statements must be prepared, consisting of:

1. Balance sheet
2. Income statement
3. Statement of cash flows
4. Statement of changes in stockholders' equity
5. Notes

Until 2008, financial statements were adjusted for inflation, that is, general price level accounting was used. The historical costs of nonmonetary assets were restated into pesos of current purchasing power. The components of stockholders' equity were also restated. The gain or loss from holding monetary assets and liabilities were included in current period income, but the effects of other restatements were in stockholders' equity. A statement of changes in financial position, similar to the statement of cash flows, was also presented. However, because it was prepared in constant pesos, the resulting amounts were not cash flows as understood under historical cost accounting. Exhibit 4-3 illustrates the difference for CEMEX, the Mexican cement company. The 2007 20F report filed with the SEC reports amounts in the statement of changes in financial position (adjusted for inflation) as well as cash flow amounts (under historical cost).[25] Under Mexican Financial Reporting Standard B-10 ("Inflation Effects"), effective 2008, inflation accounting is only used when the three-year cumulative inflation rate equals or exceeds 26 percent.

Notes are an integral part of the financial statements (covered by the auditor's report) and include the following:

- Accounting policies of the company
- Material contingencies
- Commitments for substantial purchases of assets or under lease contracts

EXHIBIT 4-3	**CEMEX Statement of Changes in Financial Position and Cash Flow Disclosures**		
	2007	**2006**	**2005**
Statement of Changes in Financial Position (adjusted for inflation)			
• Net resources provided by operating activities	Ps 45,625	47,845	43,080
• Resources provided by (used in) financing activities	130,349	(12,140)	8,450
• Resources used in investing activities	(185,798)	(24,762)	(48,302)
Cash Flows (historical cost)			
• Net cash provided by operating activities	Ps 33,431	17,484	28,909
• Net cash provided by (used in) financing activities	135,891	(5,762)	12,502
• Net cash used in investing activities	(177,707)	(1,152)	(38,818)

Source: 2007 CEMEX 20F, pp. F-7 and F-68.

---

[25] CEMEX is listed on the New York Stock Exchange and must therefore file Form 20F with the SEC.

- Details of long-term debt and foreign currency exposure
- Limitations on dividends
- Guarantees
- Employees' pension plans
- Transactions with related parties
- Income taxes

ACCOUNTING MEASUREMENTS[26]   Consolidated financial statements are prepared when a parent company controls another company. Control is indicated by the ability to determine a company's operating and financial policies. Control normally exists when more than 50 percent of a company's common stock is owned, but it can also be obtained in other ways, including the ability to appoint management or a majority of the board of directors. The equity method is used when there is influence but not control, normally meaning an ownership level between 10 and 50 percent. Joint ventures may be proportionally consolidated or accounted for using the equity method. Mexico has adopted International Accounting Standard No. 21 on foreign currency translation.[27]

The purchase method is used to account for business combinations. Goodwill is the excess of purchase price over the current value of the net assets acquired. It is not amortized, but subject to an annual impairments test. An intangible asset is amortized over its useful life (normally no more than 20 years) unless the life is indefinite, in which case it is not amortized but subject to an annual impairments test.

Research costs are expensed as incurred, while development costs are capitalized and amortized once technological feasibility has been established. Leases are classified as financing or operating. Financing leases—those transferring substantially all the benefits and risks of ownership of the asset—are capitalized, while rents from operating leases are expensed on the income statement. Contingent losses are accrued when they are likely and measurable. General contingency reserves are not acceptable under Mexican GAAP. Deferred taxes are provided for in full, using the liability method. The costs of employee pensions, seniority premiums,[28] and termination pay are accrued currently when they can be reasonably estimated based on actuarial calculations. Statutory (legal) reserves are created by allocating 5 percent of income each year until the reserve equals 20 percent of the value of the outstanding capital stock.

Japan

Japanese accounting and financial reporting reflect a mixture of domestic and international influences. Two separate government agencies have responsibility for accounting

---

[26] Because of the long-time influence of the United States and the more recent influence of the IASB, Mexican financial reporting practices have always been fairness oriented.

[27] When general price level accounting (described above) is used, it is integrated with foreign currency translation: (1) the financial statements of integrated operations are adjusted by the National Consumer Price Index after translation into pesos; (2) financial statements of "foreign entities" (i.e., subsidiaries that are not integrated operations) are first adjusted to reflect the purchasing power of the home currency, then translated into pesos using the closing exchange rate.

[28] Seniority premiums are compensation amounts paid at the termination of employment based on how long the employee has worked. Generally, employees who voluntarily retire must have worked for at least 15 years, but there is no minimum number of years for other types of termination, such as redundancy layoffs, or if an employee dies.

regulations, and there is the further influence of Japanese corporate income tax law. In the first half of the 20th century, accounting thinking reflected German influences; in the second half, U.S. ideas were pervasive. More recently, the effects of the International Accounting Standards Board have been felt, and in 2001 a profound change occurred with the establishment of a private-sector accounting standard setting organization.[29]

To understand Japanese accounting, one must understand Japanese culture, business practices, and history. Japan is a traditional society with strong cultural and religious roots. The group consciousness and interdependence in personal and corporate relationships in Japan contrast with the independent, arm's-length relationships among individuals and groups in Western nations. Japanese companies hold equity interests in each other, and often jointly own other firms. These interlocking investments yield giant industrial conglomerates—notably the *keiretsu*. Banks are often a part of these industrial groups. The widespread use of bank credit and debt capital to finance large enterprises is unusually great from a Western perspective, and corporate managers must primarily answer to banks and other financial institutions rather than shareholders. Central government also exerts tight control on many activities in Japan, which means a strong bureaucratic control over business affairs, including accounting. Knowledge of corporate activities is primarily limited to the corporation and other insiders, such as the banks and the government.

This *keiretsu* business model is being transformed as the Japanese undertake structural reforms to counteract the economic stagnation that occurred in the 1990s.[30] The financial crisis that followed the bursting of Japan's "bubble economy" also prompted a review of Japanese financial reporting standards. It became clear that many accounting practices hid how badly Japanese companies were doing. For example:

1. Loose consolidation standards allowed Japanese companies to bury loss-making operations in affiliates. Investors could not see whether a company's entire operations were really profitable.
2. Pension and severance obligations were only accrued to 40 percent of the amount owed because that was the limit of their tax deductibility. This practice led to substantial underfunding of pension obligations.
3. Securities holdings were valued at cost, not market prices. Designed to reinforce the cohesion of the *keiretsu*, these cross-holdings are vast. Companies held on to the ones with losses, but sold those with gains to prop up sagging profits.

An accounting "Big Bang" was announced in the late 1990s to make the economic health of Japanese companies more transparent and to bring Japan more in line with international standards. These accounting reforms are described later.[31]

---

[29] Until the late 1990s, external influences came to bear only gradually. In terms of what we would consider world-class reporting, accounting was slow to develop in Japan. For example, consolidated financial statements date from 1976 and requirements for segment reporting began in 1990.

[30] For example, in 1992, 46 percent of listed equities were held as cross-shareholdings by related companies. By 2004, cross-shareholdings accounted for 24 percent of shares.

[31] "Japan on the Brink," *Economist* (April 11, 1999): 15–17; "Japan Restructures, Grudgingly," *Economist* (February 6, 1999): 63–65; "The Secrets Pour Out," *Business Week* (August 2, 1999): 50–51; "Reshaping Standards," *Accountancy* (June 2000): 110; "Japan: Restoring Investor Confidence," *IASC Insight* (September 2000): 8; "Going International," *Accountancy* (March 2002): 102–103; "The Sun Also Rises: A Survey of Japan," *Economist* (October 8, 2005): 1–18.

ACCOUNTING REGULATION AND ENFORCEMENT   The national government has a significant influence on accounting in Japan. Accounting regulation is based on three laws: the Company Law, the Securities and Exchange Law, and the Corporate Income Tax Law. These three laws are linked and interact with each other. A leading Japanese scholar refers to the situation as a "triangular legal system."[32]

The Company Law is administered by the Ministry of Justice (MOJ). Developed from German commercial law, the original code was enacted in 1890 but not implemented until 1899. Creditor and shareholder protection is its fundamental principle, with an unequivocal reliance on historical cost measurements. Disclosures on creditworthiness and the availability of earnings for dividend distribution are of primary importance. All companies incorporated under the Company Law are required to meet its accounting provisions.

Publicly owned companies must meet the further requirements of the Securities and Exchange Law (SEL), administered by the Financial Services Agency (FSA).[33] The SEL is modeled after the U.S. Securities Acts and was imposed on Japan by the United States during the U.S. occupation following World War II. The main objective of the SEL is to provide information for investment decision-making. Although the SEL requires the same basic financial statements as the Company Law, the terminology, form, and content of financial statements are more precisely defined under the SEL; certain financial statement items are reclassified for presentation, and additional detail is provided. Net income and shareholders' equity are, however, the same under the Company Law and the SEL.

Until recently, a special advisory body to the FSA was responsible for developing accounting standards under the SEL. Called the Business Accounting Deliberation Council (BADC), and now the Business Accounting Council (BAC), it was arguably the major source of generally accepted accounting principles in Japan.[34] However, a major change in accounting standard setting occurred in 2001 with the establishment of the Accounting Standards Board of Japan (ASBJ) and its related oversight foundation, the Financial Accounting Standards Foundation (FASF). The ASBJ now has sole responsibility for developing accounting standards and implementation guidance in Japan. It has 15 members, four of whom are full-time. It also has a full-time technical staff to support its activities. The FASF is responsible for funding and naming its members. Funding comes from companies and the accounting profession, not the government. As an independent private-sector organization, the ASBJ is stronger and more transparent than the BAC, and subject to fewer political and special-interest pressures.[35] The ASBJ collaborates with the IASB in developing IFRS and in 2005 launched a joint project with the IASB to reduce differences between Japanese accounting standards and IFRS. The so-called Tokyo Agreement between the ASBJ and IASB, announced in 2008, targets 2011 as the date for full convergence between

---

[32] Kiyomitsu Arai, *Accounting in Japan* (Tokyo: Waseda University, Institute for Research in Business Administration, 1994): 5.

[33] The FSA is the government regulatory agency responsible for supervising private-sector financial institutions, such as banks, insurance companies, and the securities exchanges. It took over the administration of the SEL from the Ministry of Finance when it was established in 2000. As discussed later, it also oversees the Certified Public Accountant and Auditing Oversight Board. The FSA Web site is www.fsa.go.jp/en.

[34] Before 2000, the BADC reported to the Ministry of Finance (see preceding footnote).

[35] The standard setting framework is similar to that of the U.S. Financial Accounting Foundation and Financial Accounting Standards Board, as discussed in this chapter. The FASF and ASBJ Web site is www.asb.or.jp.

the two sets of standards. The BAC still advises the FSA on accounting matters. As discussed later, the BAC is responsible for establishing auditing standards. Japanese accounting standards cannot be at variance with commercial law (or tax law, as discussed next). Thus, the triangulation of accounting standards, company law, and tax law is still a feature of Japanese financial reporting.

Finally, the influence of the tax code is important. As in France, Germany, and elsewhere, expenses can be claimed for tax purposes only if they are fully booked. Taxable income is based on the amount calculated under the Company Law.

Under the Company Law, the financial statements and supporting schedules of small and medium-sized companies are subject to audit only by statutory auditors. Both statutory and independent auditors must audit large corporations. Independent auditors must audit financial statements of publicly held companies in accordance with the Securities and Exchange Law. Statutory auditors do not need any particular professional qualification and are employed by the company on a full-time basis. Statutory audits focus mainly on the managerial actions of the directors and whether they perform their duties in compliance with legal statutes. Independent audits involve examining the financial statements and records, and must be performed by certified public accountants (CPAs).

The Japanese Institute of Certified Public Accountants (JICPA) is the professional organization of CPAs in Japan. All CPAs must belong to the JICPA.[36] In addition to providing guidance on the conduct of audits, the JICPA publishes implementation guidelines on accounting matters, and provides input to the ASBJ in developing accounting standards. Generally accepted auditing standards are promulgated by the BAC rather than the JICPA. The Certified Public Accountant and Auditing Oversight Board was established in 2003. A government agency, it is designed to monitor and oversee the auditing profession and improve the quality of Japanese audits. It was put under the FSA in 2004.

FINANCIAL REPORTING   Companies incorporated under the Company Law are required to prepare a statutory report for approval at the annual shareholders' meeting, consisting of the following:

1. Balance sheet
2. Income statement
3. Statement of changes in shareholders' equity
4. Business report
5. Supporting schedules

Notes accompanying the balance sheet and income statement describe the accounting policies and provide supporting details, as is typical in other countries. The business report contains an outline of the business and its internal control systems, and information about its operations, financial position, and operating results. A number of supporting schedules are also required, separate from the notes, including:

- Changes in bonds and other short- and long-term debt
- Changes in fixed assets and accumulated depreciation
- Collateralized assets

---

[36] The Web site is www.hp.jicpa.or.jp.

- Debt guarantees
- Changes in provisions
- Amounts due to and from the controlling shareholders
- Equity ownership in subsidiaries and the number of shares of the company's stock held by subsidiaries
- Receivables due from subsidiaries
- Transactions with directors, statutory auditors, controlling shareholders and third parties that create a conflict of interest
- Remuneration paid to directors and statutory auditors

This information is prepared for a single year on a parent-company basis and is audited by the statutory auditor. The Company Law does not require a statement of cash or funds flow.

Listed companies also must prepare financial statements under the Securities and Exchange Law, which generally requires the same basic statements as the Company Law plus a statement of cash flows. However, under the SEL, consolidated financial statements, not the parent-company statements, are the main focus. Additional footnotes and schedules are also required.[37] Financial statements and schedules submitted under the SEL must be audited by independent auditors. Beginning in 2008, listed companies must issue quarterly financial reports. Also beginning in 2008, managements of listed companies must submit an annual assessment of the company's internal controls and a letter certifying the accuracy of the annual report. The internal control report must be audited.[38]

A cash flow forecast for the next six months is included as supplemental information in filings with the FSA. Other forecast information is also reported, such as forecasts of new capital investments and production levels and activities. Overall, the amount of corporate forecast reporting is extensive in Japan. However, this information is reported in statutory filings and rarely appears in the annual report to shareholders.

ACCOUNTING MEASUREMENTS The Company Law requires large companies to prepare consolidated financial statements. In addition, listed companies must prepare consolidated financial statements under the Securities and Exchange Law. Individual company accounts are the basis for the consolidated statements, and normally the same accounting principles are used at both levels. Subsidiaries are consolidated if a parent directly or indirectly controls their financial and operational policies. Business combinations are accounted for as a purchase. Goodwill is measured on the basis of the fair value of the net assets acquired and is amortized over 20 years or less and is subject to an impairment test. The equity method is used for investments in affiliated companies when the parent and subsidiaries exert significant influence over their financial and operational policies. The equity method is also used to account for joint ventures; proportional consolidation is not allowed. Under the foreign currency translation standard, assets and liabilities of foreign

---

[37] Additional footnotes include information about such things as subsequent events and liabilities for employee retirement and severance benefits. Additional schedules detail items on the financial statements, such as marketable securities, tangible and intangible assets, investments in and loans to or from affiliated companies, bonds payable and other long-term borrowings, and reserves and allowances.

[38] The law requiring an internal control assessment and certification of the financial statements is based on the U.S. Sarbanes-Oxley Act and is informally called the "J-Sox rule." However, unlike Sarbanes-Oxley it does not require the auditor's direct assessment of the company's internal control. Rather, the auditor's opinion covers management's assessment of internal controls.

subsidiaries are translated at the current (year-end) exchange rate, revenues and expenses at the average rate, and translation adjustments are in stockholders' equity.

Inventory must be valued at cost or the lower of cost or net realizable value. FIFO, LIFO, and average are all acceptable cost-flow methods, with average the most popular.[39] Investments in securities are valued at market. Fixed assets are valued at cost. The declining-balance method is the most common depreciation method. Fixed assets are also impairments tested.

Research and development costs are expensed when incurred. Finance leases are capitalized and amortized, while the costs of operating leases are expensed. Deferred taxes are provided for all timing differences using the liability method. Contingent losses are provided for when they are probable and can be reasonably estimated. Pension and other employee retirement benefits are fully accrued as employees earn them, and unfunded obligations are shown as a liability. Legal reserves are required: Each year a company must allocate an amount equal to at least 10 percent of cash dividends and bonuses paid to directors and statutory auditors until the legal reserve reaches 25 percent of capital stock.

Many of the accounting practices described above were implemented as a result of the accounting Big Bang referred to earlier. These changes include: (1) requiring listed companies to report a statement of cash flows; (2) extending the number of subsidiaries that are consolidated based on control rather than ownership percentage; (3) extending the number of affiliates accounted for using the equity method based on significant influence rather than ownership percentage; (4) valuing investments in securities at market rather than cost; (5) valuing inventory at the lower of cost or net realizable value rather than cost; (6) full provisioning of deferred taxes; and (7) full accrual of pension and other retirement obligations. In December 2009, the Financial Services Agency announced that listed Japanese companies may voluntarily adopt IFRS for fiscal periods starting on or after March 31, 2010. This is seen as a step toward full adoption of IFRS, expected around 2015.

China

China has one-fifth of the world's population, and market-oriented reforms have helped generate rapid economic growth.[40] In the late 1970s, Chinese leaders began to move the economy from Soviet-style central planning to a system that is more market-oriented but still under Communist Party control.[41] To achieve this, they switched to a system of

---

[39] LIFO will no longer be permitted after 2010.

[40] In 1997, Great Britain ceded control of Hong Kong to China. Under the agreement between China and Britain, China has guaranteed to operate a "one country, two systems" arrangement in which Hong Kong's lifestyle will be unchanged for 50 years and basic freedoms and rights will be guaranteed by law. Accounting in Hong Kong is similar to accounting in the United Kingdom, described in Chapter 3. The discussion of China in this chapter refers to mainland China and excludes Hong Kong.

[41] China's real gross domestic product grew at an average annual rate of 10.3 percent between 1996 and 2006, one of the highest growth rates of any nation. See *The Economist Pocket World in Figures, 2009 Edition* (London: *The Economist*, 2008), p. 32. For much of recorded history, China was the largest economy in the world. Until the 15th century, China had the highest income per head and was the world's technological leader. For example, China led the world in its understanding of hydraulics, ironsmelting, and shipbuilding. Among China's inventions are the toothbrush, umbrella, playing cards, and paper. Even as late as 1820, it still accounted for 30 percent of the world's GDP. However, by 1950, its share of world output had fallen to less than 5 percent. See "The Dragon and the Eagle," *Economist* (October 2, 2004): 1–26.

household responsibility in agriculture instead of the old collectivization, increased the authority of local officials and plant managers in industry, permitted a wide variety of small-scale enterprises in services and light manufacturing, and opened the economy to increased foreign trade and investment. In 1993 China's leadership approved additional long-term reforms aimed at giving more flexibility for market-oriented institutions. Central features include the share system of ownership, privatizations, the development of organized stock exchanges, and the listing of shares in Chinese companies on Western exchanges. Nevertheless, state-owned enterprises still dominate many key industries in what the Chinese call a "socialist market economy," that is, a planned economy with market adaptations.[42]

Accounting in China has a long history. Its functioning in a stewardship role can be detected as far back as 2200 B.C. during the Hsiu Dynasty, and documents show that it was used to measure wealth and compare achievements among dukes and princes in the Xia Dynasty (2000 to 1500 B.C.). The young Confucius (551 to 479 B.C.) was a manager of warehouses, and his writings mention that the job included proper accounting—keeping the records of receipts and disbursements up-to-date. Among the teachings of Confucius is the imperative to compile a history, and accounting records are viewed as part of history.

The principal characteristics of accounting in China today date from the founding of the People's Republic of China in 1949. China installed a highly centralized planned economy, reflecting Marxist principles and patterned after the system in the Soviet Union. The state controlled the ownership, the right to use, and the distribution of all means of production, and enacted rigid planning and control over the economy. Production was the top priority of state-owned enterprises. Their sales and pricing were dictated by the state's planning authorities, and their financing and product costing were administered by the state's finance departments. Under this system, the purpose of accounting was to serve the needs of the state for economic planning and control. A uniform set of standardized accounts was developed to integrate information into the national economic plan. The uniform accounting system contained all-inclusive accounting rules that were mandatory for state-owned enterprises across the country.

Financial reporting was frequent and detailed. The main feature was a fund-management orientation where *funds* meant the property, goods, and materials used in the production process. Financial reporting emphasized the balance sheet, which reflected the source and application of funds. It focused on stewardship and accountability, or the fulfilling of production and other goals, as well as compliance with governmental policies and regulations. Accounting emphasized counting quantities and comparing costs and quantities. Although accounting focused more on managerial than financial objectives, its role in decision-making by the managers of individual enterprises was nevertheless subordinated to the central authorities.

China's economy today is best described as a hybrid economy in which the state controls strategic commodities and industries, while other industries, as well as the

---

[42] The Chinese economy is now the fourth-largest in the world, after the United States, Japan, and Germany. A central feature of China's reforms is a gradualist approach to economic liberalization. See Robert J. Barro, "China's Slow Yet Steady March to Reform, *Business Week* (September 30, 2002): 28; Fareed Zakaria, "The Big Story Everyone Missed," *Newsweek* (January 6, 2003): 52.

commercial and private sectors, are governed by a market-oriented system.[43] The recent economic reforms involve privatizations, including the conversion of state-owned enterprises into share-issuing corporations. New accounting rules have had to be developed for newly privatized companies and other independent limited liability companies, as well as for foreign business entities, such as joint ventures. The role of the government has been changing from managing both the macro- and microeconomy to one managing at the macro level only.[44] Accounting standards were needed to reflect this new reality.

ACCOUNTING REGULATION AND ENFORCEMENT   The Accounting Law, last amended in 2000, covers all enterprises and organizations, including those not owned or controlled by the state. It outlines the general principles of accounting and defines the role of the government and the matters that require accounting procedures. The State Council (an executive body corresponding to a cabinet) has also issued Financial Accounting and Reporting Rules for Enterprises (FARR). These focus on bookkeeping, the preparation of financial statements, reporting practices, and other financial accounting and reporting matters. FARR apply to all enterprises other than very small ones that do not raise funds externally. The Ministry of Finance, supervised by the State Council, formulates accounting and auditing standards. Besides accounting and auditing matters, the ministry is responsible for a wide range of activities affecting the economy. Generally, these activities include formulating long-term economic strategies and setting the priorities for the allocation of government funds. More specifically, the ministry's responsibilities include:

- formulating and enforcing economic, tax, and other finance-related policies
- preparing the annual state budget and fiscal report
- managing state revenue and expenditure
- developing the financial management and tax system[45]

Accounting and auditing matters fall into the last category.

In 1992 the Ministry of Finance issued Accounting Standards for Business Enterprises (ASBE), a conceptual framework designed to guide the development of new accounting standards that would eventually harmonize domestic practices and harmonize Chinese practices with international practices. The ASBE was a landmark event in China's move to a market economy. Before the ASBE, more than 40 different uniform accounting systems were in use, varying across industries and types of ownership. Although each one of these could individually be labeled as *uniform*, taken together they resulted in inconsistent practices overall. Thus, one motive for issuing the ASBE was to harmonize domestic accounting practices. Moreover, existing practices were incompatible with international practices and unsuited for a market-oriented economy. Harmonizing Chinese accounting

---

[43] State-owned enterprises dominate key sectors, such as banking, telecoms, energy, and the media. Non-state-owned enterprises now produce two-thirds of China's manufacturing output.
[44] The ownership relationship between the government and state-owned enterprises has been redefined. Regulations issued by the Ministry of Finance in 1994 announced for the first time that the state is an investor in the enterprise and is responsible for the enterprise's debts limited to the amount of its capital; the enterprise has its own legal status, enjoying its own property rights and bearing independent civil responsibilities. See Zezhong Xiao and Aixiang Pan, "Developing Accounting Standards on the Basis of a Conceptual Framework by the Chinese Government," *International Journal of Accounting* 32, no. 3 (1997): 282. For further discussion of China's reforms of state-owned enterprises, see "The Longer March," *Economist* (September 30, 2000): 71–73. China has 120,000 state-owned enterprises.
[45] "Role of the Ministry of Finance," Ministry of Finance Web site (www.mof.gov.cn), December 16, 2000.

to international practices served to remove barriers of communication with foreign investors and helped meet the needs of the economic reforms already under way.

After the issuance of the ASBE, the Ministry of Finance replaced the more than 40 uniform accounting systems mentioned previously with 13 industry-based and two ownership-based accounting systems. These systems were viewed as transitional until specific accounting standards could be promulgated that would apply to all enterprises operating in China. A revised ASBE was issued in 2001.

The China Accounting Standards Committee (CASC) was established in 1998 as the authoritative body within the Ministry of Finance responsible for developing accounting standards.[46] The standard-setting process includes assigning necessary research to task forces, the issuance of exposure drafts, and public hearings. CASC members are experts drawn from academia, accounting firms, government, professional accounting associations, and other key groups concerned with the development of accounting in China. After it was formed, the CASC began issuing standards on such issues as the cash flow statement, debt restructuring, revenue, nonmonetary transactions, contingencies, and leases. All of these standards were aimed at converging Chinese accounting standards with International Financial Reporting Standards.

Finally, in 2006, in a Big Bang approach to convergence, a new set of Accounting Standards for Business Enterprises was issued. This new ASBE consists of one basic ASBE and 38 specific ASBE. The basic standard established the framework, and the specific standards set out broad principles and detailed implementation guidance on such areas as fixed and intangible assets, inventories, leases, income taxes, consolidations, and segment reporting. Together they represent a comprehensive set of Chinese accounting standards that are substantially in line with IFRS. The new ASBE applies to all Chinese companies (except small ones), phasing out the industry and ownership standards referred to above. Exhibit 4-4 summarizes the basic ASBE. Forty-eight new auditing standards, similar to the International Standards on Auditing issued by the International Auditing and Assurance Standards Board (see Chapter 8), were issued at the same time. All Chinese accounting firms and CPAs are required to follow these audit standards.

The China Securities Regulatory Commission (CSRC) regulates China's two stock exchanges: Shanghai, which opened in 1990, and Shenzhen, which opened in 1991.[47] It

---

EXHIBIT 4-4   **China's Accounting Standards for Business Enterprises—Basic Standard**

- **General provisions:** stewardship, economic decision-making, going concern, accrual basis.
- **Qualitative requirements of accounting information:** faithful representation, relevance, understandability, comparability, substance over form, prudence.
- **Definitions of elements:** assets, liabilities, owners' equity, revenue, expenses, profit.
- **Accounting measurement:** Generally, historical cost; if elements are measured at replacement cost, net realizable value, present value, or fair value, the enterprise shall ensure that such amounts are available and can be reliably measured.
- **Financial reports:** balance sheet, income statement, cash flow statement, and notes.

---

[46] The CASC Web site is www.casc.gov.cn.
[47] The CSRC Web site is www.csrc.gov.cn.

sets regulatory guidelines, formulates and enforces market rules, and authorizes initial public offers and new shares. A code of corporate governance was introduced in 2002. The CSRC also issues additional disclosure requirements for listed companies. Thus, disclosure requirements for listed companies are established by two government bodies, the Ministry of Finance and the CSRC.[48]

Until 1995 China had two professional accounting organizations. The Chinese Institute of Certified Public Accountants (CICPA), established in 1988 under the jurisdiction of the Ministry of Finance, regulated the audit of private-sector enterprises. The Chinese Association of Certified Public Auditors (CACPA) was responsible for auditing state-owned enterprises and was under the authority of a separate agency, the State Audit Administration. In 1995 CICPA and CACPA merged, keeping the name of the CICPA. The CICPA sets the requirements for becoming a CPA, administers the CPA examination, develops auditing standards, and is responsible for the code of professional ethics.[49]

FINANCIAL REPORTING   The accounting period is required to be the calendar year. Financial statements consist of:

1. Balance sheet
2. Income statement
3. Cash flow statement
4. Statement of changes in equity
5. Notes

Additional statements are required disclosing asset impairments, changes in capital structure, appropriations of profits, and business and geographical segments. The notes include a statement of accounting policies. As applicable, they discuss such matters as contingencies, important post-balance sheet events, and related-party transactions. A management discussion and analysis is required discussing the enterprise's operations, financial position, results, cash flows, and items affecting them. Financial statements must be consolidated, comparative, in Chinese, and expressed in the Chinese currency, the renminbi. The annual financial statements must be audited by a Chinese CPA. Listed companies must assess their internal controls and engage an

---

[48] China's stock markets rank second in the world in terms of market capitalization. Around 1,500 companies are listed, and there are officially nearly 70 million individual investors. Nevertheless, the state holds roughly two-thirds of the shares of listed companies, meaning that two-thirds of the market capitalization is not traded. Most companies are listed for political rather than economic reasons, and almost all of them benefit from government favoritism. Since the state is the dominant shareholder of most listed companies, there are few incentives for managers to maximize shareholder value, and thus managers have relatively little market discipline. Controlling shareholders tend to engage in related-party transactions that are not in the interest of minority shareholders. (China has a *guanxi* ["relationship"] culture based on mutuality and mutual duties. *Guanxi* creates obligations for a continual exchange of favors, which in the extreme can lead to corruption.) Disclosures are still poor, and enforcement of market rules is weak. Much of the individual trading is based on rumor rather than reliable information. The stock markets are not yet effective as a way to allocate capital. See "Fools in Need of Institutions," *Economist* (June 30, 2001): 65–66; "Banking on Growth," *Economist* (January 18, 2003): 67–68; "A Survey of Asian Finance: Casino Capital," *Economist* (February 8, 2003): 10–12; P. Lupton, "Corporate Governance and Business Ethics in the Asia-Pacific Region," *Business and Society* (June 2005): 178–210.

[49] China faces a huge shortage of qualified accountants. There are approximately 70,000 bilingual market-oriented accountants trying to do the work of 300,000 to one million. See Katie Hunt, "China: Currency of Change," *Accountancy* (June 2007): 35–36.

external auditor to evaluate the controls and comment on the self-assessment report.[50] A quarterly balance sheet, income statement, and notes are required for listed companies.

ACCOUNTING MEASUREMENTS   The purchase method must be used to account for business combinations. Goodwill is the difference between the cost of the acquisition and the fair values of the assets and liabilities acquired. It is tested for impairment on an annual basis. The equity method is used for investments in associates, those over which the investee has significant influence. The equity method is also used to account for joint ventures. All subsidiaries under the control of the parent are consolidated. The financial statements of an overseas subsidiary are translated based on the primary economic environment in which it operates. If it is the local (overseas) environment, the balance sheet is translated at the year-end exchange rate, the income statement is translated at the average-for-the-year exchange rate, and any translation difference is shown in equity. If it is the parent's environment, monetary items are translated at the year-end exchange rate, nonmonetary items are translated at the relevant transaction-date exchange rate, and revenues and expenses are translated at the transaction-date rate (or the appropriate average rate for the period). The translation difference is included in income.

Historical cost is the basis for valuing tangible assets; revaluations are not allowed. They are depreciated over their expected useful lives, normally on a straight-line basis. Accelerated and units-of-production depreciation are also acceptable. FIFO and average are acceptable costing methods, and inventory is written down for price declines and obsolescence. Acquired intangibles are also recorded at cost. Those with a finite life are amortized over the periods benefited based on the pattern in which the benefits are consumed. Intangibles with an indefinite life are not amortized but are impairments tested at least annually. Because land and much of the industrial property in China are owned by the state, companies that acquire the right to use land and industrial property rights show them as intangibles. Assets are revalued when a change in ownership takes place, as when a state-owned enterprise is privatized. Certified asset assessment firms or CPA firms determine these valuations.

Research costs are expensed, but development costs are capitalized if technological feasibility and cost recovery are established. Finance leases are capitalized. Deferred taxes are provided in full for all temporary differences. Employee benefits are expensed as they are earned rather than when paid. Contingent obligations are provided for when they are both probable and their amount can be reliably estimated.

India

India occupies much of the South Asian subcontinent, with Pakistan to the west, China, Nepal, and Bhutan to the north, and Bangladesh to the east. The Himalaya Mountains, the tallest mountain system in the world, are located on India's northern

---

[50] This requirement is similar to Section 404 of the Sarbanes-Oxley Act discussed in the section on the United States.

border.[51] Coastal India has the Arabian Sea to the west, the Indian Ocean to the south, and the Bay of Bengal to the east. India has 17 percent of the world's population, the second most populous nation in the world after China.[52] India is also one of the most ethnically diverse countries in the world. It is home to several hundred languages, 18 of which have official status. Hindi is the official language and the most widely spoken, but English is widely used in government, business, science, and education.

The people of India have had a continuous civilization for more than 5,000 years. Extensive urbanization based on commerce and agricultural trade appears to have begun in the Indus River Valley (in the northwest) around 3000 B.C. Since this time, numerous empires have ruled various portions of South Asia, often assimilating a rich array of peoples, each adding its own contribution to the region's increasingly diverse cultures, ideas, and technologies. The political map of ancient and medieval India was made up of myriad kingdoms with fluctuating boundaries. In the 4th and 5th centuries A.D., northern India was unified under the Gupta Dynasty. During this period, known as India's Golden Age, science, literature, and the arts flourished under Hindu culture. The south also experienced several great empires. Arab, Turkic, and Afghan Muslims ruled successively from the 8th to the 18th century A.D.[53]

European economic competition in India began soon after the Portuguese arrived in 1498. The first British outpost was established by the East India Company in 1619, and permanent trading stations were opened in other parts of the country over the rest of the 17th century. The British expanded their influence from these footholds until, by the 1850s, they controlled—politically, militarily, and economically—most of present-day India, Pakistan, Sri Lanka, and Bangladesh. A mass campaign against British colonial rule began in the 1920s under the leadership of Mohandas Gandhi and Jawaharlal Nehru. Rising civil disobedience and World War II eventually rendered India too costly and difficult to administer, and the British government granted independence in 1947. British India was immediately partitioned into two separate states: India, with a Hindu majority; and East and West Pakistan—now Bangladesh and Pakistan—with Muslim majorities. The British legacy in India is substantial, including its common law legal system, its parliamentary system of central government, and the widespread use of the English language.

From 1947 to the late 1970s, the Indian economy was characterized by central government socialist-style planning and import-substitution industries. Economic production was transformed from primarily agriculture, forestry, fishing, and textile manufacturing to various heavy industries and transportation. However, the lack of competition contributed to poor product quality and inefficiencies in production. Facing an economic crisis, the government began opening up the economy in 1991.[54] The market-oriented economic reforms adopted since then include the privatization of

---

[51] The country's exact size is subject to debate because some of its borders are disputed.
[52] India has 41 cities with more than one million people. It is also a young nation: 30 percent of the world's children are in India.
[53] Hinduism, Buddhism, Jainism, and Sikhism were born in India.
[54] Community and family networks have a long tradition in India and have affected the structuring of businesses. Family-controlled businesses are very common. In general, ownership in Indian companies is concentrated, either by families or the government.

some state-owned industries, liberalized foreign investment and exchange regimes, reductions in tariffs and other trade barriers, reform and modernization of the financial sector, significant adjustments in government monetary and fiscal policies, and safeguarding intellectual property rights. However, a large proportion of heavy industry is still state-owned, and high tariffs and limits on foreign direct investment are still in place.[55] The services sector has proved to be India's most dynamic sector in recent years, with telecommunications and information technology recording particularly rapid growth.[56]

Future economic growth is constrained by an inadequate infrastructure, a cumbersome bureaucracy and red tape, labor market rigidities, and corruption. The lack of reliable and affordable infrastructure, especially roads and electricity, is viewed by many as the single most important brake on future growth. Red tape also imposes heavy costs on business in many parts of the country—for example, in bribes paid to inspectors.[57] Finally, labor laws impose extra costs.[58] The reforms that began in 1991 have cut away bureaucratic controls and encouraged the creation of a more competitive marketplace. Most observers agree that further reforms and additional investment in infrastructure are needed to make India a leading economic player, but as noted at the beginning of this chapter, the same observers are optimistic about India's growth prospects.

ACCOUNTING REGULATION AND ENFORCEMENT   The British influence extends to accounting: Financial reporting is aimed at fair presentation, and there is an independent accounting profession that sets accounting and auditing standards. The two major sources of financial accounting standards in India are companies law and the accounting profession. The first companies act was legislated in 1857, and the first law relating to the maintenance and audit of accounting records was enacted in 1866, along with the first formal qualifications of auditors. Both were based on British law.

The current Companies Act 1956 is administered and updated by a government agency, the Ministry of Company Affairs. The act provides a broad framework for keeping so-called books of account and the requirements for an audit. According to the act, books of account

- must give a true and fair view of the state of affairs of the company
- must be kept on an accrual basis according to the double-entry system of accounting.

---

[55] U.S. Department of State, "Background Notes: India" (October 2006), www.state.gov; Library of Congress – Federal Research Division, "Country Profile: India" (December 2004), http://lcweb2.loc.gov/frd/cs/profiles/India.pdf; "Now for the Hard Part: A Survey of India," *Economist* (June 3, 2006): 1–18.

[56] The industry barely existed in India in 1991, when the economic reforms began. It is said that India's telecommunications and information technology sector is successful because it has always competed in a global marketplace. It never benefited from government favors or suffered distorted incentives of government protection. See "Now for the Hard Part: A Survey of India," *Economist* (June 3, 2006): 4.

[57] Priya Basu of the World Bank is quoted as saying, "Entrepreneurs have to spend significant time in dealing with permits, clearances and inspections, and end up paying substantial 'rents' to the inspectors." See *Economist*, "Now for the Hard Part: A Survey of India" (June 3, 2006): 14. The article goes on to say that collusion between contactors and vendors is so common that it is probably not even recognized as corrupt. See also *Economist*, "An Elephant, Not a Tiger" (December 2008): 1–18.

[58] Chapter 5B of the 1947 Industrial Disputes Act prohibits companies with more than 100 employees from laying off workers without the permission of the state government. This law discourages hiring and encourages the substitution of capital for labor in a country that is people rich.

The act requires an audited balance sheet and profit and loss account, approved by the board of directors.[59] An accompanying directors' report must address the state of affairs of the company, its material commitments, recommended dividends, and other information necessary for understanding the nature of the company's business and subsidiaries.

The Institute of Chartered Accountants of India (ICAI), established in 1949, regulates the profession of chartered accountancy and is responsible for developing both accounting and auditing standards.[60] Chartered accountants were previously known as registered accountants and the institute was preceded by other organizations of professional accountants, such as the Society of Auditors, founded in Madras in 1927. The institute prescribes the qualifications for becoming a chartered accountant, holds examinations and training programs for candidates, issues certificates to practice, and disciplines members for professional misconduct and breaches of ethical behavior. Its Accounting Standards Board issues Indian Accounting Standards (AS), and its Auditing and Assurance Standards Board issues Auditing and Assurance Standards (AAS). AS have statutory authority, and AAS are mandatory for the practice of auditing. The institute is supervised by the Ministry of Company Affairs. In 2007, the ICAI announced that it will adopt IFRS in 2011.

There are 22 stock exchanges in India, the oldest of which is the Mumbai (Bombay) Stock Exchange, established in 1875 and now listing more than 6,000 stocks.[61] The regulatory agency that oversees the functioning of stock markets is the Securities and Exchange Board of India (SEBI), an agency of the Ministry of Finance established in 1988 and given statutory authority in 1992. In general, the accounting and disclosure requirements for listed companies are similar to those in the AS.

FINANCIAL REPORTING   Financial statements consist of two-year balance sheets, income statements, cash flow statements, and accounting policies and notes. Companies that are not listed are only required to prepare parent-only statements, but listed companies must prepare both consolidated and parent-only statements. Neither a statement of shareholders' equity nor a statement of comprehensive income is required. Financial statements must present a true and fair view, but there is no true and fair override as there is in the United Kingdom. As noted above, the Companies Act requires that a directors' report accompany the financial statements. Companies listed on a stock exchange must also provide a management discussion and analysis covering such topics as the industry structure and development, opportunities and threats faced by the company, internal controls, and risks that affect the performance of business segments or products. Listed companies must also provide interim financial results on a quarterly basis.

ACCOUNTING MEASUREMENTS   Subsidiaries are consolidated when the parent owns more than half of the entity's voting power or controls the composition of its board of directors. Subsidiaries may be excluded from consolidation if control is temporary or if there are long-term restrictions on the subsidiary's ability to transfer funds to

---

[59] As noted later, Indian accounting standards also require a cash flow statement.
[60] The Institute's Web site is www.icai.org.
[61] The combined market capitalization of India's stock exchanges is the eighth largest in the world.

the parent. There are no standards on accounting for business combinations, but most of them are accounted for as a purchase. However, the uniting-of-interests (pooling) method is used for mergers (called amalgamations). Goodwill is the difference between the consideration given and the existing carrying amounts of the assets and liabilities acquired. Practice varies between no amortization of goodwill to amortization over no more than 10 years. Goodwill is also reviewed for impairment. Proportional consolidation is used for jointly controlled entities (joint ventures). The equity method is used to account for associates—entities over which there is significant influence but not control.

Translation of the financial statements of a foreign operation depends on whether it is integral or nonintegral to the operations of the reporting (parent) entity. For integral foreign operations, monetary assets and liabilities are translated at the closing (year-end) exchange rate, nonmonetary items carried at historical cost are translated at the exchange rate at the date of the transaction, and nonmonetary items carried at fair value are translated at the exchange rate when fair value was determined. Income statement amounts are translated at the exchange rate on the date of transaction or weighted average rate for the period. Exchange differences are reported in income. Assets and liabilities of nonintegral foreign operations are translated at the closing exchange rate, income and expense items are translated at the exchange rates at the dates of the transactions, and the resulting exchange difference is accumulated in a foreign currency exchange reserve on the balance sheet. AS have no provisions for subsidiaries in hyperinflationary economies.

Fixed assets are valued at either historical cost or revalued (fair) value. Revaluations must be applied to the entire class of fixed asset, but there is no requirement that revaluations be performed at regular intervals. Depreciation is allocated on a systematic basis over the life of the asset. If assets are revalued, depreciation is based on the revalued amount. Intangible assets are normally amortized over no more than 10 years. Internally generated goodwill or other intangibles (e.g., brand names) are not recognized as assets. Research costs are expensed as incurred, but development costs may be deferred if the technical feasibility of the product or process has been demonstrated and the recoverability of the costs is reasonably certain. Inventory is valued at the lower of cost or net realizable value. FIFO and average are acceptable cost-flow methods.

Finance leases are capitalized at fair market value and depreciated over the life of the lease. Operating leases are expensed on a straight-line basis over the lease term. The costs of employee benefits are accounted for as the employee earns them rather than when they are paid. Contingent losses are provided for when they are probable (likely) and a reasonable estimate of the amount can be made. Deferred taxes are provided for all timing differences. Deferred tax assets and liabilities are not discounted to their present values.

As noted earlier, the Institute of Chartered Accountants of India has announced the adoption of IFRS in 2011. However, adoption will likely be rolled out gradually, with the largest Indian companies adopting IFRS in 2011 and the rest of them implementing IFRS by 2014.

Exhibit 4-5 summarizes the significant accounting practices in the countries surveyed in this chapter.

EXHIBIT 4-5 Summary of Significant Accounting Practices

	United States	Mexico	Japan	China	India
1. Business combinations: purchase or pooling	Purchase	Purchase	Purchase	Purchase	Both
2. Goodwill	Capitalize and impairments test	Capitalize and impairments test	Capitalize and amortize; and impairments test	Capitalize and impairments test	Capitalize and amortize; and impairments test
3. Associates	Equity method	Equity method	Equity method	Equity method	Equity method
4. Asset valuation	Historical cost	Historical cost[a]	Historical cost	Historical cost	Historical cost and fair value
5. Depreciation charges	Economic based	Economic based	Tax influenced	Economic based	Economic based
6. LIFO inventory valuation	Permitted	Not used	Permitted[b]	Not permitted	Not permitted
7. Probable losses	Accrued	Accrued	Accrued	Accrued	Accrued
8. Finance leases	Capitalized	Capitalized	Capitalized	Capitalized	Capitalized
9. Deferred taxes	Accrued	Accrued	Accrued	Accrued	Accrued
10. Reserves for income smoothing	No	No	No	No	Some

[a]Price-level adjusted accounting is used whenever the cumulative three-year inflation rate equals or exceeds 26 percent.
[b]Until 2010.

Discussion Questions

1. Compare and contrast the mechanisms for regulating and enforcing financial reporting in the five countries discussed in this chapter.
2. Compare and contrast the main features of financial reporting in the five countries discussed in this chapter.
3. Auditor oversight bodies have recently been established in several countries discussed in this chapter. Identify the auditor oversight bodies discussed in the chapter. What is the reason for this recent trend?
4. What is the difference between principles-based and rules-based accounting standards? What evidence indicates that U.S. GAAP is rules-based?
5. U.S. financial statements "present fairly," while U.K. financial statements are "true and fair." What is the difference between these two concepts?
6. Mexican companies traditionally guarded their information and were secretive in their financial reporting. What evidence is there that Mexican companies are becoming less secretive?
7. What was the reason for Japan's Big Bang, and what changes in accounting practice have resulted from it?
8. What important features of accounting and reporting are necessary to develop an efficient stock market with fair trading? How likely is it that China will develop such a stock market? Why do you say so?
9. China's aim is to develop accounting standards that are harmonized with international practices. Cite some examples indicating that Chinese accounting standards are consistent with "world-class" practices.
10. What evidence is there of British influence on accounting in India?

Exercises

1. This chapter provides synopses of national accounting practice systems in five countries.

   Required:
   For each country, list:
   a. The name of the national financial accounting standard-setting board or agency.
   b. The name of the agency, institute, or other organization charged with supervising and enforcing financial accounting standards.

2. The International Federation of Accountants (IFAC) is a worldwide organization of professional accounting bodies. IFAC's Web site (www.ifac.org) has links to accounting bodies around the world.

   Required: Visit IFAC's Web site. List the accounting organizations discussed in this chapter that are linked to IFAC's Web site.

3. Reread Chapter 4 and its discussion questions.

   Required:
   a. As you go through this material, prepare a list of five expressions, terms, or short phrases unfamiliar or unusual in your home country.
   b. Write a concise definition or explanation of each item.

4. Analyze the five national accounting practice systems summarized in the chapter.

   Required:
   a. For each of the five countries treated in the chapter, select the most important financial accounting practice or principle at variance with international norms.
   b. For each selection you make, briefly state your reasons for including it on your list.
   c. How does this variance affect reported earnings and the debt-to-asset ratio?
   d. How likely is it that an analyst could adjust for this variance to achieve an "apples to apples" comparison with companies from other countries?

5. Refer to Exhibit 4-5.

   Required: Which country's GAAP appears to be the most oriented toward equity investors? Which country's GAAP appears to be the least oriented toward equity investors? Why do you say so?

6. The United Kingdom and the United States have a common accounting heritage and are

linked by history and language. The term *Anglo-American accounting* is sometimes used to denote their accounting styles because of the similarities in orientation, purpose, and approach. Nonetheless, accounting differences still exist between these two countries.

Required:

a. Identify the major differences between U.K. and U.S. accounting that are discussed in Chapter 3 and this chapter.

b. Which country is likely to be systematically more conservative in measuring reported earnings? Why do you think so?

7. The following describes Japanese accounting before the Big Bang:

> The preparation of consolidated financial statements is based on the Securities and Exchange Law. Individual-company accounts are the basis for the consolidated statements, and normally the same principles are used at both levels. Subsidiaries are consolidated if a parent directly or indirectly owns more than 50 percent of the shares. (However, Japanese regulations have materiality tests that can lead to the exclusion of significant subsidiaries in consolidation.) The purchase method of accounting for business combinations is normally used for business combinations. Goodwill is measured on the basis of the book value of the net assets acquired, not the fair market value as is common in most other countries. Goodwill is amortized over five years. The equity method is used in consolidated statements for investments in nonconsolidated subsidiaries and 20 percent- to 50 percent-owned affiliated companies, but the cost method is used in individual company statements. The equity method is also used to account for joint ventures; proportional consolidation is not allowed. Under the foreign currency translation standard, assets and liabilities of foreign subsidiaries are translated at the current (year-end) exchange rate, revenues and expenses at either the

year-end or average rate, and translation adjustments are carried as an asset or liability on the balance sheet.

> Accounting measurements based on historical cost are pervasive. Inventory may be valued at cost or the lower of cost or market; cost is most often used. However, in the event of a significant and permanent decline in value, inventory must be written down to market. FIFO, LIFO, and average are all acceptable cost-flow methods, with average the most popular. Fixed assets are valued at cost and depreciated in accordance with the tax laws.

> Research and development costs may be capitalized if they relate to new products or techniques, the exploitation of resources, or the development of markets. When capitalized, research and development is amortized over five years. Finance leases, those transferring the risks and rewards of ownership to the lessee, are capitalized, while lease payments on operating leases are charged to income when incurred.

> Deferred taxes are not provided for (or needed) in individual company accounts. They are permitted in consolidated financial statements, but normally not provided there, either. Contingent losses are provided for when they are probable and can be reasonably estimated. Tax regulations limit the deductibility of employee retirement and severance benefits to 40 percent of the amount and so are normally only accrued up to this amount. Pension costs are expensed as paid, and unfunded obligations are not accrued. Legal reserves are required: Each year a company must allocate an amount equal to at least 10 percent of cash dividends and bonuses paid to directors and statutory auditors until the legal reserve reaches 25 percent of capital stock.

Required: Identify the major changes that have occurred in Japanese accounting since the Big Bang.

8. The following describes Chinese accounting in the late 1990s:

> Financial statements consist of the balance sheet, income statement, statement of changes in financial position (or cash flow statement), notes, and supporting schedules. Consolidated financial statements are required. The purchase method must be used to account for business combinations, and goodwill is amortized over the period benefited. The equity method is used when ownership of another enterprise exceeds 25 percent. When ownership exceeds 50 percent, the accounts of the subsidiary are consolidated. For overseas subsidiaries, the balance sheet is translated at the year-end exchange rate, the income statement is translated at the average-for-the-year exchange rate, and any translation difference is shown as a reserve in equity.
>
> Accounting measurements sometime have a tax orientation. For example, straight-line depreciation is used because tax laws specify this method. Tax law is also referred to in specifying the useful lives of assets and salvage value. Compared to international practice, historical cost is more strictly adhered to and the principle of conservatism is practiced on a more limited basis. These practices also reflect a tax law influence. For example,

> 1. The lower of cost or market inventory valuation method is not allowed.
> 2. Provisions for bad debts are allowed only up to 3 percent of the receivables balance.
> 3. Long-term investments are not written down for permanent declines in value.

> Historical cost is the basis for valuing tangible assets. FIFO, average, and LIFO are acceptable costing methods. Acquired intangibles are also recorded at cost and amortized over the periods benefited. Since land and much of the industrial property in China is owned by the state, companies that acquire the right to use land and industrial property rights show them as intangibles.
>
> Costs associated with research and development can be capitalized in some circumstances. Guidance is neither provided on accounting for capital versus operating leases, nor for deferred taxes. Contingent losses are not accrued; however, contingency funds may be set up as appropriations of retained earnings. Reserves for future expansion may also be appropriated out of retained earnings.

Required: Identify the major changes that have occurred in Chinese accounting since the 1990s.

9. Accounting standard setting in most countries involves a combination of private- and public-sector groups. The private sector includes the accounting profession and other groups affected by the financial reporting process, such as users and preparers of financial statements and organized labor. The public sector includes government agencies, such as tax authorities, ministries responsible for commercial law, and securities commissions. The stock market is another potential influence.

Required: Complete a matrix indicating whether each of these groups significantly influences accounting standard setting in the five countries discussed in this chapter. List the groups across the top and the countries down the side; indicate the influence of each group with a yes or no.

10. The following are financial ratios used by analysts:

- *Liquidity:* current ratio; cash flow from operations to current liabilities
- *Solvency:* debt to equity; debt to assets
- *Profitability:* return on assets; return on equity

Required: Assume that you are comparing the financial ratios of companies from two countries discussed in this chapter. Discuss how the accounting practices identified in Exhibit 4-5 would affect your comparisons for each of the six ratios listed.

CASES

Case 4-1

Standing on Principles

Recent U.S. accounting scandals, such as Enron and WorldCom, have caused some to question whether current U.S. generally accepted accounting principles (GAAP) are really protecting investors. Critics, including the U.S. Securities and Exchange Commission (SEC), charge that the rules-based approach to U.S. GAAP encourages a check-the-box mentality that inhibits transparency in financial reporting. Some observers express a preference for principles-based standards, such as International Financial Reporting Standards or those found in the United Kingdom. Both the Financial Accounting Standards Board (FASB) and the SEC have released reports on the feasibility of principles-based accounting standards in the United States.[62]

The following appeared in a leading British professional accounting journal.

> Ever since the Enron debacle first hit the news, smug U.K. accountants have found a new excuse for feeling superior to their transatlantic cousins. The U.S. Financial Accounting Standards Board's massive *oeuvre* have been scoffed at as being merely a whole bunch of rules that don't hang together. Both British and International standards, by way of contrast, are asserted to be based on principles. This essential difference, it is

argued, helps to explain why the U.S. profession has got itself into such deep trouble.

> Perhaps. But probably not. It certainly seems true that the highly detailed American standards have tended to invite legalistic interpretations and loopholing, whereas the U.K.'s paramount requirement to present a true and fair view has helped to remind us that accounting is more than a compliance activity. However, it is much too glib to characterise their accounting standards as lacking in principle compared to ours; in terms of their intellectual rigour, American accounting standards compare favourably with any others in the world.

> How is it that the U.K. and International Accounting Standards Boards appear to have found reliable principles on which to base their own standards, principles that have eluded FASB? After all, both bodies have themselves adopted conceptual frameworks that are largely copies of the FASB's version, and claim to follow them. The answer is that they haven't. Our standards aren't really more principled than the American ones, they are simply less detailed. And even that is changing—both the

---

[62] Financial Accounting Standards Board, "Proposal: Principles-Based Approach to U.S. Standard Setting," http://www.fasb.org/proposals/principles-based_approach.pdf (October 21, 2002); and Securities and Exchange Commission, "Study Pursuant to Section 108(d) of the Sarbanes-Oxley Act of 2002 on the Adoption by the United States Financial Reporting System of a Principles-Based Accounting System," www.sec.gov/news/studies/principlesbasedstand.htm#1f (July 25, 2003).

U.K. and IASB rulebooks have swollen very considerably in recent years, often inspired (if that is the word) by the content of the equivalent American standards.[63]

Required

1. What is the difference between rules-based and principles-based accounting standards, and what are the advantages and disadvantages of each?

2. Why has U.S. GAAP evolved into a rules-based approach? Would principles-based standards be effective in the United States? Why or why not?

3. What needs to change in the United States to make principles-based standards effective?

4. Are investors and analysts better served by rules-based or principles-based accounting standards? Why do you say so?

Case 4-2

Casino Capital

What conditions are necessary to develop an efficient stock market with fair trading? What role does accounting and financial reporting play in stock market development? Consider the case of China:

Those Chinese who think of themselves as street-smart tell a joke about three fools. The first is the boss who plays around with his secretary and ends up her husband. The second is the investor who plays the property market and ends up a homeowner. And the third is the punter who plays the stock market and finds himself a shareholder. This sums up the culture of China's fledgling capital markets. "Trading, not ownership," is the approach of China's investors, says Anthony Neoh, a former head of Hong Kong's Securities and Futures Commission who is now the chief outside adviser to China's regulatory body. "That's what we need to change."

This marks a shift in China's capital market reforms. So far, Beijing has focused almost entirely on the "supply side" of the securities market. This has included listing more, and better, companies, and forcing them to adopt better standards of corporate governance and disclosure. Such efforts have a long way to go.

However, the government now realizes that it also needs to work on the "demand side." At present, China's stock market, Asia's second-largest by capitalization, consists of 60m mainly clueless retail investors, driven to trade almost entirely on rumor.[64]

[T]he balance sheets of Chinese companies are, by common consent, a joke. In January [2001] the government's official auditing body admitted that more than two-thirds of the 1,300 biggest state-owned enterprises cook their books. Johnny Chen, the Beijing head of PricewaterhouseCoopers, says that even

---

[63] Ron Paterson, "A Matter of Principle," *Accountancy* (February 2003): 98.
[64] "Fools in Need of Institutions," *Economist* (June 30, 2001), p. 65.

this is an understatement. Quite simply, the SOEs' numbers are whatever the key man wants them to be. And without genuinely independent directors to chair an audit committee, that will not change.[65]

Even China's mostly hapless stock market investor (66m of them, officially) had something to cheer about this month, after the country's highest court said that shareholders could file individual or class action lawsuits against companies that lie about their accounts. There appear to be a lot of liars about. Around 900 shareholder suits are pending, in a country with 1,200 listed companies.

It remains to be seen whether these steps amount to mere tinkering, or herald the new and bolder approach to financial reform that China badly needs. Its markets for labor, goods, and services are nowadays more liberal than those in some capitalist economies. Its capital markets, by contrast, have changed only cosmetically since the days of central planning. In effect, all capital in China is allocated, one way or the other, by the government, which wastes much of it.

The decade-old stock market is dominated by state-owned enterprises that were listed for political rather than economic reasons. Some two-thirds of the market's capitalization is not traded, so the state retains total control. There is no corporate bond market to speak of.[66]

[A]ll is not what it seems in China's capital markets. For a start, growth in the domestic stock market has outstripped the efforts—game as they are—of the regulators and the legal system to police it. The authorities say that computer matching of share transactions has allowed them pretty much to stop powerful syndicates ramping up share prices. They have even sent the biggest manipulators to jail, yet insider trading is still rife on a heroic scale. Stock exchange executives reckon that the real number of investors is around half the official number: investors use multiple accounts for dodgy share dealings.

The real issue is the quality of the listed companies themselves, says one financial official. Even some of the better-regarded ones indulge in all sorts of market abuses, such as lending money raised on the stock market to the parent company rather than investing it, or speculating in the stock market on their own account. Almost all companies allowed a listing are the beneficiaries of government favoritism. Their profitability is usually abysmal, their levels of disclosure poor, and—with the state holding roughly two-thirds of the shares of companies listed in Shanghai and Shenzhen—their treatment of minority shareholders appalling.[67]

[T]he biggest problem is the poor quality of the listed companies. All but a handful are state enterprises, which are approved for an IPO by a political committee rather than by independent underwriters. A 2002 survey by the China Securities Regulatory Commission (CSRC), the top regulator, found that one in ten listed companies had doctored its books, and the finance ministry reported in January [2004] 152 firms it had surveyed had misstated their profits by a combined 2.9 billion yuan. "The stock market has been used to support national

---

[65] "Survey: Asian Business," *Economist* (April 7, 2001), p. 13.
[66] "Banking on Growth," *Economist* (January 18, 2003), p. 67.
[67] "A Survey of Asian Finance," *Economist* (February 8, 2003), pp. 10–11.

industrial policy, to subsidize SOE restructuring, not to allow private companies to raise capital," says Stephen Green of the Royal Institute of International Affairs.[68]

Required

1. Describe the conditions necessary to develop a stock market in an emerging economy.

2. How do these conditions compare to the situation in China?

3. How likely is China to develop a stock market with fair trading? Why do you say so?

4. Outline a plan of reforms necessary to achieve stock market development in China.

---

[68] "Behind the Mask: A Survey of Business in China," *Economist* (March 20, 2004): 19.

CHAPTER 5

Reporting and Disclosure

In this chapter we examine the communication of financial and nonfinancial information in an international setting. Much of the discussion addresses disclosure related to financial reporting for external users. We focus on selected topics and do not attempt to discuss every disclosure issue that applies to financial statement users, preparers, and financial professionals.

The relative importance of equity markets in national economies is growing and individual investors are becoming more active in those markets. As a result, public disclosure, investor protection, shareholder value, and stock market-driven forms of corporate governance are becoming increasingly important. Although disclosure practices vary from country to country, they are converging. However, important differences among countries will continue to affect many firms, particularly those that are not active in international capital or product markets.

Government regulators who seek to maintain or increase the credibility of their national capital markets also influence disclosure practices around the world. Stock exchanges have concluded that their continued growth and success depends on offering a high-quality market with effective investor protection. As a result, oversight by regulators and stock exchanges is increasing and disclosure requirements are becoming more stringent. The trend toward greater investor protection and enhanced disclosure will continue as stock exchanges face growing competition from each other and from less-regulated trading systems.

DEVELOPMENT OF DISCLOSURE

The development of disclosure systems closely parallels the development of accounting systems discussed in Chapter 2.[1] Disclosure standards and practices are influenced

---

[1] The terms *disclosure systems* and *accounting systems* overlap considerably. Often, as in Chapter 2 of this text, "accounting development" refers to the development of accounting standards and practices. "Disclosure development" as discussed in this chapter refers to the development of financial and nonfinancial disclosures presented in financial reports. We do not discuss disclosures made in press releases, although much of the discussion in this chapter applies to this area.

by sources of finance, legal systems, political and economic ties, level of economic development, education level, culture, and other factors.

National differences in disclosure are driven largely by differences in corporate governance and finance. In the United States, the United Kingdom, and other Anglo-American countries, equity markets have provided most corporate financing and have become highly developed. In these markets, ownership tends to be spread among many shareholders, and investor protection is emphasized. Institutional investors play a growing role in these countries, demanding financial returns and increased shareholder value. Public disclosure is highly developed in response to companies' accountability to the public.

In many other countries (such as France, Germany, Japan, and numerous emerging-market countries), shareholdings remain highly concentrated and banks (and/or family owners) traditionally have been the primary source of corporate financing. Structures are in place to protect incumbent management. Banks (which sometimes are both creditors and owners) and other insiders (such as corporate members of interlocking shareholder groups) provide discipline. These banks, insiders, and others are closely informed about the company's financial position and its activities. Public disclosure is less developed in these markets and large differences in the amount of information given to large shareholders and creditors vis-à-vis the public may be permitted.

Voluntary Disclosure

Managers have better information than external parties about their firm's current and future performance. Several studies show that managers have incentives to disclose such information voluntarily. The benefits of enhanced disclosure may include lower transaction costs in the trading of the firm's securities, greater interest in the company by financial analysts and investors, increased share liquidity, and lower cost of capital. One recent report supports the view that companies can achieve capital markets benefits by enhancing their voluntary disclosure.[2] The report includes guidance on how companies can describe and explain their investment potential to investors.

As investors around the world demand more detailed and timely information, voluntary disclosure levels are increasing in both highly developed and emerging-market countries. It is widely recognized, however, that financial reporting can be an imperfect mechanism for communicating with outside investors when managers' incentives are not perfectly aligned with the interests of all shareholders. In one classic paper, the authors argue that managers' communication with outside investors is imperfect when (1) managers have superior information about their firm, (2) managers' incentives are not perfectly aligned with the interests of all the shareholders, and (3) accounting rules and auditing are imperfect.[3] The authors state that contracting mechanisms (such as compensation linking managers' rewards to long-term share value) can reduce this conflict.

Evidence strongly indicates that corporate managers often have strong incentives to delay the disclosure of bad news, "manage" their financial reports to convey a more

---

[2] Financial Accounting Standards Board, *Improving Business Reporting: Insights into Enhancing Voluntary Disclosures,* www.fasb.org/brrp/BRRP2.PDF, 2001.
[3] See P. M. Healy and K. G. Palepu, "The Effect of Firms' Financial Disclosure Strategies on Stock Prices," *Accounting Horizons* (March 1993): 1–11.

positive image of the firm, and overstate their firm's financial performance and prospects. For example, executives face significant risks of being dismissed in firms whose financial or stock market performance is relatively poor. Seriously stressed firms may have a higher risk of bankruptcy, acquisition, or hostile takeover, leading to a management change. Also, the possible competitive disadvantage created when proprietary information is made public may offset the benefits of full disclosure.

Regulation (e.g., accounting and disclosure regulation) and third-party certification (e.g., auditing) can improve the functioning of markets. Accounting regulation attempts to reduce managers' ability to record economic transactions in ways that are not in shareholders' best interests. Disclosure regulation sets forth requirements to ensure that shareholders receive timely, complete, and accurate information. External auditors try to ensure that managers apply appropriate accounting policies, make reasonable accounting estimates, maintain adequate accounting records and control systems, and provide the required disclosures in a timely manner.

Although these mechanisms can strongly influence practice, managers occasionally conclude that the benefits of noncompliance with reporting requirements (e.g., a higher stock price due to inflated earnings) outweigh the costs (e.g., the risk of job loss and litigation resulting in criminal or civil penalties if the noncompliance is detected and reported). Thus, managers' disclosure choices reflect the combined effects of disclosure requirements and their incentives to disclose information voluntarily.

Regulatory Disclosure Requirements

To protect investors, most securities exchanges (together with professional or government regulatory bodies such as the U.S. Securities and Exchange Commission and the Financial Services Agency in Japan) impose reporting and disclosure requirements on domestic and foreign companies that seek access to their markets. These exchanges want to make sure that investors have enough information to allow them to evaluate a company's performance and prospects. Nowhere is this concern more evident than in the United States, whose disclosure standards generally are considered to be the most stringent in the world.

Stock exchanges and government regulators generally require foreign listed firms to furnish almost the same financial and nonfinancial information as that required of domestic companies. Foreign listed firms generally have some flexibility in regard to the accounting principles they use and the extent of disclosure. In many countries, foreign listed firms must file with the stock exchange any information made public, distributed to shareholders, or filed with regulators in the domestic market. However, many countries do not monitor or enforce this "cross-jurisdictional conformity of disclosure" requirement.

Shareholder protection varies substantially among countries. Anglo-American countries such as Canada, the United Kingdom, and the United States provide extensive and strictly enforced investor protection. In contrast, shareholder protection receives less emphasis in other parts of the world. For example, while China prohibits insider trading, its weak judiciary makes enforcement almost nonexistent. Shareholder protection codes in the Czech Republic, Mexico, and many other emerging-market countries also are rudimentary. Even in many developed countries, the concept of investor protection is of recent origin, and many commentators argue that it still is inadequate. For example, insider trading was not a criminal offense in Germany until the enactment of the Securities Trading Act 1994.

Frost and Lang discuss the twin objectives of investor-oriented markets: investor protection and market quality.[4]

- *Investor Protection.*   Investors are provided with material information and are protected by monitoring and enforcing market rules. Fraud is inhibited in the public offering, trading, voting, and tendering of securities. Comparable financial and nonfinancial information is sought so that investors may compare companies across industries and countries.
- *Market Quality.*   Markets are fair, orderly, efficient, and free from abuse and misconduct. Market fairness is promoted through equitable access to information and trading opportunities. Market efficiency is advanced by enhancing liquidity and reducing transactions costs. Quality markets are marked by investor confidence and they facilitate capital formation. Prices reflect investors' perceptions of value without being arbitrary or capricious.

Frost and Lang also outline four principles under which investor-oriented markets should operate:

1. *Cost effectiveness.*   The cost of market regulation should be proportionate to the benefits it secures.
2. *Market freedom and flexibility.*   Regulation should not impede competition and market evolution.
3. *Transparent financial reporting and full and complete disclosure.*
4. *Equal treatment of foreign and domestic firms.*

As Frost and Lang note, investor protection requires that investors receive timely material information and are protected through effective monitoring and enforcement. Disclosure should be sufficient to allow investors to compare companies across industries and countries. Furthermore, full and credible disclosure will enhance investor confidence, which will increase liquidity, reduce transactions costs, and improve overall market quality.

The U.S. SEC Financial Reporting Debate

The SEC generally requires foreign registrants to furnish financial information substantially similar to that required of domestic companies.[5] The SEC's financial reporting requirements are acknowledged to be the most comprehensive and rigorously enforced of any in the world. Whether the SEC's requirements help or hinder the SEC in meeting its regulatory objectives is widely debated. The SEC's reporting requirements are generally consistent with the objectives of investor protection and market quality. However, stringent reporting requirements may achieve the goal of

---

[4] Carol A. Frost and Mark Lang, "Foreign Companies and U.S. Securities Markets: Financial Reporting Policy Issues and Suggestions for Research," *Accounting Horizons* 10 (March 1996): 97.
[5] Foreign registrants' financial statements need not be prepared in accordance with U.S. GAAP if they are presented in accordance with another comprehensive body of accounting principles and are accompanied by a quantitative reconciliation to U.S. GAAP of net income, shareholders' equity, and earnings per share. Until 2007, this reconciliation requirement extended to International Financial Reporting Standards (IFRS). However, the SEC now accepts financial statements prepared using IFRS, as promulgated by the International Accounting Standards Board.

investor protection at the cost of reducing investment opportunities or imposing high transaction costs on investing.

Some commentators argue that the SEC's financial reporting requirements for foreign companies deter them from making their securities available in the United States.[6,7] As a result, it is claimed, U.S. investors are more likely to trade in markets such as the U.S. Over-the-Counter (OTC) market or overseas markets where liquidity may be relatively low, transaction costs relatively high, and investor protection less important than on the national exchanges in the United States. It then is argued that the SEC could provide U.S. investors with more investment opportunities within the regulated U.S. markets by relaxing its financial reporting requirements; this, in turn, would better balance the SEC's objectives of investor protection and market quality.

Others counter that the current accounting and disclosure system both protects investors and ensures the quality of U.S. capital markets.[8] Underlying this argument are the principles of full disclosure and equal treatment of foreign and domestic issuers. Indeed, the competitive strength of U.S. capital markets, including their substantial liquidity and high level of investor confidence, is often attributed (at least in part) to the SEC's existing disclosure system and vigorous enforcement. Research shows that cross-listing in U.S. markets can significantly reduce a foreign firm's cost of capital, particularly if the firm is from a country with weak shareholder protection.[9]

The implementation of the 2002 Sarbanes-Oxley Act (SOX) has been accompanied by new complaints about its Section 404 requiring the chief executives and chief financial officers of public companies (and their external auditors) to appraise and certify the effectiveness and adequacy of internal controls. Some foreign firms have delisted from U.S. stock exchanges (such as British companies Cable and Wireless and Rank Group). Others are apparently avoiding U.S. listings and choosing to list on other markets such as the London Stock Exchange.[10] This issue raises concerns similar to those about the SEC's reporting requirements. Sarbanes-Oxley has imposed significant new audit costs on companies (estimates range from 35 to 150 percent of pre-SOX audit fees). But the benefits of better auditing and more trustworthy financial statements are no less real.[11]

---

[6] See J. L. Cochrane, "Are U.S. Regulatory Requirements for Foreign Firms Appropriate?" *Fordham International Law Journal* 17 (1994): S58–S67; J. L. Cochrane, J. E. Shapiro, and J. E. Tobin, "Foreign Equities and U.S. Investors: Breaking Down the Barriers Separating Supply and Demand," *Stanford Journal of Law, Business and Finance* 1997.

[7] As discussed below, new regulations enacted by the 2002 Sarbanes-Oxley Act are also said to deter foreign companies from a U.S. listing. See John Rossant, "Who Needs U.S. Markets?" *Business Week* (February 16, 2004): 13.

[8] See Richard C. Breeden, "Foreign Companies and U.S. Securities Markets in a Time of Economic Transformation," *Fordham International Law Journal* 17 (1994): S77–S96; Pat McConnell,"Practical Company Experience in Entering U.S. Markets: Significant Issues and Hurdles from the Advisor's Perspective," *Fordham International Law Journal* 17 (1994): S120–S128; and remarks by SEC Commissioner Isaac C. Hunt, Jr. at the Second European FASB-SEC Financial Reporting Conference, Frankfurt, Germany (March 23, 2000), www.sec.gov/news/speech/spch363.htm.

[9] Luzi Hail and Christian Leuz, "Cost of Capital Effects and Changes in Growth Expectations around U.S. Cross-Listings," *Journal of Financial Economics* (September 2009): 428–454.

[10] See "404 Tonnes of Paper," *Economist* (December 18, 2004): 116; "Big Apple Blues," *Economist* (January 29, 2005): 73; "Escape from New York," *Accountancy Magazine* (April 2006): 52–53.

[11] There is empirical evidence that dispels the notion that SOX is responsible for recent delistings from the New York Stock Exchange. See Craig Doidge, G. Andrew Karoli, and René M. Stulz, "Has New York Become Less Competitive than London in Global Markets? Evaluation Foreign Listing Choices over Time," *Journal of Financial Economics* (March 2009): 253–277.

REPORTING AND DISCLOSURE PRACTICES

What do companies around the world actually disclose in their annual reports? Annual report disclosure practices reflect managers' responses to regulatory disclosure requirements and their incentives to provide information to financial statement users voluntarily. In many parts of the world, disclosure rules mean little, and monitoring and enforcement are largely absent. Insofar as disclosure rules are not enforced, the required disclosures are (in practice) voluntary, because corporate managers will not comply with disclosure rules if compliance is more costly than the expected costs of noncompliance. Therefore, it is important to clearly distinguish between disclosures that are "required" and disclosures that actually are made. It is misleading to focus on disclosure rules without also looking at actual disclosure practices.

For some types of disclosure (e.g., disclosures about material developments), managerial discretion plays such an important role that monitoring (and hence enforcement) is difficult. Therefore, these types of disclosure are more or less voluntary. Finally, disclosure rules vary dramatically worldwide in areas such as changes in equity statements, related party transactions, segment reporting, fair value of financial assets and liabilities, and earnings per share.

In this section we focus on (1) disclosures of forward-looking information, (2) segment disclosures, (3) social responsibility reporting, (4) corporate governance disclosures, and (5) Internet business reporting and XBRL. These disclosure and reporting items were selected because of their importance to financial statement users. For example, financial analysts and regulators have emphasized the importance of corporate disclosures of forward-looking information, such as that related to corporate goals and planned expenditures, and business-segment information. Governance disclosures have become important in recent years as a result of corporate scandals at Enron, WorldCom, Parmalot, Ahold, and other companies.

Disclosures of Forward-Looking Information

Disclosures of forward-looking information are considered highly relevant in equity markets worldwide. For example, the EU's Fourth Directive states that the annual report should include an indication of the company's likely future developments. The SEC's Regulation S-K requires companies to disclose presently known information that will materially impact future liquidity, capital resources, and operating results. As a third example, the Tokyo Stock Exchange "requests" management of listed firms to provide forecasts of sales, earnings, and dividends in their annual and semiannual press releases.

As used here, the term *forward-looking information* includes (1) forecasts of revenues, income (loss), cash flows, capital expenditures, and other financial items; (2) prospective information about future economic performance or position that is less definite than forecasts in terms of projected item, fiscal period, and projected amount;[12] and (3) statements of management's plans and objectives for future operations. These three categories of forward-looking information become more general as we move from (1) forecasts to (2) prospective information to (3) plans and objectives. Given that a primary aim of investors and analysts is assessing a

---

[12] For convenience we use the term *prospective disclosure* to refer to "softer" nonforecast disclosures.

company's future earnings and cash flows, it is reasonable to ask whether companies provide their own internal forecasts of such financial information. The practice is not very common, particularly precise forecasts. (Range forecasts are more common than precise forecasts, and directional forecasts [increase or decrease] are more common still.) One reason is that forecasts can be unreliable because they incorporate subjective estimates of uncertain future events. In addition, there can be legal repercussions for management if forecasts are not met. In the United States, the potential for lawsuits is a major deterrent to providing financial forecasts. However, as perhaps could be expected, vaguer forms of forward-looking information are more common. A study of 200 large public companies in France, Germany, Japan, the United Kingdom, and United States found that most of them disclosed information about management's plans and objectives. Softer, prospective information was also fairly common, but forecasts were much less common.[13]

An example is the forecast disclosure of Daimler, the German car company, in its 2008 annual report:

> Daimler anticipates a significant decrease in business volume in 2009. From the starting point of the currently projected unit sales, revenue is likely to be lower than in 2008 in all of the vehicle divisions. In the year 2010, we then expect at least slight growth in our business volumes, provided that the projected revival of automotive markets actually occurs. . . . . We anticipate further substantial burdens on the earnings of the Daimler Group and its divisions. . . . . With the help of our intensified efficiency-improving actions and the market success of our new products, we should be able to increase our earnings again in 2010.[14]

Segment Disclosures

Investor and analyst demand for information about firms' industry and geographic-segment operations and financial results is significant and growing. For example, financial analysts in the United States consistently request financial statement data disaggregated in much greater detail than it is now. International Financial Reporting Standards (IFRS) include highly detailed segment reporting requirements, as do accounting standards in many countries.[15] Segment disclosures help financial statement users better understand how the parts of a company make up the whole. After all, product lines and areas of the world vary in terms of risks, returns, and opportunities. A disaggregation by lines of business and geographic area should make for more informed judgments about the overall company.

Exhibit 5-1 presents the business segment and geographic area disclosure made in the 2008 Annual Report of Lafarge (a French firm). The business-segment

---

[13] Carol A. Frost and Kurt P. Ramin, "Corporate Financial Disclosure: A Global Assessment," in *International Finance and Accounting Handbook*, ed. Frederick D. S. Choi, 3rd ed. (New York: John Wiley, 2003), pp. 13–31.
[14] Refer to www.daimler.com/Projects/c2c/channel/documents/1677323_DAI_2008_Annual_Report.pdf (pp. 82–87) for Daimler's complete discussion of its outlook.
[15] See Lee H. Radebaugh and Donna L. Street, "Segmental and Foreign Operations Disclosure," in *International Finance and Accounting Handbook*, ed. Frederick D. S. Choi, 3rd ed. (New York: John Wiley, 2003), for a detailed discussion of segment and foreign operations disclosure.

EXHIBIT 5-1	Segment Disclosures by Lafarge

Consolidated Statements

Note 4 – Business Segment and Geographic Area Information

(a) Business segment information

(million euros)	Cement	Aggregates & Concrete	Gypsum	Other	Total
		2008			
STATEMENT OF INCOME					
Gross revenue	11,720	6,580	1,546	29	19,875
Less: intersegment	(809)	(7)	(25)	(1)	(842)
REVENUE	**10,911**	**6,573**	**1,521**	**28**	**19,033**
Operating income before capital gains, impairment, restricting, and other	2,964	623	36	(81)	3,542
Gains on disposals, net	228	(3)	—	4	229
Other operating income (expenses)	(294)	(70)	(9)	(36)	(409)
Including impairment on assets and goodwill	*(221)*	*(52)*	*(3)*	—	*(276)*
OPERATING INCOME	**2,898**	**550**	**27**	**(113)**	**3,362**
Finance costs					(1,157)
Finance income					216
Income from associates	15	4	13	(35)	(3)
Income taxes					(479)
NET INCOME					**1,939**
OTHER INFORMATION					
Depreciation and amortization	(700)	(260)	(80)	(36)	(1,076)
Impairment on assets and goodwill	(221)	(52)	(3)	—	(276)
Other segment noncash income (expenses) of operating income	10	—	(3)	(44)	(37)
Capital expenditures	2,109	556	144	77	2,886
Capital employed	25,547	5,503	1,484	731	33,265
BALANCE SHEET					
Segment assets	28,748	6,995	1,866	2,473	40,082
Of which investments in associates	*359*	*21*	*119*	*64*	*563*
Unallocated assets*					526
TOTAL ASSETS					**40,608**
Segment liabilities	2,601	1,273	398	1,958	6,230
Unallocated liabilities and equity**					34,378
TOTAL EQUITY AND LIABILITIES					**40,608**

Deferred tax assets and derivative instruments.

**Deferred tax liability, financial debt, derivatives instruments, and equity.*

Consolidated Statements

Note 4 – Business Segment and Geographic Area Information

(million euros)	Cement	Aggregates & Concrete	Gypsum	Other	Total
			2007		
STATEMENT OF INCOME					
Gross revenue	10,280	6,597	1,581	16	18,474
Less: intersegment	(824)	(11)	(25)	—	(860)
REVENUE	**9,456**	**6,586**	**1,556**	**16**	**17,614**
Operating income before capital gains, impairment, restricting, and other	2,481	721	116	(76)	3,242
Gains on disposals, net	156	10	—	30	196
Other operating income (expenses)	(128)	(38)	(32)	49	(149)
Including impairment on assets and goodwill	*(9)*	*(1)*	*(1)*	*(2)*	*(13)*
OPERATING INCOME	**2,509**	**693**	**84**	**3**	**3,289**
Finance costs					(652)
Finance income					126
Income from associates	13	14	19	(46)	—
Income taxes					(725)
NET INCOME FROM CONTINUING OPERATIONS					**2,038**
NET INCOME FROM DISCONTINUED OPERATIONS				**118**	**118**
NET INCOME					**2,156**
OTHER INFORMATION					
Depreciation and amortization	(578)	(258)	(73)	(32)	(941)
Other segment noncash income (expenses) of operating income	(22)	(9)	(15)	56	10
Capital expenditures	1,312	541	201	59	2,113
Capital employed	15,399	4,798	1,482	403	22,082
BALANCE SHEET					
Segment assets	18,094	6,065	1,854	2,027	28,040
Of which investments in associates	*115*	*57*	*103*	*56*	*331*
Unallocated assets*					268
TOTAL ASSETS					**28,308**
Segment liabilities	2,334	1,205	368	1,458	5,365
Unallocated liabilities and equity**					22,943
TOTAL EQUITY AND LIABILITIES					**28,308**

Deferred tax assets and derivative instruments.
**Deferred tax liability, financial debt, derivatives instruments, and equity.*

(million euros)	Cement	Aggregates & Concrete	Roofing[3]	Gypsum	Other	Total
			2006			
STATEMENT OF INCOME						
Gross revenue	9,641	6,449		1,632	14	17,736
Less: intersegment	(794)	(10)		(22)	(1)	(827)
REVENUE	**8,847**	**6,439**		**1,610**	**13**	**16,909**
Operating income before capital gains, impairment, restricting, and other	2,103	564		198	(93)	2,772
Gains on disposals, net	7	3		(8)	26	28
Other operating income (expenses)	(114)	(12)		(21)	25	(122)
Including impairment on assets and goodwill	*(3)*	*(1)*		*(19)*	—	*(23)*
OPERATING INCOME	**1,996**	**555**		**169**	**(42)**	**2,678**
Finance costs						(582)
Finance income						97
Income from associates	3	11		16		30
Income taxes						(630)
NET INCOME FROM CONTINUING OPERATIONS						**1,593**
NET INCOME FROM DISCONTINUED OPERATIONS			**(4)**			**(4)**
NET INCOME						**1,589**
OTHER INFORMATION						
Depreciation and amortization	(575)	(258)		(69)	(30)	(932)
Other segment noncash income (expenses) of operating income	(157)	(35)		(24)	142	(74)
Capital expenditures	931	436		222	50	1,639
Capital employed	15,209	4,585		1,433	163	21,390
BALANCE SHEET						
Segment assets	17,661	5,295		1,695	2,126	26,777
Of which investments in associates	*113*	*41*		*92*	*7*	*253*
Assets held for sale			2,733			2,733
Unallocated assets[1]						331
TOTAL ASSETS						**29,841**
Segment liabilities	2,316	1,174		365	1,791	5,646
Liabilities associated with assets held for sale			842			842
Unallocated liabilities and equity[2]						23,353
TOTAL EQUITY AND LIABILITIES						**29,841**

[1]*Deferred tax assets and derivative instruments.*

[2]*Deferred tax liability, financial debt, derivatives instruments, and equity.*

[3]*Discontinued operations.*

Consolidated Statements
Note 4 – Business Segment and Geographic Area Information

(b) Geographic area information

(million euros)	2008 Revenue	2008 Capital expenditure	2008 Segment assets	2007 Revenue	2007 Capital expenditure	2007 Segment assets	2006 Revenue*	2006 Capital expenditure*	2006 Segment assets
WESTERN EUROPE	6,021	669	11,236	6,285	606	10,872	5,953	501	10,266
Of which:									
France	2,721	314	4,620	2,676	264	3,628	2,524	255	3,047
United Kingdom	1,191	141	1,846	1,487	196	2,707	1,387	127	3,100
Spain	671	89	1,554	703	47	994	672	33	1,000
NORTH AMERICA	4,270	477	7,339	4,780	485	7,177	5,116	562	7,296
Of which:									
United States	2,215	286	5,634	2,709	336	5,324	3,216	430	6,192
Canada	2,055	191	1,705	2,071	149	1,853	1,900	132	1,104
MIDDLE EAST	1,611	436	6,752	527	78	878	628	44	861
Of which:									
Egypt	504	62	2,998	65	24	158	64	3	142
CENTRAL & EASTERN EUROPE	1,761	329	2,352	1,467	290	1,992	1,014	112	1,552
LATIN AMERICA	968	130	1,393	876	114	1,502	796	74	1,446
AFRICA	2,373	469	6,280	1,911	261	1,904	1,801	178	1,795
Of which:									
Algeria	361	51	3,896	9	6	14	8	1	9
ASIA	2,029	376	4,730	1,768	279	3,715	1,601	168	3,561
TOTAL	19,033	2,886	40,082	17,614	2,113	28,040	16,909	1,639	26,777

*Only from continuing operations.

disclosure reveals the most recent three years' revenue, operating income, depreciation and amortization, capital expenditures, capital employed, segment assets, and segment liabilities for Lafarge's three main product lines. The geographic area disclosure shows three years' revenue, capital expenditure, and assets by regions of the world and selected countries. Lafarge also discusses its product and geographic markets in significant detail elsewhere in the annual report.

Social Responsibility Reporting

Increasingly, companies are being called upon to answer to a wide range of "stakeholders"— employees, customers, suppliers, governments, activist groups, and the general public— who have areas of concern other than the company's ability to create economic value. Social responsibility reporting refers to the measurement and communication of information about a company's effects on employee welfare, the local community, and the environment. It reflects a belief that companies owe stakeholders an annual accounting of their social and environmental performance just like the financial information they provide shareholders. More important, as suggested by the saying "What gets measured, gets managed," social responsibility reporting is a way to demonstrate corporate citizenship. For a variety of reasons, multinational corporations are working harder than ever to protect their reputations and the environment in which they do business. Corporate scandals such as Enron, WorldCom, and Parmalat have eroded trust in business organizations and prompted new regulations. Big companies are being watched more than ever—thanks to the Internet, embarrassing news anywhere can be published everywhere. Social responsibility reporting, once mostly a side-show, is now a central part of the communication that most large companies have with outsiders.[16] "Sustainability" reports that integrate economic, social, and environmental performance are referred to as "triple-bottom-line reporting" (profits, people, and planet). Moreover, to avoid criticism that the reporting is "green-washing" (i.e., a public relations ploy without substance), such information is increasingly being verified by independent third parties.[17]

Information on employee welfare has long been of interest to labor groups.[18] Particular areas of concern relate to working conditions, job security, equal opportunity, workforce diversity, and child labor. Employee disclosures are also of interest to investors in that they provide useful insights about a firm's labor relations, costs, and productivity.

Information disclosure regarding number of employees is of great interest to national governments. Number-of-employees disclosure by geographic area gives host governments information on the employment effect of multinational companies. Employee disclosure by line of business, in turn, helps identify those industries and activities that foreign direct investors find economically attractive. If there is a conflict

---

[16] See "Just Good Business: A Special Report on Corporate Social Responsibility," *Economist* (January 19, 2008): 1–24. It is said that concern over climate change is the single biggest driver in the growth of corporate social responsibility.

[17] Mel Wilson and Rosie Lombardi, "Globalization and Its Discontent: The Arrival of Triple-Bottom-Line Reporting, *Ivey Business Journal* 66, 1 (September/October 2001): 69–72. See also P. Engardio, "Beyond the Green Corporation," *Business Week* (January 29, 2007): 50–64.

[18] For many years, workers have been considered business partners in continental Europe, with worker participation in works councils mandatory in the large companies of many countries.

between the behavior of the investors and the goals of the host government—for example, if investors invest in operations that employ low-skill workers while the government seeks to expand high-skill employment—an alert government could take steps to encourage foreign investment in the desired direction. When combined with geographical and/or line-of-business reporting, employee disclosure by function enables governments and labor groups to examine whether employment practices of multinational companies are consistent with local laws and norms.

Environmental issues include the impact of production processes, products, and services on air, water, land, biodiversity, and human health. As an example, French listed companies are now required to publish the results of their environmental activities. Among other items, information must be given on:

- Water, raw material, and energy consumption, and actions taken to improve energy efficiency
- Activities to reduce pollution in the air, water, or ground, including noise pollution, and their costs
- Amount of provisions for environmental risks

Social responsibility reporting has its critics. For example:

One problem with the triple-bottom-line is quickly apparent. Measuring profits is fairly straightforward; measuring environmental protection and social justice is not. The difficulty is partly that there is no single yardstick for measuring progress in those areas. How is any given success for environmental action to be weighed against any given advance in social justice—or, for that matter, against any given change in profits? And how are the three to be traded off against each other? . . . Measuring profits—the good old single bottom line—offers a pretty clear test of business success. The triple-bottom-line does not.

The problem is not just that there is no one yardstick allowing the three measures to be compared with each other. It is also that there is no agreement on what progress on the environment, or progress in the social sphere, actually mean—not, at least, if you are trying to be precise about it. In other words, there are no yardsticks by which different aspects of environmental protection can be compared even with each other, let alone with other criteria. And the same goes for social justice. . . .

The great virtue of the single bottom line is that it holds managers to account for something. The-triple-bottom line does not. It is not so much a license to operate as a license to obfuscate.[19]

Despite such criticisms, social responsibility reporting is now the norm among large multinational companies. A recent survey found that 80 percent of the world's largest 250 multinationals engage in such reporting, either in their annual reports or in separate sustainability reports. Reporting rates are highest among Japanese and U.K. companies and there was a sizable increase in social responsibility reporting by U.S. companies

---

[19] "The Good Company: A Survey of Corporate Social Responsibility," *Economist* (January 22, 2005): 14.

compared to earlier surveys. The Global Reporting Initiative guidelines, discussed next, are used by three-fourths of these companies as their framework for reporting. The survey also found that 40 percent of the companies have their reports audited, up from 30 percent three years earlier.[20,21]

Guidelines for sustainability reports have been issued by the Global Reporting Initiative (GRI), an independent institution affiliated with the United Nations Environment Programme. The GRI "G3" framework recommends the disclosure of performance indicators in the areas of:

- Economic performance, such as revenues, employee compensation, donations and community investments, and payments to capital providers and governments
- Environmental performance, such as energy consumption, water usage, and greenhouse emissions
- Social performance, specifically
  - Labor practices and decent work, such as employment numbers and employee turnover, labor/management relations, health and safety, training and education, and diversity and equal opportunity
  - Human rights, such as policies on nondiscrimination, child labor, and indigenous rights
  - Society, such as community impacts, anti-corruption policies, lobbying, and contributions to political parties and politicians
  - Product responsibility, such as customer health and safety, product and service labeling, advertising, and customer privacy[22]

Exhibits 5-2, 5-3, and 5-4 present examples of social responsibility reporting. They are taken from the 2008 Annual Report of the Swiss company, Roche. Exhibit 5-2 shows employment levels by region of the world and operating division. The disclosure also discusses turnover, diversity, and human rights. Exhibit 5-3 discusses health and safety issues, along with environmental protection concerns such as energy use, greenhouse gas emissions, ozone depletion, waste, and water use. Finally, Exhibit 5-4 is the auditor's report on Roche's sustainability reporting and a statement by the company's chief executive officer that Roche's sustainability reporting is aligned with GRI guidelines.[23]

Corporate Governance Disclosures

Corporate governance relates to the internal means by which a corporation is operated and controlled—the responsibilities, accountability, and relationships among shareholders, board members, and managers designed to meet corporate objectives. That is,

---

[20] *KPMG International Survey of Corporate Responsibility Reporting 2008* (October 2008), www.kpmg.com.

[21] Standards for the audit of financial information exist worldwide. However, few countries have assurance standards for sustainability reports. The Netherlands and Sweden are two European countries with such standards, while France has issued informal guidelines. For an overview of Europe refer to the Web site of the European Sustainability Reporting Association, www.sustainabilityreporting.eu.

[22] Global Reporting Initiative, *Sustainability Reporting Guidelines*, www.globalreporting.org/NR/rdonlyres/ED9E9B36-AB54-4DE1-BFF2-5F735235CA44/0/G3_GuidelinesENU.pdf.

[23] For further discussion and illustrations, see Helen Gernon and Gary K. Meek, *Accounting: An International Perspective*, 5th ed. (Boston: Irwin McGraw-Hill, 2001); and Carol Adams, Geoffrey Frost, and Sidney J. Gray, "Corporate Social and Environmental Disclosures," in *International Finance and Accounting Handbook*, ed. Frederick D. S. Choi, 3rd ed. (New York: John Wiley, 2003).

EXHIBIT 5-2	**Employment Disclosure by Roche**

People

'People are a core factor in our business success—we need people who are enthusiastic about their job and about their employer. This enthusiasm is infectious: our customers pick up on it, helping to build their trust in Roche.'

Wolfgang Troebs, General Manager of Roche Diagnostics Switzerland

Total Employees (FTE)

	2008
Number	80,080
Growth rate	+1.88%
Growth related to acquisitions	+1.01%

Employees by contract types (Headcount)

	2008	Variance
Permanent	78,216	5.2%
Temporary	2,184	−49.4%
Apprentices	931	20.1%
Full time	76,058	2.3%
Part time	4,342	0.6%

Employer of choice

Roche is determined to remain an employer of choice. We seek to attract, recruit and retain the right employees to drive the innovation on which our business is built.

Achieving this starts with our value proposition to current and prospective employees. Under the slogan 'Make your mark. Improve lives', our employer brand embodies what differentiates Roche from other employers. It presents us as a winning company offering opportunities for professional and personal growth in a collaborative and stimulating work environment. The new employer brand will be integrated in our 65 local career websites by the end of 2009.

Our Group values and leadership competencies, introduced in 2008, reinforce Roche's principles and the work environment we seek to offer. In 2009, these will be integrated into our talent management processes.

Employees (full-time equivalent , FTE) by regions | 2008

Other	1,634	*(4.0%)*
Asia	13,065	*(2.5%)*
Latin America	4,988	*(−0.4%)*
North America	25,823	*(4.3%)*
Europe	34,570	*(0.2%)*

Employees (FTE) by operating divisions | 2008		
Other	535	*(18.6%)*
Genentech	11,029	*(−0.3%)*
Chugai	6,590	*(1.9%)*
Diagnostics	25,404	*(10.2%)*
Roche Pharmaceuticals	36,522	*(−2.8%)*

Talent management

At Roche, talent management helps us identify, recruit, develop, lead and reward employees. While the focus is on identifying employees for key positions, talent management involves developing the potential of all employees to help achieve our goals.

Our Corporate Executive Committee has identified talent management as the key people priority for Roche in 2009. We will drive and measure our progress in the areas of: attraction, retention, performance management, compensation, succession management, and learning and development.

Attraction \| Competition for talent around the world is fierce. The size of the global working-age population in developed countries is decreasing and talented people from emerging markets are increasingly returning to their home countries. This shortage means that it is difficult to attract the right people.

Global standardized processes & systems

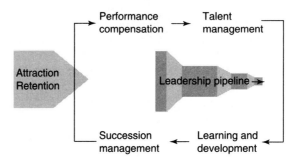

As an innovative, research-driven healthcare company, Roche operates in an industry that can have a direct benefit on the lives of millions of people worldwide. This aspect of our business can play a critical part in attracting and retaining the most motivated people. Our position as a leading multinational company, moreover, enables us to offer prospects in a growing industry with career opportunities globally.

Our careers website remains our widest-reaching and most effective tool for recruitment, with more than 10.6 million visitors in 2008.

The global careers site enables prospective and current employees to search for positions by role or by region. Roche uses the application in 37 countries to attract, source and hire candidates. In 2008 some 4,800 employees used this system to move to different positions within the Roche Group.

Approximately 65 percent of our total new hires were sourced externally. We have a talent pool of some 160,000 prospective candidates who have registered their details on our careers site.

Recruitment rate internal versus external | 2008

External 65%

Internal 35%

Career website opportunities (cumulative)

	2008	**2007**	**2006**
Registered people on the site	159,079	85,000	60,000
New employees recruited	9,192	4,100	1,700
Internal moves	4,830	451	

In 2008 we introduced a standardised recruiting process that will be rolled out across the organisation in 2009. This enables Roche to drive quality and consistency in recruiting across our operations, and helps us hire candidates in line with our renewed values and leadership competencies.

Overall, Roche had 9,192 new hires in 2008.

Retention I 2008 was a year characterised not only by acquisitions but also some significant optimisation and restructuring initiatives. Our Pharma division reduced their primary care sales force and optimised local operations such as finance, HR and other headoffice functions. Manufacturing reorganisations were also initiated in Latin America and the United States, with voluntary severance plans offered in the latter. Overall, such optimisation and restructuring initiatives accounted for 86% of employer-driven movements.

When dealing with acquisitions and reorganizations, we place an emphasis on our ability to retain valued employees. Roche offers support measures such as relocation, retention incentives and new career orientation support.

Turnover

	2008
Total	9.9%
Europe	9.5%
Latin America	14.3%
North America	10.4%
Asia	8.1%
Other	13.5%

Reasons for leaving

	2008
Employer-related	24%
Employee-related	56%
Neutral	20%

Compensation, benefits and well being | The total compensation package—pay and benefits—we offer makes a significant contribution to attracting and retaining talent within the Group. Equally important are long-term job stability, development opportunities and a good working environment.

Salaries at Roche reflect employees' contributions to the business. Pay rises and bonuses reflect business and personal performance—our 'Pay for Performance' philosophy encapsulates this. Regular benchmarks confirm that Roche offers competitive pension and benefits programmes to employees in most countries. These usually supplement local social security programmes and follow local market practices.

The remuneration packages offered by local affiliates are aligned with our Group remuneration policy, which was revised in 2004. In 2008 our total remuneration cost was 11.1 billion Swiss francs.

Through our Roche Connect programme, employees in most countries can purchase Roche's nonvoting equity securities at up to a 20% discount. In 2008 16,050 employees in 41 countries—36% of those eligible—participated in Roche Connect, up from 15,300 in 2007.

Nonvoting equity securities are awarded to managers, based on their performance, through the Roche Long-Term Plan, which was introduced in 2005. A total of 3,300 of them took part in 2008, with 880 joining for the first time.

In 2008 we moved from providing defined-benefit plans—which pay out depending on a formula defined by employees' salary, age at retirement and other factors—to defined-contribution plans—which pay out according to contributions and subsequent investments. Defined benefit plans are honoured for employees already enrolled.

We have a range of programmes to encourage our staff to look after their well-being. These include free medical check-ups, workplace ergonomic evaluations and counselling. Healthy options are available at staff restaurants.

We offer part-time, flexi-time and home-working options where appropriate. Approximately 5.4% of employees work part-time and sabbaticals are regularly arranged. Over the past year, Roche has introduced paternity leave in several countries and maternity leave is above the statutory minimum in several countries.

Performance and development | To help employees achieve their full potential, we provide regular feedback on their performance and encourage them to discuss career goals and development opportunities with their managers. In 2008 86% of our employees took part in performance management programmes and 57% in formal career development planning.

Staff performance and development is not just an employee responsibility but a management accountability. In 2008 performance management processes were reviewed to increase dialogue between managers and employees. Tight line management allows us to differentiate between high and low performers and give appropriate feedback to support employees' professional growth.

Succession management | Strengthening our talent pipeline is critical as we seek to maintain our competitive success and continue to drive a culture of innovation. In 2008 we introduced a corporate-wide approach to talent management, enabling us to nurture our high-potential employees.

Our talent framework provides us with a global approach to identify, develop and guide high-potential employees. The framework highlights talented individuals and provides access to a broad pool of employees that can take over key positions, in the short or long term.

Each step in the talent pipeline is supported by Group-wide development programmes. These programmes target the top 5% of our employees and amount to approximately 15% of total spending on learning and development.

Development opportunities are also offered through international assignments, helping to distinguish Roche as an attractive employer.

In 2008 approximately 440 employees were on long- or short-term international assignments in 50 countries. We want to ensure employees on international assignments perform successfully in their new surroundings. In 2008 we introduced cultural awareness courses to facilitate integration into the host country. Interactive training that gives employees the tools to understand the local culture from a social and business point of view were launched this year and will be rolled out widely in 2009.

We also established support programmes to help partners of employees on international assignments integrate in their new country. These programmes provide information about networks, clubs and other social organisations, and career support to enable a successful job search.

Our secondment programme gives employees the chance to work in capability and healthcare building programmes in developing countries for between 3 and 18 months. In 2008 two new secondments were approved.

Learning and development | Roche invested 139 million Swiss Francs in skills training and education in 2008 providing a total of approximately 2.4 million hours, or nearly 29 hours per employee.

Training includes technical skills programmes to meet compliance requirements, language courses, interpersonal skills training, individual coaching and programmes on leadership and change management.

Most training courses are run by the Global Functions/Business Areas or the individual affiliates and are tailored to meet local needs.

Some Roche affiliates offer comprehensive apprenticeships. Roche normally offers apprentices several alternatives, including temporary assignments, additional time at university, or a one-year internship with the company. Over half of the apprentices are hired by Roche when they finish their training. We currently have 931 apprentices working across the Group, including 156 new apprentices in 2008.

Diversity

'Having worked in different parts of the globe, I have experienced the value of diversity: it strengthens an organisation through the richness of ideas and opinions brought by people with different gender, ethnic or cultural origins.'

Pascal Soriot, Head of Commercial Operations Pharmaceuticals Division

A diverse workforce is critical to the success of a global company like Roche. Other than visible characteristics such as age, race and gender, diversity comprises experience, competencies and mindset. We believe that diversity promotes innovation. allows flexibility and inspires creativity to help Roche tackle future challenges.

We do not tolerate any form of discrimination. We foster inclusion by integrating diversity into our employee management systems.

Diversity flourishes in an environment where it exists and is acknowledged, is understood, valued and fostered, and is reflected in processes and structures.

We encourage employee diversity through formal training such as our Diversity Management Training programme and policies including the Prevention of Abuse of Power in the Workplace. We also embed inclusion into processes and daily activities.

In Basel, for example, we ensure diversity in the recruiting process through mixed gender interview panels. Ongoing improvements in family support and flexible work arrangements ensure a constant high return rate from maternity leave. For example, we opened our second day care centre in 2008 and now offer emergency day care support.

The number of women in key positions at all levels of the organisation continues to increase. In 2008, our Corporate Executive Committee welcomed its first female member, Silvia Ayyoubi, Global Head of Human Resources. Women account for 46% of our total workforce. In 2008 37% of our managers and 8% of senior managers (approximately the top 120 employees) were women, compared with 32% and 74%, respectively, in the previous year.

Gender diversity

	2008	**2007**	**2006**
Women in total workforce	46%	45%	45%
Women in management	37%	32%	31%[1]
Number (%) of women in top 120 management positions	9 (8%)	8 (7%)	4 (5%)

[1]Restated due to a reporting error in 2006 Annual Report

Being a woman has never been a career barrier to Vesna Cizej, Adriatic Management Centre Head and General Manager of Slovenia. We are all different. Intelligence is independent of race, gender and geography,' she says. 'And it is this strength of talent, with these combined differences that become the foundation for our success.'

Acknowledging diversity in Roche's workforce has allowed Vesna Cizej to adapt her leadership style to meet the needs of individual employees. She knows the importance of having an overall vision for her team but communicating that vision requires fine-tuning. 'You must be fully engaged in communicating that vision to every person in ways that are meaningful and motivational to them,' Vesna Cizej says.

Ultimately, it's all about what an employer offers its staff that keeps them inspired. At Roche, this is the opportunity to be part of something important. 'I can see where my contribution is making a real difference to people's lives. This renews the passion and energy I have for my work,' Vesna Cizej concludes.

Roche represents 139 nationalities worldwide. At our headquarters in Basel, more than half our employees do not originate from Switzerland. In the Roche affiliates, local nationals account for the majority of the workforce and for approximately 75% of their management teams. This helps to ensure that our Group policies and work reflect the diversity of our global operations.

Employee engagement

We communicate with our employees through features on our intranet and in internal newsletters, through town hall meetings and employee magazines in various languages. *Hexagon*, a worldwide employee magazine, appears quarterly in eight languages. It is also available on the Roche intranet.

We hold face-to-face lunch meetings seven or eight times a year where employees can meet members of the Corporate Executive Committee and senior managers, and ask questions. Employees from abroad can attend through live webcasts.

Human rights

Roche has a comprehensive Employment policy, which covers human rights as defined by the United Nations. The Group Compliance Officer monitors this policy throughout Roche and serves as a contact for all employees. At the end of 2008 Roche was among 230 companies recognised by Realizing Rights and Business and the Human Rights Resource Centre for our public commitment to human rights.

Roche respects the right of employees to freedom of association and collective bargaining. More than 6,600 of our employees represent their colleagues through unions memberships and over 26,160 are members of organisations that freely represent them, including the Roche Europe Forum (representing our employees across 26 countries).

Our directive on the protection of personal data protects information about employees and complies with the relevant local legislation. Where appropriate, we have negotiated data privacy agreements between different parts of the business or with works councils.

More on the web

- Employees: www.roche.com/employees
- Group policies, positions and guidelines: www.roche.com/policies_guidelines_and_posiitons
- Global careers portal: http://careers.roche.com/
- Employment policy: www.roche.com/employment_policy.pdf
- Core standards: www.roche.com/commitments

Source: 2008 Roche Annual Report

EXHIBIT 5-3   Safety and Environmental Disclosure by Roche

Safety, security, health and environmental protection

Safety, security, health and environmental protection (SHE) is integral to our business success. We take our responsibility in this area seriously throughout the lifecycle of our products. Our Corporate Principles and SHE Policy commit us to the highest standards of SHE. In 2008 we invested 218 million Swiss francs in SHE infrastructure and 295 million Swiss francs in SHE operating costs, including services and personnel.

SHE management

Everyone at Roche is responsible for ensuring the health and safety of themselves and those around them, and for minimizing the environmental impacts of our operations. We have a dedicated team of 619 full-time employees in the SHE departments across the Roche Group, including 30 people in the Corporate team, which coordinates SHE within Roche. The Corporate Security Officer appointed in 2007 within the SHE function has built up a network of local security officers to coordinate security activities across the business.

At local sites, we ensure the SHE policy and guidelines are implemented appropriately through individual site managers and SHE officers. 'Eco-delegates' working in the Diagnostics and Pharmaceuticals Divisions raise awareness of environmental issues among their colleagues.

SHE risks are identified and assessed across our businesses and affiliates, and listed in a web-based inventory. This enables us to evaluate risks and develop measures to mitigate them at Corporate level.

We monitor our SHE policy through regular site audits. In 2008 we audited 25 sites. No major deficiencies were uncovered. Most findings related to sites' risk analysis of processes requiring updates, insufficient training on emergency management or occupational hygiene assessments needing updates. We use the audits to improve our SHE performance. Recommendations are made to audited sites and their implementation is supervised by the audit team.

In 2008 we held our global conference of SHE officers to ensure our Roche Corporate SHE Policy, Guidelines and the revised Guidance notes issued in 2008 are being implemented appropriately. The conference also discussed progress towards our corporate SHE goals.

It is important for our employees to embrace our SHE standards throughout the Group. Site-specific training includes lectures and practical hands-on courses. In 2008 38,905 employees took part in 111,870 hours of SHE training.

Handling chemicals is an inherent risk in pharmaceutical and diagnostic research, development and manufacturing. Employees who handle chemicals as part of their role are trained to use them appropriately and we have published safety data sheets detailing the properties and the correct handling of over 1,000 specific chemicals.

Our three-yearly ECOmpetition encourages employees to suggest innovative ways to reduce our environmental impacts and our annual Responsible Care Network Awards ask individual sites to come up with solutions to improve energy efficiency and make them more environmentally friendly. These initiatives have led to a number of innovative proposals being implemented.

Health and safety

A safe and healthy workforce is essential to ensure employee wellbeing and productivity.

Goal: Reduce the Roche Accident Rate by 20% by 2010 to 0.079 from the 2005 baseline.

The Roche Accident Rate (RAR) measures the number of working days lost due to occupational accidents per employee per year.

In 2008 our RAR was 0.078. This represents a 2.6% increase from 2007, excluding a fatal traffic accident that year. We still remain on track to achieve our 2010 goal.

Health and Safety

	2008	2007	2006
Roche accident rate	0.078	0.076	0.083
Occupational accidents	474	482	473
Occupational illnesses	270	311	302
Work-related fatalities	0	1	0
Work-related accidents per million working hours	3.42	3.46	3.67

The number of accidents associated with contractors increased to 148. Due to the reduced number of hours worked by contractors, the associated injury frequency rate increased by 19.5%. Contractors working on our premises are obliged to follow the same safety rules as our employees.

Cases of occupational illnesses in 2008 dropped from 311 to 270 and the number of lost days reduced from 1,335 to 602. Diseases of the musculo-skeletal system accounted for more than two-thirds of these lost work days.

We strive to reduce the number and severity of occupational accidents and illnesses. All incidents are investigated and the relevant findings are communicated across the company.

Individual sites play a vital role in achieving the long-term global SHE goals we set in 2005. In 2008 sites followed up on action plans, which were developed at the SHE conference in September 2006 to help achieve the goals. The plans were assessed by Corporate SHE and the measures are continuously implemented.

Environmental footprint

We monitor our environmental footprint in research and production, packaging, transport and distribution during use and disposal.

Goal: Improve total eco-balance by 10% by 2015 from 2005 baseline (points/employee).

Performance: The environmental footprint of our business is calculated on the basis of the 'ecobalance' method designed by the Swiss Agency for the Environment (BAFU). The ecobalance reflects the total environmental impacts of our operations through the use of resources (raw materials and energy) as well as the generation of emissions and waste.

In 2008 our ecobalance was 4.95, an improvement of 3.9% from 2007. This reflects the reductions achieved across all environmental indicators, except for nitrous oxide air emissions and particulates, which have increased slightly this year. We are currently operating within our target ecobalance of 5.92 for 2015. To maintain this level we recognise the need to continuously cut resource use, and reduce the amount of waste and emissions we generate.

It is important to understand our environmental expenditure in relation to sales because this allows us to quantify the environmental impacts of our operations. We use this information to target our SHE investment in areas where we have the greatest impacts.

Our 'Eco-Efficiency Rate' (EER) combines data on energy use, waste, and emissions to air and water with expenditure on environmental protection and sales. A full explanation of the EER can be found on our website. In 2008, our EER was 77.95 an improvement of 16%

Eco-efficiency rate

	2008	2007	2006
Sales (in millions of CHF)	45,617	46,133	42,041
Environmental expenditure (in millions of CHF)	209	232	255
Environmental damage (in millions of environmental damage units)	2.80	2.96	3.30
EER	77.95	67.19	49.97

Energy and climate change

We aim to reduce energy use and emissions of green-house gases such as carbon dioxide (CO_2) from our operations.

Goal: Reduce total energy consumption by 10% by 2010 from 2005 baseline (GJ/employee)

Goal: Reduce greenhouse gas emissions by 10% by 2008 from 2003 baseline (CO_2 equivalent unit/sales)

Performance: In 2008 Roche used 13,662 terajoules of energy, a decrease of 2 terajoules from the previous year. This is equivalent to 0.718 gigajoules per employee, a slight decrease from 2007.

Energy use | terajoules

	2008	2007	2006
Total energy use	13,662	13,664	12,467
Total energy use per million CHF of sales	0.299	0.296	0.297
Total energy use per employee	0.178	0.179	0.174

Emissions from our energy use together with other greenhouse gas emissions totaled 1.06 million tonnes of CO_2 equivalent in 2008, an absolute increase on 1% from 2007. This rise in emissions despite lower energy consumption is due to increased car and plane travel.

Energy use by type in 2008 | %

Fuel used by company vehicles	9.9
Oil	1.7
Fuel due to business air travel	14.4
Waste	0.9
Grid electricity	29.0
District heating	3.9
Renewablse energy	0.5
Natural gas	39.7

Greenhouse gas emissions relative to sales have increased this year to 23.28 tonnes per million Swiss francs of sales. This equates to a total decrease of approximately 54.8% since 2003, which exceeds our 10% reduction goal by the end of 2008.

Greenhouse gas emissions | tonnes CO_2 equivalent

	2008	2007	2006
Total emissions	1,062,114	1,052,407	980,008
Total emissions per million CHF of sales	23.28	22.81	23.31

Our Group strategy for decreasing greenhouse gas emissions is guided by our position paper on Greenhouse Gases and Climate Change. The paper stresses the connection between CO_2 emissions and energy use and we are implementing measures to reduce energy consumption and improve efficiency.

We believe allowing individual sites to develop their own emissions reduction strategies maximises their efforts because they are the most familiar with local conditions. Sites are guided by our Group directive on energy conservation, which enforces a systematic approach. It includes energy efficiency standards on the design of new equipment and optimization of existing energy consuming items.

The directive requires site energy audits to be carried out. In 2008 we issued guidance to ensure a structured approach to these audits. They can be carried out by third parties or by the sites themselves. We select sites to be audited according to their circumstances and energy consumption. As a result, the audits may not cover an entire site but may concentrate on a particular system. We use the results to develop initiatives and goals to reduce future energy use.

One of the winning entries for the Roche Responsible Care Network Awards in 2008 came from our headquarters in Basel. By adjusting the site's air conditioning in IT rooms to a slightly higher temperature and a slightly lower humidity, energy use has been cut by 12% with no increased risk of damage to our IT equipment.

Some other entries shortlisted for the awards this year include:

- Roche Carolina: an energy monitoring system for data collection and data analysis allows the site to monitor, manage and optimise energy use
- Roche Burgdorf: a new heating system using wood pellets rather than fossil fuels will cut CO_2 emissions by 94%, with 28% of total energy used being renewable
- Roche Brussels: the new building includes special sun shading to prevent offices getting too hot in summer, use of rain water for toilet flushing and energy efficient lighting in the car park

We encourage employees to consolidate travel for several destinations into one trip. We invest in video and teleconferencing facilities and where travel is necessary, we promote the use of trains, rather than flights.

Changing the rules to invest in energy savings | In 2008 the World Business Council for Sustainable Development (WBCSD) exemplified Roche in a case study about our efforts to analyse the life-cycle costs and impact of energy efficiency investments. The WBCSD published the study to stimulate similar approaches in other companies. The paper highlights Roche's innovative method for calculating the value of energy-efficiency investments.

The WBCSD noted that converting the social, environmental and economic benefits over time into a single financial figure that can be compared to up-front costs is a valuable tool in promoting the business case for investment in energy-efficiency. Through this initiative, 'Roche has enabled managers throughout the business to rigorously assess the feasibility of energy efficiency investments and to pursue these opportunities for value creation.'

Ozone depletion

Halogenated hydrocarbons (such as CFCs and HCFCs) damage the ozone layer and affect the climate. Roche's directive on phasing out CFCs and HCFCs commits us to eliminate them from our cooling systems and fire extinguishing systems by 2010.

However, several projects to replace HCFCs in refrigeration units have been held up by the lack of accepted alternatives in some countries and reorganisation plans have put phasing-out projects on hold at important sites. The target date to eliminate these compounds has therefore been extended.

HFCs (hydrofluorocarbons) and PFCs (perfluorinated carbons), which are often used as replacements to HCFCs and CFCs, do not affect the ozone layer. However, they have considerable global warming potential and some are persistent in the atmosphere. We do not consider them to be a suitable long-term alternative and we aim to phase out these compounds by 2015. Appropriate plans are in place and investment projects are being implemented to meet this goal.

Ozone-depleting chemicals | tonnes

	2008	2007	2006
Halogenated hydrocarbons holdings	144.6	148.2	141.2
Halogenated hydrocarbons emissions	3.4	4.7	7.7

Emissions to air

Volatile organic compounds (VOCs) and particulates contribute to air pollution and smog, and nitrogen oxides (NO_x) and sulphur dioxide (SO_2) can contribute to acid rain. These emissions to air are included in our overall goal to reduce our total environmental impacts.

Performance: In 2008 our manufacturing processes and combustion plants emitted 213 tonnes of VOCs, down 11.3% from 2007. This means we surpassed our goal to reduce VOC emissions by 10% per tonne of unit sales from a 2003 baseline by 2008. Levels of particulates, NO, and SO_2 continue to fluctuate at a low level—with total emissions of 27 tonnes, 193 tonnes and ten tonnes, respectively, in 2008.

Emissions to air | tonnes

	2008	2007	2006
VOCs	213	240	281
Particulates	27	25	27
Nitrogen oxides	193	169	219
Sulphur dioxide	10	12	15

Waste

Roche's operations produce chemical waste that needs to be disposed of safely.

In 2008 our chemical waste amounted to 31,295 tonnes. This 18.0% decrease from 2007 reflects a smaller production volume. Incinerating this waste is the most responsible way to dispose of it, and the majority (96.8%) was dealt with in this manner.

Some waste streams originating from particular manufacturing processes can be reused by other companies. In 2008 we sold 4,940 tonnes of this waste. Our recycled chemical waste amounted to 13,811 tonnes, consisting mainly of solvents.

In 2008 we produced 42,823 tonnes of general waste, 145% more than the previous year. This considerable increase was mainly due to construction waste from building activities at different sites counting for approximately 25,000 tonnes. We incinerated 12.1% and sent 87.9% to landfill, mainly building rubble. We recycled 28,589 tonnes of general waste, down 9.8% from last year.

Landfill sites containing chemical waste from our premises are monitored regularly to make sure they do not pose a risk to human health or the environment. If necessary, landfills are sustainably remediated. We have made approximately 160 million Swiss francs available for such purposes.

Waste | tonnes

	2008	2007	2006
General waste produced	42,823	17,480	20,719
General waste per million CHF of sales	0.94	0.38	0.58
Chemical waste produced	31,295	38,167	51,155
Chemical waste per million CHF of sales	0.69	0.83	1.21

Water

Clean water is integral to Roche's manufacturing processes. In 2008 we withdrew 21 million m^3, for these purposes from various sources, approximately the same amount as last year.

The Global Reporting Initiative defines water consumption as the water used in products, cooling and air conditioning, and irrigation. We increased our consumption based on this definition by 4.3% from 2007 to 2.4 million m^3. We continually strive to reduce our water consumption globally.

Manufacturing processes often release contaminated wastewater as a by-product. We treat wastewater to ensure it is safe for the environment and humans before we release it into watercourses. We aim to increase our capacity to treat wastewater as our business continues to grow.

The extension of the biotechnological production at Roche in Penzberg, for example, required increased capacity to treat wastewater. We installed an innovative membrane technology that increases the capacity by 60% and requires less space and less energy than the previous installations. This solution was a winning entry in this year's Responsible Care Network Awards.

In 2008 we discharged 592 tonnes of organic material into water courses after treatment, a 7.6% decrease compared with 2007. Heavy metals such as chromium, copper and zinc can be removed from piping by wastewater. This year we released 545 kilograms of heavy metals, a decrease of 9.9% compared to 2007.

Water

	2008	2007	2006
Water withdrawn (million cubic meters)	21.0	21.0	22.1
Water used (million cubic meters)	2.4	2.3	4.3
Wastewater discharged to treatment plant (million cubic meters)	7.3	7.1	5.1
Organic matter discharged to watercourses after treatment (tonnes)	592	641	313
Heavy metals discharged to watercourses after treatment (kilograms)	545	605	1,086

Pharmaceuticals in the environment

Concerns have been raised about traces of pharmaceutical active ingredients detected in the environment. Current research shows that the quantities found in rivers, lakes and water supplies are generally far below the level at which they would have a therapeutic or adverse effect on human health or aquatic life in watercourses.

Manufacturing processes and improper disposal of unused medicines may lead to pharmaceuticals entering the environment but normal patient use is recognised as the main contributor. The risk of pharmaceuticals entering the environment is an important element of our life-cycle approach to environmental protection in product development.

Roche aims to minimise the release of pharmaceuticals into the environment wherever possible. All our manufacturing sites are designed and operated to ensure that, as far as practicable, active pharmaceutical ingredients are not discharged into the wastewater.

We offer financial incentives to encourage retailers and others in our value chain to return unused or outdated products. This ensures these are incinerated rather than disposed of in landfills. We promote new take-back programmes where they do not already exist.

In 2008 Roche published a global position statement on pharmaceuticals in the environment, outlining our intentions to monitor risks to human health and the environment.

We acknowledge that long-term effects of pharmaceuticals in the environment need to be researched further. We participate in international and local bodies dedicated to study the impact of trace chemicals, including pharmaceuticals, in surface and groundwater.

Compliance and incidents

Goal: Receive no significant SHE-related fines.

Performance: No significant fines have been reported for 2008.

The integrity of our business is compromised when we fail to comply with relevant legislation and regulations. Our Group policies often surpass local laws and regulations but as a minimum Roche is committed to comply with local requirements.

Some substances, as well as biological materials, used in pharmaceutical manufacturing are regulated because there is potential for them to be misused, for example in the production of narcotics, toxins or chemical weapons. We keep these substances in small quantities, under rigorous control and in line with all applicable legislation.

More on the web

- SHE performance: www.roche.com/key_figures_and_facts
- Safety, security, health and environmental protection: www.roche.com/environment
- Safety, security, health and environmental protection (SHE) policy: www.roche.com/reporting_and_indices
- Group fact sheets, positions, policies and guidelines: www.roche.com/policies_guidelines_and_positions

Source: 2008 Roche Annual Report

EXHIBIT 5-4   **Auditor's Report on Sustainability Reporting by Roche**

Independent Assurance Report

To the Corporate Sustainability Committee of Roche Holding Ltd, Basel ('Roche').

We have performed assurance procedures to provide assurance on the following aspects of the 2008 sustainability reporting of Roche.

Subject matter

Data and information disclosed with the sustainability reporting of Roche and its consolidated subsidiaries. excluding Chugai Pharmaceutical Co. Ltd. and Genentech Inc., for the year ended December 31, 2008 on the following aspects:

- The management and reporting processes with respect to the sustainability reporting and to the preparation of SHE and people key figures as well as the control environment in relation to the data aggregation of these key figures
- The SHE key figures in the tables on the pages 108 to 114 and some selected people key figures disclosed on the pages 100 to 105 of the Roche Business Report 2008

Criteria

- The Roche Group internal sustainability reporting guidelines based on the Responsible Care, Health, Safety and Environmental reporting guidelines published by the European Chemical Industry Council (CEFiC) and the 'Sustainability Reporting Guidelines G3' published on October 2006 by the Global Reporting Initiative (GRI)
- The defined procedures by which the SHE and people key figures are gathered, collated and aggregated internally

Responsibility and methodology

The accuracy and completeness of sustainability indicators are subject to inherent limitations given their nature and methods for determining, calculating and estimating such data. Our Assurance should therefore be read in connection with Roche's internal guidelines, definitions and procedures on the reporting of its sustainability performance.

   The Roche Corporate Sustainability Committee is responsible for both the subject matter and the evaluation criteria. Our responsibility is to provide a conclusion on the subject matter based on our assurance procedures in accordance with the International Standard on Assurance Engagements (ISAE) 3000.

Main assurance procedures

Our assurance procedures included the following work:

- **Evaluation of the application of group guidelines** | Reviewing the application of the Roche internal sustainability reporting guidelines
- **Site visits** | Visiting selected sites of Roche's Pharmaceuticals and Diagnostics Divisions in Switzerland, France. UK, Canada, Mexico and Brazil. The selection was based on quantitative and qualitative criteria; Interviewing personnel responsible for internal reporting and data collection at the sites we visited and at the Group level to determine the understanding and application of the guidelines
- **Assessment of the key figures** | Performing tests on a sample basis of evidence supporting selected SHE and people key figures (Roche accident rate, energy consumption, CO_2 emissions related to energy consumption, general wastes, use of water, fines in relation to safety and environmental protection, headcount data, staff turnover, women in senior management positions and cost of training) concerning completeness, accuracy, adequacy and consistency
- **Review of the documentation and analysis of relevant policies and basic principles** | Reviewing the relevant documentation on a sample basis including group sustainability policies, management and reporting structures and documentation
- **Assessment of the processes and data consolidation** | Reviewing the appropriateness of the management and reporting processes for sustainability reporting Assessing the consolidation process of data at the Group level.

Conclusions

In our opinion

- The internal sustainability reporting guidelines are being applied properly
- The internal reporting system to collect and aggregate the SHE and people key figures is functioning as designed and provides an appropriate basis for its disclosure

Based on our work described in this report and the assessment of criteria, nothing has come to our attention that causes us to believe that the data and information mentioned in the subject matter and disclosed with the Sustainability Reporting in the Roche Business Report 2008 does not give a fair picture of Roche's performance.

Zurich, 23 January 2009
PriceWaterhouseCoopers AG
Dr. Thomas Scheiwiller   Juerg Hutter

The Global Reporting Initiative sustainability reporting guidelines
    As in previous years we have once again aligned our sustainability reporting to the guidelines of the Global Reporting Initiative (GRI).
    For the second time, Roche is of the opinion that the A+ level of the GRI G3 guidelines applies to its Annual Report 2008. This was checked with and confirmed by the GRI.
    Details of how we report against each indicator can be found at www.roche.com/reporting_and_indices
    Severin Schwan

Source: 2008 Roche Annual Report

corporate governance is the system by which companies are directed and controlled. Among corporate governance issues are the rights and treatment of shareholders, the responsibilities of the board, disclosure and transparency, and the role of stakeholders.

Dallas provides a framework for understanding and assessing corporate governance mechanisms that exist in individual countries.[24] The four components of his framework are the market infrastructure, legal environment, regulatory environment, and informational infrastructure.

1. *Market infrastructure*   includes ownership patterns (concentrated vs. dispersed), the extent to which companies are publicly listed, ownership rights, and the market for corporate control (takeovers). The structure of the board, traditions of board independence, and whether the chairperson and CEO roles are separated are related issues.

2. *Legal environment*   includes the type of legal system and whether shareholder/stakeholders' rights are clearly defined and consistently and effectively enforced. Company laws and securities laws are part of the legal environment. Company laws cover how companies are formed and managed, and the rights and responsibilities of managers, directors, and shareholders. Securities laws relate to the issuance and trading of securities, including filing and disclosure requirements. In addition, general commercial laws are important in ensuring the rights of owners (including minority shareholders), creditors, and other stakeholders.

3. *Regulatory environment*   is closely linked to the legal environment. Regulatory agencies are responsible for regulating markets to conform to existing laws. They ensure orderly and efficient markets and enforce public disclosure requirements.

4. *Informational infrastructure*   pertains to the accounting standards used and whether they result in accurate, complete, and timely financial reporting. It also includes the structure of the auditing profession and professional standards for auditing practice and independence. The timely disclosure of reliable, publicly available information enables stakeholders to judge a company's governance effectiveness and its operating and financial performance.

[24] George S. Dallas, *Governance and Risk* (New York: McGraw-Hill, 2004).

Exhibit 5-5 summarizes the relationships of Dallas's governance framework. Note that the four components are interconnected.

As implied by Exhibit 5-5, corporate governance structures and practices vary around the world, reflecting differences in culture, traditional sources of finance, patterns of corporate ownership concentration, and legal systems and frameworks. To illustrate, Exhibit 5-6 lists some broad generalizations about Germany and Japan on the one hand, and the United Kingdom and the United States on the other. Because of these differences, governance mechanisms are historically weaker in Germany and Japan than in the United Kingdom and United States. However, corporate governance is being improved in many countries around the world, including Germany and Japan, as companies' governance practices receive increased attention from regulators, investors, and analysts.

The United States, United Kingdom, and Australia are among the growing number of countries that require listed companies to make specific corporate governance disclosures in their annual reports. The EU Fourth and Seventh Directives (see Chapter 8) require publicly traded European companies to provide corporate governance statements. The Organisation for Economic Cooperation and Development (OECD, also discussed in Chapter 8) issued its revised *Principles of Corporate Governance* in 2004, enunciating six basic principles of corporate governance.[25] Disclosure and transparency are covered in the fifth principle, shown in Exhibit 5-7.

EXHIBIT 5-5	Framework for Understanding Corporate Governance Mechanisms in Countries (Dallas 2004)

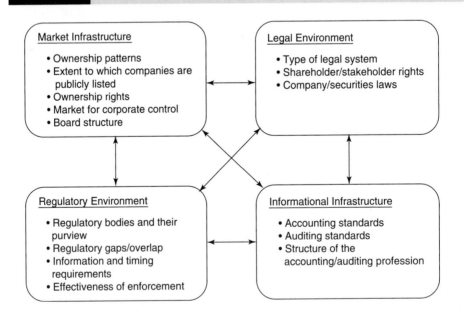

---

[25] Organisation for Economic Cooperation and Development, *OECD Principles of Corporate Governance* (2004), www.oecd.org/dataoecd/32/18/31557724.pdf. The six principles are (1) ensuring the basis for an effective corporate governance framework, (2) the rights of shareholders and key ownership functions, (3) equitable treatment of shareholders, (4) the role of stakeholders in corporate governance, (5) disclosure and transparency, and (6) the responsibilities of the board.

EXHIBIT 5-6	**Comparison of Germany and Japan vs. the United Kingdom and United States**

Germany and Japan	United Kingdom and United States
• Consensus culture; cooperative relationships	• Competition; arm's-length relationships
• Network-oriented	• Market-oriented
• Bank-oriented: relatively more reliance on debt; stock exchange less important as source of finance	• Stock market-oriented: relatively more reliance on equity; stock exchange more important as source of finance
• Insider-dominated; concentrated ownership and relatively more influence of controlling shareholder(s)	• Outsider-dominated; dispersed ownership and relatively less influence of controlling shareholder(s)
• Stakeholder focused	• Shareholder focused
• Code (civil) law legal system	• Common law legal system

EXHIBIT 5-7	**OECD Fifth Principle of Corporate Governance: Disclosure and Transparency**

The corporate governance framework should ensure that timely and accurate disclosure is made on all material matters regarding the corporation, including the financial situation, performance, ownership and governance of the company.

A. Disclosure should include, but not be limited to, material information on:
  1. The financial and operating results of the company.
  2. Company objectives.
  3. Major share ownership and voting rights.
  4. Remuneration policy for members of the board and key executives, and information about board members, including their qualifications, the selection process, other company directorships and whether they are regarded as independent by the board.
  5. Related party transactions.
  6. Foreseeable risk factors.
  7. Issues regarding employees and other stakeholders.
  8. Governance structures and policies, in particular, the content of any corporate code of policy and the process by which it is implemented.
B. Information should be prepared and disclosed in accordance with high quality standards of accounting and financial and nonfinancial disclosure.
C. An annual audit should be conducted by an independent, competent, and qualified auditor in order to provide an external and objective assurance to the board and shareholders that the financial statements fairly present the financial position and performance of the company in all material respects.
D. External auditors should be accountable to the shareholders and owe a duty to the company to exercise due professional care in the conduct of the audit.
E. Channels for disseminating information should provide for equal, timely, and cost-efficient access to relevant information by users.
F. The corporate governance framework should be complemented by an effective approach that addresses and promotes the provision of analysis or advice by analysts, brokers, rating agencies and others, that is relevant to decisions by investors, free from material conflicts of interest that might compromise the integrity of their analysis or advice.

Source: OECD Principles of Corporate Governance (2004): 22–23
(www.oecd.org/dataoecd/32/18/31557724.pdf).

Disclosure is a key element in any system of good corporate governance. Exhibit 5-8 presents an example of a corporate governance disclosure from the annual report of the Swedish company Volvo. Included in its disclosure are statements about how governance is carried out, information about the board of directors, and a discussion of internal controls. Board of directors disclosures include the names of board members, how often the board meets, statements about independent directors, and the workings of the audit and remuneration committees. Volvo's disclosures are typical of many large multinational corporations.

EXHIBIT 5-8   Volvo Governance Disclosure

Corporate Governance Report

During 2008, the Board focused specifically on adapting the Group's operations to the present market conditions, initially to a very strong demand for the Group's products and during the second half to a significantly weaker development. The Board has furthermore focused specifically on issues pertaining to the continuous integration of newly acquired operations and on issues relating to the continuous renewal of the Group's product portfolio.

Corporate bodies in corporate governance

The governance and control of the Volvo Group is carried out through a number of corporate bodies. At the Annual General Meeting, the shareholders exercise their voting rights with regard, for example, to the composition of the Board of Directors of AB Volvo and election of external auditors. An Election Committee proposes candidates to serve as Board members, Board Chairman and external auditors. The Board is responsible for the Group's long-term development and strategy as well as controlling and evaluating the company's operations. In addition, the Board appoints the President of AB Volvo, who is also the Chief Executive Officer (CEO). The duties of the Board are partly exercised through its Audit Committee and its Remuneration Committee. The CEO is in charge of the daily management of the Group in accordance with guidelines and instructions provided by the Board.

The CEO is in charge of the daily management of the Group through primarily two different bodies, the Group Executive Committee and the business areas' and business units' Boards of Directors. The Group Executive Committee comprises those who report directly to the CEO. The Group Executive Committee meetings, which are led by the CEO, deal with Group-wide issues and issues affecting more than one business area/unit, and sharing of information concerning the Group's performance. The CEO or another member of the Group Executive Committee is the Chairman of the Boards of all business areas and business units and these comprise mainly of other members of the Group Executive Committee. The Boards of the business areas and business units effect control and follow-ups of business areas' and business units' financial development, business plans and goals as well as make decisions regarding, for example, investments.

Swedish Code of Corporate Governance

Volvo applies the Swedish Code of Corporate Governance, revised as of July 1, 2008 (the Code), in accordance with which this Corporate Governance Report has been prepared. The Board's report of the key aspects of the company's system for internal controls and risk management regarding financial reports is included as a special section of this Corporate Governance Report.

Between January 1, 2008 and December 31, 2008 Volvo did not deviate from any of the regulations set forth in the Code.

This Corporate Governance Report has not been reviewed by the company's auditors.

Election Committee

The Election Committee is the shareholders' body responsible for submitting to the Annual General Meeting the names of candidates to serve as Chairman and other members of the Board as well as proposal for fees and other compensations to be paid to the Board members. In the years in which election of auditors for Volvo shall be held, the Election Committee presents proposals for election of auditors and proposal for fees to be paid to the auditors based on the preparations carried out by Volvo's Audit Committee.

The Election Committee's proposal shall be presented to Volvo in sufficient time to be able to be included in the notice to attend the Annual General Meeting and at the same time to be published on Volvo's website. In conjunction with the notice to attend the Annual General Meeting is published, the Election Committee shall among other things comment on whether those persons who are proposed to be elected as Board members are to be considered as independent in relation to the company and company management as well as to large shareholders in the company and further to comment on their material assignments and holding of shares in Volvo. At Volvo's Annual General Meeting in 2007, new instructions for the Election Committee were adopted. According to these instructions, the Annual General Meeting shall select five members for the Election Committee, of which four shall represent the largest shareholders in the company, in terms of the number of votes, who have expressed their willingness to participate in the Election Committee. In addition, one of the members shall be the Chairman of the AB Volvo Board. Additionally, the Election Committee can offer other larger shareholders to appoint one representative as a member of the Election Committee. If such an offer is made, it should be directed in turn to the largest shareholder in terms of voting rights not already being represented on the Election Committee. The number of members on the Election Committee may not exceed seven however.

The Election Committee, which was appointed at Volvo's Annual General Meeting in 2008 in accordance with the new instructions, comprised Volvo's Chairman Finn Johnsson, Carl-Olof By, representing AB Industrivärden, Lars Förberg, representing Violet Partners LP, Anders Oscarsson, representing SEB Fonder / Trygg Försäkring and Thierry Moulonguet, representing Renault. The Election Committee elected Thierry Moulonguet as Chairman. Later during 2008, the Election Committee offered Svenska Handelsbanken together with SHB Pension Fund, SHB Pensionskassa, SHB Employee Fund and Oktagon and AMF Pension to appoint one representative each as a member of the Election Committee. Handelsbanken and others appointed Häkan Sandberg and AMF Pension appointed Christer Elmehagen. When Christer Elmehagen in December 2008 retired from AMF Pension, he also retired from the Election Committee.

The Election Committee has proposed reelection of Peter Bijur, Leif Johansson, Finn Johnsson (Chairman of the Board), Louis Schweitzer, Ravi Venkatesan, Lars Westerberg and Ying Yeh as members of the AB Volvo Board. In addition, the Election Committee proposed election for the first time of Jean-Baptiste Duzan and Anders Nyrén. Tom Hedelius and Philippe Klein have declined reelection.

The Board

In 2008, AB Volvo's Board of Directors consisted of nine members elected by the Annual General Meeting. In addition, the Board had three members and two deputy members appointed by employee organizations. The CEO, Leif Johansson, was a member of the Board.
During 2008, six regular meetings, one statutory meeting and one extraordinary meeting were held.

The Board has adopted work procedures for its activities that contain rules pertaining to the distribution of work between the Board members, the number of Board meetings, matters to be handled at regular meetings of the Board and duties incumbent on the Chairman.

In addition thereto, the work procedures contain directives concerning the tasks of the Audit Committee and the Remuneration Committee respectively. The Board has also issued

The Board's composition and attendance at meetings January 1, 2008, to December 31, 2008

	Board	Audit Committee	Remuneration Committee
Finn Johnsson	8		4
Peter Bijur	7	3	
Per-Olof Eriksson[1]	3	1	
Tom Hedelius	7		3
Leif Johansson	8		
Philippe Klein	5		
Louis Schweitzer	7		3
Ravi Venkatesan[2]	2		
Lars Westerberg	8	3	
Ying Yeh	7	3	
Martin Linder, employee rep.	8		
Olle Ludvigsson, employee rep.	8		
Johnny Rönnkvist, employee rep.	7		
Total number of meetings	**8**	**3**	**4**

[1]*Resigned from the Board in conjunction with the 2008 Annual General Meeting.*
[2]*Elected to the Board at the 2008 Annual General Meeting.*

written instructions specifying how financial information should be reported to the Board as well as the distribution of duties between the Board and the President.

The Annual General Meeting decides on the fees to be paid to the Board members elected by the shareholders. The Annual General Meeting held on April 9, 2008 approved a total fee to the Board, for the time until the end of the next Annual General Meeting, of SEK 5,725,000 to be distributed among the Board Members according to the following. The Chairman of the Board should receive a fee of SEK 1,500,000 and each of the remaining members should receive a fee of SEK 500,000, with the exception of the President. In addition, the Chairman of Audit Committee should receive SEK 250,000 and the other two members of the Audit Committee SEK 125,000 each and the members of the Remuneration Committee SEK 75,000 each.

During the year, the Board reviewed the business plans and strategies for the various businesses in the Volvo Group. The Board also reviewed the financial positions of AB Volvo and the Volvo Group on a regular basis and acted in order to ascertain that there are efficient systems in order to follow-up and control the business and financial position of the Volvo Group. In connection therewith, the Audit Committee was responsible for preparing for the Board's work to assure the quality of the company's financial reporting through reviewing the interim reports and the annual report. In connection therewith, the Board met with the company's auditors during 2008. The Board continuously evaluated the performance of the CEO.

During 2008, the Board focused specifically on adapting the Group's operations to the present market conditions; initially to a very strong demand for the Group's products and during the second half to a significantly weaker development. The Board has furthermore focused specifically on issues pertaining to continuation of the integration of newly acquired operations and on issues relating to the continuous renewal of the Group's product portfolio.

The Board's work is mainly performed through Board meetings and through meetings in the respective committees of the Board. In addition thereto, the Chairman of the Board is in regular contact with the CEO in order to discuss on-going business and to ensure that the decisions taken by the Board are executed. An account of each Board member's age, main education, professional experience, assignments in the Company and other important board memberships, own and related parties ownership of shares in Volvo as of March 4, 2009, and the years of membership on the Volvo Board, is presented on the Board and auditors page.

During 2008, the Board performed its yearly evaluation of the Board's work. The Chairman has informed the Election Committee on the result of the evaluation.

Independence requirements

The Board of Directors of Volvo must meet independence requirements pursuant to the rules of the OMX Nordic Exchange Stockholm (the "Stockholm Exchange"), and the Code. Below follows a short description of the rules of the Stockholm Exchange and the Code. The independence requirements mainly mean that only one person from the company's management may be a member of the Board, that a majority of the Board members elected by the General Meeting shall be independent of the company and the company management and that at least two of the Board members elected by the General Meeting that are independent from the company and the company's management shall also be independent of the company's major shareholders. In addition, the Code demands that a majority of the members in the Audit Committee shall be independent of the company and the company management and that at least one member shall be independent of the company's major shareholders. A member of the Board who is a member of the company management shall not be a member of the Audit Committee. With regard to the Remuneration Committee, the Code sets the requirement that members of the Remuneration Committee, with the exception of the Board Chairman if a member of the Remuneration Committee, shall be independent of the company and company management.

Considering the above demands regarding the Board's independence, the Election Committee has reported to the company the following understanding about the independence from the company and the company management as well as the company's largest shareholders with regard to the Board members who were elected at the Annual General Meeting in 2008:

Finn Johnsson, Peter Bijur, Tom Hedelius, Philippe Klein, Louis Schweitzer, Ravi Venkatesan, Lars Westerberg and Ying Yeh are all independent from the company and company management.

Leif Johansson, as Volvo's CEO, is not independent from the company and company management.

Louis Schweitzer and Philippe Klein are Chairman of the Board and employee, respectively, of Renault and represent Renault on the company's Board of Directors. Since Renault controls more than 10% of the shares and votes in Volvo, these persons may not, pursuant to the Code and the rules of the Stockholm Exchange, be considered as independent in relation to one of the company's major shareholders.

Also the Election Committee must meet independence requirements pursuant to the Code. According to the Code the majority of the members of the Election Committee are to be independent of the company and the company management. Neither the CEO nor other members of the executive management are to be members of the Election Committee. At least one member of the nomination committee is to be independent of the company's largest shareholder in terms of votes or any group of shareholders that act in concert in the governance of the company. All members of the Election Committee have been considered to be independent of Volvo and Volvo's management. All members of the Election Committee except Thierry Moulonguet have been considered to be independent of Volvo's largest shareholder in terms of votes, since Thierry Moulonguet represents Renault in the Election Committee and Renault is Volvo's largest shareholder in terms of votes.

Audit Committee

In December 2002, the Board established an Audit Committee primarily for the purpose of overseeing the accounting and financial reporting processes and the audit of the financial statements. The Audit Committee is responsible for preparing the Board's work to assure the quality of the company's financial reporting through reviewing the interim reports and the annual report. In addition, the Audit Committee's task is to establish guidelines specifying what other services than audit the company may procure from the company's auditors and to provide guidelines for and decisions on transactions with companies and persons closely associated with Volvo. The Audit Committee is also responsible for evaluating the internal and external auditors' work as well as to provide the Election Committee with the results of the evaluation and to assist in preparing proposals for auditors. Finally the Audit Committee shall evaluate the quality, relevance and efficiency of the Group's system for internal controls, internal audit and risk management.

At the statutory Board meeting following the 2008 Annual General Meeting, Peter Bijur, Lars Westerberg and Ying Yeh were appointed members of the Audit Committee. Lars Westerberg was appointed Chairman of the Audit Committee.

The Audit Committee met with the external auditors and Head of Internal Audit at the meetings of the Audit Committee. The Audit Committee has also met separately with the external auditors and the Head of Internal Audit without the presence of the company management. The Audit Committee and the external auditors have among other things discussed the external audit plan and risk management. The Audit Committee held three meetings during 2008.

Remuneration Committee

In April 2003, the Board established a Remuneration Committee primarily for the purpose of preparing and deciding on issues relating to remuneration to senior executives in the Group. The duties of the Committee include presenting recommendations for resolution by the Board regarding terms of employment and remuneration for the President of AB Volvo, principles for remuneration, including pensions and severance payment for other members of the Group Executive Committee, and principles for variable salary systems, share-based incentive programs, pensions and severance payment for other senior executives in the Group. In addition, the Remuneration Committee decides the individual terms of employment for the other members of the Group Executive Committee in accordance with the principles established by the Board.

In 2008, the Remuneration Committee comprised Board members Tom Hedelius, Louis Schweitzer and Finn Johnsson, Chairman. The Remuneration Committee held four meetings during the year.

Group Executive Committee

An account of their respective age, principal education, Board memberships, own and related parties' ownership of shares in Volvo as of March 4, 2009, and year of joining Volvo for the CEO and each member of the Group Executive Committee is presented in the Group Executive Committee section.

External auditing

Volvo's auditors are elected by the Annual General Meeting, for a period of three or four years. The current auditor is PricewaterhouseCoopers AB (PwC), which was elected at the 2007 Annual General Meeting for a period of three years. The next election of auditors will thus be at the 2010 Annual General Meeting. Two PwC partners, Göran Tidström and Olov Karlsson, are responsible for the audit of Volvo. Göran Tidström is the Lead Partner.

The external auditors discuss the external audit plan and risk management with the Audit Committee. The Auditors review the interim report for the period January 1 to June 30 and the annual report. The auditors report their findings as regards the annual report to the shareholders through the audit report, which they present to the Annual General Meeting of the shareholders. In addition, the auditors report detailed findings from their reviews to the Audit Committee twice a year and, once a year, to the full Board of Directors.

When PwC is retained to provide services other than the audit, it is done in accordance with rules decided by the Audit Committee pertaining to pre-approval of the nature of the services and the fees.

Disclosure Committee

A Disclosure Committee was established in 2004. The Committee contributes to ensuring that Volvo fulfills its obligations according to applicable legislation as well as to listing rules to timely disclose to the financial market all share price sensitive information.

The Committee comprises the heads of the departments Corporate Finance, Internal Audit, Investor Relations, Corporate Legal, Business Control and Financial Reporting. Chairman of the Disclosure Committee is the company's Senior Vice President of Corporate Communications.

Outstanding share- and share-price-related incentive programs

An account of outstanding share- and share-price-related incentive programs is provided in Note 34 Employees in the Group's notes.

The Board's report on the key aspects of the company's system for internal controls and risk management regarding financial reports

The Board is responsible for the internal controls according to the Swedish Companies Act and the Swedish Code of Corporate Governance (the Code). The purpose of this report is to provide shareholders and other interested parties an understanding of how internal control is organized at Volvo with regard to financial reporting.

The report has been prepared in accordance with the Code and the guidance issued by the Confederation of Swedish Enterprise and FAR SRS and is thus limited to internal control over financial reporting. This report is included as a section in the Corporate Governance Report, but does not comprise a portion of the formal annual report. This report has not been reviewed by the company's external auditors.

Introduction

Until March 2008 AB Volvo's Series B shares were registered with the Securities and Exchange Commission (SEC) in the US. Volvo was subject to the Sarbanes-Oxley Act (SOX) until the B shares were deregistered from the SEC. SOX includes, among other things, comprehensive regulations regarding the evaluation of the internal control over the financial reporting.

Also after the deregulation from the SEC Volvo has maintained many principles for the internal controls of the financial reporting which were implemented when the Group had to comply with the SOX regulations. Volvo primarily applies internal control principles introduced by the Committee of Sponsoring Organizations of the Treadway Commission (COSO). The COSO principles consist of five interrelated components. The components are: control environment, risk assessment, control activities, information and communication and follow-up.

Volvo has had a specific department for internal control since 2005. The aim of the Internal Control function is to provide support for management groups within business areas and business units, so that they are able to continuously provide good and improved internal controls relating to financial reporting. Work that is conducted through this function is based primarily on an evaluation methodology that has been developed for the purpose of complying with SOX requirements. The methodology is aimed at ensuring both compliance with directives and policies, as well as to create good conditions for specific control activities in key processes related to financial reporting. The Audit Committee is informed of the result of the work performed by the Internal Control function within Volvo with regard to risks, control activities and follow-up on the financial reporting.

Volvo also has an Internal Audit function with the primary task of independently verifying that companies in the Group follow the principles and rules that are stated in the Group's directives, policies and instructions for financial reporting. The head of the Internal Audit function reports directly to the CEO, the Group's CFO and the Audit Committee.

Control environment

Fundamental to Volvo's control environment is the business culture that is established within the Group and in which managers and employees operate. Volvo works actively on communications and training regarding the company's basic values as described in The Volvo Way, an internal document concerning Volvo's business culture, and the Group's Code of Conduct, to ensure that good morals, ethics and integrity permeate the organization.

The foundation of the internal control process relating to the financial reporting is built up around the Group's directives, policies and instructions, and the responsibility and authority structure that has been adapted to the Group's organization to create and maintain a satisfactory control environment. The principles for internal controls and directives and policies for the financial reporting are contained in Volvo Financial Policies & Procedures (FPP), an internal book comprising all important instructions, rules and principles.

Risk assessment

Risks relating to the financial reporting are evaluated and monitored by the Board through the Audit Committee inter alia through identifying what types of risks that typically could be considered as material and where they would typically occur. The annual evaluation of internal control activities conducted by the Internal Control and Internal Audit functions, are based on a risk-based model. The evaluation of the risk that errors will appear in the financial reporting is based on a number of criteria. Complex accounting principles can, for example, mean that the financial reporting risks being inaccurate for those posts that are covered by such principles. Valuation of a particular asset or liability according to various evaluation criteria can also constitute a risk. The same is true for complex and/or changing business circumstances.

Control activities

In addition to the Board of AB Volvo and its Audit Committee, the Boards and management groups of Group companies constitute the overall supervisory body.

Several control activities are applied in the ongoing business processes to ensure that potential errors or deviations in the financial reporting are prevented, discovered and corrected. Control activities range from review of outcome results in management group meetings to specific reconciliation of accounts and analyses of the ongoing processes for financial reporting. CFOs in Group companies are ultimately responsible for ensuring that control activities in the financial processes are appropriate and in accordance with the Group's policies and instructions. They are also responsible for ensuring that authority structures are designed so that one person can't perform an activity and then perform the control of the same activity. Control activities within IT security and maintenance are a key part of Volvo's internal control over financial reporting.

Information and communication

Policies and instructions relating to the financial reporting are updated and communicated on a regular basis from management to all affected employees. In addition, there are a number of committees and networks within Volvo that serve as forums for information and discussions regarding issues relating to the financial reporting and application of internal rules. Included in these committees and networks are representatives from the business areas and the Group's staff units who are responsible for financial reporting. Work in these committees and networks is aimed, among other things, at ensuring a uniform application of the Group's policies, principles and instructions for the financial reporting and to identify and communicate shortcomings and areas of improvement in the processes for financial reporting.

Follow-up

Ongoing responsibility for follow-up rests with the business area's management groups and accounting and controller functions. In addition, the Internal Audit and the Internal Control functions conduct follow-up and supervision in accordance with what is adopted in the introduction of this report. The outcome of evaluation activities shall be reported to Group management and to the Audit Committee.

Source: 2008 Volvo Annual Report

Internet Business Reporting and XBRL

The World Wide Web is increasingly being used as an information dissemination channel, with print media often playing a secondary role. Electronic information dissemination is often less expensive than print media and offers instantaneous communication. The Web also allows interactive information dissemination in a manner not possible in print form.[26] Securities trading using the Internet has increased the demand for Web-based business and financial reporting. Individual investors are increasingly using the Web to trade and make investment decisions, and use the Web as an important source of information. Most companies listed on a stock exchange post their annual, interim, sustainability, and other reports of interest to investors on their Web sites (Investor Relations tab). Many stock exchanges have links to the Web sites of their listed companies. Many stock exchanges also use electronic news services to provide immediate access to all announcements by listed companies. The benefit to companies and investors is that all announcements, not just the ones deems "newsworthy" by the financial press, are made publicly available on a single Web site.

One important development that will facilitate Web-based business reporting is eXtensible Business Reporting Language (XBRL). XBRL is a system for labeling information or data. Data "tags," which work like barcodes, describe the financial information to which they are attached. Taxonomies are then developed for distributing, exchanging, and summarizing the information. This standard will be built into nearly all future releases of accounting and financial reporting software, and most users will not need to learn how to manipulate it directly in order to enjoy its benefits.[27] XBRL is on the verge of revolutionizing financial reporting. According to the Financial Executive Research Foundation, "XBRL will have as big an impact on commerce in the 21st century as double-entry bookkeeping had on the Industrial Revolution."[28]

The concept of a universal financial reporting computer language emerged in 1999. Soon after, Microsoft and IBM recognized both its potential and the need to develop a single standard cooperatively rather than each software company develop its own standard, which would undermine the very idea of making the language universal. Because it has been developed cooperatively, XBRL is free to software companies that wish to use it in their software, and extensions of XBRL developed for specific industries are free for downloading from the Internet.

---

[26] See International Accounting Standards Committee, "Business Reporting on the Internet: A Discussion Paper Issued by the IASC Staff" (London: November 1999).
[27] See Kurt Ramin, "Fair Values," *Business Excellence for the Intellectual Capital Investor* 1 (Summer 2000): 13–16; Stanley Zarowin and Wayne E. Harding, "Finally, Business Talks the Same Language," *Journal of Accountancy* (August 2000): 24–30.
[28] Glenn Cheney, "XBRL: A Technology Whose Time Is Now," *Financial Executive* (March 2005): 45.

XBRL automatically translates any desired item of business information—words or numbers—so that the information need be entered only once. Once entered, this information can be used and worked with in many ways without being reformatted. Reporting in an electronic XBRL format makes data interactive, enabling anyone using financial statements to pick and choose as much or as little information as they want.[29] To quote one observer:

> Everyone along the information supply chain—investors, creditors, analysts, stock exchanges, auditors, regulators, policymakers and others—can quickly, accurately, easily and inexpensively access, validate, compare, analyze, slice, dice, mix, match, and manipulate information for any number of companies. It also allows the same body of data to automatically—instantly—find its proper place in spreadsheets, tax returns, business reports, annual reports, pie charts, government forms, Web sites and financial statements. No manual transcription. No mistakes along the way.[30]

XBRL taxonomies have already been developed for U.S. and German GAAP and for IFRS, enabling financial statement preparation according to these accounting standards. Taxonomies of other national GAAP are also being developed. In 2009, the U.S. SEC began implementing requirements for XBRL-based financial reports and schedules as an exhibit to registration statements and periodic filings.

ANNUAL REPORT DISCLOSURES IN EMERGING-MARKET COUNTRIES

Disclosures in the annual reports of companies from emerging-market countries are generally less extensive and less credible than those of companies from developed countries. Insufficient and misleading disclosure and lax investor protection have been cited as factors contributing to the East Asia financial crisis of 1997.

The low disclosure levels in emerging-market countries are consistent with their systems of corporate governance and finance. Equity markets are not well developed, banks and insiders such as family groups supply most of the financing, and so in general there has been less demand for credible, timely public disclosure than in more developed economies.

However, investor demand for timely and credible information about companies in emerging-market countries has been growing. Regulators have responded to this demand by making disclosure requirements more stringent, and by stepping up their monitoring and enforcement efforts.

A recent study presents evidence supporting the view that disclosure levels and quality are lower in emerging-market countries than in developed countries.[31] The study is concerned with the "opacity" of earnings in 34 countries around the world. Opacity, the opposite of transparency, may be thought of as the extent to which an earnings amount obscures real economic performance. Exhibit 5-9 ranks countries in

---

[29] Further information is available at www.xbrl.org.
[30] Glenn Cheney, "XBRL: A Technology Whose Time Is Now," *Financial Executive* (March 2005): 45.
[31] See Utpal Bhattacharya, Hazem Daouk, and Michael Welker, "The World Price of Earnings Opacity," *Accounting Review* 78, No. 3 (July 2003): 641–678.

EXHIBIT 5-9	**Earnings Opacity Ranking of Countries from Least to Most**

1. United States	13. Switzerland	25. South Africa[a]
2. Norway	14. Sweden	26. Malaysia[a]
3. Portugal	15. Germany	27. Italy
4. Brazil[a]	16. The Netherlands	28. Pakistan[a]
5. Belgium	17. Finland	29. Japan
6. Mexico[a]	18. Austria	30. Chile[a]
7. Canada	19. Thailand[a]	31. India[a]
8. France	20. Ireland	32. Indonesia[a]
9. Australia	21. Hong Kong[a]	33. South Korea[a]
10. Spain	22. Singapore[a]	34. Greece[a]
11. United Kingdom	23. Taiwan[a]	
12. Denmark	24. Turkey[a]	

[a]*Emerging market country*

Source: Utpal Bhattacharya, Hazem Daouk, and Michael Welker, "The World Price of Earnings Opacity," *Accounting Review* 78, no. 3 (July 2003): 660.

terms of their overall earnings opacity from least to most opaque. Emerging-market countries tend to have the most opaque earnings. A further issue is having adequate numbers of accountants and auditors to monitor and enforce sound financial reporting systems. In general, there are far fewer accountants and auditors per capita in emerging-market countries than in developing countries, suggesting potential enforcement difficulties in emerging markets.[32]

Empirical evidence on disclosure practices in emerging-market countries was limited until recently. However, as these countries' stock markets and listed companies seek to increase their presence, researchers are developing more evidence on what these practices are and how they differ from those in developed countries.

IMPLICATIONS FOR FINANCIAL STATEMENT USERS AND MANAGERS

Financial statement users should expect wide variation in disclosure levels and financial reporting practices. Although managers in many firms continue to be strongly influenced by the costs of disclosing proprietary information, the levels of both mandatory and voluntary disclosure are increasing worldwide. Managers in traditionally low-disclosure countries should consider whether adopting a policy of enhanced disclosure might provide significant benefits for their firms. In addition, managers who decide to provide enhanced disclosures in areas investors and analysts consider important, such as segment and governance disclosures, might obtain a competitive advantage over firms with restrictive disclosure policies. Further study of the costs and benefits of enhanced disclosure in international settings should provide important evidence in this area.

---

[32] Shahrokh M. Saudagaran and Joselito G. Diga, "Financial Reporting in Emerging Capital Markets: Characteristics and Policy Issues," *Accounting Horizons* 11 (June 1997): 41–64. Chapter 4 discusses this issue in the case of China.

Discussion Questions

1. The chapter discusses the objectives of investor-oriented markets: investor protection and market quality. Transparent financial reporting is important for achieving these objectives. What is transparent financial reporting? Explain how transparent financial reporting protects investors and improves market quality.

2. Why are multinational corporations increasingly being held accountable to constituencies other than traditional investor groups?

3. Should foreign companies seeking to issue securities in the United States be required to disclose as much as U.S. companies issuing securities in the United States? Critically evaluate the arguments presented in this chapter.

4. What is the difference between voluntary disclosure and mandatory disclosure? Provide at least two explanations for the differences in managers' *voluntary* disclosure practices. Provide at least two explanations for the differences in managers' *mandatory* disclosure practices.

5. What is triple-bottom-line reporting, and why is it a growing trend among large multinational corporations? There are now few requirements for this type of reporting. Is more regulation necessary? Why or why not?

6. Do you expect to observe more or less voluntary disclosure by companies in emerging-market countries than in developed countries? Why? Do you expect to observe more or less regulatory disclosure requirements in emerging-market countries than in developed countries? Why?

7. What are the two broad objectives for investor-oriented markets? Which of these do you think is more important? Present reasons for your response.

8. From the perspective of a securities market regulator, is more required disclosure always better than less? Why or why not?

9. Why are forecasts of revenues and income relatively uncommon?

10. What is corporate governance? Listed companies in some countries are required to disclose information about their corporate governance practices. Why might investors and analysts find such information useful?

Exercises

1. The Outlook section in Daimler's 2008 annual report may be found at http://ar2008.daimler. com/daimler/annual/2008/gb/English/pdf/ 04_DAI_AR2008_Management-Report.pdf (pp. 82–87).

   Required: Provide (1) a list of items forecasted (e.g., sales, profits, economic growth), (2) the forecast horizon (e.g., one year ahead, six months ahead, not stated), and (3) the amount forecasted (e.g., growth of €10 million, 10 percent growth). How might an investor or analyst use such forecast information? Overall, how useful is Daimler's forecast disclosure? Why do you say so?

2. Exhibit 5-1 presents the business-segment and geographic-segment information of Lafarge, a French company that uses International Financial Reporting Standards (IFRS) in its consolidated financial statements.

   Required: Go to the Web site of the International Accounting Standards Board (www.iasb.org) and find the technical summary of IFRS 8, "Operating Segments." Compare the segment disclosures of Lafarge to the requirements of IFRS 8. Does Lafarge voluntarily report any information beyond the requirements of IFRS 8?

3. Exhibit 5-2 presents the employment disclosure of Roche.

   Required:
   a. How do the employment levels compare between the periods presented? Where are Roche's employees located?
   b. Which regions of the world have the highest turnover rates and what are the reasons for this turnover?
   c. What is Roche's policy on diversity in the workplace, and what is the evidence that its policy is being achieved?

d. What is the relevance of the above information for outside investors?

4. Exhibit 5-3 presents the safety and environmental disclosure of Roche.

   Required: Comparing the three years: (1) Which measures show an improved record of safety and environmental protection? (2) Which measures show a worse record of safety and environmental protection? What is your overall conclusion about Roche's safety and environmental record for the years presented?

5. Exhibit 5-4 presents the independent assurance report on Roche's sustainability reporting. The auditor's engagement was carried out "in accordance with International Standards on Assurance Engagements (ISAE) 3000."

   Required:
   a. Go to the World Wide Web and learn about the International Auditing and Assurance Standards Board (www.ifac.org/IAASB).
   b. What is the difference between auditing and assurance engagements?
   c. Has Roche earned a "clean opinion" on its sustainability reporting?

6. Corporate social responsibility (CSR), as practiced by business, means many different things. Consider the following: "At one end of the broad span of CSR lie corporate policies that any well-run company ought to have in place anyway, policies that are called for on any sensible view of business ethics or good management practice. These include not lying to your employees, for instance, not paying bribes, and looking farther ahead than the next few weeks. At the other end of the range are the more ambitious and distinctive policies that differentiate between leaders and laggards in the CSR race—large expenditures of time and resources on charitable activities, for instance, or binding commitments to 'ethical investment,' or spending on environmental protection beyond what regulators demand."[33]

   Required:
   a. Discuss the meaning of corporate social responsibility.
   b. Do companies have an obligation to do more than the law requires? Why or why not?
   c. Should companies report on their social responsibility activities? Why or why not?

d. What is the relevance of CSR disclosures for outside investors?

7. The Global Reporting Initiative (GRI) has developed a set of guidelines for social responsibility reporting.

   Required: Go to the GRI Web site (www.globalreporting.org) and find its guidelines. The disclosure guidelines are categorized as indicators of economic, environmental, and social performance.
   a. List the performance indicators recommended in the GRI guidelines.
   b. Which category requires the most extensive disclosures?
   c. Which areas of disclosure are likely to be the easiest and which areas are likely to be the most difficult to provide?

8. Exhibit 5-8 is the corporate governance disclosure of the Volvo Group. Some of the disclosures relate to independence requirements for the board of directors and audit committee.

   Required:
   a. What is the independence requirement for the board of directors?
   b. How many Volvo board members are independent? Does this number meet the requirement?
   c. Certain board members are considered not independent. What criteria were used to determine that these board members are not independent? What rationale can you think of for viewing these board members as not independent?
   d. How many members does the audit committee have? What percentage of these members is independent?

9. The Organisation for Economic Cooperation and Development (OECD) published its revised Principles of Corporate Governance in 2004.

   Required: Obtain the document from the OECD Web site (www.oecd.org).
   a. Outline the six sections of the OECD's corporate governance principles.
   b. Discuss how these principles contribute to better corporate governance.

10. Exhibit 5-9 ranks 34 countries on earnings opacity. Which five countries have the most surprising placement? Why do you say so?

---

[33] "The Good Company: A Survey of Corporate Social Responsibility," *Economist* (June 22, 2005): 8.

CASES

Case 5-1

In the Green

O.J. Sanders works in the financial reporting section of a large U.S. pharmaceutical company. The company has recently committed to "go green" and O.J.'s boss wants to add some environmental disclosures in the company's annual report. O.J. is charged with recommending the contents of the environmental disclosure. In his research, O.J. learns that U.S. companies have generally lagged European companies in environmental reporting, but that more and more U.S. companies are now disclosing environmental matters. He believes that his company should at least "match the competition" in the disclosures it makes. Toward that end, he obtains the annual report of Roche, a Swiss competitor. O.J. also learns about the G3 sustainability reporting guidelines of the Global Reporting Initiative.

Required:

1. Discuss why financial statement users find environmental disclosures informative.
2. Obtain the G3 sustainability reporting guidelines of the Global Reporting Initiative (GRI, www.globalreporting.org). List the environmental performance indicators that the GRI recommends for disclosure.
3. How closely do Roche's environmental disclosures match the GRI recommendations (see Exhibit 5-3)? What are the areas of nondisclosure?
4. Describe the environmental disclosures that O.J. should recommend his company make.

Case 5-2

Seeing Is Believing

Tyler Poland is a stock picker responsible for recommending Mexican securities for his brokerage firm's clients. He is often frustrated about the lack of credible information on companies in Mexico. "Everything is always so top secret," he says. "Any time I try to learn about a company's activities, all I hear is 'I wouldn't know what to tell you'." In Mexico, it seems, information is power.

Trivial or not, information seems to be off-limits to anyone who is not an insider.

Tyler knows that this secretiveness goes way back in Mexico's history. The Aztec rulers kept their subjects amazed by powerful deities who were both unpredictable and hard to understand. The Spanish followed many detailed bureaucratic rules but hardly ever shared them with ordinary Mexicans.

After independence, the ruling political parties made sure that compromising information never got in the wrong hands.

Historian and novelist Hector Aguilar Camin has written, "In Mexico, powerful people have traditionally kidnapped information. Part of the process of democratization is freeing it." But "there is still a tendency to want to hold it hostage for some kind of benefit."[34]

Most economists believe that government secrecy made the 1994 currency collapse more severe because the Mexican government withheld vital macroeconomic statistics from the international banking community. Many worry now that secrecy will limit Mexico's economic growth. Yet pressure for transparency has grown along with an influx of foreign investors doing business in Mexico. The rise of opposition political parties and the growth of a free press have fueled a new debate over access to information.

"What good are all of these trends to me?" complains Tyler. "I need better information now."

---

[34] *Wall Street Journal*, September 10, 1998, p. 1a.

Required

1. Discuss at least five characteristics that predict relatively *low* disclosure levels in Mexico. Your response should be based on a review of the material presented in Chapters 2 and 4 and this chapter, in addition to the case information above.
2. Discuss characteristics or features that predict relatively *high* levels of disclosure in Mexico.
3. Accounting measurement and disclosure practices are improving (from an investor-protection viewpoint) in many emerging-market economies. What are some of the recent improvements in these areas in Mexico? Discuss the underlying factors that help explain why the improvements are occurring. Again, refer to the material presented in Chapters 2 and 4 in addition to the case information above.

CHAPTER 6

Foreign Currency Translation

Examine the following financial performance commentary. It is extracted from Rio Tinto, a leading multinational company engaged in metal and mineral production. The company operates in over 50 countries and employs in excess of 106,000 people.

> Rio Tinto's shareholders' equity, earnings and cash flows are influenced by a wide variety of currencies due to the geographic diversity of the Group's sales and the countries in which it operates. The U.S. dollar, however, is the currency in which the great majority of the Group's sales are denominated. Operating costs are influenced by the currencies of those countries where the Group's mines and processing plants are located and also by those currencies in which the costs of imported equipment and services are determined. The Australian and Canadian dollars and the Euro are the most important currencies (apart from the US dollar) influencing costs. In any particular year, currency fluctuations may have a significant impact on Rio Tinto's financial results. A strengthening of the US dollar against the currencies in which the Group's costs are partly determined has a positive effect on Rio Tinto's underlying earnings.
>
> The following sensitivities give the estimated effect on underlying earnings assuming that each exchange rate moved in isolation. The relationship between currencies and commodity prices is a complex one and movements in exchange rates can cause movements in commodity prices and vice versa. Where the functional currency of an operation is that of a country for which production of commodities is an important feature of the economy, such as the Australian dollar, there is a certain degree of natural protection against cyclical fluctuations, in that the currency tends to be weak, reducing costs in US dollar terms, when commodity prices are low, and vice versa.

Earnings sensitivities – exchange rates	Average exchange rate for 2008	Effect on net and underlying earnings of 10% change in full year average +/– US$m
Australian dollar	US$0.86	502
Canadian dollar	US$0.94	214
Euro	US$1.47	34
Chilean peso	US$0.0019	17
New Zealand dollar	US$0.71	29
South African rand	US$0.12	47
UK sterling	US$1.86	22

The exchange rate sensitivities quoted above include the effect on operating costs of movements in exchange rates but exclude the effect of the revaluation of foreign currency financial asssets and liabilities. They should therefore be used with care.

Given the dominant role of the US currency in the Group's affairs, the US dollar is the currency in which financial results are presented both internally and externally. It is also the most appropriate currency for borrowing and holding surplus cash, although a portion of surplus cash may also be held in other currencies, most notable Australian dollars, Canadian dollars and the Euro. This cash is held in order to meet short term operational and capital commitments and, for the Australian dollar, dividend payments. The Group finances its operations primarily in US dollars, either directly or using cross currency interest rate swaps. A substantial part of the Group's US dollar debt is located in subsidiaries having a US functional currency.

However, certain US dollar debt and other financial assets and liabilities including intragroup balances are not held in the functional currency of the relevant subsidiary. This results in an accounting exposure to exchange gains and losses as the financial assets and liabilities are translated into the functional currency of the subsidiary that accounts for those assets and liabilities. These exchange gains and losses are recorded in the Group's income statement except to the extent that they can be taken to equity under the Group's accounting policy. Gains and losses on US dollar net debt and on intragroup balances are excluded from underlying earnings. Other exchange gains and losses are included in underlying earnings.

Under normal market conditions, the group does not generally believe that active currency hedging of transactions would provide long term benefits to shareholders. The Group reviews on a regular basis its exposures and reserves the right to enter into hedges to maintain financial stability. Currency protection measures may be deemed appropriate in specific commercial circumstances and are subject to strict limits laid down by the Rio Tinto board, typically hedging of capital expenditure and other significant financial items such as tax and dividends. There is a legacy of currency forward contracts used to hedge operating cash flow exposures which were acquired with Alcan and the North companies.

Earnings sensitivities – exchange on financial assets/liabilities	Closing exchange rate US cents	Effect on net earnings of 10% US$ strengthening US$	Effect of items impacting directly on equity US$
Functional currency of business unit:			
Australian dollar	69	(12)	5
Canadian dollar	82	159	56
South African rand	11	13	—
Euro	141	249	2
New Zealand dollar	58	21	—

The functional currency of many operations within the Rio Tinto Group is the local currency of operation. The former Alcan aluminum and alumina producing operations primarily use a US dollar functional currency. Foreign currency gains or losses arising on translation to US dollars of the net assets of non US functional currency operations are taken to equity and, with effect from 1 January 2004, recorded in a currency translation reserve. A weakening of the US dollar would have a positive effect on equity. The approximate translation effects on the Group's net assets of ten per cent movements from the year end exchange rates are as follows:

Net assets' sensitivities – exchange on translation	Closing exchange rate U.S. cents	2008 Effect on net assets of 10% change in Closing rate +/– U.S. $m
Australian dollar	69	1,264
euro	141	621
Canadian dollar	82	180

The paragraphs in the preceding commentary suggest a variety of ways in which Alcan's reported performance, which the company chooses to report in U.S. dollars[1], is impacted by foreign currencies. The first paragraph suggests that the company's sales and operating costs are impacted by fluctuating exchange rates. In particular, earnings are benefitted by a strengthening of the U.S. dollar in relation to the currencies in which the company's costs are partly determined. To understand the effects of exchange rates on both revenues and expenses, assume that Rio Tinto is selling aluminum products , priced in U.S. dollars, to an importer in Italy. As Italy is a member of the European Union[2], the Italian importer must exchange euros for dollars to effect payment. Assume further that the value of the U.S. dollar unexpectedly falls in relation to the euro. The Italian buyer benefits from having to exchange less euros for dollars than would otherwise be the case,

---

[1] The dollar is the currency most used to set prices for raw materials and the currency most used to conduct trade. See, Robert J. Samuelson, "Why the Buck Is on the Edge," *Newsweek*, December 11, 2006, p. 49.
[2] Members of the European Union include Austria, Belgium, Cyprus, Czech Republic, Denmark, Estonia, Finland, France, Germany, Greece, Hungary, Ireland, Italy, Latvia, Lithuania, Luxembourg, Malta, the Netherlands, Poland, Portugal, Slovakia, Slovenia, Spain, Sweden, and the U.K.

effectively lowering the price of Rio Tinto's products. If the euro does not change in value relative to other national currencies, this would make Rio Tinto's products cheaper relative to similar aluminum products supplied from other countries. The result would be increased demand for Rio Tinto's products in Italy and other EU countries adopting the euro as their national currency, and hence, larger sales volume than originally anticipated. Similarly, an unexpected fall in the value of the dollar relative to the euro would have an adverse impact on Rio Tinto's future expenses, such as planned advertising expenditures in Italy and all EU countries mentioned above. The effect of changes in foreign currency values on a firm's future sales and future costs is referred to as *economic exposure* and is a major concern of business entities engaged in global commerce and investment. Strategies to minimize the risk of loss arising from unexpected changes in the prices of foreign currencies is the subject of Chapter 11.

In discussing the effect of exchange rate changes on earnings, the company is careful to note that these effects exclude the revaluation of foreign currency financial statements, the principle subject of this chapter. These effects relate to a process in which accounts denominated in foreign currency are translated to Rio Tinto's s reporting currency, U.S. dollars. The currency effects on Rio Tinto's sales and operating costs result from translating revenues and operating expenses denominated in say Canadian dollars to a devalued U.S. dollar. A Canadian dollar revenue and expense will translate to a higher U.S. dollar equivalent, other things remaining the same. The currency effects illustrated in the exhibits entitled, Earnings sensitivites—exchange on financial assets/liabilities, and Net assets' sensitivities—exchange on translation, respectively, occur because Rio Tinto prepares a single set of financial statements that consolidates the results of all of its subsidiaries to afford its readers a more holistic view of Rio Tinto's s total operations, both foreign and domestic. Consolidated statements, in turn, require that financial statements expressed in foreign currency be translated to the reporting currency of the parent company.

Rio Tinto's discussion of exchange rate effects raises two initial questions. First, what does the firm mean by the term, *functional currency*? Does it matter which currency is deemed functional and why? This and related terms are initially defined in Exhibit 6-2 and explained in subsequent sections of this chapter.

Second, "Do reported currency effects resulting from the translation process matter?" The evidence is mixed. Some studies suggest that they do not.[3] Recent studies suggest that they do. Bartov and Bodner, for example, provide evidence of a lagged relation between changes in currency values and stock returns but not for all translation methods employed by reporting entities.[4] Pinto initially reports that lagged values of per share foreign currency translation adjustments are useful in predicting year to year changes in earnings per share. More recently, she finds that the currency translation

---

[3] See T.D. Garlicki, F.J. Fabozzi, and R. Fonfeder, "The Impact of Earnings Under FASB 52 on Equity Returns," *Financial Management* (Autumn 1987): 36–44; B.S. Soo and L. Gilbert Soo, "Accounting for the Multinational Firm: Is the Translation Process Valued by the Stock Market?" *The Accounting Review*, Vol. 69 (October 1994): 617–637; D. Dhaliwal, K. Subra and R. Trezevant, "Is Comprehensive Income Superior to Net Income as a Measure of Firm Performance?" *Journal of Accounting and Economics*, Vol. 26 (1999): 43–67; Steven F. Cahan, Stephen M. Courtnay, Paul L. Gronewoller, and David Upton, "Value relevance of Mandated Comprehensive Income Disclosures," *Journal of Business Finance and Accounting*, Vol. 27 nos. 9&10 (2000): 1273–1301.

[4] See E. Bartov, "Foreign Currency Exposure of Multinatioinal Firms: Accounting Measures and Market Valuation," Contemporary Accounting Research, 14 (1997): 623–652.

adjustments, when measured properly, are value relevant in providing a measure of a firm's exchange rate exposure.[5]

Financial executives also attach mixed importance to gains and losses associated with foreign currency translation. While some assert that accounting gains and losses generated by accounting measurements have no impact on their operational decisions, others express great concern over the distortions they cause in reported corporate earnings. History is replete with instances of management expending resources to minimize the effects of balance sheet translation gains and losses on reported performance. Differing opinions notwithstanding, all agree that foreign currency translation can have significant effects on repoted earnings.

What are the implications of the foregoing discussion? To properly interpret the reported performance of multinational companies, statement readers must understand the nature of foreign exchange gains and losses, how these numbers are derived, and what they mean. To facilitate this understanding, we begin with an examination of why foreign currency translation is necessary.

REASONS FOR TRANSLATION

To reiterate, companies with significant overseas operations prepare consolidated financial statements that afford their statement readers an aggregate view of the firm's global operations. To accomplish this, financial statements of foreign subsidiaries that are denominated in foreign currencies are restated to the reporting currency of the parent company. This process of restating financial information from one currency to another is called translation.

Many of the problems associated with currency translation stem from the fact that the relative value of foreign currencies are seldom fixed. Variable rates of exchange, combined with a variety of translation methods that can be used and different treatments of translation gains and losses, make it difficult to compare financial results from one company to another, or in the same company from one period to the next. In these circumstances, it becomes a challenge for multinational enterprises to make informative disclosures of operating results and financial position as per Rio Tinto's example. Financial analysts find that interpreting such information can also be quite challenging and these troubles extend to evaluating managerial performance.

There are three additional reasons for foreign currency translation. These include recording foreign currency transactions, measuring a firm's exposure to the effects of currency gyrations, and communicating with foreign audiences-of-interest.

Foreign currency transactions, such as the purchase of merchandise from China by a Canadian importer, must be translated because financial statements cannot be prepared from accounts that are expressed in more than one currency. How, for example,

---

[5] Jo Ann M. Pinto, "Foreign Currency Translation Adjustments as Predictors of Earnings Changes," *Journal of International Accounting, Auditing and Taxes* (2001): 51–69 and "How Comprehensive is Comprehensive Income? The Value Relevance of Foreign Currency Translation Adjustments," *Journal of International Financial Management and Accounting*, Vol. 16, no. 2 (2005): 97–122.

is one to prepare cost of goods sold when purchases are denominated in Chinese renminbi, Russian rubles, and Argentine pesos?

For accounting purposes, a foreign currency asset or liability is said to be exposed to currency risk if a change in the rate at which currencies are exchanged causes the parent (reporting) currency equivalent to change. The measurement of this exposure will vary depending on the translation method a firm chooses to employ.

Finally, the expanded scale of international investment increases the need to convey accounting information about companies domiciled in one country to users in others. This need occurs when a company wishes to list its shares on a foreign stock exchange, contemplates a foreign acquisition or joint venture, or wants to communicate its operating results and financial position to its foreign stockholders. Many Japanese companies translate their entire financial statements from Japanese yen to U.S. dollars when reporting to interested American audiences. This practice is often called a *convenience translation* and is described more fully in Chapter 9.

BACKGROUND AND TERMINOLOGY

Translation is not the same as conversion, which is the physical exchange of one currency for another. Translation is simply a change in monetary expression, as when a balance sheet expressed in British pounds is restated in U.S. dollar equivalents. No physical exchange occurs, and no accountable transaction takes place as it does in conversion.

Foreign currency balances are translated to domestic currency equivalents by the foreign exchange rate: the price of a unit of one currency expressed in terms of another. The currencies of major trading nations are bought and sold in global markets. Linked by sophisticated telecommunications networks, market participants include banks and other currency dealers, business enterprises, individuals, and professional traders. By providing a venue for buyers and sellers of currencies, the foreign exchange market facilitates the transfer of international payments (e.g., from importers to exporters), allows international purchases or sales to be made on credit (e.g., bank letters of credit that permit goods to be shipped in advance of payment to an unfamiliar buyer), and provides a means for individuals or businesses to protect themselves from the risks of unstable currency values. (Chapter 11 gives a fuller discussion of exchange risk management.)

Foreign currency transactions take place in the spot, forward, or swap markets. Currency bought or sold spot normally must be delivered immediately, that is, within 2 business days. Thus, an American tourist departing for Paris can purchase and immediately receive euros by paying the spot rate in dollars. Spot market rates are influenced by many factors, including different inflation rates among countries, differences in national interest rates, and expectations about the direction of future rates. Spot market exchange rates may be direct or indirect.[6] In a direct quote, the exchange rate specifies the number of domestic currency units needed to acquire a unit of foreign currency. For example, on a given day, the U.S. dollar price of a euro might be $1.4116. An indirect quote is the reciprocal of the direct quote: the price of a unit of the domestic currency in terms of the foreign currency. In this example, it would take approximately € 0.7084 euros to acquire 1 U.S. dollar.

Translation of foreign currency balances is straightforward with either direct or indirect quotes. Domestic currency equivalents are obtained by multiplying foreign

---

[6] For a daily listing of foreign exchange rates, visit www.ozforex.com.

currency balances by direct exchange rate quotations or dividing foreign currency balances by indirect quotations. To illustrate, suppose that the cash balance of a U.S. subsidiary located in Bombay, India, on July 15 is INR1,000,000. The direct (spot) exchange rate on that date is $.020546. The U.S. dollar equivalent of the rupee cash balance on January 31 is $20,546, calculated by translating INR1,000,000 in either of the following ways:

$$INR1,000,000 \times \$0.020546 = \$20,546 \text{ or}$$

$$INR1,000,000 \div INR\ 48.6700 = \$20,546$$

Transactions in the forward market are agreements to exchange a specified amount of one currency for another at a future date. Quotations in the forward market are expressed at either a discount or a premium from the spot rate, or as outright forward rates. We will illustrate the latter. Moreover, spot and forward rates may often include bid and ask quotes. The bid quote is what the foreign exchange dealer would pay you for foreign currency; the ask quote is the rate that the dealer would sell you foreign currency. If spot roubles (Russian) are quoted at $0.031584, while the 6-month forward rouble is offered at $0.030807, forward roubles are selling at a discount of 9.8 percent in the United States, calculated as follows: forward premium (discount) = (forward rate − spot rate)/spot rate × 12/n, where n is the number of months in the forward contract. Thus, ($0.030807 − $0.031584)/$0.031584 × 12/3 = −0.098. Had the euro been quoted indirectly, the premium would have been determined as: forward premium (discount) = (spot rate − forward rate)/forward rate × 12/n, or rouble (31.6615 −32.4597)/32.4597 × 12/3 = −0.098. Spot and forward quotes for major foreign currencies on any business day can be found in the business section of many major newspapers. Exhibit 6-1 contains spot and forward quotes for selected currencies. A more comprehensive listing can be found on www.fxstreet.com.

EXHIBIT 6-1 **Sample of Spot and Forward Foreign Exchange Quotes**

Currency	(Foreign Currency in Dollars)			
	Spot	1 month	3 month	1 year
Czech Rep. koruna	18.3840	18.3890	18.4245	18.5240
Russian rouble	31.6615	31.9015	32.4597	35.5515
Swedish krona	7.8173	7.8157	7.8126	7.7942
Swiss franc	1.0752	1.0748	1.0739	1.0673
Turkish new lira	1.5295	1.5402	1.5625	1.6674
U.K. pound	0.6480	0.6086	0.6087	0.6090
EU euro	0.7084	0.7084	0.7084	0.7080
Brazilian real	1.9386	1.9504	1.9727	2.0668
Mexican pesos	13.5955	13.6548	13.7708	14.2855
Hong Kong dollar	7.7503	7.7483	7.7442	7.7328
Indian rupee	48.6700	48.7650	48.9475	49.6875
Japanese yen	93.6250	93.5935	93.5283	93.0020
Saudi Arabian riyals	3.7504	3.7499	3.7489	3.7452
South African rands	8.0884	8.1393	8.2347	8.6545
South Korean won	1265.65	1265.25	1263.35	1256.15

A swap transaction involves the simultaneous spot purchase and forward sale, or spot sale and forward purchase, of a currency. Investors often use swap transactions to take advantage of higher interest rates in a foreign country while simultaneously protecting themselves against unfavorable movements in the foreign exchange rate. As an example, should interest rates in the United States exceed those in Switzerland, Swiss investors could purchase dollars in the spot market and invest them in higher yielding U.S. dollar debt instruments, say 6-month U.S. Treasury notes. In doing so, however, Swiss investors would lose this yield advantage if the U.S. dollar loses value relative to the Swiss franc in the 6-month period. To protect against this possibility, Swiss investors could simultaneously sell the dollars they expect to receive in 6 months at the guaranteed forward rate. Such swap transactions work well when the U.S./Swiss interest rate differential is greater than the discount on forward dollars (i.e., the difference between spot and 6-month forward dollars). Over time, foreign currency traders will eliminate this difference, thereby creating interest rate parity.

Exhibit 6-2 defines the foreign currency translation terms used in this chapter.

| EXHIBIT 6-2 | Glossary of Foreign Currency Translation Terms |

attribute. The quantifiable characteristic of an item that is measured for accounting purposes. For example, historical cost and replacement cost are attributes of an asset.

conversion. The exchange of one currency for another.

current rate. The exchange rate in effect at the relevant financial statement date.

discount. When the forward exchange rate is below the current spot rate.

exposed net asset position. The excess of assets that are measured or denominated in foreign currency and translated at the current rate over liabilities that are measured or denominated in foreign currency and translated at the current rate.

foreign currency. A currency other than the currency of the country being referred to; a currency other than the reporting currency of the enterprise being referred to.

foreign currency financial statements. Financial statements that employ foreign currency as the unit of measure.

foreign currency transactions. Transactions (e.g., sales or purchases of goods or services or loans payable or receivable) whose terms are stated in a currency other than the entity's functional currency.

foreign currency translation. The process of expressing amounts denominated or measured in one currency in terms of another currency by use of the exchange rate between the two currencies.

foreign operation. An operation whose financial statements are (1) combined or consolidated with or accounted for on an equity basis in the financial statements of the reporting enterprise and (2) prepared in a currency other than the reporting currency of the reporting enterprise.

forward exchange contract. An agreement to exchange currencies of different countries at a specified rate (forward rate) at a specified future date.

functional currency. The primary currency in which an entity does business and generates and spends cash. It is usually the currency of the country where the entity is located and the currency in which the books of record are maintained.

(continued)

EXHIBIT 6-2   Glossary of Foreign Currency Translation Terms (Continued)

historical rate. The foreign exchange rate that prevailed when a foreign currency asset or liability was first acquired or incurred.

local currency. Currency of a particular country being referred to; the reporting currency of a domestic or foreign operation being referred to.

monetary items. Obligations to pay or rights to receive a fixed number of currency units in the future.

reporting currency. The currency in which an enterprise prepares its financial statements.

settlement date. The date on which a payable is paid or a receivable is collected.

spot rate. The exchange rate for immediate exchange of currencies.

transaction date. The date at which a transaction (e.g., a sale or purchase of merchandise or services) is recorded in a reporting entity's accounting records.

translation adjustments. Translation adjustments result from the process of translating financial statements from the entity's functional currency into the reporting currency.

unit of measure. The currency in which assets, liabilities, revenue, and expenses are measured.

THE PROBLEM

If foreign exchange rates were relatively stable, currency translation would be no more difficult than translating inches or feet to their metric equivalents. However, exchange rates are seldom stable. The currencies of most industrialized countries are free to find their own values in the currency market. For an illustration of the volatility of exchange rates of selected countries, examine the data compiled by the Federal Reserve Bank of St. Louis at www.research.stlouisfed.org/fred2.

Fluctuating exchange values are particularly evident in Eastern Europe, Latin America, and certain parts of Asia. Currency fluctuations increase the number of translation rates that can be used in the translation process and create foreign exchange gains and losses. Currency movements are also closely tied to local rates of inflation, the subject of Chapter 7.

FINANCIAL STATEMENT EFFECTS OF ALTERNATIVE TRANSLATION RATES

The following three exchange rates can be used to translate foreign currency balances to domestic currency. First, the *current rate* is the exchange rate prevailing as of the financial statement date. Second, the *historical rate* is the prevailing exchange rate when a foreign currency asset is first acquired or a foreign currency liability first incurred. Finally, the *average rate* is a simple or weighted average of either current or historical exchange rates. As average rates are simply variations of current or historical rates, the following discussion focuses on the latter two.

What then are the financial statement effects of using historical as opposed to current rates of exchange as foreign currency translation coefficients? Historical exchange rates generally preserve the original cost equivalent of a foreign currency item in the domestic currency statements. Suppose that a foreign subsidiary of a U.S. parent company acquires an item of inventory for 1,000 foreign currency (FC) units when the exchange rate (indirect quote) is FC2 = $1. This asset would appear in the U.S. consolidated statements at $500. Now assume that the exchange rate changes from FC2 = $1 to FC4 = $1 by the next financial statement date and that the inventory item is still on hand. Will the U.S. dollar equivalent of the inventory now change to $250? It would not. As long as we translate the original FC1,000 cost at the rate that prevailed when the asset was acquired (historical rate), it will appear in the U.S. financial statements at $500, its historical cost expressed in U.S. dollars. *Use of historical exchange rates shields financial statements from foreign currency translation gains or losses,* that is, from increases or decreases in the dollar equivalents of foreign currency balances due to fluctuations in the translation rate between reporting periods. *The use of current rates causes translation gains or losses.* Thus, in the previous example, translating the FC1,000 piece of inventory at the current rate (FC4 = $1) would yield a translation loss of $250 [(FC1,000 ÷ 2) − (FC1,000 ÷ 4)].

Here we must distinguish between *translation* gains and losses and *transaction* gains and losses, both of which fall under the label exchange gains and losses. Foreign currency transactions occur whenever an enterprise purchases or sells goods for which payment is made in a foreign currency or when it borrows or lends foreign currency. Translation is necessary to maintain the accounting records in the currency of the reporting enterprise.

Of the two types of transaction adjustments, the first, *gains and losses on settled transactions,* arises whenever the exchange rate used to book the original transaction differs from the rate used at settlement. Thus, if a U.S. parent company borrows FC1,000 when the exchange rate is FC2 = $1 and then converts the proceeds to dollars, it will receive $500 and record a $500 liability on its books. If the foreign exchange rate rises to FC1 = $1 when the loan is repaid, the U.S. company will have to pay out $1,000 to discharge its FC1,000 debt. The company has suffered a $500 conversion loss.

The second type of transaction adjustment, *gains or losses on unsettled transactions,* arises whenever financial statements are prepared before a transaction is settled. In the preceding example, assume that the FC1,000 is borrowed during year 1 and repaid during year 2. If the exchange rate prevailing at the financial statement date (end of year 1) is FC1.5 = $1, the dollar equivalent of the FC1,000 loan will be $667, creating an exchange loss of $167. Until the foreign currency debt is actually repaid, however, this *unrealized* exchange loss is similar in nature to a translation loss as it results from a restatement process.

Exhibit 6-3 lays out the distinction between transaction and translation gains and losses. Differences in exchange rates in effect at the various dates shown cause the various types of exchange adjustments.

When considering exchange gains and losses, it is critical to distinguish between transaction gains and losses and translation gains and losses. A realized (or settled) transaction creates a real gain or loss. Accountants generally agree that such a gain or loss should be reflected immediately in income. In contrast, translation adjustments (including gains or losses on unsettled transactions) are unrealized or paper items. The appropriate accounting treatment of these gains or losses is less obvious.

EXHIBIT 6-3	**Types of Exchange Adjustments**

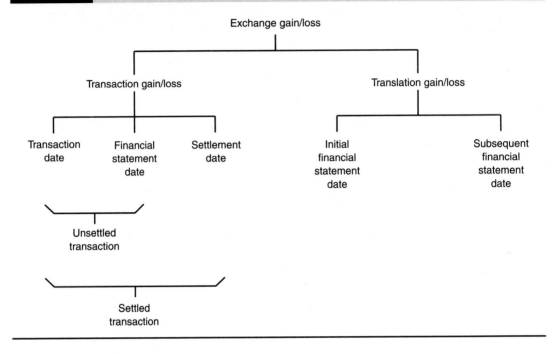

An informed reader of consolidated financial statements must understand three major issues associated with fluctuating exchange rates:

1. What exchange rate was used to translate foreign currency balances to domestic currency?
2. Which foreign currency assets and liabilities are exposed to exchange rate changes?
3. How are translation gains and losses accounted for?

These issues are examined in the rest of this chapter.

Foreign Currency Transactions

The distinguishing feature of a foreign currency transaction is that settlement is effected in a foreign currency. Thus, foreign currency transactions occur whenever an enterprise purchases or sells goods for which payment is made in a foreign currency or when it borrows or lends foreign currency. As an example, a company purchasing inventories denominated in Saudi Arabian riyals on account suffers an exchange loss should the riyal gain in value before settlement.

A foreign currency transaction may be *denominated* in one currency but *measured* in another. To understand why, consider first the notion of the *functional currency*. The functional currency of an entity is the primary currency in which it transacts business and generates and spends cash. If a foreign subsidiary's operation is relatively self-contained and integrated within the foreign country (i.e., one that manufactures a product for local distribution), it will normally generate and spend its local (country-of-domicile's) currency. Hence, the local currency (e.g., euros for the Belgian subsidiary of a U.S. parent) is its functional currency. If a foreign entity keeps its accounts in a currency other than the functional currency (e.g., the Indian accounts of a U.S. subsidiary whose functional currency is really British pounds, rather than Indian rupees), its functional currency is the third-country currency (pounds). If a foreign entity is merely an extension of its parent company (e.g., a Mexican assembly operation that receives components from its U.S. parent and ships the assembled product back to the United States), its functional currency is the U.S. dollar. Exhibit 6-4 identifies circumstances justifying use of either the local or parent currency as the functional currency.

To illustrate the difference between a transaction being denominated in one currency but measured in another, assume that a U.S. subsidiary in Hong Kong purchases merchandise inventory from the People's Republic of China payable in renminbi. The subsidiary's functional currency is the U.S. dollar. In this instance, the subsidiary would measure the foreign currency transaction—denominated in renminbi—in U.S. dollars, the currency in which its books are kept. From the parent's point of view, the subsidiary's liability is denominated in renminbi but measured in U.S. dollars, its functional currency, for purposes of consolidation.

FAS No. 52, the U.S. authoritative pronouncement on accounting for foreign currency, mandates the following treatment for foreign currency transactions:

1. At the date the transaction is recognized, each asset, liability, revenue, expense, gain, or loss arising from the transaction shall be measured and recorded in the

EXHIBIT 6-4 Functional Currency Criteria

Economic Factors	Circumstances Favoring Local Currency as Functional Currency	Circumstances Favoring Parent Currency as Functional Currency
Cash flows	Primarily in the local currency and do not impact parent's cash flows	Directly impact parent's cash flows and are currently remittable to the parent
Sales price	Largely irresponsive to exchange rate changes and governed primarily by local competition	Responsive to changes in exchange rates and determined by worldwide competition
Sales market	Largely in the host country and denominated in local currency	Largely in the parent country and denominated in parent currency
Expenses	Incurred primarily in the local environment	Primarily related to productive factors imported from the parent company
Financing	Primarily denominated in local currency and serviced by local operations	Primarily from the parent or reliance on parent company to meet debt obligations
Intercompany transactions	Infrequent, not extensive	Frequent and extensive

Adapted from: Financial Accounting Standards Board, *Statement of Financial Accounting Standards No. 52,* Stamford, CT: FASB, 1981, Appendix A.

functional currency of the recording entity by use of the exchange rate in effect at that date.

2. At each balance sheet date, recorded balances that are denominated in a currency other than the functional currency of the recording entity shall be adjusted to reflect the current exchange rate.

On this basis, a foreign exchange adjustment (i.e., gain or loss on a settled transaction) is necessary whenever the exchange rate changes between the transaction date and the settlement date. Should financial statements be prepared before settlement, the accounting adjustment (i.e., gain or loss on an unsettled transaction) will equal the difference between the amount originally recorded and the amount presented in the financial statements.

The FASB rejected the view that a distinction should be drawn between gains and losses on settled and unsettled transactions, because such distinctions cannot be applied in practice. Two accounting treatments for transactions gains and losses are possible.

Single-Transaction Perspective

Under a single-transaction perspective, exchange adjustments (both settled and unsettled) are treated as an adjustment to the original transaction accounts on the premise that a transaction and its settlement are a single event. The following example illustrates this treatment.

On September 1, 2011, a U.S. manufacturer sells, on account, goods to a Swedish importer for 1 million Swedish krona (SEK). The dollar/krona exchange rate is $0.12 = SEK 1, the krona receivable are due in 90 days, and the U.S. company operates on a calendar-year basis. The krona begins to depreciate before the receivable is collected. By the end of the month, the dollar/krona exchange rate is $0.11 = SEK 1; on December 1, 2011, it is $0.09 = SEK 1. (These transactions are posted in Exhibit 6-5.)

EXHIBIT 6-5   U.S. Company's Record: Single-Transaction Perspective

		Foreign Currency	U.S. Dollar Equivalent
Sept. 1, 2011	Accounts receivable	SEK 1,000,000	120,000
	Sales	SEK 1,000,000	120,000
	(To record credit sale)		
Sept. 30, 2011	Sales		10,000
	Accounts receivable		10,000
	(To adjust existing accounts for initial exchange rate change: SEK 1,000,000 × $0.12 minus SEK 1,000,000 × $0.11)		
Dec. 1, 2011	Retained earnings		20,000
	Accounts receivable		20,000
	(To adjust accounts for additional rate change: SEK 1,000,000 × $0.11 minus SEK 1,000,000 × $0.09)		
Dec. 1, 2011	Foreign currency	SEK 1,000,000	90,000
	Accounts receivable	SEK 1,000,000	90,000
	(To record settlement of outstanding foreign currency receivables)		

In this illustration, until the account is collected, the initial dollar amount recorded for both accounts receivable and sales is considered an estimate to be subsequently adjusted for changes in the dollar/krona exchange rate. Further depreciation of the krona between the financial statement date (September 1) and the settlement date (December 1) would require additional adjustments. In the Rio Tinto example at the beginning of this chapter, the effect of exchange rate changes illustrated in Exhibit 6-5 would have impacted consolidated revenues.

Two-Transaction Perspective

Under a two-transaction perspective, collection of the krona receivable is considered a separate event from the sale that gave rise to it. In the previous illustration, the export sale and related receivable would be recorded at the exchange rate in effect at that date. Depreciation of the krona between September 1 and December 1 would result in an exchange loss (i.e., loss on an unsettled transaction) and currency receivable on December 1, 2011, at the even lower exchange rate would result in a further exchange loss (i.e., loss on a settled transaction). See Exhibit 6-6.

In the interest of uniformity, FAS No. 52 requires the two-transaction method of accounting for foreign currency transactions. Gains and losses on settled and unsettled transactions are included in the determination of income; for example, the gains and losses illustrated in Exhibit 6-6 are the foreign currency effects explained in the first exhibit of the Rio Tinto example (Earnings sensitivities—exchange rates). Major exceptions to this requirement occur whenever (1) exchange adjustments relate to certain long-term intercompany transactions and (2) transactions are intended and effective as hedges of net investments (i.e., hedges of foreign operations' exposed net asset/liability positions) and foreign currency commitments. (The notion of an exposed asset or liability position is described shortly.)

EXHIBIT 6-6	**U.S. Company's Record: Two-Transaction Perspective**		
		Foreign Currency	U.S. Dollar Equivalent
Sept. 1, 2011	Accounts receivable	SEK 1,000,000	$120,000
	Sales	SEK 1,000,000	$120,000
	(To record credit sale at Sept. 1, 2011 exchange rate)		
Sept. 30, 2011	Foreign exchange loss		10,000
	Accounts receivable		10,000
	(To record effect of initial rate change)		
Dec. 1, 2011	Foreign currency	SEK 1,000,000	90,000
	Foreign exchange loss		20,000
	Accounts receivable	SEK 1,000,000	110,000
	(To record settlement of foreign currency receivable)		

FOREIGN CURRENCY TRANSLATION

Companies operating internationally use a variety of methods to express, in terms of their domestic currency, the assets, liabilities, revenues, and expenses that are stated in a foreign currency. These translation methods can be classified into two types: those that use a single translation rate to restate foreign balances to their domestic currency equivalents and those that use multiple rates. Exhibit 6-7 summarizes the treatment of specific balance sheet items under these translation methods.

Single Rate Method

The single rate method, long popular in Europe, applies a single exchange rate, the current or closing rate, to all foreign currency assets and liabilities. Foreign currency revenues and expenses are generally translated at exchange rates prevailing when these items are recognized. For convenience, however, revenues and expenses are typically translated by an appropriately weighted average of current exchange rates for the period.

Under the single, or current, rate method, the financial statements of a foreign operation (viewed by the parent as an autonomous entity) have their own reporting domicile: the local currency environment in which the foreign affiliate does business. The consolidated statements preserve the original financial statement relationships (such as financial ratios) of the individual consolidated entities as all foreign currency financial statement items are translated by a constant. That is, consolidated results reflect the currency perspectives of each entity whose results go into the consolidated

EXHIBIT 6-7	**Exchange Rates Employed in Different Translation Methods for Specific Balance Sheet Items**			
	Current	**Current Noncurrent**	**Monetary Nonmonetary**	**Temporal**
Cash	C	C	C	C
Accounts receivable	C	C	C	C
Inventories				
Cost	C	C	H	H
Market	C	C	H	C
Investments				
Cost	C	H	H	H
Market	C	H	H	C
Fixed assets	C	H	H	H
Other assets	C	H	H	H
Accounts payable	C	C	C	C
Long-term debt	C	H	C	C
Common stock	H	H	H	H
Retained earnings	*	*	*	*

Note: C, current rate; H, historical rate; and *, residual, balancing figure representing a composite of successive current rates.

totals, not the single-currency perspective of the parent company. Some people fault this method on the ground that using multiple currency perspectives violates the basic purpose of consolidated financial statements.

For accounting purposes, a foreign currency asset or liability is said to be *exposed* to exchange rate risk if its parent currency equivalent changes owing to a change in the exchange rate used to translate that asset or liability. Given this definition, the current rate method presumes that all local currency assets are exposed to exchange risk as the current (vs. the historical) rate changes the parent currency equivalent of all foreign currency assets every time exchange rates change. This seldom accords with economic reality as inventory and fixed asset values are generally supported by local inflation.

Consider the following example. Suppose that a foreign affiliate of a U.S. multinational corporation (MNC) buys a tract of land at the beginning of the period for FC1,000,000. The exchange rate (historical rate) was FC1 = $1. Thus, the historical cost of the investment in dollars is $1,000,000 (FC1,000,000 ÷ FC1). Due to changing prices, the land rises in value to FC1,500,000 (unrecognized under U.S. GAAP) while the exchange rate declines to FC1.4 = $1 by the end of the period. If this foreign currency asset were translated to U.S. dollars using the current rate, its original dollar value of $1,000,000 would now be recorded at $714,286 (FC1,000,000 ÷ FC1.4) implying an exchange loss of $285,714. Yet the increase in the fair market value of the land indicates that its current value in U.S. dollars is actually $1,071,285 (FC1,500,000 ÷ FC1.4). This suggests that translated asset values make little sense without making local price-level adjustments first. Also, translation of a historical cost number by a current market-determined exchange rate (e.g., FC1,000,000 ÷ FC1.4 = $714,286) produces a result that resembles neither historical cost ($1,000,000) nor current market value ($1,071,285).

Finally, translating all foreign currency balances by the current rate creates translation gains and losses every time exchange rates change. Reflecting such exchange adjustments in current income could significantly distort reported measures of performance. Many of these gains and losses may never be fully realized, as changes in exchange rates often reverse direction.

Multiple Rate Methods

Multiple rate methods combine current and historical exchange rates in the translation process.

CURRENT–NONCURRENT METHOD   Under the current–noncurrent method, a foreign subsidiary's current assets (assets that are usually converted to cash within a year) and current liabilities (obligations that mature within a year) are translated into their parent company's reporting currency at the current rate. Noncurrent assets and liabilities are translated at historical rates. Income statement items (except for depreciation and amortization charges) are translated at average rates applicable to each month of operation or on the basis of weighted averages covering the whole period being reported. Depreciation and amortization charges are translated at the historical rates in effect when the related assets were acquired.

Unfortunately, this method does not often square with reality. Using the year-end rate to translate current assets implies that all foreign currency cash, receivables, and inventories are equally exposed to exchange risk; that is, will be worth more or less in parent currency if the exchange rate changes during the year. This is simply not true.

For example, if the local price of inventory can be increased after a devaluation, its value is protected from currency exchange risk. On the other hand, translation of long-term debt at the historical rate shifts the impact of fluctuating currencies to the year of settlement. Many consider this to be at odds with reality as analysts are always assessing the current realizable values of a firm's long-run obligations. Moreover, current and noncurrent definitions are merely a classification scheme, not a conceptual justification, of which rates to use in translation.

MONETARY–NONMONETARY METHOD[7]   The monetary–nonmonetary method also uses a balance sheet classification scheme to determine appropriate translation rates. Monetary assets and liabilities; that is, claims to and obligations to pay a fixed amount of currency in the future are translated at the current rate. Nonmonetary items—fixed assets, long-term investments, and inventories—are translated at historical rates. Income statement items are translated under procedures similar to those described for the current–noncurrent framework.

Unlike the current–noncurrent method, this method views monetary assets and liabilities as exposed to exchange rate risk. Since monetary items are settled in cash, use of the current rate to translate these items produces domestic currency equivalents that reflect their realizable or settlement values. It also reflects changes in the domestic currency equivalent of long-term debt in the period in which exchange rates change, producing a more timely indicator of exchange rate effects.

Note, however, that the monetary–nonmonetary method also relies on a classification scheme to determine appropriate translation rates. This may lead to inappropriate results. For example, this method translates all nonmonetary assets at historical rates, which is not reasonable for assets stated at current market values (such as investment securities and inventory and fixed assets written down to market). Multiplying the current market value of a nonmonetary asset by a historical exchange rate yields an amount in the domestic currency that is neither the item's current equivalent nor its historical cost. This method also distorts profit margins by matching sales at current prices and translation rates against cost of sales measured at historical costs and translation rates.

TEMPORAL METHOD[8]   With the temporal method, currency translation does not change the *attribute* of an item being measured; it only changes the *unit of measure.* In other words, translation of foreign balances restates the currency denomination of these items, but not their actual valuation. Under U.S. GAAP, cash is measured in terms of the amount owned at the balance sheet date. Receivables and payables are stated at amounts expected to be received or paid when due. Other assets and liabilities are measured at money prices that prevailed when the items were acquired or incurred (historical prices). Some, however, are measured at prices prevailing as of the financial statement date (current prices), such as inventories under the lower of cost or market rule. In short, a time dimension is associated with these money values.

---

[7] This method was originally proposed in Samuel R. Hepworth, Reporting Foreign Operations, Ann Arbor: University of Michigan, 1956.
[8] This method was originally proposed in Leonard Lorensen, "Reporting Foreign Operations of U.S. Companies in U.S. Dollars," Accounting Research Study No. 12, New York: American Institute of Certified Public Accountants, 1972.

In the temporal method, monetary items such as cash, receivables, and payables are translated at the current rate. Nonmonetary items are translated at rates that preserve their original measurement bases. Specifically, assets carried on the foreign currency statements at historical cost are translated at the historical rate. Why? Because historical cost in foreign currency translated by a historical exchange rate yields historical cost in domestic currency. Similarly, nonmonetary items carried abroad at current values are translated at the current rate because current value in foreign currency translated by a current exchange rate produces current value in domestic currency. Revenue and expense items are translated at rates that prevailed when the underlying transactions took place, although average rates are suggested when revenue or expense transactions are voluminous.

When nonmonetary items abroad are valued at historical cost, the translation procedures resulting from the temporal method are virtually identical to those produced by the monetary–nonmonetary method. The two translation methods differ only if other asset valuation bases are employed, such as replacement cost, market values, or discounted cash flows.

Because it is similar to the monetary–nonmonetary method, the temporal method shares most of its advantages and disadvantages. In deliberately ignoring local infla-tion, this method shares a limitation with the other translation methods discussed. (Of course, historical cost accounting ignores inflation as well!).

All four methods just described have been used in the United States at one time or another and can be found today in various countries. In general, they produce noticeably different foreign currency translation results. The first three methods (i.e., the current rate, current–noncurrent, and monetary–nonmonetary) are predicated on identifying which assets and liabilities are exposed to, or sheltered from, currency exchange risk. The transla-tion methodology is then applied consistent with this distinction. The current rate method presumes that the entire foreign operation is exposed to exchange rate risk since all assets and liabilities are translated at the year-end exchange rate. The current–noncurrent rate method presumes that only the current assets and liabilities are so exposed, while the monetary–nonmonetary method presumes that monetary assets and liabilities are exposed. In contrast, the temporal method is designed to preserve the underlying theoret-ical basis of accounting measurement used in preparing the financial statements being translated. See Chapter 11 for a further discussion of exposure.

Financial Statement Effects

Exhibits 6-8 and 6-9 highlight the financial statement effects of the major translation meth-ods described. The balance sheet of a hypothetical Mexican subsidiary of a U.S.-based multinational enterprise appears in pesos in the first column of Exhibit 6-9. The second column depicts the U.S. dollar equivalents of the Mexican peso(MXN) balances when the exchange rate was MXN1 = $0.13. Should the peso depreciate to MXN1 = $0.11, several different accounting results are possible.

Under the current rate method, exchange rate changes affect the dollar equivalents of the Mexican subsidiary's total foreign currency assets (TA) and liabilities (TL) in the current period. Since their dollar values are affected by changes in the current rate, they are said to be *exposed* (in an accounting sense) to foreign exchange risk. Accordingly, under the current rate method, an exposed net asset position (TA > TL) results in a

EXHIBIT 6-8	Mexican Subsidiary Balance Sheet					
	U. S. Dollars before Peso Devaluation		U. S. Dollars after Peso Depreciation ($ 0.11 = MXN1)			
	Pesos	**($ 0.13 = MXN1)**	**Current Rate**	**Current– Noncurrent**	**Monetary– Nonmonetary**	**Temporal**
Assets						
Cash	3,000	$ 390	$ 330	$ 330	$ 330	$ 330
A/R	6,000	780	660	660	660	660
Inventories	9,000	1,170	990	990	1,170	990[a]
F/A (net)	18,000	2,340	1,980	2,340	2,340	2,340
Total	36,000	$4,680	$3,960	$4,320	$4,500	$4,320
Liabilities and Owners' Equity						
S-T payables	9,000	$1,170	$ 990	$ 990	$ 990	$ 990
L-T debt	12,000	1,560	1,320	1,560	1,320	1,320
O/E	15,000	1,950	1,650	1,770	2,190	2,010
Total	36,000	$4,680	$3,960	$4,320	$4,500	$4,320
Accounting exposure (MXN)			15,000	9,000	(12,000)	(3,000)
Translation gain (loss) ($)			(300)	(180)	240	60

Note: If the exchange rate remained unchanged over time, the translated statements would be the same under all translation methods.

[a] Assume inventories are carried at lower of cost or market. If they were carried at historical cost, the temporal balance sheet would be identical to the monetary–nonmonetary method.

translation loss if the Mexican peso loses value, and an exchange gain if the peso gains value. An exposed peso net liability position (TA < TL) produces a translation gain if the Mexican peso loses value and a loss if the peso gains value. In our example, current rate translation yields a $300 translation loss, since the dollar equivalent of the Mexican subsidiary's net asset position *after* the peso depreciation is $1,650 (MXN15,000 × $0.11), whereas the dollar equivalent *before* the depreciation was $1,950 (MXN15,000 × $0.13). These translation gains and losses are those depicted at the start of this chapter in its exhibit entitled, "Net assets' sensitivities—exchange on translation."

Under the current–noncurrent method, the U.S. company's accounting exposure is measured by its peso net current asset or liability position (a positive MXN9,000 in our example). Under the monetary–nonmonetary method, exposure is measured by its net peso monetary asset or liability position (a negative MXN12,000). Accounting exposure under the temporal principle depends on whether the Mexican subsidiary's inventories or other nonmonetary assets are valued at historical cost (and therefore not exposed) or some other valuation basis (a negative MXN3,000 in our example).

To summarize, the different translation methods in our example give a wide array of accounting results, ranging from a $300 loss under the current rate method to a $240 gain under the monetary–nonmonetary method. This difference is large given that all the results are based on the same facts. What is more, operations reporting respectable

EXHIBIT 6-9	Mexican Subsidiary Income Statement

	U. S. Dollars before Peso Devaluation		U. S. Dollars after Peso Depreciation ($ 0.11 = MXN1)			
	Pesos	($ 0.13 = MXN1)	Current Rate	Current–Noncurrent	Monetary–Nonmonetary	Temporal
Sales	40,000	$5,200	$4,400	$4,400	$4,400	$4,400
Cost of sales	20,000	2,600	2,200	2,200	2,600	2,200[a]
Depreciation[b]	1,800	234	198	234	234	234
Other expenses	8,000	1,040	880	880	880	880
Pre-tax income	10,200	1,326	1,122	1,086	686	1,086
Income tax (30%)	3,060	(398)	(337)	(337)	(337)	(337)
Translation g/l[c]	—	—	(300)	(180)	240	60
Net income/(loss)	7,140	$ 928	$ 485	$ 569	$ 589	$ 809

Note: This example assumes that the income statement is prepared the day after devaluation.
[a]Assumes that inventories were written down to market at period's end.
[b]Estimated life of fixed assets is assumed to be 10 years.
[c]This example reflects what reported earnings would look like if all translation gains or losses were immediately reflected in current income.

profits before currency translation may well report losses or much lower earnings after translation (the converse is also true). To protect themselves against the financial statement effects of currency swings, financial managers may execute protective maneuvers known as *hedging* strategies. Chapter 11 covers hedging options and foreign exchange risk management in greater detail.

Which Is Best?

We begin by asking whether a single translation method is appropriate for all circumstances in which translations occur and for all purposes that translation serves. Our answer would be, no. Circumstances underlying foreign exchange translation differ widely. Translating accounts from a stable to an unstable currency is not the same as translating accounts from an unstable currency to a stable one. Likewise, there is little similarity between translations involving import- or export-type transactions and those involving a permanently established affiliate or subsidiary company in another country that reinvests its local earnings and does not intend to repatriate any funds to the parent company in the near future.

Second, translations are made for different purposes. Translating the accounts of a foreign subsidiary to consolidate those accounts with those of the parent company has very little in common with translating the accounts of an independent company mainly for the convenience of various foreign audiences-of-interest.

We pose two additional questions:

1. What are acceptable foreign currency translation methods and under what conditions?
2. Are there situations in which currency translation may be inappropriate?

Regarding the first question, we think that there are three different translation approaches that make sense from a reader's viewpoint: (1) the historical method, (2) the current method, and (3) no translation at all. Financial accounts of foreign entities can be translated either from a parent company perspective or from a local perspective. Under the parent company perspective, foreign operations are extensions of parent company operations and are, in large measure, sources of domestic currency cash flows. Accordingly, the object of translation is to change the unit of measure for financial statements of foreign subsidiaries to the domestic currency, and to make the foreign statements conform to accounting principles generally accepted in the country of the parent company. We think these objectives are best achieved by translation methods that use historical rates of exchange. We prefer the temporal principle, as it generally maintains the accounting principles used to measure assets and liabilities originally expressed in foreign currency units.[9] Because foreign statements under a parent company perspective are first adjusted to reflect parent company accounting principles (before translation), the temporal principle is appropriate, as it changes a measurement in foreign currency into a measurement in domestic currency without changing the basis of measurement. The temporal translation method is easily adapted to processes that make accounting adjustments during the translation. When this is so, adjustments for differences between two or more sets of accounting concepts and practices are made along with the translation of currency amounts. For example, inventories or certain liabilities may be restated according to accounting practices different from those originally used. The temporal principle can accommodate any asset valuation framework, be it historical cost, current replacement price, or net realizable values.

The current rate method of translation is a straightforward translation (restatement) from one currency language to another. There is no change in the nature of the accounts; only their particular form of expression is changed. The current rate method is appropriate when the translated accounts of foreign subsidiaries keep the local currency as the unit of measure; that is, when foreign entities are viewed from a local (as opposed to a parent) company perspective. Translation at the current rate does not change any of the initial relationships (e.g., financial ratios) in the foreign currency statements, as all account balances are simply multiplied by a constant. This approach is also useful when the accounts of an independent company are translated for the convenience of foreign stockholders or other external user groups.

The current rate method is also appropriate when price-level-adjusted accounts are translated to another currency. If reliable price-level adjustments are made in a given set of accounts and if domestic price-level changes for the currency are reflected closely in related foreign exchange rate movements, the current rate translation of price-level-adjusted data yields results that are comparable to translating historical cost accounts under the historical rate translation method.[10] This topic is covered in Chapter 7.

---

[9] Frederick D.S. Choi and Gerhard G. Mueller, *An Introduction to Multinational Accounting*, Upper Saddle River, NJ: Prentice-Hall, 1978.

[10] Alas, empirical evidence suggests that exchange rate changes and differential inflation are seldom perfectly negatively correlated. Distortions caused by this market anomaly are discussed by David A. Ziebart and Jong-Hag Choi, "The Difficulty of Achieving Economic Reality Through Foreign Currency Translation," *International Journal of Accounting* 33, no. 4 (1998): 403–414.

Are there situations in which currency translations can confuse rather than enlighten? We think so. No translation is appropriate between highly unstable and highly stable currencies. Translation of one into the other will not produce meaningful information using any translation method. No translation also means nonconsolidation of financial statements. We think this is reasonable. If a currency is unstable enough to put account translations out of the question, financial statement consolidation should also be out of the question. No translation is necessary when financial statements of independent companies are issued for purely informational purposes to residents in another country that is in a comparable stage of economic development and has a comparable national currency situation. Finally, certain special management reports should not be translated. Effective international managers should be able to evaluate situations and reach decisions in terms of more than one currency unit. (These and related issues are discussed in Chapter 10.) Some internal company reports may have several different columns of monetary amounts, each in a different currency unit. Translation may be impossible for certain other reports (such as those on a possible international acquisition) because historical foreign exchange rate information may not be available. Still other types of reports may translate current or monetary items only and leave other items untranslated.

Appropriate Current Rate

Thus far we have referred to rates of exchange used in translation methods as either historical or current. Average rates are often used in income statements for expediency. The choice of an appropriate exchange rate is not clear-cut because several exchange rates are in effect for any currency at any time. There are buying and selling (bid and ask) rates, spot rates and forward rates, official rates and free-market rates, and so on. We believe that an appropriate translation rate should reflect economic and business reality as closely as possible. The free-market rate quoted for spot transactions in the country where the accounts to be translated originate is a rate that appropriately measures current transaction values.

Sometimes a country applies different exchange rates to different transactions. In these situations, one must choose among several existing rates. Several possibilities have been suggested: (1) dividend remittance rates, (2) free-market rates, and (3) any applicable penalty or preference rates, such as those associated with imports or exports. Your authors believe that free-market rates are preferable, with one exception: Where specific exchange controls are in effect (i.e., when certain funds are definitely earmarked for specific transactions to which specific foreign exchange rates apply), the applicable rates should be used. For instance, if a Latin American subsidiary of a U.S. parent has received permission to import certain goods from the United States at a favorable rate and has set aside certain funds to do so, the ear-marked funds should be translated to dollars at the special preference rate. The current year-end free-market rate should then be applied to the balance of the foreign cash account. This procedure translates portions of a foreign currency cash account at two or more different translation rates. That is fine as long as it properly and fully reflects economic reality.

Translation Gains and Losses

Exhibit 6-8 illustrated four translation adjustments resulting from applying various translation methods to foreign currency financial statements. Internationally, accounting treatments of these adjustments have been as diverse as the translation procedures.

Approaches to accounting for translation adjustments range from deferral to no deferral with hybrid approaches in between.

Deferral

Exclusion of translation adjustments in current income is generally advocated because these adjustments merely result from a restatement process. Changes in the domestic currency equivalents of a foreign subsidiary's net assets are unrealized and have no effect on the local currency cash flows generated by the foreign entity. Therefore, it would be misleading to include such adjustments in current income. Under these circumstances, translation adjustments are accumulated separately as a part of consolidated equity. Parkinson offers additional reasons to support deferral:

> It can be argued that the gain or loss relates to a very long-term investment—perhaps even a permanent investment—of a . . . parent in a foreign subsidiary; that the gain or loss will not become realized until the foreign operation is closed down and all the net assets are distributed to the parent; that at or before such time the change in the exchange rate may have reversed— i.e., that no gain or loss will ever be realized. It can also be argued that operating results recorded in the periods following the currency revaluation (and translated at the then current exchange rate) will indicate the increased or decreased worth of the foreign operation and that in these circumstances there is no need to record a one-time translation gain or loss in the income statement—that in fact the recording of such a gain or loss might be misleading.[11]

Some analysts are opposed to deferral on the grounds that exchange rates may not reverse themselves. Even if they do, deferral of exchange adjustments is premised on predicting exchange rates, a most difficult task. Some argue that deferring translation gains or losses masks the behavior of exchange rate changes; that is, rate changes are historical facts and financial statement users are best served if the effects of exchange rate fluctuations are accounted for when they occur.

Deferral and Amortization

Some firms, like those in Japan, defer translation gains or losses and amortize these adjustments over the life of related balance sheet items. As an example, assume that the acquisition of a fixed asset is financed by issuing debt. It can be argued that principal and interest payments on the debt are covered by cash flows generated from using the fixed asset. Here, the translation gain or loss associated with the debt would be deferred and amortized over the life of the related fixed asset, that is, released to income in a manner compatible with depreciation expense. Alternatively, the translation gain or loss arising from the debt could be deferred and amortized over the remaining life of the debt as an adjustment to interest expense.

---

[11] MacDonald R. Parkinson, Translation of Foreign Currencies, Toronto: Canadian Institute of Chartered Accountants, 1972, 101–102.

Such approaches are criticized by some on theoretical and practical grounds. For example, finance theory tells us that capital budgeting decisions about fixed asset investments are independent of decisions about how to finance them. Linking the two looks more like a device to smooth income. Adjusting interest expense is also suspect. Domestic borrowing costs are not adjusted to reflect changes in market interest rates or the fair value of the debt. Thus, the argument goes, why should fluctuations in currency values have such an effect?

Partial Deferral

A third option in accounting for translation gains and losses is to recognize losses as soon as they occur, but to recognize gains only as they are realized. This was common practice in the United States at one time. Although conservative, deferring a translation gain solely because it is a gain denies that a rate change has occurred. Moreover, deferral of translation gains while recognizing translation losses is logically inconsistent. This approach also lacks any explicit criteria to determine when to realize a translation gain. Also, those who favor deferral of translation gains are at a loss to determine how much to defer. In the past, companies have netted current gains against prior losses and deferred the difference. This implies that translation gains or losses are not period items and will "wash out" in the long run. If this were so, deferrals would be a questionable practice.

No Deferral

A final reporting option utilized by many firms around the world today is to recognize translation gains and losses in the income statement immediately. This option views deferral of any type as artificial and misleading. Deferral criteria are often attacked as internally inconsistent and impossible to implement. However, including translation gains and losses in current income introduces a random element to earnings that could result in significant earning fluctuations whenever exchange rates change. Moreover, including such paper gains and losses in reported earnings can mislead statement readers, because these adjustments do not always provide information compatible with the expected economic effects of rate changes on an enterprise's cash flows.

Where Are We?

The objectives of translation have an important bearing on the nature of any potential translation adjustment. If a local currency perspective is maintained (local company perspective), reflecting a translation adjustment in current income is unwarranted. Recall that a local company perspective requires the current rate translation method in order to preserve relationships existing in the foreign currency statements. In our opinion, including translation gains or losses in income distorts original financial relationships and may mislead users of the information. Management, for example, is interested in how a particular affiliate is faring in its local currency, and translation gains and losses generated from a restatement process does not shed much light on local performance. In this instance, it makes sense to treat translation gains or losses as adjustments to consolidated equity.

If the reporting currency of the parent company is the unit of measure for the translated financial statements (parent company perspective), it is advisable to recognize translation gains or losses in income immediately. The parent company perspective views a foreign subsidiary as an extension of the parent. Translation gains and losses reflect increases or decreases in the domestic currency equity of the foreign investment and should be recognized.

TRANSLATION ACCOUNTING DEVELOPMENT

Translation accounting practices have evolved over time in response to the increasing complexity of multinational operations and changes in the international monetary system. To provide some historical perspective on the current state of translation accounting, we briefly chronicle financial reporting initiatives in the United States as they are representative of experiences elsewhere.

Pre-1965

Before 1965 the translation practices of many U.S. companies were guided by Chapter 12 of Accounting Research Bulletin No. 43.[12] This statement advocated the current–noncurrent method. Transaction gains or losses were taken directly to income. Translation gains or losses were netted during the period. Net translation losses were recognized in current income, while net translation gains were deferred in a balance sheet suspense account and used to offset translation losses in future periods.

1965–1975

ARB No. 43 allowed certain exceptions to the current–noncurrent method. Under special circumstances, inventory could be translated at historical rates. Long-term debt incurred to acquire long-term assets could be restated at the current rate when there was a large (presumably permanent) change in the exchange rate. Any accounting difference caused by debt restatement was treated as part of the asset's cost. Moreover, translating all foreign currency payables and receivables at the current rate was allowed after Accounting Principles Board Opinion No. 6 was issued in 1965.[13] This change to ARB No. 43 gave companies another translation option.

1975–1981

To end the variety of treatments allowed under previous translation standards, the Financial Accounting Standards Board(FASB) issued FAS No. 8 in 1975.[14] This statement significantly changed U.S. practice and that of foreign companies subscribing to U.S. GAAP by requiring the temporal method of translation. Equally important,

---

[12] American Institute of Certified Public Accountants, Committee on Accounting Procedure, "Restatement and Revision of Accounting Research Bulletins," Accounting Research Bulletin No. 43, New York: AICPA, 1953.

[13] American Institute of Certified Public Accountants, "Status of Accounting Research Bulletins," Accounting Principles Board Opinion No. 6, New York: AICPA, 1965.

[14] Financial Accounting Standards Board, "Accounting for the Translation of Foreign Currency Transactions and Foreign Currency Financial Statements," Statement of Financial Accounting Standards No. 8, Stamford, CT: FASB, 1975.

deferral of translation gains and losses was no longer permitted. Translation and transaction exchange gains and losses had to be recognized in income during the period of the rate change.

FAS No. 8 proved controversial. While some applauded it for its theoretical merits, many condemned it for the distortions it caused in reported corporate earnings. The pronouncement was criticized for producing accounting results not in accord with economic reality. The yo-yo effect of FAS No. 8 on corporate earnings also caused concern among executives of multinational companies. They worried that their companies' reported earnings would appear more volatile than those of domestic companies, and thereby depress their stock prices.

1981–Present

In May 1978, the FASB invited public comment on its first 12 pronouncements. Most of the 200 letters received related to FAS No. 8, urging that it be changed. Responding to the dissatisfaction, the FASB reconsidered FAS No. 8 and, after many public meetings and two exposure drafts, issued Statement of Financial Accounting Standards No. 52 in 1981.[15]

FEATURES OF STANDARD NO. 52/INTERNATIONAL ACCOUNTING STANDARD 21

The objectives of translation under FAS No. 52 differ substantially from those of FAS No. 8. FAS No. 8 adopted a parent company perspective by requiring that foreign currency financial statements be presented as if all transactions had taken place in parent currency. Standard No. 52 recognizes that both the parent company and the local company perspectives are valid reporting frameworks. At the international level, the IASB issued a parallel pronouncement, IAS 21, that was recently amended to clarify its requirements and to resolve certain implementation concerns.[16] Both FAS No. 52 and the current version of IAS 21 seek to

1. Reflect, in consolidated statements, the financial results and relationships measured in the primary currency in which each consolidated entity does business (its *functional currency*).
2. Provide information that is generally compatible with the expected economic effects of an exchange rate change on an enterprise's cash flows and equity.

These objectives are based on the concept of a functional currency. Recall that the functional currency of an entity is the currency of the primary economic environment in which it operates and generates cash flows. Moreover, the functional currency designation determines the choice of translation method employed for consolidation purposes and the disposition of exchange gains and losses.

---

[15] Financial Accounting Standards Board, "Foreign Currency Translation," Statement of Financial Accounting Standards No. 52, Stamford, CT: FASB, 1981.
[16] Comments on the paper are available at www.iasb.org/news.

Translation When *Local* Currency Is the Functional Currency

If the functional currency is the foreign currency in which the foreign entity's records are kept, its financial statements are translated to dollars using the current rate method. Resulting translation gains or losses are disclosed in a separate component of consolidated equity. This preserves the financial statement ratios as calculated from the local currency statements. The following current rate procedures are used:

1. All foreign currency assets and liabilities are translated to dollars using the exchange rate prevailing as of the balance sheet date; capital accounts are translated at historical rates.
2. Revenues and expenses are translated using the exchange rate prevailing on the transaction date, although weighted average rates can be used for expediency.
3. Translation gains and losses are reported in a separate component of consolidated stockholders' equity. These exchange adjustments do not go into the income statement until the foreign operation is sold or the investment is judged to have permanently lost value.

Translation When the *Parent* Currency Is the Functional Currency

When the parent currency is a foreign entity's functional currency, its foreign currency financial statements are remeasured to dollars using the temporal method. All translation gains and losses resulting from the translation process are included in determining current period income. Specifically:

1. Monetary assets and liabilities and nonmonetary assets valued at current market prices are translated using the rate prevailing as of the financial statement date; other nonmonetary items and capital accounts are translated at historical rates.
2. Revenues and expenses are translated using average exchange rates for the period except those items related to nonmonetary items (e.g., cost of sales and depreciation expense), which are translated using historical rates.
3. Translation gains and losses are reflected in current income.

Translation When *Foreign* Currency Is the Functional Currency

A foreign entity may keep its records in one foreign currency when its functional currency is another foreign currency. In this situation, the financial statements are first remeasured from the local currency into the functional currency (temporal method) and then translated into U.S. dollars using the current rate method. Assume a German parent company owns a wholly-owned affiliate in Mexico. The Mexican affiliate subcontracts most of its production to Brazilian vendors. Hence, the Mexican affiliate's functional currency is deemed to be the Brazilian real. In consolidating the accounts of its Mexican affiliate, the German parent company would first remeasure the Mexican accounts from pesos to reals using the temporal method with any translation gains and losses reflected in the reported earnings of the Mexican concern. These real balances would then be translated to German marks using the current rate method with any translation adjustments arising from this process reflected in consolidated equity.

Exhibit 6-10 charts the translation procedures described here, and the appendix to this chapter demonstrates the mechanics of foreign currency translation.

EXHIBIT 6-10   Translation Procedure Flowchart

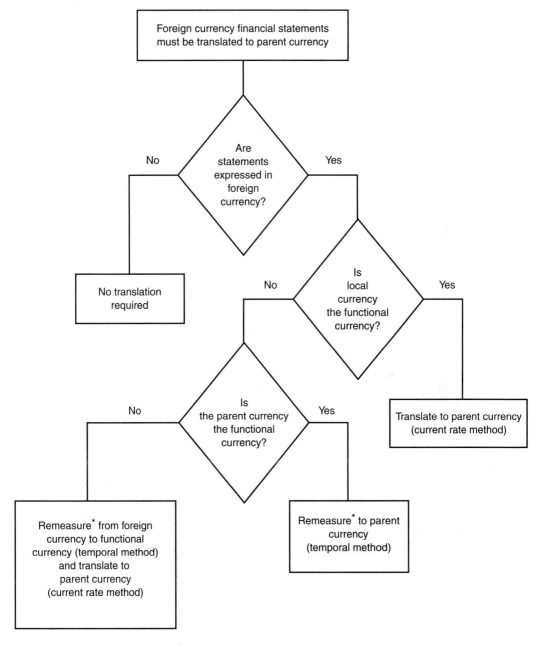

*The term *remeasure* means to translate so as to change the unit of measure from a foreign currency to the functional currency.

An exception to the current rate method is required for subsidiaries located in places where the cumulative rate of inflation during the preceding three years exceeds 100 percent. In such hyperinflationary conditions, the dollar (the stronger currency) is considered the functional currency, requiring use of the temporal translation method.

Where an entity has more than one distinct and separable operation (e.g., a branch or division), each operation may be considered as a separate entity with its own functional currency. Thus, a U.S. parent might have a self-contained manufacturing operation in Mexico designed to serve the Latin American market and a separate sales outlet for the parent company's exported products. Under these circumstances, financial statements of the manufacturing operation would be translated to dollars using the current rate method. The peso statements of the Mexican sales outlet would be remeasured in dollars using the temporal method.

Once the functional currency for a foreign entity is determined, that currency designation must be used consistently unless changes in economic circumstances clearly indicate that the functional currency has changed. If a reporting enterprise can justify the change, analysts should note that the accounting change need not be accounted for retroactively.

MEASUREMENT ISSUES

Readers of consoliated accounts must address several issues if they are to properly interpret the financial statement effects of foreign currency translation. The following sections discuss several of them.

Reporting Perspective

In adopting the notion of functional currency, FAS No. 52 and IAS 21 accommodate both local and parent company reporting perspectives in the consolidated financial statements. But are financial statement readers better served by incorporating two different reporting perspectives and, therefore, two different currency frameworks in a single set of consolidated financial statements? Is a translation adjustment produced under the temporal method any different in substance from that produced under the current rate method? If not, is any useful purpose served by disclosing some translation adjustments in income and others in stockholders' equity? Is FAS No. 8's concept of a single unit of measure (the parent company's reporting currency) the lesser of two evils? Should we stop translating foreign currency financial statements altogether? Doing so would avoid many of the pitfalls associated with current translation methods, including the problem of incorporating more than one perspective in the translated results.

It has also been suggested that FAS No. 52 is inconsistent with the theory of consolidation, which is to show the statements of a parent company and its subsidiaries as if the group were operating as a single company. Yet subsidiaries whose functional currency is the local currency operate relatively independently of the parent. If the multinational doesn't operate as a single company, then why consolidate those parts that are independent?[17]

---

[17] C. W. Nobes, "An Analysis of the Use of 'Theory' in the UK and US Currency Translation Standards," reprinted in C. W. Nobes, Issues in International Accounting, New York: Garland, 1986, pp. 129–130.

What Happened to Historical Cost?

As noted earlier in the chapter, translating a balance measured under historical cost at the current exchange rate produces an amount in U.S. dollars that is neither the item's historical cost nor its current value equivalent. Such a translated amount defies theoretical description. Historical cost is the basis of U.S. GAAP and most overseas assets of most multinationals will have historical cost measurements. Yet the current rate method is used for translation whenever a local currency is deemed to be the functional currency. Even if financial statement users can still make sense of the consolidated amounts, the theoretical incoherence remains.

Concept of Income

Under the currency translation pronouncements already described, adjustments arising from the translation of foreign currency financial statements and certain transactions are made directly to shareholders' equity, thus bypassing the income statement. The apparent intention of this was to give statement readers more accurate and less confusing income numbers. Some, however, dislike the idea of burying translation adjustments that were previously disclosed. They fear readers may be confused as to the effects of fluctuating exchange rates on a company's worth.

Managed Earnings

Currency translation pronouncements such as those just described provide opportunities to manage earnings. Consider the choice of functional currencies. An examination of the functional currency criteria shown in Exhibit 6-4 suggests that the choice of a functional currency is not straightforward. A foreign subsidiary's operations could satisfy opposing criteria. For example, a foreign subsidiary may incur its expenses primarily in the local country and make its sales primarily in the local environment and denominated in local currency. These circumstances would favor selection of the local currency as the functional currency. Yet the same operation may be financed entirely by the parent company with cash flows remitted to the parent. Therefore, the parent currency could be selected as the functional currency. The different possible outcomes involved in selecting functional currencies may be one reason why Exxon-Mobil Oil chooses the local currency as the functional currency for most of its foreign operations, while Chevron-Texaco and Unocal choose the dollar. When choice criteria conflict and the choice can significantly affect reporting outcomes, there are opportunities for earnings management.

Research to date is inconclusive as to whether managers manipulate income (and other financial statement amounts) by the choice of functional currency.[18] Some evidence

---

[18] For example, see J. H. Amernic and B. J. B. Galvin, "Implementing the New Foreign Currency Rules in Canada and the United States: A Challenge to Professional Judgement," *International Journal of Accounting* (Spring 1984): 165–180; Thomas G. Evans and Timothy S. Doupnik, Determining the Functional Currency Under Statement 52, Stamford, CT: FASB, 1986, 11–12; Dileep R. Mehta and Samanta B. Thapa, "FAS 52, Functional Currency, and the Non-Comparability of Financial Reports," *International Journal of Accounting* 26, no. 2 (1991): 71–84; Robert J. Kirsch and Thomas G. Evans, "The Implementation of FAS 52: Did the Foreign Currency Approach Prevail?" *International Journal of Accounting* 29, no. 1 (1994): 20–33; and M. Aiken and D. Ardern, "Choice of Translation Methods in Financial Disclosure: A Test of Compliance with Environmental Hypotheses," *British Accounting Review*, 35 (2003): 327–348.

of earnings management appears when one looks at when companies choose to adopt a new currency translation pronouncement. For example, evidence regarding adoption dates for the U.K.'s currency translation pronouncement, SSAP 20 shows that companies chose to defer adoption of the standard to influence their financial performance and, achieve certain corporate financial objectives.[19] Such motives as these reduce the credibility of multinationals' consolidated financial statements.

FOREIGN CURRENCY TRANSLATION AND INFLATION

An inverse relationship between a country's rate of inflation and its currency's external value has been empirically demonstrated.[20] Consequently, use of the current rate to translate the cost of nonmonetary assets located in inflationary environments will eventually produce domestic currency equivalents far below their original measurement bases. At the same time, translated earnings would be greater because of correspondingly lower depreciation charges. Such translated results could easily mislead rather than inform. Lower dollar valuations would usually understate the actual earning power of foreign assets supported by local inflation, and inflated return on investment ratios of foreign operations could create false expectations of future profitability.

The FASB decided against inflation adjustments before translation, believing such adjustments to be inconsistent with the historical cost valuation framework used in basic U.S. statements. As a solution, FAS No. 52 requires use of the U.S. dollar as the functional currency for foreign operations domiciled in hyperinflationary environments (those countries where the cumulative rate of inflation exceeds 100 percent over a three-year period). This procedure would hold constant the dollar equivalents of foreign currency assets, as they would be translated at the historical rate (by the temporal method). This method has its limitations. First, translation at the historical rate is meaningful only if differential rates of inflation between the subsidiary's host country and parent country are perfectly negatively correlated with exchange rates. If not, the dollar equivalents of foreign currency assets in inflationary environments will be misleading. Should inflation rates in the hyperinflationary economy fall below 100 percent in a future three-year period, switching to the current rate method (because local currency would become the functional currency) could produce a significant translation adjustment to consolidated equity, as exchange rates may change significantly during the

---

[19] George Emmanuel Iatrides and Nathan Lael Joseph, "Characteristics of UK firms Related to Timing of Adoption of Statement of Standard Accounting Practice No. 20," *Accounting and Finance*, Vol. 46 (2006): 429–455. For evidence of earnings motivation for switching currency translation methods, see Dahli Gray, "Corporate Preferences for Foreign Currency Accounting Standards," *Journal of Accounting Research* (Autumn 1984): 760–764; James J. Benjamin, Steven Grossman, and Casper Wiggins, "The Impact of Foreign Currency Translation on Reporting During the Phase-in of SFAS No. 52," *Journal of Accounting, Auditing, and Finance* 1, no. 3 (1996): 174–184; Frances L. Ayres, "Characteristics of Firms Electing Early Adoption of SFAS 52," *Journal of Accounting and Economics* (June 1986): 143–158; and Robert W. Rutledge, "Does Management Engage in the Manipulation of Earnings?" *Journal of International Accounting, Auditing, and Taxation* 4, no. 1 (1995): 69–86.

[20] B. Balassa, "The Purchasing Power Parity Doctrine: A Reappraisal," *Journal of Political Economy* (1964): 145–154; R. Z. Aliber and C. P. Stickney, "Accounting Measures of Foreign Exchange Exposure: The Long and Short of It," *Accounting Review* (January 1975): 44–57; and W. Beaver and M. Wolfson, "Foreign Currency Translation in Perfect and Complete Markets," *Journal of Accounting Research* (Autumn 1982): 528–560.

interim. Under these circumstances, charging stockholders' equity with translation losses on foreign currency fixed assets could have a significant effect on financial ratios with stockholders' equity in the denominator. The issue of foreign currency translation cannot be separated from the issue of accounting for foreign inflation, which is treated at greater length in the next chapter.[21]

FOREIGN CURRENCY TRANSLATION ELSEWHERE

We now look briefly at foreign currency translation in other parts of the world. The Canadian Institute of Chartered Accountants (CICA), the U.K.'s Accounting Standards Board, and the International Accounting Standards Board all participated in the deliberations that led to FAS No. 52. It is not surprising, therefore, to find that their corresponding standards are largely compatible with FAS No. 52.[22]

A distinctive feature of Canada's standard (CICA 1650) concerns foreign long-term debt. In Canada, gains and losses from translation are deferred and amortized as opposed to being recognized in income immediately. Canada has issued a second exposure draft proposing to eliminate its defer and amortize approach.

A major difference between the U.K. and U.S. relates to self-contained subsidiaries in hyperinflationary countries. In the United Kingdom, financial statements must first be adjusted to current price levels and then translated using the current rate; in the United States, the temporal method is used.

Finally, there is an important distinction between IAS 21 (as revised) and FAS No. 52. Under IAS 21, the financial statements of subsidiaries in highly inflationary environments must be adjusted to reflect changes in the general price level before translation, a treatment like that in the U.K. standard.

The Australian foreign currency translation standard calls for revaluing noncurrent, nonmonetary assets for subsidiaries in high inflation countries prior to translation. The New Zealand standard is silent on the issue. The New Zealand standard also calls for the monetary–nonmonetary method of translation for subsidiaries with operations integrated with the parent, producing results very similar to the temporal method.

Japan recently changed its standard to require the current rate method in all circumstances, with translation adjustments shown on the balance sheet in stockholders' equity. The EU Fourth and Seventh Directives (see Chapter 8) have no provisions on foreign currency translation. As a result, currency translation practices varied considerably. However, foreign currency translation practices in Europe have narrowed as International Financial Reporting Standards has become the reporting norm for listed EU companies. Observation suggests that foreign currency translation standards globally are converging on FAS No. 52 and IAS 21.

---

[21] For a recent examination of this relationship, see John Huges, Jing Liu, and Mingshan Zhang, "Valuation and Accounting for Inflation and Foreign Exchange," *Journal of Accounting Research*, Vol. 42, no. 4 (2004): 731–754.

[22] All three standards were issued in 1983, roughly 18 months after FAS No. 52. The Canadian standard is Accounting Recommendation 1650 and the British standard is Statement of Standard Accounting Practice 20; both are titled "Foreign Currency Translation." The original International Accounting Standard 21 was modified in 1993 and is now called, "The Effects of Changes in Foreign Exchange Rates."

Appendix 6-1

Translation and Remeasurement Under FAS No. 52

Exhibit 6-11 presents comparative foreign currency balance sheets at December 31, 2010 and 2011, and a statement of income for the year ended December 31, 2011, for CM Corporation, a wholly-owned foreign subsidiary of a U.S. company. The statements conform with U.S. generally accepted accounting principles before translation to U.S. dollars.

Capital stock was issued and fixed assets acquired when the exchange rate was FC1 = $.17. Inventories at January 1, 2011, were acquired during the fourth quarter of 2010. Purchases (FC6,250), sales, other expenses, and dividends (FC690) occurred evenly during 2011. Retained earnings in U.S. dollars at December 31, 2010, under the temporal method were $316. Exchange rates for calendar 2011 were as follows:

January 1, 2011	FC1 = $.23
December 31, 2011	FC1 = $.18
Average during 2011	FC1 = $.22
Average during fourth quarter, 2011	FC1 = $.23
Average during fourth quarter, 2011	FC1 = $.19

EXHIBIT 6-11 **Financial Statements of CM Corporation**		
Balance Sheet	**12/31/10**	**12/31/11**
Cash	FC 300	FC 500
Accounts receivable (net)	1,300	1,000
Inventories (lower of FIFO cost or market)	1,200	1,500
Fixed assets (net)	9,000	8,000
Total assets	FC 11,800	FC 11,000
Accounts payable	FC 2,200	FC 2,400
Long-term debt	4,400	3,000
Capital stock	2,000	2,000
Retained earnings	3,200	3,600
Total liabilities and owners' equity	FC 11,800	FC 11,000

Income Statement		**Year ended 12/31/11**
Sales		FC 10,000
Expenses		
Cost of sales	5,950	
Depreciation (straight-line)	1,000	
Other	1,493	8,443
Operating income		FC 1,557
Income taxes		467
Net income		FC 1,090

Current Rate Method

Translation adjustments under the current rate method arise whenever (1) year-end foreign currency balances are translated at a current rate that differs from that used to translate ending balances of the previous period, and (2) foreign currency financial statements are translated at a current rate that differs from exchange rates used during the period. The translation adjustment is calculated by (1) multiplying the beginning foreign currency net asset balance by the change in the current rate during the period, and (2) multiplying the increase or decrease in net assets during the period by the difference between the average exchange rate and the end-of-period exchange rate. Exhibit 6-12 depicts how the FAS No. 52 translation process applies to these figures.

EXHIBIT 6-12	Current Rate Method of Translation (Local Currency is Functional Currency)		
	Foreign Currency	Exchange Rate	Dollar Equivalents
Balance Sheet Accounts			
Assets			
Cash	FC 500	$.18	$ 90
Accounts receivable	1,000	.18	180
Inventories	1,500	.18	270
Fixed assets	8,000	.18	1,440
Total	FC 11,000		$1,980
Liabilities and Stockholders' Equity			
Accounts payable	FC 2,400	.18	$ 432
Long-term debt	3,000	.18	540
Capital stock	2,000	.17	340
Retained earnings	3,600	a	404
Translation adjustment (cumulative)		b	264
Total	FC 11,000		$1,980
Income Statement Accounts			
Sales	FC 10,000	.22	$2,200
Cost of sales	(5,950)	.22	(1,309)
Depreciation	(1,000)	.22	(220)
Other expenses	(1,493)	.22	(328)
Income before income taxes	FC 1,557		$ 343
Income taxes	(467)	.22	(103)
Net income	FC 1,090		$ 240
Retained earnings, 12/31/10	3,200		316
Less: dividends	(690)	.22	(152)
Retained earnings, 12/31/11	FC 3,600		$ 404

[a] *See statement of income and retained earnings.*

[b] *The cumulative translation adjustment of $264 is comprised of two parts: (1) the cumulative translation adjustment at the beginning of the year and (2) the translation adjustment for the current year and would be disclosed as a component of Other Comprehensive Income.*

As can be seen, translation procedures under the current rate method are straightforward. However, the derivation of the beginning cumulative translation adjustment merits some explanation. Assume that calendar 2011 is the first year in which the current rate method is adopted (e.g., the previous translation method was the temporal method, as the U.S. dollar was considered functional before 2011). Under this scenario, a one-time translation adjustment would be calculated as of January 1, 2011. This figure approximates the amount by which beginning stockholders' equity would differ in light of the switch from the temporal to the current rate method. It is calculated by translating CM Corporation's January 1, 2011, foreign currency net asset position at the current rate prevailing on that date. (This result simulates what CM's beginning net asset position would be had it used the current rate method all along.) The difference between this amount and the amount of net assets under the temporal method constitutes CM Corporation's beginning-of-period cumulative translation adjustment, as illustrated here.

Net assets, 12/31/10		FC 5,200
Multiplied by exchange rate as of 1/1/11 (FC1 = $.23)		X $0.23
Less: As reported stockholders' equity, 12/31/10 :		1,196
Capital stock	$340	
Retained earnings (per temporal method)	316	656
Cumulative translation adjustment, 1/1/10		$ 540

Given this information, the following steps yield a translation adjustment of $(276) for calendar 2011.

1. Net assets, 12/31/10			FC 5,200
Multiplied by change in current rate:			
Rate, 12/31/10	FC1 = $.23		
Rate, 12/31/11	FC1 = $.18	X $(.05)	$(260)
2. Change in net assets during year (net income less dividends)		FC 400	
Multiplied by difference between average and year-end rate:			
Average rate	FC1 = $.22		
Year-end rate	FC1 = $.18	X $(.04)	$ (16)
Total			$(276)

The final cumulative translation adjustment for 2011 of $264 is reached by adding the $(276) translation adjustment for 2011 to the beginning balance of $540.

Temporal Method

Exhibit 6-13 illustrates the FAS No. 52 remeasurement process when the dollar is the functional currency.

EXHIBIT 6-13	**Temporal Method of Translation (U.S. Dollar is Functional Currency)**		
	Foreign Currency	**Exchange Rate**	**Dollar Equivalents**
Balance Sheet Accounts			
Assets			
Cash	FC 500	$.18	$ 90
Accounts receivable	1,000	.18	180
Inventories	1,500	.19	285
Fixed assets	8,000	.17	1,360
Total	FC 11,000		$1,915
Liabilities and Stockholders' Equity			
Accounts payable	FC 2,400	.18	$ 432
Long-term debt	3,000	.18	540
Capital stock	2,000	.17	340
Retained earnings	3,600	a	603
Translation adjustment	—	b	—
Total	FC 11,000		$1,915
Income Statement Accounts			
Sales	FC 10,000	.22	$2,200
Cost of sales	(5,950)	c	(1,366)
Depreciation	(1,000)	.17	(170)
Other expenses	(1,493)	.22	(328)
Aggregate exchange gain (loss)	—	d	206
Income taxes	467	.22	(103)
Net income	FC 1,090		$ 439
Retained earnings, 12/31/10	3,200		316
Dividends	(690)	.22	(152)
Retained earnings, 12/31/11	FC 3,600		$ 603

[a] See statement of income and retained earnings.

[b] Under the temporal method, translation adjustments ("gains and losses") appear directly in consolidated income as opposed to stockholders' equity.

[c] The dollar equivalent of cost of sales is derived by translating the components of cost of sales—namely, purchases or cost of production plus beginning and ending inventories by appropriate exchange rates as follows:

Beginning inventories	FC 1,200 at $.23 = $ 276
Purchases	FC 6,250 at $.22 = $1,375
Cost of goods available for sale	$1,651
Ending inventories	FC 1,500 at $.19 = $ 285
Cost of sales	$1,366

[d] The aggregate exchange gain or loss figure combines both transaction and translation gains and losses.

In contrast to the current rate method, the temporal method translates foreign currency balances using historical as well as current exchange rates. Calculation of the exchange adjustment, which aggregates both transaction and translation gains and losses, also differs. In this example, the first component of the translation adjustment is found by multiplying the beginning net monetary asset position by the change in the current rate during the year. Thus:

> (12/31/10 Monetary assets
> − monetary liabilities)
> × change in current rate
> = (FC1,600 − FC6,600)
> × ($.18 − $.23)
> = $250

The second component is found by first identifying the variables (i.e., sources and uses of monetary items) that caused the foreign subsidiary's net monetary asset position (exposure) to change, and then multiplying these items by the difference between the year-end exchange rate and the rates that pertain to them. This is illustrated here.

Change in net monetary asset position:

12/31/10	FC (5,000)
12/31/11	FC (3,900)
	FC 1,100

Composition of change:
Sources of monetary items multiplied by difference between year-end and average rate:

Net income	FC 1,090
Depreciation	FC 1,000

$$2,090 \times (.18 - .22) = \$ (84)$$

Uses of monetary items multiplied by the difference between the year-end and average rate:

Increase in inventories	FC 300
Dividends	FC 690

$$900 \times (.18 - .22) = \$40$$

The aggregate exchange adjustment is the sum of any transaction gain or loss together with the individual translation components derived, that is, $250 + ($84) + $40 = $206.

Discussion Questions

1. What is the difference between the spot, forward, and swap markets? Illustrate each description with an example.
2. What do current, historical, and average exchange rates mean in the context of foreign currency translation? Which of these rates give rise to translation gains and losses? Which do not?
3. A foreign currency transaction can be denominated in one currency, yet measured in another. Explain the difference between these two terms using the case of a Canadian dollar borrowing on the part of a Mexican affiliate of a U.S. parent company that designates the U.S. dollar as the functional currency.
4. What is the difference between a transaction gain or loss and a translation gain or loss?
5. Briefly explain the nature of foreign currency translation as (a) a restatement process and (b) a remeasurement process.
6. Compare and contrast features of the major foreign currency translation methods introduced in this chapter. Which method do you think is best? Why?
7. Under what set of conditions would the temporal method of currency translation be appropriate . Under what set of conditions would the current rate method be appropriate?
8. What lessons, if any, can be learned from examining the history of foreign currency translation in the United States?

9. In what way is foreign currency translation tied to foreign inflation?

10. How does the treatment of translation gains and losses differ between the current and temporal translation methods under FAS No. 52, and what is the rationale for the differing accounting treatments?

Exercises

1. Assume that your Japanese affiliate reports sales revenue of 250,000,000 yen. Referring to Exhibit 6-1, translate this revenue figure to U.S. dollars using the direct bid spot rate. Do the same using the indirect spot quote.

2. On April 1, A. C. Corporation, a calendar-year U.S. electronics manufacturer, buys 32.5 million yen worth of computer chips from the Hidachi Company paying 10 percent down, the balance to be paid in 3 months. Interest at 8 percent per annum is payable on the unpaid foreign currency balance. The U.S. dollar/ Japanese yen exchange rate on April 1 was $1.00 = ¥93.6250; on July 1 it was $1.00 = ¥93.5283.

   Required: Prepare dated journal entries in U.S. dollars to record the incurrence and settlement of this foreign currency transaction assuming:
   a. A. C. Corporation adopts a single-transaction perspective, and
   b. it employs a two-transactions perspective.

3. On January 1, the wholly-owned Mexican affiliate of a Canadian parent company acquired an inventory of computer hard drives for its assembly operation. The cost incurred was 15,000,000 pesos when the exchange rate was MXN11.3 = C$1. By year-end, the Mexican affiliate had used three-fourths of the acquired hard drives. Due to advances in hardware technology, the remaining inventory was marked down to its net realizable value of MXN1,750,000. The year-end exchange rate was MXN12.3 = C$1. The average rate during the year was MXN11.8 = C$1.

   Required:
   a. Translate the ending inventory to Canadian dollars assuming the Mexican affiliate's functional currency is the Mexican peso.
   b. Would your answer change if the functional currency were the Canadian dollar? Please explain.

4. U.S. Multinational Corporation's subsidiary in Bangkok has on its books fixed assets valued at 7,500,000 baht. One-third of the assets were acquired two years ago when the exchange rate was THB40 = $1. The other fixed assets were acquired last year when the exchange rate was THB38 = $1. Each layer of fixed assets is being depreciated straight-line with an estimated useful life of 20 years. Relevant exchange rates for the current year are:

   Year-end rate: THB34 = $1
   Average rate: THB35 = $1

   Required:
   a. Calculate the Thai subsidiary's depreciation expense for the current year, assuming the baht is the functional currency.
   b. Repeat requirement a., assuming instead that the U.S. dollar is the functional currency.

5. Sydney Corporation, an Australian-based multinational, borrowed 10,000,000 euros from a German lender at the beginning of the calendar year when the exchange rate was EUR.60 = AUD1. Before repaying this one-year loan, Sydney Corporation learns that the Australian dollar has depreciated to EUR.55 = AUD1. It also discovers that its Frankfurt subsidiary has an exposed net asset position of EUR30,000,000, which will produce a translation gain upon consolidation. What is the exchange gain or loss that will be reported in consolidated income if
   a. The euro is the foreign operation's functional currency?
   b. The Australian dollar is the foreign operation's functional currency?

6. Shanghai Corporation, the Chinese affiliate of a U.S. manufacturer, has the balance sheet shown below. The current exchange rate is $.0.15 = CNY1.

Balance Sheet of Shanghai Corporation (000's)

Assets		Liabilities	
Cash	CNY 5,000	Accounts payable	CNY21,000
Accounts receivable	14,000	Long-term debt	27,000
Inventories[a] (cost = 24,000)	22,000		
Fixed assets, net	39,000	Stockholders' equity	32,000
Total assets	CNY80,000	Total liab & SE	CNY80,000

[a]*Inventories are carried at the lower of cost or market.*

Required:
a. Translate the Chinese dollar balance sheet of Shanghai Corporation into U.S. dollars at the current exchange rate of $.0.15 12 = CNY1. All monetary accounts in Shanhai's balance sheet are denominated in Chinese yuan.
b. Assume the Chinese yuan revalues from $0.15 = CNY1 to $0.1875 = CNY1. What would be the translation effect if Shanghai's balance sheet is translated by the current–noncurrent method? By the monetary–nonmonetary method?
c. Assume instead that the Chinese yuan weakens from $0.15 = CNY1 to $0.1125 = CNY1. What would be the translation effect under each of the two translation methods?

7. Use the information provided in Exercise 6.

Required:
a. What would be the translation effect if Shanghai Corporation's balance sheet were translated by the temporal method assuming the Chinese yuan appreciates by 25 percent? By the current rate method?
b. If the Chinese yuan depreciates by 25 percent, what would be the translation effects under each of the two methods in requirement a?
c. Based on your previous calculations and in Exercise 6, which translation method—current–noncurrent, monetary–nonmonetary, temporal, or current—gives statement readers the most meaningful information?

8. Company A is headquartered in Country A and reports in the currency unit of Country A, the Apeso. Company B is headquartered in Country B and reports in the currency unit of Country B, the Bol. Company A and B hold identical assets, Apeso100 and Bol100, at the beginning and end of the year. At the beginning of the year, the exchange rate is Apeso1 = Bol1.25. At the end of the year, the exchange rate is Apeso1 = Bol 2. No transactions occur during the year.

Required:
a. Calculate total assets reported by Company A and Company B at the beginning and at the end of the year. Which company has a gain and which has a loss for the year?
b. Does your answer to part a. make sense? Would it matter if Companies A and B intended to repatriate their respective foreign assets rather than keep them invested permanently abroad?
c. What is the lesson for statement readers from all of this? Is it all a shell game?

9. A 100 percent–owned foreign subsidiary's trial balance consists of the accounts listed as follows. Which exchange rate—current, historical, or average—would be used to translate these accounts to parent currency assuming that the foreign currency is the functional currency? Which rates would be used if the parent currency were the functional currency?

Trial Balance Accounts	
Cash	Common stock
Marketable securities (cost)	Premium on common stock
Accounts receivable	Retained earnings
Inventory (market)	Sales
Equipment	Purchases
Accumulated depreciation	Cost of sales
Prepaid expenses	General and administrative expenses
Goodwill	Selling expenses
Accounts payable	Depreciation
Due to parent (denominated in dollars)	Amortization of goodwill
Bonds payable	Income tax expense
Income taxes payable	Intercompany interest expense
Deferred income taxes	

10. On December 15, MSC Corporation acquires its first foreign affiliate by acquiring 100 percent of the net assets of the Armaselah Oil Company based in Saudi Arabia for 930,000,000 Saudi Arabian riyals.(SAR). At the time, the exchange rate was $1.00 = SAR3.750. The acquisition price is traceable to the following identifiable assets:

Cash	SAR 60,000,000
Inventory	120,000,000
Fixed assets	750,000,000

As a calendar-year company, MSC Corporation prepares consolidated financial statements every December 31. However, by the consolidation date, the Saudi Arabian riyal depreciates such that the new spot rate is $1.00 = SAR4.125.

Required:

a. Assuming no transactions took place before consolidation, what would be the translation gain or loss if Armaselah's balance sheet were translated to dollars by the temporal rate method?

b. How does the translation adjustment affect MSC's cash flows?

c. What adjustments to Armaselah's accounts would you make to enable you to compare its financial statements with another company of comparable size in the same industry that is employing the current rate translation method per IAS 21?

CASES

Case 6-1

Regents Corporation

Regents Corporation is a recently acquired U.S. manufacturing subsidiary located on the outskirts of London. Its products are marketed principally in the United Kingdom with sales invoiced in pounds and prices determined by local competitive conditions. Expenses (labor, materials, and other production costs) are mostly local, although a significant quantity of components is now imported from the U.S. parent. Financing is primarily in U.S. dollars provided by the parent.

Headquarters management must decide on the functional currency for its London operation: Should it be the U.S. dollar or the British pound? You are asked to advise management on the appropriate currency designation and its relative financial statement effects. Prepare a report that supports your recommendations and identify any policy issues your analysis uncovers.

Exhibit 6-14 presents comparative balance sheets for Regents Corporation at December 31, 2010 and 2011 , and a statement of income for the year ended December 31, 2011 . The statements conform with U.S. generally accepted accounting principles prior to translation to dollars.

EXHIBIT 6-14 Regents Corporation Financial Statements		
Balance Sheet	**12/31/10**	**12/31/11**
Assets		
Cash	£ 1,060	£ 1,150
Accounts receivable	2,890	3,100
Inventory (FIFO)	3,040	3,430
Fixed assets	4,400	4,900
Accumulated depreciation	(420)	(720)
Intangible asset (patent)		70
Total	£10,970	£11,930
Liabilities and Stockholders' Equity		
Accounts payable	£ 1,610	£ 1,385
Due to parent	1,800	1,310
Long-term debt	4,500	4,000
Deferred taxes	80	120
Common stock	1,500	1,500
Retained earnings	1,480	3,615
Total	£10,970	£11,930

(continued)

EXHIBIT 6-14	Regents Corporation Financial Statements (Continued)		
Balance Sheet		**12/31/10**	**12/31/11**
Income Statement Year Ended 12/31/11			
Sales			£16,700
Expenses			
Cost of sales		£11,300	
General and administrative		1,600	
Depreciation		300	
Interest		480	13,680
Operating income			£ 3,020
Transaction gain (loss)			125
Income before taxes			£ 3,145
Income taxes Current		£ 670	
Deferred		40	710
Net income			£ 2,435
Retained earnings at 12/31/10 (residual)			1,480
			3,915
Dividends			300
Retained earnings at 12/31/11			£ 3,615

Exchange rate information and additional data:

1. Exchange rates:

    December 31, 2010 $1.80 = £1
    December 31, 2011 $1.90 = £1
    Average during 2011 $1.86 = £1
    Average during fourth quarter 2010 $1.78 = £1
    Average during fourth quarter 2011 $1.88 = £1

2. Common stock was acquired, long-term debt issued, and original fixed assets purchased when the exchange rate was $1.70 = £1.

3. Due to parent account is denominated in U.S. dollars.

4. Exchange rate prevailing when the intangible asset (patent) was acquired and additional fixed assets purchased was $1.82 = £1.

5. Purchases and dividends occurred evenly during 2011.

6. Of the £300 depreciation expense for 2011 , £20 relates to fixed assets purchased during 2011.

7. Deferred taxes are translated at the current rate.

8. Inventory represents approximately three months of production.

Case 6-2

Managing Offshore Investments: Whose Currency?

The Offshore Investment Fund (OIF) was incorporated in Fairfield, Connecticut, for the sole purpose of allowing U.S. shareholders to invest in Spanish securities. The fund is listed on the New York Stock Exchange. The fund custodian is the Shady Rest Bank and Trust Company of Connecticut ("Shady Rest"), which keeps the fund's accounts. The question of which currency to use in keeping the fund's books arose at once. Shady Rest prepared the fund's books in euros, since the fund was a country fund that invested solely in securities listed on the Madrid Stock Exchange. Subsequently, the fund's auditors stated that, in their opinion, the functional currency should be the U.S. dollar. This case is based on an actual occurrence. Names and country of origin have been changed to ensure anonymity.

Effects of the Decision

The decision to possibly adopt the U.S. dollar as the functional currency for the fund created considerable managerial headaches. For one thing, the work of rewriting and reworking the accounting transactions was a monumental task that delayed the publication of the annual accounts. The concept of the functional currency was a foreign concept in Spain, and the effects of the functional currency choice were not made clear to the managers. Consequently, they continued to manage the fund until late in November without appreciating the impact the currency choice had on the fund's results.

Additional difficulties caused by the functional currency choice were:

a. Shady Rest, with some $300 billion in various funds under management, still had not developed an adequate multicurrency accounting system. Whereas accounting for a security acquisition would normally be recorded in a simple bookkeeping entry, three entries were now required. In addition, payment for the purchase itself could impact the income statement in the current period.

b. More serious problems related to day-to-day operations. When a transaction was initiated, the fund manager had no idea of its ultimate financial effect. As an example, during the first year of operations, the Fund manager was certain that his portfolio sales had generated a profit of more than $1 million. When the sales finally showed up in the accounts, the transaction gain was offset by currency losses of some $7 million!

Reasons Given for Choosing the Dollar as Functional

The auditors gave the following reasons for choosing the dollar as the fund's functional currency:

a. Incorporation in the United States
b. Funded with U.S. shareholder capital
c. Dividends determined and paid in U.S. dollars
d. Financial reporting under U.S. GAAP and in U.S. dollars
e. Administration and advisory fees calculated on U.S. net assets and paid in U.S. dollars

f. Most expenses incurred and paid in U.S. dollars

g. Accounting records kept in U.S. dollars

h. Subject to U.S. tax, SEC, and 1940 Exchange Act regulations

Since the fund was set up to invest in Spain, it is assumed that U.S. shareholders are interested in the impact of an exchange rate change on the fund's cash flows and equity; that is, the shareholders do not invest in Spanish securities only because of attractive yields, but also are making a currency play that directly affects the measurement of cash flow and equity.

Management's Viewpoint

Management disagreed with the auditors. Following is its rebuttal:

a. Incorporation in the United States with U.S. shareholders. FAS 52 clearly states that the functional currency should be determined by "the primary economic environment in which that entity operates rather than by the technical detail of incorporation." Similarly, nowhere does FAS 52 state that the facts that the company has U.S. shareholders and pays dividends in U.S. dollars are relevant. In fact, FAS 52 concerns itself throughout with the firm and its management rather than its shareholders.

b. Financial reporting in U.S. dollars under U.S. GAAP. The auditors fail to differentiate between reporting currency and functional currency. It is clear that the U.S. dollar should be the reporting currency, but that alone does not mean that the U.S. dollar is the functional currency.

c. Payment of certain expenses in dollars. The payment of expenses in U.S. dollars is no reason to make the dollar the functional currency. While expenses of some $8 million for calendar year 2010 were incurred in U.S. dollars, income of over $100 million was earned in euros.

d. U.S. tax and SEC regulations. These considerations are relevant for the reporting currency, not the functional currency.

The decisive argument against identifying the dollar as the functional currency is that doing so does not provide information that is, in the words of FAS 52, "generally compatible with the expected economic effect of a rate change on an enterprise's cash flow and equity." Specifically, the operating cash flow of the Fund is located entirely in Spain once the initial transfer of funds raised by the issue of capital is made. The Fund buys and sells investments in Spain, and receives all its income from Spain. If the functional currency is euros, then realized currency fluctuations are recognized only when money is repatriated to the United States. The present practice of "realizing" an exchange profit or loss when, for example, cash in Spain is exchanged for an investment purchased in Spain is wrong and misleading.

Consider an example. Suppose that the fund deposits EUR100,000,000 in a Spanish bank when the exchange rate is EUR1 = $1.4090. One month later, when the exchange rate is EUR1 = $1.3988, the fund purchases and pays for an investment of EUR100,000,000, which it sells for cash on the same day, having decided the investment was unwise. Ignoring transaction costs, the fund has EUR100,000,000 in cash in Madrid at both the beginning and the end of the week. If the functional currency is euros, there is no realized gain or loss. However, translation to dollars generates an unrealized currency loss of $1,020,000 , which would be realized only when the amount in question is repatriated to the United States. This is analogous to the purchase of a stock whose price later falls. If the U.S. dollar is the functional currency, the transaction in question would result in a realized loss on exchange of $1,020,000. This result is absurd in terms of any commonsense view of cash flow; indeed, it highlights that, given the fund's purpose, the effect on the reporting of income of adopting the U.S. dollar as the functional currency is equally absurd.

The net asset value of the fund is determined each week in U.S. dollars, and reported to stockholders in U.S. dollars. This is entirely consistent with having the U.S. dollar as the appropriate reporting currency. Using the dollar as the functional currency implies that there is a realistic and practical option on each transaction of moving between the dollar and the euro. This assumption is patently wrong; the fund will only repatriate its base capital under two circumstances: (1) liquidation or (2) as a temporary expedient if Spanish yields fall below U.S. yields.

General Thrust of FAS 52

The language of FAS 52 indicates that its authors did not write it with direct reference to a situation such as that of the Offshore Investment Fund, that is, a company that raises money for the single purpose of investing it in a foreign country. FAS 52 seems rather to be written from the viewpoint of an operating holding company owning a separate, distinct foreign operating subsidiary.

FAS 52 defines the functional currency of an entity as the currency of the primary economic environment in which that entity operates. Had the fund been incorporated in Malta and, as a separate entity, borrowed the funds from its U.S. parent, use of the local currency would have been automatic. If substance is to prevail over form, one must conclude that the euro should still be used.

Paragraph 6 of FAS 52 states, "for an entity with operations that are relatively self-contained and integrated within a particular country, the functional currency generally would be the currency of that country." This statement reinforces the operational aspect that governs the choice of the functional currency; it is surely wrong to argue that the operations of the fund are conducted anywhere but in Spain.

Paragraph 8 reinforces the contention that "management's judgment will be required to determine the functional currency in which financial results and relationships are measured with the greatest degree of relevance and reliability."

Finally, paragraphs 80 and 81 draw a very clear distinction that reinforces our (management's) contention. Paragraph 80 reads:

In the first class are foreign operations that are relatively self-contained and integrated within a particular country or economic environment. The day-to-day operations are not dependent upon the economic environment of the parent's functional currency; the foreign operation primarily generates and expends foreign currency. The foreign currency net cash flows that it generates may be reinvested and converted and distributed to the parent. For this class, the foreign currency is the functional currency.

This definition should be contrasted with paragraph 81, which states:

In the second class . . . the day-to-day operations are dependent on the economic environment of the parent's currency, and the changes in the foreign entity's individual assets and liabilities impact directly on the cash flows of the parent company in the parent's currency. For this class, the U.S. dollar is the functional currency.

Since the purpose of single-country funds is to create entities of the first rather than the second class, paragraph 80 precisely describes the operations of the Overseas Investment Fund.

Required

1. Based on the arguments presented, what do you think should be the functional currency in this case?

CHAPTER 7

Financial Reporting and Changing Prices

Fluctuating currencies and changes in money prices of goods and services are integral features of international business. Chapter 6 focused on the former. This chapter dwells on the financial statement effects of changing prices.

The global economy is presently experiencing one of its most serious economic downturns since the 1930s. During times such as these, national governments are often tempted to adopt expansive fiscal stimulus and monetary measures designed to lift their economies out of recession. Disproportionate stimulus measures, however, are sure to stoke the flames of inflation as too much stimulus money chases the same goods and labor. It is too early to tell what path governments, affected by the current recession, will follow or how soon economic recovery will manifest itself. Recent reports, however, suggest that inflation worries are heating up.[1] Developing economies, some of which fought serious battles to tame inflation in the 1980s and 1990s, are especially worrisome. In several large emerging markets, such as India, Indonesia, the Philippines, Russia, Turkey, and South Africa, double digit inflation has already arrived. Given the distortive effects of changing prices on financial statements and their interpretation, it is important that financial statement readers understand what these effects are and how to cope with this reporting conundrum.

Grupo Modello S.A., the largest manufacturer of Corona beer in Mexico, operates in an environment where changing prices have been nontrivial in the recent past. To see how price changes have been reflected in the company's published accounts, examine Exhibit 7-1, which contains selected excerpts from Grupo Modello S.A.'s financial statements and related notes.[2]

---

[1] Mark Whitehouse, "Inflation is Tempting to Indebted Nations," *Wall Street Journal*, March 30, 2009.
[2] As the cumulative rate of inflation in Mexico no longer exceeds 28 percent, the country has discontinued for the moment, mandated inflation adjusted accounting.

EXHIBIT 7-1   **Selected Excerpts from Grupo Modelo's Financial Accounts**

Grupo Modelo S.A. de C.V. and Subsidiaries

Consolidated Income Statements
For the years ended December 31, 2007 and 2006
(Amounts expressed in thousands of pesos of December 31, 2007 purchasing power

	2007	**2006**
Operating profit	MXP20,587,851	MXP16,860,640
Other (expenses), net	(466,444)	(605,676)
Comprehensive financing income:		
Interest earned, net	1,442,608	1,287,970
Exchange profit(loss), net	87,591	115,807
Loss on monetary position	(868,786)	(958,700)
	661,413	445,077
Profit before provisions	20,782,820	16,700,041
Provisions for (Note 12)		
Income, asset and flat rate corporate		
tax 5,513,9814,962,626		
Consolidated net income for the year	MXP15,268,8395	MXP11,737,415

Consolidated Balance Sheets

As of December 31, 2007 and 2006 (Notes 1, 2, and 15)
(Amounts in thousands of pesos of December 31, 2007 purchasing power)

Assets	**2007**	**2006**
Current		
Cash and marketable securities	MXP20,716,601	MXP22,923,116
Accounts and notes receivable (Note 3)	5,413,848	3,724,554
Inventories (Note 4)	9,504,555	6,961,732
Prepaid expenses and other current items	2,632,200	2,213,179
Total current assets	38,267,204	35,822,581
Long-term accounts and notes receivable (Note 3)	1,724,593	1,437,690
Investment in shares of associated companies (Note 5)	4,177,386	3,360,961
Property, plant and equipment (Note 6)	79,031,553	76,171,558
Accumulated depreciation	(26,721,013)	(25,126,654)
Other assets (Note 7)	3,244,524	2,491,059
Total assets	MXP99,724,247	MXP94,157,195
Total liabilities	MXP17,712,993	MXP14,795,092
Stockholders' equity		
Common stock (Note 10)	16,377,411	16,377,411
Premium on share subscription	1,090,698	1,090,698
Earned surplus (Notes 11 and 12):		
Legal reserve	3,213,558	2,767,938
Reserve for acquisition of own shares	242,596	688,923

(continued)

Assets	2007	2006
Retained earnings	39,622,514	38,022,111
Net income	9,503,111	8,997,526
	52,581,779	50,476,498
Accumulated effect of deferred tax	(5,472,843)	(5,472,843)
Adjustment to capital for retirement obligations	(464,807)	(430,181)
Deficit in the restatement of stockholders' equity	(1,051,534)	(1,044,944)
Total majority stockholders' equity	MXP63,060,704	MXP60,966,640

Notes to the Consolidated Financial Statements

As of December 31, 2007 and 2006 (Amounts in thousands of pesos of December 31, 2007 purchasing power)

2. Accounting policies—The Group accounting policies used in preparing these consolidated financial statements comply with the requirements for reasonable presentation set forth by Mexican Financial Information Standards (NIF) and are expressed in pesos of December 31, 2007 purchasing power through application of National Consumer Price Index (NCPI) factors. Those standards require that the Group's Management make certain estimates and assumptions in determining the valuation of some items included in the consolidated financial statements.

Following is a summary of the most significant accounting policies, methods and criteria for recognizing the effects of inflation on the financial information:

d) Inventories and cost of sales—This item is originally recorded through the last-in first-out method and is subsequently restated to replacement cost. Values thus determined do not exceed market value.

f) Property, plant and equipment—These items are recorded at acquisition cost, restated by applying inflation factors derived from the NCPI according to the antiquity of the expenditure.

h) Depreciation—This item is calculated based on the restated values of property, plant and equipment, based on the probable useful life as determined by independent appraisers and the technical department of the group. Annual depreciation rates are shown in Note 6.

n) Stockholders' equity—The capital stock, legal reserve, contributions for future capital increases, and retained earnings represent the value of those items in terms of December 31, 2007 purchasing power and are restated by applying NCPI factors to historical amounts.

Deficit in the restatement of stockholders' equity—The balance of this account represents the sum of the items "Cumulative gain or loss from holding non-monetary assets" and "Cumulative monetary gain or loss," described below:

Cumulative gains or loss from holding non-monetary assets—This item represents the cumulative change in the value of non-monetary assets due to causes other than inflation. It is determined only when the specific cost method is used, since those costs are compared to restatements determined using the NCPI. If the specific costs are higher than the indexes, there is a gain from holding non-monetary assets; otherwise, there is a loss.

Cumulative monetary gain or loss—This item is the net effect arising on the initial restatement of the financial statement figures.

o) Gains or loss on monetary position—This account represents the effect of inflation on monetary assets and liabilities, even when they continue to have the same nominal value. When monetary assets exceed monetary liabilities, a monetary loss is generated, since assets maintain their nominal value, they lose purchasing power. When liabilities are greater, a profit arises, since they are settled with money of lower purchasing power. These effects are charged or credited to the income statement and form part of comprehensive financing income.

6. Property, Plant, and Equipment—Net

a) The balance of this account is made up as follows:

		2007		2006
Item	Net historical cost	Net restatement	Net total value	Net total value
Land	MXP 1,620,065	MXP 3,236,266	MXP 4,856,331	MXP5,032,597
Machinery and equipment	14,301,114	7,947,178	22,248,292	23,051,551
Transportation equipment	2,522,857	344,500	2,867,357	3,103,914
Building and other structures	6,875,008	6,730,890	13,605,898	14,543,722
Computer equipment	506,973	41,263	548,236	584,053
Furniture and other equipment	1,646,293	91,438	1,737,731	476,486
Antipollution equipment	538,773	317,032	855,805	902,937
Construction in progress	5,378,716	212,174	5,590,890	3,349,644
	MXP33,389,799	MXP18,920,741	MXP52,310,540	MXP51,044,904

A quick scan of Modello's income statement reveals an account labeled "Comprehensive Financing Income." Two of its components should be familiar to you. The first relates to interest on the firm's receivables and payables. The second, discussed in Chapter 6, is the translation gains or losses resulting from the currency translation process. The third component, "Loss from monetary position," is probably new to you and stems from Modello's attempts to reflect the effects of changing prices on its financial accounts. But what does this figure mean, and how is it derived?

Grupo Modello's balance sheet also introduces financial statement items that are unfamiliar to most statement readers. The first relates to its fixed assets. Footnote 6 suggests that the 2007 balance of MXP52,310,540 for Property, Plant, and Equipment, net of accumulated depreciation, consists of two components: one labeled "Net historical cost," the other, "Net restatement." While the former may be a familiar term, the latter probably is not. Another novel balance sheet account appears in Stockholders' Equity, labeled "Deficit in the Restatement of Stockholders' Equity."

Finally, the first paragraph of its accounting policy description states that all figures disclosed in Modello's comparative statements, and the notes thereto, are expressed in December 2007 purchasing power. What does "December 2007 purchasing power" mean, and what is its rationale? And, more important, do statement readers actually impound the foregoing information in their security pricing and managerial decisions?

Subsequent sections of this chapter are devoted to answering these and related questions. The managerial implications of changing prices are covered in Chapter 10. To make informed decisions, financial analysts must understand the contents of financial accounts that have been adjusted for changing prices. This is especially germane for those interested in emerging markets. Informed analysts must also have some facility for adjusting accounts for changing prices in those instances where (1) companies choose not to account for inflation or

(2) have recently stopped producing inflation-adjusted numbers so as to facilitate apple-to-apple comparisons over time and/or with companies that do. The International Accounting Standards Board's IAS 29 currently mandates that companies inflation adjust their accounts when the cumulative rate of inflation for the preceding three years exceeds 100 percent. Accordingly, companies subscribing to IASB standards (see Chapter 8) will stop adjusting their accounts for inflation when the inflation rate is less than this threshold and resume inflation accounting when annual inlfation rates exceed this benchmark.

Depreciation for the year amounted to MXP3,120,777 (MXP2,897,764 in 2006).

CHANGING PRICES DEFINED

To understand what *changing prices* means, we must distinguish between general and specific price movements, both of which are embraced by the term. A *general price level* change occurs when, on average, the prices of all goods and services in an economy change. The monetary unit gains or loses purchasing power. An overall increase in prices is called *inflation*; a decrease, *deflation*. What causes inflation? Evidence suggests that aggressive monetary and fiscal policies designed to achieve high economic growth targets, excessive spending associated with national elections, and the international transmission of inflation are causal explanations.[3] The issue, however, is complex.

A *specific price* change, on the other hand, refers to a change in the price of a specific good or service caused by changes in demand and supply. Thus, the annual rate of inflation in a country may average 5 percent, while the specific price of one-bedroom apartments may rise by 50 percent during the same period. Exhibit 7-2 defines additional terminology used in this chapter.

EXHIBIT 7-2   **Glossary of Inflation Accounting Terms**

attribute. The quantifiable characteristic of an item that is measured for accounting purposes. For example, historical cost and replacement cost are attributes of an asset.

current-cost adjustments. Adjusting asset values for changes in specific prices.

disposable wealth. The amount of a firm's net assets that could be withdrawn without reducing its beginning level of net assets.

gearing adjustment. The benefit to shareholders' purchasing power gain from debt financing and signals that the firm need not recognize the additional replacement cost of operating assets to the extent they are financed by debt. The U.S. expression for gearing is *leverage.*

general purchasing power equivalents. Currency amounts that have been adjusted for changes in the general level of prices.

general purchasing gains and losses. See **monetary gains and losses**.

historical cost-constant currency. See **general purchasing power equivalents**.

holding gain. Increase in the current cost of a nonmonetary asset.

hyperinflation. An excessive rate of inflation, as when the general level of prices in an economy increases by more than 25 percent per annum.

inflation. Increase in the general level of prices of all goods and services in an economy.

---

[3] John F. Boschen and Charles L. Weise, "What Starts Inflation: Evidence from the OECD Countries," *Journal of Money, Credit and Banking* 35 (June 2003): 323.

monetary asset. A claim to a fixed amount of currency in the future, like cash or accounts receivable.

monetary gains. Increases in general purchasing power that occur when monetary liabilities are held during a period of inflation.

monetary liability. An obligation to pay a fixed amount of currency in the future, such as an account payable or debt that bears a fixed rate of interest.

monetary losses. Decreases in general purchasing power that occur when monetary assets are held during a period of inflation.

monetary working capital adjustment. The effect of specific price changes on the total amount of working capital used by the business in its operation.

nominal amounts. Currency amounts that have not been adjusted for changing prices.

nonmonetary asset. An asset that does not represent a fixed claim to cash, such as inventory or plant and equipment.

nonmonetary liability. A debt that does not require the payment of a fixed sum of cash in the future, such as a customer advance. Here the obligation is to provide the customer a good or service whose value may change because of inflation.

parity adjustment. An adjustment that reflects the difference in inflation between the parent and host countries.

permanent assets. A Brazilian term for fixed assets, buildings, investments, deferred charges and their respective depreciation, and depletion or amortization amounts.

price index. A cost ratio where the numerator is the cost of a representative "basket" of goods and services in the current year and the denominator is the cost of the same basket of goods and services in a benchmark year.

purchasing power. The general ability of a monetary unit to command goods and services.

real profit. Net income that has been adjusted for changing prices.

replacement cost. The current cost of replacing the service potential of an asset in the normal course of business.

reporting currency. The currency in which an entity prepares its financial statements.

restate-translate method. Used when a parent company consolidates the accounts of a foreign subsidiary located in an inflationary environment. With this method, the subsidiary's accounts are first restated for local inflation and then translated to the parent currency.

specific price change. The change in the price of a specific commodity, such as inventory or equipment.

translate-restate method. A consolidation method that first translates a foreign subsidiary's accounts to parent currency and then restates the translated amounts for parent-country inflation.

As consumers, we are well aware of inflation's effects on our material standard of living. We immediately feel its impact in our pocketbooks when the price of oil or our favorite fast-food selection increases. The social and political devastation resulting from bouts of *hyperinflation* (e.g., when the inflation rate soars by more than 50 percent per month) can be extreme. Consider the following commentary offered by Steve H. Hanke, former economic adviser to the president and state counselor of the Republic of Montenegro.

> Voters in Montenegro recently turned out in record numbers to denounce their republic's loose union with Serbia. This action followed a bizarre history of monetary policy that wreaked havoc with people's lives. Following a 20-year period of double-digit inflation (annualized rates averaging 75%), the

Serbian Parliament, controlled by Slobodan Milosevic, secretely ordered the Serbian National Bank (a regional central bank) to issue $1.4 billion in credits to Milosevic's friends and political allies. This illegal move doubled the quantity of money the National Bank of Yugoslavia had planned to create and fanned the flames of inflation. Beginning in 1992, Yugoslavia experienced one of the highest and longest periods of hyperinflation in history. When it peaked in 1994, prices had increased by 313,000,000% in one month! There were a total of 14 maxi-devaluations during the hyperinflation, completely wiping out the Yugoslav dinar's value. To appreciate the impact of this hyperinflation on the local population, first, assume you had the equivalent of $10,000 in the bank, next, move the decimal point of the dollar 22 places to the left, and finally, try to buy something to eat. Little wonder why stable prices are a national priority for much of the world. Businesses also feel inflation's effects when the prices of their factor inputs rise.[4]

While changing prices occur worldwide, their business and financial reporting effects vary from country to country. Europe and North America, for instance, have enjoyed relatively modest general price-level increases, averaging less than 3 percent per year during the last decade. By contrast, Eastern Europe, Latin America, and Africa have experienced much higher inflation rates. Annual rates of inflation have been as high as 106 percent in Turkey, 2,076 percent in Brazil, and, most recently, 231,000,000 percent in Zimbabwe![5]

Local inflation affects the exchange rates used to translate foreign currency balances to their domestic currency equivalents. As we shall see, it is hard to separate foreign currency translation from inflation when accounting for foreign operations.

WHY ARE FINANCIAL STATEMENTS POTENTIALLY MISLEADING DURING PERIODS OF CHANGING PRICES?

During a period of inflation, asset values recorded at their original acquisition costs seldom reflect the assets' current (higher) value. Understated asset values result in understated expenses and overstated income. From a managerial perspective, these measurement inaccuracies distort (1) financial projections based on unadjusted historical time series data, (2) budgets against which results are measured, and (3) performance data that fail to isolate the uncontrollable effects of inflation. Overstated earnings may, in turn, lead to:

- Increases in proportionate taxation
- Requests by shareholders for more dividends
- Demands for higher wages by workers
- Disadvantageous actions by host governments (e.g., imposition of excess profit taxes)

Should a firm distribute all of its overstated earnings (in the form of higher taxes, dividends, wages, and the like), it may not keep enough resources to replace specific assets whose prices have risen, such as inventories and plant and equipment.

---

[4] Steve H. Hanke, "Inflation Nation," *Wall Street Journal*, May 24, 2006, p. A14.
[5] Chris McGreal, "Zimbabwe's Inflation Rate Surges to 231,000,000%," guardian.co.uk, October 9, 2008.

Failure to adjust corporate financial data for changes in the purchasing power of the monetary unit also makes it hard for financial statement readers to interpret and compare reported operating performances of companies. In an inflationary period, revenues are typically expressed in currency with a lower general purchasing power (i.e., purchasing power of the current period) than applies to the related expenses. Expenses are expressed in currency with a higher general purchasing power because typically they reflect the consumption of resources that were acquired a while back (e.g., depreciating a factory purchased ten years ago) when the monetary unit had more purchasing power. Subtracting expenses based on historical purchasing power from revenues based on current purchasing power results in an inaccurate measure of income.

Conventional accounting procedures also ignore purchasing power gains and losses that arise from holding cash (or equivalents) during an inflationary period. If you held cash during a year in which the inflation rate was 100 percent, it would take twice as much cash at the end of the year to have the same purchasing power as your original cash balance. This further distorts business-performance comparisons for financial statement readers.

Therefore, it is useful to recognize inflation's effects explicitly for several reasons:

1. The effects of changing prices depend partially on the transactions and circumstances of the enterprise. Users do not have detailed information about these factors.
2. Managing the problems caused by changing prices depends on an accurate understanding of the problems. An accurate understanding requires that business performance be reported in terms that allow for the effects of changing prices.
3. Statements by managers about the problems caused by changing prices are easier to believe when businesses publish financial information that addresses the problems.[6]

Even when inflation rates slow, accounting for changing prices is useful because the cumulative effect of low inflation over time can be significant. As examples, the cumulative inflation rate during the last ten years was approximately 22 percent in highly industrialized countries like the Eurozone, Japan, the United Kingdom, and the United States, approximately 61 percent for emerging economies in Asia, 575 percent for Latin America, and 804 percent for Central and Eastern Europe.[7] The distorting effects of prior inflation can persist for many years, given the long lives of many assets. And, as mentioned earlier, specific price changes may be significant even when the gen()eral price level does not change much.

TYPES OF INFLATION ADJUSTMENTS

Statistical series that measure changes in both general and specific prices do not generally move in parallel.[8] Each type of price change has a different effect on measures of a firm's financial position and operating performance and is accounted for with different

---

[6] Financial Accounting Standards Board, *Financial Reporting and Changing Prices: Statement of Financial Accounting Standards No. 33* (Stamford, CT: FASB, September 1979).
[7] Bank for International Settlements 76th Annual Report (June 2006).
[8] Carlos Dabus, "Inflationary Regimes and Relative Price Variability: Evidence from Argentina," *Journal of Development Economics* 62 (2000): 535–547.

objectives in mind. Hereinafter, accounting for the financial statement effects of general price-level changes is called the *historical cost-constant purchasing power* model. Accounting for specific price changes is referred to as the *current-cost* model.

GENERAL PRICE-LEVEL ADJUSTMENTS

Currency amounts adjusted for general price-level (purchasing power) changes are called *historical cost-constant currency* or *general purchasing power equivalents*. Currency amounts that have not been so adjusted are called *nominal* amounts. For example, during a period of rising prices, a long-lived asset that is on the balance sheet at its original acquisition cost is expressed in nominal currency. When its historical cost is allocated to the current period's income (in the form of depreciation expense), revenues, which reflect current purchasing power, are matched with costs that reflect the (higher) purchasing power of the earlier period when the asset was bought. Therefore, nominal amounts must be adjusted for changes in the general purchasing power of money to match them appropriately with current transactions.

Price Indexes

General price-level changes are measured by a price-level index of the form $\Sigma p_1 q_1 / \Sigma p_0 q_0$, where $p =$ the price of a given commodity and $q =$ quantity consumed. A price index is a cost ratio. For example, if a family of four spends $20,000 to buy a representative basket of goods and services at the end of year 1 (the base year = start of year 2) and $22,000 to buy the same basket a year later (start of year 3), the year-end price index for year 2 is $22,000/$20,000, or 1.100. This figure implies a 10 percent rate of inflation during year 2. Similarly, if the basket in question costs our family of four $23,500 two years later (end of year 3), the general price-level index would be $23,500/$20,000, or 1.175, implying 17.5 percent inflation since the base year. The index for the base year is $20,000/$20,000, or 1.000.

Use of Price Indexes

Price index numbers are used to translate sums of money paid in past periods to their end-of-period purchasing power equivalents (i.e., historical cost-constant purchasing power). The method used is as follows:

$$\text{GPL}_c / \text{GPL}_{td} \times \text{Nominal amount}_{td} = \text{PPE}_c$$

where

GPL = general price index

c   = current period

td   = transaction date

PPE = general purchasing power equivalent

For example, suppose that $500 is spent at the end of the base year, and $700 one year later. To restate these expenditures at their year 3 purchasing power equivalents, using price index numbers from our example, we would do the following:

		Year 3	
End of:	**Nominal Expenditure**	**Adjustment Factor**	**Purchasing Power Equivalent**
Year 1	$500	1.175/1.000	$587.50
Year 2	$700	1.175/1.100	$747.73

It would take $587.50 at the end of year 3 to buy (in general) what $500 would have bought at the end of year 1. Similarly, it would take $747.73 at the end of year 3 to buy (in general) what $700 would have bought a year earlier. Alternatively, during a period of inflation, the nominal expenditures of $500 at the end of year 1, and $700 a year later, are not comparable unless they are expressed in terms of a common denominator, which is year 3 general purchasing power equivalents. This is why Grupo Modello, cited earlier in the chapter, restates all of its trend data to December 31, 2007, purchasing power.

Price-level adjusted figures do not represent the current cost of the items in question; they are still historical cost numbers. The historical cost numbers are merely restated in a new unit of measure: general purchasing power at the end of the period. When transactions occur uniformly throughout a period (such as revenues from the sale of goods or services), a shortcut price-level adjustment can be used. In expressing revenues as end-of-period purchasing power equivalents rather than price-level adjusting each day's revenues (365 calculations!), one could multiply total annual revenues by the ratio of the year-end index to the average general price-level index (such as a monthly weighted average) for the year. Thus:

$$GPL_c/GPL_{avg} \times Total\ revenues = PPE_c$$

Object of General Price-Level Adjustments

Let us briefly review the conventional notion of enterprise income. Traditionally, income (disposable wealth) is that portion of a firm's wealth (i.e., net assets) that the firm can withdraw during an accounting period without reducing its wealth beneath its original level. Assuming no additional owner investments or withdrawals during the period, if a firm's beginning net assets were 10,000 Russian rubles and its ending net assets increased to RUB25,000 due to profitable operations, its income would be RUB15,000. If it paid a dividend of RUB15,000, the firm's end-of-period wealth would be exactly what it was at the beginning. Hence, conventional accounting measures income as the maximum amount that can be withdrawn from the firm without reducing its original money capital.

If we cannot assume stable prices, the conventional measure of income may not accurately measure a firm's disposable wealth. Assume that the general price level rises by 21 percent during a year. To keep up with inflation, a firm that begins the year with RUB10,000 would want its original investment to grow to at least RUB12,100, because it would take that much at year's end to buy what RUB10,000 would have bought at the beginning. Suppose that, using conventional accounting, the firm earns RUB15,000 (after tax). Withdrawing RUB15,000 would reduce the firm's nominal end-of-period wealth to the original RUB10,000. But this is less than it needs to keep up with inflation (RUB12,100). The historical cost-constant purchasing power model takes this discrepancy into account by measuring income so that the firm could pay out its entire income as dividends while having as much purchasing power at the end of the period as at the beginning.

As another illustration, suppose that an Argentine merchandiser begins the calendar year with ARS100,000 in cash (no debt), which is immediately converted into salable inventory (e.g., 10,000 compact discs of an Argentinian rock star at a unit cost of 10 pesos). The firm sells the entire inventory uniformly during the year at a 50 percent markup. Assuming no inflation, enterprise income would be ARS50,000, the difference between ending and beginning net assets ($150,000 – $100,000), or as revenue minus expenses (cost of CDs sold). Withdrawal of ARS50,000 would leave the firm with ARS100,000, as much money capital as at the start of the year, maintaining its original investment.

Suppose instead that the period had a 21 percent inflation rate, with the general price level (1.21 at year-end) averaging 1.10 during the year. Inflation-adjusted income would be measured (in thousands) as follows:

	Nominal Pesos	Adjustment Factor	Constant Pesos
Revenues	ARS150,000	1.21/1.10	ARS165,000
– Expenses	100,000	1.21/1.00	121,000
Operating income	ARS 50,000		ARS 44,000
– Monetary loss	=		15,000
Net income	ARS 50,000		ARS 29,000

In these calculations, sales took place at the same rate throughout the year, so they are adjusted by the ratio of the end-of-year index to the year's average price index. Because the inventory sold during the year was bought at the beginning of the year, cost of sales is adjusted by the ratio of the year-end index to the beginning-of-year index.

Where did the monetary loss come from? During inflation, firms will have changes in wealth that are unrelated to operating activities. These arise from monetary assets or liabilities—claims to, or obligations to pay, a fixed amount of currency in the future. Monetary assets include cash and accounts receivable, which generally lose purchasing power during periods of inflation. Monetary liabilities include most payables, which generally create purchasing power gains during inflation. In our example, the firm received and held cash during a period when cash lost purchasing power. As inventory was sold for cash, cash was received uniformly throughout the year. The firm's cash balance at the end of the year, if expressed in terms of year-end purchasing power, should be ARS165,000 (150,000×1.21/1.10). It is actually only ARS150,000, resulting in an ARS15,000 loss in general purchasing power (a monetary loss). This explains the Loss from monetary position figure in Grupo Modelo's income statement cited earlier. During 2006 and 2007, Modelo had more monetary assets on its books than monetary liabilities, giving rise to a purchasing power loss each year.

In contrast to conventional accounting, income using the historical cost-constant purchasing power model is only $29,000. However, withdrawing ARS29,000 makes the firm's end-of-period wealth ARS121,000 (ARS150,000 – AP 29,000), giving it as much purchasing power at the end of the period as at the beginning.

IAS 29 is consistent with this approach to accounting for changing prices. Reproduced in Exhibit 7-3 is a financial reporting example for VESTEL, a leader in the

Turkish and global markets for consumer electronics, white goods, and digital products. It is for the most recent year in which the company applied the tenets of IAS 29 as explained below:

VESTEL has price-level adjusted all revenues and expenses to December 31, 2005 purchasing power equivalents, using the year-end WPI over the relevant index that prevailed when each revenue and expense transaction occurred. The monetary loss of YTL9, 296,000 occurs because VESTEL held an excess of monetary assets over monetary losses during 2005. The company calculated this loss by multiplying the change in a general price-level index by the weighted average of the difference between monetary assets and liabilities for the year. The company wisely cautions

---

EXHIBIT 7-3   Inflation-Adjusted Income Statement of Vestel and Related Note

---

VESTEL ELEKTRONIK SANAYI VE TICARET A.S. GROUP OF COMPANIES
CONSOLIDATED INCOME STATEMENTS FOR THE YEARS ENDED 31 DECEMBER 2005 AND 2004
(Currency show in thousands of New Turkish Lira ("YTL") in equivalent purchasing power at 31.12.2005 unless otherwise indicated.)

	Note	01.01-31.12.2005	01.01-31.12.2004
Net sales		4.456.229	4.604.903
Cost of sales		(3.798.115)	(3.854.366)
Gross profit		658.114	750.537
Selling expenses		(337.763)	(318.197)
General and administrative expenses		(141.642)	(138.089)
Warranty expenses		(30.972)	(30.327)
Other income/(expenses), net	20	22.265	5.224
Income from operations		170.002	269.148
Financing income/(expense), net	21	(36.085)	(74.057)
Income before taxation		133.917	195.091
Taxation charge			
Current		(54.699)	(41.036)
Deferred		43.592	(2.428)
Taxation on income	15	(11.107)	(43.464)
Income before minority interest		122.810	151.627
Minority interest		(30.168)	(45.979)
Monetary loss	27	(9.296)	(18.710)
Net income for the year		83.346	86.938
Basic and fully diluted earnings per share (in full TL)	4	524	546

The accompanying notes are an
    integral part of these statements.

EXHIBIT 7-3	Inflation-Adjusted Income Statement of Vestel and Related Note (Continued)

Vestel Elektronik Sanayi ve Ticaret Anonim Sirketi
Notes to Consolidated Financial Statements for the Year Ended 31, December 2008
2.1 Measurement currency and reporting currency
    The financial statements have been prepared under the historical cost convention, other than financial assets which are stated at fair value.
    The restatement for the changes in the general purchasing power of TL (Turkish lira) as of 31, December 2005 is based on IAS 29 ("Financial Reporting in Hyperinflationary Economies"). IAS 29 requires that financial statements prepared in the currency of a hyperinflationary economy be stated in terms of the measuring unit current at the balance sheet date and the corresponding figures for previous periods be restated in the same terms. One characteristic (but not limited to) that necessitates the application of IAS 29 is a cumulative three year inflation rate approaching or exceeding 100%. As of 31 December 2005, the three year cumulative rate was 36% (31 December 2004: 70% - 31 December 2003: 181%) based on the Turkish countrywide wholesale price index published by the State Institute of Statistics.
    As from 1 January 2006 it has been decided to discontinue the adjustment of financial statements for inflation after taking into account that hyperinflation period has come to an end as indicated by existing objective criteria and that other signs indicating the continuance of hyperinflation have largely disappeared.
    The effects of ending the adjustments for inflation on financial statements are summarized as follows:
    The financial statements as of 31 December 2006, 2007 and 2008 have not been subjected to any inflation adjustment whereas the financial statements for previous periods have been adjusted for inflation on the basis of the measuring unit current at the preceding balance sheet date namely 31 December 2005.

the reader that its price-level-adjusted amounts do not reflect current costs. To quote VESTEL:

> Restatement of balance sheet and income statement items through the use of a general price index and relevant conversion factors does not necessarily mean that the Company could realize or settle the same values of assets and liabilities as indicated in the balance sheets. Similarly, it does not necessarily mean that the Company could returns or settle the same values of equity to its shareholders.

CURRENT-COST ADJUSTMENTS

The current-cost model differs from conventional accounting in two major respects. First, assets are valued at their current cost rather than their historical cost. As an asset is conceptually equal to the discounted present value of its future cash flows, current-cost advocates argue that current values provide statement readers with a better measure of a firm's future earnings and cash-flow potential. Second, income is defined as a firm's *disposable wealth*—the amount of resources the firm could distribute during a period (not counting tax considerations) while maintaining its productive capacity or physical capital. One way to maintain capital is to adjust the firm's original net asset position (using appropriate specific price indexes or direct pricing, such as current invoice prices, supplier price lists, etc.) to reflect changes in the asset's current-cost equivalent during the period. Continuing our previous example, the transactions of our hypothetical merchandiser under the current-costing framework can be illustrated using the accounting equation as our analytical framework (figures given in thousands):

	Assets =	**Liabilities + Owners' Equity**	
	Cash	Inventory	Capital
1.	100,000		100,000
2.	(100,000)	100,000	
3.	150,000		150,000 (revenue)
4.		40,000	40,000 OE reval.
5.		(140,000)	(140,000) exp.

Line 1 depicts the financial statement effects of the initial ARS100,000 investment into the firm. Line 2 depicts the exchange of cash for inventory. Assuming a 50 percent markup, line 3 shows the sale of inventory for cash, which increases owners' equity by the same amount. To reflect the current cost of the sale, the merchandiser increases the carrying value of inventories by 40 percent, as depicted in line 4. The offset to the 40 percent writeup of inventory is an ARS40,000 increase in the owners' equity revaluation account. This adjustment does two things. The owners' equity revaluation amount tells statement readers that the firm must keep an additional ARS40,000 in the business to enable it to replace inventories whose replacement costs have risen. The inventory revaluation, in turn, increases the cost of resources consumed (cost of sales), line 5. Thus, current revenues are matched against the current economic cost (not the historical cost) incurred to generate those revenues. In our example, current-cost-based net income is measured as ARS150,000 − (ARS100,000 × 140/100) = ARS10,000. The current-cost profit of ARS10,000 is the amount the firm could spend without reducing its business operations. Thus, the current-cost model attempts to preserve a firm's physical capital or productive capacity.

An example of current-cost reporting is provided by Infosys, the world-class information technology and consulting group headquartered in India. Its inflation-adjusted accounts appear in Exhibit 7-4.

In the commentary that precedes the finacial statements, Infosys explains the purpose of its current-cost information. That purpose is to maintain its operating capability. It also emphasizes that its current-cost disclosures account for the changes in specific prices as they affect the enterprise. This last statement provides the rationale for the "gearing adjustment" that Infosys includes in its income statement. The gearing adjustment will be explained in more detail on page 229 of this chapter. The current-cost reserve appearing in the equity section of Infosys' consolidated balance sheet represents an amount that is not available for dividends in order to provide for the replacement of assets whose specific prices have increased.

EXHIBIT 7-4	**Current-Cost Financial Statements of Infosys**

Current-cost-adjusted financial statements

Current Cost Accounting ("CCA") seeks to state the value of assets and liabilities in a balance sheet at their value, and measure the profit or loss of an enterprise by matching current costs against current revenues. CCA is based on the concept of "operating capability", which may be viewed as the amount of goods and services that an enterprise is capable of providing with the existing resources during a given period. In order to maintain its operating capability, an enterprise should remain in command of resources that form the basis of its acticities. Accordingly, it becomes necessary to take into account the rising cost of assets consumed in generating these revenues. CCA takes into account the changes in specific prices of assets as they affect the enterprise.

The consolidated balance sheet and profit and loss account of Infosys and its subsidiary companies for fiscal year 2007, prepared in substantial compliance with the current-cost basis, are presented below. The methodology prescribed by the Guidance Note on Accounting for Changing Prices issued by the Institute of Chartered Accontants of India is adopted in preparing the statements.

Consolidated balance sheet as of March 31, 2007

		in Rs. crore
	2007	**2006**
ASSETS EMPLOYED		
Fixed assets		
Original cost	5,039	3,222
Accumulated depreciation	(2,082)	(1,519)
	2.957	1,703
Capital work-in-progress	965	571
Net fixed assets	3,922	2,274
Investments	25	755
Deferred tax assets	92	65
Current assets, loans and advances		
Cash and bank balances	5,871	3,429
Loans and advances	1,214	1,297
Monetary working capital	829	613
	7,914	5,339
Less: Other liabilities and provisions	(681)	(1,412)
Net current assets	7,233	3,927
	11,272	7,021
FINANCED BY:		
Share capital and reserves		
Share capital	286	138
Minority interest	4	68
Reserves:		
Capital reserve	5	54
Share premium	2,768	1,543
Current-cost reserve	178	165
General reserve	8,031	5,053
	10,982	6,815
	11,272	7,021

Current-cost-adjusted financial statements

Consolidated profit and loss account for the year ended March 31, 2007

		in Rs. crore
	2007	**2006**
Total income	13,893	9,521
Historic cost profit before tax	4,247	2,792
Add/Less: Current-cost operating adjustments	(111)	(43)
	4,136	2,749
Less: Gearing adjustment	–	–
Current-cost profit before tax, exceptional items and minority interest	4,136	2,749
Provision for taxation		
Previous years	–	–
Current year	(386)	(313)
Current-cost profit after tax, before exceptional items and minority interest	3,750	2,436
Exceptional item—Income from sale of investments (net of taxes)	6	–
Current-cost profit after tax and exceptional items, before minority interest	3,756	2,436
Minority interest	(11)	(21)
Current-cost profit after tax, exceptional items and minority interest	3,745	2,415
Appropriations		
Dividend		
Interim	278	177
Final (proposed)	371	234
Silver jubilee special dividend	–	827
Dividend tax	102	174
Amount transferred—general reserve	2,994	1,003
	3,745	2,415
Statement of retained profits / reserves		
Operating balance of reserves	5,217	4,206
Retained current-cost profit for the year	2,994	1,003
Movements in current-cost reserve during the year	(2)	8
	8,209	5,217

Note:
1. The cost of technology assets, like computer equipment, decreases over time. This is offset by an accelerated depreciation charge to the financial statements. Accordingly, such assets are not adjusted for changes in prices.
2. The above data is provided solely for information purpose. The Management accepts no responsibility for any direct, indirect, or consequential losses or damages suffered by any person relying on the same.

GENERAL PRICE-LEVEL ADJUSTED CURRENT COSTS

This third reporting option to account for changing prices combines features of the general price-level model and the current-cost framework discussed in the preceding paragraphs.[9] This measurement construct, referred to here as the *price-level-adjusted*

---

[9] For detailed guidance see, Financial Accounting Standards Board, "Financial Reporting and Changing Prices," *Statement of Financial Accounting Standards No. 89*, Stamford, CT: FASB, December 1986.

current-cost model, employs both general and specific price indexes. Consistent with the general price-level model, one of its objectives is to express a firm's earnings and net assets in terms of their end-of-period purchasing-power equivalents. The income statement would also include information on purchasing-power gains or losses on holding net monetary items. In keeping with the current-cost framework, another set of objectives is to report the firm's net assets in terms of their current cost and to report an earnings number that represents the firm's disposable wealth.

A distinctive feature of the price-level-adjusted current-cost framework is that it discloses the changes in the current costs of a firm's nonmonetary assets, net of inflation. The idea here is to show that portion of the change in a nonmonetary asset's value that exceeds or falls short of a change in the general purchasing power of monetary. To illustrate, assume that the current cost of a piece of machinery was $1,000 at the beginning of the year. Its current replacement cost at the end of the year rises to $1,250. The general price level over that same period rises from a level of 100 to 110; that is, it would take $110 dollars at the end of the year to command what $100 would at the beginning. In this example, the current cost of the machinery increased by $250($1,250 − $1,000). The portion of the increase that was due merely to a change in the purchasing power of money is determined by first restating the beginning current cost to end-of-period purchasing-power equivalents, $1,000 × 110/100 = $1,100. Thus, the change in the machinery's replacement cost that was simply due to a change in the purchasing power of money was $100 ($1,100 − $1,000), and the real change in the machinery's current cost was $250 − $100, or $150. As asset values are used by analysts to estimate a firm's future earnings and cash flows (e.g., multiplying asset values by past return on asset ratios), isolating the changes in asset values that are real as opposed to illusionary is important. These two disclosures that usually appear in stockholders' equity are usually interpreted as follows: The increase in nonmonetary assets due to general inflation is the amount that must be retained in the firm just to enable it to keep up with general inflation. The second component—for example, the increase in current costs that exceeds general inflation—is viewed by some as the unrealized real holding gain on nonmonetary assets. We argue that the latter is not a gain but an increase in the cost of doing business that should be retained in the business to allow the firm to preserve its productive capacity, à la our Infosys example.

The financial statements of Grupo Modello, highlighted at the beginning of this chapter, provide a good example of the price-level-adjusted current-cost model. Footnotes to those statements help explain that Modell's consolidated financial statements and notes thereto are stated consistently in Mexican pesos of December 31, 2005 purchasing power by applying factors derived from the National Consumer Price Index (NCPI).

The account *Loss from monetary position* appearing in the income statement section entitled "Comprehensive Financing Income" is the general purchasing loss from holding an excess of monetary assets over monetary losses during the year. The property, plant, and equipment schedule appearing in note 6 of Exhibit 7-1 and related expenses have been adjusted to their end-of-period general-price-level adjusted current costs. Ditto for inventories and cost of sales. Finally, the account "Deficit in the restatement of stockholders' equity" appearing in shareholders' equity consists of two parts: the gain in current costs that exceed or fall short of general inflation, and the change in the nonmonetary asset's carrying value that is due to general inflation. In this case, the change in the general price level exceeded the increase in the current costs of Modello's nonmonetary assets. The portion of the change in current costs that fall short of the change in the general price level is viewed as an unrealized holding loss.

NATIONAL PERSPECTIVES ON INFLATION ACCOUNTING

Other countries have experimented with different inflation accounting approaches. Actual practices also reflect pragmatic considerations, such as the severity of national inflation and the views of those directly affected by inflation accounting numbers. Examining additional national approaches to inflation accounting is helpful in understanding current practice.

United States

In 1979, the FASB issued Statement of Financial Accounting Standards (SFAS) No. 33. Entitled "Financial Reporting and Changing Prices," this statement required U.S. enterprises with inventories and property, plant, and equipment (before deducting accumulated depreciation) of more than $125 million, or total assets of more than $1 billion (after deducting accumulated depreciation), to experiment for five years with disclosing both historical cost-constant purchasing power and current-cost constant purchasing power. These disclosures were to supplement rather than replace historical cost as the basic measurement framework for primary financial statements.[10]

Many users and preparers of financial information that complied with SFAS No. 33 found that (1) the dual disclosures required by the FASB were confusing, (2) the cost of preparing the dual disclosures was excessive, and (3) historical cost-constant purchasing power disclosures were less useful than current-cost data. Since then, the FASB has decided to encourage but no longer require U.S. reporting entities to disclose either historical cost-constant purchasing power or current-cost constant purchasing power information. The FASB published guidelines (SFAS 89) to assist enterprises that report the statement effects of changing prices and to be a starting point for any future inflation accounting standard.[11]

Reporting enterprises are encouraged to disclose the following information for each of the five most recent years:

- Net sales and other operating revenues
- Income from continuing operations on a current-cost basis
- Purchasing power (monetary) gains or losses on net monetary items
- Increases or decreases in the current cost or lower recoverable amount (i.e., the net amount of cash expected to be recoverable from use or sale) of inventory or property, plant, and equipment, net of inflation (general price-level changes)
- Any aggregate foreign currency translation adjustment, on a current-cost basis, that arises from the consolidation process
- Net assets at year-end on a current-cost basis
- Earnings per share (from continuing operations) on a current-cost basis

---

[10] Financial Accounting Standards Board, "Financial Reporting and Changing Prices," Statement of Financial Accounting Standards No. 33, Stamford, CT: FASB, 1979.
[11] Financial Accounting Standards Board, "Financial Reporting and Changing Prices," Statement of Financial Accounting Standards No. 89, Stamford, CT: FASB, December 1986.

- Dividends per share of common stock
- Year-end market price per share of common stock
- Level of the Consumer Price Index (CPI) used to measure income from continuing operations

To increase the comparability of these data, information may be presented either in (1) average (or year-end) purchasing-power equivalents, or (2) base period dollars used in calculating the CPI. Whenever income on a current-cost constant purchasing-power basis differs significantly from historical-cost income, firms are asked to provide more data.

The SFAS No. 89 disclosure guidelines also cover foreign operations included in the consolidated statements of U.S. parent companies. Enterprises that adopt the dollar as the functional currency for measuring their foreign operations view these operations from a parent-currency perspective. Accordingly, their accounts should be translated to dollars, then adjusted for U.S. inflation (the translate-restate method). Multinational enterprises adopting the local currency as functional for most of their foreign operations adopt a local-currency perspective. The FASB allows companies to either use the translate-restate method or adjust for foreign inflation and then translate to U.S. dollars (the restate-translate method). Accordingly, adjustments to current-cost data to reflect inflation may be based on either the U.S. or the foreign general-price-level index. Exhibit 7-5 summarizes these provisions.

EXHIBIT 7-5 Restatement Methodology for Foreign Operations

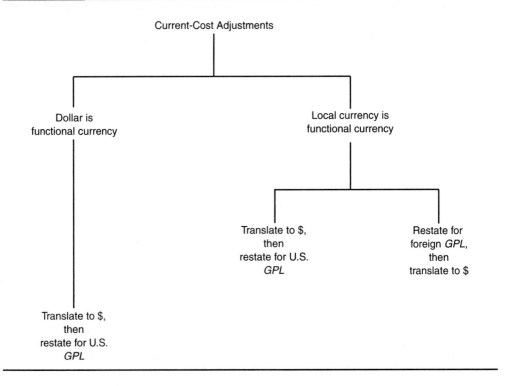

United Kingdom

The U.K. Accounting Standards Committee (ASC) issued Statement of Standard Accounting Practice No. 16 (SSAP No. 16), "Current-Cost Accounting," on a three-year experimental basis in March 1980. Although SSAP No. 16 was withdrawn in 1988, its methodology is recommended for companies that voluntarily produce inflation adjusted accounts.[12]

SSAP No. 16 differs from SFAS No. 33 in two major respects. First, whereas the U.S. standard required both constant dollar and current-cost accounting, SSAP No. 16 adopted only the current-cost method for external reporting. Second, whereas the U.S. inflation adjustment focused on the income statement, the U.K. current-cost statement required both a current-cost income statement and a balance sheet, with explanatory notes. The U.K. standard allowed three reporting options:

1. Presenting current-cost accounts as the basic statements with supplementary historical-cost accounts.
2. Presenting historical-cost accounts as the basic statements with supplementary current-cost accounts.
3. Presenting current-cost accounts as the only accounts accompanied by adequate historical-cost information.

In its treatment of gains and losses related to monetary items, FAS No. 33 required separate disclosure of a single figure. SSAP No. 16 required two figures, both reflecting the effects of specific price changes. The first, called a monetary working capital adjustment (MWCA), recognized the effect of specific price changes on the total amount of working capital used by businesses in their operations. Similar in nature to the monetary gain or loss figure required under the general price-level model, this adjustment acknowledges the fact that the baskets of goods and services that companies acquire are much more firm-specific in regard to supplies, inventories, and the like than those consumed by the general public. The second, called the gearing adjustment, allowed for the impact of specific price changes on a firm's nonmonetary assets (e.g., depreciation, cost of sales, and monetary working capital). As a formula, the gearing adjustment equals:

$$[(TL - CA) / (FA + I + MWC)] (CC \text{ Dep. Adj.} + CC \text{ Sales Adj.} + MWCA)$$

where

TL	=	total liabilities other than trade payables
CA	=	current assets other than trade receivables
FA	=	fixed assets including investments
I	=	inventory
MWC	=	monetary working capital
CC Dep. Adj.	=	current-cost depreciation adjustment
CC Sales Adj.	=	current cost of sales adjustment
MWCA	=	monetary working capital adjustment

---

[12] Accounting Standards Committee, *Handbook on Accounting for the Effects of Changing Prices* (London: Chartac Books, 1986).

The gearing adjustment acknowledges that such expenses as cost of goods sold and depreciation need not be inflated to recognize the higher replacement cost of these assets to the extent that they are financed by debt. The latter normally gives rise to "monetary gains" computed using specific as opposed to general price indexes.

Brazil

Inflation is often an accepted part of the business scene in Latin America, Eastern Europe, and Southeast Asia. Brazil's past experience with hyperinflation makes its inflation accounting initiatives informative.

Although no longer required, recommended inflation accounting in Brazil today reflects two sets of reporting options—Brazilian Corporate Law and the Brazil Securities and Exchange Commission.[13] Inflation adjustments complying with corporate law restate permanent assets and stockholders' equity accounts using a price index recognized by the federal government for measuring devaluation of the local currency. Permanent assets include fixed assets, buildings, investments, deferred charges and their respective depreciation, and amortization or depletion accounts (including any related provisions for losses).[14] Stockholders' equity accounts comprise capital, revenue reserves, revaluation reserves, retained earnings, and a capital reserves account used to record the price-level adjustment to capital. The latter results from revaluing fixed assets to their current replacement costs less a provision for technical and physical depreciation.

Inflation adjustments to permanent assets and stockholders' equity are netted, with the excess being disclosed separately in current earnings as a monetary correction gain or loss. Exhibit 7-6 and related commentary provide an illustration of this inflation accounting methodology and the rationale for the monetary correction account.

The price-level adjustment to stockholders' equity (BRL275) is the amount by which the shareholders' beginning-of-period investment must grow to keep up with inflation. A permanent asset adjustment that is less than the equity adjustment causes a purchasing power loss reflecting the firm's exposure on its net monetary assets (i.e., working capital). To illustrate, let:

M = monetary assets

N = nonmonetary assets

L = liabilities

E = equity

i = inflation rate

Then

$$M + N = L + E \tag{7.1}$$

---

[13] Financial analysts and Brazilian financial executives we have interviewed continue to adjust Brazilian accounts for changing prices to facilitate their analyses. Should significant inflation recur in Brazil, the inflation adjustments we describe will likely be reinstated.

[14] Permanent assets do not include inventories, which is a conceptual shortcoming of this inflation accounting model.

EXHIBIT 7-6   Inflation Adjustments, Brazilian Style

Inflation-Corrected Amounts

Historical Amounts			Assuming a 25% Rate of Inflation		
Balance Sheet	1/1/X7	12/31/X7			12/31/X7
Current assets	BRL 150	BRL 450	Current assets		BRL 450
Permanent assets	1,600	1,600	Permanent assets		2,000[a]
Provision for depreciation	(200)	(300)	Provision for depreciation		(300)
			Monetary correction	(75)[b]	
			Correction of historical charge to P&L	(25)[c]	(100)
Total	BRL1,550	BRL1,750	Total		BRL2,050
Current liabilities	BRL 50	BRL 50	Current liabilities		BRL 50
Long-term debt	400	400	Long-term debt		400
Equity:			Equity:		
Capital	800	800	Capital		800
			Capital reserve		200[d]
Reserves	300	300	Reserves		375[e]
Profit of period		200	Profit of period		225
Total	BRL1,550	BRL1,750	Total		BRL2,050
Income Statement Year Ended 12/31/X7			Year Ended 12/31/X7		
Operating profit		BRL 500	Operating profit		BRL 500
Depreciation of period (historical)		100	Depreciation of period	100	
			Correction of depreciation	25	
Trading profit		400	Trading profit Inflationary loss:		125
Inflationary loss on foreign debt		(100)	Exchange loss on foreign debt	(100)	375
Monetary correction on local debt		(100)	Monetary correction on local debt	(100)	
			Gain on correction of balance sheet	50[f]	(150)
Net profit		BRL 200	Net profit		BRL 225

[a]Represents the original BRL1,600 plus a 25 percent (BRL400) adjustment.
[b]25 percent of the original BRL300.
[c]25 percent of the period's depreciation expense (typically based on the average value of fixed assets).
[d]25 percent of the original capital balance of BRL800.
[e]Represents the original R$300 plus a 25 percent (BRL75) adjustment.
[f]Gain on correction of the balance sheet:

Correction of permanent assets	BRL400	
Correction of depreciation allowance	75	325
Correction of capital	200	
Correction of reserves	75	275
		50

Multiplying both sides of Equation (7.1) by $(1+i)$ quantifies the impact of inflation on the firm's financial position. Thus

$$M(1+i) + N(1+i) = L(1+i) + E(1+i) \qquad (7.2)$$

Equation (7.2) can be reexpressed as

$$M + Mi + N + Ni = L + Li + E + Ei \qquad (7.3)$$

Regrouping Equation (7.3) as

$$M + \underbrace{N + Ni}_{\substack{\text{permanent} \\ \text{asset} \\ \text{adjustment}}} = L + \underbrace{E + Ei}_{\substack{\text{owner's} \\ \text{equity} \\ \text{adjustment}}} + \underbrace{(L - Mi)}_{\substack{\text{monetary} \\ \text{gain or loss}}} \qquad (7.4)$$

Since $M + N = L + E$,

$$Ni = Ei + (L - Mi) \qquad (7.5)$$

Or

$$\underbrace{Ni}_{\substack{\text{inflation} \\ \text{adjustment to} \\ \text{nonmonetary} \\ \text{(permanent)} \\ \text{assets}}} - \underbrace{Ei}_{\substack{\text{inflation} \\ \text{adjustment} \\ \text{to owners'} \\ \text{equity}}} = \underbrace{(L - Mi)}_{\substack{\text{monetary} \\ \text{gain or loss}}} \qquad (7.6)$$

Conversely, a permanent asset adjustment greater than the equity adjustment produces a purchasing power gain, suggesting that some of the assets have been financed by borrowing. For example, suppose that a firm's financial position before monetary correction is

Permanent assets	1,000	Liabilities	500
		Owners' equity	500

With an annual inflation rate of 30 percent, a price-level adjusted balance sheet would show:

Permanent assets	1,300	Liabilities	500
		Capital	500
		Capital reserve	150
		Monetary gain	150[15]

---

[15]This analysis (monetary gain) assumes that liabilities are of the fixed-rate variety or are floating-rate obligations where the actual rate of inflation exceeds the expected rate that is incorporated into the terms of the original borrowing.

The Brazilian Securities Exchange Commission requires another inflation accounting method for publicly traded companies.[16] Listed companies must remeasure all transactions during the period using their functional currency. At the end of the period, the prevailing general price-level index converts units of general purchasing power into units of nominal local currency. Also,

- Inventory is included as a nonmonetary asset and is remeasured with the functional currency.
- Noninterest-bearing monetary items with maturities exceeding 90 days are discounted to their present values to allocate resulting inflationary gains and losses to appropriate accounting periods (the discount on trade receivables is treated as a reduction of sales, the discount on accounts payable reduces purchases, etc.).
- Balance sheet adjustments are similarly reclassified to appropriate line items in the income statement (e.g., the balance sheet adjustment to accounts receivable is reclassified as a reduction of sales).

To relieve Brazilian firms from having to present two sets of financial statements in their annual reports, the Securities Exchange Commission blended features of the corporate law methodology into its price-level accounting methodology.

INTERNATIONAL ACCOUNTING STANDARDS BOARD

The IASB has concluded that reports of financial position and operating performance in local currency are not meaningful in a hyperinflationary environment. IAS 29,[17] mentioned in conjunction with VESTEL's inflation-adjusted financial statements (see Exhibit 7-3) requires (rather than recommends) the restatement of primary financial statement information. Specifically, financial statements of an enterprise that reports in the currency of a hyperinflationary economy, whether based on a historical or current-cost valuation framework, should be reexpressed in terms of constant purchasing power as of the balance sheet date. This rule also applies to corresponding figures for the preceding period. Purchasing-power gains or losses related to a net monetary liability or asset position are to be included in current income. Reporting enterprises should also disclose

1. The fact that restatement for changes in the general purchasing power of the measuring unit has been made
2. The asset-valuation framework employed in the primary statements (i.e., historical or current-cost valuation)
3. The identity and level of the price index at the balance sheet date, together with its movement during the reporting period
4. The net monetary gain or loss during the period

---

[16] Coopers & Lybrand, *1993 International Accounting Summaries* (New York: John Wiley, 1993), B32–B33.
[17] International Accounting Standards Committee, "Financial Reporting in Hyperinflationary Economies," International Accounting Standard No. 29, London: IASC, 1989.

INFLATION ISSUES

Analysts must address the following issues when reading inflation-adjusted accounts: (1) whether constant dollars or current costs better measure the effects of inflation, (2) the accounting treatment of inflation gains and losses, (3) accounting for foreign inflation, and (4) the combined effects of inflation and foreign exchange rates. We discuss the first and third issues together.

Inflation Gains and Losses

Treatment of gains and losses on monetary items (i.e., cash, receivables, and payables) is controversial. Our survey of practices in various countries reveals important variations in this respect.

In the United States are determined by restating, in constant dollars, the beginning and ending balances of, and transactions in, all monetary assets and liabilities (including long-term debt). The resulting figure is disclosed as a separate item. This treatment views gains and losses in monetary items as different in nature from other types of earnings.

In the United Kingdom, gains and losses on monetary items are partitioned into monetary working capital and a gearing adjustment. Both figures are determined in relation to specific (not general) price changes. The gearing adjustment indicates the benefit (or cost) to shareholders from debt financing during a period of changing prices. This figure is added (deducted) to (from) current-cost operating profit to yield a disposable wealth measure called "current-cost profit attributable to shareholders."

The Brazilian approach, no longer required, does not adjust current assets and liabilities explicitly, as these amounts are expressed in terms of realizable values. However, as Exhibit 7-6 shows, the adjustment from netting price-level adjusted permanent assets and owners' equity represents the general purchasing-power gain or loss in financing working capital from debt or equity. A permanent asset adjustment that exceeds an equity adjustment represents that portion of permanent assets being financed by debt, creating a purchasing-power gain. Conversely, an equity adjustment greater than the permanent asset adjustment denotes the portion of working capital financed by equity. A purchasing-power loss is recognized for this portion during an inflationary period.

SSAP No. 16 has great merit in dealing with the effects of inflation. Along with inventories and plant and equipment, an enterprise needs to increase its net nominal monetary working capital to maintain its operating capability with increasing prices. It also benefits from using debt during inflation. However, the magnitude of these phenomena should not be measured in general purchasing power terms because a firm rarely, if ever, invests in an economy's market basket. We believe that the purpose of inflation accounting is to measure the performance of an enterprise and enable anyone interested to assess the amounts, timing, and likelihood of future cash flows.

A firm can measure its command over specific goods and services by using an index to calculate its monetary gains and losses.[18] Because not all enterprises can construct firm-specific purchasing-power indexes, the British approach is a good

---

[18] Frederick D. S. Choi, "Foreign Inflation and Management Decisions," *Management Accounting* **58** (June 1977): 21–27.

practical alternative. However, rather than disclose the gearing adjustment (or some equivalent), we prefer to treat it as a reduction of the current-cost adjustments for depreciation, cost of sales, and monetary working capital. We think that current-cost charges from restating historical-cost income during inflation are offset by the reduced burden of servicing debt used to finance these operating items.

Holding Gains and Losses

Current value accounting divides total earnings into two parts: (1) operating income (the difference between current revenues and the current cost of resources consumed) and (2) unrealized gains that result from the possession of nonmonetary assets whose replacement value rises with inflation. The measurement of holding gains is straightforward, but their accounting treatment is not. Should portions of raw materials inventory gains be realized in periods when the respective inventories are turned into finished goods and sold? Are there ever unrealized adjustment gains or losses that should be deferred? Or should all such gains or losses be lumped together and disclosed in a special new section within stockholders' equity?

We think that increases in the replacement cost of operating assets (e.g., higher projected cash outflows to replace equipment) are not gains, realized or not. Whereas current-cost-based income measures a firm's approximate disposable wealth, changes in the current cost of inventory, plant, equipment, and other operating assets are revaluations of owners' equity, which is the portion of earnings that the business must keep to preserve its physical capital (or productive capacity). Assets held for speculation, such as vacant land or marketable securities, do not need to be replaced to maintain productive capacity. Hence, if current-cost adjustments include these items, increases or decreases in their current-cost (value) equivalents (up to their realizable values) should be stated directly in income.

Foreign Inflation

When consolidating the accounts of subsidiaries located in inflationary environments, should management first restate these accounts for foreign inflation, then translate to parent currency? Or should it first translate the unadjusted accounts to the parent currency, then restate them for parent-country inflation? In the United States, the FASB tried to cope with inflation by requiring large reporting entities to experiment with both historical cost-constant purchasing power and current-cost disclosures. FAS No. 89, which encourages (but no longer requires) companies to account for changing prices, leaves the issue unresolved at two levels. First, companies may continue to maintain the value of their nonmonetary assets at historical cost (restated for general price-level changes) or may restate them to their current-cost equivalents. Second, companies that elect to provide supplementary current-cost data for foreign operations have a choice of two methods for translating and restating foreign accounts in U.S. dollars. They can either restate for foreign ininflation, then translate to the parent currency (the restate-translate method), or they can translate to the parent currency, then restate for inflation (translate-restate). How do we choose between these two methods? We can choose with a decision-oriented framework.

Investors care about a firm's dividend-generating potential, because their investment's value ultimately depends on future dividends. A firm's dividend-generating potential is directly related to its capacity to produce goods and services. Only when a firm preserves its productive capacity (and thus its earning power) will there be future dividends to consider.

Therefore, investors need specific, not general, price-level-adjusted statements. Why? Because specific price-level adjustments (our current-cost model) determine the maximum amount that the firm can pay as dividends (disposable wealth) without reducing its productive capacity.

This conclusion implies that the restate-translate and translate-restate methods are both deficient. They are both based on a valuation framework that has little to recommend it—historical cost. Neither method changes that framework. No matter how it is adjusted, the historical-cost model is still the historical-cost model!

We favor the following price-level adjustment procedure:

1. Restate the financial statements of all subsidiaries, both domestic and foreign, and the statements of the parent to reflect changes in specific prices (e.g., current costs).
2. Translate the accounts of all foreign subsidiaries into domestic currency equivalents using a constant (e.g., the current or a base-year foreign exchange rate).
3. Use specific price indexes that are relevant to what the firm consumes in calculating monetary gains or losses. A parent-company perspective requires domestic price indexes; a local-company perspective requires local price indexes.

Restating both foreign and domestic accounts to their specific current-price equivalents produces decision-relevant information. This information provides investors the greatest possible amount of information concerning future dividends. It would be much easier to compare and evaluate the consolidated results of all firms than it is now. This reporting philosophy was stated by Dewey R. Borst, comptroller of Inland Steel Company:

> Management seeks the best current information to monitor how they have done in the past, and to guide them in their current decision making. Outsiders value financial statements for the same general purpose of determining how the firm has done in the past and how it is likely to perform in the future. Therefore, there is no legitimate need to have two distinct sets of data and methods of presentation of financial information. The same data now available through the development of managerial accounting is also suitable for outsiders.[19]

Avoiding the Double-Dip

When restating foreign accounts for foreign inflation, firms sometimes double-count for the effects of inflation, the *double-dip*. This problem exists because local inflation directly affects the exchange rates used in translation. While economic theory assumes an inverse relationship between a country's internal rate of inflation and the external value of its currency, evidence suggests that this relationship seldom holds (at least in

---

[19] Dewey R. Borst, "Accounting vs. Reality: How Wide Is the 'GAAP'?" *Week in Review* (July 13, 1982): 1.

the short run).[20] Accordingly, the size of the resulting adjustment to eliminate the double-dip will vary depending on the degree to which exchange rates and differential inflation are negatively correlated.

As noted before, inflation adjustments to cost of sale or depreciation expense are designed to reduce "as reported" earnings to avoid overstating income. However, due to the inverse relationship between local inflation and currency values, changes in the exchange rate between successive financial statements, generally caused by inflation (at least over a period of time), will make at least part of the impact of inflation (i.e., currency translation adjustments) affect a company's "as reported" results. Thus, to avoid adjusting for the effects of inflation twice, the inflation adjustment should take into account the translation loss already reflected in a firm's "as reported" results.

This adjustment is relevant to U.S.-based multinational corporations (MNCs) that have adopted the dollar as the functional currency for their foreign operations under FAS No. 52 and that translate inventories using the current exchange rate. It is also germane to non-U.S.-based MNCs that recognize translation gains and losses in current income. Absent any offsetting adjustments, such companies could reduce or increase earnings twice when accounting for foreign inflation.

The following inventory accounting example shows the relationship between inflation and foreign currency translation. The company in question uses the FIFO inventory costing method and translates inventory to dollars at the current exchange rate. We assume the following:

- Local country inflation was 20 percent in the year just ended. U.S. inflation was 6 percent during the year.
- The opening exchange rate on January 1 was LC1 = $1.00.
- The closing exchange rate on December 31 was LC1 = $0.88.
- Currency devaluation during the year to maintain purchasing power parity was 12 percent.
- Local currency inventory was LC200 on January 1 and LC240 on December 31.
- No change occurred in the physical quantity of inventory during the year.

The dollar equivalent of beginning and ending inventory is calculated as follows:

	LC Amount	Exchange Rate	$ Amount
Jan. 1 FIFO inventory	200	LC = $1.00	$200
Dec. 31 FIFO inventory	240	LC = $0.88	$211

"As reported" income will reflect a translation loss of $29 (assuming that the currency was devalued at year-end), the difference between translating LC240 inventory on December 31 at $0.88 versus $1.00.

During the next inventory turnover period, "as reported" cost of sales will, therefore, be LC240 in local currency, $211 in dollars.

---

[20] Michael Adler and Bernard Dumans, "International Portfolio and Corporation Finance: A Synthesis," *Journal of Finance* 38 (June 1983): 925–984.

If cost of sales was adjusted for inflation by the restate-translate method, the company might do as follows:

- Remove the year's 20 percent inflation from the December 31 local currency inventory (240/1.20), reducing it to LC 200—the same as it was on January 1 (before inflation).
- The local currency cost of sales adjustment would then be LC40, the amount required to change the December 31 inventory from LC240 to LC200.
- Translate the local currency cost of sales adjustment (LC40) to dollars at $1.00, making a $40 cost of sales adjustment (LC40 × $1.00 = $40).

Note that on an inflation-adjusted basis, the company has reduced earnings by a $29 translation loss and a $40 cost of sales inflation adjustment—a total of $69, or 34 percent of what began as $200 of inventory on January 1. Yet inflation was only 20 percent! Double-dipping caused this difference. The dollar calculations include a partial overlap between the currency devaluation loss, which results from inflation, and the cost of sales adjustment for inflation, which is a root cause of the currency devaluation. The restate-translate cost of sales inflation adjustment alone was enough. It would offset not only the U.S. inflation rate (6 percent in this example) but also the 12 percent inflation differential between the country's 20 percent rate and the U.S. 6 percent rate—which led to the 12 percent devaluation. We conclude that if cost of sales is adjusted to remove local country inflation, it is necessary to reverse any inventory translation loss that was reflected in "as reported" earnings. Appendix 7-1 provides a case analysis.

Appendix 7-1

Accounting for Foreign Inflation: A Case Analysis

The following case study highlights how a leading U.S.-based MNE, the General Electric Company (GE), accounts for foreign inflation. Most of our discussion will be limited to inventory and cost of sales, as well as monetary gains and losses. The procedures for inventories and cost of sales also apply to fixed assets and their related cost expirations when these accounts are translated using the current rate.[21]

GE uses the temporal method of foreign currency translation because the U.S. dollar is its functional currency for most of its foreign operations. Inventories are generally translated at the current rate to signal that they are exposed to exchange-rate risk. GE management believes that it needs the restate-translate method of accounting for inflation, using specific local price indexes for fixed assets and inventory, to properly measure its foreign operations on an inflation-adjusted basis. Accordingly,

GE adjusts the local currency cost of foreign fixed assets and inventory for local specific price changes and then translates at the current exchange rate. Restatement of fixed assets, from which restated depreciation expense is derived, uses generally understood practices (i.e., restate for current cost and then translate to dollars) and is not repeated here. For inventory, however, the cost of sales inflation adjustment cannot be derived from the restated balance sheet inventory value. Therefore, we will explain these two inflation adjustments separately.

Current-Cost Inventory Adjustment

For FIFO inventories that are not material in amount or that turn over very frequently, GE assumes that current cost and FIFO book cost are essentially equivalent. Accordingly, the historical book cost is reported as current cost.

---

[21] The following discussion is excerpted from Frederick D. S. Choi, "Resolving the Inflation/Currency Translation Dilemma," *Management International Review* 27, no. 2 (1987): 28–33.

With LIFO inventories, and FIFO inventories not excluded by the previous criteria, GE restates ending inventories to their current-cost equivalents using local specific price indexes before translation to dollars at the current rate. If the inventory input rate is relatively constant, the current-cost inventory adjustment is approximated by applying one-half of the local inflation rate during the inventory accumulation period. Thus, assuming a four-month accumulation period, an annual inflation rate of 30 percent, an ending inventory balance of LC1,000,000, and an ending exchange rate of LC1 = $0.40, the dollar FIFO inventory value restated to a current-cost basis would be:

$$[(2.5\% \text{ per mo.} \times 4 \text{ mos.})/2] \times$$
$$LC1,000,000 = LC50,000$$

$$LC1,000,000 + LC50,000 =$$
$$LC1,050,000 \times \$0.40 = \$420,000$$

If the foreign subsidiary carries its inventories on a LIFO basis, its restated FIFO value is calculated in the same manner, using its LIFO cost index as the inflation rate.

Current Cost of Sales Adjustment: Simulated LIFO

When a foreign operation uses LIFO accounting for its "as reported" results, the cost of sales is close to market. Therefore, no cost of sales inflation adjustment is made. For foreign operations that use FIFO accounting, GE's inflation adjustment simulates what would have been charged to cost of sales under LIFO accounting. However, to avoid the double-dip effect, the company also takes into account any inventory translation loss that is already reflected in "as reported" results. To illustrate, suppose that the December 31 FIFO inventory balance is LC5,000, that the year's inflation rate was 30 percent (January 1 = index 100, December 31 index = 130), and that the currency devalued by 20 percent from LC1 = $0.50 at January 1 to LC1 = $0.40 at December 31.

The following sequential analysis shows how the double-counting phenomenon is minimized. Steps 1 through 3 illustrate how the current cost of sales adjustment is derived in local currency. Step 4 expresses this inflation adjustment in the parent currency (i.e., U.S. dollars). Step 5 identifies the translation loss that has already been booked as a result of having translated inventories to dollars at a current rate that fell during the year. Finally, step 6 subtracts the translation loss already reflected in "as reported" results from the current cost of sales adjustment.

Usually, when inflation outpaces devaluation, the dollar current cost of sales adjustment will be positive (i.e., a deduction from "as reported"

1. December 31 FIFO inventory subject to simulated LIFO charge	LC5,000
2. Restate line 1 to January 1 cost level (LC5,000 × 100/130)	LC3,846
3. The difference between line 1 and line 2 inventory values represents current year local currency FIFO inventory inflation	LC1,154
4. Translate line 3 to dollars at the January 1 exchange rate (LC1 = $0.50). The result is simulated dollar LIFO expense for the current year	$ 577
5. Calculate the translation loss on FIFO inventory (line 1) that was already reflected in "as reported" results:	
a. Translate line 1 to January 1 exchange rate (LC5,000 × $0.50)	$2,500
b. Translate line 1 at December 31 exchange rate (LC5,000 × $0.40)	$2,000
c. The difference is the inventory translation loss already reflected in "as reported" results	$(500)
6. The net of lines 4 and 5c is the cost of sales adjustment in dollars:	
a. Simulated dollar LIFO expense from line 4	$ 577
b. Less: Inventory translation loss already reflected in "as reported" results (from line 5c)	$(500)
c. The difference is the net dollar current cost of sales adjustment	$ 77

earnings). However, if devaluation outpaces infla-tion, the adjustment will be negative (i.e., the dollar cost of sales adjustment would be sub-tracted from, rather than added to, "as reported" dollar cost of sales).

Current-Cost Monetary Adjustment

The final inflation adjustment described here relates to the fact that debtors typically gain during inflation because typically they repay fixed monetary obligations in currencies of reduced purchasing power. Accordingly, if a for-eign affiliate has used debt to finance part of its fixed assets and inventory, its inflation-adjusted data include a monetary adjustment (i.e., a pur-chasing power gain). However, because GE lim-its its inflation adjustments to inventories, fixed assets, and their related cost expirations, it limits the monetary adjustment to that portion of liabilities used to finance fixed assets and inven-tories—hereinafter known as applied liabilities. As a debtor's gain, the monetary adjustment recognizes that the interest expense being paid on applied liabilities includes compensation to the lender for the eroding purchasing power of the funds loaned. It also partly offsets the income-reducing inflation adjustments for depreciation expense and cost of sales due to the impact of inflation on fixed assets and inventory replacement costs.

Calculation of the monetary adjustment involves two steps, because local inflation impacts

exchange rates used to translate local currency liabilities to their dollar equivalents. Thus, the purchasing power gain on local currency liabili-ties used to finance fixed assets and inventories during an inflationary period is partly or fully offset by a reversal of any translation gains (or losses) on these liabilities already reflected in "as reported" results. These gains result from having translated monetary liabilities by an exchange rate that fell during the period.

In the following illustration, assume that a foreign subsidiary's local currency cost of fixed assets and FIFO inventory add up to LC10,600, that its net worth is LC7,500, that differential inflation between the parent and host country is 30 percent, and that the local currency devalued by 20 percent from LC1 = $0.50 at January 1 to LC1 = $0.40 at December 31. The current-cost monetary adjustment is calculated as follows.

Steps 1 through 5 identify the portion of mone-tary liabilities employed to finance assets whose values have been adjusted for inflation. Steps 6 and 7 calculate the monetary gains on these applied liabilities in local currency. Step 8 reexpresses this gain in U.S. dollars. Step 9 identifies the translation gain resulting from having translated monetary liabilities to dollars by an exchange rate (the current rate) that depreciated during the year. Finally, step 10 subtracts the translation gain on the monetary liabilities from the purchas-ing power gain on the same accounts to yield (in this example) a net monetary gain from chang-ing prices.

1. Local currency cost fixed assets at December 31	LC 5,600
2. FIFO inventory at December 31	LC 5,000
3. Total of lines 1 and 2	LC 10,600
4. Subtract net worth at December 31	LC (7,500)
5. The balance represents "applied liabilities"	LC 3,100
6. Restate December 31 applied liabilities to their January 1 purchasing power equivalent (i.e., multiply LC 3,100 by 100/130)	LC 2,385
7. The difference between lines 5 and 6 is the purchasing power gain on applied liabilities	LC 715
8. Translate line 7 to dollars at the January 1 exchange rate. The result is the debtor's gain from inflation in dollars (LC 715 × $0.50)	$ 358
9. Calculate the year's translation gain (loss) on applied LC liabilities already reflected in "as reported" results:	
a. Line 5 times January 1 exchange rate (LC 3,100 × $0.50)	$1,550
b. Line 5 times December 31 exchange rate (LC 3,100 × $0.40)	$1,240

    c. The difference is the translation gain $310

    d. The difference between line 8 and line 9c. is the dollar current-cost monetary adjustment

10.

    a. Line 8 (debtor's gain from inflation) $358

    b. Less: translation gain already reflected in as reported results (from line 9.c.) $(310)

    c. The difference is the net purchasing power gain from the use of debt to finance nonmonetary assets. $ 48

Discussion Questions

1. From a user's perspective, what is the inherent problem in attempting to analyze historical cost-based financial statements of a company domiciled in an inflationary, devaluation-prone country?

2. Examine the income statements of Modello, Vestel, and Infosys, referenced earlier in this chapter. Which earnings number do you feel provides the better earnings metric for an investment analyst, and why?

3. Consider the statement: "The object of accounting for changing prices is to ensure that a company is able to maintain its operating capability." How accurate is it?

4. Following are the remarks of a prominent member of the U.S. Congress. Explain why you agree or disagree.

> The plain fact of the matter is that inflation accounting is a premature, imprecise, and underdeveloped method of recording basic business facts. To insist that any system of inflation accounting can afford the accuracy and fairness needed for the efficient operation of our tax system is simply foolish. My years on the Ways and Means Committee have exposed me to the many appeals of business—from corporate tax "reform" to the need for capital formation—which have served as a guise for reducing the tax contributions of American business. In this respect, I see inflation accounting as another in a long line of attempts to minimize corporate taxation through backdoor gimmickry.

5. As more and more companies span the globe in terms of their operating, financing, and investing activities, they will increasingly turn to international financial reporting standards when communicating with domestic and non-domestic financial statement readers. What approaches to inflation accounting does IAS 29 sanction when a firm is domiciled or has major operations in a hyperinflationary environment? Why should analysts understand the requirements of this pronouncement?

6. Briefly describe the historical-cost-constant purchasing power and current-cost models. How are they similar? How do they differ?

7. As a potential investor in the shares of multinational enterprises, which inflation method, restate-translate or translate-restate, would give you consolidated information most relevant to your decision needs? Which information set is best from the viewpoint of the foreign subsidiary's shareholders?

8. What is a gearing adjustment, and on what ideas is it based?

9. How does accounting for foreign inflation differ from accounting for domestic inflation?

10. What does double-dipping mean in accounting for foreign inflation?

Exercises

1. Sobrero Corporation, a Mexican affiliate of a major U.S.-based hotel chain, starts the calendar year with 1 billion pesos (P) cash equity investment. It immediately acquires a refurbished hotel in Acapulco for P 900 million. Owing to a favorable tourist season, Sobrero Corporation's rental revenues were P 144 million for the year. Operating expenses of P 86,400,000 together with rental revenues were incurred uniformly throughout the year. The building, comprising 80 percent of the original purchase price (balance attributed to land), has an estimated useful life of 20 years and is being depreciated in straight-line fashion. By year-end, the Mexican consumer price index rose to 420 from an initial level of 263, averaging 340 during the year.

Required:
a. Prepare financial statements for Sobrero Corporation's first year of operations in terms of the historical-cost model and the historical-cost-constant dollar model.
b. Compare and evaluate the information content of rate-of-return statistics computed using each of these models.

2. The comparative historical-cost balance sheets of Majikstan Enterprises for 2010 and 2011 are reproduced below. The accounts are expressed in 000's of renges (MJR's).

Balance Sheet	2010	2011
Cash	MJR 2,500	MJR 5,100
Equipment, net	4,000	3,500
Total assets	MJR 6,500	MJR 8,600
Current liabilities	MJR 1,000	MJR 1,200
Long-term debt	3,000	4,000
Owners' equity	2,500	3,400
Total	MJR 6,500	MJR 8,600

Required: What was the change in Majikstan's net monetary asset or liability position?

3. Using the information provided in Exercise 2. Calculate Majikstan Enterprises' net monetary gain or loss in local currency for 2011 based on the following general price-level information.

12/31/10	30,000
Average	32,900
12/31/11	36,000

4. Revisit Sobrero Corporation in Exercise 1. In addition to the information provided there, assume that Mexico's construction cost index increased by 80 percent during the year, while the price of vacant land adjacent to Sobrero Corporation's hotel increased in value by 90 percent.

Required: Use the new information to restate the value of Sobrero's nonmonetary assets. What would Sobrero Corporation's financial statements look like under the current-cost model?

5. Majikstan Enterprises has equipment on its books that it acquired at the start of 2009 . The equipment is being depreciated in straight-line fashion over a 10-year period and has no salvage value. The current cost of this equipment at the end of 2010 was MJR8,000,000,000. During 2011 , the specific price index for equipment increased from 100 to 137.5. General price-level index information for the period was as follows:

12/31/10	30,000
Average	32,900
12/31/11	36,000

Required: Using this information, calculate the increse in the current cost of Majikstan Enterprise's equipment, net of inflation.

6. Now assume that Majikstan Enterprises is a foreign subsidiary of a U.S.-based multinational corporation and that its financial

statements are consolidated with those of its U.S. parent. Relevant exchange rate and general price-level information for the year are given here:

Exchange rate:		General Price Level Index:	
		Majikstan	**U.S.**
12/31/10	MJR 4,400 = $1	30,000	281.5
Average 2011	MJR 4,800 = $1	32,900	292.5
12/31/11	MJR 5,290 = $1	36,000	303.5

Required: What would be the increase in the current cost of Majikstan Enterprise's equipment, net of inflation, when expressed in U.S. dollars under the restate-translate methodology? Under the translate-restate method?

7. The balance sheet of Rackett & Ball plc., a U.K.-based sporting goods manufacturer, is presented here. Figures are stated in millions of pounds (£m). During the year, the producers' price index increased from 100 to 120, averaging

110. The aggregate current cost of sales, depreciation, and monetary working capital adjustment is assumed to be £216m.

Required: Assuming that changes in the producer's price index are a satisfactory measure of the change in R&B's purchasing power, calculate, as best as you can, R&B's monetary working capital adjustment and its gearing adjustment.

	£2010 m	£2011 m
Fixed Assets:		
Intangible assets	56	150
Tangible assets	260	318
Investments	4	5
	320	479
Current Assets:		
Inventory	175	220
Trade receivable	242	270
Marketable securities	30	50
Cash	25	25
	472	565
Current Liabilities:		
Trade payables	(170)	(160)
Net current assets	302	405
Total assets less current liabilities	622	884
Long-term liabilities	85	128
Total net assets	237	356
Owner's Equity:		
Common stock	42	42
Premium on common stock	87	87
Retained earnings	108	227
Total owner's equity	237	356

8. Ninsuvaan Corporation, a U.S. subsidiary in Bangkok, Thailand, begins and ends its calendar year with an inventory balance of BHT500 million. The dollar/baht exchange rate on January 1 was $0.02 = BHT1. During the year, the U.S. general price level advances from 180 to 198, while the Thai general price level doubles. The exchange rate on December 31 was $0.015 = BHT1.

Required:

a. Using the temporal method of translation, calculate the dollar equivalent of the inventory balance by first restating for Thai inflation, then translating to U.S. dollars.

b. Repeat part (a), but translate the nominal baht balances to dollars before restating for U.S. inflation.

c. Which dollar figure do you think provides the more useful information?

d. If you are dissatisfied with either result, suggest a method that would provide more useful information than those in parts (a) and (b).

9. Doosan Enterprises, a U.S. subsidiary domiciled in South Korea, accounts for its inventories on a FIFO basis. The company translates its inventories to dollars at the current rate. Year-end inventories are recorded at 10,920,000 won. During the year, the replacement cost of inventories increases by 20 percent. Inflation and exchange rate information are as follows:

January 1:   Specific price index = 100; $1 = KRW900

December 31:   Specific price index = 120; $1 = KRW1,170

Required: Based on this information, calculate the dollar current-cost adjustment for cost of sales while avoiding a double-charge for inflation.

10. The year-end balance sheet of Helsinki Corporation, a wholly owned British affiliate in Finland, is reproduced here. Relevant exchange rate and inflation information is also provided.

Balance Sheet Year Ended 2011

Cash	EUR2,000	Short-term debt	EUR8,000
Inventory	8,000	Long-term debt	25,000
Plant & equipment, net	20,000		
Other assets	5,000	Owners' equity	2,000
Total	EUR35,000		EUR35,000

Exchange rate and price information:

January 1:   General price index = 300
                      EUR1.5 = £1

December 31:   General price index = 390
                      EUR1.95 = £1

Required: Using this information, calculate the monetary adjustment without double-counting for the effects of foreign inflation (assume that the U.K inflation rate is negligible).

CASES

Case 7-1

Kashmir Enterprises

Kashmir Enterprises, an Indian carpet manufacturer, begins the calendar year with the following Indian rupee (INR) balances:

Cash	920,000	Accounts payable	420,000
Inventory	640,000	Owners' equity	1,140,000
	$1,560,000		$1,560,000

During the first week in January, the company acquires additional manufacturing inventories costing INR 2,400,000 on account and a warehouse for INR3,200,000 paying INR800,000 down and signing a 20-year, 10 percent note for the balance. The warehouse (assume no salvage value) is depreciated straight-line over the period of the note. Cash sales were INR6,000,000 for the year; selling and administrative expenses, including office rent, were INR1,200,000. Payments on account totaled INR2,200,000, while inventory on hand at year-end was INR480,000. Except for interest expense paid on December 31, all other cash receipts and payments took place uniformly throughout the year.

On January 1, the U.S. dollar/rupee exchange rate was $.025 = INR 1; at year-end it was $.02 = INR 1. The average exchange rate during the year was $.022. The Indian consumer price index rose from 128 to 160 by December 31, averaging 144 during the year. At the new financial statement date, the cost to replace inventories had increased by 30 percent; the cost to rebuild a comparable warehouse (based on the construction cost index) was approximately INR4,480,000.

Required

1. Assuming beginning inventories were acquired when the general price index level was 128, prepare Kashmir Enterprises' financial statements (i.e., income statement and balance sheet) under the (a) conventional original transactions cost model, (b) historical-cost constant rupee model, and (c) current-cost model.

2. Comment on which financial statement set gives financial analysts the most useful performance and wealth measures.

3. Now assume that management at Kashmir Enterprises' U.S. headquarters wants to see the Indian rupee statements in U.S. dollars. Two price-level foreign currency translation procedures are requested. The first is to translate Kashmir's unadjusted rupee statements to dollars (use the current-rate method) and then restate the resulting dollar amounts accounting for U.S. inflation (the U.S. general price level at the financial statement date was 108, up 8 percent from the previous

year). The second is to restate the Indian rupee statements accounting for inflation (using the historical-cost constant rupee model), then translate the adjusted amounts to dollars using the current rate.

Comment on which of the two resulting sets of dollar statements you prefer for use by American readers. (The U.S. general price level averaged 104 during the year.)

Case 7-2

Icelandic Enterprises, Inc.

In 1993 Icelandic Enterprises was incorporated in Reykjavik to manufacture and distribute women's cosmetics in Iceland. All of its outstanding stock was acquired at the beginning of 2001 by International Cosmetics, Ltd. (IC), a U.S.-based MNE headquartered in Shelton, Connecticut.

Competition with major cosmetics manufacturers both within and outside Iceland was very keen. As a result, Icelandic Enterprises (now a wholly-owned subsidiary of International Cosmetics) was under constant pressure to expand its product offerings. This required frequent investment in new equipment. Competition also affected the company's pricing flexibility. As the demand for cosmetics was price elastic, Icelandic lost market share every time it raised its prices. Accordingly, when Icelandic increased selling prices, it did so in small increments while increasing its advertising and promotional efforts to minimize the adverse effects of the price increase on sales volume.

International Cosmetics' financial policies with respect to Icelandic were dictated by two major considerations:

the continued inflation and devaluation of the Icelandic krona (ISK). To counter these, headquarters management was eager to recoup its dollar investment in Icelandic Enterprises through dollar dividends. If dividends were not possible, subsidiary managers were instructed to preserve IC's original equity investment in Icelandic krona. Due to the unstable krona, all financial management analyses were made in dollars. International Cosmetics designated the dollar as Icelandic Enterprise's functional currency. Accordingly, it adopted the temporal method when translating Icelandic's krona accounts to their dollar equivalents. All monetary assets and liabilities were translated to dollars using the current exchange rate. All nonmonetary items, except those assets that were carried at current values, were translated using historical rates. Income and expense accounts were translated at the average exchange rates prevailing during the year, except depreciation and amortization charges related to assets translated at historical exchange rates. Translation gains and losses were taken directly to consolidated earnings.

Adjusting Icelandic's accounts for inflation was not attempted. Management believed that such restatements were too costly and subjective. IC's management also claimed that translating Icelandic's accounts to dollars automatically approximated the impact of inflation. The following is a comparative balance sheet and income statement for Icelandic Enterprises, along with relevant foreign exchange and general price-level indexes.

Required

1. Comment on International Cosmetics' policies on the basis of "as reported" earnings.
2. Is management correct in stating that by translating their financial reports into dollars they "automatically approximate the impact of inflation"?
3. What revised actions/policies would you recommend based on inflation-adjusted figures?

Balance Sheet	2001		2002	
(000's)	Dollars	Krona	Dollars	Krona
Cash	7,715	221,176	9,086	368,414
Accounts receivable	18,000	516,078	21,202	859,633
Inventory	118,706	2,949,017	154,988	4,912,187
PP&E, net[a]	283,252	1,221,237	265,706	3,057,000
Other assets	22,022	272,013	28,838	1,024,950
Total	449,695	5,179,521	479,820	8,172,284
Current liabilities	94,748	2,716,438	82,673	3,351,980
Due to parent	50,000	1,433,500	50,000	2,027,250
Capital stock[b]	98,758	713,430	98,758	713,430
Retained earnings	206,189	316,153	248,389	2,079,624
Total	449,695	5,179,521	479,820	8,172,284

Income Statement	2001		2002	
	Dollars	Krona	Dollars	Krona
Net sales	328,805	8,168,500	462,248	14,650,500
Cost of sales	150,012	3,726,750	199,874	6,334,800
Gross margin	178,793	4,441,750	262,354	8,315,700
Selling expenses	78,493	1,950,000	110,841	3,513,000
General and administrative expenses	28,680	712,500	49,647	1,573,500
Depreciation	44,056	122,124	47,002	305,700
Operating income	27,564	1,657,126	54,864	2,923,500
Interest expense	7,064	175,500	11,453	363,000
Income before taxes[c]	20,500	1,481,626	43,411	2,560,500

	1997	1998	1999	2000	2001	2002
National Inflation and Exchange Rates[d]						
Consumer price index:						
Iceland	63.1	100.0	150.6	224.7	418.2	547.0
United States	88.1	100.0	110.4	117.1	120.9	126.1
Krona per dollar:						
Year-end	3.949	6.239	8.173	16.625	28.670	40.545
Average	3.526	4.798	7.224	12.352	24.843	31.694

[a]Plant and equipment were acquired at the beginning of each period as follows: 1998, ISK 1,250,000; 1999, ISK 427,500; 2000, ISK 375,000; 2001, ISK 160,000; 2002, ISK 844,500. Depreciation is calculated at 10 percent per annum. A full year's depreciation is charged in the year of acquisition. Assume there were no disposals during any of the years.
[b]Common stock was acquired when the exchange rate was ISK 7.224 = $1.
[c]Inclusive of translation gains and losses.
[d]The inflation and exchange rate relationships used here are based on actual data for an earlier period.

CHAPTER 8

Global Accounting and Auditing Standards

Efforts to "harmonize" accounting around the world began even before the creation of the International Accounting Standards Committee (IASC) in 1973.[1] Companies seeking capital outside of their home markets and investors attempting to diversify their investments internationally faced increasing problems resulting from national differences in accounting measurement, disclosure, and auditing. International accounting harmonization efforts accelerated during the 1990s, matching the growing globalization of international business and securities markets, and the increased cross-listings by companies. The harmonization efforts involved accounting standard setters, securities market regulators, stock exchanges, and those who prepare or use financial statements. The substantial differences in financial reporting requirements and practices around the world, and the increasing need of financial statement users to compare information of companies from different countries, were, and continue to be, the driving forces behind the movement to harmonize accounting.

Harmonized standards are compatible, that is, they do not contain conflicts. The term *convergence* is associated with the International Accounting Standards Board (IASB), discussed later in this chapter. As envisioned by the IASB, the convergence of international and national accounting standards involves the gradual elimination of differences through the cooperative efforts of the IASB, national standard setters, and other groups seeking best solutions to accounting and reporting issues. Thus, the notions behind harmonization and convergence are closely aligned. However, harmonization was generally taken to mean the elimination of differences between existing accounting standards, while convergence might also involve coming up with a new accounting treatment not in any current standard. *Convergence* is now the term most commonly used, and *harmonization* is used much less. It is important to note that neither

---

[1] The IASC was the predecessor body to the International Accounting Standards Board (IASB).

process necessarily implies replacing national standards with international ones; national and international accounting standards can coexist.[2]

Accounting convergence includes the convergence of (1) accounting standards (which deal with measurement and disclosure), (2) disclosures made by publicly traded companies in connection with securities offerings and stock exchange listings, and (3) auditing standards.[3]

A SURVEY OF INTERNATIONAL CONVERGENCE

Advantages of International Convergence

Proponents of international convergence claim that it has many advantages. Donald T. Nicolaisen, former chief accountant of the U.S. Securities and Exchange Commission, said the following in September 2004:

> At a conceptual level, supporting convergence is easy. An accounting treatment that transparently reflects the economics of a transaction to readers of financial statements in the U.K., will also do so for readers in France, Japan, the U.S. or any other country. Similarly, the auditing requirements and procedures that are the most effective are likely to be the same in the U.S., Canada, China, or Germany. Disclosures relevant to investors in Italy, Greece or the Middle East, are likely to be just as useful to investors in the U.S. and elsewhere. Having high-quality standards for accounting, auditing, and disclosure benefits investors and reduces the cost of accessing the capital markets around the world. In short, convergence is good business and good for investors.[4]

In April 2005, Nicolaisen wrote the following:

> Key forces favoring a single set of globally accepted accounting standards are the continued strong expansion of the capital markets across national borders and the desire by countries to achieve strong, stable and liquid capital markets to fuel economic growth. A thriving capital market requires a high degree of investor understanding and confidence. Converging with or embracing a common set of high quality accounting standards contributes immensely to this investor understanding and confidence.
>
> If a company's financial statements are prepared using accounting standards which are not viewed as being of high quality or with which the investor is unfamiliar, then investors may not be able to fully understand a company's prospects and thus may insist on a risk premium for an

---

[2] Thus, one should distinguish between convergence and adoption. Some countries, such as the United States and China discussed in Chapter 4, are converging their national GAAP with International Financial Reporting Standards (IFRS). Other countries, such as those of the European Union discussed in Chapter 3 are adopting IFRS. Some people use the term standardization interchangeably with harmonization and convergence. However, standardization generally means imposing a rigid and narrow set of rules—a one-size-fits-all approach. Harmonization and convergence are more flexible approaches to achieving compatibility.

[3] This is just a partial listing. For example, efforts are also under way to converge auditor education and requirements for offering and listing securities on stock markets.

[4] D. T. Nicolaisen, "Remarks Before the IASB Meeting with World Standard-Setters" (September 28, 2004), www.sec.gov/news/speech/spch092804dtn.htm.

investment in that company. The relative cost of obtaining capital will thereby increase for those companies. And, at the extreme, if as a result of companies using weak or incomplete accounting standards it becomes excessively time-consuming or difficult for investors to distinguish good investment opportunities from bad, investors may choose instead to invest in what they consider to be safer opportunities rather than in particular securities which may actually offer greater reward.

Financial statements prepared using a common set of accounting standards help investors better understand investment opportunities as opposed to financial statements prepared under differing sets of national accounting standards. Without common standards, global investors must incur the time and effort to understand and convert the financial statements so that they can confidently compare opportunities. This process is time-consuming and can be difficult, sometimes causing investors to resort to educated guesses as to content and comparability. Additionally, if investors are presented with financial information that varies substantially depending on which accounting standards are employed, that can cause investors to have doubt about the actual financial results of a company, resulting in a correspondingly adverse effect on investor confidence. . . .

Embracing a common set of accounting standards can also lower costs for issuers. When companies access capital markets beyond their home jurisdiction, they incur additional costs of preparing financial statements using different sets of accounting standards. These include the costs for company personnel and auditors to learn, keep current with and comply with the requirements of multiple jurisdictions. Similarly, use of resources dedicated to standards writing could potentially be optimized if fewer separate accounting models are pursued.[5]

Finally, a recent paper argued for "global GAAP." Among the benefits cited are:

- High-quality financial reporting standards that are used consistently around the world improve the efficiency with which capital is allocated. The cost of capital will be reduced.
- Investors can make better investment decisions. Portfolios are more diverse and financial risk is reduced. There is more transparency and comparability between competitors in the global markets.
- Companies can improve their strategic decision-making in the merger and acquisition area.
- Accounting knowledge and skills can be transferred seamlessly around the world.
- The best ideas arising from national standard-setting activities can be leveraged in developing global standards of the highest quality.[6]

To summarize, most arguments for accounting convergence relate in one way or another to increasing the operational and allocational efficiency of capital markets.

---

[5] D. T. Nicolaisen, "A Securities Regulator Looks at Convergence," *Northwestern University Journal of International Law and Business* (April 2005), www.sec.gov/news/speech/spch040605dtn.htm.
[6] PricewaterhouseCoopers, *Global GAAP: The Future of Corporate Reporting* (2003), www.pwcglobal.com.

Criticisms of International Standards

The internationalization of accounting standards has also had critics. As early as 1971 (before the IASC was formed), some said that international standards were too simple a solution for a complex problem. Arguing that accounting, as a social science, has built-in flexibility, critics maintained that the ability to adapt to widely different situations is one of its most important values. They doubted that international standards could be flexible enough to handle differences in national backgrounds, traditions, and economic environments, and some thought that internationalization would be a politically unacceptable challenge to national sovereignty. Many of these doubts and fears continue to be expressed today.

Critics also question whether comparability is the right goal of financial reporting. They worry that reflecting the underlying reality of a company's performance and financial position (that is, achieving a fair presentation) may be sacrificed in pursuit of achieving comparability. They also fear that a global monopoly standard-setter will inhibit innovation and the development of better quality standards. Finally, there are questions about whether comparability can be achieved without proper enforcement and as long as firms' reporting incentives differ across countries.[7]

Other observers claim that large international accounting service firms are using international accounting standards as a tool with which to expand their markets. Multinational accounting firms, they say, are indispensable to apply international standards in national environments where such standards might seem distant and complex. As international financial institutions and international markets insist on the use of international standards, only large international accounting firms will be able to meet the demand.

Finally, some critics maintain that international standards are not suitable for small and medium-sized companies, particularly unlisted ones with no public accountability. Standards written to meet the needs of users in the world's capital markets are unnecessarily complex and require too much detailed disclosure for these types of companies. In such firms, there is often no separation between ownership and management, and shares change hands infrequently—perhaps only on succession in a family business.[8]

Reconciliation and Mutual Recognition

As international equity issuance and trading grow, problems related to distributing financial statements in nondomestic jurisdictions become more important. As already noted, supporters argue that international convergence will help resolve problems associated with filings of cross-border financial statements.

Two other approaches have been advanced as possible solutions to the problems related to cross-border financial statement filings: (1) reconciliation, and (2) mutual recognition (also known as "reciprocity"). With reconciliation, foreign firms can prepare financial statements using home-country accounting standards, but also must provide a reconciliation between critical accounting measures of the home country and the

---

[7] For example, institutional differences as discussed in Chapters 2, 3, and 4 shape financial reporting incentives such as meeting earnings forecasts, underreporting liabilities, and smoothing earnings.
[8] See B. Shearer, "In Support of a GAAP Gap," *Accountancy Magazine* (September 2005): 96–97. "Big GAAP/ little GAAP" is a familiar theme in accounting. Here, it means international standards for global companies and simplified standards for the others. As noted later in this chapter, *IFRS for SMEs* was issued in 2009 in response to this concern.

country where the financial statements are being filed. For example, the U.S. Securities and Exchange Commission (SEC) permits foreign registrants to file their financial statements using another comprehensive body of accounting principles besides U.S. GAAP or International Financial Reporting Standards (IFRS). However, companies that do so must reconcile net income, shareholders' equity, and earnings per share to U.S. GAAP, if materially different. Reconciliations are less costly than preparing a full set of financial statements under a different set of accounting principles. However, they only provide a summary, not the full picture of the enterprise.

Mutual recognition exists when regulators outside the home country accept a foreign firm's financial statements based on home-country principles. For example, the London Stock Exchange accepts U.S. GAAP-based financial statements in filings made by foreign companies. Reciprocity does not improve the cross-country comparability of financial statements and can create an "unlevel playing field" in that it may allow foreign companies to apply standards less rigorous than those that apply to domestic companies.

Evaluation

The harmonization/convergence debate may never be completely settled. Some arguments against harmonization have merit. However, increasing evidence shows that the goal of international harmonization of accounting, disclosure, and auditing has been so widely accepted that the trend toward international convergence will continue or even accelerate. Debates aside, all dimensions of accounting *are* becoming harmonized worldwide. Many companies are voluntarily adopting International Financial Reporting Standards (IFRS). Growing numbers of countries have adopted IFRS in their entirety, base their national standards on IFRS, or allow the use of IFRS. Leading international organizations and standard-setting bodies throughout the world (the European Commission, World Trade Organization, and Organization for Economic Cooperation and Development, among others) endorse the goals of the International Accounting Standards Board (IASB). Progress in harmonizing disclosure and auditing has been impressive.

Finally, national differences in the underlying factors that lead to variation in accounting, disclosure, and auditing practice are narrowing as capital and product markets become more integrated. As already mentioned, many companies have voluntarily adopted IFRS. They have done so because they see economic benefit in adopting accounting and disclosure standards that are credible internationally. Moreover, as discussed in Chapter 5, companies are voluntarily expanding their disclosures in line with IFRS in response to demand from institutional investors and other financial statement users. The success of recent convergence efforts by international organizations may indicate that convergence is happening as a natural response to economic forces.

SOME SIGNIFICANT EVENTS IN THE HISTORY OF INTERNATIONAL ACCOUNTING STANDARD SETTING

1959—Jacob Kraayenhof, founding partner of a major European firm of independent accountants, urges that work on international accounting standards begin.

1961—Groupe d'Etudes, consisting of practicing accounting professionals, is established in Europe to advise European Union authorities on matters concerning accounting.

1966—Accountants International Study Group is formed by professional institutes in Canada, United Kingdom, and United States.

1973—International Accounting Standards Committee (IASC) is created.

1976—Organization for Economic Cooperation and Development (OECD) issues Declaration on Investment in Multinational Enterprises containing guidelines on "Disclosure of Information."

1977—International Federation of Accountants (IFAC) is founded.

1977—Group of Experts appointed by United Nations Economic and Social Council issues four-part report on *International Standards of Accounting and Reporting for Transnational Corporations.*

1978—Commission of European Community issues Fourth Directive as first move toward European accounting harmonization.

1981—IASC establishes consultative group of nonmember organizations to widen input to international standard setting.

1984—London Stock Exchange states that listed companies not incorporated in United Kingdom or Ireland are to comply with international accounting standards.

1987—International Organization of Securities Commissions (IOSCO) resolves at annual conference to promote use of common standards in accounting and auditing practices.

1989—IASC issues Exposure Draft 32 on comparability of financial statements and publishes *Framework for the Preparation and Presentation of Financial Statements.*

1995—IASC Board and IOSCO Technical Committee agree on work plan whose successful completion will result in IAS forming a comprehensive core set of standards. Successful completion of these standards will allow IOSCO Technical Committee to recommend endorsement of IAS for cross-border capital raising and listing purposes in all global markets.

1995—European Commission adopts new approach to accounting harmonization that allows use of IAS by companies listing on international capital markets.

1996—U.S. Securities and Exchange Commission (SEC) announces that it "supports the IASC's objective to develop, as expeditiously as possible, accounting standards that could be used for preparing financial statements that could be used in cross-border offerings."

1998—IOSCO publishes "International Disclosure Standards for Cross Border Offerings and Initial Listings by Foreign Issuers."

2000—IOSCO accepts all 40 core standards prepared by IASC in response to IOSCO's 1993 wish list.

2000—European Commission proposes regulation requiring all EU companies listed on regulated markets to prepare consolidated accounts in accordance with IAS by 2005.

2001—International Accounting Standards Board (IASB) succeeds IASC and assumes its responsibilities. IASB standards, designated International Financial Reporting Standards (IFRS), include IAS issued by the IASC.

2002—European Parliament endorses Commission proposal that virtually all EU listed companies must follow IASB standards starting no later than 2005 in their consolidated financial statements. Member states may extend requirement to nonlisted companies and to individual company statements. European Council later adopts enabling regulation.

2002—IASB and FASB sign the "Norwalk Agreement" committing them to convergence of international and U.S. accounting standards.

2003—European Council approves amended EU Fourth and Seventh Directives removing inconsistencies between old directives and IFRS.

2004—Australian Accounting Standards Board announces intent to adopt IFRS as Australian accounting standards.

2005—SEC proposes "roadmap" to eliminate requirement for reconciliation between IFRS and U.S. GAAP. SEC and EU Commission later agree on roadmap to eliminate requirement no later than 2009.

2005—Chinese Ministry of Finance commits to converging Chinese accounting standards to IFRS by 2007. Canadian Accounting Standards Board proposes eliminating Canadian GAAP in favor of IFRS by 2011. IASB and Accounting Standards Board of Japan launch convergence project.

2006—FASB and IASB sign memorandum of understanding setting out milestones the two boards must reach in order to demonstrate acceptable level of convergence between U.S. GAAP and IFRS to SEC and EU Commission.

2006—IASB publishes statement on its working relationships with other accounting standard setters.

2006—EU issues Statutory Audit Directive, replacing the Eighth Directive.

2007—Accounting Standards Board of Japan and IASB sign the "Tokyo Agreement" committing them to convergence of Japanese GAAP and IFRS.

2007—SEC eliminates reconciliation requirement for companies using IFRS as promulgated by IASB.

2008—SEC proposes "roadmap" outlining milestones that, if achieved, could lead to mandatory transition to IFRS by U.S. issuers starting in 2014, later changed to 2015.

OVERVIEW OF MAJOR INTERNATIONAL ORGANIZATIONS PROMOTING ACCOUNTING CONVERGENCE

Six organizations have been key players in setting international accounting standards and in promoting international accounting harmonization:

1. International Accounting Standards Board (IASB)
2. Commission of the European Union (EU)
3. International Organization of Securities Commissions (IOSCO)
4. International Federation of Accountants (IFAC)

5. United Nations Intergovernmental Working Group of Experts on International Standards of Accounting and Reporting (ISAR), part of United Nations Conference on Trade and Development (UNCTAD)
6. Organization for Economic Cooperation and Development Working Group on Accounting Standards (OECD Working Group)

The IASB represents private-sector interests and organizations. The EU Commission, referred to as the European Commission (EC), the OECD Working Group, and the ISAR are political entities that derive their powers from international agreements. IFAC's main activities include issuing technical and professional guidance and promoting the adoption of IFAC and IASB pronouncements. IOSCO promotes high standards of regulation, including harmonized accounting and disclosure standards for cross-border capital raising and trading.

Also important is the World Federation of Exchanges (WFE), the trade organization for regulated securities and derivative markets worldwide. The WFE promotes the professional business development of financial markets. One of the WFE's goals is to establish harmonized standards for business processes (including financial reporting and disclosure) in cross-border trading in securities, including cross-border public offerings.

Many regional accounting organizations (e.g., the ASEAN Federation of Accountants, the Nordic Federation of Accountants) participate in cross-country standard setting within their respective regions. The Fédération des Experts Comptables Européens (FEE: Federation of European Accountants) represents national accounting bodies in Europe. Other regional organizations include the Fédération des Bourses Européennes (FESE: Federation of European Securities Exchanges) and the Committee of European Securities Regulators (CESR), consisting of securities market regulators from EU member nations.

Refer to Exhibit 8-1 for Web sites offering information about major international organizations. Exhibit 8-2 presents the Web site addresses of national regulatory and accountancy organizations, many of which are actively involved in accounting convergence activities.

INTERNATIONAL ACCOUNTING STANDARDS BOARD

The International Accounting Standards Board (IASB), formerly the IASC, is an independent private-sector standard-setting body founded in 1973 by professional accounting organizations in nine countries and restructured in 2001. (The restructuring made IASC into an umbrella organization under which the IASB carries out its work.)[9] Before the restructuring, the IASC issued 41 International Accounting Standards (IAS) and a Framework for the Preparation and Presentation of Financial Statements. The IASB's objectives are:

1. To develop, in the public interest, a single set of high-quality, understandable, and enforceable global accounting standards that require high-quality, transparent, and comparable information in financial statements and other financial reporting to help participants in the world's capital markets and other users make economic decisions.
2. To promote the use and rigorous application of those standards.

---

[9] The IASC Foundation will be renamed the International Financial Reporting Standards Foundation sometime during 2010.

EXHIBIT 8-1	Web Sites Offering Information about Major International Organizations and International Convergence Activities

Organization	Web Site Address
Bank for International Settlements	www.bis.org
Committee of European Securities Regulators	www.cesr-eu.org
Confederation of Asian & Pacific Accountants (CAPA)	capa.com.my
Deloitte IAS Plus Web site	www.iasplus.com
European Union (EU)	europa.eu
European Commission—Internal Market and Financial Services	ec.europa.eu/internal_market/index_en.htm
Fédération des Experts Comptables Européens (FEE) a/k/a European Federation of Accountants	www.fee.be
Federation of European Securities Exchanges a/k/a Fédération des Bourses Européennes (FESE)	www.fese.be/en/
International Accounting Standards Board (IASB)	www.iasb.org
International Federation of Accountants (IFAC)	www.ifac.org
International Monetary Fund (IMF)	www.imf.org
International Organization of Securities Commissions (IOSCO)	www.iosco.org
Organization for Economic Cooperation and Development (OECD)	www.oecd.org
United Nations Conference on Trade and Development (UNCTAD)	www.unctad.org
World Bank	www.worldbank.org
World Federation of Exchanges (WFE)	www.world-exchanges.org
World Trade Organization (WTO)	www.wto.org

Note: These listings were correct when this book went to press.

3. In fulfilling the objectives associated with (1) and (2), to take account of, as appropriate, the special needs of small and medium-sized entities and emerging economies.
4. To bring about convergence of national accounting standards, and International Accounting Standards and International Financial Reporting Standards to high-quality solutions.[10]

The IASB represents accounting organizations from every part of the world. With a remarkably broad base of support, the IASB is the driving force in international accounting standard setting. Exhibit 8-3 lists the current IASB standards (as of April

---

[10] See the IASB Web site (www.iasb.org).

EXHIBIT 8-2	Web Site Addresses of Selected Regulatory and Accountancy Organizations

Organization	Web Site Address
Government and Regulatory Organizations	
U.K. Financial Services Authority (FSA)	www.fsa.gov.uk
U.S. Public Company Accounting Oversight Board	www.pcaobus.org
U.S. Securities and Exchange Commission (SEC)	www.sec.gov
U.S. Securities and Exchange Commission (SEC) Edgar Database	www.sec.gov/edgar.shtml
French Autorité des Marché Financiers (AMF)	www.amf-france.org
National Professional Accountancy Organizations	
Argentina—Federación Argentina de Consejos Profesionales de Ciencias Económicas	www.facpce.org.ar
Barbados—Institute of Chartered Accountants of Barbados	www.icab.bb
Belgium—Institut des Experts Comptables	www.accountancy.be
Belgium—Institut des Réviseurs d'Entreprises	www.accountancy.be
Canada—Society of Management Accountants of Canada	www.cma-canada.org
Canada—Chartered Accountants of Canada	www.cica.ca
Canada—Certified General Accountants Association of Canada	www.cga-canada.org
China—Chinese Institute of Certified Public Accountants	www.cicpa.org.cn
Cyprus—Institute of Certified Public Accountants of Cyprus	www.icpac.org.cy
Czech Republic—Union of Accountants of the Czech Republic	www.svaz-ucetnich.cz
France—Conseil Supérieur de l'Ordre des Experts-Comptables	www.experts-comptables.com
Georgia—Georgian Federation of Professional Accountants and Auditors	www.gfpaa.ge
Germany—Institut der Wirtschaftsprüfer in Deutschland	www.idw.de
Hong Kong—Hong Kong Institute of Certified Public Accountants	www.hksa.org.hk
Hong Kong—Hong Kong Institute of Accredited Accounting Technicians	www.hkaat.org.hk
India—Institute of Chartered Accountants of India	www.icai.org
Ireland—Institute of Chartered Accountants in Ireland	www.icai.ie
Japan—Japanese Institute of Certified Public Accountants	www.hp.jicpa.or.jp
Jordan—Arab Society of Certified Accountants	www.ascasociety.org
Kenya—Institute of Certified Public Accountants of Kenya	www.icpak.com
Korea—Korean Institute of Certified Public Accountants	www.kicpa.or.kr
Malaysia—Malaysian Institute of Accountants	www.mia.org.my
Malta—Malta Institute of Accountants	www.miamalta.org
Mexico—Instituto Mexicano de Contadores Públicos	www.imcp.org.mx
Nepal—Institute of Chartered Accountants of Nepal	www.ican.org.np
Netherlands—Koninklijk Nederlands Instituut van Registeraccountants	www.nivra.nl

(continued)

EXHIBIT 8-2	Web Site Addresses of Selected Regulatory and Accountancy Organizations (Continued)

Organization	Web Site Address
New Zealand—Institute of Chartered Accountants of New Zealand	www.nzica.com
Nigeria—Institute of Chartered Accountants of Nigeria	www.ican-ngr.org
Norway—Den norske Revisorforeningen (DnR)	www.revisorforeningen.no
Pakistan—Institute of Cost and Management Accountants of Pakistan	www.icmap.com.pk
Pakistan—Institute of Chartered Accountants of Pakistan	www.icap.org.pk
Philippines—Philippine Institute of Certified Public Accountants	www.picpa.com.ph
Romania—Corpul Expertilor Contabili si Contabililor Autorizati din Romania	www.ceccar.ro
Singapore—Institute of Certified Public Accountants of Singapore	www.accountants.org.sg
South Africa—South African Institute of Chartered Accountants (SAICA)	www.saica.co.za
South Africa—South African Institute of Professional Accountants	www.saipa.co.za
Sri Lanka—Institute of Chartered Accountants of Sri Lanka	www.icasrilanka.com
Sweden—Branchorganisationen för revisorer och rådgivare	www.farsrs.se
U.K.— Institute of Chartered Accountants in England & Wales	www.icaew.com
U.K.—Chartered Institute of Management Accountants	www.cimaglobal.com
U.K.—Association of Chartered Certified Accountants	www.acca.org.uk
U.K.—Chartered Institute of Public Finance and Accountancy	www.cipfa.org.uk
U.K.—Institute of Chartered Accountants of Scotland	www.icas.org.uk
U.K.—Association of Accounting Technicians	www.taaieem.org
U.S.—American Institute of Certified Public Accountants	www.aicpa.org
U.S.—National Association of State Boards of Accountancy	www.nasba.org
U.S.—Institute of Management Accountants	www.imanet.org
U.S.— Institute of Internal Auditors	www.theiia.org
Zimbabwe—Institute of Chartered Accountants of Zimbabwe	www.icaz.org.zw

Accounting Standard-Setting Bodies

Australia—Australian Accounting Standards Board (AASB)	www.aasb.com.au
Canada—Accounting Standards Board (ASB)	www.acsbcanada.org
France—Conseil National de la Comptabilité (CNC)	www.minefi.gouv.fr/directions _services/CNCompta
Germany—German Accounting Standards Committee (GASC)	www.drsc.de
Japan—Accounting Standards Board (ASBJ)	www.asb.or.jp
Netherlands— Dutch Accounting Standards Board	www.rjnet.nl
New Zealand—Accounting Standards Review Board	www.asrb.co.nz
United Kingdom—Accounting Standards Board (ASB)	www.frc.org.uk/asb
United States—Financial Accounting Standards Board (FASB)	www.fasb.org

Note: These listings were correct when this book went to press.

EXHIBIT 8-3	Current IASB Standards
Standard	**Description**
IAS 1	Presentation of Financial Statements
IAS 2	Inventories
IAS 3	No longer effective. Replaced by IAS 27 and IAS 28.
IAS 4	No longer effective. Replaced by IAS 16, 22, and IAS 38.
IAS 5	No longer effective. Replaced by IAS 1.
IAS 6	No longer effective. Replaced by IAS 15.
IAS 7	Cash Flow Statements
IAS 8	Accounting Policies, Changes in Accounting Estimates and Errors
IAS 9	No longer effective. Replaced by IAS 38.
IAS 10	Events Occurring after the Balance Sheet Date
IAS 11	Construction Contracts
IAS 12	Income Taxes
IAS 13	No longer effective. Replaced by IAS 1.
IAS 14	No longer effective. Replaced by IFRS 8.
IAS 15	No longer effective. Withdrawn December 2003.
IAS 16	Property, Plant, and Equipment
IAS 17	Leases
IAS 18	Revenue
IAS 19	Employee Benefits
IAS 20	Accounting for Government Grants and Disclosure of Government Assistance
IAS 21	The Effects of Changes in Foreign Exchange Rates
IAS 22	No longer effective. Replaced by IFRS 3.
IAS 23	Borrowing Costs
IAS 24	Related Party Disclosures
IAS 25	No longer effective. Replaced by IAS 39 and IAS 40.
IAS 26	Accounting and Reporting by Retirement Benefit Plans
IAS 27	Consolidated and Separate Financial Statements
IAS 28	Investments in Associates
IAS 29	Financial Reporting in Hyperinflationary Economies
IAS 30	No longer effective. Replaced by IFRS 7.
IAS 31	Interests in Joint Ventures
IAS 32	Financial Instruments: Disclosures and Presentation
IAS 33	Earnings Per Share
IAS 34	Interim Financial Reporting
IAS 35	No longer effective. Replaced by IFRS 5.
IAS 36	Impairment of Assets
IAS 37	Provisions, Contingent Liabilities, and Contingent Assets

(continued)

EXHIBIT 8-3	Current IASB Standards (Continued)
Standard	**Description**
IAS 38	Intangible Assets
IAS 39	Financial Instruments: Recognition and Measurement. Partially replaced by IFRS 9.
IAS 40	Investment Property
IAS 41	Agriculture
IFRS 1	First-time Adoption of International Financial Reporting Standards
IFRS 2	Share-Based Payment
IFRS 3	Business Combinations
IFRS 4	Insurance Contracts
IFRS 5	Non-Current Assets Held for Sale and Discontinued Operations
IFRS 6	Exploration for and Evaluation of Mineral Resources
IFRS 7	Financial Instruments: Disclosure
IFRS 8	Operating Segments IFRS 9 Financial Instruments

Note: As of April 2010. Consult IASB Web site, www.iasb.org, for current list.

2010).[11] The IASB Web site (www.iasb.org) makes IASB standards freely available to registered users. IASB standards follow the principles of fair presentation and full disclosure (see Chapter 2). Financial reporting and accounting measurement principles are described in Chapter 3. Simplified reporting standards have been issued for small and medium-sized entities.[12]

During the first decade of the IASC, international accounting standards were more descriptive than prescriptive. These early standards codified similar national practices and excluded outlier practices. The IASC began to address more difficult issues during its second 10 years and responded to concerns that its standards included too many alternative accounting treatments and were not rigorous enough.

IASC's Core Standards and the IOSCO Agreement

The IASB (like the former IASC) has been striving to develop accounting standards that will be accepted by securities regulators around the world. As part of this effort, the IASC adopted a work plan to produce a comprehensive core set of high-quality standards. In July 1995, the IOSCO Technical Committee stated its agreement with the work

---

[11] Standards issued by the IASB are referred to as International Financial Reporting Standards (IFRS); those issued by the IASC are called International Accounting Standards (IAS). The IASB has adopted all previously issued IAS. All references to IFRS include IAS.
[12] Issued in 2009, *IFRS for SMEs* simplifies recognition and measurement requirements. For example, (a) property, plant, and equipment and intangibles are valued at historical cost—the revaluation option is removed; (b) all intangible assets, including goodwill, are presumed to have a ten-year life and are amortized over that period; (c) development costs are expensed; and (d) the cost model is permitted for investments in associates and joint ventures. Disclosure requirements are also reduced. For example, the disclosure of earnings per share and operating segment reporting are not required. The volume of accounting guidance is reduced by more than 85 percent compared to full IASB standards.

plan. The Core Standards were completed with the approval of IAS 39 in December 1998. IOSCO's review of the Core Standards began in 1999, and in 2000 it endorsed the use of IASC Standards for cross-border offerings and listings.

The IASB Structure

The IASC board formed a Strategy Working Party (SWP) to consider what the IASC's strategy and structure should be after completion of the core standards work program. In 1998, the SWP approved a discussion paper, "Shaping IASC for the Future," to encourage and focus discussion. In 1999, the IASC board unanimously approved a resolution supporting a proposed new structure with the following main features: (1) IASC would be established as an independent organization; (2) the organization would have two main bodies, the trustees and the board, as well as a Standing Interpretations Committee (now called the International Financial Reporting Interpretations Committee) and a Standards Advisory Council (now called the IFRS Advisory Council); and (3) the trustees would appoint the board members, exercise oversight, and raise the funds needed, whereas the board would have sole responsibility for setting accounting standards. A monitoring board of securities market regulators was established in 2009 to oversee the activities of the trustees.

The IASB includes the following bodies.[13]

1. *Trustees.*   The IASB has 22 trustees: six from North America, six from Europe, six from the Asia/Oceania region, and four from any area ("subject to establishing overall geographic balance").[14] The trustees appoint the members of the board, the International Financial Reporting Interpretations Committee, and the IFRS Advisory Council. The trustees are responsible for raising funds, and supervise and review the priorities and operations of the IASB.

2. *Monitoring Board.*   The Monitoring Board was recently established to provide a formal link between the trustees and capital market authorities. The Monitoring Board has one representative from the European Commission, two from the International Organization of Securities Commissions, one from the Japanese Financial Services Agency, and one from the U.S. Securities and Exchange Commission. There is also an observer, representing the Basel Committee on Banking Supervision.[15] The Monitoring Board appoints the trustees and provides oversight over their activities.

3. *IASB Board.*   The board establishes and improves standards of financial accounting and reporting for businesses. Its responsibilities include "complete responsibility for all IASB technical matters including the preparation and issuing of International Accounting Standards, International Financial Reporting Standards, and exposure drafts . . . and final approval of Interpretations by the

---

[13] Much of this section is based on information published on the IASB Web site (www.iasb.org). The IASB structure is modeled after the U.S. accounting standard-setting structure, as described in Chapter 4.

[14] All direct quotations in this section are from the IASB constitution (revised February 2009), found on its Web site (www.iasb.org).

[15] The European Commission and the International Organization of Securities Commissions are discussed later in this chapter. The Japanese Financial Services Agency and the U.S. Securities and Exchange Commission are discussed in Chapter 4.

International Financial Reporting Interpretations Committee," and approving the technical agenda and the conduct of its work. The board consists of 15 members, appointed by the trustees to provide "the best available combination of technical expertise and diversity of international business and market experience."[16] All board members are paid IASB employees. Up to three members may be part-time; the rest are full-time. To ensure geographic diversity, the board will normally have four members from North America, four from Europe, four from the Asia/Oceania region, one from Africa, one from South America, and the rest from any area ("subject to maintaining overall geographic balance"). The board maintains liaison with national standard setters and other official bodies concerned with standard setting. (The purpose is to partner with these national bodies to achieve the convergence of national and international accounting standards.)[17] Members are appointed for a five-year term, renewable once.

4. *International Financial Reporting Interpretations Committee (IFRIC).* The IFRIC consists of 14 members appointed by the trustees. The IFRIC interprets "the application of International Accounting Standards and International Financial Reporting Standards and provides timely guidance on financial reporting issues not specifically addressed in IAS and IFRS, in the context of IASB's Framework," publishes draft interpretations and reviews public comments on them, and obtains board approval for final interpretations.

5. *IFRS Advisory Council.* The IFRS Advisory Council, appointed by the trustees, is made up of "thirty or more members, having a diversity of geographic and professional backgrounds, appointed for renewable terms of three years." The council was reconstituted in 2009 so that it is made up of individuals representing a wide range of investor groups relevant to the accounting standard-setting process.[18] The IFRS Advisory Council normally meets three times each year. Its responsibilities are to give the board advice on its agenda and priorities, inform the board of the views "of the organizations and individuals on the council on major standard setting projects," and give "other advice" to the board or the trustees.

The IASB follows due process in setting accounting standards. For each standard, the board normally publishes a discussion paper that sets out the possible requirements for the standard and the arguments for and against each one. Subsequently, the board publishes an exposure draft for public comment, and it then examines the arguments put forward in the comment process before deciding on the final form of the standard. An exposure draft and final standard can be issued only when nine members of the board have voted in favor of doing so.[19]

---

[16] By July 1, 2012, there will be 16 IASB Board members.

[17] The IASB has formal liaison relationships with standard setters in Australia and New Zealand, Canada, France, Germany, Japan, the United Kingdom, the United States, and the Technical Expert Group of the European Financial Reporting Advisory Group (EFRAG, discussed later in this chapter).

[18] For example, there are representatives from the major accounting firms, the World Bank, the International Monetary Fund, Financial Executives International, Committee of European Securities Regulators, and the International Organization of Securities Commissions. A complete list of SAC members is available on the IASB Web site, www.iasb.org.

[19] The number increases to ten when the board becomes 16 members.

Recognition and Support for the IASB

International Financial Reporting Standards are now widely accepted around the world. They are (1) used by many countries as the basis for national accounting requirements or are adopted entirely; (2) accepted by many stock exchanges and regulators that allow foreign or domestic companies to file financial statements prepared in conformance with IFRS; and (3) recognized by the EC and other supranational bodies. In 1995, the EC endorsed IFRS. Rather than amend existing directives, the EC determined that the EU should associate with IASC/IASB and IOSCO efforts toward a broader international harmonization of accounting standards. EU companies listed on recognized stock exchanges now use IFRS in preparing consolidated financial statements.

The signing of the 2002 "Norwalk Agreement" by the IASB and U.S. Financial Accounting Standards Board symbolized the commitment of national standard setters to converge toward a single set of international accounting standards worldwide. The Australian Accounting Standards Board has adopted IFRS as Australia's accounting standards. China and Japan have committed to converging their respective national accounting standards to IFRS. The Canadian Accounting Standards Board will replace Canadian accounting standards with IFRS in 2011. Standard setters from Australia/New Zealand, Canada, France, Germany, Japan, the United Kingdom, and the United States actively partner with the IASB in its standard-setting activities.

U.S. Securities and Exchange Commission Response to IFRS

During the 1990s, the SEC came under increasing pressure to make U.S. capital markets more accessible to non-U.S. issuers. At the time, the SEC expressed support for the IASB's objective to develop accounting standards for use in financial statements used in cross-border offerings. However, the SEC also stated that three conditions must be met for it to accept IASB standards.[20]

1. The standards must include a core set of accounting pronouncements that constitutes a comprehensive, generally accepted basis of accounting.
2. The standards must be of high quality—they must result in comparability and transparency, and they must provide for full disclosure.
3. The standards must be rigorously interpreted and applied.

Later, senior officials of the SEC indicated that if the IASB and FASB make sufficient progress in converging their standards, and if sufficient progress is made in creating an infrastructure for interpreting and enforcing accounting standards, the SEC would consider allowing foreign registrants to file in the United States using IFRS without reconciling to U.S. GAAP.

In 2005, the SEC issued a "roadmap" setting out the steps for eliminating the requirement to reconcile IFRS to U.S. GAAP. The SEC roadmap reaffirmed that sufficient convergence must have been achieved between the two sets of standards and that the SEC has confidence in auditing and enforcement practices. The SEC and the EU Commission (discussed next) signed an agreement on the roadmap later that same year. In 2006, the FASB and IASB signed a memorandum of understanding on how they will achieve convergence

---

[20] U.S. Securities and Exchange Commission, "News Release—SEC Statement Regarding International Accounting Standards" (Washington, DC: U.S. Securities and Exchange Commission, April 11, 1996).

between U.S. GAAP and IFRS in order for the SEC to eliminate the reconciliation requirement. This memorandum of understanding is essentially their own roadmap containing a "to do" list and milestones for achieving equivalence between the two sets of standards. In 2007, the SEC eliminated the reconciliation requirement for companies using IFRS. The SEC's decision indicates confidence in the quality and application of IFRS and in the convergence process between the FASB and IASB. The FASB/IASB memorandum of understanding was updated in 2008, setting out major convergence goals to be achieved by 2011.

The SEC is currently studying whether to allow, or even require, U.S. companies to use IFRS. Opponents of the idea question whether principles-based IFRS would be workable in the litigious U.S. environment. Opponents believe that U.S. interests are best served by keeping U.S. GAAP for U.S. companies and continuing the effort to converge U.S. GAAP and IFRS. They worry about accounting standards that are not "made in America." However, proponents argue that a single set of high-quality global standards is the right goal. They argue that IFRS will continue to improve over time and that the convergence process—already long, difficult, and costly—is unlikely to be wholly successful in eliminating differences between U.S. GAAP and IFRS. An SEC proposal issued in 2008 could eventually lead to the mandatory transition to IFRS by U.S. registrants. (The originally proposed start date of 2014 was later changed to 2015.)

EUROPEAN UNION (EU)

The Treaty of Rome established the European Economic Community (EEC, later called the European Community) in 1957, with the goal of harmonizing the legal and economic systems of its member states. The EEC was absorbed into the European Union (EU) when it came into existence in 1993, as a result of the (1992) Maastricht Treaty. The EU now comprises 27 member countries (Austria, Belgium, Bulgaria, Cyprus, Czech Republic, Denmark, Estonia, Finland, France, Germany, Greece, Hungary, Ireland, Italy, Latvia, Lithuania, Luxembourg, Malta, the Netherlands, Poland, Portugal, Romania, Slovakia, Slovenia, Spain, Sweden, and the United Kingdom). In contrast to the IASB, which has no authority to require implementation of its accounting standards, the European Commission (EC, the governing body of the EU) has full enforcement powers for its accounting directives throughout the member states.

One of the EU's goals is to achieve integration of European financial markets. Toward this end, the EC has introduced directives and undertaken major initiatives to achieve a single market for:

- raising capital on an EU-wide basis
- establishing a common legal framework for integrated securities and derivatives markets
- achieving a single set of accounting standards for listed companies

The EC embarked on a major program of company law harmonization soon after it was formed.[21] EC directives now cover all aspects of company law. Several have a

---

[21] EU directives become the law of member states through a complex, lengthy process. Preliminary work leads to the issuance of a draft directive (i.e., exposure draft) by the EU. When a draft directive is broadly acceptable (after hearings and other evaluation procedures), it is submitted to the member states for ratification after approval from the European Council. After the EU adopts a directive, each member state adopts and implements it. Directives are binding on member states, but the method of implementation is left to the discretion of national authorities.

direct bearing on accounting. Many observers consider the Fourth, Seventh, and Eighth Directives to be historically and substantively the most important.

Fourth, Seventh, and Eighth Directives

The EU's Fourth Directive, issued in 1978, is the broadest and most comprehensive set of accounting rules within the EU framework. Both public and private companies above certain minimum size criteria must comply. Fourth Directive requirements apply to individual company accounts and include format rules for financial statements, disclosure requirements, and valuation rules. The true and fair view is the overriding requirement and holds for footnote disclosures just as it does for financial statements. The Fourth Directive also requires that financial statements be audited. It aims to ensure that European companies disclose comparable and equivalent information in their financial statements.

The Seventh Directive, issued in 1983, addresses the issue of consolidated financial statements. At the time, consolidated financial statements were the exception rather than the rule. They were the norm in Ireland, the Netherlands, and the United Kingdom, and Germany required consolidation of German subsidiaries (only). Elsewhere in Europe consolidated statements were rare. The Seventh Directive requires consolidation for groups of companies above a certain size, specifies disclosures in notes and the directors' report, and requires an audit. Because of the newness of consolidations as a legal requirement, member states were given wide latitude and many options for incorporating the Seventh Directive into their individual national company laws.

The Eighth Directive, issued in 1984, addresses various aspects of the qualifications of professionals authorized to carry out legally required (statutory) audits. Essentially, this directive lays down minimum qualifications for auditors. It covers requirements for the education and training of auditors and independence. The Eighth Directive was substantially amended in 2006 and is now referred to as the Statutory Audit Directive. The new directive is a response to accounting scandals involving European companies such as Parmalat, the Italian dairy company, and Ahold, the Dutch grocery chain, as well as to the American accounting scandals involving WorldCom, Global Crossing, and Enron, and others. It includes requirements for the appointment and removal of auditors, audit standards, continuing professional education, auditor rotation, and public oversight. It requires that all statutory audits in the EU observe International Standards on Auditing (discussed later). Among its more important provisions is one requiring each member state to establish a public oversight body for the audit profession and the establishment of the European Group of Auditors' Oversight Bodies (EGAOB) to coordinate their activities. Exhibit 8-4 compares certain features of the Statutory Audit Directive to the U.S. Sarbanes-Oxley Act (see Chapter 4).

Transparency Directive

The 2007 Transparency Directive harmonized certain requirements for annual and interim reporting for listed companies. Among the provisions are requirements that the annual report must be released no later than four months after year-end and the half-yearly (financial) report must be released within two months of the half-year date. Both reports must contain a "responsibility statement" by which the board of directors confirms that the financial statements give a true and fair view. A narrative management

EXHIBIT 8-4	Comparison of EU Statutory Audit Directive and U.S. Sarbanes-Oxley Act	
Issue	**EU Statutory Audit Directive**	**U.S. Sarbanes-Oxley Act**
Audit committees	Required for listed companies. Appoints or dismisses the auditor. At least one member must be independent. At least one member must have financial expertise.	Required for listed companies. Appoints or dismisses the auditor. Committee must be independent. At least one member must have financial expertise. Also requires procedures for complaints from whistleblowers.
Internal controls	Audit firm must report on key matters that arise from the audit, especially weaknesses in internal controls.	Same. Requirements are more detailed.
Public oversight of auditors	Each member state must appoint an oversight body for auditors.	Public Company Accounting Oversight Board (PCAOB) oversees audit of public companies, establishes standards for auditing, quality control, ethics, and independence of audit firms.
Firm vs. partner rotation	Key audit partner rotation every seven years, with member-state option of rotation of audit firm.	Lead audit partner must rotate every five years.
Auditing standards	International Standards on Auditing.	PCAOB standards.

report discussing the company's material evens and transactions, performance, and financial position must be released quarterly.

Have EU Harmonization Efforts Been Successful?

The Fourth and Seventh Directives had a dramatic impact on financial reporting throughout the EU, bringing accounting in all the member states up to a good and reasonably uniform level. It harmonized the presentation of the profit and loss account (income statement) and balance sheet and added minimum supplementary information in the notes, in particular a disclosure of the impact of tax regulations on reported results. It accelerated accounting development in many EU countries and also influenced accounting in neighboring, non-EU countries.

However, the success of EU harmonization efforts has been debated. For example, member states generally did not scrap their existing accounting rules when adopting EU directives. Instead, they adapted the new rules to their existing ones. Another issue is the extent to which member states enforced compliance with the directives. Thus, some question whether the directives harmonized accounting as much as had been intended when they were issued.[22]

---

[22] Peter Walton, "European Harmonization," in *International Finance and Accounting Handbook*, ed. Frederick D. S. Choi, 3rd ed. (New York: John Wiley, 2003).

Karel van Hulle, former head of the accounting and audit unit at the European Commission, described some of the difficulties.

It must be admitted that the comparability achieved through the harmonisation process is far from perfect. First of all, the Accounting Directives contain primarily minimum rules. They are *not* dealing with a number of important accounting issues. Secondly, the provisions of the Directives are not always interpreted in the same way by Member States. A number of questions relating to the interpretation of the Directives have been dealt with by the Contact Committee on the Accounting Directives.[23] Other questions have remained on the table. It has been difficult to arrive at an agreed position on these questions because the text of the Directives often leaves much scope for interpretation and Member States were not prepared to compromise on the interpretation. The general wording of some of the provisions in the Accounting Directives has been an important reason why the Commission has not brought some of these questions before the European Court of Justice for a final ruling.[24]

The EU's New Approach and the Integration of European Financial Markets

In 1995, the EC adopted a new approach to accounting harmonization, referred to as the New Accounting Strategy. The commission announced that the EU needed to move promptly in order to give a clear signal that companies seeking listings in the United States and other world markets will be able to remain within the EU accounting framework. The EC also stressed that the EU needed to strengthen its commitment to the international standard-setting process that offers the most efficient and rapid solution for the problems of companies operating on an international scale.

In 2000, the EC adopted a new financial reporting strategy. The cornerstone of this strategy was a proposed regulation that all EU companies listed on regulated markets, including banks, insurance companies, and SMEs (small and medium-sized companies), prepare consolidated accounts in accordance with IFRS. (Unlisted SMEs are not covered, but may find it in their interest to adopt IFRS voluntarily, especially if they seek international capital.) The EU Parliament endorsed this proposal, and the EU Council adopted the necessary enabling legislation in 2002.[25]

This regulation affected some 7,000 listed EU companies (compared with nearly 300 listed EU companies that used IFRS in 2001). It is designed "to encourage cross-border trade in financial services and so create a fully-integrated market, by helping to make financial information more transparent and easily comparable."[26]

---

[23] European Commission Contact Committee on the Accounting Directives, *The Accounting Harmonisation* in the European Community: *Problems of Applying the Fourth Directive on the Annual Accounts of Limited Companies* (Luxembourg: Office for Official Publications of the European Communities, 1990).

[24] Karel van Hulle, "International Harmonisation of Accounting Principles: A European Perspective," *Wirtschaftsprüferkammer—Mitteilungen,* special edition (June 1997): 44–50.

[25] Regulation (EC) No. 1606/2002. Member states may extend this requirement to all companies, not just listed ones, including individual company accounts.

[26] "International Accounting Standards: Mandatory for Listed Companies by 2005," *Single Market News,* no. 25 (March 2001): 18–19.

To become legally binding, IFRS must be adopted by the EC. Included in the above regulation is a two-tiered "endorsement mechanism" and the establishment of the Accounting Regulatory Committee (ARC), an EU body with representatives from member states. An IFRS is first given a technical review and opinion by the European Financial Reporting Advisory Group (EFRAG), a private-sector organization of auditors, preparers, national standard setters, and others.[27] The Standards Advice Review Group, an EU body of independent experts and representatives of national standard setters, next assesses whether EFRAG's endorsement advice is well balanced and objective. Then the ARC recommends that the IFRS be endorsed (or not) based on whether it is compatible with European directives and conducive to the European public good. EC endorsement completes the process. The entire endorsement process normally takes around 10 months. To date, all IFRS have been endorsed, with the exception of one "carve-out" to IAS 39.[28] The Fourth and Seventh Directives were also amended in 2003 to remove inconsistencies between the old directives and IFRS. Auditor's reports refer to IFRS "as adopted by the European Union."

Finally, there have been developments designed to strengthen enforcement of IRFS in Europe. In 2003, the Committee of European Securities Regulators adopted Standard 1 on Financial Information. This standard contains 21 principles aimed at developing and implementing a common approach to the enforcement of IFRS throughout the EU.[29] Standard 2 on Financial Information Coordination and Enforcement Activities was issued to provide a framework for coordinating enforcement in the EU.[30]

INTERNATIONAL ORGANIZATION OF SECURITIES COMMISSIONS (IOSCO)

The International Organization of Securities Commissions (IOSCO) consists of securities regulators from more than 100 countries. The objectives of IOSCO's member agencies are:

- To cooperate together to promote high standards of regulation in order to maintain just, efficient, and sound markets
- To exchange information on their respective experiences in order to promote the development of domestic markets
- To unite their efforts to establish standards and an effective surveillance of international securities transactions
- To provide mutual assistance to promote the integrity of the markets by a rigorous application of the standards and by effective enforcement against offenses

Together, IOSCO members are responsible for regulating more than 90 percent of global securities markets. As financial markets have become increasingly global,

---

[27] The EFRAG Web site is www.efrag.org.
[28] A carve-out is an exception to one or more provisions of a particular standard. The EC has endorsed IAS 39 with the exception of its provisions on hedge accounting. This carve-out allows entities to use hedge accounting in circumstances that are not permitted by IAS 39.
[29] *Standard No. 1 on Financial Information: Enforcement of Standards on Financial Information in Europe,* CESR 03–073 (March 12, 2003). CESR was established in 2001 as an EC advisory group on securities market regulation. Its Web site is www.cesr-eu.org.
[30] *Standard No. 2 on Financial Information Coordination and Enforcement Activities* CESR 03-317c (April 2004).

cross-border cooperation among securities regulators has become an increasingly important objective for the organization.

IOSCO has worked extensively on international disclosure and accounting standards to facilitate the ability of companies to raise capital efficiently in global securities markets. In 1998, IOSCO published a set of nonfinancial disclosure standards that may eventually enable companies to use a single prospectus to offer or list shares on any of the world's major capital markets. Securities regulators worldwide are increasingly adopting these standards.

An IOSCO technical committee focuses on multinational disclosure and accounting. Its main objective is to facilitate the process whereby world-class issuers can raise capital in the most effective and efficient way on all capital markets where investor demand exists. It cooperates with the IASB by, among other activities, providing input on IASB projects. It has endorsed IFRS for cross-border securities offerings. A working-party study completed in 1998 presented recommendations for facilitating multinational equity offerings. The report recommended "that regulators be encouraged, where consistent with their legal mandate and the goal of investor protection, to facilitate the use of single disclosure documents, whether by harmonisation of standards, reciprocity or otherwise."[31]

Exhibit 8-5 presents a brief summary of the 10 disclosure standards. The summary is important because it indicates the comprehensiveness proposed by the working party. The disclosure standards proposed are also highly detailed.

In 2002, a companion disclosure document for ongoing disclosures was published. Excerpts from this document are reproduced in Exhibit 8-6.

EXHIBIT 8-5	Summary of International Disclosure Standards for Cross-Border Offerings and Initial Listings by Foreign Issuers

1. **Identity of Directors, Senior Management, and Advisers and Responsibility Statement**

   This standard identifies the company representatives and other individuals involved in the company's listing or registration, and indicates the persons responsible. The definition of the persons covered by this standard may vary in each country and would be determined by host country law.

2. **Offer Statistics and Expected Timetable**

   This standard provides key information regarding the conduct of any offering and the identification of important dates relating to the offering. It is understood that listings do not always involve offerings.

3. **Key Information**

   This standard summarizes key information about the company's financial condition, capitalization, and risk factors.

4. **Information on the Company**

   This standard provides information about the company's business operations, the products it makes or the services it provides, and the factors that affect the business.

5. **Operating and Financial Review and Prospects**

   This standard provides management's explanation of factors that have affected the company's financial condition and results of operations, and management's assessment of factors and trends

(continued)

---

[31] International Organization of Securities Commissions, *International Disclosure Standards for Cross-Border Offerings and Initial Listings by Foreign Firms*, 1998.

EXHIBIT 8-5	Summary of International Disclosure Standards for Cross-Border Offerings and Initial Listings by Foreign Issuers (Continued)

that are anticipated to have a material effect on the company's financial condition and results of operations in future periods. In some countries, a forecast or statement of the company's prospects for the current year and/or other future periods may be required.

6. Directors and Officers

This standard provides information concerning the company's directors and managers that will allow investors to assess their experience, qualifications, and levels of compensation, as well as their relationship with the company. The definition of the persons covered by this disclosure standard may vary in each country and would be determined by host country law. Information is also required concerning the company's employees.

7. Major Shareholders and Related-Party Transactions

This standard provides information regarding the major shareholders and others that control or may control the company. The standard also provides information regarding transactions the company has entered into with persons affiliated with the company and whether the terms of such transactions are fair to the company.

8. Financial Information

This standard specifies which financial statements must be included in the document, as well as the periods to be covered, the age of the financial statements, and other information of a financial nature. The country in which the company is listed (or is applying for listing) will determine the comprehensive bodies of accounting and auditing principles that will be accepted for use in preparation and audit of the financial statements.

9. The Offer

This standard provides information regarding the offer of securities, the plan for distribution of the securities, and related matters.

10. Additional Information

This standard provides information, most of it of a statutory nature, that is not covered elsewhere in the document.

Source: International Organization of Securities Commissions (IOSCO), *International Disclosure Standards for Cross-Border Offerings and Initial Listings by Foreign Issuers,* 1998 (public document).

EXHIBIT 8-6	Principles for Ongoing Disclosure and Reporting of Material Developments

1. The Key Elements of an Ongoing Disclosure Obligation

Listed entities should have an ongoing disclosure obligation requiring disclosure of all information that would be material to an investor's investment decision.

2. Timeliness

The listed entity shall disclose ongoing information on a timely basis, which could require disclosure on:

a. an immediate basis for disclosure of material developments, where such a term could be defined as "as soon as possible" or prescribed as a maximum of specified days; and

b. a periodic basis, prescribed by law or listing rules, such as quarterly or annual reports. Such information would also include management discussion and analysis (MD&A), where required, which can be disclosed in a separate report or included in a periodic report.

(continued)

EXHIBIT 8-6	Principles for Ongoing Disclosure and Reporting of Material Developments (Continued)

The disclosure obligation may require disclosure of relevant information on an immediate basis even when it belongs to periodic reporting.

3. **Simultaneous and Identical Disclosure**

   If the entity is listed in more than one jurisdiction, the information released under the ongoing disclosure obligation of one jurisdiction where it is listed should be released on an identical basis and simultaneously in all the other jurisdictions where it is listed. This obligation should not be dependent on where the listed entity is principally listed.

4. **Dissemination of Information**

   Under the ongoing disclosure obligation, listed entities should ensure that full information is promptly made available to the market by using efficient, effective, and timely means of dissemination.

5. **Disclosure Criteria**

   Ongoing disclosure of information should be fairly presented, not be misleading or deceptive, and contain no material omission of information.

6. **Equal Treatment of Disclosure**

   The information to be disclosed in compliance with the ongoing disclosure obligation should not be disclosed to selected investors or other interested parties before it is released to the public. Certain narrow exceptions may be permitted to this principle to allow communications with advisers and rating agencies or, in the ordinary course of business, communications with persons with whom the listed entity is negotiating, or intends to negotiate, a commercial, financial, or investment transaction or representatives of its employees or trade unions acting on their behalf. In all these cases, the recipients have a duty to keep the information confidential.

Source: International Organization of Securities Commissions, *Principles for Ongoing Disclosure and Material Development Reporting by Listed Entities: A Statement of the Technical Committee,* October 2002 (public document).

INTERNATIONAL FEDERATION OF ACCOUNTANTS (IFAC)

High-quality auditing standards are necessary to ensure that accounting standards are rigorously interpreted and applied. Auditors validate and add credibility to external financial reports. Credible financial reporting is at the core of the efficient functioning of capital markets. International accounting and auditing standards are interrelated. Accounting standards define what is useful accounting information. Auditing standards guide the auditor in determining whether the information is reliable. Useful and reliable accounting information puts investors, creditors, and others in a position to make better decisions. It therefore makes sense that the development of international accounting and auditing standards should be aligned.

External auditing in 10 countries of Europe, the Americas, and Asia was discussed in Chapters 3 and 4. From this discussion, the following points about (independent, external) auditing may be discerned:

1. The main purpose of an external audit varies around the world. For example,
   a. In the United States, auditors attest to whether financial statements "present fairly" a company's financial position and results. The test of fair presentation is compliance with (U.S.) GAAP.

b. In the United Kingdom, auditors attest to whether financial statements present a "true and fair view" of a company's financial position and results. There is a "true and fair override" of U.K. GAAP.

c. In Germany, auditors primarily attest to whether financial statements comply with the law.

2. Auditor responsibility varies around the world. For example,

   a. In France, auditors must report criminal acts they become aware of to the state prosecutor, in addition to their other responsibilities.

   b. In Germany, auditors must provide a private report to the company's managing board of directors and supervisory board on the company's future prospects, in addition to their other responsibilities.

3. Who can conduct an audit varies around the world. For example,

   a. In the United States, only certified public accountants may do so.

   b. In the United Kingdom, members of four professional associations are allowed to do so: chartered accountants in England and Wales, chartered accountants in Scotland, chartered accountants in Ireland, and chartered certified accountants.

   c. In the Netherlands, administrative accountants may audit smaller companies, while *registeraccountants* may audit all companies.

   d. In Germany, sworn book examiners audit small and medium-sized companies, while *wirtschaftsprüfer* may audit all companies.

4. Nations have taken steps to tighten control over the auditing profession. Recently established oversight bodies include:

   a. The Public Company Accounting Oversight Board in the United States. It is a government agency established as a result of the Sarbanes-Oxley Act.

   b. The Haut Counseil du Commissariat aux Comptes (High Council of External Auditors) in France. It is overseen by the Ministry of Justice.

   c. The Professional Oversight Board in the United Kingdom. It is overseen by the Financial Reporting Council, an independent private-sector body.

   d. The Certified Public Accountant and Auditing Oversight Board in Japan. It is overseen by the Financial Services Agency, a government agency.

5. Auditors are facing increasing responsibility for improving corporate governance. For example,

   a. In the United States, auditors express an opinion on internal controls (for listed companies).

   b. In Japan, auditors express an opinion on management's assessment of the internal controls (for listed companies).

The rationale for converging accounting standards was made earlier in this chapter. Comparability is necessary so that investors can make "apples to apples" comparisons. The reason for converging auditing standards is subtler. Fundamentally, an audit assures users that they can trust the information communicated by the financial statements. However, if auditors around the world are not comparably trained or do not observe comparable standards, then their work varies in quality. As a result, the inherent reliability of financial statements also varies. (See Chapter 9 for further discussion on international auditing issues, both internal and external.)

IFAC is a worldwide organization with 157 members and associates in 123 countries, representing more than 2.5 million accountants. Organized in 1977, its mission is "to strengthen the accountancy profession worldwide and contribute to the development of strong international economies by establishing and promoting adherence to high-quality professional standards, furthering the international convergence of such standards, and speaking out on public interest issues where the profession's expertise is most relevant."[32]

IFAC is governed by the IFAC Council, which is made up of one representative from each member organization. The council elects the IFAC board, which is responsible for setting policy and overseeing IFAC operations, the implementation of programs, and the work of IFAC's standard-setting groups and committees. The Public Interest Oversight Board (PIOB) is an independent body that provides additional oversight. Day-to-day administration is provided by the IFAC chief executive located in New York, which is staffed by accounting professionals from around the world.

IFAC's professional work is done through its standard-setting boards and standing committees. The IFAC standard-setting boards are:

- International Accounting Education Standards Board
- International Auditing and Assurance Standards Board
- International Ethics Standards Board for Accountants
- International Public Sector Accounting Standards Board

The IFAC standing committees are the following:

- Compliance Advisory Panel
- Developing Nations Committee
- Nominating Committee
- Professional Accountants in Business Committee
- Small and Medium Practices Committee
- Transnational Auditors Committee

IFAC's International Auditing and Assurance Standards Board issues International Standards on Auditing (ISA), which are organized into the following groups:

- General Principles and Responsibilities
- Risk Assessment and Response to Assessed Risk
- Audit Evidence
- Using Work of Others
- Audit Conclusions and Reporting
- Specialized Areas[33]

IFAC has close ties with other international organizations, such as IASB and IOSCO. The financial statements of an increasing number of companies are being audited in conformity with IFAC's International Standards on Auditing. As noted earlier, all financial statement audits in the EU must follow ISA.

---

[32] IFAC 2008 Annual Report (www.ifac.org).
[33] The *Handbook of International Standards on Auditing and Quality Control* is available at the IFAC Web site (www.ifac.org).

UNITED NATIONS INTERGOVERNMENTAL WORKING GROUP OF EXPERTS ON INTERNATIONAL STANDARDS OF ACCOUNTING AND REPORTING (ISAR)

ISAR was created in 1982 and is the only intergovernmental working group devoted to accounting and auditing at the corporate level. "ISAR assists developing countries and economies in transition to implement best practices in corporate transparency and accounting in order to facilitate investment flows and economic development. ISAR achieves this through an integrated process of research, intergovernmental consensus building, information dissemination, and technical cooperation."[34] ISAR discusses and publishes best practices, including those recommended by the IASB.

ISAR was an early proponent of environmental reporting, and recent initiatives have focused on IFRS implementation, corporate governance, disclosure, corporate responsibility reporting, and accounting by small and medium-sized enterprises. It has also conducted technical assistance projects in a number of areas, such as accounting reform and retraining in the Russian Federation, Azerbaijan, and Uzbekistan, and designing and developing a long-distance learning program in accountancy for French-speaking Africa. Its *ISAR Update* is published twice a year.

ORGANIZATION FOR ECONOMIC COOPERATION AND DEVELOPMENT (OECD)

The OECD is the international organization of 30 (mostly industrialized) market-economy countries. It functions through its governing body, the OECD Council, and its network of about 200 committees and working groups. Its journal *Financial Market Trends,* issued twice a year, assesses trends and prospects in the international and major domestic financial markets of the OECD area. Descriptions and analyses of the structure and regulation of securities markets are often published either as OECD publications or as special features in *Financial Market Trends.* An important activity is promoting good governance in the public and private sectors. (See Chapter 5 for a discussion of *OECD Principles of Corporate Governance.*) With its membership consisting of mostly larger, industrialized countries, the OECD is often a counterweight to other bodies (such as the United Nations and the International Trade Union Confederation) that have built-in tendencies to act contrary to the interests of its members.[35]

CONCLUSION

Most people now believe that international convergence is necessary to reduce the regulatory barriers to cross-border capital-raising efforts. The debate is no longer *whether* to converge, nor even *how* to converge. Although national differences in environmental factors that affect accounting development (such as systems of corporate governance and finance) will persist for some time, financial reporting systems are converging

---

[34] ISAR Web site (www.unctad.org/Templates/Startpage.asp?intItemID=2531&lang=1), June 2009.
[35] From the OECD Web site (www.oecd.org), April 1, 1998.

as international capital markets become more investor oriented. The International Accounting Standards Board is at the center of this movement. These days it is impossible to address capital market and stock exchange regulatory issues without considering international convergence of accounting principles, disclosure, and auditing.

Discussion Questions

1. Distinguish between the terms "harmonization" and "convergence" as they apply to accounting standards.
2. Compare and contrast the following proposed approaches for dealing with international differences in accounting, disclosure, and auditing standards: (1) reciprocity, (2) reconciliation, and (3) international standards.
3. What are the key rationales that support the development and widespread application of International Financial Reporting Standards?
4. What are the key rationales *against* the development and widespread application of International Financial Reporting Standards?
5. What evidence is there that International Financial Reporting Standards are becoming widely accepted around the world? Do you believe that worldwide convergence of accounting standards will end investor concerns about cross-national differences in accounting practices? Why or why not?

6. Describe the structure of the International Accounting Standards Board and how it sets International Financial Reporting Standards.
7. What is the purpose of accounting harmonization in the European Union (EU)? Why did the EU abandon its approach to harmonization via directives to one favoring the IASB?
8. Why is the concept of auditing convergence important? Will international harmonization of auditing standards be more or less difficult to achieve than international harmonization of accounting principles? Describe IFAC's work on converging auditing standards.
9. Describe IOSCO's work on harmonizing disclosure standards for cross-border offerings and initial listings by foreign issuers. Why is this work important to securities regulators around the world?
10. What role do the United Nations and the Organization for Economic Cooperation and Development play in harmonizing accounting and auditing standards?

Exercises

1. Three solutions have been proposed for resolving the problems associated with filing financial statements across national borders: (1) reciprocity (also known as mutual recognition), (2) reconciliation, and (3) use of international standards.

   Required: Present a complete but concise evaluation of each of the three approaches. What do you expect would be the preferred approach from the perspective of each of the following: (1) investors, (2) company management, (3) regulatory authorities, (4) stock exchanges, and (5) professional associations? Discuss your reasons for each response. Which approach do you predict will eventually prevail?

2. Exhibit 8-1 presents the Web site addresses of many major international organizations involved in international accounting harmonization. Consider the following three: the International Federation of Accountants (IFAC), the United Nations Intergovernmental Working Group of Experts on International Standards of Accounting and Reporting (ISAR), and the Organization for Economic Cooperation and Development (OECD).

   Required: For each of these three organizations, describe its membership, its organizational focus, and why it is concerned with international financial accounting standard setting.

3. Exhibit 8-2 presents the Web site addresses of national accountancy organizations, many of which are involved in international accounting standard-setting and convergence activities.

   Required: Select one of the accounting organizations and search its Web site for information about its involvement in international accounting standard setting and convergence. Describe the organization's activities in these areas.

4. The text discusses the many organizations involved with international convergence activities, including the IASB, EU, and IFAC.

   Required:
   a. Compare and contrast these three organizations in terms of their standard-setting procedures.
   b. At what types and sizes of enterprises are their standards *primarily* directed?
   c. Briefly critique the following statement: "Acceptance of international accounting standards (accounting principles, disclosures, and auditing), as far as it has come and is likely to come in the near future, is significantly centered in companies operating in multiple countries."

5. The chapter contains a chronology of some significant events in the history of international accounting standard setting.

   Required: Consider the 1995 European Commission adoption of a new approach to accounting harmonization. Consult some literature references about this event; prepare a short essay describing it and indicating why it is deemed significant.

6. Exhibit 8-3 identifies current IASB standards and their respective titles.

   Required: Using information on the IASB Web site (www.iasb.org) or other available information, prepare an updated list of IASB standards.

7. The biographies of current IASB board members are on the IASB Web site (www.iasb.org).

   Required: Identify the current board members (including the chair and vice-chair). Note each member's home country and prior affiliation(s). Which board members have previously served on national accounting standard-setting bodies?

8. Chapter 3 discusses financial reporting and accounting measurements under International Financial Reporting Standards (IFRS). Chapter 4 discusses the same issues for U.S. GAAP and Exhibit 4-2 summarizes some of the significant differences between IFRS and U.S. GAAP.

   Required: How would each difference affect the balance sheet and income statement? How would each difference affect the following financial ratios used by analysts?
   a. Liquidity: *current ratio*
   b. Solvency: *debt to equity; debt to assets*
   c. Profitability: *return on assets; return on equity*

9. The U.S. Securities and Exchange Commission (SEC) roadmap issued in 2008 may eventually move U.S. issuers to report under International Financial Reporting Standards (IFRS). Consider the following critical questions of such a move:
   a. IFRS lack detailed rules when compared to U.S. GAAP. Shouldn't IFRS be further developed and improved before mandating them?
   b. An effort is already under way to converge U.S. GAAP and IFRS. Why not just keep converging?
   c. How will U.S. interests be protected if standard setting is the responsibility of a non-U.S. organization?

   Required: As one who believes that U.S. companies should use IFRS instead of U.S. GAAP in their financial statement filings with the SEC, how would you answer each of the above critical questions?

10. The IASB Web site (www.iasb.org) summarizes each of the current International Financial Reporting Standards.

    Required: Answer each of the following questions.
    a. In measuring inventories at the lower of cost or net realizable value, does net realizable value mean:
       i. estimated replacement cost, or
       ii. estimated selling price less estimated costs to complete and sell the inventory?
    b. Under International Financial Reporting Standards, which of the following methods is (or are) acceptable to account for an investment in a joint venture?
       i. cost method
       ii. equity method

   iii. proportionate consolidation
   iv. consolidation
c. Which of the following would be classified as an extraordinary item?
   i. loss from settlement of a product liability lawsuit
   ii. claims paid by an airline as a result of a plane crash
   iii. destruction of a communications satellite during launch
   iv. none of the above
d. In Year 1, an enterprise accrued its warranty obligation based on its best estimate of the expected cost to repair defective products during the three-year warranty coverage period. During Year 2, warranty claims were significantly more than expected due to unrecognized quality-control problems in Year 1. Is it appropriate to restate the financial statements for Year 1 to reflect the revised estimate of the warranty obligation?
e. True or false: An enterprise with a December 31 year-end declares a dividend on its common shares on January 5. The dividend is recognized as a liability at year-end.

f. After initial recognition, which of the following financial assets is (are) not remeasured at fair value?
   i. options on unquoted equity securities
   ii. marketable securities (equities)
   iii. derivative financial instruments that are financial assets
   iv. fixed maturity instruments the enterprise intends to hold to maturity
g. Which of the following is true? An enterprise that follows the policy of revaluing its property, plant, and equipment may apply that policy:
   i. to all assets within a single country on a country-by-country basis
   ii. to all assets within a single broad class, such as to land and buildings
   iii. to all assets of a certain age, such as all assets 10 years old or older.
h. True or false: Interest costs on funds borrowed by an enterprise to finance the construction of a new building must be capitalized as part of the cost of the building.

CASES

Case 8-1

PetroChina Company Limited

PetroChina Company Limited (PetroChina) was established as a joint stock company under the company law of the People's Republic of China in 1999 as part of the restructuring of China National Petroleum Corporation. PetroChina is an integrated oil and gas company with operations in virtually every aspect of China's oil and gas industry, including exploration and production, refining and marketing, natural gas transmission, and petrochemicals. PetroChina manages some 70 percent of China's oil and gas reserves and 45 percent of its oil-refining capacity. Its shares were listed on the Hong Kong and New York Stock Exchanges in 2000.

You are an equity research analyst and have been asked to prepare a research report on PetroChina. Your business strategy analysis indicates that PetroChina's sales growth and financial performance can probably be sustained. However, although your qualitative analysis has yielded promising results, you are concerned that your financial analysis will be difficult due to accounting and audit-quality issues.

You start your analysis by becoming familiar with the accounting principles used to prepare PetroChina's financial statements filed with the U.S. Securities and Exchange Commission. You are encouraged that the company states that its financial statements conform to IASB standards, but realize that how accounting standards are applied is as important as the standards themselves.

Required

PetroChina's financial statements filed with the U.S. Securities and Exchange Commission may be found at www. petrochina.com.cn/resource/EngPdf/ annual/20-f_2008.pdf. Examine Petro China's Note 3, "Summary of Principal Accounting Policies," and read about the IASB Standards on the IASB Web site (www.iasb.org) and the IAS Plus Web site (www.iasplus.com).

1. As much as possible, assess the extent to which PetroChina's accounting principles conform to IASB standards.
2. How reliable is your assessment?
3. What further information would help your assessment?
4. Does the auditor's report provide information useful in your assessment? Explain.

Case 8-2

Whither The Withering Standard Setters?

Sir David Tweedie, chairman of the International Accounting Standards Board, is quoted as saying that the IASB and the FASB will eventually merge. "U.S. standards and ours will become so close that it will be senseless having two boards, and they will merge eventually. . . . Ultimately, it doesn't make sense having two standard setters producing the same standards."[36]

Required

1. Go to the Web sites of the International Accounting Standards Board (www.iasb.org) and the U.S. Financial Accounting Standards Board (www.fasb.org). Compare and contrast the two boards in terms of their composition and standard-setting processes.

2. Why is so much attention paid to convergence between International Financial Reporting Standards (IFRS) and U.S. GAAP and not to convergence between IFRS and other national accounting standards? What evidence is there of the direction of convergence: Is U.S. GAAP converging to IFRS, are IFRS converging to U.S. GAAP, or are they converging toward each other?

3. U.S. companies must use U.S. GAAP in their financial statements, not IFRS. Why should U.S. accountants, analysts, and others involved in financial reporting need to know about IFRS?

4. Will the IASB and FASB eventually merge, or will they remain separate accounting standard-setting bodies? Why do you say so?

---

[36] L. Bolton, "IASB and FASB Will Eventually Merge, Says Tweedie," *Accountancy Magazine* (October 2005): 6.

CHAPTER 9

International Financial Statement Analysis

INTRODUCTION

Trends in global trade, investment, and external finance, documented in Chapter 1, imply that financial managers, vendors, investors, equity research analysts, bankers, and other financial statement users have a growing need to read and analyze nondomestic financial statements. Cross-border financial comparisons are vital when assessing the financial promise and soundness of a foreign direct or portfolio investment. There has been tremendous growth in international capital issuance and trading in recent years due to privatizations, economic growth, relaxation of capital controls, and continued advances in information technology.

The need to use, and therefore understand, nondomestic financial statements has also increased as merger and acquisition activities have become more international. The value of cross-border mergers grew steadily during the 1990s, and this growth shows no signs of abatement.

Finally, as business becomes more global, financial statements become more important than ever as a basis for competitive analysis, credit decisions, business negotiations, and corporate control. Continued reduction in national trade barriers, the emergence of Europe as a unified market, convergence of consumer tastes and preferences, and a growing sophistication of business firms in penetrating nondomestic markets have significantly intensified multinational business competition. All this creates a further need for international financial statement analysis and valuation.

This chapter synthesizes information presented in Chapters 1 through 8. It examines opportunities and challenges encountered in analyzing foreign financial statements, and provides suggestions for the analyst.

CHALLENGES AND OPPORTUNITIES IN CROSS-BORDER ANALYSIS

Cross-border financial analysis involves multiple jurisdictions. An analyst, for example, may have occasion to study a company outside her home country or to compare companies from two or more countries. Unique challenges face those doing international analysis.

Nations vary dramatically in their accounting and auditing practices, disclosure quality, legal and regulatory systems, nature and extent of business risk, and modes of conducting business. This variation means that analytical tools that are effective in one jurisdiction may be less so in another. The analyst often faces daunting challenges in obtaining credible information. In many emerging market economies, financial analyses often have limited reliability.

International financial analysis and valuation are characterized by many contradictions. On the one hand, the rapid pace of harmonization of accounting standards is leading to enhanced comparability of financial information worldwide. However, vast differences in financial reporting practices remain. An examination of international financial reporting standards (IFRS's) issued by the IASB to date suggest that definitions of corporate transparency are not necessarily consistent with the notion of transparency that analysts are accustomed to. To wit, IASB/IFRSB pronouncements focus on the extent of disclosure as opposed to disclosures that help reveal the economics of underlying transactions. Restatement of prior year financial statements for first-time adopters of IFRS's are limited to one year thereby complicating trend analysis. And, some standards continue to permit reporting options. As one example, in adjusting their accounts for changing prices, reporting entities are allowed the option of accounting for general price level changes or specific price changes. As Chapter 7 illustrates, the information content of both measurement options are very different. Some analysts question the extent to which greater uniformity in accounting standards will actually result in the provision of comparable information by leading companies in an industry.[1]

As discussed in Chapter 5, companies around the world are disclosing more information voluntarily, and more credible information. At the national level, many countries are striving to improve the availability and quality of information about public companies. Empirical research has validated the benefits of doing so. Specifically, the strength of a country's disclosure system, including disclocure requirements, monitoring, and enforcement, is positively associated with market development.[2] Moreover, access to freely available information relevant for financial analysis is growing dramatically with dissemination of company information on the Internet. However, in many countries there continues to be a great gulf between expectations based on these advances and reality. Financial analysts are often frustrated in their attempts to gather information. Also, many governments continue to publish highly suspect information.

Despite the foregoing contradictions, the environment of international financial analysis and valuation are improving, and the overall outlook for the analyst is positive. Globalization of capital markets, advances in information technology, and increasing competition among national governments, stock exchanges, and companies for investors and trading activity continue. Together these forces are creating incentives for companies to voluntarily improve their external financial reporting practices.

---

[1] For example, see Hope, Ole-Kristan, "Variations in the Financial Reporting Environment and Earnings Forecasting," *Journal of International Financial Management and Accounting* 15, no. 1 (2004): 22.
[2] Carol Ann Frost, Elizabeth A. Gordon, and Andrew F. Hayes, "Stock Exchange Disclosure and Market Development: An Analysis of 50 International Exchanges," *Journal of Accounting Research*, Vol. 44, no. 3 (2006): 437–483.

With the implementation of the euro, together with continued advances in European corporate disclosure practices, distinctions between cross-border and within-border financial analysis are blurring. Portfolio diversification strategies in Europe are increasingly based on industry sectors rather than countries. Rather than balancing stock picks among strong and weak currency countries, portfolio managers are increasingly focusing on picking the best companies in an industry regardless of country of origin. Globalization also means that strictly domestic analyses are becoming less relevant. Interdependencies are growing and no company is insulated from events happening worldwide.

BUSINESS ANALYSIS FRAMEWORK

Palepu, Bernard, and Healy provide a useful framework for business analysis and valuation using financial statement data.[3] The framework's four stages of analysis (discussed in more detail in the following pages) are: (1) business strategy analysis, (2) accounting analysis, (3) financial analysis (ratio analysis and cash flow analysis), and (4) prospective analysis (forecasting and valuation). The relative importance of each stage depends on the purpose of the analysis. The business analysis framework can be applied to many decision contexts including securities analysis, credit analysis, and merger and acquisition analysis.

INTERNATIONAL BUSINESS STRATEGY ANALYSIS

Business strategy analysis is an important first step in financial statement analysis. It provides a qualitative understanding of a company and its competitors in relation to its economic environment. This ensures that quantitative analysis is performed using a holistic perspective. By identifying key profit drivers and business risks, business strategy analysis helps the analyst make realistic forecasts.[4] Standard procedures for gathering information for business strategy analysis include examining annual reports and other company publications, and speaking with company staff, analysts, and other financial professionals. The use of additional information sources, such as the World Wide Web, trade groups, competitors, customers, reporters, lobbyists, regulators, and the trade press is becoming more common. The accuracy, reliability, and relevance of each type of information gathered also needs to be evaluated.[5]

Business strategy analysis is often complex and difficult in an international setting. As noted previously, key profit drivers and types of business risk vary among countries. Understanding them can be daunting. Business and legal environments and corporate objectives vary around the world. Many risks (such as regulatory risk, foreign exchange risk, and credit risk, among others) need to be evaluated and brought together coherently. In some countries, sources of information are limited and may not be accurate.

---

[3] Krishna G. Palepu, Victor L. Bernard, and Paul M. Healy, Business Analysis and Valuation Using Financial Statements, Cincinnati, Ohio: South-Western College Publishing, 1996.
[4] Profit drivers are principal financial and operating elements that affect a firm's profitability.
[5] Financial analysts are increasingly using techniques developed in the fast-growing business discipline of competitive intelligence (CI).

Information Availability

Business strategy analysis is especially difficult in some countries due to lack of reliable information about macroeconomic developments. Governments in developed countries are sometimes accused of publishing faulty or misleading economic statistics. The situation is much worse in many emerging economies. For example, one reason the 1994/95 Mexican currency crisis was a surprise was that the government concealed information about its shrinking foreign reserves and exploding money supply. Some countries delay publishing statistics when the numbers are unfavorable, or even falsify their economic figures.

Obtaining industry information is also difficult in many countries and the quantity and quality of company information varies greatly. The availability of company-specific information has been strikingly low in many developing economies.[6] Recently, many large companies that list and raise capital in overseas markets have been expanding their disclosures and have voluntarily switched to globally recognized accounting principles such as International Financial Reporting Standards.

EXHIBIT 9-1	Country Information Freely Available on the Internet	
Organization	**Web Site Address**	**Description**
Canada Department of Foreign Affairs and International Trade	http://www.dfait-maeci.gc.ca/english/menu.htm	Market information
China's Official Gateway to News and Information	www.china.org.cn	Country information on a variety of fronts.
CRUISE	www.cranfield.ac.uk/cils/Library/subjects/country.htm	Country reports including economic and market data.
CIA-The World Factbook	www.cia.gov/cia/publications/Factbook/geos/fm.html	Information on government, economy, communications, and transnational issues.
Financial Times	http://ft.com	Country reports (also industry reports, company news, and financial information)
Political and Economic Risk Consultancy, Ltd. (PERC)	http://www.asiarisk.com/	Country outlooks; connection to other WWW sites
UNCTAD	www.unctad.org	Data for analysis of international trade, foreign direct investment commodities and development
U.S. Federal Reserve	www.federalreserve.gov	Foreign exchange rates
U.S. State Department	http://travel.state.gov/	Travel warnings
World Bank	www.dev.data.worldbank.org	Country development data
World Tourism Organization	http://www.world-tourism.org	Newsletters, press releases

---

[6] See Chapter 5 for further discussion. Also see S. M. Saudagaran, and J. G. Diga, "Financial Reporting in Emerging Capital Markets: Characteristics and Policy Issues," *Accounting Horizons* (June 1997): 41–64.

Recommendations for Analysis

Data constraints make it difficult to perform business strategy analyses using traditional research methods. Very often, travel is necessary to learn about local business climates and how industries and companies actually operate, especially in emerging market countries. The World Wide Web also offers quick access to information that recently was unavailable or difficult to obtain. Exhibit 9-1 presents a sampling of freely available Web resources that can be used to learn about country risks and travel conditions.

Country information can also be found in "international briefings" publications distributed by large accounting firms, banks, and brokerages.[7] The International Federation of Stock Exchanges (FIBV, http://www.fibv.com) and the Federation of European Stock Exchanges (FESE, http://www.fese.be) publish highly informative international newsletters and *Accountancy, the Economist, Financial Analysts Journal, Euromoney* articles highly relevant for international financial analysis.

Enormous risks may follow an inadequate business strategy analysis. Consider the Parmalat affair, representing the largest fraud in European financial history. In this case, at least $13 billion in missing assets of Italy's fastest growing dairy group could not be accounted for, resulting in huge losses for the company's investors and creditors alike. Commentators attribute this financial debacle to several causes. Foreign investors reportedly invested in a company that did not provide complete or credible disclosures. They did not know much about the business environment in which they were investing and participated in a market in which financial reporting rules were not strictly enforced.[8]

ACCOUNTING ANALYSIS

The purpose of accounting analysis is to assess the extent to which a firm's reported results reflect economic reality. The analyst needs to evaluate the firm's accounting policies and estimates, and assess the nature and extent of a firm's accounting flexibility. The latter refers to management's discretion in choosing which accounting policies and estimates to apply to a particular accounting event. To reach reliable conclusions, the analyst must adjust reported accounting amounts to remove distortions caused by the use of accounting methods the analyst deems inappropriate. Examples might include marking trading assets to market and not recording the gains or losses in income but in an allowance account, prematurely recognizing revenues, or reversing estimated liability accruals to smooth earnings.

Corporate managers are allowed to make many accounting-related judgments because they know the most about their firm's operations and financial condition. Flexibility in financial reporting is important because it allows managers to use accounting measurements that best reflect the company's particular operating circumstances.

---

[7] For example, PricewaterhouseCoopers LLC publishes International Briefings every month, which reports on notable business, political, and economic developments worldwide.

[8] Gail Edmondson, David Fairlamb, and Nanette Byrnes, "The Milk Just Keeps on Spilling," *BusinessWeek* (January 26, 2004): 54, 55, 58.

However, managers have incentives to distort operating reality by using their accounting discretion to distort reported profits. One reason is that reported earnings are often used to evaluate their managerial performance.[9]

Healy and colleagues suggest the following process for evaluating a firm's accounting quality:

1. Identify key accounting policies
2. Assess accounting flexibility
3. Evaluate accounting strategy
4. Evaluate the quality of disclosure
5. Identify potential red flags (e.g., unusually large asset write-offs, unexplained transactions that boost profits, or an increasing gap between a company's reported income and its cash flow from operations)
6. Adjust for accounting distortions

To illustrate this process, consider the accounting quality of WorldCom, a large U.S. company whose accounting policies resulted in a major Wall Street scandal. In formally indicting the company on its faulty accounting practices, the following questions might be asked: (1) How did WorldCom account for its major operating expenditures? (2) What options does U.S. GAAP allow for such expenditures? (3) Did WorldCom adopt an overly aggressive or conservative approach to accounting for these expenditures? (4) Did WorldCom capitalize an expenditure that should have been expensed to manage its earnings? (5) Did WorldCom disclose sufficient information for investors to undo the company's aggressive accounting treatment? (6) Would reversal of WorldCom's selected accounting posture have a significant depressing effect on reported earnings?

In this case, WorldCom chose to capitalize what were in effect operating expenses. While this practice is in clear violation of U.S. GAAP, management chose to conceal this information from investors by disguising operating expenses as capital expenditures. The financial statement effects of capitalizing versus expensing its major expenditures had a significant effect on reported earnings as the amounts involved approached $2 billion!

Two major issues confront those doing accounting analysis in an international setting. The first is cross-country variation in accounting measurement quality, disclosure quality, and audit quality; the second concerns the difficulty in obtaining information needed to conduct accounting analysis.

Cross-country variation in quality of accounting measurement, disclosure, and auditing is dramatic. National characteristics that cause this variation include required and generally accepted practices, monitoring and enforcement, and extent of managerial discretion in financial reporting.[10] Chapters 3 and 4 of this text present summaries of significant accounting practices in five European countries and five countries of the

---

[9] Additional influences on corporate managers' accounting decisions include: (1) accounting-based debt covenants; (2) management compensation; (3) corporate control contests; (4) tax considerations; (5) regulatory considerations; (6) capital market considerations; (7) stakeholder considerations; and (8) competitive considerations. Palepu, Bernard, and Healy, op. cit.

[10] While faulty application of accounting principles is frequently touted as the leading cause of low accounting quality, some argue that the application of faulty accounting principles is the root cause. See Paul Rosenfield, "What Drives Earnings Management?" *Journal of Accountancy* [October 2000]: 5.

Americas and Asia, respectively. These chapters, which summarize only a subset of major accounting topics, show that significant managerial discretion may be used in many countries, including France, Germany, and China.

Consider accounting practices in Germany. As discussed in Chapter 3, German financial accounting is closely aligned with tax reporting. Creditor protection is a second goal of financial reporting. As a result, financial reports are prepared with a creditor focus rather than an investor focus. The resulting conservative reporting bias may generate accounting amounts that do not reflect actual operating performance. German managers have great discretion in their use of reserves and in implementing many accounting policies. Even where specific procedures are mandated, monitoring and enforcement of compliance with reporting requirements is far short of what investors can expect in the United States.

Disclosure quality and the level of audit assurances must also be closely scrutinized when analyzing the financial statements of a German company. Footnote disclosure of accounting policies is quite limited in some German annual reports. Identifying the components of large financial statement items (such as reserve accounts) can be difficult. Auditing issues are so important that we discuss international auditing in a separate section of this chapter.

Financial reporting in China provides a second example of how accounting measurement, disclosure, and audit quality can vary dramatically from accounting practices in Anglo-American countries. Although China is implementing major accounting reform as part of its transition from a planned economy to a controlled market economy, until recently it did not have financial reporting and external auditing in forms that would be familiar to Westerners.[11] Private investors and creditors were virtually nonexistent for three decades after the People's Republic was founded in 1948, and The Accounting Law, which sets forth accounting and reporting requirements, was adopted only in 1985. Accounting Standards for Business Enterprises, which specifies that such basic accounting practices as double-entry bookkeeping and the accrual basis should be used, became effective in 1993. The auditing profession is also very new in China.

Suggestions for the Analyst

Especially when analyzing companies in emerging market countries, the analyst should meet often with management to evaluate their financial reporting incentives and accounting policies. Many companies in emerging market countries are closely held, and managers may not have strong incentives for full and credible disclosure. Accounting policies in some countries may be similar or identical to IAS (or other widely accepted standards), but managers often have great discretion in how those policies are applied. Finally, as noted earlier, new communications technology (including the World Wide Web) is having a great impact on all stages of financial research. Many companies and countries now have Web sites that make it much easier for anyone interested to gather information. Refer to the section entitled "Information Access" later in this chapter for a discussion of useful information sources for accounting analysis.

---

[11] For further discussion, see Chapter 4; Ajay Adhikari and Shawn Z.Wang, "Accounting for China," *Management Accounting* (April 1995): 27–32.

INTERNATIONAL FINANCIAL ANALYSIS

The goal of financial analysis is to evaluate a firm's current and past performance, and to judge whether its performance can be sustained. Ratio analysis and cash flow analysis are important tools in financial analysis. Ratio analysis involves comparison of ratios between the firm and other firms in the same industry, comparison of a firm's ratios across years or other fiscal periods, and/or comparison of ratios to some absolute benchmark. It provides insights into the comparative and relative significance of financial statement items and can help evaluate the effectiveness of managements' operating, investing, financing, and earnings retention policies. A summary of commonly used financial ratios appears in Exhibit 9-2.

Cash flow analysis focuses on the cash flow statement, which provides information about a firm's cash inflows and outflows, classified among operating, investing, and financing activities, and disclosures about periodic noncash investing and financing activities. Analysts can use cash flow analysis to address many questions about the firm's performance and management. For example, has the firm generated positive cash flows from operations? How have cash flow components changed across time in relation to changes in income statement components, sales, and cost of sales in particular? What have been the cash flow consequences of management decisions about financial policy, dividend policy, and investment? When used in conjunction with the income statement, cash flow information also informs analysts about the validity of the going concern assumption, a firm's liquidity, and management's use of measurement options to manage earnings.

Ratio Analysis

Two issues must be addressed in analyzing ratios in an international setting. First, do cross-country differences in accounting principles cause significant variation in financial statement amounts of companies from different countries? Second, how do differences in local culture and economic and competitive conditions affect the interpretation of accounting measures and financial ratios, even if accounting measurements from different countries are restated to achieve "accounting comparability"?

Extensive evidence reveals substantial cross-country differences in profitability, leverage, and other financial statement ratios and amounts that result from both accounting and nonaccounting factors. (The next section discusses cross-country differences in two valuation ratios, the price-to-earnings and price-to-book ratios.) In one study, sales revenue, net income, and leverage (total debt/shareholders' equity) were compared among firms domiciled in France, Germany, Japan, the United Kingdom, and the United States.[12] The five 80-firm country samples were matched according to size (market value of equity), with all firms belonging to the manufacturing industry group (SIC codes 20 through 39). All three financial measures varied substantially among the country samples. For example, median net income was

---

[12] Carol A. Frost, "Characteristics and Information Value of Corporate Disclosures of Forward-Looking Information in Global Equity Markets," Dartmouth College Working Paper, July 2002.

EXHIBIT 9-2	Summary of Financial Ratios

Ratio	Formula for Computation
I. Liquidity	
1. Current ratio	Current assets
	Current liabilities
2. Quick or acid-test ratio	Cash, marketable securities, and receivables
	Current liabilities
3. Current cash debt ratio	Net cash provided by operating activities
	Average current liabilities
II. Efficiency	
4. Receivables turnover	Net sales
	Average trade receivables (net)
5. Inventory turnover	Cost of goods sold
	Average inventory
6. Asset turnover	Net sales
	Average total assets
III. Profitability	
7. Profit margin on sales	Net income
	Net sales
8. Rate of return on assets	EBIT[1]
	Average total assets
9. Rate of return on common stock equity	Net income minus preferred dividends
	Average common stockholders' equity
10. Earnings per share	Net income minus preferred dividends
	Weighted common shares outstanding
11. Payout ratio	Cash dividents
	Net income
IV. Coverage	
12. Debt to total assets ratio	Debt
	Total assets or equities
13. Times interest earned	Income before interest charges and taxes
	Interest charges
14. Cash debt coverage ratio	Net cash provided by operating activities
	Average total liabilities
15. Book value per share	Common stockholders' equity
	Outstanding common shares

[1] *EBIT = earnings before interest and taxes. Some analysts prefer to use EBITDA, which also includes depreciation and amortization charges in the numerator.*

much greater in the United Kingdom and the United States than in Germany and Japan. Variation in net income was partially explained by accounting principle differences because financial reporting is generally less conservative in the United Kingdom and the United States than in Germany and Japan. Nonaccounting factors also affected reported net income. For example, the creditor focus in France, Germany, and Japan accounted for lower net income than in the United States and the United Kingdom as there is less pressure on managers in those countries to report steadily increasing net income.

In the foregoing study, Frost found median leverage in the United Kingdom and the United States to be lower than in Germany and Japan. This is partially attributed to the fact that conservative accounting in Germany and Japan results in lower reported shareholders' equity than in the United Kingdom and the United States. Higher leverage in Germany, Japan, and France is also attributed to higher debt in capital structures, reflecting the heavy dependence on bank financing in those countries.

How large are the differences in financial statement items caused by differences among national accounting principles? Although no longer required,[13] hundreds of non-U.S. companies listed on U.S. stock exchanges provided footnote reconciliation disclosures that provide evidence on this question, at least in the context of differences between U.S. GAAP-based and non-U.S. GAAP-based accounting amounts.

An earlier survey of financial statement reconciliations by foreign registrants prepared by the U.S. SEC is informative.[14] Approximately one-half of the 528 non-U.S. registrants surveyed disclosed material differences between net income as reported in their financial statements and U.S. GAAP-based net income. The five types of financial statement differences disclosed by the largest number of registrants were (in descending order): (1) depreciation and amortization, (2) deferred or capitalized costs, (3) deferred taxes, (4) pensions, and (5) foreign currency translation.

The study also shows that more than two-thirds of the registrants that disclosed material differences in net income reported that income under U.S. GAAP was lower than under non-U.S. GAAP. Nearly half of them reported income differences greater than 25 percent. Twenty-five of the 87 registrants that reported that income under U.S. GAAP was greater than under non-U.S. GAAP reported differences greater than 25 percent. Similar results were found for reconciliations of shareholders' equity. Overall, the evidence in the SEC study shows that financial statement differences under U.S. versus non-U.S. GAAP are highly material for many companies.

Evidence from SEC registrants' reconciliation disclosures therefore indicates that GAAP differences can cause significant variation in financial statement numbers. Even as the world marches toward adoption of IFRS issued by the IASB, measurement options permitted by IFRS, differences in national enforcement policies and differences in flavors of IFRS (see Chapter 8), suggest that measurement and disclosure differences will not disappear. Accordingly, an analyst will often choose to make financial statements more comparable by making accounting principle adjustments to the financial statements being analyzed. Appendix 9-1 illustrates the restatement of an income and balance sheet

---

[13] The U.S. Securities and Exchange Commission relaxed its U.S. GAAP reconciliation requirements for non-U.S. registrants in 2007.

[14] U.S. Securities and Exchange Commission, Division of Corporation Finance, Survey of Financial Statement Reconciliations by Foreign Registrants, May 1, 1993.

from Japanese GAAP to U.S. GAAP. Even after financial statement amounts are made reasonably comparable (by adjusting for accounting principle differences), interpretation of those amounts must consider cross-country differences in economic, competitive, and other institutional differences. Analysis of Japanese companies provides a good illustration. Brown and Stickney argue that the relation between financial and tax reporting, the importance in Japan of operating through corporate groups (keiretsu), and the tolerance in Japan for heavy use of short-term financial leverage must all be considered when analyzing the profitability and risk of Japanese companies.[15] For example, Japanese-reported earnings tend to be lower than earnings reported in Anglo-American countries, even after adjusting for GAAP differences. The close linkage between tax and financial reporting gives Japanese companies an incentive to be conservative in determining their income. Also, because high intercorporate stock holdings reduce the percentage of shares held by outsiders, Japanese companies are under less pressure to report ever-increasing earnings than are companies in the United States and other Anglo-American countries.[16] Refer to Appendix 9-2 for further detailed discussion of international ratio analysis. The appendix focuses on comparison of Japanese and U.S. financial ratios and their interpretation.

Cash Flow Analysis

As discussed earlier, cash flow analysis provides insights into a company's cash flows and management. Highly detailed cash flow statements are required under U.S. GAAP, U.K. GAAP, IFRS, and accounting standards in a growing number of other countries. Cash flow–related measures are especially useful in international analysis because they are less affected by accounting principle differences than are earnings-based measures. When cash flow statements are not presented, it is often difficult to compute cash flows from operations and other cash flow measures by adjusting accrual-based earnings. Many companies simply do not disclose the information needed to make the adjustments. As one example, German balance sheets often contain surprisingly large reserve accounts that reflect many different types of accrual. Few (if any) details are presented that might allow the financial statement user to assess the implications for operating, investment, and financing cash flows.

Coping Mechanisms

How do financial statement users cope with cross-country accounting principle differences? Several approaches are used. Some analysts restate foreign accounting measures to an internationally recognized set of principles, or to some other common basis. Others develop a detailed understanding of accounting practices in a limited set of countries and restrict their analysis to firms located in those countries.

---

[15] Paul R. Brown and Clyde P. Stickney, "Instructional Case: Tanaguchi Corporation," *Issues in Accounting Education* 7 (Spring 1992): 57–68.

[16] Jill L. McKinnon, "Application of Anglo-American Principles of Consolidation to Corporate Financial Disclosure in Japan," *ABACUS* 20 (1984): 16–33 provides further detail on corporate groups in Japan versus those in Anglo-American countries. She argues that the Anglo-American consolidation methods adopted by Japan in 1977 may reflect international pressure for accounting conformity more than the inherent desirability of those methods. She implies that as a result, Japanese consolidated financial statements are less useful than they might be. The McKinnon study provides an important illustration that knowing what accounting principles are used is only the first step in interpreting financial statements from different countries.

Brown, Soybel, and Stickney illustrate the use of a restatement algorithm to enhance cross-border comparisons of financial performance.[17] They restate the operating performance of U.S. and Japanese companies to a similar reporting basis. Rather than convert U.S. data to a Japanese financial reporting basis, or Japanese data to a U.S. financial reporting basis, they adjust (as necessary) both U.S. and Japanese data to achieve uniform accounting principles.

Appendix 9-1 illustrates another approach, in which the financial statements of a hypothetical Japanese business (Toyoza Enterprises) are restated from a Japanese GAAP basis to a U.S. GAAP basis. The restatement algorithm used in Appendix 9-1 involves a detailed analysis of numerous financial statement items.

Relatively simple restatement algorithms can be effective. One approach is to focus on a few of the most material financial statement differences for which enough information is available to make reliable adjustments. For example, Brown and colleagues, mentioned above, summarize many differences between Japan and U.S. GAAP, but their restatement algorithm focuses on only four accounting principle differences: (1) inventory cost assumptions, (2) depreciation method, (3) bonuses to directors and statutory auditors, and (4) deferred taxes and special tax reserves.

INTERNATIONAL PROSPECTIVE ANALYSIS

Prospective analysis involves two steps: forecasting and valuation. In forecasting, analysts make explicit forecasts of a firm's prospects based on its business strategy, accounting, and financial analysis. It addresses questions such as, How will a company's change in business strategy affect future sales volume and profits? Has the company recently adopted new accounting policies that will make current earnings appear stronger, perhaps at the cost of lower earnings next year? Will financial relationships evidenced in an analyst's ratio analysis continue?

In valuation, analysts convert quantitative forecasts into an estimate of a firm's value. Valuation is used implicitly or explicitly in many business decisions. For example, valuation is the basis of equity analysts' investment recommendations. In analyzing a possible merger, the potential acquirer will estimate the value of the target firm. Many different valuation approaches are used in practice, ranging from discounted cash flow analysis to simpler techniques based on price-based multiples.[18] Experts in international valuation give this warning to those doing international prospective analysis: "Any rules you've learned in your home country will fall apart overseas." Exchange rate fluctuations, accounting differences, different business practices and customs, capital market differences, and many other factors will have major effects on international forecasting and valuation.

For example, discounted cash flow analysis values a business as the present value of its expected cash flows, discounted at a rate that reflects the riskiness of those cash flows. While this valuation principle is no different for developed and

---

[17] See Paul R. Brown, Virginia E. Soybel, and Clyde P. Stickney, "Achieving Comparability of U.S. and Japanese Price-Earnings Ratios," in Frederick D. S., Choi, ed., *International Accounting and Finance Handbook*, 2nd ed., New York: John Wiley & Sons, 1997, pp. 7.1–7.18.
[18] See Aswath Damodaran, *Investment Valuation*, 2nd ed., New York: John Wiley & Sons, 2000.

emerging markets alike, many of the inputs taken for granted in the former may not be as accessible in emerging economies.[19] For example, the government bond rate, often used as a surrogate for the risk-free rate, assumes that governments do not default, at least on local borrowing. This is often not the case internationally. Other inputs including risk parameters and premiums are typically more difficult to estimate owing to the paucity of historical data. And earnings forecasts, as a basis for estimating future cash flows, are less reliable. Hope attributes this to several factors.[20] One factor is the greater choice that managers have in choosing among accounting methods. Greater choice makes it more difficult to do cross-section analyses and makes it easier for managers to distort economic reality in reporting firm performance. Forecast accuracy is also positively related to the extent to which accrual accounting is prescribed in a country. Accruals provide a better measure of a firm's future cash generating ability than cash receipts and disbursements and irons out discontinuities in reported revenues and expenses. Finally, the accuracy of analysts' earnings forecasts are positively related to the strength of a country's enforcement standards. This is attributed to the notion that enforcement narrows the range of permitted accounting choices. This, in turn, reduces analysts' uncertainty about the degree of firms' reporting discretion.[21]

Consider next the use of price-based (valuation) multiples in an international setting. Valuation multiples such as price-to-earnings (P/E) and price-to-book (P/B) ratios are often used to estimate a firm's value. One common approach is to calculate the desired multiple for a group of comparable firms (such as other firms in the same industry), and then apply that multiple to the firm being valued to get a reasonable price. For example, if the price-to-earnings ratio of the industry group is 15, and the firm's earnings are forecast to be $1.80/share, then $27.00 per share is a reasonable price for the firm being analyzed. One might use the valuation multiples approach to determine the bid price for an acquisition candidate. If the candidate is a European company, comparable firms might be chosen from selected European countries.

Reliance on valuation multiples assumes that market prices reflect future prospects and that pricing of firms with similar operating and financial characteristics (such as firms in the same industry) is applicable to the firm being analyzed because of its similarity to those firms. Application of price multiples in a cross-border setting is challenging because it requires that the determinants of each multiple, and reasons why multiples vary across firms, be thoroughly understood.

Exhibit 9-3 displays mean price to earnings ratios for stock indexes in 17 countries at the end of 2007.

Exhibit 9-3 shows that P/E ratios vary across countries. At the end of 2007 P/E multiples ranged from 9.5 in South Africa to 41.2 for firms listed on the stock exchange in China. But what accounts for these variations across national boundaries?

National differences in accounting principles are one potential source of cross-country ratio variations. Such differences, for example, cause P/E ratios in Japan to be generally higher than those in the United States (recall that reported earnings in Japan

---

[19] Aswath Damodaran, "Valuation in Emerging Markets," in Frederick D. S. Choi, ed., International Finance and Accounting Handbook, 3rd ed., New York: John Wiley & Sons, 2003, p. 9.3.
[20] Hope, op. cit., pp. 21–39.
[21] Hope, op. cit., p. 23.

EXHIBIT 9-3	International Price/Earnings Ratios	
Country	**Index**	**P/E**
Canada	SPTSX	17.8
China (PRC)	SHCOMP	41.2
France	CAC	16.8
Hong Kong	HIS	15.74
India	SENSEX	22.97
Italy	MIB30	15.3
Japan	NKY	37.7
Mexico	MEXBOL	19.1
Netherlands	AEX	11.9
Russia	RTSI$	11.1
Singapore	STI	14.4
South Africa	TOP40	9.5
Spain	IBEX	14.8
Sweden	OMX	14.9
Switzerland	SMI	15.5
UK	UKX	13.6
US	SPX	17.7

Source: "Global P/E Ratios, Ticker Sense Blogger," Birinyi Associates, Inc., July 20–24, 2009.

are lower than in the United States for comparable companies with similar financial performance). However, even after adjusting for accounting differences, P/E ratios in Japan are still much higher than in the United States.

French and Poterba examined disparities between Japanese and U.S. P/E ratios and the steep increase in Japanese P/E ratios during the late 1980s.[22] They made several accounting adjustments to the Japanese data and found that their adjustments reduced but did not eliminate the difference between Japanese and U.S. P/E ratios. French and Poterba concluded that accounting differences explain about half of the long-term differences between U.S. and Japanese P/E ratios.

Brown, Soybel, and Stickney also investigated why Japanese P/E ratios are higher than U.S. P/E ratios.[23] They found that adjusting for different accounting principles explains only a small part of the difference. A comparison of their study with French and Poterba's shows how different approaches and assumptions can lead to very different conclusions about valuation ratios.

The substantial variation in valuation ratios shown in Exhibit 9-3 reflects changes in financial performance and in market prices across time and countries. As discussed

---

[22] Kenneth R., French and James M. Poterba, "Were Japanese Stock Prices Too High?" Journal of Financial Economics 29 (1991): 337–362.

[23] See Paul R. Brown, Virginia E., Soybel, and Clyde P. Stickney, "Achieving Comparability of U.S. and Japanese Price-Earnings Ratios," op. cit., for a review of comparative analyses of Japanese and U.S. P/E ratios. For further comparative evidence on cross-country differences in P/E and P/B ratios, see Peter Joos and Mark Lang, "The Effects of Accounting Diversity: Evidence from the European Union," Journal of Accounting Research 32 (Suppl., 1994): 141–175.

previously, even French and Poterba's rigorous analysis of the changes in P/E ratios in Japan during the late 1980s yielded only partial answers. Thus, accounting offers only a partial explanation for differences among P/E ratios in different countries and over time. An understanding of additional environmental considerations (see Appendix 9-2) is necessary for meaningful analysis and interpretation.

FURTHER ISSUES

All four stages of business analysis (business strategy, accounting, financial, and prospective analysis) may be affected by the following factors: (1) information access, (2) timeliness of information, (3) language and terminology barriers, (4) foreign currency issues, and (5) differences in types and formats of financial statements.

Information Access

Information about thousands of companies from around the world has become more widely available in recent years. Countless information sources are appearing on the World Wide Web. Companies around the world now have Web sites, and their annual reports are available free of charge from various Internet and other sources. Refer to Exhibit 9-4 for Web sites that provide information highly relevant for company research.

Many companies also respond to written and telephone requests for their annual reports and other financial documents. However, the amount of company information available varies considerably from country to country.

Many commercial databases provide access to financial and stock market data for tens of thousands of companies around the world. Companies covered by commercial databases tend to be large companies that are of most interest to financial statement users and investors. It is striking that even in emerging market countries such as China and the Czech Republic, data for many firms are now available.

Other valuable information sources include (1) government publications, (2) economic research organizations, (3) international organizations such as the United Nations, and (4) accounting, auditing, and securities market organizations. Web site addresses appear throughout this text and are only a starting point for gathering information.

TIMELINESS OF INFORMATION   The timeliness of financial statements, annual reports, regulatory filings, and accounting-related press releases varies dramatically by country. Whereas quarterly financial reporting is a generally accepted practice in the United States, this is not always the case elsewhere.[24] Financial reporting lags can also be estimated by comparing a company's fiscal year-end with its audit report date. The latter is often considered a reasonable indication of when corporate financial information first becomes publicly available. For Brazil, Canada, Chile, Colombia, Mexico, the Philippines, South Korea, Taiwan, Thailand, and the United States, this reporting lag reportedly averaged between 30–60 days. It averaged 61–90 days in Argentina, Australia, Denmark, Finland, Ireland, Israel, Japan, the Netherlands, New Zealand, Norway, Portugal, Singapore, South Africa, Spain, Sweden, Switzerland, the United

---

[24] An informal survey of many world-class company Web sites suggests that more and more companies are voluntarily choosing to provide quarterly reports owing to capital market pressures to do so.

EXHIBIT 9-4	Freely Available Web Sites for Company Research (all Web sites begin with the prefix http://www)	

Name of Web Site	Web Site Address	What It Provides
Annual Reports Library	zpub.com/sf/arl/	Alphabetical listing of U.S. corporations with links to home pages and annual reports that can be downloaded free of charge with Adobe Acrobat Reader.
Asian Business Watch	asianbusinesswatch. com	Company and stock market news for Japan and Asia.
Babel	babel.altavista.com	Translates text files; only does first few pages of long documents.
Bank of England	bank of england.co.uk/	United Kingdom monetary and financial statistics, working papers, and other publications, information on the bank's structure and functions, and much more.
BFA-NET: Bureau of Financial Analysis Network	bfanet.com	South African company and stock market information; check out "Little Facts."
Bloomberg News Service	bloomberg.com/	Highlights from the Bloomberg news service.
Businessjeeves.com	businessjeeves.com	Good starting place; many links.
Business Week Online	businessweek.com	Current issue, archives, and an assortment of worthwhile data.
CAROL: Company Annual Reports Online	carolworld.com	Online annual reports for some European companies.
Cross Border Capital	liquidity.com/	Reports on equity, fixed income, and currency markets in over 70 developed and emerging markets. Reports over six months old available for free (with registration).
Daiwa Securities	dir.co.jp/Reception/ research.html	Research reports and forecasts on the Japanese economy.
Edgar—U.S. Securities & Exchange Commission	sec.gov/edgar.shtml	Most SEC filings since 1996.
Emerging Markets Companion	emgmkts.com/	Many useful links and resources on Asia, Latin America, Africa, and Europe.
EnterWeb: The Enterprise Development Web site	enterweb.org/ welcome.htm	Meta-index to business and finance globalization, and more. "The focus is on micro, small, and medium-sized enterprise development both in developed and developing countries."
Europages—European Business Directory	europages.com/	Lists 500,000 companies in 30 countries; includes some manufacturers' catalogs.
Financial Times of London	ft.com/	Online edition of the Financial Times; current articles, market information, and more.

(continued)

EXHIBIT 9-4	Freely Available Web Sites for Company Research (all Web sites begin with the prefix http://www) (Continued)	
Name of Web Site	**Web Site Address**	**What It Provides**
FT Interactive Data	turboguide.com/ data2/cdprod1/ doc/cdrom frame/ 002/686.pub.FT. Excel.html	Good sampling from FT Excel databases; must register.
Hong Kong Securities and Futures Commission	hksfc.org.hk	Information on Hong Kong securities markets.
Hoover's Online	hoovers.com	Some information, such as press releases, is free. Links to company home pages and other information. Includes more than 800 of the most important non-U.S. companies.
INO Global Market	ino.com/	Information for traders in futures and options markets worldwide.
International Business (Michigan State University Center for International Business Education and Research)	ciber.bus.msu.edu/ busres.htm	Links to good investment and macro sites.
International Monetary Fund	imf.org/	IMF news, publications, and more.
Internet Corruption Rankings	gwdg.de/~uwww/ icr_serv.htm	Provides the TI-Corruption Perception Index, a comparative assessment of the integrity of many countries, along with many other links and services.
National Corporate Services, Inc. International Investing	natcorp.com/	Excellent start point; many links to sites providing free information.
NIRI Useful Investor Relations Sites	niri.org	Links to interesting Web sites.
Public Register's Annual Report, The companies.	prars.com	Annual reports, prospectuses, or 10-Ks on over 32,000 U.S. companies.
Rutgers Accounting Network (RAW)	rutgers.edu/ Accounting/ raw.html	Excellent starting place.
Stewart Mayhew's Directory of Worldwide Securities Exchanges	voltaire.is.tcu.edu/ ~vmihov/ exchanges/xlinks. Htm	Links to official home pages of stock markets and derivatives exchanges around the world.
Stock City	stockcity.com	ADR profiles, organized by sector, region, and country. Profiles require Adobe Acrobat Reader.

(continued)

EXHIBIT 9-4	Freely Available Web Sites for Company Research (all Web sites begin with the prefix http://www) (Continued)	
Name of Web Site	**Web Site Address**	**What It Provides**
Streetlink Investor Information Center	streetlink.com	Financial reports available online; U.S. companies only.
United Nations System	unsystem.org	Spotty coverage of companies and Accounting information; good information on communications and country background.
USA Today Money	usatoday.com/ money/ mfront.htm	Comprehensive assortment of news and data.
VIBES: Virtual International Business and Economic Sources	uncc.edu/lis/library/ reference/intbus/ vibehome.htm	Great for linking to regional sites; excellent starting place, especially good for macro data.
Wright Investor' Service	wisi.com	Can search alphabetically by country or by industry.
Yahoo! Finance	finance.yahoo.com	Extensive data, news, and stock quotes.

Kingdom, and Zimbabwe. In Austria, Belgium, France, Germany, Greece, Hong Kong, India, Italy, Malaysia, Nigeria, and Sri Lanka, information lags averaged 91–120 days. And for Pakistan, the average lag exceeded 120 days.[25]

Frost documents further international variations in the timeliness of earnings-related press releases.[26] She defined disclosure lags as the average number of days between a company's fiscal year-end and the date of the press release. These lags were 73 days for companies domiciled in France, 82 days for Germany, 46 days for Japan, 72 days for the United Kingdom, and 26 days for the United States.

Variability in the timeliness of accounting information places additional burdens on readers of foreign financial statements. This burden is especially pronounced for firms whose operating circumstances are changing over time. Meaningful valuations require constant updates of reported numbers using both conventional and unconventional means.

Foreign Currency Considerations

Accounts denominated in foreign currency present financial analysts with two types of problems. The first relates to reader convenience, the second to information content.

The vast majority of companies around the world denominate their financial accounts in the currency of their national domicile. To a U.S. reader accustomed to

---

[25] See International Accounting and Auditing Trends, 4th ed., Center for International Financial Analysis & Research, Princeton, NJ: CIFAR Publications, Inc., 1995.
[26] Carol A. Frost, "Characteristics and Information Value of Corporate Disclosures of Forward-Looking Information in Global Equity Markets," Dartmouth College Working Paper, February 1998.

dealing in dollars, analysis of accounts expressed in euros may be discomforting. A normal inclination is to translate foreign currency balances to domestic currency. However, foreign currency reports are, for the most part, troublesome in appearance only. Financial ratios that transform nominal (interval) measurements to percentage relationships are independent of currency. A current ratio computed from a Dutch balance sheet expressed in euros is the same as one computed from the same financial statement translated into dollars. Consider the following year-end balance sheet accounts of a British company.

	2009	2010	2011
Current assets	£12,500	£12,200	£12,800
Current liabilities	£8,333	£7,625	£8,000

Assuming year-end dollar/pound exchanges rates of $1.70, $1.80, and $1.60 for 2009, 2010, and 2011, respectively, the current ratio will be 1.5 to 1 for 2009, 1.6 to 1 for 2010, and 1.6 to 1 for 2011, whether expressed in British pounds or U.S. dollars. Local currency (e.g., pound) balances are especially appropriate when analyzing financial trends.

Readers who prefer a domestic currency framework when analyzing foreign currency accounts may apply a convenience translation using year-end exchange rates. One must be careful, however, when analyzing translated trend data. Use of convenience rates to translate foreign currency accounts can distort underlying financial patterns in local currency. To illustrate, assume the following three-year sales revenue patterns for our British concern.

	2009	2010	2011
Sales revenue	£23,500	£28,650	£33,160

Convenience translations using the year-end exchange rates employed earlier (i.e., $1.70 for 2009, $1.80 for 2010, and $1.60 for 2011) yield a U.S. dollar sales increase of 7.5 percent [($53,056–$39,950)/$39,950] over the three-year period. The sales gain in pounds, however, is 41 percent [(£33,160–£23,500)/£23,500].

An alternative approach is to translate foreign currency data to domestic currency using a single base year's exchange rate. But which base-year exchange rate should be used? In our example, should the sales figures be translated using the 2009 exchange rate, the 2010 exchange rate, or the 2011 exchange rate?

Although we prefer to analyze foreign statements in local currency, we favor the use of the most recent year's exchange rate as a convenience translator for readers who prefer domestic currency statistics. An exception is warranted, however, if the foreign currency financial statements have been adjusted for changes in the general purchasing power of the foreign currency unit (see Chapter 7 for a discussion of this treatment). If foreign currency balances are expressed in base-year purchasing power equivalents, year-end exchange rates associated with the given base year should be employed. In our example, if sales revenues were expressed in pounds of 2009 general purchasing power, the 2009 exchange rate would have been an appropriate translation rate.

While translated statements give readers the convenience of viewing foreign currency accounts in a familiar currency, they may give a distorted picture. Specifically, exchange rate changes and accounting procedures together often produce domestic currency equivalents that conflict with underlying events. We illustrate this problem using the statement of cash flows as an example.

Recall from Chapter 6 that consolidated financial statements allow a multinational company to report the results of its worldwide operations in a single currency. Also recall that a variety of currency translation methods are in use internationally. Regardless of the currency translation method employed, it is not always clear to readers of consolidated funds flow statements, whether reported fund sources or uses reflect the results of an operational decision or simply an exchange rate change.

To illustrate, the translated statements of earnings, financial position, and cash flows for the Norwegian affiliate of a U.S.-based multinational company appear in Exhibit 9-5. The parent company employs the current rate method and defines the krone as its functional currency for consolidation purposes. Assume that capital stock is translated at the historical rate.

A cursory examination of the translated statement of cash flows shows that major sources of cash were operations (net income plus depreciation), the issuance of long-term debt, and a translation adjustment. In turn, cash was used to increase the company's investment in fixed assets.

The pattern of cash flow shown in Exhibit 9-5 differs from that experienced by a purely domestic company due to the presence of an aggregate translation adjustment. However, examination of this component of the translated funds statement reveals that it does not really constitute a source or use of cash. The translation adjustment is calculated by multiplying the beginning foreign currency net asset balance by the change in the current rate during the period and, second, by multiplying the increase or decrease in net assets during the period by the difference between the average exchange rate and end-of-period exchange rate. This procedure, together with the dual nature of the accounting equation, suggests that most components of the translated funds statement are a mix of translation effects and actual cash flows. In our current example, a statement reader needs to figure out whether the increase of long-term debt in the amount of $1,584,000 is an indication of the Norwegian affiliate's financing activities or is largely an accounting adjustment. Similar considerations apply to the purported $2,695,000 investment in fixed assets.

Assume that the translated statements appearing in Exhibit 9-5 are based on the Norwegian krone balances appearing in Exhibit 9-6 and that the relevant exchange rate information is as stated.

A cash flow comparison between the functional currency (krone) and the reporting currency (dollars) yields some striking contrasts. While the cash flow statement generated from the translated balance sheet and income statement (Exhibit 9-5) shows long-term debt as a source of funds, the krone statement (Exhibit 9-6) suggests that this was not the case. Likewise, what appears to be an investment in fixed assets from a dollar perspective turns out to be a pure translation phenomenon.

Closer analysis provides insight into the magnitude of the translation effects. An analysis of the fixed asset account reveals that there was no purchase, sale, or retirement of fixed assets during the year. Thus, the year-end balance should have been the beginning book value, $11,050,000 (NOK85,000,000), less depreciation of $720,000

EXHIBIT 9-5 Translated Financial Statements of Norwegian Subsidiary

Translated Balance Sheets as of 12/31/10 and 12/31/11

	December 31	
	2010	2011
Assets (000's)		
Cash	$ 3,120	$ 5,190
Net fixed assets	11,050	13,840
Total assets	$14,170	$19,030
Liabilities and owners' equity		
U.S. $500 payable	$ 650	$ 650
Long-term franc debt	6,240	8,304
Capital stock	4,968	4,968
Retained earnings	2,312	2,636
Translation adjustment	—	2,472
Total liabilities and stockholders' equity	$14,170	$19,030

Translated Statement of Income for the Year 2011 (000's)

Sales		$ 1,728
Expenses		
Operating costs	$ 864	
Depreciation	720	
Foreign exchange gain	(180)	1,404
Net income		$ 324

Translated Statement of Cash Flows (000's)

Sources		
Net income	$ 324	
Depreciation	720	
Increase in long-term debt	2,064	
Translation adjustment	2,472	$ 5,580
Uses		
Increase in fixed assets		3,510
Net increase in cash		$ 2,070

(NOK5,000,000), or $10,330,000. The actual ending balance was $13,840,000, suggesting that the entire increase in fixed assets ($13,840,000 – 10,330,000) was due to an exchange rate effect. Similarly, there was no change in Norwegian krone long-term debt during the year. Because this monetary liability was translated by an exchange rate that revalued during the year, the entire increase in long-term debt ($8,304,000 – 6,240,000) also arose from a translation adjustment. Similar transactional analyses account for additional translation effects related to the Norwegian subsidiary's working capital accounts. These effects are summarized in Exhibit 9-7.

Note that the sum of all the translation effects appearing in Exhibit 9-6 equals the aggregate translation adjustment appearing in the shareholders' equity section of the translated balance sheet. An informed reader can better determine the influence of exchange rate changes from a firm's financing and investing activities using the foregoing analysis.

EXHIBIT 9-6   **Financial Statements for Wholly-Owned Norwegian Subsidiary**

Local Currency Balance Sheet as of 12/31/10 and 12/31/11

	December 31	
	2010	2011
Assets		
Cash	NOK 24,000	NOK 30,000
Net fixed assets	85,000	80,000
Total assets	NOK 109,000	NOK 110,000
Liabilities and owners' equity		
U.S. $500 payable	NOK 5,000	NOK 3,750
Long-term krona debt	48,000	48,000
Capital stock	46,000	46,000
Retained earnings	10,000	12,250
Total liabilities and owners' equity	NOK 109,000	NOK 110,000
Statement of Cash Flows		
Sources		
Net income		NOK 2,250
Depreciation		5,000
Less: Krone foreign-exchange gain		1,250
Uses:		
None		—
Net increase in cash		NOK 6,000
Relevant Exchange Rates		
December 31, 2010		NOK1 = $.130
Average during 2011		NOK1 = $.144
December 31, 2011		NOK1 = $.173

EXHIBIT 9-7   **Analysis of Exchange Rate Effects**

	Debit	Credit
Cash	$1,206	
Fixed assets	3,519	
Intercompany payable		$ 180
Long-term debt		2,064
	$4,716	$2,244
Aggregate translation adjustment		2,472
	$4,716	$4,716

Differences in Statement Format

Balance sheet and income statement formats vary from country to country. For example, in contrast to the United States, where most companies adopt the balance sheet account format with assets appearing on the left and equity claims on the right, the format is often the reverse in the United Kingdom. As a second example, in contrast to U.S. balance sheets, which display assets in decreasing order of liquidity and liabilities in increasing order of maturity, in many countries the most liquid assets and the shortest term liabilities appear at the foot of the balance sheet.

Classification differences also abound internationally. For example, accumulated depreciation is reported as a contra-asset account in the United States. In Germany, depreciable assets are usually reported net of accumulated depreciation, but all current period changes in long-term asset accounts are shown directly in the balance sheet. In most countries, the distinction between a current and noncurrent liability is one year. In Germany it is often four years. Handbooks like *Transactional Accounting*[27] may be consulted for a detailed treatment of other classification differences prevailing in individual countries.

Financial statement format differences, while troublesome, are seldom critical because the underlying structure of financial statements is quite similar around the world. Accordingly, most format differences can usually be reconciled with a little effort.

Language and Terminology Barriers

Language differences among countries can present information barriers to financial statement users. Most companies domiciled in non-English-speaking countries publish their annual reports in the home country language. However, growing numbers of the relatively large companies in developed economies provide English-language versions of their annual reports.

Accounting terminology differences can also cause difficulty.[28] For example, U.S. readers associate the term stock with certificates of corporate ownership. Readers in the United Kingdom, on the other hand, associate the term with a firm's inventory of unsold goods. Other examples of terminology differences between the United Kingdom and the United States include turnover (sales revenue), and debtors and creditors (accounts receivable and payable).

In summary, many substantial issues confront the user of international financial statements. Perhaps the most difficult issues concern foreign currency and the availability and credibility of financial information. Difficulties with foreign currency will probably have a pervasive influence on international accounting for some time. In contrast, problems related to information availability and credibility are gradually decreasing as more and more companies, regulatory authorities, and stock exchanges recognize the the importance of improving investors' access to timely and credible information.

FINANCIAL STATEMENT ANALYSIS AND AUDITING

In our earlier section on accounting analysis, we noted the importance of assessing the quality of the information contained in a firm's published accounts. Thoughtful readers must judge the adequacy of accounting measurements employed and remove distortions caused by the use of accounting methods deemed inappropriate. A corollary of this quality assessment is an assessment of the credibility of the information provided,

---

[27] Dieter Ordelheide and KPMG, Transactional Accounting, 2nd ed., Hampshire, U.K.: Palgrave, 2001.
[28] Lisa Evans, "Language, Translation and the Problem of International Accounting Communication," *Accounting, Auditing and Accountability Journal*, Vol. 17, no. 2 (2004): 248.

irrespective of the measurement rules employed. In addition to questions of information quality and quantity, financial analysts must be relatively free from undue risk due to fraud or deception on the part of those making the financial representations. We now discuss the attest or audit function and the role it plays in international financial statement analysis.

The Attest Function

Independent auditors perform the attest function in financial reporting. As competent outside experts they review financial information provided by a firm's management and then attest to its reliability, fairness, and other aspects of quality. This process establishes and maintains the integrity of financial information.

While auditing processes are rooted in antiquity, the growth of auditing as a separate and distinct profession during the nineteenth century was encouraged by the enactment in the United Kingdom, circa 1845, of a requirement that companies keep accounts which had to be audited by persons other than directors. The earliest accounting body was the Society of Accountants in Edinburgh.

Investors and other readers of financial statements have a big stake in the attestation of professional auditors. They can make decisions with better expected outcomes if they have relatively better information available. The public is also better served. Incomplete, unreliable, or even misleading financial information may well have a negative effect on capital formation processes within an economy. Moreover, scarce resources may be misdirected to socially less desirable channels or wasted through excessive rates of bankruptcy. Sensitivity to the importance of the attest function is probably higher in multinational settings than it is in single-country situations.

Aside from decision and public interest effects, independent audits introduce efficiency into the financial reporting process. If users of financial information had to obtain firm information on their own and verify this information item by item and user by user, an immensely costly process would ensue. In this regard, division of responsibilities produces net benefits. Management has a comparative advantage in preparing and offering financial information needed by outsiders. Auditors, in turn, have a comparative advantage in ensuring that management's financial representations are relatively free of bias. Their independent attestations enable statement readers around the world to discriminate among generally acceptable and unacceptable accounting practices and to assess the overall quality of financial reports at a lower cost than would otherwise be the case.

The Audit Report

The auditors' attestation is typically communicated to financial statement readers by way of an audit report. This report either follows, or in some cases, precedes the firm's principal financial statements appearing in its annual report. But, what is included in such a report? Do auditors in all countries employ identical reporting formats? Exhibit 9-8 contains a taxonomy of audit reporting requirements in a sample of countries.[29]

---

[29] Exhibit 9-8 and subsequent exhibits on various facets of international auditing practice draw on an excellent survey conducted by Belverd Needles. For greater detail, see his chapter "Taxonomy of Auditing Standards," in Frederick D.S. Choi, *International Finance and Accounting Handbook*, 3rd ed., New York: John Wiley & Sons, 2003.

EXHIBIT 9-8	**Selected Reporting Requirements for Audit Reports**

United Kingdom

The auditor's report discloses the responsibilities of company directors and the scope of the audit; basis of opinion and statement of opinion. The balance sheet, income statement, and related notes must be covered by statute; auditing standards extend this coverage to the cash flow statement. The auditors' opinion must state whether the financial statements give a true and fair view and that the statements comply with statutory requirements. Auditors must state that they have read other information contained in the audit report, including the corporate governance statement, and describe implications for the audit report if the auditors become aware of any inconsistencies. The scope section also explains the auditor's responsibilities in relation to the separate directors' report, the accounting records, information and explanations required, and rules regarding the disclosure of directors' remuneration.

United States

A standard three paragraph report identifies the company and the principal financial statements being audited (scope) and states the responsibilities of management and the auditor. The auditor must indicate whether or not the audit complied with generally accepted auditing standards. The auditor must express an opinion as to whether the financial statements are presented fairly in accordance with GAAP and whether GAAP has been consistently observed in relation to reports in previous years. If an opinion cannot be expressed this must be stated.

Sweden

The Swedish Companies Act requires the auditor statements about:

1. The preparation of the annual report is in accordance with the Act.
2. The adoption of the balance sheet and income statement.
3. The proposal included in the administration report for disposition of the unappropriated earnings or deficit.
4. The discharge from the liability of members of the board of directors and the managing director.

Germany

The German Commercial Code specifies that the auditor's report contain a description of the process and result of the audit, including management's report, a forecast of future developments, a statement of compliance with legal regulation, and a statement describing the company's risk management system. The auditor must provide a summary of the content, type, and volume of the audit in the Bestaetigungsvmerk, an evaluation of the audit results, and statements as to whether or not the financial statements and management's report present a true and fair view.

Based on the sample data provided in Exhibit 9-8, it should be evident that auditors reports vary internationally in terms of the information they contain. Both the U.K. and U.S. audit reports identify the scope of the audit, identify the auditing and accounting standards adhered to, and set forth the auditor's opinion. The German report expands the information set to include information on future developments as well as description of the company's risk management system, both useful pieces of information for statement readers. The reports differ most markedly in terms of the opinions that are expressed. Exhibit 9-9 focuses on the wording of auditor opinions selected randomly from company annual reports in the United Kingdom, United States, Sweden, Switzerland, and Norway.

In documenting the diversity of audit opinions internationally, Exhibit 9-9 raises information issues for analysts. U.K. auditors state that the financial statements they audit give a true and fair view of a company's affairs. In this instance, does the term *true* mean "the truth, the whole truth and nothing but the truth?" Does inclusion of the term "fair" imply that the truth has somehow been compromised? U.S. auditors take a less absolute stance and state that the audited statements present fairly and in accordance with a set of U.S. measurement rules. Does this wording connote the same meaning as true and fair? The Swedish opinion is more informative than the requirements set forth in Exhibit 9-8 where Swedish auditors are allowed to opine to nothing. However, are Swedish GAAP and the Annual Accounts Act synonymous? The wording in Exhibit 9-9 seems to suggest this. If so, does this imply that Swedish GAAP is legally based, which normally differs from standards promulgated by private professional groups? Or, does it mean that the Companies Act prescribes adherence to

---

EXHIBIT 9-9   **Diversity of Audit Opinions**

United Kingdom

In our opinion, the financial statements give a **true** and **fair** view of the state of affairs of the company and of the group as at December 31 and of the profit and cash flows of the group for the year then ended and have been properly prepared in accordance with the Companies Act 1985.

United States

In our opinion, the financial statements referred to above present **fairly,** in all material respects, the consolidated financial position of the company at December 31, 2009 and, and the consolidated results of its operations and its cash flows for each of the three years in the period ended December 31 in conformity with U.S. GAAP.

Sweden

The annual accounts and the consolidated accounts have been prepared in accordance with the Annual Accounts Act and, thereby, give a true and fair view of the Company's and the Group's financial position and results of operations in accordance with generally accepted accounting principles in Sweden.

Switzerland

In our opinion, the accounting records and financial statements and the proposed appropriation of available earnings comply with **Swiss law** and the company's **articles of incorporation**.

Norway

The parent company's financial statements are prepared in accordance with law and regulations and give a true and fair view of the financial position of the Company as of December 31, and the results of its operations and its cash flows for the year then ended, in accordance with generally accepted accounting principles in Norway. The financial statements of the group are prepared in accordance with law and regulations and give a true and fair view of the financial position of the group as of December 31 and the results of its operations, its cash flows, and changes in equity for the year then ended in accordance with International Financial Reporting Standards as adopted by the EU.

generally accepted auditing stndards promulgated by the Swedish accounting profession? If it means the former, does compliance with the law (also read the Swiss opinion) assure that the statements provide a true and fair view of a company's affairs? Finally, observe that the Norwegian example provides two audit reports; one for the parent company, the other for the group. Do duel audit opinions suggest that one set of measurement principles is somehow superior to the other? This question is especially germane for those relying on parent company financials for their analysis as the latter are normally the basis for taxation which has real cash flow effects.

Auditing and Credibility

The credibility of the audit report rests on several platforms. These include, but are not limited to, the source of auditing standards, their enforcement, and the professionalism of the individual or individuals performing the audit.

Exhibit 9-7 suggests that auditing standards emante from national legislation such as Companies Acts and/or private professional accounting associations. In many cases it is a matter of degree. Auditing standards are primarily promulgated by private professional groups in most countries. Notable exceptions are Austria, Germany, and Switzerland, where auditng standards are largely influenced by legislation. Countries such as France, Japan, Korea, Kenya, Sweden, and the United Kingdom rely on a combination of legal and professional standards.[30] In some cases, standards promulgated by private professional groups are much more rigorous than those crafted by the government; in other cases, just the opposite may be true. Accordingly, credibility of the attest function is also a function of enforcement mechanisms and the extent of auditor liability.

Enforcement of auditing standards and auditing lapses has proved difficult at the international level. Professionally developed standards generally lack the force of law, the possibility of economic sanction, and, more generally, international political and diplomatic recognition. Hence, enforcement of standards is by and large left to the profession itself. Insistence upon strict or tightening auditing standards invariably produces adverse economic consequences for clients (i.e., increased audit service fees) which, in turn, leads to competitive pressures among independent auditors. At the national level, the effectiveness of enforcing auditing and ethical standards varies from country to country. In most of the countries he surveyed, Needles finds that an auditor who violates auditing standards may be disciplined either by law or by professional sanctions. Penalties include reprimands, fines, and in some cases expulsion from the professional bodies of which the auditor or audit firm is a member. Professional bodies in the United Kingdom have experienced difficulty in obtaining evidencce of wrong doing as they lack subpeona power. In the United States, an expelled member from a state society of accountants or the American Institute of CPA's does not necessarily prevent the expelled member from conducting audits. Only individual states, operating through their state boards of accounting, have the authority to revoke a license to practice. Press coverage often reveals that boards often fail to impose sanctions or to follow up on imposed sanctions. Governments in countries such as France, Japan, Germany, Kenya, and the Netherlands often take a formal role in enforcement actions. Hence, enforcement at the national level has proved uneven.

---

[30] Needles, ibid.

Auditor liability to third parties for wrongful acts represents a form of market enforcement. Here too, market practices vary. At one end of the spectrum, in countries such as Germany and the United States, simple negligence on the part of the auditor is usually insufficient for aggrieved third parties to previal in their litigation claims. In countries such as Hong Kong, Japan, Kenya, Saudi Arabia, Sweden, and the United Kingdom, just the opposite may be the case. In most countries, auditors can be held liable for gross negligence or fraud.

In the final analysis, the credibility of auditing is a function of who is doing the audit. Here, statement readers must distinguish between two classes of accountants. Assume you are examining the annual report of a French firm as a basis for an investment decision. Being removed from the local scene, one of the first things you would now do would be to look to see if the annual report contains an audit report by an independent account. You find the report and it is signed by the Commissaires aux Comptes. Can you conclude that managements financial representations have been subject a rigorous independent audit? Not necessarily. The Commissaires is a statutory auditor, whose appointment is mandatory under French commercial law. Statutory auditors in France are required to oversee in very general terms a company's bookkeeping and accounting and then to report annually to the stockholders' meeting. The law does not specify any professional qualifications for the Commissaires which may range from very minimal to substantial. Often one or several stockholders serve in this capacity. Consequently, a statement of an opinion by a Commissaire has a completely different meaning and premise from a possibly similar statement or opinion by an Expert des Comptable. The latter is a well-trained professional accountant who is comparable in stature to a U.K. chartered accountant or an American certified public accountant. Exhibit 9-10 contains examples of auditor distinctions in selected countries.

EXHIBIT 9-10	Differing Auditor Status in Selected Countries

France
    Commissaires aux Compte
    Expert des Comptable

Japan
    Statutory Auditor
    Accounting Auditor

Unites Kingdom
    Certified Accountant
    Chartered Accountant

United States
    Public Accountant
    Certified Public Accountant

Mexico
    Comisario
    Contador Publico

Then there is the issue of auditor qualifications and licensure. Educational requirements for professional qualification are modest in the United Kingdom and fairly substantial in the United States. Indeed, most countries require academic training and candidates applying for auditor certification must meet various licensing requirements, including passing comprehensive professional exams. On the other hand, practical experience requirements for professional qualification are substantial in Germany and the Netherlands but are no longer required at all in some jurisdictions of the United States. Once certified as a professional auditor, continuing education to keep an auditor abreast of current business and professional developments are required in Australia, Japan, Korea, Mexico, the Netherlands, the United Kingdom, and the United States. This is seldom the case elsewhere.

Ultimately, the value of an auditor lies in his or her independence from the firm he or she is auditing. Most would agree that CPA's in the United States are subject to the most stringent independence standards that exist internationally. In some countries, such as Hong Kong, auditors may sit on corporate boards of directors, or as is the case in South Korea, may own small financial interests in companies their firms audit. On the European Continent, many large audit firms are owned, at least in part, by large banks that they may very well audit. This does not mean that European auditors are necessarily dependent in fact or in appearance. Rather, it means that a thoroughly different organization of the independent auditing profession prevails. While a non-U.S. person may hold that an audit firm performing management advisory services and tax advocacy for a client cannot possibly be independent, U.S. auditors whose activities in these areas have recently been constrained would argue that bank equity ownership of an audit firm (although separated from audit operations) impairs independence. Who is right?

The auditor independence question often raises operational problems in multinational engagements. Auditor independence is a concept not only entrenched in professional ethics codes in the United States but also anchored in administrative SEC regulations such as their basic Regulation SX and Accounting Series Release No. 126. Therefore, international affiliates of publicly held U.S. parent companies are all audited by persons who meet U.S. definitions of auditor independence. This is not always a simple matter when audits abroad are conducted by associated or correspondent firms rather than by an audit firm's own branch offices. The situation may be even more vexing in those countries where local rules require that independent audits be performed only by local nationals.

Coping Mechanisms

We have now seen that audit reports internationally are varied in their information content. We have also documented variations in the platforms that help to give the attest function credibility. These differences support the case for strong international harmonization efforts in auditing. A leading organization that has as its mission the harmonization of global auditing standards is the International Federation of Accountants (IFAC).[31] A description of this organization and its activities are described

---

[31] Additional information on IFAC is available at www.ifac.org. Also see, Anne Loft, Christopher Humphrey, and Stuart Turley, "In Pursuit of Global Regulation: Changing Governance and Accountability Structures at the International Federation of Accountants (IFAC)," *Accounting, Auditing and Accountability Journal*, Vol. 19, no. 3 (2006), p. 451.

in Chapter 8. At the same time, differences in audit conditions described in the previous sections, especially in the area of independence standards and audit standards that are anchored to legal systems, suggest that global harmonization efforts will not be easy.

The European Community is also pursuing harmonization of audit standards at the regional level. This effort, however, is complicated by the diversity that characterizes organizational structures of the accounting profession in various EU countries. For example, the United Kingdom currently has six accounting bodies four of which have ministerial approval to serve as statutory auditors. France has two accountancy bodies while Germany has three. This diverse range of acounting structures makes it very difficult to secure agreement in the audit area. Suffice it to say that tangible progress toward harmonized auditing standards in Europe has been slow.[32]

In the absence of harmonized audit standards, financial analysts must make it a point to understand the audit conditions that exist in the country that hosts the business entity whose financial statements are under scrutiny. Failing this, restricting financial analyses to those companies whose statements have been audited by reputable audit firms known for their professional expertise and integrity is one coping option. If the stakes are sufficiently high, as they are for institutional investors, insisting on or paying for a second audit opinion by a world-class international audit firm is another.

Internal Auditing

A sound external audit of a reporting entity's financial statements is a *necessary* condition to assure the credibility of managements communications with external parties. However, it is not *sufficient*. The effectiveness of a firm's internal control system is equally important as it provides a more timely system of "checks and balances" than can be provided by a firm's outside auditors. The service activity that crafts and monitors a firm's internal control system is the internal audit function.

Many explanations have been advanced concerning the recent rise of internal auditing. One is the phenomenal growth of audit committees of corporate boards of directors. These audit committees, which play an active role in corporate governance, often rely on internal audit functions as their direct instrumentality. This has enhanced the stature of internal auditors as well as given them direct access to top management.

Another contributing factor to the growing importance of internal auditing is the unprecedented growth in corporate control needs. For example, at the leading French bank, Societe Generale, a rogue trader took unauthorized positions resulting in a stunning $7.2 billion loss for the firm.[33] The question of illicit payments by MNC's has ushered in yet another generation of specific tasks for internal auditing. A case in point is the recent corporate governance scandal surrounding 160-year-old German conglomerate Siemens, involving the common and highly organized payment of bribes to prospective customers.[34]

In the United States, the importance of internal auditing was highlighted by the spate of corporate scandals which began during the late 1990s. The roots of these scandals are

---

[32] See Peter Walton, "European Harmonization," in Frederick D.S. Choi, *International Finance and Accounting Handbook*, 3rd ed., New York: John Wiley & Sons, 2003.
[33] Elizabeth Charnock, "Holistic Compliance: The Future of Financial Risk Management," *Financial Executive*, April 2009, pp. 55–57.
[34] Dionne Searcey, "In Antibribery Law, Some Fear Inadvertent Chill on Business," *Wall Street Journal*, August 6, 2009, p. A9.

directly attributed to lax corporate governance sytems in which management placed their personal interests above the interests of their shareholders.[35] To bolster investor confidence, the U.S. Congress enacted the Sarbanes-Oxley Act (SOX). This act puts the onus on both management and their auditors to create an operating environment that (1) minimizes conflicts of interest, (2) fosters greater corporate transparency, reliability, and accuracy in financial reporting, and (3) increases the independence among management, the board of directors, and the auditors, key players in any system of corporate governance. Regarding the latter, sections 205 and 301 of the the Act highlight key roles for audit committees, a subset of a company's board of directors. First, audit committees must oversee the accounting and financial reporting processes and the financial statement audits of the companies they serve. Second, they must appoint, compensate, and evaluate the effectiveness of the external auditor. Third, they must establish procedures for the receipt and follow-up of complaints regarding questionable accounting or auditing procedures. SOX also increases the enforcment tools available to market regulators and attempts to minimze conflict of interest inherent in securities market transactions (i.e., putting investor interests ahead of transactions-driven behavior of investment advisors and investment banks).[36]

Two sections of SOX that merit special note are sections 303 and 404. Section 303 states that both the CFO and CEO must personally sign off on all required financial statements, attesting that the statements are complete and accurate and comply with all relevant regulations and accounting standards. Section 404 mandates that management include a written statement assuring the reader that they have designed and tested adequate internal controls and that these controls are working. These controls must be audited by the company's outside auditors, thus formalizing the relationship between a firm's external and internal auditors. SOX also created the Public Company Accounting Oversight Board (PCAOB) which, among other things, provides guidance for auditing a company's internal controls and establishes the content of the auditor's report.

To show how the Sarbanes-Oxley Act has been operationalized, we provide excerpts from the annual report of the world's recognized soft drink provider, Coca-Cola. Exhibit 9-11 reproduces the additional paragraph that is now included in U.S. audit reports. This paragraph follows the paragraphs describing audit scope, audit standards, and the audit opinion. The Committee of Sponsoring Organizations

---

EXHIBIT 9-11   **Coca-Cola's Enhanced Audit Report**

We also have audited, in accordance with the standards of the Public Company Accounting Oversight Board (United States), the effectiveness of The Coca-Cola Company's internal control over financial reporting as of December 31, 2008, based on criteria established in *Internal Control-Integrated Framework* issued by the Committee of Sponsoring Organizations of the Treadway Commission and our report dated February 24, 2009, expressed an unqualified opinion thereon.

Ernst & Young LLP

---

[35] This is known in agency theory as asymmetric behavior whereby the agent (management) maximizes its own personal interest at the expense of the principal (shareholders) to whom they owe their primary fiduciary responsibility.

[36] R. Trent Gazzaway, "Audit Committees: Expanded Roles, Responsibilities and Focus," *Financial Executive*, July/August, 2008, pp. 22–25.

(COSO) mentioned in Coke's audit report is an organization that was established in the 1970s to study how to combat fraudulent financial reporting. Its sponsoring organizations include the American Accounting Association, American Institute of Certified Public Accountants, Financial Executives Institute, the Institute of Internal Auditors, and the Institute of Management Accountants.[37] Exhibit 9-12 contains management's responsibility report for the firm's internal controls and Exhibit 9-13 illustrates the new internal control responsibilities of the company's external auditors.

Additional factors that help to explain the growth and recognition and importance of internal auditing include:

1. Ever-increasing corporate management accountability
2. Increasing organizatinal complexities, especially in multinational enterprises
3. Growth of corporate mergers, acquisitions, and restructurings
4. Growing use of electronic funds remittances and other transfers for illicit purposes (i.e., money laundering)
5. Increased reliance on internal auditing by external auditors (i.e., greater reliance on the work of an internal auditor improves the economics of the attest function.)
6. Increase of regulatory requirements for the performance of internal audits the likes of Sarbanes-Oxley (SOX)

Evidence from Asia (e.g., Japan recently enacted its own version of SOX) and Europe also points to expansion of internal auditing within larger corporations worldwide.

Still another explanation is probably found in the world economic environment. The phenomenon of global competition, described in Chapter 1, has resulted in thinning corporate profit margins highlighting the importance of cost and expense controls. Internal auditing plays an important role in monitoring such controls.

Professional Organization

Professional focus for internal auditing is provided by the Institute of Internal Auditors (IIA), which is headquartered in the United States and has an international membership. Established in 1941, IIA is committed to:

- Providing, on an international scale, comprehensive professional development activities, standards for the practice of internal auditing, and certification
- Researching, disseminating, and promoting to its members and to the public throughout the world, knowledge and information concerning internal auditing, including internal control and related subjects
- Establishing meetings worldwide in order to educate members and others as to the practice of internal auditing as it exists in various countries throughout the world
- Bringing together internal auditors and promoting education in the field of internal auditing

The professional examination and certification activites of IIA leads to qualification as a Certified Internal Auditor (CIA). The CIA designation is the only globally accepted

---

[37] Major tenets of COSO's new guidance for monitoring internal control systems is reproduced in Edith Orenstein's, "COSO's New Guidance for Monitoring Internal Control," *Financial Executive*, January/February, 2009, p. 58. Details are available on COSO's website at www.coso.org.

EXHIBIT 9-12 Report of Coca-Cola's Management on Internal Control

Report of Management on Internal Control Over Financial Reporting

The Coca-Cola Company and Subsidiaries

Management of the Company is responsible for the preparation and integrity of the Consolidated Financial Statements appearing in our Annual Report on Form 10-K. The financial statements were prepared in conformity with generally accepted accounting principles appropriate in the circumstances and, accordingly, include certain amounts based on our best judgments and estimates. Financial information in this Annual Report on Form 10-K is consistent with that in the financial statements.

Management of the Company is responsible for establishing and maintaining adequate internal control over financial reporting as such term is defined in Rules 13a-15(f) under the Securities and Exchange Act of 1934 ("Exchange Act"). The Company's internal control over financial reporting is designed to provide reasonable assurance regarding the reliability of financial reporting and the preparation of the Consolidated Financial Statements. Our internal control over financial reporting is supported by a program of internal audits and appropriate reviews by management, written policies and guidelines, careful selection and training of qualified personnel and a written Code of Business Conduct adopted by our Company's Board of Directors, applicable to all Company Directors and all officers and employees of our Company and subsidiaries. In addition, our Company's Board of Directors adopted a written Code of Business Conduct for Non-Employee Directors which reflects the same principles and values as our Code of Business Conduct for officers and employees but focuses on matters of most relevance to non-employee Directors.

Because of its inherent limitations, internal control over financial reporting may not prevent or detect misstatements and even when determined to be effective, can only provide reasonable assurance with respect to financial statement preparation and presentation. Also, projections of any evaluation of effectiveness to future periods are subject to the risk that controls may become inadequate because of changes in conditions, or that the degree of compliance with the policies or procedures may deteriorate.

The Audit Committee of our Company's Board of Directors, composed solely of Directors who are independent in accordance with the requirements of the New York Stock Exchange listing standards, the Exchange Act and the Company's Corporate Governance Guidelines, meets with the independent auditors, management and internal auditors periodically to discuss internal control over financial reporting and auditing and financial reporting matters. The Audit Committee reviews with the independent auditors the scope and results of the audit effort. The Audit Committee also meets periodically with the independent auditors and the chief internal auditor without management present to ensure that the independent auditors and the chief internal auditor have free access to the Audit Committee. Our Audit Committee's Report can be found in the Company's 2009 Proxy statement.

Management assessed the effectiveness of the Company's internal control over financial reporting as of December 31. In making this assessment, management used the criteria set forth by the Committee of Sponsoring Organizations of the Treadway Commission (COSO) in *Internal Control-Integrated Framework*. Based on our assessment, management believes that the Company maintained effective internal control over financial reporting as of December 31, 2008.

The Company's independent auditors, Ernst & Young LLP, a registered public accounting firm, are appointed by the Audit Committee of the Company's Board of Directors, subject to ratification by our Company's shareholders. Ernst & Young LLP has audited and reported on the Consolidated Financial Satements of the Coca-Cola Company and subsidiaries, and the Company's internal control over financial reporting. The reports of the independent auditors are contained in this annual report.

Muhtar Kent
President and Chief Executive Officer
Harry L. Anderson
Vice President and Controller
Gary P. Fayard
Executive Vice President and Chief Financial Officer

| EXHIBIT 9-13 | Report of Coca-Cola's Independent Auditors on Internal Control |

Report of Independent Registered Public Accounting Firm on Internal Control over Financial Reporting Board of Directors and Shareholders

The Coca-Cola Company

We have audited the Coca-Cola Company's internal control over financial reporting as of December 31, 2008, based on criteria established in Internal Control-Integrated Framework issued by the Committee of Sponsoring Organizations of the Treadway Commission (the COSO criteria). The Coca-Cola Company's management is responsible for maintaining effective internal control over financial reporting and for its assessment of the effectiveness of internal control over financial reporting. Our responsibility is to express an opinion on the Company's internal control over financial reporting based on our audit.

We conducted our audit in accordance with the standards of the Public Company Accounting Oversight Board (United Sates). Those standards require that we plan and perform the audit to obtain reasonable assurance about whether effective internal control over financial reporting was maintained in all material respects. Our audit included obtaining an understanding of internal control over financial reporting, assessing the risk that a material weakness exists, testing and evaluating the design and operating effectiveness of internal control based on the assessed risk, and performing such other procedures as we considered necessary in the circumstances. We believe that our audit provides a reasonable basis for our opinion.

A company's internal control over financial reporting is a process designed to provide reasonable assurance regarding the reliability of financial reporting and the preparation of financial statements for external purposes in accordance with generally accepted accounting principles. A company's internal control over financial reporting includes those policies and procedures that (1) pertain to the maintenance of records that, in reasonable detail, accurately and fairly reflect the transactions and dispositions of the assets of the company; (2) provide reasonable assurance that transactions are recorded as necessary to permit preparation of financial statements in accordance with generally accepted accounting principles, and that receipts and expenditures of the company are being made only in accordance with authorizations of management and directors of the company; and (3) provide reasonable assurance regarding prevention or timely detection of unauthorized acquisition, use, or disposition of the company's assets that could have a material effect on the financial statements.

Because of its inherent limitations, internal control over financial reporting may not prevent or detect misstatements. Also projections of any evaluation of effectiveness to future periods are subject to the risk that controls may become inadequate because of changes in conditions, or that the degree of compliance with the policies or procedures may deteriorate.

In our opinion, The Coca-Cola Company maintained, in all material respects, effective internal control over financial reporting as of December 31, 2008, based on the COSO criteria.

We also have audited, in accordance with the standards of the Public Company Accounting Oversight Board (United States), the consolidated balance sheets of The Coca-Cola Company and subsidiaries as of December 31, 2008 and 2007, and the related consolidated statements of income, shareholders' equity, and cash flows for each of the three years in the period ended December 31, 2008, and our report dated February 24, 2009, expressed an unqualified opinion thereon.

Ernst & Young LLP

certification for internal auditors. At present, the IIA boasts a membership approaching 130,000 from 165 countries.

Evolving Role of Internal Auditing

The role of internal auditors has evolved over time. Initial growth of internal auditing was initially evidenced in Europe where many countries enacted regulations specifically referring to internal audit functions and requirements. Early auditors adopted a "traffic cop" mentality in their work. They were largely concerned with ascertaining the extent of compliance with established policies, plans and procedures, verifying a firm's assets, and reconciling inventory and cash to accounting records. It is not suprising that management views of internal auditing were generally guarded, with internal auditors being regarded as necessary evils. Your authors have personally observed instances where managers were loathe to communicate with auditors. In turn, internal auditors were always trying to catch managers doing something wrong. This type of situation is wasteful and detrimental to the health of the organization and its stakeholders, including financial statement users.

In an environment of global competition, managers today are looking to internal auditors for expertise that transcends traditional control functions. The major international public accounting firm of PricewaterhouseCoopers offers 10 imperatives to internal auditors to improve their value to companies operating in a post-Enron world.[38] They are:

1. Sharpen dialog with top management and directors in order to clearly establish the value-added objectives of internal audit (i.e., strategic issues, risk management, and protection of company assets).
2. Realign to meet key stakeholders' expectations (stockholders, executive management, external auditors, and market regulators).
3. Think and act strategically.
4. Expand audit coverage to include "tone set at the top," the conduct of executive management in protecting the company.
5. Assess and strengthen expertise for complex business auditing.
6. Leverage technology in high-risk areas.
7. Focus on enterprise risk management capabilities.
8. Make the audit process dynamic.
9. Strengthen quality assurance processes.
10. Measure the enhanced performance against expectations of shareholders.

The idea here is that if the internal audit function is considered a mere policing function, management support will continue to be lukewarm as manifested by their continual questioning of internal audit costs. This will not serve the organization or its major constituents well. If auditors are viewed as contributing members of the management team and provide helpful managerial advice, for example, on how to control a firm's risk exposures, they will be valued and their costs deemed more than acceptable.

Being a valued advisor to management need not and should not compromise an auditor's independence. Compromising one's integrity does not earn management's respect. Doing so would increase the risk that management would violate their fiduciary

---

[38] Seymour Jones, "Internal Auditing," in Frederick D.S. Choi, *International Finance and Accounting Handbook*, 3rd ed., New York: John Wiley & Sons, 2003, p. 32.13.

responsibility to maintain a sound system of internal controls which is now mandated by law. Rather management would value and embrace auditors who (1) fulfill their responsibiltiies to their key constituents, that is, readers of the firm's financial reports and (2) are talented enough to offer advice that helps a firm to maintain its international competitiveness.

Appendix 9-1

Illustration of Restatement of Japanese GAAP Financial Statements to a U.S. GAAP Basis

In this appendix we show how GAAP restatements might be used to reduce the effects of accounting diversity that persist in a post-IASB world. Exhibit 9-14 contains the year-end financial statements of Toyoza Enterprises (Japan) and Lincoln Corporation (United States), with relevant notes.

Comparative financial ratios for Toyoza and Lincoln Enterprises are provided in Exhibit 9-15. Based on this preliminary analysis, Toyoza appears less liquid, less efficient, less profitable, and financially less solvent than Lincoln Enterprises. But is it? A good analyst will attempt

EXHIBIT 9-14 Year-End Unadjusted Financial Statements and Related Notes		
	Toyoza Enterprises (¥Thousands)	**Lincoln Enterprises ($Thousands)**
Income Statements		
Sales	¥1,400,000	$12,000
Operating expenses:		
Cost of sales	1,120,000	10,044
Selling and administrative	100,000	575
Other operating	114,200	319
Goodwill amortization		10
Operating income	¥ 65,800	$ 1,052
Gains (losses)		
Interest expenses	28,000	130
Income before taxes	37,800	922
Income taxes	23,800	258
Income after taxes	14,000	664
Equity in earnings of unconsolidated subsidiaries		116
Net income	¥ 14,000	$ 780
Balance Sheets		
Cash	¥ 124,500	$ 1,920
Accounts receivable, net	510,000	1,660
Marketable securities	45,000	500
Inventory	390,000	1,680
Investments	150,000	1,000
Plant and equipment, net	280,600	5,160

(continued)

EXHIBIT 9-14   Year-End Unadjusted Financial Statements and Related Notes (Continued)

	Toyoza Enterprises (¥Thousands)	Lincoln Enterprises ($Thousands)
Goodwill	—	80
Total assets	¥1,500,000	$12,000
Short-term payables	¥ 165,000	$ 1,800
Short-term debt	525,000	2,160
Deferred taxes	—	—
Other current liabilities	90,000	—
Long-term debt	520,000	2,400
Reserves	90,000	—
Capital stock	75,000	960
Retained earnings	35,000	4,680
Total liabilities and owners' equity	¥1,500,000	$12,000

Notes to Toyoza's Financial Statements:

1. The balance sheet and income statement were prepared in accordance with the Japanese Commercial Code and related regulations.
2. Investments in subsidiaries and affiliated companies are accounted for using the equity method.
3. Inventories are stated at average cost. Ending inventories restated to a FIFO basis would have been ¥198 million higher.
4. Plant and equipment are carried at cost. Depreciation, with minor exceptions, is computed by the sum-of-the-years-digits method. Plant and equipment, purchased 2 years ago, have an estimated life of 4 years.
5. Operating expenses include lease rental payments of ¥40 million. The average term of the lease contracts is 4 years. All leases transfer ownership to the lessor at the end of the least term. Lincoln Enterprises' cost of capital is estimated to be 8 percent.
6. A translation gain of ¥20 million relating to consolidation of foreign operations with a net monetary liability position is being deferred under long-term debt.
7. Purchased goodwill is amortized over 20 years. The current period's amortization expense is ¥12 million for the year and is included under other operating expenses. Under a U.S. GAAP impairments test, it would have been 10% of that amount.
8. Toyoza Enterprises is allowed to set up special-purpose reserves (i.e., government-sanctioned charges against earnings) equal to a certain percentage of total export revenues. This year's charge (including other operating expenses) was ¥26,400,000. Similarly, this year's addition to Toyoza's general-purpose reserves was ¥30,800,000.
9. The ¥/$ exchange rate at year-end was ¥110 = $1.
10. Toyoza Enterprise's marginal income tax rate is 35 percent.

Notes to Lincoln Enterprises' financial statements:

1. The balance sheet and income statement are based on U.S. GAAP.
2. Inventories are carried at FIFO cost.
3. Plant and equipment are depreciated in straight-line fashion.
4. Foreign operations are consolidated with those of the parent using the temporal method of currency translation as Lincoln adopts the U.S. dollar as its functional currency.

EXHIBIT 9-15	Comparative Financial Ratios Based on Unadjusted Data	
	Toyoza	**Lincoln**
Liquidity		
Current ratio	1.37x	1.45x
Acid-test ratio	.87x	1.03x
Efficiency		
Receivables turnover	2.75x	7.23x
Inventory turnover	2.87x	5.98x
Asset turnover	.93x	1.00x
Profitability		
Profit margin	1.0%	6.5%
Return on assets	4.4%	9.7%
Return on equity	12.7%	13.8%
Coverage		
Debt to total assets	92.7%	53.0%
Times interest earned	2.4x	8.9x

to ascertain to what extent these observed differences are due to real economic differences versus differences in accounting measurements and other environmental influences.

To aid comparison with Lincoln, we restate Toyoza's statements to a U.S. GAAP basis. Based on the information provided and examining the notes in sequence, the following adjustments are required:

1. Inventories are adjusted to reflect differences in costing methods. Adjustments would increase inventories and decrease cost of sales by ¥198,000.
2. The difference between straight-line and sum-of-the-year's-digits depreciation for the current year yields an adjustment to cost of sales and net plant and equipment of ¥46,750. The difference in depreciation for the preceding year is ¥140,250. Based on a marginal tax rate of 35 percent, the ¥140,250 increase in reported pretax earnings would create ¥49,088 in deferred taxes with the balance credited to retained earnings.
3. Under U.S. GAAP the lease transaction would be capitalized. Discounting the

stream of ¥40,000,000 rental payments for 5 years at 8 percent yields a present value of ¥159,600,000 attributed to both a leased asset and a lease obligation. Based on this amount, we can break down the ¥40,000,000 lease payment into an interest payment of ¥12,768,000 and a ¥27,232,000 reduction of the lease obligation. Straight-line depreciation would yield an expense of ¥31,920,000.
4. Under SFAS No. 52 the translation gain would be removed from long-term debt and included in income.
5. Compared to U.S. GAAP, the goodwill amortization expense is ¥10,800,000 larger. We would make an adjusting entry to recognize an asset and reduce operating expenses.
6. As the United States does not permit discretionary reserves, these reserves would be removed and included in income. Moreover, they would be reclassified as equity as opposed to debt.
7. These adjustments, which Exhibit 9-16 summarizes in spreadsheet form, increase Toyoza's restated earnings by ¥220,240,000. Of this, ¥20,000,000 relating to the translation gain is not recognized for tax purposes. This yields a tax expense of ¥107,822,000 and a balance of ¥107,822,000 currently payable.

Exhibit 9-17 shows a ratio comparison of Toyoza and Lincoln Enterprises based on data adjusted for accounting differences. As can be seen, adjusted ratios show a much improved profitability picture for Toyoza. However, liquidity and efficiency ratios have worsened. While solvency (coverage) ratios have improved, the debt to total assets ratio remains exceedingly high by U.S. standards.

If accounting principle differences were the only differences among countries, adjustments such as those illustrated above would be sufficient to enable anyone to analyze and interpret foreign financial statements without ambiguity. Unfortunately, institutional and cultural differences among countries are not constant. If these differences are major, further analysis is necessary to ensure proper analysis and understanding. Appendix 9-2 amplifies this important point.

EXHIBIT 9-16   **Adjustment Spreadsheet**

	Unadjusted	Adjustments	Adjusted	Dollars
Sales	¥1,400,000		¥1,400,000	$12,727
-Operating expenses:				
Cost of sales	1,120,000	1) (198,000)		
		2a) (46,750)		
		3) 31,920	907,170	8,247
Selling and administrative	100,000		100,000	909
Other operating	114,200	3) (40,000)		
		5) (10,800)		
		6) (26,400)		
		7) (30,800)	6,200	56
Losses (gains)	—	4) (20,000)	(20,000)	(182)
Interest	28,000	3) 12,768	40,768	371
Taxes	23,800	7) 107,822	131,622	1,197
Net income	¥ 14,000	8) 220,240	¥ 234,240	$ 2,129
Cash	¥ 124,500		¥ 124,500	$ 1,132
Accounts receivable	510,000		510,000	4,636
Marketable securities	45,000		45,000	409
Inventory	390,000	3) 198,000	588,000	5,345
Investments	150,000		150,000	1,364
Plant and equipment, net	280,500	2a) 46,750		
		2b)140,250		
		3) 127,680	595,180	5,411
Goodwill		7) 10,800	10,800	98
Total assets	¥1,500,000		¥2,023,480	$18,395
Short-term payables	¥ 165,000		¥ 165,000	$ 1,500
Short-term debt	525,000		525,000	4,773
Deferred taxes	—			
Other current liabilities	90,000	2b) 49,088		
		7) 107,822	246,910	2,244
Long-term debt	520,000	4) (20,000)		
		3) 132,368	632,368	5,749
Reserves	90,000	6) 26,400		
		6) 30,800	32,800	298
Capital stock	75,000		75,000	682
Retained earnings	35,000	2b) 91,162		
		8) 220,240	346,402	3,149
Total liabilities and owners' equity	¥1,500,000		¥2,023,480	$18,395

EXHIBIT 9-17	Comparative Financial Ratios Based on Adjusted Data	
	Toyoza	Lincoln
Liquidity		
Current ratio	1.35x	1.45x
Acid-test ratio	.73x	1.03x
Efficiency		
Receivables turnover	2.75x	7.23x
Inventory turnover	1.54x	5.98x
Asset turnover	.69x	1.00x
Profitability		
Profit margin	16.7%	6.5%
Return on assets	20.1%	9.7%
Return on equity	51.5%	13.8%
Coverage		
Debt to total assets	77.6%	53.0%
Times interest earned	9.9x	8.9x

Appendix 9-2

International Ratio Analysis[39]

Financial ratio analysis is a well-established tool for financial performance evaluation, credit analysis, and security analysis. While financial ratios may correctly measure liquidity, efficiency, and profitability in within-country comparisons, they are often misused when applied to cross-border financial comparisons, due in part to accounting principle differences. A more serious problem is that investors may misinterpret these ratios because they do not understand a foreign environment, even when financial statements have been restated to a common set of accounting principles.

Consider Japan. An initial comparison of aggregate financial ratios for Japanese and U.S. firms reveals striking differences. Japanese companies generally appear less liquid, less solvent, less efficient, and less profitable than their U.S.

counterparts. However, after Japanese ratios are adjusted for differences between Japanese and U.S. GAAP, they are still very different from ratios found in comparable U.S. companies.

Environmental Considerations

Japanese companies appear to have very high leverage. For example, an earlier study conducted by the SEC found that mean leverage (total debt/shareholders' equity) in their Japan sample was 2.032, compared to 0.514 in the U.S. sample. However, high debt ratios traditionally have not been major sources of concern in Japan. Part of the reason is historical.

When the Japanese government (under pressure from the United States) ended 200 years of

---

[39] The following discussion is taken from a three-nation study by collaborators in Japan, Korea, and the United States. Participants in that study were Messers. Hisaaki Hino of Morgan Guaranty Trust Company, Junichi Ujiie of Nomura Securities Company, Ltd., Professors Sang Kee Min and Sang Oh Nam of Seoul National University, and Professor Arthur I. Stonehill of Oregon State University and Frederick D.S. Choi of New York University.

isolation in the mid-19th century, it made rapid economic growth and development a major national goal. To achieve this goal, the government established an extensive banking infrastructure to supply industry with most of its financing. The dependence of industrial companies on the banking system increased after World War II. Large, new industrial groupings called keiretsu evolved with major commercial banks at their core. Linked through business and personal ties, banks and their associated companies are very close. When loans become delinquent, banks (often) extend the terms of repayment or (occasionally) refinance the loan. A bank might even install a key bank official as president or board member of a troubled company to help it out.

Other companies in the keiretsu can prepay receivables owed to the distressed firm and allow longer periods for that firm to repay its receivables. With this ability to manipulate and postpone interest and principal payments, long-term debt in Japan works more like equity in the United States.[40]

Because long-term debt in Japan has many of the characteristics of preferred stock, interest payments in Japan can be likened to dividends.

Accordingly, interest coverage ratios, which are generally much lower in Japan than in the United States, are not viewed with much concern. Earnings in Japan beyond those needed to make loan payments benefit the bank little. When loans are negotiated, the borrower makes (and seldom discloses) a general agreement to give the bank collateral or guarantees upon the bank's request. Also at the bank's request, borrowing companies must submit their year-end proposed appropriation of revenue (including dividends) to the bank before it can be submitted to shareholders for approval. Banks customarily insist on compensating balances even though they are illegal, with 20 to 50 percent of company borrowings reportedly kept with the bank as time (or other) deposits. Under these conditions, low interest coverage usually does not mean a high risk of default.

Institutional and cultural factors also affect liquidity ratios without necessarily changing the financial risk that the ratios are designed to measure. For example, an American reader who sees the relatively low current ratios of Japanese companies (resulting from relatively high short-term debt) might conclude that Japanese companies have a relatively lower ability to cover their short-term debt. In Japan, however, high short-term debt seldom indicates a lack of liquidity. Short-term debt is attractive to companies because short-term obligations typically have lower interest rates than long-term obligations. Moreover, short-term borrowings in Japan are seldom repaid but normally are renewed or rolled over. Banks are happy to renew these loans as this allows them to adjust their interest rates to changing market conditions. Thus, short-term debt in Japan works like long-term debt elsewhere. In fact, the use of short-term debt to finance long-term assets appears to be the rule, not the exception, in Japan.

Longer average collection periods also reflect differences in business customs. Purchases in Japan are rarely made in cash. Postdated checks with maturities ranging between 60 and 90 days are common. The Japanese tradition of lifetime employment has some influence on collection policies. Companies often go to great lengths to accommodate their commercial customers. During business downturns, companies extend repayment terms to avoid placing their customers in a financial bind that might force them to discharge employees. In return, continued patronage ensures stability in employment (and other respects) for the selling company. Inventory turnover numbers are similarly affected.

During slack periods, manufacturing companies prefer to continue production and build inventories rather than idle workers. Japanese managers are not as concerned with short-term profits as their U.S. counterparts. They have more job security than prevails in the United States. Equity shares in Japanese companies are largely held by related commercial banks, suppliers, and customers. These shareholders are more interested in maintaining their close business ties than in stock market gains, and will hold shares on a long-term basis regardless of short-term market performance.

Corporate managers in Japan believe that increased market share will ensure long-run profits. For this reason, sales growth is a main objective. Growing sales contribute to higher employment

---

[40] The gradual liberalization of Japan's financial system is increasing the exceptions to this practice.

and greater job security, and as such are consistent with the tradition of lifetime employment. Because all Japanese enterprises seek sales growth, price competition is intense, resulting in low profit margin and profitability statistics. This is especially so for large companies that usually sell heavily in extremely competitive export markets.

So, are Japanese companies truly more risky, less efficient, and less profitable than their U.S. counterparts? Not necessarily.

In Europe, national characteristics also appear to strongly influence profit measurement. Large companies in France and Germany tend to be more conservative in measuring profits than large companies in the United Kingdom. Also important are tax laws and reliance on lenders rather than investors for capital.

Thus, when analyzing foreign financial statements, readers must be careful to determine whether observed differences in firm performance result from: (a) accounting measurement differences; (b) economic, cultural, or institutional differences; or (c) real differences in the attributes being measured.

Discussion Questions

1. What are the four main steps in doing a business strategy analysis using financial statements? Why, at each step, is analysis in a cross-border context more difficult than a single-country analysis?
2. One interpretation of the popular efficient markets hypothesis is that the market fully impounds all public information as soon as it becomes available. Thus, it is supposedly not possible to beat the market if fundamental financial analysis techniques are applied to publicly available information such as a firm's published accounts. Why might this hypothesis be more tenable in the United States than in other international capital markets?
3. Describe the impact on accounting analysis of cross-country variations in accounting measurement and disclosure practices.
4. Investors can cope with accounting principles in different ways. Can you suggest two methods of coping and which of the two you find most appealing?
5. What are common pitfalls to avoid in conducting an international prospective analysis?

6. How does the translation of foreign currency financial statements differ from the foreign currency translation process described in Chapter 6?
7. If you were asked to provide the five most important recommendations you could think of to others analyzing nondomestic financial statements, what would they be?
8. ABC Company, a U.S.-based MNC, uses the temporal translation method (see Chapter 6) in consolidating the results of its foreign operations. Translation gains or losses incurred upon consolidation are reflected immediately in reported earnings. Company XYZ, a Dutch MNC, employs the current rate method with translation gains and losses going into owners' equity. What financial ratios are most likely to be affected by these different accounting principles, and what are the implications for security analysts?
9. What role does the attest function play in international financial statement analysis?
10. What is internal control, how do internal auditors relate to it, and how does this process relate to the analysis of financial statements?

Exercises

1. Condensed comparative income statements of Señorina Panchos, a Mexican restaurant chain, for the years 2009 through 2011 are presented in Exhibit 9-18 (000,000's pesos). You are interested in gauging the past trend in dividends paid by Señorina Panchos from a dollar perspective. The company's payout ratio (ratio of dividends paid to reported earnings) has averaged 30 percent. Foreign exchange rates during the three-year period are found in Exhibit 9-19.

EXHIBIT 9-18	**Comparative Income Statements: Señorina Panchos**		
	2009	**2010**	**2011**
Sales	91,600	114,300	138,900
Gross margin	15,500	20,500	27,700
Net income	8,500	10,800	15,900

EXHIBIT 9-19	**Foreign Exchange Rates**		
	2009	**2010**	**2011**
Year-end rates	$1 = P 12.112	$1 = P 12.640	$1 = P 13.000

EXHIBIT 9-20	**Statement of Cash Flow Worksheet**		
	Beginning Balance	**Debit**	**Credit**	**Ending Balance**
Balance sheet items (detailed)				
		Sources of funds	Uses of funds	
Net change in cash				

Required: Prepare a trend analysis of dividends paid by Señorina Panchos from a U.S. perspective assuming (a) there are no restrictions on the payment of dividends to U.S. investors and (b) Señorina Panchos' accounting practices are similar to those in the United States.

2. Based on the balance sheet and income statement data contained in Exhibit 9-5, and using the suggested worksheet format shown in Exhibit 9-20 or one of your own choosing, show how the statement of cash flows appearing in Exhibit 9-5 was derived.

3. Refer again to Exhibits 9-5 and 9-6. Show how you would modify the consolidated funds statement appearing in Exhibit 9-5 to enable an investor to get a better feel for the actual investing and financing activities of the Norwegian subsidiary.

4. Infosys Technologies, introduced in Chapter 1, regularly provides investors with a performance measure called *economic value-added* (EVA). Originally pioneered by GE, EVA measures the profitability of a company after deducting not just the cost of borrowing but also the firm's cost of equity capital. So EVA is the after-tax return *on* capital employed (adjusted for the tax shield on debt) less the cost *of* capital employed. Companies that earn a higher return on capital employed than its cost of capital create value for its shareholders. Those that do not destroy shareholder value.

Reproduced below is EVA calculations for Infosys for 2006.

Required:
1. Did Infosys create value for its shareholders?
2. Is EVA a useful performance metric relative to net income? (Compare PAT or profit after tax, and EVA to average capital employed.)

Cost of capital:	
Cost of risk-free debt (%)	7.50
Market premium	7.00
Beta variant	0.78
Cost of equity (%)	12.96
Average debt/Total capital (%)	—
Cost of debt – net of tax (%)	NA
Weighted average cost of capital (%)	12.96
Average capital employed	6,177
PAT as a percentage of average capital employed (%)	40.14
Economic Value Added:	
Operating profit (excluding extraordinary income)	2,654
Less: Taxes	313
Less: Cost of capital	801
EVA	1,540
Ratios:	
EVA as a percentage of average capital employed (%)	24.93

5. Read Appendix 9-1. Referring to Exhibit 9-14 and related notes, assume instead that Toyoza's inventories were costed using the FIFO method and that Lincoln Enterprises employed the LIFO method. Provide the adjusting journal entries to restate Toyoza's inventories to a LIFO basis, assuming that ending inventories would have been ¥250 million lower under the LIFO method.

6. The following sales revenue pattern for a British trading concern was cited earlier in the chapter:

	2009	2010	2011
Sales revenue	£23,500	£28,650	£33,160

Required:

a. Perform a convenience translation into U.S. dollars for each year given the following year-end exchange rates:

2009	£1 = $2.10
2010	£1 = $2.20
2011	£1 = $1.60

b. Compare the year-to-year percentage changes in sales revenues in pounds and in U.S. dollars. Do the two time series move in parallel fashion? Why or why not?

c. Suggest a method for minimizing the effect of exchange rate changes on foreign currency trend data.

7. Refer to Exhibit 9-3. This exhibit presents P/E ratios for public companies in various countries. What factors might explain the differences in P/E ratios that you observe?

8. Assume you are a member of an international policy setting committee and are responsible for harmonizing audit report requirements internationally. Examine Exhibit 9-8. Based on the varying requirments you observe, what minimum set of requirements would you advocate for on behalf of the international investing community? Your committee also includes delegates from Austria, Bahrain, France, Finland, Malaysia, Nigeria, Scotland, and Chile.

9. Examine Exhibit 9-9. On the basis of the information provided there, which opinion gives you the most comfort as an investor in nondomestic securities?

10. Identify three to four criteria that you would personally use to judge the merits of any corporate database. Use these criteria to rate the information content of any Web site appearing in exhibit 9-4 as excellent, fair, or poor.

CASES

Case 9-1

Sandvik

One of the accounting development patterns that was introduced in Chapter 2 was the macroeconomic development model. Under this framework accounting practices are designed to enhance national macroeconomic goals. A national policy advocating stable employment by avoiding major swings in business cycles would sanction accounting practices that smooth income. Similarly, national policies supporting growth in certain industries would sanction rapid write-offs of fixed assets to encourage capital formation. Sweden is a good example of this reporting pattern. Assets may be revalued upwards if they are deemed to have "enduring value," the tax law permits shorter asset lives, and ceiling tests for depreciation charges include the higher of 130 percent declining balance method or 20 percent straight line. Companies are also permitted to allocate a portion of pre-tax earnings to special tax equalization reserves which are not available for dividends until reversed.

Reproduced below are the parent company financial statements of Sandvik for the years 2006 and 2007 and selected notes. Sandvik is a global high technology company headquartered in Sweden, with advanced products and well-known brands. Its core areas of competence include high speed tools for metal working, machinery, tools and services for rock excavation, and specialty steels.

The company states that it applies all IFRS and IFRIC interpretations approved by the EU to the extent possible within the framework of the Swedish Annual Accounts Act and considering the close tie between financial reporting and taxation. Examine the data presented and answer the following questions.

1. What advantages and disadvantages arise for firms that chose to employ the Swedish system of special reserves?
2. What are the potential benefits of the system of special reserves to the Swedish government?
3. In what way does the existence of the Swedish reserve system affect the ability of a financial analyst to evaluate a Swedish firm vis-à-vis a non-Swedish firm?
4. In what way does the use of "reserves" affect Sandvik's financial statements for the year 2007? How does this compare with the effect of reserves in the previous year?
5. Show the accounting entry used to create the 2007 *Appropriations* figure in the income statement.
6. If you were to unwind the effect of reserves for 2007, how would Sandvik's key profitability ratios, such as return on sales and return on assets change?

Parent Company Income Statement

Amounts in SEK M		2007	2006
Revenue	Note 2	20682	17932
Cost of sales and services		−16111	−13646
Gross profit		4571	4286
Selling expenses		−621	−577
Administrative expenses		−1982	−1719
Research and development costs	Note 4	−1019	−778
Other operating income	Note 5	488	455
Other operating expenses	Note 6	−916	−1344
Operating profit	Note 3, 7, 8	521	323
Income from shares in group companies	Note 9	5997	9264
Income from shares in associated companies	Note 9	5	1
Income from investments held as non-current assets	Note 9	—	0
Interest income and similar items	Note 9	638	657
Interest expenses and similar items	Note 9	−1165	−898
Profit after financial items		5996	9347
Appropriations	Note 10	3063	305
Income tax expense	Note 11	−745	−29
Profit for the year		8314	9623

Parent Company Balance Sheet

Amounts in SEK M		2007	2006
ASSETS			
Non-current assets			
Intangible assets			
Patents and similar rights	Note 14	26	51
Total		26	51
Property, plant and equipment			
Land and buildings	Note 14	484	473
Plant and machinery	Note 14	3624	3492
Equipment, tools and installations	Note 14	305	309
Construction in progress and advance payments	Note 14	1352	974
Total		5765	5248
Financial assets			
Shares in group companies	Note 15	13762	11723
Advances to group companies		48	34
Investmments in associated companies	Note 16	4	4
Advances to associated companies		—	0
Other investments		1	1
Non-current receivables	Note 18	20	23

(continued)

Parent Company Balance Sheet (Continued)

Amounts in SEK M		2007	2006
Deferred tax assets	Note 11	22	17
Total		13857	11802
Total non-current assets		19648	17101
Current assets			
Inventories	Note 19	6242	4599
Current receivables			
Trade receivables		1255	1150
Due from group companies		16311	15846
Due from associated companies		131	474
Income tax receivables	Note 11	393	16
Other receivables	Note 18	518	456
Prepaid expenses and accrued income		679	423
Total		19287	18365
Cash and cash equivalents		6	19
Total current assets		25535	22983
TOTAL ASSETS		45183	40084
EQUITY AND LIABILITIES			
Equity			
Non-distributable equity			
Share capital		1424	1424
Legal reserve		1611	1611
Total		3035	3035
Distributable equity			
Profit brought forward		1552	1637
Profit for the year		8314	9623
Total		9866	11260
Total equity	Note 20	12901	14295
Untaxed reserves			
Accelerated depreciation	Note 21	—	2430
Tax allocation reserves	Note 22	—	639
Other untaxed reserves	Note 22	19	15
Total		19	3084
Provisions			
Provisions for pensions and similar obligations	Note 23	108	106
Provisions for taxes	Note 11	55	42
Other provisions	Note 24	154	127
Total		317	275
Non-current interest-bearing liabilities			
Loans from financial institutions	Note 25	1718	1669
Loans from group companies	Note 25	30	3
Other liabilities	Note 25	10131	2511
Total		11879	4183

(continued)

Parent Company Balance Sheet (Continued)

Noncurrent non–interest-bearing liabilities

Other liabilities		—	9
Total		—	9

Current interest-bearing liabilities

Loans from group companies		10902	12766
Other liabilities		1080	1324
Total		11982	14090

Current noninterest-bearing liabilities

Advance payments from customers		159	53
Accounts payable		1721	1734
Due to group companies		3655	27
Due to associated companies		82	125
Other liabilities		136	205
Accrued expenses and deferred income	Note 28	2332	2004
Total		8085	4148
TOTAL EQUITY AND LIABILITIES		45183	40084
Pledged assets	Note 29	—	—
Contingent liabilities	Note 29	16068	11929

Note 10. Appropriations

Parent Company	2007	2006
Accelerated depreciation	2429	−143
Changes in tax allocation reserves	638	437
Changes in other untaxed reserves	−4	11
Total	3063	305

Note 11. Income tax

Reported in Income Statement

	Group		Parent Company	
Income tax expense	2007	2006	2007	2006
Current tax	−4396	−3135	−829	−115
Adjustment of taxes attributable to prior years	229	−16	67	64
Total current tax expense	−4167	−3151	−762	−51
Deferred taxes relating to temporary differences and unused tax losses	763	145	17	22
Total tax expense	−3404	−3006	−745	−29

The Group's tax expense for the year was SEK 3,404 M (3.006) or 26.2% (27.0) of the profit after financial items.

The adjustment of taxes attributable to prior years mainly relates to favorable tax litigation resolutions and advance rulings in Sweden and reversal of tax provisions upon finalization of tax audits of foreign subsidiaries.

Reconciliation of the Group's tax expense   The Group's weighted average tax based on the tax rates in each country,

is 29. 6% (27.0). The nominal tax rate in Sweden is 28.0% (28.0).

Reconciliation of the Group's weighted average tax rate, based on the tax rates in each country, and the Group's actual tax expense:

Reconciliation of the Parent Company's tax expense   The Parent Company's effective tax rate of 8.2% (0.8) is less than the nominal tax rate in Sweden, mainly due to tax-exempt dividend income from subsidiaries and associated companies:

	2007		2006	
Group	SEK M	%	SEK M	%
Profit after financial items	12997		11113	
Weighted average tax based on each				
country's tax rate	−3849	−29.6	−3001	−27.0
Tax effect of:				
Non-deductible expenses	−195	−1.5	−179	−1.6
Tax exempt income	199	1.5	244	2.2
Adjustments relating to prior year	229	1.8	−16	−0.1
Effects of unused tax losses, net	75	0.6	−22	−0.2
Other	137	1.1	−32	−0.3
Total reported tax expense	−3404	−26.2	−3006	−27.0

Reconciliation of the Parent Company's nominal tax rate and actual tax expense:

	2007		2006	
Parent Company	SEK M	%	SEK M	%
Profit before tax	9059		9652	
Tax based on the nominal tax rate for the				
Parent Company	−2537	−28.0	−2703	−28.0
Tax effects of:				
Non-deductible expenses	−33	−0.4	−59	−0.6
Tax-exempt income	1758	19.4	2669	27.6
Adjustments relating to prior years	67	0.7	64	0.7
Total reported tax expense	−745	−8.2	29	−0.3

Tax items recognized directly in equity

Group	2007	2006
Deferred tax relating to hedging reserve	31	34
Total	31	34
Parent Company	2007	2006
Current tax relating to taxable group contributions	843	−95
Total	843	−95

Reported in the balance sheet

Deferred tax assets and liabilities   The deferred tax assets and liabilities reported in the balance sheet are attributable to the following assets and liabilities (liabilities shown with a minus sign):

	2007			2006		
Group	Deferred tax assets	Deferred tax liabilities	Net	Deferred tax assets	Deferred tax liabilities	Net
Intangible assets	34	−666	−632	39	−282	−243
Property, plant, and equipment	96	−965	−869	195	−1573	−1378
Financial non-current assets	58	−2	56	26	−31	−5
Inventories	1445	−62	1383	1034	−30	1004
Receivables	66	−335	−269	95	−237	−142
Interest-bearing liabilities	325	−263	62	549	−184	365
Noninterest-bearing liabilities	513	−761	−248	393	−444	−51

	2007			2006		
Group	Deferred tax assets	Deferred tax liabilities	Net	Deferred tax assets	Deferred tax liabilities	Net
Other	19	−49	−30	20	−261	241
Unused tax losses	84	—	84	—	—	—
Total	2640	−3103	−463	2351	−3042	−691
Offsetting within companies	−1317	1317	—	−1031	1013	—
Total deferred tax assets and liabilities	1323	−1786	−463	1338	−2029	−691
Parent Company						
Property, plant and equipment	—	−37	−37	—	−38	−38

Note 21. Parent Company's Accelerated Depreciation

	Land and buildings	Plant and machinery	Equipment, tools and installations	Patents and similar rights	Total
Balance at 1 January 2006	1	2075	182	29	2287
Accelerated depreciation for the year	0	127	13	3	143
Balance at 31 December 2006	1	2202	195	32	2430
Balance at 1 January 2007	1	2202	195	32	2430
Accelerated depreciation for the year	−1	−2202	−195	−32	−2430
Balance at December 2007	—	—	—	—	—

Note 22. Parent Company's Other Untaxed Reserves

	2007	2006
Tax allocation reserves		
Appropriated at 2002 tax assessment	—	435
Appropriated at 2004 tax assessment	—	204
Balance at 31 December	—	639
Other untaxed reserves	19	15

Case 9-2

Continental A.G.

Marissa Skye and Alexa Reichele, tire analysts for a global investment fund located in Manhattan, are examining the 20X0 earnings performance of two potential investment candidates. Reflecting the company's investment philosophy of picking the best stocks wherever they are located in the world, both junior analysts have adopted an approach of undertaking matched comparisons of leading firms in the tire industry. For starters, Dietrich and Marissa focused on Goodyear Tire & Rubber Company (United States) and Continental A.G. (Germany) as their first screen.

ALEXA: Well, what do you think, Marissa?

MARISSA: Looking at the income trends (see Exhibit 9-21), I sort of like Continental.

ALEXA: Yes, I agree. Goodyear's results are much more volatile.

MARISSA: I always look to see how a company has done in an off year. Owing to the continued consolidation of the tire industry, excess capacity created by reduced demand for autos and trucks, as well as reduced consumer spending for replacement tires in light of economic and political uncertainties, 20X0 was a disastrous year for every major company in the industry. Given that environment, Continental's performance was stellar!

ALEXA: Maybe we'd better check with Kazuo, our accountant, to see if we're reading the tea leaves correctly.

MARISSA: I'll give him a call.

(After a 5-minute conversation)

ALEXA: Well, what did he say?

MARISSA: He said, we're probably correct in our overall assessment (I think he's just being polite), but that we'd better check the company's accounting policies. He says German accounting principles tend to impart a conservative bias to corporate earnings. He'll send us an e-mail attachment summarizing some major GAAP differences between the United States and Germany very soon.

(The e-mail attachment is reproduced as Exhibit 9-22.)

MARISSA: (Having examined the attachment) Looks like there are some major differences in reporting rules between Germany and the United States.

ALEXA: Do you think we should attempt to restate Continental's accounts to a U.S. GAAP basis?

MARISSA: Why don't we try?

ALEXA: Where should we start?

MARISSA: Let's examine Continental's financial statements (see Exhibit 9-23) to see if we can detect any unusual accounting practices that may have a distorting effect on the company's reported performance. I notice that Continental follows the European practice of including both parent company (Consolidated A.G.) and consolidated numbers. Let's just focus on the consolidated figures for now.

ALEXA: Right. And if we find some disparities, maybe we should just attempt one or two adjustments, particularly those for which we have sufficient information.

If these adjustments have a significant earnings impact, then let's press the right buttons and see if we can't get the company to give us some additional information so that we can do a more comprehensive analysis.

MARISSA: Sounds good. Let's get started.

EXHIBIT 9-21 Comparative Performance Data Goodyear ($ millions)

	19X6	19X7	19X8	19X9	20X0
Sales	9,040	9,905	10,810	10,869	11,273
Net income (loss)	124	771	350	207	(38)

Continental (Euro millions)

	19X6	19X7	19X8	19X9	20X0
Sales	4,969	5,098	7,906	8,382	8,551
Net income (loss)	115	139	195	228	93

EXHIBIT 9-22 Major Accounting Differences between Germany and the United States

	Germany	United States
Goodwill	Written off against reserves or amortized; commercial law prescribes four years; most companies amortize over 15 years for tax purposes.	Capitalized and amortized subject to an impairments test.
Long-term leases	Generally no lease capitalization.	Capitalization required when specific criteria met.
Depreciation	Highest rates allowable for tax purposes.	Generally straight-line over estimated useful lives.
Inventory	Costing must mirror physical flow of goods. Average costing is common.	LIFO costing method is common.
Reserves	Use of discretionary reserves to smooth earnings are not uncommon.	Use of discretionary reserves to smooth earnings are discouraged.

EXHIBIT 9-23	Continental's Financial Statements and Related Notes

Continental Aktiengesellschaft
Consolidated Balance Sheet at December 31, 20X0

Assets	See Note No.	12/31/20X0 euro 000	12/31/19X9 euro 000
Fixed assets and investments			
Intangible assets	(1)	430,920	11,944
Property, plant and equipment	(2)	2,196,724	1,797,125
Investments	(3)	225,729	189,428
		2,853,373	1,998,497
Current assets			
Inventories	(4)	1,611,566	1,506,771
Receivables and other assets	(5)	1,475,557	1,386,212
Marketable securities	(6)	51,426	339,219
Liquid assets	(7)	144,625	134,079
		3,283,174	3,366,281
Prepaid expenses	(8)	31,070	41,092
		6,167,617	5,405,870

Shareholders' equity and liabilities	See Note No.	12/31/20X0 euro 000	12/31/19X9 euro 000
Shareholders' equity			
Subscribed capital	(9)	439,097	435,022
Capital reserves	(10)	962,275	956,240
Retained earnings	(11)	137,788	133,770
Minority interests	(12)	94,286	46,692
Reserve for retirement benefits	(13)	2,861	3,691
Net income available for distribution		36,383	70,984
		1,672,690	
Special reserves	(14)	80,552	118,103
Provisions	(15)	1,733,440	1,386,799
Liabilities	(16)	2,680,935	2,254,569
		6,167,617	5,405,570

Continental Aktiengesellschaft
Consolidated Statement of Income for the period from January 1 to December 31, 20X0

	See Note No	20X0 euro 000	19X9 euro 000
Sales	(17)	8,551,015	8,381,880
Cost of sales[*]	(18)	6,490,128	6,256,858
Gross profit on sales		2,060,887	2,125,002
Selling expenses	(19)	1,255,474	1,174,268
Administrative expenses	(20)	504,277	474,932

(continued)

EXHIBIT 9-23	Continental's Financial Statements and Related Notes	(Continued)	
	See Note No	20X0 euro 000	19X9 euro 000
Other operating income	(21)	194,266	164,076
Other operating expenses	(22)	140,218	91,351
Net income from investments and financial activities	(23)	2138,777	2116,536

Continental Aktiengesellschaft
Consolidated Statement of Income for the period from January 1 to December 31, 20X0

	See Note No	20X0 euro 000	19X9 euro 000
Net income from regular business activities		216,407	431,991
Taxes	(24)	122,972	204,153
Net income for the year		93,435	227,838
Balance brought forward from previous year		1,380	1,199
Minority interests in earning	(25)	288	258
Withdrawal from the reserve for retirement benefits		+830	+544
Change in reserves		259,174	2158,539
Net income available for distribution		36,383	70,984

Based on an audit performed in accordance with our professional duties, the consolidated financial statements comply with the legal regulations. The consolidated financial statements present, in compliance with required accounting principles, a true and fair view of the net worth, financial position, and results of the corporation. The management report for the corporation is in agreement with the consolidated financial statements.

Berlin/Hanover, April 8,19X1

Accounting policies:
Assets
Acquired intangible assets are carried at acquisition cost and amortized by the straight-line method over their anticipated useful life. Capitalized goodwill resulting from the acquisition of companies is deducted in installments from retained earnings on the balance sheet, over periods estimated individually from 10 to 20 years.

Property, plant, and equipment is valued at acquisition or manufacturing costs, less scheduled depreciation.

Continental Aktiengesellschaft uses the declining balance method to depreciate movable fixed assets, while the straight-line method is used for all other fixed assets. We change over from the declining balance method to the straight-line method as soon as this leads to higher depreciation. In the financial statements of Continental Aktiengesellschaft, the special depreciation permitted by the tax laws is taken insofar as necessary in view of the fact that the commercial balance sheet is the basis for the balance sheet prepared in accordance with the tax regulations.

Since 1989, pursuant to internationally accepted accounting principles, additions have been depreciated exclusively by the straight-line method in the consolidated financial statements.

(continued)

EXHIBIT 9-23   Continental's Financial Statements and Related Notes   (Continued)

The following table shows the useful life taken as a basis for depreciating the major categories of property, plant, and equipment:

Buildings up to 33 years
Additions from 1990 on, up to 25 years
Technical facilities and machinery, 10 years
Plant and office equipment, 4 to 7 years

Molds up to 4 years

Additions to movable assets made during the first 6 months of the year are depreciated at the full annual rate, and those made during the last 6 months at half the annual rate. Minor fixed assets are written off completely in the year of acquisition.

These depreciation rules are applied by each of the domestic and foreign companies as of the date it became part of the Corporation.

Interests in affiliates and other companies held as investments are valued at acquisition cost, less the necessary write-downs.

Interest-bearing loans granted are shown at face value; loans that bear little or no interest are discounted to their cash value.

Inventories are carried at the lower acquisition/manufacturing cost or market.

Manufacturing cost includes direct costs, as well as a proportional part of material and production overhead and depreciation. Appropriate adjustments are made for declines in value due to reduced usability or prolonged storage.

In valuing receivables and miscellaneous assets, we make reasonable allowances to cover all perceivable risks, as well as lump-sum deductions to cover the general credit risk.

Marketable securities are valued at the lower of cost or market.

Insofar as permissible, we have continued to take all the extraordinary depreciation and write-downs, as well as the depreciation and write-downs for tax purposes, which were taken in previous years on fixed assets, investments, and current assets.

Discounts and issue costs of loans and bonds are shown as prepaid expenses and amortized over the term of the individual loans and bonds.

Shareholders' Equity and Liabilities.

Provisions based on sound business judgment are set up for all perceivable risks, undetermined obligations, and impending losses.

At our German companies, the provisions for pension plans and similar obligations are set up at a 6% interest rate, on the basis of actuarial computations in accordance with the statutory method.

Pension commitments and similar obligations of foreign companies are also computed according to actuarial principles, discounted to the present value at the interest rates prevailing in the respective countries, and covered by appropriate provisions for pension plans or by pension funds. Employee claims for severance benefits under national laws have also been taken into account.

The pension obligations of American companies are valued according to the stricter valuation rules that have been in force in the U.S.A. since 1987. The provision made for this purpose in the balance sheet is slightly higher than if the corresponding German method of computation had been applied.

The obligations of General Tire Inc., Akron, Ohio, for post-retirement medical benefits are fully covered by provisions computed according to actuarial principles. New U.S. regulations (FASB

(continued)

EXHIBIT 9-23 Continental's Financial Statements and Related Notes   (Continued)

No. 106) require that by no later than 1993, a provision must be established for not only the retirees and vested workforce, but also for the nonvested employees. Although this regulation allows a build-up of the provision over a 20-year period, we have already transferred the full additional amount required (DM270.7 million) to the provisions shown on the consolidated balance sheet. To balance this item, goodwill deducted from consolidated retained earnings at the time of the acquisition of General Tire has been capitalized in the same amount.

As a rule, provisions for repairs that have been postponed to the subsequent year are established in the amount of the probable cost.

When there are temporary differences between the values of the individual companies' assets and liabilities as determined according to the tax laws and those appearing in their balance sheets, which are prepared according to valuation principles that are uniform throughout the Corporation, deferred taxes may result. We show the latter only when they are reflected in provisions for future tax expenses. Liabilities are stated at the redemption amount.

Selected Notes:

(10) Capital reserves. This item includes amounts received upon the issuance of shares in excess of their par value totaling euro 724. 9 million, as well as the premium of euro 237.4 million paid upon the exercise of warrants attached to the bonds issued in 19X4, 19X6, and 19X7 and to the 19X8 convertible debentures. Capital reserves increased by euro 6.0 million due to the exercise of the conversion and option rights in 20X0.

(11) Retained earnings

euro 000	Continental AG	Consolidated
As of 12/31/19X9	141,699	133,770
Differences from translation	—	255,009
Other	—	2147
Allocation from net income	8,000	59,174
As of 12/31/20X0	149,699	137,788

(14) Special reserves

euro 000	12/31/20X0 Continental AG	Consolidated	12/31/19X9 Continental AG	Consolidated
Reserve per/3. Foreign Investment Act	59,766	15,000	84,312	38,265
Reserve per/6b, Income Tax Act	—	448	—	289
Reserve per/52 Par.8 Income Tax Act	705	1,069	940	1,425
Governmental capital investment subsidies	—	57,664	—	60,988
Other	2,533	6,371	4,137	17,136
	63,004	80,552	89,389	118,103

(continued)

EXHIBIT 9-23	Continental's Financial Statements and Related Notes (Continued)

The decrease in special reserves is due, in particular, to the elimination of the special reserve pursuant to /3. Foreign Investment Act, following the write-down made in connection with Semperit (Ireland) Ltd., Dublin, Ireland. The special reserves are divided into an equity portion of euro 69.5 million and a debt portion of euro 11.1 million, representing deferred taxes, which will be paid in due course, when the reserves are eliminated. Including the shareholders equity of euro 1,672.7 million shown on the balance sheet, the actual shareholders equity amounts to euro 1,742.2 million and the equity ratio to 28.2%.

---

(15) Provisions

euro 000	12/31/20X0		12/31/19X9	
	Continental AG	Consolidated	Continental AG	Consolidated
Provision for pensions	220,977	972,173	206,374	636,626
Provisions for taxes	31,937	72,210	53,144	92,265
Miscellaneous provisions	191,465	689,057	188,817	657,908
	444,379	1,733,440	448,335	1,386,799

The Corporation's provisions for pensions and similar obligations rose considerably. Apart from normal allocations, this increase was due, in particular, to an addition to cover claims for medical benefits which may be made by employees of General Tire Inc., Akron, Ohio, U.S.A., after their retirement.

At two of our retirement benefit organizations, there is a shortfall of euro 22.0 million in the coverage of pension obligations. The provisions at four other German companies have been funded only to the maximum amount permitted for tax purposes.

Lower tax liabilities permitted a reduction in provisions for taxes, which include amounts relating both to the current fiscal year and to previous years.

Provisions for deferred taxes in the individual financial statements, after deduction of the net prepaid taxes arising from consolidation procedures, amounted to euro 7.4 million.

Miscellaneous provisions cover all perceivable risks and other undetermined obligations. In addition to provisions for warranties, bonuses, and miscellaneous risks, they consist mainly of provisions for personnel and social welfare payments, deferred repairs, and service anniversaries.

(21) Other operating income

euro 000	12/31/20X0		12/31/19X9	
	Continental AG	Consolidated	Continental AG	Consolidated
Gains on the disposal of fixed assets and investments	6,179	33,423	2,435	10,733
Credit to income from the reversal of provisions	1,418	17,312	7,400	33,559
Credit to income from the reduction of the general bad debt reserve	—	1,101	—	2,014

(continued)

EXHIBIT 9-23 Continental's Financial Statements and Related Notes (Continued)

(21) Other operating income (Continued)

euro 000	12/31/20X0		12/31/19X9	
	Continental AG	Consolidated	Continental AG	Consolidated
Credit to income from the reversal of special reserves	26,385	38,824	12,645	32,456
Miscellaneous income	120,143	103,606	106,843	85,294
	154,125	194,266	129,323	164,076

In addition to current income from rentals, leasing, and miscellaneous sideline operations, other operating income includes indemnification paid by insurance companies and income attributable to other fiscal years.

For the parent company, this item consists mainly of cost apportionments received from other companies belonging to the Corporation.

(22) Other operating expenses

euro 000	12/31/20X0		12/31/19X9	
	Continental AG	Consolidated	Continental AG	Consolidated
Losses on the disposal of fixed assets and investments	2,015	6,694	306	4,315
Losses on the disposal of current assets	1,414	19,197	257	22,818
Allocation to special reserves	—	168	46,995	1,278
Miscellaneous expenses	111,504	114,161	89,374	62,940
	114,933	140,218	136,932	91,351

The miscellaneous expenses relate primarily to sideline operations and the establishment of necessary provisions; at the parent company, they include cost apportionments paid to other companies belonging to the Corporation.

(24) Taxes

euro 000	12/31/20X0		12/31/19X9	
	Continental AG	Consolidated	Continental AG	Consolidated
On income	45,747	59,884	75,612	141,476
Other taxes	14,186	63,088	17,527	62,877
	59,993	122,972	93,139	204,153

CHAPTER 10

Managerial Planning and Control

Prior chapters have largely had an external reporting orientation. This chapter focuses on internal reporting and control issues. We acknowledge that the distinction between the two is increasingly blurred.

Global competition together with continued advances in technology are significantly altering the landscape of business and its internal reporting requirements. Continued reductions in national trade barriers, floating currencies, sovereign risk, restrictions on fund remittances across national borders, differences in national tax systems, interest rate differentials, and the effects of changing commodity and equity prices on enterprise assets, earnings, and capital costs are variables that complicate management decisions. At the same time, developments such as the Internet, video conferencing, and electronic transfer are changing the economics of production, distribution, and financing. Production is increasingly awarded to the company in the world that does it, or parts of it, best. Globally coordinated value chains based on strategic alliances are replacing arms-length relationships among manufacturers, suppliers, and customers. Understandably, an increasing emphasis is being placed on information providers who understand the strategic information needs of management and who possess strong analytic skills and intellectual capital.[1]

Global competition and the speed of knowledge dissemination support the narrowing of national variations in management accounting practices.[2] Additional pressures include market and technology changes, the growth of privatization, cost and performance incentives, the coordination of global operations through joint venturing and other strategic linkages, and continual shareholder demands for value-added initiatives. These pressures are common to business organizations everywhere. They are driving management of multinational companies not only to adopt comparable internal accounting techniques, but also to use these techniques in similar fashion.[3] Managerial accounting issues discussed in this book fall into three

---

[1] Robert A. Howell, "The CFO: From Controller to Global Strategic Partner," *Financial Executive*, April 2006, pp. 20–25.
[2] Chris Guilding, Karen S. Cravens, and Mike Tayles, "An International Comparison of Strategic Management Accounting Practices," *Management Accounting Research* 9 (2000): 113–135.
[3] Ramona Dzinkowski, "Global Economic Impacts on Strategic Financial Management," *Strategic Finance*, Vol. 87, no. 6 (2005): 36–41.

broad areas: financial planning and control (this chapter), international risk management (Chapter 11), and international taxation and transfer pricing (Chapter 12). Planning topics in this chapter include business modeling, capital budgeting, and profitability management, together with the information systems needed to implement them. The balance of the chapter focuses on financial control.

BUSINESS MODELING

A recent survey finds that management accountants are spending more time on strategic planning issues than ever before. This reflects the fact that financial managers, major consumers of internal accounting data, are increasingly becoming strategic advisors to the chief executive. As Charles Noski, former CFO and Vice Chairman, AT&T states:[4]

> I think the CFO will continue to evolve, with more emphasis on the strategic issues facing the company and a requirement that the CFO be the business partner to the CEO . . . Compliance and internal controls will likely always be a part of the job, but the expectation for value-added contributions by the CFO to the growth, competitiveness and performance of the company will gain momentum.

Business modeling is big picture, and it consists of formulating, implementing, and evaluating a firm's long-range business plan. It involves four critical dimensions:[5]

1. Identifying key factors relevant to the future progress of the company
2. Formulating appropriate techniques to forecast future developments and assess the company's ability to adapt to or exploit these developments
3. Developing information systems to support strategic choices
4. Translating selected options into specific courses of action

PLANNING TOOLS

In identifying factors relevant to its future, it is helpful for a company to scan its external and internal environments to identify threats and opportunities. Systems can be set in place to gather information on competitors and market conditions. Both competitors and market conditions are analyzed for their impact on a company's competitive status and profitability. Insights gleaned from this analysis are used to plan measures to maintain or enlarge market share, or to identify and exploit new products and market opportunities.

One such tool is the WOTS-UP analysis. It is concerned with corporate strengths and weaknesses in relation to a firm's operating environment. This technique helps management generate a set of feasible strategies.[6] Exhibit 10-1 shows a WOTS-UP

---

[4] Jeffrey Marshall and Ellen M. Heffes, "What Does the Future Hold for Finance and CFOs?" *Financial Executive*, December 2006, pp. 16–20.
[5] Kiyohiko Ito and Klaus R. Macharzina, "Strategic Planning Systems," in F. D. S. Choi, ed., *International Accounting and Finance Handbook*, 2nd ed., New York: John Wiley & Sons, 1997, Ch. 25.
[6] WOTS-UP analysis is a modified version of SWOT analysis, which is constantly being improved upon as a strategic planning tool. See George Panagiotou, "Bringing SWOT into Focus," *Business Strategy Review* 14, no. 2 (2003): 8–10.

EXHIBIT 10-1	WOTS-UP Analysis of Daimler Benz AG

	Strengths (S)	**Weaknesses (W)**
	1. Product quality improved 20% from previous year 2. R & D potential higher than other automobile producers 3. 50% share of comfort limousine market 4. Daimler Benz trucks lead industry 5. Breakeven point decreased from 1.0 to 0.7 million vehicles 6. Several acquisitions (e.g., AEG, Dornier, MBB) improved the synergistic potential of Daimler Benz 7. Excellent financial situation of Daimler Benz 8. High economies of scope	1. Acquisition of high-tech firms leads to coordination problems. 2. High wage level (most of the production is located in Germany) 3. Fewer joint ventures (international alliances) than Japanese automobile producers
Opportunities (O)	**SO-Strategies**	**WO-Strategies**
1. High-tech industries (micro electronics, aerospace) growing 20% per year 2. Consumers' disposable income increasing 6% per year 3. Liberalization of Eastern European countries 4. Image and service problems of Japanese automobile firms	1. Acquire automobile producers in Eastern Germany (03/S7) 2. Extend the distribution and service net in Eastern Europe (03/S7) 3. Develop several versions of the Baby Benz (02, 03/S5, S7) 4. Use production capacity for civil products (03/S6, S8)	1. Expand transfer of managers between headquarters and subsidiaries (03/W1) 2. Produce cars in the eastern part of Germany (03/W2) 3. Intensify HR development on each level (01/W2) 4. Form international aerospace joint venture company (01/W3)
Threats (T)	**Short-Term Strategies**	**Long-Term Strategies**
1. Low value of the dollar 2. Rising interest rate 3. Foreign imports, esp. luxury cars, gaining market share 4. Gulf crisis leads to increasing gas prices 5. BMW has an excellent new line of cars 6. Rising ecological problems throughout the world 7. Military (defense) markets may break off due to peace movement	1. Place selective advertising; boost advertising expenditures 30% (T3, T5/S1, S3) 2. Strengthen basic research in new fields of technology (solar energy, biotechnology, computing and robotics, electrical car engines) (T4, T6/S7, S8)	1. Build strategic alliances (strategic networks) to reduce cost of R & D investment and to solve ecological problems (T6/W3) 2. Improve productivity and quality (in production, administration, distribution, and services) (T1,T3/W2)

Source: K. Ito and K. R. Macharzina, "Strategic Planning Systems," in F. D. S. Choi, ed., *International Accounting and Finance Handbook*, 2nd ed., New York: John Wiley & Sons, 1997, p. 25.9.

analysis done by the German automaker Daimler. For example, extending Daimler's distribution and service network in Eastern Europe is a promising strategy, given the company's strengths in product quality, truck sales, lower breakeven point, and synergistic potential. The low value of the U.S. dollar, rising foreign competition in Germany, and the perceived advantages of strengthening basic research in new technologies by building strategic alliances may explain Daimler's earlier acquisition of the Chrysler Corporation in the United States.

Decision tools currently used in strategic planning systems all depend on the quality of information regarding a firm's internal and external environment. Accountants can help corporate planners obtain data useful in strategic planning decisions. Much of the required information comes from sources other than accounting records.

CAPITAL BUDGETING

As Exhibit 10-1 reveals, one of Daimler's strategies to capitalize on its strength/opportunity set was to initially acquire automobile producers in Eastern Germany. This strategy subsequently embraced the acquisition of the Chrysler Corporation in the United States. This decision to invest abroad is a critical element in the global strategy of a multinational company.[7] Direct foreign investment typically involves large sums of capital and uncertain prospects. Investment risk is compounded by an unfamiliar, complex, constantly changing international environment. Formal planning is imperative and is normally done within a capital budgeting framework that compares the benefits and costs of the proposed investment.[8] As an example of the second dimension of corporate modeling described earlier, capital budgeting analysis helps ensure that strategic plans are financially feasible and advantageous.

Sophisticated approaches to investment decisions are available. Procedures exist to determine a firm's optimum capital structure, measure a firm's cost of capital, and evaluate investment alternatives under conditions of uncertainty. Decision rules for investment choice typically call for discounting an investment's risk-adjusted cash flows at an appropriate interest rate: the firm's weighted average cost of capital. Normally, a firm increases the wealth of its owners by making investments that promise positive net present values. When considering mutually exclusive options, a rational company will select the option that promises the maximum net present value.[9]

In the international arena, investment planning is not straightforward. Different tax laws, accounting systems, rates of inflation, risks of expropriation, currency frameworks, market segmentation, restrictions on the transferability of foreign earnings, and language and intercultural differences introduce elements of complexity seldom encountered domestically. The difficulty of quantifying such data makes the problem that much worse.

Multinational adaptations of traditional investment planning models have been made in three areas of measurement: (1) determining the relevant return from a multinational investment, (2) measuring expected cash flows, and (3) calculating the

---

[7] Cristiano Busco, Mark L. Frigo, Elena Giovannoni, Angelo Riccaboni, and Robert W. Scapens, "Integrating Global Organizations Through Performance Measurement Systems," *Strategic Finance*, January 2006, pp. 31–35.
[8] Maurice D. Levi, *International Finance*, New York: Routledge, 2005, 585 pp.
[9] The performance metric Economic Value Added (EVA) is derived from this construct.

multinational cost of capital. These adaptations provide data that support strategic choices, step 3 in the corporate modeling process.

FINANCIAL RETURN PERSPECTIVES

A manager must determine the relevant return to assess a foreign investment opportunity. But relevant return is a matter of perspective. Should the international financial manager evaluate expected investment returns from the perspective of the foreign project or that of the parent company?[10] Returns from the two perspectives could differ significantly due to (1) government restrictions on repatriation of earnings and capital, (2) license fees, royalties, and other payments that provide income to the parent but are expenses to the subsidiary, (3) differential rates of national inflation, (4) changing foreign currency values, and (5) differential taxes, to name a few.

One might argue that the return and risk of a foreign investment should be evaluated from the point of view of the parent company's domestic stockholders. However, it also can be argued that such an approach is no longer appropriate. First, investors in the parent company increasingly come from a worldwide community. Investment objectives should reflect the interests of all shareholders, not just the domestic ones. Observation also suggests that many multinational companies have long-run (as opposed to short-run) investment horizons. Funds generated abroad tend to be reinvested abroad rather than repatriated to the parent company. Under these circumstances, it may be appropriate to evaluate returns from a host country perspective. Emphasis on local project returns is consistent with the goal of maximizing consolidated group value.[11]

An appealing solution is to recognize that financial managers must meet many goals, responding to investor and noninvestor groups in the organization and its environment.[12] The host country government is one such group for a foreign investment. Compatibility between the goals of the multinational investor and the host government can be gauged through two financial return calculations: one from the host country perspective, the other from the parent country perspective. The host country perspective assumes that a profitable foreign investment (including the local opportunity cost of capital) does not misallocate the host country's scarce resources.[13] Evaluating an investment opportunity from a local perspective also gives the parent company useful information.

If a foreign investment does not promise a risk-adjusted return higher than the returns of local competitors, parent company shareholders would be better off investing directly in the local companies.

At first glance, the accounting implications of multiple rate-of-return calculations appear straightforward. Nothing could be less true. In an earlier discussion, we assumed that project rate-of-return calculations were a proxy for host country evaluation of a foreign investment. In practice, the analysis is much more complicated. Do

---

[10] This issue parallels, in many respects, the problem of currency perspectives associated with foreign currency translation discussed in Chapter 6.

[11] John C. Edmunds and David M. Ellis, A Stock Market-Driven Reformulation of Multinational Capital Budgeting, *European Management Journal* 17, no. 3 (1999): 310–317.

[12] David K. Eiteman, Arthur I. Stonehill, and Michael Moffett, *Multinational Business Finance*, 11th ed., Reading, MA: Addison-Wesley, 2007.

[13] For example, a country would probably look favorably on a proposed investment promising a 21 percent return on assets employed when investments of comparable risk elsewhere in the country yield 18 percent.

project rate of return calculations really reflect a host country's opportunity costs? Are the expected returns from a foreign investment limited to projected cash flows, or must other externalities be considered? How are any additional benefits measured? Does a foreign investment require any special overhead spending by the host government? What is the risk from a host country viewpoint, and how can it be measured? Questions such as these call for a massive increase in the amount and complexity of the information needed to calculate rates of return.

MEASURING EXPECTED RETURNS

It is challenging to measure the expected cash flows of a foreign investment. Assume, for purposes of discussion, that Daimler's U.S. manufacturing operation is considering purchasing 100 percent ownership of a manufacturing facility in Russia. The U.S. parent will finance one-half of the investment in the form of cash and equipment; the balance will be financed by local bank borrowing at market rates. The Russian facility will import one-half of its raw materials and components from the U.S. parent and export one-half of its output to Hungary. To repatriate funds to the parent company, the Russian facility will pay the U.S. parent a licensing fee, royalties for use of parent company patents, and technical service fees for management services rendered. Earnings of the Russian facility will be remitted to the parent as dividends. Exhibit 10-2 provides a diagram of prospective cash flows that need to be measured.[14]

Methods for estimating projected cash flows associated with the Russian facility are similar to those used for a domestic company. Expected receipts are based on sales projections and anticipated collection experience. Operating expenses (converted to their cash equivalents) and local taxes are similarly forecast. Additional complexities must be considered, however. They include:

1. Project versus parent cash flows
2. Parent cash flows tied to financing
3. Subsidized financing
4. Political risk

This process must also consider the impact of changing prices and fluctuating currency values on expected foreign currency returns. If local currency cash flows were fixed (e.g., if the Russian venture was in the form of a bond investment), it would be straightforward to measure exchange rate effects. Here, depreciation of the Russian ruble relative to the U.S. dollar reduces the dollar equivalent of future interest income. When an ongoing manufacturing enterprise generates foreign currency income, the analysis is more complicated. Exchange rate changes influence net operating cash flows. Accordingly, accounting measurements of exchange rate effects for each type of activity (such as domestic vs. export sales, domestic vs. imported costs, and their cumulative effects on projected cash flows) become necessary.

---

[14] For an extended discussion of this subject, see David K. Eiteman, "Foreign Investment Analysis," in F. D. S. Choi, ed., *International Finance and Accounting Handbook*, 3rd ed., New York: John Wiley & Sons, 2003, pp. 4.1– 4.19.

EXHIBIT 10-2 **Cash Flow Components**

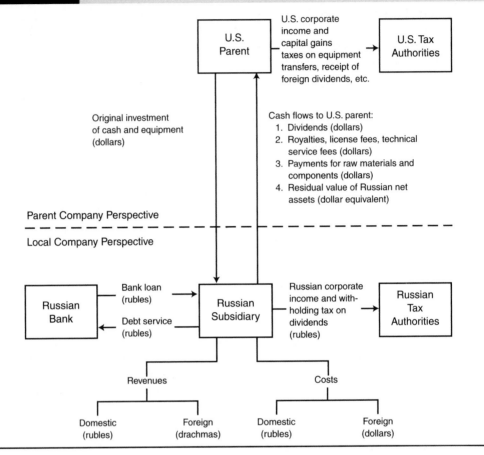

The following example illustrates the effects of changing prices and currency values on expected returns for the first two years of a six-year investment project. The Russian facility's cash flows, as shown in Exhibit 10-3, are determined under the following assumptions.

1. The Russian facility is expected to sell 100,000 units of its manufactured product in the local market at an initial unit price of 2,020 Russian roubles (RUB). Another 100,000 units will be exported to Hungary and priced in forints (HUF) reflecting the rouble base price.

2. Changes in local selling prices are tied to annual rates of inflation in Russia and Hungary, which are expected to average 20 percent and 10 percent, respectively.

3. Domestic and foreign unit sales are expected to increase each year by 10 percent.

4. The rouble is forecast to depreciate relative to the forint by 10 percent per year.

5. Variable costs of production (raw materials and labor) also reflect local inflation rates.

6. Because 50 percent of the Russian manufacturer's raw materials are imported from the United States, imported raw material prices are expected to increase by 10 percent each year in line with anticipated U.S. and Russian inflation.

EXHIBIT 10-3 **Cash Flows from Russian Subsidiary**

	Year 1	Year 2
Sales (units)		
Domestic	100,000	110,000
Foreign	100,000	110,000
Price (per unit)		
Domestic	RUB2,020	RUB2,424
Foreign	RUB2,020	RUB2,444
Gross revenues		
Domestic	RUB202,000,000	RUB266,640,000
Foreign	RUB202,000,000	RUB268,640,000
	(HUF2,020,000,000)	(HUF2,444,000,000)
Total	RUB404,000,000	RUB535,480,000
Raw materials (cost per unit)		
Domestic	RUB400	RUB480
Foreign	RUB400	RUB462
	($20)	($22)
Labor (cost per unit)	RUB200	RUB240
Variable cost (per unit)	RUB1,000	RUB1,182
Total variable costs	RUB200,000,000	RUB260,040,000
Licensing fees, royalties, etc.	RUB40,400,000	RUB53,548,000
Depreciation expense	RUB60,000,000	RUB60,000,000
Selling and administrative expenses	RUB48,000,000	RUB55,200,000
Total	RUB348,400,000	RUB428,788,000
Net operating income	RUB33,360,000	RUB64,016,000
Corporate income tax (40%)	RUB22,240,000	RUB42,676,000
Net income	RUB33,360,000	RUB64,016,000
+Depreciation	RUB60,000,000	RUB60,000,000
Net cash flow (rubles)	RUB93,360,000	RUB124,016,000
Net cash flow (dollars)	$ 4,668,000	$ 5,905,000
Exchange rates:	RUB0.1 = HUF1	RUB0.11 = HUF1
	RUB20 = $1	RUB21 = $1

7. Anticipated depreciation of the rouble relative to the U.S. dollar is 5 percent.
8. Licensing and other fees are expected to average 10 percent of gross revenues.
9. Selling and administrative expenses are expected to increase by 15 percent each year from an initial level of RUB48,000,000.
10. Depreciation expense is RUB60,000,000 a year.
11. The Russian corporate tax rate is 40 percent.
12. Projected annual cash flows will increase from RUB93,360,000 to RUB124,016,000 in local currency. Measured in U.S. dollars, net cash flows will increase from $4,668,000 to $5,905,000.

In this example, a depreciating local currency had increased projected local cash flows due to the structure of the foreign operation's product and factor markets.

When a parent company perspective is used, cash flows to the parent company seldom mirror those of its overseas affiliate. The only relevant cash flows are those with direct consequences for the parent.

Major sources of parent cash flows include debt service on loans by the parent, dividends, licensing fees, overhead charges, royalties, transfer prices on purchases from or sales to the parent (see Chapter 12 for a further discussion of this managerial topic), and the estimated terminal value of the project. Measurement of these cash flows requires an understanding of national accounting differences, governmental repatriation policies, potential future inflation and exchange rates, and differential taxes.

Differences in accounting principles are relevant if financial managers rely on locally based pro forma financial statements in estimating future cash flows. When measurement rules used in preparing these accounts differ from those of the parent country, differences in cash flow estimates could arise. One example is depreciation based on replacement values rather than historical costs (as practiced by certain large multinationals in the Netherlands and Italy). This difference could affect corporate income taxes, and consequently, cash flow. As another example, differences in inventory costing methods could influence both the measurement and the timing of total cash flow. Balance of payment concerns may prompt host governments to limit the repatriation of dividends or other cash payments to the parent company. For example, dividend remittances may be limited to a certain proportion of a company's capital base that has been formally registered with the host government. Some countries disallow repatriation of cash flows made possible by tax-deductible expenses, as these are not part of accrual-based earnings from which dividends are declared. This consideration alone would reduce the cash flows that could be repatriated in our previous Russian example by 66 and 50 percent, respectively, for the two years examined. A parent company naturally cares about the value of foreign cash flows measured in parent currency.

Accordingly, it needs estimates of future inflation and its impact on future exchange rates used to convert foreign cash flows to parent currency. Finally, provisions relating to the taxation of foreign source income must be considered. For instance, in the United States the receipt of a royalty payment on which a foreign withholding tax has been assessed gives rise to a foreign tax credit designed to minimize the double taxation of foreign source income. (International tax considerations are detailed in Chapter 12.)

MULTINATIONAL COST OF CAPITAL

If foreign investments are evaluated with this discounted cash flow model, an appropriate discount rate must be developed. Capital budgeting theory typically uses a firm's cost of capital as its discount rate; that is, a project must yield a return at least equal to a firm's capital costs to be accepted. This hurdle rate is related to the proportions of debt and equity in a firm's financial structure as follows:

$$k_a = k_e(E/S) + k_i(1 - t)(DT/S)$$

where:

k_a = weighted average (after tax) cost of capital

k_e = cost of equity

k_i = cost of debt before tax

E = value of a firm's equity

D = value of a firm's debt

S = value of a firm's capital structure (E + D)

t = marginal tax rate

It is not easy to measure a multinational company's cost of capital. The cost of equity capital may be calculated in several ways. One popular method combines the expected dividend yield with the expected dividend growth rate. Letting DVi = expected dividends per share at period's end, P_0 = the current market price of the stock at the beginning of the period, and g = expected growth rate in dividends, the cost of equity, ke, is calculated as ke = DV_i/P_0 + g. Even though it is easy to measure current stock prices, in most countries where a multinational firm's shares are listed, it is often troublesome to measure DV and g. First, DV_i is an expectation. Expected dividends depend on the operating cash flows of the company as a whole. Measuring these cash flows is complicated by environmental considerations such as those mentioned in our Russian example. Moreover, measurement of the dividend growth rate, a function of expected future cash flows, is complicated by exchange controls and other government restrictions on cross-border funds transfers.

Similar problems relate to the measurement of the debt component of the average cost of capital.[15] In a single nation, the cost of debt is the effective interest rate multiplied by (1 − t) because interest is generally a tax-deductible expense. When a multinational company borrows foreign currencies, however, additional factors enter the picture. The effective after-tax interest cost now includes foreign exchange gains or losses that arise whenever foreign exchange rates fluctuate between the transaction and settlement dates (see Chapter 6). Suppose that a U.S. multinational borrows 100,000 Israeli shekels (ILS) for 1 year at 8 percent interest when the dollar/shekel exchange rate is $0.24 = ILS1. Should the shekel appreciate to $0.264 = ILS1 before repayment, the borrowing company will incur a transaction loss of ILS108,000 × ($ 0.264 − $0.240) = $2,592. This additional cost of debt financing would be tax deductible. Assuming a corporate tax rate of 40 percent, the after-tax cost of debt would be 0.18 (1 − 0.40), or 10.8 percent, as opposed to 4 percent in a purely domestic transaction.

Additional tax considerations apply when a multinational borrows funds in several foreign capital markets. Current and prospective tax rates in each foreign market over the life of the loan must be considered. The tax-deductibe status of interest payments must be checked, because not all national taxing authorities recognize interest deductions (particularly if the associated loan is between related entities).

---

[15] In countries with underdeveloped capital markets, internal borrowing is a common substitute. Mihir A. Desai, C. Fritz Foley, and James R. Hines, "A Multinational Perspective on Capital Structure Choice and Internal Capital Markets," *Journal of Finance*, Vol. 59, no. 6 (2004): 2451–2478.

Moreover, recognition of deferred taxes, which arise whenever income for tax purposes differs from income for external reporting purposes, is becoming a generally accepted practice in many industrialized countries where MNCs operate. Because deferred taxes are considered a liability on which no interest is paid, one can ask whether they are really an interest-free source of financing and should be included in determining the cost of capital. Although this idea merits consideration, we do not believe that the cost of capital calculation should include deferred taxes.[16]

It is not always straightforward to implement international capital budgeting theory in practice. All of the capital budgeting approaches we have examined assume that the required information is readily available. Unfortunately, in actual practice, the most difficult and critical aspect of the entire capital budgeting process is obtaining accurate and timely information, especially in the international sphere, where different climates, culture, languages, and information technologies complicate matters.

MANAGEMENT INFORMATION SYSTEMS

Organization of a firm's worldwide information systems is crucial in supporting corporate strategies, including the planning processes described earlier. This task is challenging, as a multinational framework is inherently more complex than a single-country framework. Exhibit 10-4 sets forth some environmental factors that complicate the flow of business information.

Systems Issues

Distance is an obvious complication. Due to geographic circumstances, formal information communications generally substitute for personal contacts between local operating managers and headquarters management. Developments in information technology should reduce, but will not entirely eliminate, this complication.

As another example, the information requirements of regional or corporate financial planners concern both operating and environmental data. Information demanded from managerial accountants in the field depends on how much decision-making power local managers have. The greater the authority of local managers, the less information is passed on to headquarters.

In their study, "Patterns in the Organization of Transnational Information Systems," Vikram Sethi and Joseph Katz identify three global IT strategies, each related to a specific type of multinational organization. Success hinges on matching systems design to corporate strategies.[17]

Low dispersal with high centralization. Employed by smaller organizations with limited international business operations, domestic IS needs dominate. A standard platform of data and applications dominate the worldwide IT system.

---

[16] As discussed in Chapter 6, deferred taxes under the current rate method are translated at the current rate with any translation gains and losses taken to owners' equity and held in suspense until realized. Under the temporal method, they are translated at the historical rate. Because current earnings are not burdened with exchange rate effects under either treatment, neither should the costs of capital be relieved by what is, in effect, an interest-free loan from a government.

[17] Peter Gwynne, "Information Systems Go Global," *MIT Sloan Management Review*, Summer 2001, p. 14.

EXHIBIT 10-4   Framework for Systems Design

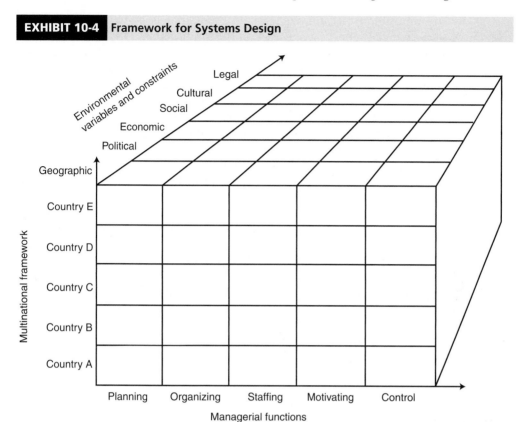

High dispersion with low centralization. This strategy is favored by multinational companies with diverse geographic operations. Local subsidiaries are afforded significant control over the development of their IT strategies and related systems.

High dispersal with high centralization. Here a "glocal" IT strategy is employed by truly global companies with strategic alliances worldwide. Information systems are designed that reflect both corporate requirements tailored to local circumstances.

Perhaps the biggest challenge facing systems specialists is designing corporate information systems that allow financial managers to respond appropriately to the phenomenon of global competition. Conditions are changing. Owing to deregulation of markets and reduction of tariff barriers, firms are increasingly able to access foreign markets either directly or indirectly through joint ventures, strategic alliances, and other cooperative arrangements. This more open access has led to competitive intensities where firms adopt strategies to (1) protect market share at home, (2) penetrate competitors' home markets to deny them market share and revenues, and (3) generate significant market share in key third-country markets.

CEOs need information systems that enable them to plan, coordinate, and control effective worldwide production, marketing, and financial strategies. To facilitate this objective, software information developers in the United States have created a new computer language, XBRL. XBRL stands for extensible business reporting language and is a standard computer programming enhancement that is being included in all accounting and financial reporting software in the United States. Once added to the software, XBRL automatically translates all numbers and words so that each data segment is identified in a standard way when viewed by a Web browser or sent to a particular spreadsheet application. Specifically, XBRL tags each segment of computerized business information with an identification marker that remains with the data when moved or changed. No matter how an application software formats or rearranges the information, the markers remain with the data. Links are created that identify the location on a financial statement where the data elements reside, instruct users as to how the data elements should be calculated in relation to other elements in the financial statements, detail descriptive lables that should be applied to the data elements including the national language in which they should be reported and specify other information such as currency of denomination, time period covered, and the like. Useful for all enterprises regardless of industry or size, XBRL reduces information processing, calculating, and formatting costs because financial data only need to be created and formatted once regardless of intended use. It will also improve a firm's investor relations as it facilitates interfirm comparisons along many dimensions, including financial accounts, accounting policies, and related footnotes in automated fashion.[18] This systems effort is being led in the United States by a consortium of accounting firms, financial service providers, and technology companies, including software giants Microsoft and IBM. Not only is this system making the distribution of financial information fast and easy, it is also eliminating the need for rewriting financial reports to accommodate incompatible accounting systems. Parallel efforts are reportedly under way in other countries along with involvement of the International Accounting Standards Board.

Information Issues

Management accountants prepare many kinds of information for corporate management, ranging from collections data to liquidity reports to operational forecasts of various types to expense disbursements. For each set of data transmitted, corporate management must determine the relevant time period of the reports, the level of accuracy required, the frequency of reporting, and the costs and benefits of timely preparation and transmission.

Here too, environmental factors affect the usage of information generated internally. Consider the influence of culture: Culture shapes the values of a given society. Citizens of these societies bring these values with them when employed by business organizations. These values, in turn, frame employees' organizational behavior and how they use information technology within the organization. Although organizations around the world are becoming more similar in their conduct of business, the people that comprise these organizations tend to maintain their cultural behavior patterns. As one example, Johns, Smith, and Strand examine the impact of uncertainty avoidance on database usage.[19] They find that cultures that are less uncomfortable with uncertainty

---

[18] Mike Willis and William M. Sinnett, "XBRL Not Just for External Reporting," *Financial Executive*, May 2008, pp. 44–47.
[19] The term uncertainty avoidance was coined by Gerte Hofstede in his oft-cited study on values as determinants of behavior. Uncertainty avoidance is a value construct that describes the degree to which one is more or less comfortable with task uncertainty and ambiguity. See discussion of Hofstede's work in Chapter 2.

and ambiguity tend to embrace information technology more readily than those who are very uncomfortable. A major implication of their study for managerial accountants is that culture is a major impediment to the international flow of data and must be explicitly dealt with in information systems design.[20]

Managers in different environments have different ways of analyzing and resolving problems, different decision time frames, and compete under different operating conditions. Different information needs are a direct consequence. Hence, we have a fundamental problem for the multinational enterprise. Local managers are likely to require different decision information than headquarters management. For example, a special feature of the U.S. consolidation process is that financial statements prepared according to foreign accounting principles are first restated to U.S. GAAP prior to being consolidated. Does this restatement somehow alter the information content of the accounts that go into a group consolidation? We provide an illustration of this reporting conundrum in the following section.

Another major information problem is the question of translation. In evaluating operations, U.S. managers generally prefer reports stated in U.S. dollars. Accordingly, reports from foreign operations of U.S. multinationals are typically translated to their U.S. dollar equivalents in order for U.S. headquarters managers to evaluate their dollar investments. However, does translating foreign currency amounts for managerial review purposes preserve the data without distortions? We address this issue empirically in Case 10-1 at the end of this chapter.

MANAGEMENT INFORMATION AND HYPERINFLATION

FAS No. 52 mandates use of the temporal translation method, described in Chapter 6, in consolidating the accounts of foreign affiliates domiciled in high-inflation environments. Even though FAS No. 52 and similar national pronouncements provide useful guidelines in preparing hard currency statements, they do not meet the information needs of firms operating in high-inflation countries. In high-inflation environments, financial reports prepared in conformity with FAS No. 52 tend to distort reality by

- Overstating or understating revenues and expenses
- Reporting large translation gains or losses that are difficult to interpret
- Distorting performance comparisons over time

Our reporting framework overcomes these limitations and is based on the following assumptions[21]:

1. Management's objective of maximizing the value of the firm is framed in terms of a currency that holds its value (i.e., a hard currency). Accordingly, the best way to

---

[20] Sharon K. Johns, L. Murphy Smith, and Carolyn A. Strand, "How Culture Affects the Use of Information Technology," *Accounting Forum* 27, no. 1 (March 2002): 84–109.
[21] Frederick D. S. Choi, "Financial Reporting in Hyperinflationary Environments: A Transactions Analysis Framework for Management," in *International Finance and Accounting Handbook*, 3rd ed., Frederick D.S. Choi, ed., New York: John Wiley & Sons, 2003, pp. 27.1–27.13.

measure the performance of an affiliate located in a high-inflation environment is in terms of hard currency.[22]

2. Our model also implicitly assumes that inflation rates, exchange rates, and interest rates are interrelated. (This assumption is not critical to the proposal.)

A common reporting convention in accounting for foreign currency transactions is to record revenues and expenses at exchange rates prevailing at the financial statement date. (Use of average rates is also common.) A better option is to report local currency transactions at the exchange rate prevailing on the payment date. Recording a transaction at any other date muddles the measurement process by introducing gains or losses in the purchasing power of money or, alternatively, implicit interest into the exchange transaction.

In a perfectly competitive market, all local currency transactions would be in cash. With inflation, it is advantageous for buyers to delay payment for as long as possible and for sellers to accelerate collections. The payment date is determined by the competitive strengths of the contracting parties. Our recommended reporting treatment produces reported numbers that are reliable, economically interpretable, and symmetric in the sense that economically similar transactions produce similar financial statement numbers when translated into a common currency. One could say that the model uses accrual accounting with a cash accounting mentality.

An example will highlight the translation gains and losses generated by FAS No. 52 reporting. While many would attribute gains or losses in our example to foreign exchange risk, they are really due to improper accounting for events that occurred above the line. Following are our working assumptions:

• Inflation and Zimbwabean dollar (ZWD) devaluation is 30 percent per month or 1.2 percent per workday.
• The exchange rate at selected intervals for months 1 and 2 are:

1/1	100.0
1/10	109.6
1/20	119.6
1/30	130.0
2/10	141.6
2/20	154.5
2/30	169.0

The real rate of interest is 1.5 percent per month or 20 percent per year.
• Cash balances are kept in hard currency (U.S. dollars).
• Month-end rates are used to record expense transactions.

Sales Revenue

Suppose that the firm sells ZWD 2,000,000 worth of merchandise in month 1, with varying invoice dates and payment terms. Assuming that financial statements are prepared

---

[22] Interviews with financial executives of U.S.-based multinationals as well as subsidiary managers suggest that this assumption is consistent with corporate practices at the micro level. It also appears consistent with practices at the macro level, as more and more Latin American countries have pegged their currencies to the U.S. dollar.

monthly, the conventional practice is to record the sales transaction at the month-end exchange rate regardless of when the sale is invoiced or when payment is received. Sales reported using the month-end exchange rate are ZWD 2,000,000/ZWD130 = $15,385.

First assume that the sale is invoiced on day 1 of month 1, with payment received immediately in cash = ZWD 2,000,000/ZWD 100 = $20,000. Conventional treatment measures the transaction at month's end rather than when cash is received, but the economic basis of the transaction is the cash that is actually received on the invoice date. Here revenues are understated by 30 percent or $4,615 determined as follows:

Cash received	$20,000
Reported sales	15,385
Variance	$ 4,615

In keeping with the temporal translation method, this $4,615 understatement of sales is offset by an equivalent nonoperating translation gain appearing below the line.[23] Next, assume instead that the sale is invoiced on day 5, and that the client receives 25 days payment terms. In our model, the transaction is booked on the same day that payment is received. From an economic point of view, there is no variance and no nonoperating translation gain or loss.

Cash received	$15,385
Reported sales	15,385
Variance	$ -0-

From a control perspective, management should be able to learn from the salesperson what the expected profit margin is on the day of sale. The salesperson does not have to wait until the books are closed to have this information, which is already at hand as invoices in hyperinflationary environments clearly state the payment due date.

In the following example, assume that the client is invoiced on day 30 with payment required a month later. From an economic point of view, the firm collects $11,834 (= ZWD 2,000,000/ZWD 169). The accounting system reports $15,385, resulting in a variance of $3,551.

Cash received	$11,834
Reported sales	15,385
Variance	$ 3,551

Here, the conventional reporting system overstates sales by 23.1 percent with the positive variance offset by an equivalent nonoperating translation loss below the line.

Exhibit 10-5 shows the magnitude of the distortions associated with differing invoicing and payment terms. Depending on sales terms, sales can be overstated or understated by significant amounts.

---

[23] Assume that the firm in question begins the period with a $10,000 equity investment and immediately converts this cash balance to saleable inventories. The goods are marked up 100 percent over cost and sold for cash the next day. In this case, the aggregate exchange adjustment would be $4,615, determined either as a plug when preparing the end-of-period translated balance sheet, or as a positive aggregate translation adjustment comprising the gain on the hard currency cash balance.

EXHIBIT 10-5	Distortions in Invoice and Payment Due Dates (ZWD2,000,000 Sales in Month 1)				
Invoice Day	Payment Terms	Today's Number	Proposed Number	Diff.	%
1	Cash	15,385	20,000	4,615	30.0%
5	5 days	15,385	18,248	2,863	18.6%
5	15 days	15,385	16,722	1,337	8.7%
5	25 days	15,385	15,385	0.000	0.0%
10	30 days	15,385	14,124	1,261	8.2%
20	30 days	15,385	12,945	2,440	−15.9%
30	30 days	15,385	11,834	3,551	−23.1%

Why do we care about these distortions? The traditional reporting system has a bad effect on the behavior of the sales force. For example, it gives the company's sales force no motivation to improve payment terms. If sales are recorded at the end-of-month rate, sales personnel do not care whether they are paid in cash or in 30 or 60 days. It is important to have a system that encourages the sales force to act in the company's best interests.

In addition, traditional reporting systems do not motivate the sales force to invoice and ship earlier in the month. When sales are recorded at end-of-month rates, the sales force does not care about the time of delivery. Yet, even one day's delay in shipment could be costly: 1.5 percent in lost interest in our example. Another glance at Exhibit 10-5 shows that bonuses and commission payments are based on inflated sales values whenever payment terms carry over to the following period.

Perhaps the most serious shortcoming of traditional reporting systems is that they encourage manipulation of results. Assume now that exchange rates at the end of each of the next 3 months are as follows:

End-of-month 1   130 = $1
End-of-month 2   169 = $1
End-of-month 3   220 = $1

Suppose that a salesperson arranges the following with a favorite customer: deliver and invoice ZWD2,000,000 of a product on day 30 of month 1 at ZWD2,500,000 with 60-day payment terms instead of invoicing at ZWD2,000,000 on the same date with 30-day payment terms. The attractiveness of this arrangement is easy to figure out. Under conventional reporting methods, the revised sales value is ZWD2,500,000/ZWD 130 = $19,231 versus ZWD2,000,000/YTL130 = $15,385 under traditional measurements. This represents an additional sales gain of almost $4,000, or 25 percent. From the customer's point of view, the actual cost of the purchase is only ZWD2,500,000/ZWD 220 = $11,364 versus ZWD2,000,000/ZWD 169 = $11,834, a savings that is hard to resist. Under these circumstances, the customer is likely to initiate such a proposal.

Under our proposed reporting system, the incentives for such arrangements are reduced. When the sales transaction is reported at the exchange rate prevailing on the payment date, the transaction is recorded at $11,364 rather than $11,834. From the selling firm's perspective, it would be better to invoice the sale at ZWD2,000,000 with 30-day payment terms. Our proposed reporting system gives the salesperson an incentive to do so. Our model thus uses the actual or forecasted exchange rate prevailing on the day of payment to record local currency transactions. Because those dates are generally in the accounts receivable system (i.e., on sales invoices), this system is readily implemented. The idea is to use *accrual* accounting while maintaining a *cash* accounting mentality. Some have correctly argued that sales and expenses in hyperinflationary environments have a built-in implicit interest rate. (Hence the need to discount local currency transactions to their present values before translation.) Our model emphasizes the difference in the exchange rate between the invoice date and the collection date, and thereby automatically incorporates the implicit interest differential (i.e., the International Fisher Effect).[24] Under our reporting framework, there is no need for management to think about what the interest rate is or worry about how to calculate an appropriate discount. After all, operating management cares about the exchange rate difference.

What happens if the customer delays payment beyond the promised date? In our reporting framework, normal payment conditions are shown in reported sales and gross margins. Thus, if a customer agrees to pay on a certain date, the transaction is booked at the exchange rate prevailing on the agreed payment date. If payment takes place after the promised date, the loss in dollars is reported below the line as a translation loss attributed to the applicable line of business or sales segment. That loss is offset by interest income as original sales terms include an explicit interest cost for delayed payments, which would appear as additional interest income below the line.

To summarize, our transactions-based reporting model

- Allocates translation gains and losses to specific revenues and expenses to which they are related
- Provides both headquarters and subsidiary management with numbers that will support better decisions
- Eliminates the need for parallel controls
- Facilitates performance comparisons over time
- Can be implemented on a cost-effective basis

ISSUES IN FINANCIAL CONTROL

Once questions of strategy and information support systems have been decided, attention shifts to the equally important area of financial control and performance

---

[24] Under a freely floating system of exchange rates, spot rates of exchange are theoretically determined by the interrelationships between national rates of inflation, interest rates, and forward rates of exchange, usually expressed as premiums or discounts from the spot rate. If the forecasted rate of inflation in Brazil one month ahead is 30 percent higher than in the United States, the real can be forecast to decline in value by 30 percent relative to the dollar. By the same token, interest rates for maturities of comparable risk can be expected to be 30 percent higher on Brazilian securities than on comparable U.S. securities. For an extended discussion of these relationships, see David K. Eiteman, Arthur I. Stonehill, and Michael H. Moffett, *Multinational Business Finance*, 11th ed., Reading, MA: Addison-Wesley, 2007.

evaluation.[25] These considerations are especially important as they enable financial managers to

1. Implement the global financial strategy of the MNE
2. Evaluate the degree to which the chosen strategies contribute to achieving enterprise goals
3. Motivate management and employees to achieve the enterprise's financial goals as effectively and efficiently as possible

Management control systems aim at accomplishing enterprise objectives in the most effective and efficient manner. Financial control systems, in turn, are quantitative measurement and communication systems that facilitate control through (1) communicating financial goals as appropriate within the organization, (2) specifying criteria and standards for evaluating performance, (3) monitoring performance, and (4) communicating deviations between actual and planned performance to those responsible.

A sound financial control system enables top management to focus the activities of its subsidiaries toward common objectives. A control system consists of operational and financial policies, internal reporting structures, operating budgets, and procedure manuals consistent with top management's goals. Thus, suboptimal behavior, which occurs when a subunit strives to achieve its own ends at the expense of the whole organization, is minimized. A timely reporting system that constantly monitors each unit is a good motivator. An efficient control system also enables headquarters management to evaluate the strategic plans of the company and to revise them when needed. Management's strategic planning tasks are aided by an information system that informs management of environmental changes that might significantly impact the company. Finally, a good control system enables top management to properly evaluate the performance of subordinates by ensuring that subordinates are held accountable only for events they can control.

If a well-designed control system is useful to a uninational company, it is invaluable to its multinational counterpart. As we have repeatedly observed, conditions that impact on management decisions abroad are not only different, but are constantly changing.

Domestic Versus Multinational Control System

How should a well-functioning control system be designed in a multinational company? Should a parent company use its domestic control system, unaltered, in its foreign operations? Early studies show that the systems used by many multinational enterprises to control their foreign operations are identical, in many respects, to those used domestically. System items commonly exported include financial and budgetary control and the tendency to apply the same standards developed to

---

[25] Corporate governance is also concerned with corporate control. However, governance issues rely on externally reported information, which is the subject of earlier chapters. For an excellent state-of-the-art piece on corporate governance, see Robert M. Bushman and Abbie J. Smith, "Financial Accounting Information and Corporate Governance," *Journal of Accounting and Economics* 32 (2001): 237–333.

evaluate domestic operations. In a now classic paper, David Hawkins offers four basic reasons for this:

1. Financial control considerations are seldom critical in the early stages of establishing a foreign operation.
2. It is normally cheaper to transplant the domestic system than to create from scratch an entire system designed for the foreign operation.
3. To simplify preparing and analyzing consolidated financial statements, the corporate controller's office insists that all operating subsidiaries use similar forms and schedules to record and transmit financial and operating data.
4. Former domestic executives working in the foreign operation and their corporate superiors are more comfortable if they can continue to use as much of the domestic control system as possible, largely because they reached the highest levels of management by mastering the domestic system.[26]

We feel that exporting domestic control systems abroad is fraught with pitfalls. It is difficult to believe that a central controller's staff could design a single and effective worldwide control system given that the multinational operating environment is so diverse. A look back at the many elements in Exhibit 10-4 illustrates this point.

Environmental diversity has an unlimited potential impact on the financial control process. Earlier, we observed that geographical distances often impede traditional methods of communicating between affiliates and company headquarters. Although better technology might overcome geographical distance, cultural distance is harder to overcome. Culture and the business environment interact to create unique sets of managerial values in a country. Language difficulties, cross-cultural differences in attitude toward risk and authority, differences in need-achievement levels, and other cultural attributes often result in unforseen consequences, including (1) misunderstood directives, (2) lower tolerance of criticism, (3) unwillingness to discuss business problems openly or to seek assistance, (4) loss of confidence among foreign managers, (5) unwillingness to delegate authority, and (6) reluctance to assume responsibility. Managers of multinational companies face many tough issues. This is especially the case for managers and employees of acquired companies in cross-border mergers and acquisitions.[27] Frequently, managers and employees steeped in one culture must often operate under management control systems designed in the context of another. Based on cultural behaviors documented by Hofstede, cited earlier, Lere and Portz offer several caveats when designing management control systems in an international context.[28] Systems designed for highly decentralized operations are less likely to be effective in countries characterized by high certainty avoidance, described earlier, and high power distance structures characteristic of socially stratified societies. Delegation of authority may be less acceptable in collectivistic societies, which tend to emphasize the authority of the group as opposed to the individual. In societies that tend to have a longer term orientation, performance measures that reflect sales growth and market share may be more meaningful than ROI and budget variances that tend to focus on the

---

[26] David F. Hawkins, "Controlling Foreign Operations," *Financial Executive*, February 1965, pp. 25–32.
[27] Yaakov Weber and Ehud Menipaz, "Measuring Cultural Fit in Mergers and Acquisitions," *International Journal of Business Performance Management* 5, no. 1 (2003): 54.
[28] John C. Lere and Kris Portz, "Management Control Systems in a Global Economy," *The CPA Journal*, September 2005, pp. 62–70.

shorter term. Hopper and Rathnasiri document the consequences of ignoring cultural mores in financial control. In their case analysis, Indian employees, accustomed to a formal bureaucratic rule-bound control system, resisted a new merit-based reward system imposed by the new Japanese owners of their company. Employees reportedly formed alliances with local politicians who were frustrated with their exclusion from organizational affairs. In the end, the Japanese managers were removed and the control system reverted back to its original bureaucratic state characterized by political interventions into operational issues.[29]

Distribution channels, credit terms, industrial policies, financial institutions, and business practices all vary from country to country. International financial managers need to adapt to these diverse business practices. In examining reward preferences in Finland and China, Chiang and Birtch find that a fuller appreciation of reward preferences entails consideration of employee characteristics and other contextual factors that transcend culture.[30]

Companies with foreign operations must also adapt to unfamiliar governmental regulations and restrictions. Exchange controls, restrictions on capital flows à la Thailand in 2007, joint ownership requirements, and many other specific business regulations are examples. The environmental considerations related to the strength of a nation's currency may be the most important for the design of overseas control systems of all those shown in Exhibit 10-4. Internal rates of inflation and fluctuating currency values are critical, and corporate control systems must allow for them. Applying financial controls designed for a stable environment to one that is less stable is a recipe for failure.

Operational Budgeting

Once strategic goals and capital budgets are in place, management next focuses on short-range planning. Short-range planning involves creating operational budgets or profit plans where needed in the organization. These profit plans are the basis for cash management forecasts, operating decisions, and management compensation schemes. Budgeted income statements of foreign affiliates are first converted to parent country accounting principles and translated from the local currency (LC) to the parent currency (PC). Periodic comparisons of actual and budgeted profit performance in parent currency require appropriate variance analyses to ensure that deviations from budget are correctly diagnosed for managerial action. While variance analysis is, in principle, the same internationally as domestically, currency fluctuations make it more complex.

The financial performance of a foreign operation can be measured in local currency, home country currency, or both. The currency used can have a significant impact in judging the performance of a foreign unit and its manager. Fluctuating currency values can turn profits (measured in local currency) into losses (expressed in home country currency).

Some favor a local currency perspective because foreign transactions take place in a foreign environment and are done in foreign currency. Foreign currency translation

---

[29] Trevor Hopper and Chandra Rathnasiri, "Japanese Cost Management Meets Sri Lankan Politics: Disappearance and Reappearance of Bureaucratic Management Controls in a Privatized Utility," *Accounting, Auditing and Accountability,* Vol. 17, no. 1 (2004): 120.

[30] Flora F.T. Chiang and Thomas A. Birtch, "An Empirical Examination of Reward Preferences within and Across National Settings," *Management International Review,* Vol. 46, no. 5 (2006): 573–596.

gains and losses are not considered when operations are evaluated in local currency. Those who favor a parent currency perspective argue that ultimately, home country shareholders care about domestic currency returns. Because they judge headquarters management by domestic currency returns, foreign managers should be judged by the same standard.

Problems remain even if parent currency is considered a better measure of performance than local currency. In theory, the exchange rate between two countries should move in proportion to changes in their differential inflation rates. Thus, if the rate of inflation is 10 percent in Italy and 30 percent in Turkey, the Turkish lira should lose approximately 20 percent of its value relative to the euro. In practice, changes in currency exchange values that lag behind foreign rates of inflation can distort performance measures. Local currency earnings and their dollar equivalents increase during excessive inflation. In the following period, when the foreign currency loses value, the dollar value of local earnings falls even if local currency earnings increase. Under these circumstances, measuring with parent currency introduces random elements in measuring the performance of foreign operations if changes in foreign exchange rates do not track differences in inflation rates.

In the long run, one must judge a foreign unit's value as an investment in terms of home country currency. A parent currency perspective is appropriate for strategic planning and long-term investment decisions. However, the currency framework used in evaluating managerial performance must depend on who is held accountable for exchange risk. (This issue is separate from who is responsible for exchange risks.) If corporate treasury manages exchange risks, then it is logical to measure foreign performance in local currency. Parent currency measures are just as valid if exchange gains and losses are removed in evaluating foreign managers. If local managers have the necessary tools to manage exchange gains and losses, measuring their performance in parent currency is justifiable.

Consider some aspects of the budgetary process. Control over a network of domestic and foreign operations requires that foreign currency budgets be expressed in parent currency for comparison. When parent currency figures are used, a change in exchange rates used to establish the budget and to monitor performance causes a variance beyond that due to other changes. Three possible rates can be used in drafting the beginning-of-period operating budget:

1. The spot rate in effect when the budget is established
2. A rate that is expected to prevail at the end of the budget period (projected rate)
3. The rate at the end of the period if the budget is updated whenever exchange rates change (ending rate).[31]

Comparable rates can be used to track performance relative to budget. If different exchange-rate combinations are used to set the budget and track performance, this creates different allocations of responsibilities for exchange rate changes and leads to different possible managerial responses. Let us consider some possibilities.

---

[31] Donald R. Lessard and Peter Lorange, "Currency Changes and Management Control: Resolving the Centralization/Decentralization Dilemma," *Accounting Review,* July 1977, pp. 628–637.

1. Budget and track performance at initial spot rate. Exchange rate changes have no effect on the evaluation of the foreign manager's performance. Local managers have little incentive to incorporate anticipated exchange rate changes into their operating decisions.
2. Budget at ending (updated) rate and track at ending rate. This combination produces similar results. Local management need not consider exchange rates because the same rate is used for budgeting and evaluation.
3. Budgeting at initial rate and track at ending rate. Local managers have full responsibility for exchange rate changes. Potential negative consequences include padding of budgets by local managers or hedging that may not be optimal for the corporation.
4. Budget and track performance using projected exchange rates. This system reflects a local currency perspective. Local managers are encouraged to incorporate expected exchange rate changes into their operating plans but are not held responsible for unexpected rate changes, which the parent company absorbs.
5. Budget at projected rate and track at ending rate. This exchange rate combination does not hold the local manager accountable for expected rate changes. Managers are responsible for (and thereby encouraged to hedge) unanticipated exchange rate changes.

Which option is best for evaluating managerial performance? All five are found in practice. We focus on the last two, the most common. As an illustration, assume the following (LC = local currency):

Projected rate of exchange:	$0.50 = LC 1	Actual end-of-period rate:	$0.25 = LC 1
Budgeted earnings in LC:	800,000	Actual earnings in LC:	1,000,000
Budget earnings in :	$400,000	Actual earnings in $:	250,000

If the projected rate is used in monitoring performance, the dollar result is $500,000 (LC 1,000,000 X $0.50), or $100,000 above budget. The manager appears to have done well. But, if the actual end-of-period rate is used, the result is $250,000 (LC 1,000,000 X $0.25), or $150,000 below budget. The manager appears to have performed poorly. Which rate should be used?

Most discussions of this problem favor option 4. Using the projected exchange rate in budgeting encourages managers to include expected exchange rate movements in their operating decisions. Use of the projected rate to monitor performance, in turn, shields local managers from unanticipated exchange rate changes they cannot control. Also, protection against exchange risk can be coordinated on a company-wide basis.

We think that use of a projected exchange rate for budgeting and the actual ending rate for tracking performance (option 5) also has merit. Like option 4, this approach encourages managers to include anticipated exchange rate changes in their plans for the budget period. Unlike option 4, holding local and corporate managers accountable for unexpected rate changes encourages them to respond to exchange rate movements. Imagine what would happen if a foreign manager, projecting a 30 percent local currency devaluation, actually experiences a 70 percent devaluation and does nothing to offset the larger than expected devaluation because his performance is measured using the projected rate.

Option 5 is especially useful when local operating plans can be changed to accommodate unanticipated currency developments. Where any remaining variances between actual and projected rates are ignored when evaluating local managers (i.e., the remaining variance is regarded as a forecasting error, which is the responsibility of corporate headquarters), this system offers additional benefits over option 4.

When responsibility for exchange variances is divided between various levels in management, budget variances need to be analyzed by responsibility level. In our previous example, the foreign subsidiary's operating variance and exchange rate variance would be analyzed as shown in Exhibit 10-6.

The total budget variance of −$150,000 (LC 800,000 X $0.50 − LC 1,000,000 X $0.25) would consist of a positive variance of $100,000 attributed to the foreign manager (LC 800,000 X $0.50 − LC 1,000,000 X $0.50) and a negative variance of −$250,000 attributed to corporate headquarters (LC 1,000,000 X $0.50 − LC 1,000,000 X $0.25). Exhibit 10-7 illustrates a framework for analyzing budget variances when the responsibility for exchange variances is divided between local management, an international division's operating management (parent currency variation), and corporate treasury (variance from budget rates). Here, the international division is responsible for

EXHIBIT 10-6 Analysis of Exchange Rate Variances

	Computation		
Responsibility	**Operating Item**	**Exchange Rate**	**Variance**
Local currency operations	LC Budget ×	Budget	Local-currency
(Foreign management)	− LC Actual ×	Budget =	operating variance
Parent currency operations	LC Actual ×	Budget	Parent-currency
(Headquarters' management)	− LC Actual ×	Actual =	exchange variance

EXHIBIT 10-7 Three-Way Analysis of Exchange Rate Variance

	Computation		
Responsibility	**Operating Item**	**Exchange Rate**	**Variance**
Local currency operations	LC Budget ×	Budget	Local-currency
(Local management)	− LC Actual ×	Budget =	operating variance
Parent currency operations	LC Actual ×	Budget	Parent-currency
(International division)	− LC Actual ×	Actual =	operating variance
Foreign exchange variance	LC Budget ×	Budget	Exchange rate
from budget (Treasury)	− LC Budget ×	Actual =	variance from budget

hedging unexpected exchange rate changes while corporate treasury is responsible for accurate rate forecasts.

Analysis of Exchange Rate Changes

We now provide a more comprehensive example of an exchange rate variance analysis.[32] Exhibit 10-8 shows the budgeted and actual condensed income statements for FC Company at the start and end of the 20X8 budget year. The profit plan for the year (expressed in parent company GAAP) is translated to parent currency at the beginning-of-period exchange rate of FC 1 = PC1. The foreign currency devalues by 20 percent by year-end.

A performance report breaking out price-, volume- and exchange-rate-induced variances appears in Exhibit 10-9.

From the perspective of the foreign affiliate, performance variances are measured in local currency and reflect the difference between budget and actual figures for each item in the income statement. These performance variances are detailed in column (7) of Exhibit 10-9. Variances for sales revenues and cost of sales can be broken down into price (cost) and volume variances. The sale volume variance of FC 1,000 is determined by multiplying the change in unit sales volume, 200 units, by the budgeted selling price of FC 5. Applying a similar methodology to cost of sales produces a volume variance of 200 units X FC 3 = FC 600. Thus, the net volume variance affecting gross margin and operating income column (9) is FC 1,000 − FC 600 = FC 400. Variances in sales revenues and cost of sales attributed to price (cost) changes during the budget period are found by multiplying the actual number of units sold by the change in selling price (production cost). This calculation yields a negative price variance of 1,200 units X −FC 0.25 = −FC 300 for sales revenue, and a positive cost variance of 1,200 units X −FC 0.60 = FC 720 for cost of sales, in column (10). Differences between budgeted and actual expenses are shown as nominal variances in column (11).

EXHIBIT 10-8	Income Statement for Exchange Rate Variance Analysis				
		Budget			**Actual**
Revenues		FC 5,000			FC 5,700[a]
Cost of goods sold		3,000[b]			2,880
Gross margin		FC 2,000			FC 2,820
Operating expenses	750			825	
Depreciation	500			500	
Interest	250	1,500		300	1,625
Operating income		FC 500			FC 1,195

[a]The company employs the FIFO costing method and production equaled sales during the year. Unit production costs dropped from a planned FC 3.00 to FC 2.40 per unit.
[b]Actual sales increased by 200 units during the year at a price of FC 4.75, FC 0.25 lower than that expected.

---

[32] Frederick D.S. Choi and Gerald F. Lewis, "Multinational Budgeting and Control Systems," in *International Finance and Accounting Handbook*, 3rd ed., F.D.S. Choi, ed., New York: John Wiley & Sons, 2003, pp. 25.1–25.22.

EXHIBIT 10-9   Performance Report FC Company (for the budget period ending 12/31/X8)

	(1)	(2)	(3)	(4)	(5)	(6)	(7)	(8)	(9)	(10)	(11)	(12)
	Budget			Actual			Variance Analysis					
							Total			Price/		Exch.
	FC	FX	PC	FC	FX	PC	FC	PC	Vol.	(Cost)	Reported	Rate
Revenue	5,000	1.0	5,000	5,700	.8	4,560	700	(440)	1,000	(300)		(1,140)
Beg. inventory	(3,000)	1.0	(3,000)	(2,800)	1.0	(2,800)	200	200				
Production	(3,000)	1.0	(3,000)	(2,880)	.8	(2,304)	120	696				
Goods available	(6,000)		(6,000)	(5,680)		(5,104)	320	896				
End. inventory	3,000	1.0	3,000	2,800	.8	2,240	(200)	(760)				
Cost of sales	(3,000)		(3,000)	(2,880)		(2,864)	120	136	(600)	720		16
Gross margin	2,000		2,000	2,820		1,696	820	(304)	400	420		(1,124)
Operating exp.	(750)	1.0	(750)	(825)	.8	(660)	(75)	90			(75)	165
Depreciation	(500)	1.0	(500)	(500)	1.0	(500)	—	—			—	—
Interest	(250)	1.0	(250)	(300)	.8	(240)	(50)	10			(50)	60
Operating income	500		500	1,195		296	695	(204)	400	420	(125)	(899)

Based on this analysis, we can see that the improvement in FC Company's operating income of FC 695 (column 7) is attributable to the following factors:

Higher volume (column 9)	FC 400
Lower selling price (column 10)	(300)
Lower production cost (column 10)	720
Higher expenses (column 11)	(125)
Increase in operating income (column 7)	FC 695

When FC Company's performance is evaluated from the parent company perspective, first its local currency results are translated to parent currency. Let us assume that Parent Company designates the parent currency as its functional currency. Accordingly, FC Company's budgeted income statement is translated to parent currency using the temporal translation method. Had the local currency been designated as functional, the current rate translation method would have been used. (See Chapter 6 for a detailed description of these methods.)

To simplify our analysis, Parent Company will analyze FC Company's budget variances using the exchange rate prevailing at the budget date (FC 1.00 = PC 1.00).[33]

With this approach, price and volume variances for sales and cost of sales will mirror those calculated under a local company perspective. The effect of exchange rate changes is calculated by multiplying actual results reported in parent currency by the change in the exchange rate during the budget period. The total variance for sales revenues in parent currency, PC 5,000 − PC 4,560 = PC 440, would be broken down into the following volume, price, and exchange rate variances:

Volume variance in col. (9) = 200 units × FC 5 = FC 1,000 × 1.0 = PC 1,000
Price variance in col. (10) = 1,200 units × −FC 0.25
$$= FC (300) \times 1.0 = PC (300)$$
Exchange rate variance in col. (12) = FC 5,700 × −PC 0.2 = PC (1,140).

Similarly, the total variance for cost of sales can be broken down as follows:

Volume variance = 200 units × FC 3 = FC 600 × 1.0 = PC (600)
Cost variance = 1,200 units × −FC 0.60 = FC (720) × 1.0 = PC 720

Exchange rate variance is computed by multiplying each component of cost of goods sold by the exchange rate change in column (12):

Beginning inventory	FC 2,800	×	-0-	=	0
Production	FC 2,880	×	PC 0.2	=	576
Ending inventory	FC 2,800	×	−PC 0.2	=	(560)
					16

---

[33] Alternative exchange rate benchmarks and their implications for performance evaluation of foreign operations are considered in a later section of this chapter.

Exchange rate variances for operating expenses and depreciation are computed by multiplying the actual figures in local currency by the exchange rate change during the period. This yields an exchange variance for operating expenses FC $825 \times -PC\ 0.2 = PC165$ and an exchange variance of FC $(300) \times -PC\ 0.2 = PC\ 60$ for interest.

In evaluating FC Company's performance in parent currency, the shortfall of $-PC\ 204$ in operating earnings can be attributed to the following factors:

Higher sales volume	PC +400
Lower selling price	(300)
Lower production cost	+720
Higher operating expenses	(75)
Higher interest expenses	(50)
Exchange rate changes (column 12)	(899)
Decrease in parent currency operating earnings (column 8)	PC (204)

A currency translation phenomenon caused by a weakening of the local currency relative to the reporting currency is a major cause of the poor operating result. We discuss the proper evaluation of this currency effect in the subsequent section of this chapter on performance evaluation of foreign operations.

STRATEGIC COSTING

While product and standard costing systems have traditionally played a major role in cost control, certain Japanese companies have introduced cost concepts that reinforce their global manufacturing strategies.[34] In doing so they have enhanced the cost control process, and more importantly, have established a direct link between management accounting practices and corporate goals.[35]

In controlling costs at the manufacturing stage, many companies around the world employ standard costing systems that basically estimate what costs of producing a product should be as a basis for arriving at a reasonable selling price. Actual costs of production are then compared with estimated costs. Resulting variances between standard and actual costs are examined as a basis for corrective actions in the production or procurement process. This process can be thought of as a cost-based pricing model.

In contrast, many Japanese companies employ a price-based costing model. Also known as target costing, this strategic costing methodology is premised on designing and building products at prices intended to ensure market success.[36] Consider the Daihatsu Motor Company. Its product development cycle (which normally lasts three years) begins with the production manager instructing Daihatsu's departments to submit design and performance specifications that they

---

[34] These manufacturing strategies embrace continuous improvement in productivity and quality. Specific practices include just-in-time (JIT) manufacturing, total quality control, and other lean production techniques.
[35] Antonio Davila and Marc Wouters, "Designing Cost-Competitive Technology Products Through Cost Management," *Accounting Horizons*, Vol. 18, no. 1 (2004): 13–26.
[36] Ibid.

believe the car should meet. This is followed by a cost estimate based not on what it will cost to build the car, but on an allowable cost per car. This allowable cost is based on subtracting a target profit margin that reflects the company's strategic plans and financial projections from a target sales price the company believes the market will accept.

While used as a target, the allowable cost is not static. During production, allowable cost is reduced every month by a cost reduction rate based on short-term profit objectives. In later years, actual costs of the previous year are the starting point for further reductions, thus assuring ongoing cost cutting for as long as the car is in production. This market-driven system, known as Kaizen costing, significantly reduces the reliance on traditional standard costing systems. Standard costing systems seek to minimize variances between budgeted and actual costs. Kaizen costing emphasizes doing what is necessary to achieve a desired performance level under competitive market conditions. Exhibit 10-10 summarizes the major differences between standard and kaizen costing concepts.

Another strategic costing concept introduced by the Japanese is behavioral costing.[37] In a process costing system, overhead is applied to goods or routine services using an overhead application rate. From a traditional cost accounting perspective, manufacturing overhead is allocated to products on a cause-and-effect basis. Despite the capital intensity of many Japanese manufacturers, the use of direct labor as an allocation base for assigning overhead costs has continued. This practice encourages production managers to reduce rather than just accumulate costs (i.e., encourage automation). A production manager wishing to reduce his overhead burden is motivated to substitute capital for labor.

EXHIBIT 10-10   **Standard versus Kaizen Costing Concepts**

Standard Cost Concepts	**Kaizen Cost Concepts**
Cost Control	Cost Reduction
Predicated on existing manufacturing conditions	Predicated on continuous manufacturing improvement
Objective: Compliance with performance standards	Objective: Achieve cost reduction targets
Standards set annually	Cost reduction targets set monthly
	Continuous improvement in manufacturing methods to attain target costs
Variance analysis based on actual vs. standard	Variance analysis based on constant cost reduction
Investigate when standards not met	Investigate when target costs not achieved

Source: Reprinted with permission from Yasuhiro Monden and John Y. Lee, "How a Japanese Auto Maker Reduces Costs," Management Accounting (Now Strategic Finance) August 1993. pp. 22–26, published by the IMA, Montvale, New Jersey, www.ima.org. For a more detailed account of Kaizen costing, see B. Modarress, A. Ansari, and D.L. Lockwood, "Kaizen Costing for Lean Manufacturing: A Case Study," *Journal of Production Research*, May 2005, pp. 1751–1760.

---

[37] T. Hiromoto, "Japanese Management Accounting," *Harvard Business review*, July–August 1988, pp. 22–26.

PERFORMANCE EVALUATION OF FOREIGN OPERATIONS

Evaluating performance is central to an effective control system. A properly designed performance evaluation system allows top management to (1) ensure managerial behavior is consistent with strategic priorities, (2) judge the profitability of existing operations, (3) spot areas that are not performing as planned, (4) allocate limited corporate resources productively, and (5) evaluate managerial performance. Developing an effective performance evaluation system is as much an art as a science. Its complexity increases with overseas operations. Performance evaluation of foreign operations must deal with such complications as exchange rate volatility, foreign inflation, transfer pricing, distinctive national cultures, and a host of other environmental effects. If these factors are ignored, headquarters risks receiving distorted measures of operating results. Inappropriate standards of performance may motivate overseas managers to take actions not in line with corporate goals. Direct consequences are reduced corporate efficiency and (possibly) reduced competitiveness.

To date, management accountants have had mixed success in creating comparable financial controls for multinational companies and their foreign operations. In addition to the many contextual variables that complicate the design of global performance evaluation systems is the more recent challenge of developing dynamic performance measurement and financial controls. The behavioral model that continues to describe extant practices is that organizations establish goals, or aspiration levels, and compare their actual performance to these goals.[38] Performance relative to aspiration tends to elicit an array of corporate responses associated with success, performance that exceeds aspirations, and failure, performance that falls short of aspirations.[39]

The remaining sections of this chapter examine some major issues associated with the performance evaluation of foreign operations, describe how leading MNCs evaluate performance, and offer some general policy guidelines.

Consistency

Survey results show that a principal goal of performance evaluation is to ensure profitability.[40] There is a potential conflict, however, when the performance evaluation system does not suit the specific nature of a foreign operation that may have purposes other than short-run profit. MNCs establish foreign operations for many reasons. Companies that depend on a steady supply of raw materials generally expand overseas to secure their supplies. Others invest abroad to lower production costs by utilizing cheaper labor and power, often establishing a local operation there. Other reasons for expanding abroad include the need to (1) avoid losing a foreign market to major competitors, (2) create markets for components and related products, (3) diversify business risks, (4) search for new markets, (5) satisfy government regulations, and (6) spread

[38] Ahmed Riahi-Belkaoui, *Behavioral Management Accounting*, Connecticut: Greenwood Publishing Group, 2002, p. 259.

[39] Stephen J. Mezias, Patrice Murphy, Ya_ru Chen, and Mikelle A. Calhoun, "Dynamic Performance Measurement Systems for a Global World: The Complexities to Come," in *International Finance and Accounting Handbook* F.D.S. Choi, ed., New York: John Wiley & Sons, 2003, Chapter 26.

[40] Survey results suggest that the one measure believed to provide reliable information for comparing operations in multiple countries is profitability. Frederick D.S. Choi, *International Finance and Accounting Handbook*, New York: John Wiley $ Sons, 2003.

overhead costs among more producing units. Many of these objectives are strategic rather than tactical in nature. Emphasis on short-term profitability and efficiency can divert attention from critical manufacturing and corporate strategy and alienate corporate personnel.

Given the uniqueness of each foreign subsidiary's mission, performance evaluation systems must allow for how the subsidiary's objectives fit in with overall corporate goals. For example, if a foreign subsidiary's purpose is to produce components for other units in the system, it should be evaluated in terms of how its prices, production, quality, and delivery timetables compare to other sources of supply. This use of nonfinancial performance measures to complement traditional financial meaures of performance is consistent with the contemporary notion of employing a *balanced scorecard*. Subsidiary managers should participate fully in establishing their objectives. Their participation helps to ensure that they will be evaluated within a framework that is sensitive to local operating conditions and consistent with overall corporate goals. Companies should be sure not to sacrifice long-term objectives because subsidiary managers are preoccupied with short-term results. This adherence to long-term goals can be accomplished by making sure that short-term performance goals and management incentives are met within the company's strategic plans.

Unit Versus Managerial Performance

CONTROLLER A   I think generally we would look upon the manager's and unit's performance as about one and the same. The operation of the foreign unit is the responsibility of the manager and how the unit does is pretty much tied in with his evaluation.[41]

CONTROLLER B   In terms of evaluating the manager, it is very much related to how he is doing against his budget because he did present his budget, which was approved by the executive office, and this was his plan of action for the coming year. Now in terms of evaluating whether his unit is one that we want to continue or invest in or whether we should be looking at other alternatives, the return on investment becomes the significant factor.[42]

Should we distinguish between the performance of the unit and the performance of its manager in evaluating a foreign operation? Although some may believe there is no distinction, this position can be held only under limited conditions.

The actions of several parties, each with a different stake in the outcome, may affect the performance of a foreign operation. These parties include (but are not limited to) local management, headquarters management, the host government, and the parent company's government.

Local managers obviously influence reported earnings through their operating decisions. Decisions made at corporate headquarters also affect foreign earnings. For example, to protect the value of assets located in devaluation-prone countries,

---

[41] Paul A. Samuelson, "Economic and Cultural Aspects of Tomorrow's Multinational Firms," *Japan and the World Economy*, December 2000, pp. 393–394.
[42] Ibid., p. 26.

corporate treasury will often instruct foreign units to transfer funds to subsidiaries located in strong-currency countries.

Host government actions and policies also directly affect the reported results of a foreign subsidiary. Required minimum capitalization ratios in various countries often enlarge the investment base against which earnings are compared. Foreign exchange controls that limit the availability of foreign currency to pay for needed imports will often depress a subsidiary's performance. Wage and price controls can also damage the reported performance of local managers.

These considerations make it clear that a distinction must be made between managerial and unit performance.[43] Evidence suggests that this is seldom the case in practice.[44] Local managers should be evaluated only on those balance sheet and income statement items they can influence. This specific evaluation can be done in practice by dividing each balance sheet and income statement item into controllable and noncontrollable components, as illustrated in Exhibit 10-11.

Under this framework, for example, a manager of a U.S. affiliate in Bogota would not be held accountable for effective interest charges incurred in connection with a Canadian dollar borrowing mandated by corporate treasury. Because the borrowing decision was made at headquarters, headquarters management is responsible for the interest cost (i.e., the nominal interest rate in Canada plus the exchange risk). Because the affiliate derives some benefit from the loan proceeds, it should pay an equitable interest charge. This related charge is called a capital charge and is based on the cost that would have been incurred had the Colombian manager borrowed locally or from the parent.

EXHIBIT 10-11	**Financial Statement Format for Control (Local Currency)**	
	Locally Controllable	**Locally Noncontrollable**
Balance Sheet		
Assets (detailed)	XX	XX
Liabilities (detailed)	XX	XX
Owners' equity (detailed)	XX	XX
Income Statement		
Revenues	XX	XX
Operating expenses	XX	XX
Interest	XX	XX
"Other"	XX	XX
Taxes	XX	XX
Net Income	XX	XX

---

[43] Business International Corporation, *Assessing Foreign Subsidiary Performance: Systems and Practices of Leading Multinational Companies*, New York: BIC, 1982, p. 10.
[44] Wagdy M. Abdallah, Nadeem M. Firoz, and Ikechi Ekeledo, "Performance Evaluation of Foreign Subsidiary Managers Using Intra Company Pricing," *The International tax Journal*, Vol. 31, no. 4 (2005): 5–12.

Performance Criteria

A single criterion is unlikely to capture all factors of performance of interest to head-quarters management.[45] Two of the more widely used financial performance criteria used by MNCs for evaluating their foreign operations are return on investment (ROI) and budgeted performance. ROI relates enterprise income to a specified investment base; budgeted performance compares operating performance to a budget. Budgetary control means that any difference between budget and actual performance can be traced to the manager or unit responsible. One classic study demonstrated that budget-ary control is better than ROI comparisons for evaluating managerial performance. ROI measures may be more appropriate for measuring unit performance, while budget comparisons may be more useful in evaluating managers.

In an earlier performance evaluation study by Business International, both U.S. and non-U.S. MNCs surveyed stated that the most important financial criterion used to evaluate the performance of overseas units is budgeted versus actual profit, followed by ROI. Also considered somewhat important were budget versus actual sales, return on sales, return on assets, budget versus actual return on investment, and operating cash flows. As for cash flows, however, U.S.-based multinationals tended to stress cash flows to the parent, whereas non-U.S. multinationals preferred cash flows to the foreign subsidiary. Interestingly, both groups gave little importance to the notion of residual income recommended in the literature. Fast growth private companies tend to favor operating income and revenue growth.[46]

Many companies do not confine their performance criteria to financial considera-tions. Nonfinancial criteria reinforce financial measures by focusing on actions that may significantly affect long-term performance. These criteria are especially important in distinguishing between managerial and unit performance.

Important nonfinancial measures include market share, product and process inno-vation, on-time performance, product reliability, customer response time, personnel development (gauged in terms of number of people promoted in relation to the number of promotable employees), employee morale (ascertained by in-house opinion surveys), and productivity measurements. No less significant is performance in social responsi-bility and host government relations. Such nonfinancial factors are vital to ensure continued success abroad.[47]

Despite difficulties in measurement, nonfinancial criteria are considered impor-tant in practice. Earlier surveys suggest that market share is important, followed by productivity improvement, relationships with host governments, quality control, and employee development and safety. Fullerton and Walters report that firms implement-ing a higher degree of just-in-time (JIT) practices such as lean manufacturing strategies and continuous quality enhancements are more likely to use nonfinancial criteria.[48]

---

[45] For example, see Rajiv D. Banker, Hsihui Chang, and Mina J. Pizzini, "Balanced Scorecard: Performance Measures Linked to Strategy," *Accounting Review*, Vol. 79, no. 1 (2004): 1–23.

[46] Trendsetter Barometer, www.barometersurveys.com

[47] Katharina Kretschmer, *Performance Evaluation of Foreign Subsidiaries*, Wiesbaden, Germany: Gabler Verlag, 2008, 363 pp.

[48] Rosemary R. Fullerton and Cheryl S. McWatters, "The Role of Performance Measures and Incentive Systems in Relation to the Degree of JIT Implementation," *Accounting, Organizations and Society* 27 (2002): 711–735.

These often include measures such as quality results, competitive benchmarking, waste and vendor quality, setup times, scrap, and downtime.[49]

Additional issues concern identifying relevant components of ROI and budget indicators and measuring them. Variations in ROI and budget comparisons relate to appropriate elements of income and the investment base. Thus, should income be the difference between revenues and expenses as they appear in a subsidiary's conventional income statement, or should it incorporate other dimensions? While conventional income measures may reflect a firm's results better than a strictly cash flow measure, they can be misleading in an international setting. To begin, net income may include allocated corporate expenses that the unit manager cannot control. It may not reflect the strategic nature of the foreign unit's mission. A subsidiary's reported results rarely reflect its total contribution.

To remedy these shortcomings, corporate accountants need to specify, as accurately as they can, the returns specifically attributable to the foreign subsidiary's existence. To report profits, therefore, they should add back things such as (1) royalty payments, service fees, and corporate allocations charged to the foreign subsidiary and (2) profits on intracorporate sales to the subsidiary. If sales to the subsidiary are not made at arms-length prices, the foreign subsidiary's profits should be adjusted for transfer pricing subsidies (transfer prices are discussed in detail in Chapter 12). Income amounts used for managerial evaluations should preferably include only those elements of revenues and expenses that unit managers can control.

What about the ROI denominator? Should it consist of shareholders' equity? Should it incorporate shareholders' equity plus total interest-bearing debt (alternatively, fixed assets plus net working capital)? Should it be total assets? If so, should assets include nonproductive resources that are carried because of local environmental constraints? Should it include assets that are allocated by corporate headquarters, such as those corporate treasury controls?

As with income, we believe that a distinction should be made. For managers, the investment base should consist of the resources they can control. Thus, excess inventories (stockpiled because of host government exchange control policies) should be eliminated, as should intracorporate receivables and cash balances over whose levels the local managers have little influence. For the subsidiary, the investment base should include all capital employed in accomplishing its stated objectives.

Assume, as an example, that a foreign unit ends the year with the following foreign currency (FC) financial position. (Current liabilities exclude any interest-paying debt including the current portion of long-term debt.)

Cash	FC 500	Current liabilities	FC 300
Accounts receivable	200	Long-term debt	800
Inventory	300		
Fixed assets	1,000	Owners' equity	900
	FC 2,000		FC 2,000

Assume further that earnings before interest and taxes (EBIT) are FC 200. Local interest rates average 12 percent.

---

[49] S. J. Daniel and W. D. Reitsperger, "Linking JIT Strategies and Control Systems: A Comparison of the United States and Japan," *The International Executive* 38 (1996): 95–121.

Many companies in the United Kingdom and the United States compute ROI by relating EBIT to fixed assets plus net working capital. In our example, this investment base yields an ROI statistic of 11.7 percent (FC 200/FC 1,700). The comparable figure for many Netherlands-based MNCs, however, is closer to 16.7 percent, because Dutch companies typically remove the ending cash balance from the definition of capital employed. (Cash on hand is considered a nonearning asset in the Netherlands).[50]

Measurement Issues and Changing Prices in Evaluation

The designer of an evaluation system for foreign operations must also face the issue of accounting measurements. Should local currency asset values be adjusted for changing prices where inflation is a significant force?[51] Such restatements directly affect measures of various ROI components and performance statistics for budgeting and performance evaluation. For example, failure to account for inflation generally overstates return-on-investment measures. As a result, corporate resources may not be directed to their most promising use within the corporation.

In Chapter 7 we said that an internal information system, sensitive to the effects of changing prices, provides a foundation for an inflation management strategy. For a closer look at such issues, we describe a case study examining the performance evaluation practices of ICI, the U.K. chemical giant and now part of the Akzo Nobel Group.

PERFORMANCE EVALUATION PRACTICES: ICI

During the oil embargo of the early 1970s, the price of oil, one of ICI's major raw materials, shot up by a factor of 5 in one year. As a result, top management was informed that even a 50 percent rate of return was inadequate! An examination of the impact of inflation on historical accounts disclosed six adverse consequences: (1) cost of goods sold was understated compared with current sales, (2) capital employed was understated in relation to its current value, (3) as a result of (1) and (2), returns on capital were doubly overstated, (4) comparisons of divisional performance based on similar assets of different ages were spurious, (5) intercountry comparisons of subsidiary performance were meaningess, and (6) performance comparisons over time were invalid.[52]

To eliminate these distortions, ICI incorporated current cost adjustments (CCA) in its internal reporting system. ICI divided its performance measures into two categories: long term (at least one year) and short term. Cash flow generation by product and ROI are the principal long-term measures. With its cash flow measure, ICI sought to determine whether a product would earn enough money to pay for replacing its plant, its share of corporate costs, and return enough profit to finance realistic growth. In modeling its operations, ICI discovered that the required rate of CCA return differed by country. For

---

[50] On the other hand, Dutch companies use cash on hand as a standard of comparison. Return on assets employed should at least exceed the return that would have been earned had cash been invested in the local capital market, 12 percent in our example.

[51] Even in countries where rates of inflation are low, the cumulative effect of changing prices on long-lived assets can be significant. This is especially true of a capital-intensive multibusiness with older fixed assets. See also Lars Oxelheim and Clas Wihlborg, *Corporate Decision-Making with Macroeconomic Uncertainty: Performance and Risk Management*, London: Oxford University Press, 2008, 244 pp.

[52] Business International, *Assessing Foreign Subsidiary Performance*, p. 124.

example, its operations in Germany needed twice the U.K. rate of return to finance the same rate of growth, primarily due to tax factors.

ICI employed as its measure of ROI the ratio of current cost operating profit (before interest, taxes, and dividends) to current cost fixed assets plus net working capital. Assets were valued at replacement cost net of depreciation for large businesses, and at gross for smaller product lines to eliminate distortions due to the age of the assets (i.e., the denominator would decrease over time simply due to depreciation, thus raising the rate of return).

In Western Europe, profit was measured before interest and taxes because these expenses were the responsibility of headquarters, and it was difficult to relate a loan to a particular project or determine the actual tax paid when a product was made in one country and sold in several others. Where performance was evaluated on a subsidiary basis (e.g., Brazil and Australia), profit was measured after interest and tax. The reason ICI chose to do this was because these subsidiaries did their own borrowing, and investment decisions there were influenced by local taxes and tax incentives. By using a current cost ROI as opposed to a historical cost return, ICI largely insulated its measure of return from local taxes, tax incentives, and inflation. As a result, ICI could compare businesses in different countries and at different times.

While ICI mainly used cash flow generation and ROI to assess long-term performance, its principal short-term performance measure was to compare actual results against budget, with particular interest in financial ratios such as gross profit margin (i.e., profit before corporate costs). The company employed a three-year plan: The first year became that period's operating budget. Performance was tracked monthly and quarterly. Quarterly results were considered more significant.

Like many MNCs, ICI incorporated inflationary expectations when budgeting local selling prices and operating costs such as expected labor expense. ICI preferred to incorporate current values in its budgeting system and forecasted a replacement value for cost of goods sold and depreciation. The stated reason for this approach was to force management's attention to the fact that if a company is in a volatile cost setup, as when the price of oil and derivatives rises or falls very fast, it has to use the cost it will incur to replace raw materials and factor that into its selling price. If it uses historic cost, profits may not be adequate to continue purchasing oil at current prices.

Thus, performance was tracked using the actual cost of goods incurred each month. The unit's manager was held accountable for the variance (if any), because unexpected (i.e., greater than forecasted) increases in cost could be countered by raising prices.[53]

The budget also included a forecasted depreciation expense based on local indexes reflecting the asset's replacement cost. The local manager was not responsible for any variance (calculated quarterly) between forecasted and actual depreciation. It was not considered feasible for a local manager to discern and react to a change in forecasted depreciation. However, the product manager was expected to achieve his budgeted profit after actual depreciation.

ICI also included a forecasted monetary working capital adjustment (MWCA) in its budget. (See Chapter 7 for a discussion of this concept.) ICI did not consider the difference between forecasted and actual MWCA to be very meaningful because this

---

[53] This assumed that competitors suffered the same cost increases, which might not always be true due to exchange rate factors.

variance was considered to be caused by changes in costs and selling prices and would show up elsewhere in the profit and loss account.[54]

ICI's solution to inflation reporting largely focused on aggregate balance sheets and income statements. We next offer an internal reporting system that allows management to examine reported numbers in more disaggregated fashion.

Foreign Currency Effects

The foreign exchange variance analysis earlier in the chapter assumes that local managers are responsible for domestic operating results. Ideally, the local manager's responsibility for exchange variances should be in line with the ability to react to exchange rate changes.

The economic impact of changes in exchange rates on performance can be more profound than can be seen through accounting measures alone. To more fully assess the impact of inflation and currency volatility, and gauge their own ability to react, companies need to analyze their competitive market position and the impact of currency changes on their costs and revenues and those of their competition. To shed more light on this issue, we return to ICI's handling of exchange rates and budgetary control. Like many MNCs, ICI uses a forecasted rate of exchange to set budgets and the actual end-of-period rate to measure performance. Unlike many MNCs, ICI believes that the variance that results when the actual exchange rate differs from the budget rate is not meaningful by itself. For example, the company may have budgeted a rate for the euro for its subsidiary in France and the end-of-the-month exchange rate turns out to be identical to the forecasted rate. There is no arithmetic variance, but ICI may have lost some sales volume in France. The reason may be that its competitors are exporters from Canada and the Canadian dollar has weakened against the euro. As a result, the Canadians may have a margin advantage against ICI and can lower their prices in euros to maintain the same level of profits when converting to Canadian dollars.

Thus, ICI believes that exchange rate changes have more impact than accounting measures convey. It finds that further analysis is necessary to determine the real impact of currency fluctuations on performance, to arrive at effective reactions, and to determine how far the local manager is to be held accountable for protecting his budgeted profit in pounds sterling.

To achieve these objectives, ICI looks at the currencies in which its costs and revenues arise in relation to those of its competitors. Here is a view from within the company:

We buy oil and oil-related products, which are basically dollar denominated, and we are not a price-maker but are in competition with other producers in Europe. Our oil costs are dollar denominated and our revenues are denominated in other European currencies. If the pound appreciates against all other currencies, then revenues arising from foreign sales, and even those from U.K. sales subject to competitive pressures, will be reduced. As partial compensation, raw material costs (dollar-denominated oil) will be lower, but on balance ICI is worse off because the decrease in raw material costs is less than the decrease in sales revenue in absolute terms. The figure can be significant because ICI is the U.K.'s largest single exporter. Currency movements in the opposite

---

[54] The gearing adjustment on net, nontraded monetary liabilities (a form of purchasing power gain) was not incorporated into budgeting because raising funds was the responsibility of the headquarters.

direction are, of course, possible and in fact have recently occurred. An appreciation of the U.S. dollar against all other currencies puts the same raw material cost pressures on our European competitors as on U.K. manufacturing operations so we will not suffer a comparative disadvantage. The comparative disadvantage would arise if there was a depreciation of the pound versus the dollar coupled with a depreciation of other European currencies against the pound. This would both reduce our income and increase our costs.[55]

This approach to analyzing the economic impact of currency movements affects ICI's evaluation of its managers, whose freedom to react to such external circumstances is limited. In measuring the manager's performance, the company takes into account the extent to which he has been affected by factors beyond his control and also his reaction to them.

PERFORMANCE STANDARDS

Once questions of measurement are resolved, companies must develop meaningful standards with which to evaluate performance. But what standards are appropriate for a company with operations all over the world? Let's look at some possibilities.

A company may have certain corporate-wide standards, such as a minimum required ROI, that it applies to individual subsidiaries or product lines; or it may set different ROI levels or other benchmarks (such as gross margin) for different subsidiaries or product lines. These standards may be incorporated into budgets and can later be compared with results. Performance can also be measured over time. Companies may require stated improvement in specific ratios or income. Past performance is usually significant in developing the next period's budget. Finally, firms can compare their own overseas performance with that of competitors or compare its own units with one another.

Comparing the performance of foreign units against that of their competitors can be useful. At the same time, these comparisons have many pitfalls. (See Chapter 9 for a more extensive discussion of problems involved in analyzing foreign financial statements.) For example, when competitors are local firms, the problem of data availability and adequacy may be considerable, especially if competitors are privately held. When data is available, comparisons might be difficult. Competitors' transfer pricing policies and accounting principles may be impossible to determine. Cross-border comparisons compound these problems even further.

Comparing subsidiaries with other units of the parent company, either at home or abroad, must also be done cautiously as questions of comparability again arise. Differences in subsidiary objectives will automatically bias performance comparisons unless directly accounted for. Even if subsidiary objectives are the same, differences in country risk profiles must be considered. If higher levels of risk are to be offset by higher levels of return, it is reasonable to expect higher profitability from operations in riskier countries. To date, however, no single agreed-upon formula guides how to incorporate these country risks in assessing subsidiary performance.

Many firms require a shorter payback period, adjust cash flow projections for risk, or raise the required rate of return when considering investments in riskier

---

[55] Ibid., p. 127.

countries.[56] ROI is readily adjusted for political risk because one can set a desired ROI to include a premium in line with risk in a given country (offset to some extent by lower risk that results from geographical diversification of a firm's portfolio of foreign operations).

Applying risk premiums to an ROI goal is unavoidably subjective, but the process can be made systematic. One approach is to adjust the corporate-wide ROI by a numerical risk index developed for each country. For example, assume that a country-by-country risk assessment service, such as Business International, assigns a total score of 65 out of 100 possible points to Country Y. (A higher number indicates a lower country risk.) If a company's worldwide target ROI is 15 percent, Country Y's risk-adjusted target ROI is about 23 percent (15 divided by 65 percent). If Country Z's risk index is 75, its target ROI will be 20 percent (15 divided by 75 percent). Under this system, differences between a subsidiary's actual ROI and its budgeted ROI are calculated and used to compare the performance of subsidiaries in different countries. In this example, if one subsidiary's actual ROI in Country Y was 23.5 percent and the ROI of another subsidiary in Country Z was 21 percent, the subsidiary in Country Z will have performed better, as its variance from budgeted ROI was a positive 1 percent versus 0.5 percent for the subsidiary in Country Y. An overall risk index may not reflect the risk to which a particular foreign subsidiary is exposed. For example, the risk exposure of an oil company's subsidiary may differ from that of a consumer goods manufacturer in the same country. Thus, the risk index should be modified to reflect the specific risk to each unit. A more critical issue, however, is whether a company-wide ROI standard should be applied at all.

Performance evaluations based on a single company-wide standard are generally unsatisfactory. A performance budget is a more useful standard of comparison for multinational operations. Realistic budgets enable performance targets to incorporate considerations that are unique to a particular unit. Comparisons of actual performance to a budget also enables headquarters management to distinguish those results for which subsidiary managers can be held responsible from those that are beyond their control.

Following are seven caveats that may be useful guidelines for those who evaluate the results of foreign operations:

1. Foreign subsidiaries should not be evaluated as independent profit centers when they are really strategic components of a multinational system.
2. Company-wide return on investment criteria should be supplemented by performance measures tailored to the specific objectives and environments of each foreign unit.
3. Specific goals that consider each subsidiary's internal and external environment should be incorporated in performance budgets.
4. A subsidiary's performance should be evaluated in terms of departures from these objectives, the reasons for those departures, and managerial responses to unforeseen developments.

---

[56] For an analysis of the impact of political risk on the cost of capital, see Kirt C. Butler and Domingo Castelo Joaquin, "A Note on Political Risk and the Required Return on Foreign Direct Investment," *Journal of International Business Studies* 29, no. 3 (1998): 599–608.

5. Subsidiary managers should not be held responsible for results that are beyond their control (at home and abroad).
6. Subsidiary managers whose performance is being measured should participate fully in setting the goals by which they will be judged.
7. Multiple measures of performance, financial and nonfinancial, should be used in evaluating foreign operations.

Value Reporting

We end this chapter with a recent management accounting development that attempts to bridge the gap between internal and external users of accounting information. It acknowledges that financial managers have a responsibility not only to assure compliance with stated objectives but to engage in value creation. It entails reporting both financial and nonfinancial measures and processes that provide both company managers and their shareholders with historical and predictive indicators of shareholder value. It also recognizes that information useful to management are also of interest to investors in enabling them to assess future enterprise value.[57]

A company that embraces value reporting is Infosys Technologies, alluded to in earlier chapters. What follows is a case description of the company's value reporting platform. To increase its transparency with the investing community, Infosys provides investors with data that are used internally to manage its affairs. The conceptual framework that guides its discloures is mapped below:

Value creation $\rightarrow$ Value Preservation $\rightarrow$ Value Realization

Value is created by developing and executing operating strategies that generate positive net present values of expected future cash flows. Value is preserved by implementing sound financial controls and engaging in the effective management of enterprise risks. By consistently delivering on its promises, management helps to assure investors that they will reap the benefits that the business has created.

As the firm's traditional financial statements have a historical orientation, Infosys provides a range of nonfinancial information that is related to creating long-term shareholder value. These reports are organized among four themes diagrammed in Exhibit 10-12.

Specific information provided to investors that is consistent with the disclosure framework in Exhibit 10-12 includes information on brand valuation, economic value-added, intangible assets, financial position statement including intangible assets, current cost financial statements(see Chapter 7), human resource accounting and a value-added statement. The company adopts similar measures for its internal measurement of business performance. This assures congruence between financial and nonfinancial measures used internally and those used by the market. This information model has been used by Infosys before it went public in 1993. Infosys is a good example of a company that has excelled by constantly adapting to the ever-changing environment of international business.

---

[57] Robert Eccles, Robert Herz, Mary Keegan, and David Phillips, *The Value Reporting Revolution: Moving Beyond the Earnings Game*, New York: John Wiley & Sons, 2001.

EXHIBIT 10-12 ValueReporting™ Disclosure Model

External Market Overview	**Internal Value Strategy**

External Market Overview
- Competitive environment
- Regulatory environment
- Macroeconomic environment

Internal Value Strategy
- Goals
- Objectives
- Governance
- Organization

Value Platform
- Innovation
- Brands
- Customers
- Supply chain
- People

Managing for Value
- Financial information
- Financial position
- Risk management
- Segment performance

Discussion Questions

1. This chapter identifies four dimensions of the strategic planning process. How does Daihatsu's management accounting system, described in this chapter, conform with that process?

2. Explain the difference between a standard costing system and the Kaizen costing system popularized in Japan.

3. Companies must decide whose rate of return (i.e., local vs. parent currency returns) to use when evaluating foreign direct investment opportunities. Discuss the internal reporting dimensions of this decision in a paragraph or two.

4. As an employee on the financial staff of Multinational Enterprises, you are assigned to a three-person team that is assigned to examine the financial feasibility of establishing a wholly owned manufacturing subsidiary in the Czech Republic. You are to compute an appropriate hurdle (discount) rate with which to conduct a discounted cash flow analysis. List all the parameters you would consider in measuring your company's cost of capital (discount rate).

5. Refer to Exhibit 10-7 which presents the methodology for analyzing exchange rate variances. Describe in your own words what this methodology accomplishes.

6. State the unique difficulties involved in designing and implementing performance evaluation systems in multinational companies.

7. Foreign exchange rates are used to establish budgets and track actual performance. Of the various exchange rate combinations mentioned in this chapter, which do you favor? Why? Is your view the same when you add local inflation to the budgeting process?

8. WOTS-UP analysis fails to identify a best strategy. Refer to Exhibit 10-1 and examine the strategies Daimler Benz identified in its two-by-two matrix. What other strategies would you have considered?

9. List six arguments that support a parent company's use of its domestic control systems for its foreign operations, and six arguments against this practice.

10. How does value reporting differ from the financial reporting model you learned in your basic accounting course? Do you think this is a good reporting innovation?

Exercises

1. Slovenia Corporation manufactures a product that is marketed in North America, Europe, and Asia. Its total manufacturing cost to produce 100 units of product X is € 2,250, detailed as follows:

Raw materials	€ 500
Direct labor	1,000
Overhead	750
Total	€ 2,250

The company bases its selling price on a cost-plus formula.

Required:

a. What would be Slovenia Corporation's selling price per unit if it wants a gross profit of 10 percent above cost?

b. Slovenia Corporation wants to be price competitive on an international basis. To accomplish this it must be able to price its product no higher than $21.50. Using the target costing methodology described in this chapter, what would be Slovenia Corporation's allowable costs? Assume that the company still wants a profit margin of 10 percent of its allowable costs. What does your calculation imply about its manufacturing costs?

2. Review the operating data incorporated in Exhibit 10-3 for the Russian subsidiary of the U.S. parent company.

Required: Using Exhibit 10-3 as a guide, prepare a cash flow report from a parent currency perspective identifying the components of the expected returns from the Russian investment for the first two years of its operations. The U.S. parent company is only allowed to receive 70 percent of its affiliate's reported net income, after Russian corporate income taxes, as dividends. However, U.S. tax law provides a credit against U.S. taxes for any foreign income taxes paid.

3. Assume that management is considering whether to make the foreign direct investment described in Exercise 3. Investment will require $6,000,000 in equity capital. Cash flows to the parent are expected to increase by 5 percent over the previous year for each year after year 2 (through year 6). Exchange rate forecasts are as follows:

Year	Rate
1	RUB 26 = $1
2	RUB 27 = $1
3	RUB 29 = $1
4–6	RUB 31 = $1

Management insists on a risk premium of 10 percent when evaluating foreign projects.

Required: Assuming a weighted average cost of capital of 10 percent and no expected changes in differential tax rates, evaluate the desirability of the Russian investment using a traditional discounted cash flow analysis.

4. Do a WOTS-UP analysis for your school or firm relative to its major competitor. Based on your analysis, suggest several countermeasures your dean or CEO might consider to maintain or improve your organization's competitive standing.

5. Assume the following:

- Inflation and Zambian kwacha (ZMK) devaluation is 30 percent per month, or 1.2 percent per workday.

- Foreign exchange rates at selected intervals for the current month are:

1/1	100.0
1/10	109.6
1/20	119.6
1/30	130.0

- The real rate of interest is 1.5 percent per month, or 20 percent per year.

- Cash balances are kept in hard currency (dollars).

- Month-end rates are used to record expense transactions.

Required: Based on these assumptions, prepare a table showing the distortions that can occur when expense transactions totaling ZMK 1,000,000 are recorded using conventional measurement rules (i.e., month-end rates in this example) instead of the internal reporting structure recommended in this chapter.

Transactions:	
Invoice Date	**Payment Terms**
1	Cash
5	15 days
5	25 days

6. Global Enterprises, Inc. uses a number of performance criteria to evaluate its overseas operations, including return on investment. Compagnie de Calais, its Belgian subsidiary,

EXHIBIT 10-13	Compagnie de Calais Performance Report	
Sales		$4,200,000
Other income		120,000
		$4,320,000
Costs and expenses:		
Cost of sales	$3,200,000	
Selling and administrative	330,000	
Depreciation	160,000	
Interest	162,000	
Exchange losses	368,000	4,220,000
Income before taxes		$ 100,000
Income taxes		42,000
Net income		$ 58,000

submits the performance report shown in Exhibit 10-13 for the current fiscal year (translated to U.S. dollar equivalents). Included in sales are $500,000 worth of components sold by Compagnie de Calais to its sister subsidiary in Brussels at a transfer price set by corporate headquarters at 40 percent above an arms-length price. Cost of goods sold includes excess labor costs of $150,000 owing to local labor laws. Administrative expenses include $50,000 of headquarters expenses, which are allocated by Global Enterprises to its Belgian affiliate.

The parent company holds all of its subsidiaries responsible for their fair share of corporate expenses. Local financing decisions are centralized at corporate treasury, as are all matters related to tax planning. At the same time, Global Enterprises thinks that all subsidiaries should be able to cover reasonable financing costs. Moreover, it thinks that foreign managers should be motivated to use local resources as efficiently as possible. Hence, Compagnie de Calais is assessed a capital charge based on its net assets and the parent company's average cost of capital. This figure, which amounts to $120,000, is included in the $162,000 interest expense figure. One-half of the exchange gains and losses figure is attributed to transactions losses resulting from the Belgian subsidiary's export activities. The balance is due to translating the Belgian accounts to U.S. dollars for consolidation purposes. Exchange risk management is also centralized at corporate treasury.

Required: Based on the foregoing information, prepare a performance report that isolates those elements that should be included in performance appraisals of the foreign unit.

7. In evaluating the performance of a foreign manager, a parent company should never penalize a manager for things the manager cannot control. Given the information provided in Exercise 6, prepare a performance report identifying the relevant elements for evaluating the manager of Compagnie de Calais.

8. To encourage its foreign managers to incorporate expected exchange rate changes into their operating decisions, Vancouver Enterprises requires that all foreign currency budgets be set in Canadian dollars using exchange rates projected for the end of the budget period. To further motivate its local managers to react to unexpected rate changes, operating results at period's end are translated to dollars at the actual spot rate prevailing at that time. Deviations between actual and budgeted exchange rates are discarded in judging the manager's performance.

At the start of the 2010 fiscal year, budgeted results for a Mexican affiliate, the Cuernavaca Corporation, were as follows (amounts in thousands):

Sales	MXP 8,000,000	CAD 2,560
Expenses	6,400,000	2,048
Income	MXP 1,600,000	CAD 512

Actual results for the year in dollars were: sales, CAD2,160,000; expenses, CAD1,680,000; and net income, CAD480,000. Relevant exchange rates for the peso during the year were as follows:

Jan. 1, 2010 spot rate:	CAD.00040
Global Enterprise's one-year forecast	CAD.00032
Dec. 31, 2010 spot rate	CAD.00024

Required: Based on the foregoing information, did the Mexican manager perform well? Support your answer using the variance analysis suggested in the chapter. (Refer to Exhibit 10-6.)

9. Exhibit 10-9 contains a performance report that breaks out various operating variances of a foreign affiliate, assuming the parent currency is the functional currency under FAS No. 52. Using the information in Exhibit 10-9, repeat the variance analysis, assuming instead that the parent company defines the local currency as its functional currency.

10. Parent Company establishes three wholly owned affiliates in countries X, Y, and Z. Its total investment in each of the respective affiliates at the beginning of the year, together with year-end returns in parent currency (PC), appear here:

Subsidiary	Total Assets	Returns
X	PC 1,000,000	PC 250,000
Y	PC 3,000,000	PC 900,000
Z	PC 1,500,000	PC 600,000

Parent Company requires a return on its domestic investments of 10 percent and is evaluating the annual performance of its three foreign affiliates. To establish an appropriate performance benchmark, Parent Company subscribes to a country risk evaluation service that compiles an unweighted risk index for various countries around the world. The risk scores for each of the n countries are:

Country Risk Score (out of 60)	
X	30
Y	21
Z	15

Other things being equal, the higher the score, the lower the country's risk.

Required: Prepare an analysis for Parent Company's management indicating which affiliate performed best.

CASES

Case 10-1

Foreign Investment Analysis: A Tangled Affair

You are the CFO of Marisa Corporation, a major electronics manufacturer headquartered in Shelton, Connecticut. To date, your company's operations have been confined to the United States and you are interested in diversifying your operations abroad. One option would be to begin establishing wholly owned subsidiaries in Europe, Latin America, and Asia. Another option is to acquire a multinational company that already has a major international presence. You are leaning toward the latter course of action as you are interested in diversifying your company's operating risk and enhancing its bottom line as soon as possible. You also have a significant stock option package and will benefit greatly if the price of Marissa Corporation's common stock were to rise over the next year.

You are particularly interested in MBI International, a U.S.-based multinational with operations in a significant number of countries. You estimate that approximately 60% of the company's earnings are from abroad. Foreign operations performance statistics, provided in MBI Corporation's consolidated financial statements, are included in Exhibit 10-14 for the years 2008, 2007, and 2006. Relevant notes are also appended.

Unfortunately, MBI does not disclose data explaining the movement of the major currencies in which it conducts its businesses. You do a Google search and uncover a trade-weighted index supplied by the U.S. government. Given MBI's large-scale operations, you decide to use the trade-weighted index as a proxy for MBI's currency experience (see Exhibit 10-15). (In using such a proxy, you are assuming that the currency mix of MBI's activities parallel the currency mix in the trade-weighted index.)

Required

1. On the basis of the information provided, together with what you have learned in Chapter 6, does MBI represent an attractive acquisition candidate?

EXHIBIT 10-14 MBI Data on Non-U.S. Operations

Non-U.S. Operations (Dollars in millions)	2008	2007	2006
At year-end:			
Net assets employed:			
Current assets	$24,337	$20,361	$20,005
Current liabilities	15,917	12,124	11,481
Working capital	$8,420	$8,237	$8,524
Plant and equipment, net	11,628	9,879	9,354

(continued)

EXHIBIT 10-14	**MBI Data on Non-U.S. Operations (Continued)**		

Non-U.S. Operations (Dollars in millions)	**2008**	**2007**	**2006**
Investments and other assets	9,077	6,822	5,251
	$29,125	$24,938	$23,129
Long-term debt	$5,060	$3,358	$2,340
Other liabilities	2,699	2,607	2,505
Deferred taxes	2,381	1,184	1,580
	$10,140	$7,779	$6,425
Net assets employed	$18,985	$17,159	$16,704
Number of employees	168,283	167,291	163,904
For the year:			
Revenue	$41,886	$36,965	$34,361
Earnings before income taxes	$7,844	$7,496	$7,088
Provision for income taxes	3,270	3,388	3,009
Net earnings	$4,574	$4,108	$4,079

Notes: Non-U.S. subsidiaries that operate in a local currency environment account for approximately 90 percent of the company's non-U.S. revenue. The remaining 10 percent of the company's non-U.S. revenue is from subsidiaries and branches that operate in U.S. dollars or whose economic environments are highly inflationary.

As the value of the dollar weakens, net assets recorded in local currencies translate into more U.S. dollars than they would have at the previous year's rates. Conversely, as the dollar becomes stronger, net assets recorded in local currencies translate into fewer U.S. dollars than they would have at the previous year's rates. The translation adjustments, resulting from the translation of net assets, amounted to $3,266 million at December 31, 2008, $1,698 million at December 31, 2007, and $1,917 million at December 31, 2006. The changes in translation adjustments since the end of 2006 are a reflection of the strengthening of the dollar in 2007 and the weakening of the dollar in 2008.

EXHIBIT 10-15	**Dollar's Trade–Weighted Exchange Index, 2006–2008 (1990 = 100)**

December 31	**Index**
2006	92.8
2007	93.7
2008	83.7
Average Rates for Years, 2002–2008	
2002	138.2
2003	143.0
2004	112.2
2005	96.9
2006	92.7
2007	98.6
2008	89.1

Case 10-2

Assessing Foreign Subsidiary Performance in a World of Floating Exchange Rates

General Electric Company's worldwide performance evaluation system is based on a policy of decentralization. The policy reflects its conviction that managers will become more responsible and their business will be better managed if they are given the authority and necessary tools to budget and achieve a targeted net income in dollar terms. Moreover, decentralization permits the company to overcome the difficulty of centrally exercising detailed control over its large and diverse operations. Foreign affiliate managers, like their domestic counterparts, are accountable for dollar income, a practice not followed by many MNCs.

In the words of one financial executive, "Although many U.S. corporations are decentralized in their U.S. operations, they seem to be less so with regard to their foreign operations. One reason may be the concern as to whether foreign managers are sufficiently trained in some aspects of international finance, such as foreign exchange exposure management. We feel this is essential training, and our people get that training."

General Electric does not have any rigid standards for comparing the performance of its affiliates. Strategic and operating plans are agreed upon for each business, including financial targets. Like most other companies, GE generally requires a higher rate of return from investment proposals in riskier countries and has a system of ranking countries according to relative risk. A proposed investment in a high-risk area will have more difficulty being approved and will generally require a higher ROI, but approval depends on both the forecasted

ROI and the company's total strategic objectives in each country.

The system of budgeting and forecasting extends five years into the future. The first year of the long-range forecast becomes a preliminary budget for the year ahead. A year later the budget is revised, a comparison is made between it and the original forecast, and changes are accounted for.

Measurement of an affiliated company's performance is related to the objectives of its strategic plan and the annual budgets that are derived from the plan. The primary financial measure is success in achieving the affiliates' committed dollar net income. Other measurements include ROI (calculated as the sum of reported net income plus after-tax interest expense, divided by the sum of net worth plus borrowings), net income to sales ratios, market share, inventory and receivable turnover rates, and currency exposure.

While the performance of both an affiliate and its manager are measured primarily on bottom-line results, the review of the manager includes other measurements. Assessments include how well the manager has dealt with government relations, the progress made toward achieving certain targets such as increasing market share, and success in maintaining good employee relationships. These measurements are based on the strategic plan and targets that were established between the manager and parent company supervisor at the start of a period.

GE conducts periodic operating reviews where each manager is reviewed by the level above. The focus is on planning, results, and most recent estimates. This evaluation process provides corporate management with an opportunity to determine whether short-term actions are being taken at the expense of long-range goals.

To minimize currency exposure, GE finances fixed assets with equity and holds the affiliate responsible for maintaining a balanced position on working capital. The policy is modified as necessary for varying circumstances.

Unlike MNCs that have centralized the financing and exposure management functions at the head office, GE makes exposure management a responsibility of its local managers, overseen by sector and corporate personnel. To avoid the transaction costs of having, for example, a French affiliate hedge its position by buying French francs forward, GE has provisions for internal hedging arrangements. Corporate treasury obtains currency exposure data from all affiliates and provides needed information on offsets. Therefore, units can execute a hedging agreement between themselves without going to outside sources.

In setting the budget, the affiliate's manager uses the exchange rate he expects to prevail. General Electric believes that, although predicting rates of exchange is not an exact science, the managers of its foreign businesses have the necessary authority and tools to take those actions that will enable them to achieve their budgeted income. These tools include hedging and pricing decisions. The manager can not only raise prices, cut

costs, lead payments, lag receivables, borrow locally, and remit dividends quickly but he can also take out forward contracts if they are available.

The affiliate manager has the responsibility and authority to protect the unit against currency fluctuations and, therefore, is accountable for dollar profits regardless of exchange rate changes. According to a company spokesperson:

If an unexpected devaluation occurs, the affiliate's performance is still measured in terms of dollar income vis à vis budget. GE considers changes in the rate of exchange in the same way as other risks that occur in a country. For example, if an affiliate's sales are less than those budgeted for because of a recession in that economy, countermeasures are available to the affiliate. If one contends that these things are not controllable, how does one manage a company? We're not saying it's controllable in the sense that it can be prevented from happening, but it is susceptible to countermeasures before and after the event occurs.

Required

1. Compare GE's approach to performance evaluation with that of ICI (mentioned in the chapter).
2. Critically evaluate the strengths and weaknesses of each company's approach to the performance evaluation of its foreign managers as it relates to the problem of fluctuating currency values.
3. Which approach to performance evaluation do you support and why?

CHAPTER 11

Financial Risk Management

While business is normally associated with the production and distribution of goods and services, the real contribution of business to society is the assumption and management of risk. Producers of nonfinancial products assume the risk of contracting human, physical, and financial capital to fabricate a product or service that may or may not prove acceptable to society. If their enterprise proves unsuccessful, the firm ceases to exist; if successful, the firm earns a profit. On the other side of the coin, financial institutions that provide the external funding desired by business producers assume risks of collectibility and changes in the cost and availability of loanable funds. Risk management is especially challenging at the international level owing to the larger number of variables that must be considered.

The management of risk at the enterprise level, ERM, views individual risks in the context of a firm's business strategy. Risks today are increasingly viewed from a portfolio perspective with risks of various business functions being coordinated by a senior financial manager who keeps the CEO and board of directors apprised of critical risks and devises risk optimization strategies.[1] The variables that management accountants must track to supply risk managers with relevant and timely data span a variety of dimensions that varies from company to company. Exhibit 11-1 provides a corporate example of actual practice. Infosys Technologies, introduced in Chapter 1, begins by identifying its stragegic objectives and then identifying external and internal risk factors that could affect the achievement of these objectives. These risk factors are measured by managerial accountants and formally reported to responsible managers by way of operating reviews, subsidiary reviews, disclosure committee meetings, and regular updates to its corporate risk council. Information contained in risk management performance reports then cycle back and reaffirm or alter strategic objectives and risk identification processes.[2] Infosys' Risk Management Report provides an excellent example of the kinds of information that make up an enterprise risk management system. External risk factors encompass data on macroeconomic factors, exchange rate fluctuations, political intelligence, competitive

---

[1] David L. Olson and Desheng Dask Wu, *Enterprise Risk Management*, New Jersey: World Scientific Publishing Co., 2008, 252 pp.
[2] Infosys Annual Report.

EXHIBIT 11-1   Risk Management Cycle Employed by Infosys

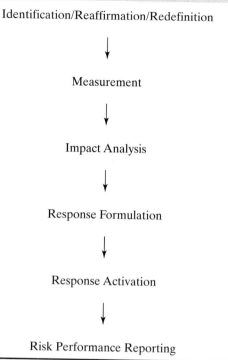

Identification/Reaffirmation/Redefinition

↓

Measurement

↓

Impact Analysis

↓

Response Formulation

↓

Response Activation

↓

Risk Performance Reporting

environment, revenue concentration, inflation and cost structure, immigration regulations for countries where company personnel are employed, physical security, data security and business continuity, and the risk of technology obsolence. Internal risk factors that are formally monitored include financial reporting risks, including compliance with Sarbanes-Oxley (see Chapter 9), liquidity and leverage, contractual compliance, legal compliance, intellectual property rights, engagement execution to assure high quality and timely product and service deliveries, integration and collaboration to ensure acquistions and joint ventures are good organizational fits, human resource management and, perhaps most important, culture, values, and leadership. The latter includes building a culture of ethical core values and leadership training.

While the management of individual risks is increasingly a coordinated affair, this does not in any way minimize the importance of managing individual risks. At the individual risk level, corporate treasurers around the world value new and imaginative ways to minimize their exposures to market risks[3]; that is, the volatility of foreign exchange rates, commodity prices, interest rates, and equity prices. The financial services industry now offers many financial hedge products, including currency swaps, interest rate swaps, and options. Accounting standard setters around the world are working on appropriate measurement and reporting principles for these financial products. Many of

---

[3] The term *market risk* is sometimes used synonymously with the term *value-at-risk*. In this chapter, the latter refers to the chance of loss on a firm's trading portfolio, which could include hedging instruments, caused by changes in asset prices, interest rates, market volatility, or market liquidity.

these financial instruments are treated as off-balance sheet items by international financial reporting entities. Accordingly, the risks inherent in their use are often masked.

Exhibit 11-2 is a glossary of risk management terms used in this chapter. We now examine internal reporting and control issues associated with the management of individual risks.

EXHIBIT 11-2   **Glossary of Risk Management Terms**

accounting risk. The risk that the preferred accounting treatment for a transaction is not available.

balance sheet hedge. Reducing foreign exchange (FX) exposure by varying the mix of a firm's foreign currency assets and liabilities.

counterparty. The individual or institution with whom an exchange is effected.

credit risk. The risk that a counterparty will default on its obligations.

derivative. Contractual arrangements creating special rights or obligations that derive their value from another financial instrument or commodity.

economic exposure. The effect of FX rate changes on a firm's future costs and revenues.

exposure management. Structuring a company's affairs to minimize the adverse effects of exchange rate changes on earnings.

foreign currency commitments. Firm sales or purchase commitments that are denominated in foreign currency.

inflation differential. Difference in the inflation rate between two or more countries.

liquidity risk. The inability to trade a financial instrument in a timely fashion.

market discontinuities. Sudden and significant changes in market value.

market risk. Risk of loss owing to unexpected changes in the prices of foreign exchange, credit, commodities, and equities.

net exposed asset position. An excess of exposed assets over exposed liabilities (also called a positive exposure).

net exposed liability position. An excess of exposed liabilities over exposed assets (also called a negative exposure).

net investment. A firm's net exposed asset or liability position.

notional amount. The principal amount specified in a contract to determine settlement.

operational hedge. FX risk protection that focuses on variables that impact a firm's foreign currency revenues and expenses.

option. The right but not the obligation to buy or sell a financial contract at a specified price on or before a specified date in the future.

regulatory risk. The risk that a public law will constrain the intended use of a financial product.

risk mapping. Examining the temporal relationship of various market risks to financial statement variables that affect a firm's value and assessing their likelihood of occurrence.

structural hedges. Selecting or relocating operations to reduce a firm's overall FX exposure.

tax risk. The risk that a desired tax treatment is not available.

translation exposure. Measuring the parent currency effects of FX changes on foreign currency assets, liabilities, revenues, and expenses.

transaction exposure. Exchange gains and losses that arise from the settlement (conversion) of foreign currency transactions.

value at risk. Risk of loss on an entity's trading portfolio caused by changes in market conditions.

value driver. Balance sheet and income statement accounts that impact firm value.

ESSENTIALS

The main goal of financial risk management at the individual risk level is to minimize the chance of loss arising from unexpected changes in the prices of currencies, credit, commodities, and equities. Exposure to price volatility is known as market risk. For example, a corporation in Sweden that issues new stock to domestic investors might view market risk as exposure to rising share prices. An unexpected rise in stock prices is undesirable if the issuer could have issued fewer shares for the same amount of cash by waiting. A Swedish investor, on the other hand, would view risk as the possibility of a fall in equity prices. If stock prices were to fall significantly in the near term, the investor would rather wait before buying.

Market participants tend to be risk averse. Thus, many will trade some potential profits for protection from adverse price changes. Financial intermediaries and market makers have responded by creating financial products that enable a market participant to transfer the risk of unexpected price changes to someone else—a counterparty. For example, a financial intermediary might sell a corporate issuer an option (i.e., the right but not the obligation) to buy stock and the investor (the counterparty) an option to sell the stock short.

Market risk has many dimensions. Although we will focus on price or rate volatility, management accountants consider other risks enumerated under ERM above. Liquidity risk exists because not all financial risk management products can be freely traded. Highly illiquid markets include real estate and small capitalization stocks.[4] Market discontinuities refer to the risk that markets may not always produce gradual price changes. The stock market plunge at the start of this decade is a case in point. Credit risk is the likelihood that a counterparty to a risk management contract will not meet their obligations. For example, a counterparty agreeing to exchange euros for Canadian dollars may fail to deliver euros on the promised date. Regulatory risk is the risk that a public authority may prevent a financial product from being used for its intended purpose. For example, the Kuala Lumpur stock exchange does not permit the use of short sales as a hedge against declines in equity prices. Tax risk is the risk that certain hedge transactions will not receive the desired tax treatment. An example is the treatment of foreign exchange losses as capital gains when ordinary income is preferred. Accounting risk is the chance that a hedge transaction will not be accounted for as part of the transaction it is intended to hedge. An example of this is when the gain on the hedge of a purchase commitment is treated as "other income" instead of a reduction of the cost of the purchase.

WHY MANANGE FINANCIAL RISKS?

The rapid growth of risk management services suggests that management can increase firm value by controlling financial risks.[5] Moreover, investors and other stakeholders increasingly expect financial managers to identify and actively manage market risk

---

[4] Many would agree that the current financial crisis was triggered by a liquidity crisis. Recent financial innovations such as credit default swaps proved ineffective in maintaing the liquidity of the market for subprime credit.

[5] For empirical evidence on this, see James M. Nelson, Jacquelyn Sue Moffitt, and John Affleck-Graves, "The Impact of Hedging on the Market Value of Equity," *Journal of Corporate Finance*, Vol. 11, no. 5 (2005): 851–881.

exposures. If the value of the firm equals the present value of its future cash flows, active exposure management is justified on several grounds.

First, exposure management helps stabilize a firm's expected cash flows. A more stable cash flow stream helps minimize earnings surprises, thereby increasing the present value of expected cash flows. Stable earnings also reduce the likelihood of default and bankruptcy risk, or the risk that earnings may not cover contractual debt service payments. Second, active exposure management enables firms to concentrate on their primary business risks. Thus, a manufacturer can hedge its interest rate and currency risks and concentrate on production and marketing. Similar benefits are available to financial institutions. Third, debt holders, employees, and customers also gain from exposure management. As debt holders generally have a lower risk tolerance than shareholders, limiting the firm's risk exposure helps align the interests of shareholders and bondholders. Fourth, derivative products allow employer-administered pension funds to enjoy higher returns by permitting them to invest in certain instruments without having to actually buy or sell the underlying instruments. Fifth, because losses caused by certain price and rate risks are passed on to customers in the form of higher prices, exposure management limits customers' exposure to these risks.[6]

ROLE OF ACCOUNTING

Management accountants play an important role in the risk management process. They help identify potential market risks, quantify trade-offs associated with alternative risk response strategies, measure a firm's exposure to specific risks, account for specific hedge products, and evaluate the effectiveness of hedging programs. In the current economic meltdown, deemed by many to be the biggest financial crisis since the Great Depression, a major limitation of quantitative risk models was the failure of management and their accountants to adjust their risk models for changes in the environment that made their data inputs questionable.[7]

Identifying Market Risks

A useful framework for identifying various types of potential market risks may be called risk mapping. This framework begins with an examination of the relationship of various market risks to the value drivers of a firm and its competitors. Exhibit 11-3 illustrates a framework first developed by J. P. MorganChase. We call it the risk-mapping cube.[8]

The term value drivers in Exhibit 11-3 refers to major financial condition and operating performance items that impact a firm's value. Market risk encompasses foreign exchange and interest rate risk, as well as commodity and equity price risk. The third dimension of the risk-mapping cube examines the relationship of market risks and value drivers for each of the firm's principal competitors.

---

[6] J. P. Morgan & Co., Inc., Arthur Andersen & Co., SC, and Financial Engineering Limited, "The J. P. Morgan/Arthur Andersen Guide to Corporate Exposure Management," Risk Magazine (1994).

[7] Jeffrey Marshall and Gregory J. Millman, "Lessons from the Abyss: The Credit Meltdown and Risk Management," *Financial Executive*, May 2008, p. 38.

[8] Ibid.

EXHIBIT 11-3 **Risk-Mapping Cube**

Value drivers	Market risks				
	Foreign exchange	Interest rates	Commodity prices	Equity prices	Other
Revenue					
Cost of sales					
Operating expenses					
Taxes					
Current assets					
Current liabilities					
Fixed assets					
Other					

(Cube dimensions: Your company, Competitor Y, Competitor Z)

Source: J. P. Morgan et al., "The J. P. Mohan/Arthur Andersen Guide to Corporate Exposure Management." *Risk Magazine,* 1994, 19.

To illustrate, let us examine the first row of the exposure management cube. Interest rate risk may affect the revenue of the firm in the following manner. Credit sales are normally collected after a certain period, depending on the credit terms offered the client (e.g., 30, 60, or 90 days). The firm usually relies on short-term loans to finance current operations, such as wages and other operating expenses. Rising interest rates before the receivables are collected would reduce the firm's return from sales. Credit sales denominated in foreign currency would yield less than expected parent currency should the foreign currency lose value before collection. Fluctuating commodity prices can have a significant impact on revenues as well as cost of sales. Finally, as managers of investment funds know all too well, falling equity prices immediately worsen fund performance statistics.

How does the third dimension of the exposure management cube work? This dimension examines how a competitor's exposure to market risk might impact the firm. Suppose you decide to sell baseball caps of the team you expect to win the next World Series. You decide to buy and sell these caps locally. Are you exposed to foreign exchange risk? You might not think so, but if a competitor buys baseball caps from abroad and the currency of its source country loses value relative to your home currency, this change may allow your competitor to sell at a lower price than you. This is called competitive currency exposure.

As the object of this exercise is to identify potential risks, we add two other dimensions to the risk management construct in Exhibit 11-3. For each cell of the cube management accountants should incorporate a probability density function associated with a range of possible outcomes for each value driver. To illustrate, unexpected foreign exchange rate changes could have a range of effects on a firm's revenues. Each of these outcomes would, in turn, be associated with a certain likelihood based on objective, or more likely, subjective, probability assessments. These probability scenarios, in turn, would be estimated over various time frames. Intervals such as three months, six months, and so forth add a temporal dimension to risk mapping. Accountants are well positioned to provide such data.[9]

Quantify Trade-offs

Another role that accountants play in the risk management process involves quantifying trade-offs associated with alternative risk response strategies. Management may prefer to keep some risk exposures rather than hedge whenever the costs of risk protection are deemed higher than the benefits. As an example, an importer who has a firm purchase commitment denominated in foreign currency may prefer not to hedge if he believes the foreign currency will weaken before the delivery date. Accountants would measure the benefits from hedging against its costs plus the opportunity costs of foregone gains from speculating in market movements.

Risk Management in a World of Floating Exchange Rates

Many of the market price movements we have been discussing are interrelated. In this chapter, we confine our analysis to a specific price exposure: foreign exchange rate changes. We do this for three reasons. First, a scrutiny of annual report disclosures suggest that exchange rate or FX risk is one of the most common forms of risk that multinational firms encounter. Second, influential financial executives state that one of the most difficult external risks that financial managers must cope with is foreign exchange risk.[10] Third, the risk management concepts and associated accounting treatments for foreign exchange risk parallel those for interest rate, commodity, and equity price risks.

In a world of floating exchange rates, risk management includes (1) anticipating exchange rate movements, (2) measuring a firm's exposure to exchange risk, (3) designing appropriate protection strategies, and (4) establishing internal risk management controls. These are discussed in turn.

Forecasting Exchange Rate Changes

In developing an exchange risk management program, financial managers must have information on the potential direction, timing, and magnitude of exchange rate changes. Forewarned of exchange rate prospects, financial managers can more efficiently and effectively arrange appropriate defensive measures. Whether it is possible to accurately predict currency movements, however, remains an issue.

---

[9] A booklet on this subject prepared by the American Institute of Certified Public Accountants can be found at www.aicpa.org/assurance/index.htm.
[10] Quote from John Connors, former CFO of Microsoft, *Treasury and Risk*, p.mailzeen.com, December 2006.

Information frequently used in making exchange rate forecasts (e.g., currency depreciation) relates to changes in the following factors:

Inflation differentials.   Evidence suggests that a higher rate of inflation in a given country tends, over time, to be offset by an equal and opposite movement in the value of its currency.

Monetary policy.   An increase in a country's money supply that exceeds the real growth rate of national output fosters inflation, which affects exchange rates.

Balance of trade.   Governments often use currency devaluations to cure an unfavorable trade balance (i.e., when exports < imports).

Balance of payments.   A country that spends (imports) and invests more abroad than it earns (exports) or receives in investments from abroad experiences downward pressure on its currency's value.

International monetary reserves and debt capacity.   A country with a persistent balance of payments deficit can forestall a currency devaluation by drawing down its savings (i.e., level of international monetary reserves) or drawing on its foreign borrowing capacity. As these resources decrease, the probability of devaluation increases.

National budget.   Deficits caused by excessive government spending also worsen inflation.

Forward exchange quotations.   A foreign currency that can be acquired for future delivery at a significant discount signals reduced confidence in that currency.

Unofficial rates.   Increases in the spread between official and unofficial or black market exchange rates suggest increased pressure on governments to align their official rates with more realistic market rates.

Behavior of related currencies.   A country's currency will normally behave in a fashion similar to currencies of countries with close economic ties to it.

Interest rate differentials.   Interest rate differentials between any two countries predict future change in the spot exchange rate.

Foreign equity option prices.   Since arbitrage links a foreign equity's price in its home market with its domestic currency value, changes in the domestic currency option price of a foreign equity signals a change in the market's expectations of future FX rates.[11]

These items help predict the direction of currency movements. However, they are usually not enough to predict the timing and magnitude of currency changes. Politics strongly influences currency values in many countries. Political responses to devaluation or revaluation pressures frequently result in temporary measures rather than exchange rate adjustments. These temporary measures include selective taxes, import controls, export incentives, and exchange controls. Awareness of the politics of a country whose currency is under pressure is important. It helps financial managers discern whether the government will lean toward market intervention or rely on free-market solutions.

---

[11] Chu and Swidler confirm this using the case of Telmex options around the 1994 Mexican peso devaluation. Ting-Heng Chu and Steve Swidler, "Forecasting Emerging Market Exchange Rates from Foreign Equity Options," *Journal of Financial Research*, no. 3 (2002): 353–366.

Some claim that exchange rate forecasting is a futile exercise. In a world where exchange rates are free to fluctuate, FX markets are said to be efficient.[12] Current market rates (i.e., forward exchange rates) represent the consensus of all market participants about future FX rates. Information that is generally available is immediately impounded in current FX rates. Thus, such information has little value in predicting future exchange rates. Under these conditions, FX rate changes are random responses to new information or unforeseen events. Forward exchange rates are the best available estimates of future rates. The randomness of FX rate changes reflect the diversity of opinions on exchange values by participants.

What do all of these factors imply for management accountants? For one thing, accountants must develop systems that gather and process comprehensive and accurate information on variables correlated with exchange rate movements. These systems can incorporate information provided by external forecasting services, financial publications that track currency movements, and daily contacts with foreign currency dealers. They should be online and computer-based to ensure managers a superior source of information on which to base their currency forecasts. Financial managers must also understand the consequences of not using other forecasting methods.

If exchange rate forecasting is not possible or too expensive to undertake, then financial managers and accountants should arrange their company's affairs to minimize the detrimental effects of rate changes. This process is known as exposure management.

EXPOSURE MEASUREMENT   Structuring a company's affairs to minimize the adverse effects of exchange rate changes requires information on its exposure to FX rate risk. FX exposure exists whenever a change in FX rates changes the value of a firm's net assets, earnings, and cash flows.[13] Traditional accounting measures of FX exposure center on two major types of exposure: translation and transaction.

Translation Exposure

Translation exposure measures the impact of FX rate changes on the domestic currency equivalents of a firm's foreign currency assets and liabilities. For example, a U.S. parent company operating a wholly owned subsidiary in Ecuador (whose functional currency is the U.S. dollar) experiences a change in the dollar value of its Ecuadorean net monetary assets whenever the exchange value of the Ecuadorean sucre changes relative to the dollar. Because foreign currency amounts are typically translated to their domestic currency equivalents for either management review or external financial reporting purposes (see Chapter 6), translation effects have a direct impact on reported profits. A foreign currency asset or liability is exposed to exchange rate risk if a change in the exchange rate causes its parent currency equivalent to change. Based on this definition, foreign currency balance sheet items exposed to exchange rate risks are those items that are translated at current (as opposed to historical) exchange rates. Accordingly,

---

[12] Gunter Dufey and Ian H. Giddy, "Management of Corporate Foreign Exchange Risk," in F. D. S. Choi, ed., International Finance and Accounting Handbook, New York: John Wiley & Sons, 2003, pp. 6.1–6.31. For instructional insights on this subject see: ian.giddy @stern.nyu.edu.

[13] See Niclas Hagelin and Bengt Pramborg, "Hedging Foreign Exchange Exposure: Risk Reduction from Transaction and Translation Hedging," *Journal of International Financial Management and Accounting,* Fall 2004, pp. 1–20. For recent corporate examples of FX exposure management, see Coline Sume Emadione, "Foreign Exchange Exposure and Management: Case Study of Two Large Multinationals," (2009) at www.essays.se.

translation exposure is measured by taking the difference between a firm's exposed foreign currency assets and liabilities. This process is depicted in Exhibit 11-4.

An excess of exposed assets over exposed liabilities (i.e., those foreign currency items translated at current exchange rates) causes a net exposed asset position. This is sometimes referred to as a positive exposure. Devaluation of the foreign currency relative to the reporting currency produces a translation loss. Revaluation of the foreign currency produces a translation gain. Conversely, a firm has a net exposed liability position or negative exposure whenever exposed liabilities exceed exposed assets. In this instance, devaluation of the foreign currency causes a translation gain. Revaluation of the foreign currency causes a translation loss.

Accounting measures of exposure vary depending on the translation method adopted. (Chapter 6 distinguished four major translation options.) Exhibit 11-5 illustrates

EXHIBIT 11-4 **Translation Exposure**

Exposed assets > Exposed liabilities = Positive exposure

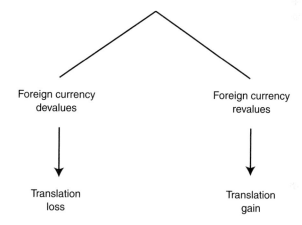

Exposed assets < Exposed liabilities = Negative exposure

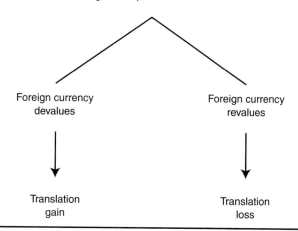

EXHIBIT 11-5	Accounting Exposure Illustrated (in thousands)						
		U.S. Dollars Before Pesos Devaluation ($.03 = PHP1)	U.S. Dollars After Philippine Peso Devaluation ($.02 = PHP1)				
	Peso		Current Rate	Current–Noncurrent	Monetary–Nonmonetary	Temporal	
Assets							
Cash	PHP 500,000	$15,000	$10,000	$10,000	$10,000	$10,000	
Accounts receivable	1,000,000	30,000	20,000	20,000	20,000	20,000	
Inventories	900,000	27,000	18,000	18,000	27,000	18,000	
Fixed assets (net)	1,100,000	33,000	22,000	33,000	33,000	33,000	
Total	PHP 3,500,000	$105,000	$70,000	$81,000	$90,000	$81,000	
Liabilities & Owners' Equity							
Short-term payables	PHP 400,000	$ 12,000	$ 8,000	$ 8,000	$ 8,000	$ 8,000	
Long-term debt	800,000	24,000	16,000	24,000	16,000	16,000	
Stockholders' equity	2,300,000	69,000	46,000	49,000	66,000	57,000	
Total	PHP 3,500,000	$105,000	$70,000	$81,000	$90,000	$81,000	
Accounting exposure (PHP)			2,300,000	2,000,000	300,000	1,200,000	
Translation gain (loss) ($)			(23,000)	(20,000)	(3,000)	(12,000)	

the major translation options described in Chapter 6. The year-end balance sheet is that of a hypothetical Philippine subsidiary of a U.S. parent company. The second column depicts the U.S. dollar equivalents of the Philippine peso (PHP) amounts at an exchange rate of $0.03 = PHP1. The peso is expected to devalue by 33⅓ percent during the coming period. As inventories are stated at market values under the lower of cost or market rule, the monetary–nonmonetary and temporal translation methods produce different exposure measures and are treated separately. Assuming the U.S. parent designates the U.S. dollar as the subsidiary's functional currency, its potential foreign exchange loss on a positive exposure of PHP1,200 million would be $12 million, determined as shown in Exhibit 11-6.

EXHIBIT 11-6	Caculation of Potential Foreign Exchange Loss (in millions)		
Exposed Assets			
Cash		PHP 500	
Accounts receivable		1,000	
Inventories		900	PHP 2,400
Exposed Liabilities			
Short-term payables		PHP 400	
Long-term debt		800	1,200
Positive exposure			PHP 1,200
Pre-depreciation rate ($0.03 = PHP1)		PHP 1,200	=	$36
Post-depreciation rate ($0.02 = PHP1)		PHP 1,200	=	24
Potential foreign exchange loss			($12)

Alternatively, if the parent company designates the Philippine peso as the subsidiary's functional currency, the potential exchange loss is $23 million. This is based on a positive exposure of PHP2,300 million using the current rate method mandated by FASB No. 52. An exposure report format for the income statement based on similar concepts (suggested by the Management Accounting Practices Committee of the International Federation of Accountants) appears in Exhibit 11-7.

Exhibit 11-6 assumed that the Philippine subsidiary's transactions were denominated solely in pesos. In most foreign operations, however, transactions are done in more than one currency. FX risk is a multidimensional issue: For example, a receivable denominated in New Zealand dollars is unlikely to have the same future value as a receivable in Singapore dollars, even if both have the same face value at the time of sale. To account for these situations, management accountants prepare a variety of exposure reports that distinguish among foreign currency assets and liabilities according to the currencies in which they are denominated. Exhibit 11-8 illustrates a multicurrency exposure report for the Philippine subsidiary, which manufactures a durable good for sales in local, Australian, and American markets. Supplies are imported from Indonesia.

EXHIBIT 11-7	Format for an Income Statement Exposure Forecast

	Items Translated at Current Exchange Rates				Items Translated at Historic Exchange Rates				Total Exposure
Income Statement Category	Local Currency (amount)	Foreign Currency (amount)	Conver- sion Rate	Local Equivalent Rate	Local Currency (amount)	Foreign Currency (amount)	Conversion Rate	Local Equivalent Rate	
Revenues (By Category)									
Less: Cost of Sales (By Category)									
Gross Profit									
Less: Expenses (By Category) Earnings Before Interest and Tax Expense									
Earnings Before Tax									
Tax									
Net Income									
Net Exposed Position									
Net Covered Position									
Net Uncovered Position									

EXHIBIT 11-8	Multicurrency Translation Exposure (in thousands)				
	Philippine Pesos	Australian Dollars	Indonesian Rupiahs	U.S. Dollars	Total[1]
Exposed Assets					
Cash	$ 50,000	–	–	–	$ 50,000
Receivables	45,000	$15,000	–	$40,000	100,000
Inventories	90,000			–	90,000
Total	185,000	$14,000		$40,000	$240,000
Exposed Liabilities					
Short-term payables	$ 20,000	$ 2,500	$ 12,500	$ 5,000	$ 40,000
Long-term debt	50,000			30,000	80,000
Total	$ 70,000	$ 2,500	$ 12,500	$35,000	120,000
Net exposure	$115,000	$12,500	$ (12,500)		

[1]Stated in U.S. dollars at the spot rate effective on the date of the report.

The format of the exposure report in Exhibit 11-8 resembles that in Exhibit 11-5 except that Exhibit 11-8 segregates exposed assets and liabilities by currency of denomination. Balance sheet items are typically expressed in U.S. dollars to facilitate an assessment of the relative magnitudes of the various items.

A multicurrency exposure reporting format offers many advantages over its single currency counterpart. For one thing, the information provided is more complete. Rather than disclosing a single net positive exposure figure of $120 million, the report in Exhibit 11-8 shows that this figure is comprised of several different currency exposures.

Each connotes different exchange risk consequences for the U.S. parent. Also, under a single currency perspective, the positive exposure of $12,500,000 in Australian dollars is combined with the negative exposure of $12,500,000 in Indonesian rupiahs, suggesting a natural offset. This offset is true only if the Australian dollar and Indonesian rupiah move in tandem relative to the U.S. dollar. If they do not, the translation effects could be significantly different.

A multicurrency report also enables the parent company to aggregate similar exposure reports from all its foreign subsidiaries and analyze, on a continual basis, its worldwide translation exposure by national currency. This type of analysis is particularly helpful when local managers are responsible for protection against translation exposure. One can easily imagine a situation where local managers in two foreign subsidiaries may face opposite exposures in the same currency. Multicurrency exposure reports enable a parent company to make sure its local managers avoid hedging activities that are disadvantageous to the company as a whole.

Transaction Exposure

Transaction exposure concerns exchange gains and losses that arise from the settlement of transactions denominated in foreign currencies. Unlike translation gains and losses, transaction gains and losses have a direct effect on cash flows as they result from a currency conversion process.

EXHIBIT 11-9	Multicurrency Transaction Exposure ($ thousands)				
	Philippine Pesos	Australian Dollars	Indonesian Rupiahs	U.S. Dollars	Total
Exposed Assets					
Receivables	$ 45,000	$ 15,000	—	$40,000	$100,000
Inventories	90,000	—	—	—	$ 90,000
Future sales commitments	—	10,000	—	—	10,000
Total	$135,000	$ 25,000		$40,000	$200,000
Exposed Liabilities					
Short-term payables	$ 20,000	$ 2,500	$ 12,500	5,000	$ 40,000
Long-term debt commitments	50,000	—	—	30,000	80,000
Future purchase	—	—	10,000	—	10,000
Leases	—	$ 5,000	—	—	5,000
Total	$ 70,000	$ 7,500	$ 22,500	$35,000	$135,000
Net exposure		$ 17,500	$(22,500)	$ 5,000	

A multicurrency transaction exposure report for our Philippine subsidiary appears in Exhibit 11-9. It includes items that normally do not appear in conventional financial statements but cause transaction gains and losses, such as forward exchange contracts, future purchase and sales commitments, and long-term leases.[14] The exposure report excludes items that do not directly relate to foreign currency transactions (such as cash on hand). A transaction exposure report also has a different perspective than a translation exposure report. A translation exposure report takes the perspective of the parent company. A transaction exposure report takes the perspective of the foreign operation. Exhibit 11-9 focuses on what happens on the books of the Philippine affiliate if the peso changes value relative to the Australian dollar, the Indonesian rupiah, and the U.S. dollar. The peso column is of no concern, as peso transactions are recorded and settled in pesos. A devaluation of the peso relative to the Australian and U.S. dollars will produce transaction gains owing to positive exposures in both currencies. A devaluation of the peso relative to the rupiah would produce a transaction loss, as more pesos would be required to settle the Philippine subsidiary's foreign currency obligations. These transaction gains or losses (net of tax effects) directly impact U.S. dollar earnings upon consolidation.

Centralized control of a firm's overall exchange exposures is possible. This entails having each foreign affiliate send its multicurrency exposure reports to corporate headquarters continually. Once exposures are aggregated by currency and by country, the company can implement centrally coordinated hedging policies to offset potential losses.

Accounting Versus Economic Exposure

The reporting frameworks previously described highlight a firm's exposure to FX risk at a given time. Both translation and transaction exposure reports, however, do not

---

[14] These items are normally disclosed in footnotes to the financial statements.

measure a firm's economic exposure. This is the effect of currency value changes on the future operating performance and cash flows of the firm.

Exhibit 11-9 indicates that the Philippine subsidiary is long on Australian dollars. That is to say, exposed Australian dollar assets exceed exposed Australian dollar liabilities. Based on this report, a financial manager might decide to hedge this position by selling 17.5 million Australian dollars in the forward exchange market. Would this be the right decision? Probably not. Although the Philippine subsidiary is long on Australian dollars, not all the items in the exposure report require an immediate inflow or outflow of Australian dollars. The future sales commitment of $10 million will probably not bring in cash until a later accounting period. Also, the exposure report does not include all Australian dollar receipts or disbursements because future sales denominated in Australian dollars are not considered. Although Australian dollar receivables currently total $15 million, this figure will not stay the same for long. From an external reporting perspective, these future cash flows should not be considered. From an internal reporting perspective, they cannot be ignored.

More and more companies differentiate between exposures that are static and those that are fluid in nature. They prepare multicurrency cash flow statements that enable them to monitor monthly cash receipts and disbursements for each currency in which they do business (see Exhibit 11-10). A traditional exposure report considers the effects of exchange rate changes on account balances as of the financial statement date. A multicurrency cash flow statement emphasizes exposures generated by exchange rate changes during the forthcoming budget period. Cash receipts for each national currency include the collection of current and anticipated credit sales, asset disposals, and other cash-generating activities. Multicurrency cash disbursements incorporate those required for current and anticipated obligations, debt service, and other cash purchases.

EXHIBIT 11-10	Budgeted Cash Flows by Country

Unit/Country: _____ Date: _____

Currency			Budget Periods				
		January	February	March	April	May	June
Philippine pesos	Receipts						
	Payments						
	Net						
Australian dollars	Receipts						
	Payments						
	Net						
Indonesian rupiahs	Receipts						
	Payments						
	Net						
Other	Receipts						
	Payments						
	Net						

The notion of economic exposure recognizes that exchange rate changes affect the competitive position of firms by altering the prices of their inputs and outputs relative to those of their foreign competitors. For example, assume that our hypothetical Philippine subsidiary obtains its labor and material locally. Devaluation of the Philippine peso relative to all other foreign currencies could improve rather than worsen the subsidiary's position. It could increase its exports to Australia and the United States as the devalued peso would make its goods cheaper in terms of the Australian and U.S. dollar. Domestic sales could also rise, because the peso devaluation would make imported goods more expensive in local currency. The devaluation would have no appreciable effect on the cost of local-source inputs. Thus, the future profitability of the Philippine subsidiary might increase because of the currency depreciation. Under these circumstances, booking a transaction loss on a positive translation exposure would distort the economic implications of the peso devaluation.

Alternatively, a German manufacturing affiliate of a U.K. parent, organized to serve the German market, may have a positive translation exposure. Appreciation of the euro relative to the pound would produce a translation gain upon consolidation. If the German affiliate were to source all of its inputs in Germany, its economic exposure would appear to be shielded from exchange risk. Yet, if a major German competitor obtained some of its manufacturing components from Russia, this competitor may enjoy a cost advantage if the rouble were undervalued relative to the deutsche mark.

These examples suggest that economic or operating exposure bears little or no relation to translation and transaction exposure. Accordingly, the management of such exposure will require hedging technologies that are more strategic than tactical in nature.[15]

Companies may opt for structural hedges that involve selecting or relocating manufacturing sites to reduce the operating exposure of the business as a whole. Such actions, however, may require foregoing economies of scale, which could reduce the expected rate of return of the business.

Alternatively, parent companies could take a portfolio approach to risk reduction by selecting businesses that have offsetting exposures.[16] In so doing, the operating exposure of the firm as a whole is minimized. This strategy will necessitate careful review of individual business units' operating results after correcting for the effects of operating exposure. A company may opt to exploit exchange rate volatility by reconfiguring its businesses. The object is to preserve maximum flexibility by being able to increase production and sourcing in countries where currencies become strongly undervalued in real terms. This entails additional costs of relocating production facilities and building excess capacity. On the other hand, these strategic moves reduce average operating costs across a range of exchange rates.

The notion of economic or operating exposure places new burdens on management accountants. Traditional sources will not contain much of the required information. The proper measurement of operating exposure will require an understanding of the structure of the market in which a company and its competitors do business, as well as the

---

[15] Peijie Wang, *The Economics of Foreign Exchange and Global Finance*, Berlin: Springer Publishing Company, 2005.

[16] This portfolio approach is a subset of the portfolio strategy associated with enterprise risk management systems described at the start of this chapter.

effects of real (as opposed to nominal) exchange rates. These effects are hard to measure. As operating exposures tend to be long in duration, uncertain in terms of measurables, and not based on explicit commitments, accountants will have to provide information that spans multiple operating functions and time periods.

PROTECTION STRATEGIES   Once foreign exchange exposures are quantified, the next step is to design hedging strategies that minimize or eliminate such exposures. These strategies include balance sheet, operational, and contractual hedges.

Balance Sheet Hedges   A balance sheet hedge reduces a firm's exposure by adjusting the levels and monetary denomination of a firm's exposed assets and liabilities. For example, increasing cash balances in foreign currency can offset declines in interest rates and income on domestic fixed income instruments. In Exhibit 11-8, a natural hedge against the $115 million positive exposure would be to increase the Philippine subsidiary's peso borrowings by $115 million. In this case the borrowed cash must be remitted to the parent or invested in nonexposed assets, otherwise the net exposed asset position would not change. Other methods of hedging a firm's positive exposure in a subsidiary located in a devaluation-prone country include:

1. Keeping local currency cash balances at the minimum level required to support current operations
2. Remitting profits above those needed for capital expansions back to the parent company
3. Speeding up (leading) the collection of outstanding local currency receivables
4. Deferring (lagging) payments of local currency payables
5. Speeding up the payment of foreign currency payables
6. Investing excess cash in local currency inventories and other assets less subject to devaluation loss
7. Investing in strong currency foreign assets

Operational Hedges   This form of risk protection focuses on variables that impact foreign currency revenues and expenses. Raising selling prices (for sales invoiced in a devaluation-prone currency) in proportion to the anticipated currency depreciation helps protect targeted gross margins. One variation of this theme is invoicing sales in hard currencies. Tighter control of costs affords a larger margin of safety against potential currency losses. A final example includes structural hedges. These entail relocating manufacturing sites to reduce operating exposures of the firm or changing the country in which raw materials or manufacturing components are sourced.

Balance sheet and operational hedging are not costless. Foreign subsidiaries in devaluation-prone countries are frequently urged to minimize their local currency working capital balances (cash and receivables in particular), simultaneously increasing holdings of local currency debt. Such actions, unfortunately, are often disadvantageous. Increased export potential resulting from a devaluation might call for more working capital rather than less. The opportunity cost in lost sales could far exceed any translation loss. Also, local currency borrowing before a devaluation can be extremely expensive. Other foreign subsidiaries usually have similar ideas at the same time and, consequently, the local banking system may accommodate such credit demands only at an excessive cost. Furthermore, bank credit during such periods is usually scarce because most countries impose severe credit restraints to counter the problems that cause devaluation pressures in the first place. The cost of borrowing under these circumstances often exceeds any protection provided.

Strategic hedges also have their limits. One strategy, for example, is to vertically integrate operations to minimize a firm's exposure to exchange rate-sensitive resources. This course of action, however, exposes the firm to additional costs connected with setting up a new foreign affiliate and the potential loss of scale economies. Vertical integration also takes a long time to carry out.

Contractual Hedges   A variety of contractual hedge instruments have been developed to afford managers greater flexibility in managing foreign exchange exposures. Exhibit 11-11 shows some foreign exchange hedge products that have recently appeared. As you can see, managers have plenty of choices to consider.

EXHIBIT 11-11   **Exchange-Related Financial Instruments**

alternative currency option. A currency option that, if exercised, can be settled in one of several alternative currencies at the choice of the option holder.

basket hedging. The use of a basket of currencies (comprising fewer currencies than the hedged portfolio) to offset the risk of all the nonbase currencies in a portfolio.

break forward. An option that allows the buyer to fully participate in the movement of a currency beyond a specified level without having to pay an explicit option premium.

combined interest rate and currency swap (CIRCUS). A transaction in which two counterparties exchange interest payment streams denominated in two different currencies (i.e., exchanging fixed interest payments in one currency for floating rate interest in another).

contingent hedge with an agreement for rebate at maturity (CHARM). A currency option that (1) is exercisable if a bidding company wins the contract or (2) is void if the company loses the contract, where the issuer of the option rebates a portion of the premium. The value of the payoff depends on (1) the buyer's ability to obtain business requiring currency protection and (2) the movement of the underlying currency.

convertible option contract. An option to purchase or sell foreign currency that converts to a forward contract if the forward exchange rate falls below a certain price.

covered option securities (COPS). Short-term obligations that give the issuer the option to repay principal and interest in the original, or a mutually acceptable, currency.

covered interest arbitrage. An agreement in which two counterparties exchange currencies at both the spot and forward rates simultaneously.

cross-currency basis swap. A floating interest rate swap in two currencies.

cross-currency cap. An option in which the holder is paid the positive difference between the spread on two different currency base rates and a strike spread.

currency coupon swap. A fixed to floating coupon swap in two different currencies.

currency option. The right but not the obligation to buy or sell another currency at an agreed-upon strike price within a specified time period.

currency swap. The initial exchange of two currencies and subsequent reexchange of the same currencies at the end of a certain time period.

(continued)

EXHIBIT 11-11	**Exchange-Related Financial Instruments (Continued)**

currency swap option (swaption). An option to buy or sell a currency swap at a specified exchange rate.

dual option bonds. A bond giving the investor the choice of currencies in which to receive interest and principal repayments.

exchange rate agreement (ERA). A synthetic agreement for forward exchange whose value is correlated with the spread between two forward currency exchange rates.

forward exchange contract. A contractual agreement between two parties to exchange a specified amount of currency for another at a fixed date in the future.

futures contract. An exchange-traded contract calling for delivery of a specified amount of currency at a fixed date in the future.

foreign equity option. The right but not the obligation to buy or sell a foreign equity at a specified price on or before a specified date in the future.

indexed currency option notes (ICONS). Bonds that are denominated and pay interest in one currency with redemption value linked to the exchange rate of another currency.

look-back option. The retroactive right to buy a currency at its low point or sell a currency at its high point within the option period.

principal exchange-rate-linked securities (PERLS). Debt instruments paying interest and principal in U.S. dollars where the principal is pegged to the exchange rate between the dollar and another currency.

range forwards. A forward exchange contract specifying a range of exchange rates at which currencies will be exchanged at maturity.

synthetic position. A combined transaction to produce a security with features that could not be obtained directly (e.g., combining a fixed rate debt with a currency swap).

tailored swap. A currency swap in which the notional principle can be adjusted to meet the changing risk exposure of a business.

Source: Adapted from Gary L. Gastineau, Swiss Bank Corporation Dictionary of Financial Risk Management, Chicago: Probus, 1992.

Most of these financial instruments are derivative as opposed to basic in nature. Basic financial instruments, such as repurchase agreements (receivables), bonds, and capital stock, meet conventional accounting definitions of assets, liabilities, and owners' equity. Derivative instruments are contractual arrangements giving rise to special rights or obligations and that derive their value from another financial instrument or commodity. Many are based on contingent events. Accordingly, they do not have the same characteristics as the instrument on which they are based. An example would be a cross-currency basis swap on a principal amount of $100 million. Here the derivative product is the promise to exchange interest payment differentials based upon, but independent of, the underlying principle or notional amount of the respective borrowings. If floating rates were higher than fixed rates, one counterparty would owe the other counterparty the difference. Any amounts owing would depend upon the movement in interest rates. The market for derivatives is a 24-hour global trading market comprised largely of banks. Derivatives traders around the world are interconnected through highly sophisticated electronic and telecommunications systems.

In recent years, numerous surprises occurred in the market for derivatives that dominated the financial headlines. Names such as Long-Term Capital Management,

Merrill Lynch, AIG, UBS, Bear Stearns, and Orange County gained instant notoriety because of the magnitude of the losses they sustained. Prestigious financial institutions such as Goldman Sachs, Morgan Stanley, and Bank of America also made the front page. Reported losses ranged from hundreds of millions of dollars to the billions. While losses related to derivatives have occurred in the past, what is truly distinctive about the current experience is that is is truly global. Reasons for such losses include inadequate control over trader behavior, pricing models that do not incorporate the risks of extreme market movements (discontinuities), market illiquidity, and ultimately the naiveté of directors and senior management as to the nature and risks of these instruments.[17]

Despite these debacles, the derivatives market, currently in excess of $100 trillion in size, continues to grow in sophistication and use. Financial managers of multinational enterprises use these instruments to manage their exposures to exchange risk, especially transactions and economic, as these exposures directly impact a firm's current and future cash flows. Allayannis and Ofek find a strong negative association between foreign currency derivative use and a firm's exchange rate exposure. This suggests that firms use derivatives primarily to hedge rather than speculate in foreign currencies. It also implies that usage of foreign currency derivatives does indeed reduce foreign exchange rate risk.[18] Although we express a preference for hedging transaction and economic exposures, executives appear interested in managing translation exposure as well. They voice concern over reporting lower earnings to shareholders. In a comparative study of derivative usage among German and U.S. companies, minimizing the variability of reported earnings was rated most important among German companies. While U.S. companies tend to use financial derivatives to minimize the variability of cash flow, minimizing the variability of reported earnings was a close second.[19] In a related study, Swedish companies' use of derivatives to hedge the balance sheet (translation exposure) was as prevalent as their use of derivatives for committed and anticipated transactions.[20]

Accounting for Hedge Products

Contractual hedge products are financial contracts or instruments that enable users to minimize, eliminate, or otherwise transfer market risks to someone else's shoulders. They include, but are not limited to, forward contracts, futures, swaps, options, and combinations of these. While many of these derivative instruments have grown in complexity, user surveys document management's preference for the most basic, or vanilla, varieties.[21]

---

[17] Rene M. Stulz, "Risk Management Failures: What Are They and When Do They Happen?" *Journal of Applied Corporate Finance*, Fall 2008, pp. 58–67.
[18] George Allayannis and Eli Ofek, "Echange Rate Exposure, Hedging and the Use of Foreign Currency Derivatives," Journal of International Money and Finance 20 (2001): 273–296.
[19] Reasons for the U.S. emphasis on reported earnings relate to analysts' perceptions and prediction of future earnings and management compensation. In Germany, reported earnings play an important role in taxation and dividend distribution. Gordon M. Bodner and Gunther Gebhardt, "Derivative Usage in Risk Management by US and German Non-Financial Firms: A Comparative Study," Journal of International Financial Management and Accounting 10, no. 3 (1999): 153–187.
[20] Hagelin and Pramborg, op. cit.
[21] Ed McCarthy, "Derivatives Revisited," Journal of Accountancy (May 2000). Also available at www.aicpa. org/pubs/jofa/may 2000/mccarthy.htm.

Knowledge of accounting measurement rules for derivatives is especially important when designing an effective hedge strategy for the firm. To understand the importance of hedge accounting, we illustrate some basic hedge accounting practices.

First, review the basic components of an income statement (absent taxes).

Operating revenues	XXX
− Operating expenses	XXX
= Operating income	XXX
+ Other income	XXX
− Other expense	XXX
= Net income	XXX

Analysts usually focus on operating income in evaluating how well management has operated its core business. Net income includes the confounding effects of extraordinary or nonrecurring events.

The accounting treatment for financial derivatives that is gaining acceptance internationally is to mark that product to market with any gains or losses recognized as a component of nonoperating income. In the United States at least, an exception is permitted in certain instances if the transaction meets appropriate hedge criteria, including the following:

1. The item being hedged exposes the firm to a market risk.
2. The firm describes its hedging strategy.
3. The firm designates the instrument to be employed as a hedge.
4. The firm documents its rationale as to why the hedge is likely to be effective.

If the appropriate criteria are met, the firm can use the gains or losses recognized on marking the hedge product to market to offset the gains or losses on the transaction that is being hedged (e.g., sales or purchases). To illustrate, assume that an Irish manufacturer of stout (a dark malt beverage) has a sales commitment to deliver X barrels to a buyer in the United States in two months. Fearing that the U.S. dollar will devalue before delivery, the Irish manufacturer buys a forward exchange contract that will allow it to sell U.S. dollars in two months' time at a price close to the current price. If the dollar devalues before delivery, the gain on the foreign exchange contract will offset the loss on the sales contract. If the hedging requirements listed above are met, operating income will meet its target. If the criteria are not met, the gain on the forward contract will appear as other income and operating income will come in below target.

Accounting issues associated with FX hedging products relate to recognition, measurement, and disclosure. Recognition centers on whether hedging instruments should be recognized as assets or liabilities in the body of financial statements. There is also the question of whether the hedge product should receive the same accounting treatment as the item being hedged.

Closely related to the recognition issue is the question of measurement. How, for example, should an FX derivative be valued? Should it take on the same measurement basis as the hedged instrument or transaction, or should it reflect an independent valuation? If an independent valuation, which valuation model historical cost, market value, lower of cost or market, net realizable value, or discounted present value is preferable? How should gains or losses related to the FX instrument be reflected in the income statement? Should they be reflected in income at all? Can and should risks associated with financial instruments be recognized and measured? This last question is especially important because risks attaching to many of the newer financial instruments, such as options and futures, are symmetric. Someone's gain is another's loss. Finally, to what extent should buyers and sellers of financial instruments detail the nature and amounts of financial instruments to which they are a party? What attributes of financial instruments should be disclosed in general-purpose financial statements? How much disclosure is necessary to sufficiently inform readers of the nature and magnitude of off-balance-sheet risks associated with corporate financial instruments? We now examine some basic FX risk management products. This is followed by a discussion of appropriate accounting treatments.

FX FORWARD CONTRACTS   Importers and exporters generally use forward exchange contracts when goods invoiced in foreign currencies are purchased from or sold to foreign parties. The forward contract offsets the risk of transaction gains or losses as exchange rates fluctuate between the transaction and settlement dates. Forward contracts also hedge anticipated foreign currency payables or receivables (foreign currency commitments) and can be used to speculate in foreign currencies. These contracts are not traded on any organized exchange and are consequently less liquid than other contracts. On the other hand, they are flexible in contract amount and duration.

A forward exchange contract is an agreement to deliver or receive a specified amount of foreign currency in exchange for domestic currency, on a future date, at a fixed rate called the forward rate. Differences between the forward rate and the spot rate prevailing at the date of the forward contract give rise to a premium (forward rate > spot rate) or a discount (forward rate < spot rate). The premium or discount rate multiplied by the amount of the foreign currency to be received or delivered, the notional amount of the contract, produces a recognizable premium or discount on the forward contract. The forward contract will also give rise to transaction gains or losses whenever the exchange rate prevailing at the transaction date differs from those prevailing at interim financial statement or settlement dates.

The accounting issue here is whether premiums, discounts, gains, or losses on foreign exchange contracts should receive similar or differing treatment for each use identified. Exhibit 11-12 summarizes how these accounting adjustments should be reported under FAS No. 52, now amended by FAS No. 133.

FINANCIAL FUTURES   A financial futures contract is similar in nature to a forward contract. Like a forward, it is a commitment to purchase or deliver a specified quantity of foreign currency at a future date at a set price. Alternatively, it may provide for cash settlement instead of delivery and can be cancelled before delivery by entering into an offsetting contract for the same financial instrument. In contrast to a forward contract, a futures agreement is a standardized contract, involves standardized provisions with respect to size and delivery date, is traded on an organized exchange,[22] is marked to market at the end of each day, and must meet periodic margin requirements. Losses on a

---

[22] Examples include the International Monetary Market in Chicago and newer exchanges such as the New York Futures Exchange, the London International Financial Futures Exchange, the Singapore Money Exchange (SIMEX), the Sydney Futures Exchange, and the MATIF in Paris.

EXHIBIT 11-12	Accounting Treatment of Forward Contracts	
	Gains/Losses	**Discount/Premium[a]**
Unsettled foreign currency transaction	Recognize in current income	Recognize in current income
Identifiable foreign commitment	Recognize in current income	Recognize in current income
Exposed net asset (liability) position		
a. Foreign currency is functional currency	Disclose in separate component of consolidated equity	Same treatment as related gains/losses, or current income
b. Parent currency is functional currency	Recognize in current income	Recognize in current income
Speculation	Recognize in current income[b]	N/A[c]

[a]Normally amortized over the life of the underlying instrument/activity.

[b]Gains/losses in this category are a function of the difference between the forward rate available for the remaining period of the contract and the contracted forward rate (or the forward rate last used to measure a gain or loss on that contract for an earlier period).

[c]Not applicable.

futures contract give rise to a margin call; gains normally give rise to a cash payment. Exhibit 11-13 documents the growing size of this market.[23]

Corporate treasurers generally use futures contracts to shift the risk of price changes to someone else. They can also be used to speculate in anticipated price movements and to exploit short-term anomalies in the pricing of futures contracts.

EXHIBIT 11-13	Currency Derivatives

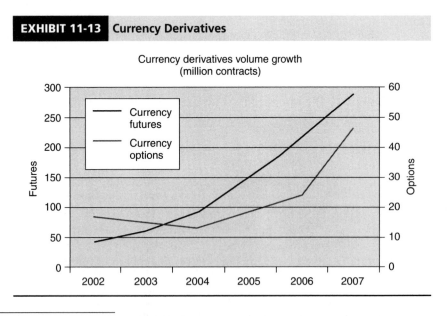

Currency derivatives volume growth
(million contracts)

---

[23] Source: World Federation of Exchanges.

How does a financial futures contract work? If Alpha Corporation borrows yen for three months and wants to protect itself against an appreciation of the yen before maturity, it could buy a futures contract to receive an equal amount of yen in 90 days. Appreciation of the yen causes a gain on the futures contract, offsetting the loss on the yen borrowing.

CURRENCY OPTIONS   A currency option gives the buyer the right to buy (call) or sell (put) a currency from the seller (writer) at a specified (strike) price on or before a specified expiration (strike) date. A European-type option may be exercised only at the expiration date. An American-type option may be exercised any time up to and including the expiration date. The buyer of a call pays a premium for the option and benefits if the price of the underlying asset exceeds the strike price at maturity; the buyer of a put benefits if the price falls below the strike price at the expiration date. Exhibit 11-13 also illustrates the growing size of this market.

To illustrate, suppose a U.S. contractor bids for a CAD100 million construction project in Canada. The outcome of the bid will not be known for three months. Should the Canadian dollar lose value during that time, the contractor will suffer a loss if it wins the fixed price contract. The U.S. contractor therefore buys an option to receive the difference between the future US$/CAD spot rate in 90 days at a strike price of $0.90 per Canadian dollar. The contract details are as follows:

Contract Type	FX CAD Put/U.S.$ Call Option
Maturity	90 days
Strike rate	$0.90 /CAD
Contract amount	$100 million
Option premium	$0.03

If, at maturity, the foreign exchange rate falls to $0.80, the contract holder gains 10 cents per CAD face value of the put contract. In this example, the change in value of the Canadian dollar yields an option payoff of $10,000,000 [($.80 − $0.90) × CAD100 million]. The option premium, which can be viewed as the cost of insuring against a falling Canadian dollar, is $3 million ($0.03 × CAD100 million). By buying the put option, the contractor makes a gain in the value of the option that offsets the potential currency loss (minus the option premium). If the value of the Canadian dollar is unchanged at the strike date, the contractor would simply let the option expire, treating the option premium as a cost of insurance.

Currency options can also be used to manage earnings. Assume an option trader believes the euro will gain in value in the near term. She would buy a naked call. Should the euro appreciate in value by the exercise date, the buyer would exercise the option and pocket the difference between the current and strike price, less the call premium. To limit downside risk, the buyer would obtain a bull call spread. This trading strategy involves buying a call and simultaneously selling an identical call with a higher strike price. The premium paid for the lower strike call will be partly offset by the amount received from the sale of the higher priced call. The maximum profit here is the difference between strike prices less the net premium. The net premium is, in effect, the maximum potential loss on the spread, ignoring transaction costs.

Straddles involve the sale of a call and a put with identical terms. Here the writer of the options bets that exchange rates will not change much during the life of the options. The writer gains revenue from premiums received for writing the options. It is a high-risk strategy, however. If exchange rates change enough to cause one or both of the options to be exercised, the writer's potential loss is unlimited.

CURRENCY SWAPS   A currency swap involves a current and future exchange of two different currencies at predetermined rates. Currency swaps enable companies to access an otherwise inaccessible capital market at a reasonable cost. It also allows a firm to hedge against exchange rate risks arising from international business. Suppose, for example, that Alpha Corporation (a U.S.-based multinational) wishes to raise $10,000,000 of fixed-rate debt in British pounds to fund a newly formed London affiliate. Alpha is relatively unknown to British investors. Similarly, Beta Company, Ltd., domiciled in the United Kingdom, would like to fund a New York subsidiary with a similar amount of dollar financing. It is relatively unknown in the United States. Under these circumstances, Gamma Bank may accommodate both companies by arranging a U.S. dollar/U.K pound currency swap. Assume the following: the swap exchange rate is $1.00 = £ .66 (both at inception and maturity); the swap term is five years; and the swap specifies interest rates of 10 percent in pounds and 8 percent in dollars. The following cash flow pattern would take place. At inception, Alpha Corporation exchanges $10,000,000 for £6,600,000 from Beta Company, Ltd. Assuming interest is paid annually, Alpha pays £660,000 to Beta each year and Beta pays $800,000 to Alpha. At the end of the five-year term, each company would reexchange the principal amounts of $10,000,000 and £6,600,000.

As a result of this swap transaction, both Alpha Corporation and Beta Company, Ltd. have been able to access funds in a relatively inaccessible market. They have done so without incurring exchange rate risk. And, owing to their comparative advantage in borrowing in their home markets, they have achieved their foreign currency borrowings at a lower cost than they could otherwise obtain.

ACCOUNTING TREATMENTS   The FASB issued FAS No. 133, as amended by FAS 138 and clarified by FAS 149, to provide a single comprehensive approach to accounting for derivative and hedge transactions.[24] IAS 39, recently revised, contains similar guidelines providing, for the first time, universal guidance on accounting for financial derivatives.[25] While these two pronouncements are similar in tenor, they differ in terms of the degree of detail in implementation guidance (see Chapter 8 on accounting harmonization).

Before these pronouncements, global accounting standards for derivative products were incomplete, inconsistent, and developed in piecemeal fashion. Most derivative instruments, being executory in nature, were treated as off-balance sheet items.

---

[24] FAS No. 133 supercedes FAS No. 80 and amends FAS No. 52. Financial Accounting Standards Board, "Accounting for Derivative Instruments and Hedging Activities," Statement of Financial Accounting Standards 133, Stamford, CT: FASB, October 1994. FAS No 149 amends and clarifies FAS 133, resulting in more consistent reporting of contracts as either derivatives or hybrid instruments. Financial Accounting Standards Board, "Amendment of Statement 133 on Derivative Instruments and Hedging Activities," Statement of Financial Accounting Standards No. 149, Stamford, CT: FASB, April 2003. Also see FASB's Web site at www.fasb.org.
[25] International Accounting Standards Committee, "Financial Instruments: Recognition and Measurement," International Accounting Standard 39, London: IASC, December 1998. Also see their Web site at http://iasc.org.

An atmosphere of caveat emptor prevailed for statement readers attempting to gauge the volume and risks of derivative usage.

The basic provisions of these standards are as follows:

- All derivative instruments are to be recorded on the balance sheet as assets and liabilities. They are to be recorded at fair value, including those that are embedded in host contracts that are themselves not carried at fair value.
- Gains and losses from changes in the fair value of derivative instruments are not assets or liabilities. They are automatically recognized in earnings if they are not designated as hedges. There are three types of hedging relationships to be recognized, measured, and disclosed: fair value (FV) hedges that include recognized foreign currency assets and liabilities and firm foreign currency commitments, hedges of a net investment in a foreign operation (NI), and cash flow (CF) hedges that include FX-denominated forecasted transactions.
- Hedges must be highly effective to qualify for special accounting treatment; that is, gains or losses on hedging instruments should exactly offset gains or losses on the item being hedged.
- Hedging relationships must be fully documented for the benefit of statement readers. For hedges of recognized foreign currency assets or liabilities and unrecognized firm foreign currency commitments, gains or losses stemming from changes in the fair value of a derivative instrument (and nonderivative financial instruments) are included immediately in earnings. Changes in the value of the foreign currency asset, liability, or firm commitment being hedged are also recognized in current income.
- Gains or losses on hedges of a foreign currency net investment (an exposed net asset or liability position) are initially reported in other comprehensive income. It is subsequently reclassified into current earnings when the subsidiary is sold or liquidated.
- Gains or losses on hedges of uncertain future cash flows, such as forecasted export sales, are initially recognized as an element of comprehensive income. Gains or losses are recognized in earnings when the forecasted transaction affects earnings.

Practice Issues

While authoritative guidelines issued by the FASB and IASB have done much to clarify the recognition and measurement of derivatives, issues remain. The first relates to the determination of fair value. Wallace estimates 64 possible calculations for measuring change in the fair values of the risk being hedged and of the hedging instrument. He identifies four ways to measure changes in the fair value of the risks being hedged: fair market value, use of spot-to-spot exchange rates, use of forward-to-forward exchange rates, and use of an option pricing model. There are as many ways of calculating the change in value of the hedging instrument. Finally, these calculations can be done either before or after taxes.[26]

Financial reporting complexities also arise if hedges are not deemed "highly effective" in offsetting FX risk. However, the term highly effective is a subjective notion. In theory,

---

[26] Jeffrey B. Wallace, "FAS 133: Accounting for Derivative Instruments," in Frederick D.S. Choi, ed., Handbook of International Finance and Accounting, New York: John Wiley and Sons, 2003, pp. 19-1–19-24.

highly effective means a perfect negative correlation between changes in the value or cash flow of a derivative and changes in the value or cash flow of the item being hedged. This implies a range of acceptable value changes for the derivative. The FASB recommends an 80–120% range. If these bounds are violated, the hedge is terminated and deferred gains or losses on the derivative are recognized in current earnings. This, in turn, reintroduces undesired volatility into a firm's reported earnings stream.

Actually, a highly effective hedge may not entirely eliminate the earnings effect of FX changes. To illustrate, assume that the dollar equivalent of a Japanese yen denominated receivable falls by $10,000,000. The forward contract used to offset this FX risk experiences a gain of $10,800,000. Since the gain on the forward falls within the bounds of 80–120%, the forward has been an effective hedge. However, the $800,000 excess gain would be recognized in current income.[27]

Next we illustrate selected accounting treatments for forward contracts used as hedging instruments.

HEDGE OF A RECOGNIZED ASSET, LIABILITY, OR AN UNRECOGNIZED FIRM COMMITMENT

On September 1, a Canadian manufacturer sells, on account, goods to a Mexican importer for 1 million Mexican pesos (MXP). The Canadian dollar/peso exchange rate is CAD0.11 = MXP1. The peso receivable is due in 90 days. The peso begins to depreciate before the receivable is collected. By the end of the month, the Canadian dollar/peso exchange rate is CAD0.10 = MXP1; on December 1 it is CAD0.08 = MXP1. The Canadian exporter expects to receive CAD140,000 for the MXP1,000,000 owed if the spot rate remains unchanged through December 1. To avoid the risk of receiving less than CAD140,000 should the peso lose value before December 1, the Canadian exporter acquires a forward contract on September 1 to deliver MXP1,000,000 for Canadian dollars on December 1 at a forward rate of CAD0.10 = MXP 1. In this example, pesos can be sold only at a discount, as the spot rate is greater than the forward rate. The total discount on the forward contract is CAD10,000 [(CAD0.11 spot rate − CAD0.10 forward rate) X MXP1,000,000 notional amount] and is the price of reducing uncertainty. In effect, the Canadian exporter turns an uncertain receipt of C$140,000 to a certain receipt of CAD130,000. At later financial statement dates before maturity, the forward contract amount (peso liability) is multiplied by the spot rate in effect on those dates. Changes in spot rates cause transaction gains or losses on the forward contract. Thus, if the exchange rate prevailing on December 1 is CAD0.08 = MXP1, the Canadian exporter realizes a gain of CAD30,000 (CAD0.11 spot rate − CAD0.08 future spot rate = MXP1,000,000 liability). Had the forward contract not been purchased, the exporter would have received only CAD110,000 upon conversion of the MXP1,000,000 account receivable. Thus, the forward contract offsets a transaction loss on the foreign currency receivable with a transaction gain on the foreign currency payable.

Exhibit 11-14 provides accounting entries for the forward exchange contract just described, assuming that financial statements are prepared on September 30

---

[27] There are several ways of testing for hedging effectiveness. Details of the dollar offset, variability reduction, and regression methods are described in Finnerty, John D., and Dwight Grant, "Testing Hedging Effectiveness Under SFAS 133," www.nysscpa.org/cpajournal/2003/0403/features/f044033.htm.

EXHIBIT 11-14	Hedge of a Foreign Currency Transaction

Sept. 1	(CAD) Contract receivable	C$130,000	
	Deferred discount	10,000	
	MXP Contract payable		140,000
	(To record agreement with foreign currency dealer to exchange MXP1,000,000 worth CAD140,000 for CAD130,000 in three months.)		
Sept. 30	MXP Contract payable	10,000	
	Transaction (hedge) gain		10,000
	(To record transaction gain from reduced dollar equivalent of forward contract payable CAD0.11 − CAD0.10 × MXP1,000,000)		
Sept. 30	Discount expense	3,333	
	Deferred discount		3,333
	(Amortize deferred discount for one month.)		
Dec. 1	MXP Contract payable	20,000	
	Transaction (hedge) gain		20,000
	(To record additional transaction gain by adjusting contract to new current rate CAD0.10 − CAD0.08 × MXP1,000,000.)		
Dec. 1	Discount expense	6,667	
	Deferred discount		6,667
	(Amortize deferred discount balance)		
Dec. 1	MXP Contract payable	110,000	
	Mexican pesos		110,000
	(To record delivery of MXP1,000,000 to foreign currency dealer; this MXP1,000,000 is obtained from collecting the amount owed by the Mexican importer.)		
Dec. 1	Cash	130,000	
	(CAD) Contract receivable		130,000
	(To record receipt of CAD130,000 cash per forward contract.)		

prior to settlement of the peso transaction. The exchange rate on September 30 is CAD 0.10 = MXP1.

Assuming that the discount is treated as an element of operating expense, the net effect of the hedge transaction on operating income (ignoring any foreign exchange commissions) is determined as follows:

Dollar equivalent of receivable collected from Mexican importer	CAD110,000
Transaction gains on forward contract	30,000
Proceeds from sales commitment	140,000
Discount on forward contract	(10,000)
Operating income	CAD130,000

Gains on the forward contract have effectively offset the devaluation of the peso. Expected gross margins and operating income are attained. The discount on the forward contract represents the cost of hedging FX risk.

A similar accounting treatment would prevail if our Canadian exporter were to make a sales agreement on September 1 to deliver goods and receive payment of MXP1,000,000 from the Mexican importer three months in the future rather than immediately delivering goods and waiting for payment. This type of executory contract is known as a foreign currency commitment.

Alternatively, the preceding illustration might have taken the form of a forecasted export sale. This expectation is not the result of a past transaction nor is it the result of a firm sales commitment. It represents an uncertain future cash flow (an anticipated transaction). Hence, the gains or losses on the forward contract to hedge the forecasted peso receipts would initially be recorded in equity as a part of comprehensive income. These amounts would be reclassified into current earnings in the period in which the export sales are actually recognized.

HEDGE OF A NET INVESTMENT IN A FOREIGN OPERATION

As discussed in Chapter 6, whenever a foreign subsidiary with an exposed net asset position is consolidated with its parent, a translation loss results if the foreign currency loses value relative to the parent currency. A translation loss also occurs if the foreign subsidiary has an exposed net liability position and the foreign currency appreciates relative to the parent currency. One way to minimize such losses is to buy a forward contract. The strategy here is to have transaction gains realized on the forward contract offset translation losses.

To illustrate, suppose that a U.S. calendar-year foreign affiliate in Japan has a net exposed liability position of JPY135,000,000 at September 30. Its functional currency is the dollar. To minimize any translation loss triggered by an unexpected appreciation of the yen, the U.S. parent buys a forward contract to receive 135,000,000 yen in 90 days at the forward rate of $.010692. Exchange rates to the end of the year are as follows:

September 30 spot =	$.010680
September 30 90-day forward =	$.010692
December 31 spot =	$.010762

A transactions analysis of this hedge appears in Exhibit 11-15.

This example abstracts from tax effects. The expected translation loss of $11,070 (net exposed liabilities of [JPY135,000,000 X ($.010762 − $.010680)] is offset by a transaction gain on the forward contract of $11,070 minus the premium expense of $1,620. If the foreign currency had been the functional currency, any exchange adjustment arising from consolidation would bypass income and appear in other comprehensive income. Under these circumstances, transaction gains and losses on forward hedges and related premiums/discounts would also be reflected in other comprehensive income.

EXHIBIT 11-15	Hedge of a Net Exposed Liability Position	

September 30	JPY Contract receivable	$1,441,800
	Deferred premium	1,620
	$ Contract payable	$1,443,420
	(To record contract with foreign currency dealer to exchange $1,443,420 for JPY135,000,000 in 90 days)	
December 31	JPY Contract receivable	11,070
	Transaction hedge gain	11,070
	(To record transaction gain from increased dollar equivalent of forward contract receivable; $.010762 − $.010680 × JPY135,000,000.)	
December 31	Premium expense	1,620
	Deferred premium	1,620
	(Amortization of deferred premium.)	
December 31	$ Contract payable	1,443,420
	Cash	1,443,420
	(To record purchase of JPY135,000,000.)	
December 31	Foreign currency	1,452,870
	JPY Contract receivable	1,452,870
	Cash	1,452,870
	Foreign currency	1,452,870
	(To record receipt of JPY135,000,000 from foreign currency dealer and its conversion.)	

SPECULATING IN FOREIGN CURRENCY

Opportunities exist for enhancing reported earnings using forward and option contracts in FX markets.[28] The forward contract in the previous example would not qualify for hedge accounting treatment had it been purchased solely to profit from an expected appreciation of the yen. Forward contracts bought as speculations are initially recorded at the forward rate. (The forward rate is the best indicator of the spot rate that will apply when the contract matures.) Transaction gains or losses recognized prior to settlement depend on the difference between the initial forward rate and the rate available for the remaining period of the contract.

Suppose that our speculator in yen (Exhibit 11-15) prepares monthly and year-end financial statements. All facts remain the same except that the 60-day forward rate for yen is $.010688 at the end of October. The Contract receivable would be initially recorded at the 90-day forward rate, or $1,443,420. At the end of October, the transaction gain on the forward contract would be $540 or JPY135,000,000 X [$.010692 (90-day forward rate on September 30) − $.010688 (60-day forward rate on October 31)]. It is

---

[28] Dilip K. Ghosh and Augustine C. Arize, "Profit Possibilities in Currency Markets: Arbitrage, Hedging and Speculation," The Financial Review 38 (2003): 473–496.

recognized in current income. As the foreign currency contract is recorded at the forward rate, no discounts or premiums are recognized.

Accounting treatments for the other foreign currency instruments discussed are similar to that for forward contracts. The accounting treatment prescribed is based on the nature of the hedging activity; that is, whether the derivative hedges a firm commitment, a forecasted transaction, a net investment in a foreign operation, and so on.

A measurement complication arises in measuring the fair value and changes in fair values of hedging instruments when financial derivatives are not actively traded. For example, measurement of the gains or losses associated with an option contract depends on whether the option is traded on or off a major exchange. Valuation of an option is readily done when the option is quoted on a major exchange. Valuation is more difficult when the option is traded over-the-counter. Here, one must generally rely on mathematical pricing formulas. The so-called Black–Scholes options pricing model makes it possible to value an option at any time.

DISCLOSURE

Prior to pronouncements such as FAS 133 and IAS 39, corporate financial disclosures did not tell statement readers whether, or the extent to which, management had employed derivative contracts. Assessing their potential impact on reported performance and a firm's risk complexion was difficult. Required disclosures under FAS 133 and IAS 39 remedy this to a large extent. They include the following:

- Risk management objective and strategy for undertaking hedge transactions.
- Description of the item being hedged.
- Identification of the hedged items market risk.
- Description of the hedge instrument.
- Amounts that are excluded from the assessment of a hedge's effectiveness.
- A priori justification that a hedging relationship will be highly effective in minimizing market risk.
- Ongoing assessment of the actual hedging effectives of all derivatives used during the period.

Selected excerpts from Coca-Cola's recent annual report appear in Exhibit 11-16. It illustrates corporate disclosure practices with respect to hedge instruments.

EXHIBIT 11-16   **Coca-Cola's Risk Management Disclosures**

Our Company recognizes all derivative instruments as either assets or liabilities in our consolidated balance sheets at fair value. The accounting for changes in fair value of a derivative instrument depends on whether it has been designated and qualifies as part of a hedging relationship and, further, on the type of hedging relationship. At the inception of the hedging relationship, the Company must designate the instrument as a fair value hedge, a cash flow hedge, or a hedge of a net investment in a foreign operation. This designation is based upon the exposure being hedged.

We have established strict counterparty credit guidelines and enter into transactions only with financial institutions of investment grade or better. We monitor counterparty exposures daily and review any downgrade in credit rating immediately. If a downgrade in the credit rating of a counterparty were to occur, we have provisions requiring collateral in the form of U.S. government securities for substantially all of our transactions. To mitigate presettlement risk, minimum credit standards become more stringent as the duration of the derivative financial instrument increases. To minimize the concentration of credit risk, we enter into derivative transactions with a portfolio of financial institutions. The Company has master netting agreements with most of the financial institutions that are counterparties to the derivative instruments. These agreements allow for the net settlement of assets and liabilities arising from different transactions with the same counterparty. Based on these factors, we consider the risk of counterparty default to be minimal.

Interest Rate Management

Our Company monitors our mix of fixed-rate and variable-rate debt as well as our mix of short-term debt versus long-term debt. This monitoring includes a review of business and other financial risks. From time to time, in anticipation of future debt issuances, we may manage our risk to interest rate fluctuations through the use of derivative financial instruments. During 2008, the Company discontinued a cash flow hedging relationship on interest rate locks, as it was no longer probable that we would issue the long-term debt for which these hedges were designated. As a result, the Company reclassified a previously unrecognized gain of approximately $17 million from AOCI to earnings as a reduction to interest expense. Additionally, during 2008 the Company recognized losses of approximately $9 million related to the portion of cash flow hedges deemed to be ineffective as an increase to interest expense.

Any ineffective portion, which was not significant, of these instruments during 2007 and 2006 was immediately recognized in net income.

Foreign Currency Management

The purpose of our foreign currency hedging activities is to reduce the risk that our eventual U.S. dollar net cash inflows resulting from sales outside the United States will be adversely affected by changes in foreign currency exchange rates.

We enter into forward exchange contracts and purchase foreign currency options (principally euro and Japanese yen) and collars to hedge certain portions of forecasted cash flows denominated in foreign currencies. The effective portion of the changes in fair value for these contracts, which have been designated as foreign currency cash flow hedges, was reported in AOCI and reclassified into earnings in the same financial statement line item and in the same period or periods during which the hedged transaction affects earnings. The Company did not discontinue any foreign currency cash flow hedging relationships during the years ended December 31, 2008, 2007 and 2006. Any ineffective portion, which was not significant in 2008, 2007 or 2006, of the change in the fair value of these instruments was immediately recognized in net income.

Additionally, the Company enters into forward exchange contracts that are effective economic hedges and are not designated as hedging instruments under SFAS No. 133. These instruments are used to offset the earnings impact relating to the variability in foreign currency exchange rates on certain monetary assets and liabilities denominated in nonfunctional currencies. Changes in the fair value of these instruments are immediately recognized in earnings in the line item other income (lose)—net of our consolidated statements of income to offset the effect of remeasurement of the monetary assets and liabilities.

The Company also enters into forward exchange contracts to hedge its net investment position in certain major currencies. Under SFAS No. 133, changes in the fair value of these instruments are recognized in foreign currency translation adjustment, a component of AOCI, to offset the change in the value of the net investment being hedged. For the years ended December 31, 2008, 2007 and 2006, we recorded net gain (loss) in foreign currency translation adjustment related to those instruments of approximately $3 million, $(7) million and $3 million, respectively.

Commodities

The Company enters into commodity futures and other derivative instruments to mitigate exposure to fluctuations in commodity prices and other market risks.

We purchase commodity futures to hedge forecasted cash flows related to future purchases of certain commodities. The effective portion of the changes in fair value for these contracts, which have been designated as commodity cash flow hedges, are reported in AOCI and reclassified into earnings in the same financial statement line item and in the same period or periods during which the hedged transaction affects earnings. The Company did not discontinue any commodity cash flow hedging relationships during the years ended December 31, 2008, 2007 and 2006. Any ineffective portion, which was not significant in 2008, 2007 and 2006, of the change in the fair value of these instruments was immediately recognized in net income.

The following tables present the carrying values, fair values and maturities of the Company's derivative instruments outstanding as of December 31, 2008 and 2007 (in millions):

	Carrying Values Assets/(Liabilities)[1]	Fair Values Assets/(Liabilities)[1]	Maturity
2008			
Foreign currency forward contracts	$(124)	$(124)	2009–2010
Foreign currency options and collars	12	12	2009–2010
Interest rate locks	(43)	(43)	2009
Commodity futures	(42)	(42)	2009–2010
Other derivative instruments	(17)	(17)	2009
	$(214)	$(214)	

[1] Does not include the impact of approximately $8 million of cash collateral held or placed with the same counterparties.

	Carrying Values Assets/(Liabilities)	Fair Values Assets/(Liabilities)	Maturity
2007			
Foreign currency forward contracts	$(58)	$(58)	2008–2009
Foreign currency options and collars	46	46	2008
Interest rate locks	—	—	N/A
Commodity futures	1	1	2008
Other derivative instruments	28	28	2008
	$17	$17	

The Company estimates the fair values of its derivatives based on quoted market prices or pricing models using current market rates, and records them as prepaid expenses and other assets or accounts payable and accrued expenses in our consolidated balance sheets. The amounts recorded reflect the effect of legally enforceable master netting agreements that allow the

Company to settle positive and negative positions and cash collateral held or placed with the same counterparties. As of December 31, 2008, we had approximately $5 million reflected in prepaid expenses and other assets and $211 million reflected in accounts payable and accrued expenses. Refer to Note 12.

Summary of AOCI

For the years ended December 21, 2008, 2007 and 2006, we recorded a net gain (loss) to AOCI of approximately $(6) million, $(59) million and $(31) million, respectively, net of both income taxes and reclassifications to earnings, primarily related to gains and losses on foreign currency cash flow hedges. These items will generally offset the variability of the cash flows relating to the underlying exposures being hedged in future periods. The Company estimates that it will reclassify into earnings during the next 12 months losses of approximately $31 million from the after-tax amount recorded in AOCI as of December 31, 2008, as the anticipated cash flows occur.

The following table summarizes the activity in AOCI related to derivatives designated as cash flow hedges held by the Company during the applicable periods (in millions):

	Before-Tax Amount	Income Tax	After-Tax Amount
2008			
Accumulated derivative net gains (losses) as of January 1, 2008	$(112)	$43	$(69)
Net changes in fair value of derivatives	(62)	23	(39)
Net reclassification from AOCI into earnings	53	(20)	33
Accumulated derivative net gains (losses) as of December 31, 2008	$(121)	$46	$(75)

	Before-Tax Amount	Income Tax	After-Tax Amount
2007			
Accumulated derivative net gains (losses) as of January 1, 2007	$(16)	$6	$(10)
Net changes in fair value of derivatives	(158)	61	(97)
Net reclassification from AOCI into earnings	62	(24)	38
Accumulated derivative net gains (losses) as of December 31, 2007	$(112)	$43	$(69)

	Before-Tax Amount	Income Tax	After-Tax amount
2006			
Accumulated derivative net gains (losses) as of January 1, 2006	$35	$(14)	$21
Net changes in fair value of derivatives	(38)	15	(23)
Net reclassification from AOCI into earnings	(13)	5	(8)
Accumulated derivative net gains (losses) as of December 31, 2006	$(16)	$6	$(10)

FINANCIAL CONTROL

Any financial risk management strategy must evaluate the effectiveness of hedging programs. Feedback from a thoughtful evaluation system helps to build institutional experience in risk management practices. Performance assessment of risk management programs also provides information on when existing strategies are no longer appropriate.

FINANCIAL CONTROL POINTS   There are several areas where performance evaluation systems are fruitful. These include, but are not limited to, corporate treasury, purchasing, and foreign subsidiaries. Control of corporate treasury includes assessing the performance of the total exchange risk management program. This assessment includes quantifying all exposures that were managed, identifying the hedges that were applied, and reporting on hedging results. Such an evaluation system also includes documentation of how and to what extent corporate treasury assisted other business units in the organization.

To illustrate, suppose the sales manager for the consumer markets division of Worldwide Company wishes to grant customer X a line of credit. Corporate treasury, which secures the needed funds, would quote the sales manager an internal transfer price. This price is based on current market rates for loans of comparable risk. Assume this rate is 8 percent. The sales manager can then quote customer X a borrowing rate of 8 percent plus a markup as compensation for assessing the client's credit risk. In the meantime, corporate treasury will enter the money markets and try to obtain a more favorable rate than it quoted the sales manager. The total return on this transaction includes the profit margin on the sale plus the financing spread. Management accountants need to set up a responsibility accounting system that credits the sales manager and corporate treasury for their fair share of the total profit on the sales transaction.[29]

Similar considerations apply to the purchasing function. Here, exchange risk management services are just one piece of the total risk management program. Controls are also necessary to monitor the performance of programs designed to hedge commodity price risk and mix.

In many organizations, foreign exchange risk management is centralized at corporate headquarters. This allows subsidiary managers to concentrate on their core business. However, when comparing actual to expected results, evaluation systems must have benchmarks against which to compare the success of corporate risk protection. (See Chapter 10 for more on multinational performance evaluation systems.)

APPROPRIATE BENCHMARKS

The object of risk management is to achieve an optimal balance between risk reduction and costs. Hence, appropriate standards against which to judge actual performance are necessary ingredients in any performance appraisal system. These benchmarks need to be specified in advance of any protection program and should be based on the concept

---

[29] If, for example, corporate treasury tries to beat the 8 percent benchmark rate but instead pays 9 percent, the sales manager should not be charged for the reduced spread.

of opportunity cost. In foreign exchange risk management, the following questions should be considered when selecting a benchmark:[30]

- Does the benchmark represent a policy that could have been followed?
- Can the benchmark be specified in advance?
- Does the benchmark provide a lower cost strategy than some other alternative?

When FX risk-management programs are centralized, appropriate benchmarks against which to compare the success of corporate risk protection would be programs that local managers could have implemented. In other cases, firms that are averse to foreign exchange risk might automatically hedge any foreign exposure in the forward market or borrow local currency. These strategies would also be natural benchmarks against which to appraise financial risk management. The performance of a certain hedge product (e.g., a currency swap), or that of a risk manager, would be judged by comparing the economic return earned on the actively hedged transaction against the economic return that would have been earned had the benchmark treatment been used.

REPORTING SYSTEMS   Financial risk reporting systems must be able to reconcile both internal reporting and external reporting systems. Risk management activities (typically managed by corporate treasury) have a future orientation. However, they must eventually reconcile with exposure measurements and financial accounts for external reporting purposes. These normally fall under the jurisdiction of the corporate controller's department. A team approach is most effective in formulating financial risk objectives, performance standards, and monitoring and reporting systems. Financial risk management is a prime example of where corporate finance and accounting are closely connected.

Discussion Questions

1. What is market risk? Illustrate this risk with a foreign exchange example.
2. Your company has just decided to purchase 50 percent of its inverntory from China and purchases will be invoiced in Chinese yuan. What four processes do you need to consider in designing a foreign exchange risk protection system?
3. Compare and contrast the terms translation, transaction, and economic exposure. Does FAS No. 52 resolve the issue of accounting versus economic exposure?
4. List 10 ways to reduce a firm's foreign exchange exposure for a foreign affiliate located in a devaluation-prone country. In each instance, identify the cost–benefit trade-offs that need to be measured.
5. Explain, in your own words, the difference between a multicurrency translation exposure report and a multicurrency transactions exposure report.
6. Explain how a company might use a currency swap to hedge its foreign exchange risk on a foreign currency borrowing.
7. What is a financial futures contract? How does it differ from a forward exchange contract?
8. Identify three major types of hedges recognized by IAS 39 and FAS 133 and describe their accounting treatments.
9. All hedging relationships must be "highly effective" to qualify for special accounting treatment. What is meant by the term highly

---

[30] Ian Cooper and Julian Franks, "Treasury Performance Measurement," The Treasurer (February 1988): 56.

effective and why is its measurement important for financial managers?

10. The notion of an "opportunity cost" was perhaps first introduced to you in your first course in microeconomics. Explain how this notion can be applied in evaluating the effectiveness of FX risk hedging programs.

Exercises

1. Refer to Exhibit 11-1 which discloses the risk management paradigm for Infosys Technologies. Explain in your own words what each step of the cycle entails, including the feedback loop from the last to the first step.

2. Reexamine the Risk-Mapping Cube in Exhibit 11-3. Provide examples of how the various market risks—foreign exchange, interest rate, commodity price, and equity price—might affect the value driver: current assets.

3. As one of your first assignments as a new hire on the corporate treasurer's staff of Global Enterprises, Ltd., you are asked to prepare an exchange rate forecast for the Zonolian ecru (ZOE). Specifically, you are expected to forecast what the spot rate for the ecru is likely to be at the end of 2011. Selected information on which to base your forecast follows. Be sure to identify any additional bases underlying your forecast and any assumptions.

4. Exhibit 11-5 contains a hypothetical balance sheet of a foreign subsidiary of a U.S. MNC. Exhibit 11-6 shows how the foreign exchange loss is determined assuming the parent company employs the temporal method of currency translation.

   Required: Demonstrate how the exchange gains or losses would be computed under each of the other translation methodologies.

5. Following is the consolidated balance sheet (000s omitted) of Worberg Bank, a U.S. financial institution with wholly owned corporate affiliates in London and Jerusalem. Cash and due from banks includes ILS100,000 and a £ 40,000 bank overdraft. Loans consist entirely of Israeli shekel receivables while consolidated deposits include ILS40,000 and £ 15,000. Worberg Bank adopts the local currency as the functional currency for its foreign affiliates and so translates all assets and liabilities (including owners' equity) using the current

Worberg Bank Consolidated Balance Sheet as of Year-End (000)

	2006	2007	2008	2009	2010	2011
Visible trade balance (ZOEbn)	7.1	6.5	0.6	27.7	25.4	
Current account balance (ZOEbn)	21.6	21.9	27.3	215.8	213.8	
Foreign direct investment (ZOEbn)	9.5	9.2	12.8	11.3	11.6	
Portfolio flows (ZOEbn)	29.7	13.4	5.0	20.6	9.6	
Foreign exchange reserves (ZOEbn)	15.25	19.18	28.14	31.46	30.99	
Real GDP growth (% change yoy)	26.20	5.09	6.80	4.80	3.70	
Consumer prices (% changes yoy)	51.97	27.70	15.72	18.60	12.32	
Nominal GDP (ZOEbn)	266.0	335.0	412.0	415.0	479.0	
Nominal exchange rate to U.S.$	6.42	7.60	7.92	9.15	9.55	?

Cash and due from banks	$ 20,000	Deposits	$ 50,000
Loans	100,000		
Fixed assets	30,000	Owners' equity	100,000
Total	150,000		150,000

rate. The exchange rate prevailing as of the balance sheet date was (£/$/ILS= 1/2/4).

Required: Prepare a multicurrency exposure report for Worberg Bank.

6. Refer to Exercise 5. Assume that the shekel is forecast to devalue such that the new exchange relationship after the devaluation is (£ /$/ILS = 1/2/8).

Required: Calculate the consolidated gain or loss that would result from this exchange rate movement.

7. Trojan Corporation USA borrowed 1,000,000 New Zealand dollars (NZ$) at the beginning of the calendar year when the exchange rate was $0.60 = NZ$1. Before repaying this one-year loan, Trojan learns that the NZ dollar has appreciated to $0.70 = NZ$1. It discovers, also, that its New Zealand subsidiary has an exposed net asset position of NZ$ 3,000,000, which will produce a translation gain upon consolidation. What is the amount of the exchange gain or loss that will be reported in consolidated income if:
   a. the U.S. dollar is the foreign operation's functional currency?
   b. the New Zealand dollar is the foreign operation's functional currency and Trojan Corporation. designates the New Zealand dollar borrowing as a hedge of the New Zealand affiliate's positive exposure?

8. On April 1, Anthes Corporation, a calendar-year U.S. electronics manufacturer, invests 30 million yen in a three-month yen-denominated CD with a fixed coupon of 8 percent. To hedge against the depreciation of the yen prior to maturity, Anthes designates its accounts payable due to the Sando Company as a hedge. Anthes Corporation. purchased 32.5 million yen worth of computer chips on account paying 10 percent down, the balance to be paid in three months. Interest at 8 percent per annum is payable on the unpaid foreign currency balance. The U.S. dollar/Japanese yen exchange rate on April 1 was $1.00 = ¥100; on July 1 it was $ 1.00 = ¥90.

Required: Prepare dated journal entries in U.S. dollars to record the incurrence and settlement of this foreign currency transaction assuming that the hedge is deemed highly effective in reducing Alexaa's FX risk.

9. On June 1, ACL International, a U.S. confectionery products manufacturer, purchases on account bulk chocolate from a Swiss supplier for 166,667 Swiss francs (CHF) when the spot rate is $0.90 = CHF 1. The Swiss franc payable is due on September 1. To minimize its exposure to an exchange loss should the franc appreciate relative to the dollar prior to payment, ACL International acquires a forward contract to exchange $103,334 for francs on September 1 at a forward rate of $0.92 = CHF 1.

Required: Given the following exchange rate information, provide journal entries to account for the forward exchange contract on June 1, June 30, and September 1. The company closes its books quarterly.

June 30 spot rate $0.91 =	CHF 1
September 1 spot rate $0.93 =	CHF 1

What is the effective dollar cost of the Swiss chocolate purchase in Exercise 7? Show your calculations.

10. In June, Mu Corporation, a U.S. manufacturer of specialty confectionery products, submits a bid to supply a prestigious retail merchandiser with boxed chocolates for the traditional Valentine's Day. At the time the spot rate for francs was $0.89 = CHF1. If it secures the contract, it will sign a contract with a large Swiss chocolate manufacturer to buy the necessary raw material. The outcome of the bidding will not be known for two months and the treasurer of Mu Corporation is concerned that the franc may rise in value during the interim, thus reducing (or possibly even eliminating) its planned profit on the fixed-price bid.

To protect his company against an appreciation of the franc, the treasurer buys 25 CHF September 30 option calls at 1.80 (i.e., a premium of 1.8 cents per franc) on a standard contract amount of CHF 62,500. His prediction proves accurate as the franc rises in value to 91.6 cents by the end of August. Rather than await the outcome of the bid, Mu Corporation exercises its call options at the end of August.

Required: Provide the nessary journal entries to record the acquisition and exercise of the options.

CASES

Case 11-1

Exposure Identification

You have just landed a summer internship (congratulations) with the management information services group of Pirelli, the Italian global tire manufacturer. Management is acutely aware of the importance of risk management and the market's concern with enterprise risk. Although the firm has an active hedging program, management is interested in an impartial assessment of the company's risk exposure from a layman's point of view. Accordingly, your supervisor asks you to take a look at the company's published financial statements and accompanying notes appearing in its 2008 annual report. You are to identify as many exposures as you can that impact the company using the worksheet format provided below. To sensitize you to the company's current risk management programs, you are also asked to identify the exposures that the company is currently hedging. Pirelli's annual report can be assessed online at www. Pirelli.com.

Annual report page number	Value driver	Market Risk

Case 11-2

Value at Risk: What Are Our Options?

The scene is a conference room on the 10th floor of an office building on Wall Street, occupied by Anthes Enterprises, a small, rapidly growing manufacturer of electronic trading systems for equities, commodities, and currencies.

The agenda for the 8:00 A.M. meeting concerns reporting issues associated with a potential sales contract for the stock exchange in the Slovak Republic, which wants to upgrade its technology to effectively participate in the globalization of financial markets. In attendance are Anthes Enterprise's COO Shevon Estwick, Controller Sy Jones, Treasurer, Bebi Karimbaksh, and Vice President of Marketing Autherine Allison.

SHEVON: Thank you for agreeing to meet on such short notice. Autherine, are you ready to give us an update on Slovakia?

AUTHERINE: You mean the Slovak Republic.

SHEVON: Yes.

AUTHERINE: I think there is a 90 percent chance we'll land the contract. Things move a little slowly over there and they're still concerned about some of the legal details of our sales contract. I think they find the legalese a bit intimidating and I can't say I blame them. I've scheduled another trip next month to go over contract details. This time I'm taking our legal counsel and have asked him to prepare another draft expressed in terms that are easier to understand. They're also waiting for approvals from their Central Bank, which has to approve major transactions such as this one.

SHEVON: Good. Are we prepared to deliver on the contract?

AUTHERINE: Yes, we've lined up the financing, have done our credit checks, and the equipment and installation teams are ready to proceed on two week's notice.

SHEVON: Given the size of the contract, are we hedged against the possibility of a devaluation?

BEBI: Yes, we've written a put option on the koruna for 90 days.

SHEVON: Do we think we'll close on the deal before then?

BEBI: Autherine doesn't think so, but you never know. The problem is no one will write an option for a longer term. We'll renew the option as we have other transactions of this extended duration.

SHEVON: Sy, are we all right on the reporting front?

SY: Not really.

SHEVON: How's that?

SY: It looks like we're up against a reporting standard that requires that gains or losses on cash flow hedges whose maturities do not match that of the underlying be recognized in current earnings.

SHEVON: Come again?

SY: The bottom line is that we won't be able to treat gains or losses on our put options as a part of comprehensive income, but we'll have to recognize them in current earnings.

SHEVON: Won't that mess up our bottom line?

SY: I'm afraid so. There would be no offsetting gain or loss from our anticipated sale.

BEBI: It's taken me a whole year to get to know the right people

SY: That may be, but we just can't find anyone who's willing to write an option for more than 90 days at a time.

SHEVON: I don't want to think about what the accounting will do to our stock price! I mean, we're about to float our first Euro-equity issue. A lower offering price would be disastrous at this stage of our development, not to mention the effect on our shareholders.

AUTHERINE: Given the nature of our business, I don't think the transactions side of our business will change much.

SHEVON: Do you think it would be worthwhile having a consultant advise us on this one?

SY, AUTHERINE, AND BEBI (IN UNISON)
Why not?

SHEVON: When you do, would you show that individual the following pages that I ripped out from an nnual report I just received as a shareholder and see if it has any information value? (see attachment)

Required

As a consultant for Anthes Enterprises, identify what you believe are promising hedge accounting options.

Attachment: Torn Pages from the Annual Report of a Major U.S. Manufacturer

First page: Note 10:

We are exposed to the risk of loss arising from adverse changes in:

- commodity prices, affecting the cost of our raw materials and energy,
- foreign exchange risks,
- interest rates,
- stock prices, and
- discount rates affecting the measurement of our pension and retiree medical liabilities.

In the normal course of business, we manage these risks through a variety of strategies, including the use of derivatives. Certain derivatives are designated as either cash flow or fair value hedges and qualify for hedge accounting treatment, while others do not qualify and are marked to market through earnings.

For cash flow hedges, changes in fair value are deferred in accumulated other comprehensive loss within shareholders' equity until the underlying hedged item is recognized in net income. For fair value hedges, changes in fair value are recognized immediately in earnings, consistent with the underlying hedged item. Hedging transactions are limited to an underlying exposure. As a result, any change in the value of our derivative financial instruments would be substantially offset by an opposite change in the value of the underlying hedged items. Hedging ineffectiveness and a net earnings impact occur when the change in the value of the hedge does not offset the change in the value of the underlying hedged item. If the derivative instrument is terminated, we continue to defer the related gain or loss and include it as a component of the cost of the underlying hedged item. Upon determintation that the hedged item will not be part of an actual transaction, we recognize the related gain or loss in net income in that period. We also use derivatives that do not qualify for hedge accounting treatment. We account for such derivatives at market value with the resulting gains and losses reflected in our income statement. We do not use derivative instruments for trading or speculative purposes and we limit our exposure to individual counterparties to manage credit risk.

Commodity Prices We are subject to commodity price risk because our ability to recover increased costs through higher pricing may be limited in the competitive environment in which we operate. This risk is managed through the use of fixed-price purchase orders, pricing agreements, geographic diversity and derivatives. We use derivatives, with terms of no more than two years, to economically hedge price fluctuations related to a portion of our anticipated commodity purchases, primarily for natural gas and diesel fuel. For those derivatives that are designated as cash flow hedges, any ineffectiveness is recorded immediately. However our commodity cash flow hedges have not had any significant ineffectiveness for all periods presented. We classify both the earnings and cash flow impact from these derivatives consistent with the underlying hedged item. During the next 12 months, we expect to reclassify gains of $24 million related to cash flow

hedges from accumulated other comprehensive loss into net income.

Foreign Exchange Our operations outside of the U.S. generate over a third of our net revenue of which Mexico, the United Kingdom and Canada comprise nearly 20%. As a result, we are exposed to foreign currency risks from unforeseen economic changes and political unrest. On occasion, we enter into hedges, primarily forward contracts with terms of no more than two years, to reduce the effect of foreign exchange rates. Ineffectiveness on these hedges has not been material. *(rest of page torn off)*

Partial second page:

Our Divisions We manufacture or use contract manufacturers, market and sell a variety of slaty, sweet and grain-based snacks, carbonated and non-carbonated beverages, and foods through our North American and international business divisions. Our North American divisions include the United States and Canada. The accounting policies for the divisions are the same as those described in Note 2, except for certain allocation methodologies for stock-based compensation expense and pension and retiree medical expense, as described in the unaudited information in "Our Critical Accounting Policies." Additionally, beginning in the fourth quarter of 2005, we began centrally managing commodity derivatives on behalf of our divisions. Certain of the commodity derivatives, primarily those related to the purchase of energy for use by our divisions, do not qualify for hedge accounting treatment. These derivative hedge underlying commodity price risk and were not entered into for speculative purposes. Such derivatives are marked to market with the resulting gains and losses recognized as a component of corporate unallocated expense. These gains and losses are reflected in division results when the divisions take delivery of the underlying commodity. Therefore, division results reflect the contract purchase price of the energy or other commodities.

Division results are based on how our Chairman and Chief Executive Officer evaluates our divisions. Division results exclude certain Corporate-initiated restructuring and impairment charges, merger related costs and divested businesses. For addition unaudited information on our divisions, see "Our Operations" in Management's Discussion and Analysis.

International Taxation and Transfer Pricing

Consider the case of a manufacturing company that was evaluating sites for new European operations. The decision came down to three locations in different countries, all roughly equal from a pretax viewpoint. Management made the final choice, but didn't consult with their tax specialist team until after the deal was done.

Bad move. Turns out they picked the very worst of the three from a tax perspective, ending up with a two percentage point increase in their effective tax rate—two points of gross margin down the drain. And because their tax specialists weren't consulted until the last minute, there was no turning back. Space had already been procured, employees hired and contracts signed.[1]

Of all the environmental variables that financial managers must contend with in multinational operations, only foreign exchange is as influential as taxation. Tax considerations strongly influence decisions on where to invest, what form of business organization to use, how to finance, when and where to recognize elements of revenues and expense, and what transfer prices to charge.

With the possible exception of cost of goods sold, taxation is the largest expense of most businesses. Thus, it makes sense for management to minimize international taxes whenever possible. Financial managers must also contend with special rules regarding the taxation of foreign-source income. Moreover, international tax agreements, laws, and regulations are constantly changing. Changes in one country's tax provisions have complex and wide-ranging effects in a multinational tax-planning system, and computer-based simulation systems are essential aids to management.

Because it is not possible in a single chapter to provide a working knowledge of the major tax provisions in all of the world's economically important countries, we limit our discussion here to some of the major variables that financial managers need to consider in tax planning for multinational operations. These variables include major differences

---

[1] Deloitte, "Breathing Lessons: Make Time for Taxes. It's Worth It." (May 8, 2007), www.deloitte.org/dtt/cda/doc/content/Breathing%20Lessons(1).pdf.

in national tax systems (i.e., how countries tax businesses operating in their jurisdictions), national attempts to address the issue of double taxation (i.e., how countries tax the foreign-source income of their business entities), and arbitrage opportunities between national tax jurisdictions for multinational firms. Transfer pricing, in addition to its role in minimizing multinational corporate taxes, should be considered in the broader context of strategic planning and control.

INITIAL CONCEPTS

The maze of laws and regulations that govern the taxation of foreign corporations and profits earned abroad rests on a few basic concepts. These include notions of tax neutrality and tax equity. *Tax neutrality* means that taxes have no effect (are neutral) on resource-allocation decisions. That is, business decisions are driven by economic fundamentals, such as rate of return, rather than tax considerations. Such decisions should result in an optimal allocation of resources: When taxes influence the allocation of resources, the result will probably be less than optimal. In reality, taxes are seldom neutral.[2]

Tax equity means that taxpayers who are similarly situated should pay the same tax, but there is much disagreement over how to interpret this concept. For example, is a foreign subsidiary simply a domestic company that happens to operate abroad? If so, then foreign- and domestic-source income should be taxed at the same parent-country rate. Or is a foreign subsidiary a foreign company that happens to be owned by a domestic one? In this case, foreign-source income should be taxed the same as other companies in that country, that is, at the foreign country's tax rate. We shall find that actual international tax practices waver between these two extremes.

DIVERSITY OF NATIONAL TAX SYSTEMS

A firm can conduct international business by exporting goods and services or by making direct or indirect foreign investments. Exports seldom trigger a tax exposure in the importing country, because it is difficult for importing countries to enforce taxes levied on foreign exporters. On the other hand, a company that operates in another country through a branch or an incorporated affiliate subjects itself to that country's taxes. The effective management of this tax exposure requires an understanding of national tax systems, which differ greatly among countries. Differences range from types of taxes and tax burdens to differences in tax assessment and collection philosophies.

Types of Taxes

A company operating abroad encounters a variety of taxes. *Direct taxes*, such as income taxes, are easy to recognize and normally are disclosed on companies' financial statements. *Indirect taxes*, such as consumption taxes, are not so clearly recognized or as frequently disclosed. Typically they are buried in "other" expenses. Exhibit 12-1 illustrates the differential impact of direct and indirect taxes on pretax and after-tax

---

[2] See, for example, PriceWaterhouseCoopers, *Paying Taxes 2009: The Global Picture* (2008), www.pwc.com/extweb/pwcpublications.nsf/docid/E3885850CC074F43852574F80055639C/$File/Paying_Taxes_2009.pdf.

EXHIBIT 12-1	Income Effects of Direct vs. Indirect Taxes	
	Direct	**Indirect**
Revenues	250	250
Expenses	150	190
Pretax income	100	60
Direct taxes (40%)	40	-0-
After-tax income	60	60

income. In comparing investment performance between countries, the focus should be on after-tax income.

The *corporate income tax* is probably more widely used to generate government revenue than any other major tax, with the possible exception of customs duties. Since the mid-1980s, however, the international trend has been a lowering and converging of income tax rates. Fueling this trend is the recognition that reduced tax rates increase the global competitiveness of a country's business enterprises and create an attractive environment for international business. Indeed, the integration of the world economy and the increasing ability of businesses to move from high-tax environments to low-tax ones constrain a country's ability to set higher rates than elsewhere. Exhibit 12-2 shows national income tax rates for selected countries.

Withholding taxes are taxes imposed by governments on dividend, interest, and royalty payments to foreign investors. For example, assume that a country has a 10 percent withholding tax on interest paid to foreign investors. The investors would receive only 90 percent of the interest paid by the bonds. While legally imposed on the foreign recipient, these taxes are typically withheld at the source by the paying corporation, which remits the proceeds to tax collectors in the host country. Because withholding taxes may hinder the international flow of long-term investment capital, they are often modified by bilateral tax treaties.

The *value-added tax* is a consumption tax found in Europe and Canada. This tax is typically levied on the value added at each stage of production or distribution. It applies to total sales less purchases from any intermediate sales unit. Thus, if a Norwegian merchant buys 500,000 krone of merchandise from a Norwegian wholesaler and then sells it for 600,000 krone, the value added is 100,000 krone, and a tax is assessed on this amount. Companies that pay the tax in their own costs can reclaim them later from the tax authorities. Consumers ultimately bear the cost of the value-added tax. Exhibit 12-3 shows how the value-added tax works.

Border taxes, such as customs or import duties, generally aim at keeping domestic goods price competitive with imports. Accordingly, taxes assessed on imports typically parallel excise and other indirect taxes paid by domestic producers of similar goods.

The *transfer tax* is another indirect tax. It is imposed on transfers of items between taxpayers and can have important effects on such business decisions as the structure of acquisitions. For example, business acquisitions in Europe are often made through the purchase of shares rather than the underlying net assets. More variations in structure are found in U.S. acquisitions because transfer taxes are less important in the United States.

EXHIBIT 12-2	Corporate Income Tax Rates				

Country	(%)	Country	(%)	Country	(%)
Argentina	35	Greece	22/29	Philippines	30
Australia	30	Honduras	30	Poland	19
Austria	25	Hong Kong	16.5	Portugal	25
Bahrain	0	Hungary	16	Romania	16
Bangladesh	30	Iceland	15	Russia	20
Belgium	33.99	India	33.99	Saudi Arabia	20
Bolivia	25	Indonesia	28	Singapore	18
Brazil	34[a]	Ireland	12.5	Slovak Republic	19
Bulgaria	10	Israel	26	Slovenia	21
Canada	33.5[b]	Italy	31.4[d]	South Africa	28[g]
Cayman Islands	0	Japan	40.69[e]	Spain	30
Chile	17	Korea, Republic of	27.5	Sri Lanka	35
China	33	Latvia	15	Sweden	28
Colombia	33	Lithuania	20	Switzerland	19.2[h]
Costa Rica	30	Luxembourg	21[f]	Taiwan	25
Croatia	20	Malaysia	26	Thailand	30
Cyprus	10	Malta	35	Tunisia	30
Czech Republic	20	Mexico	28	Turkey	20
Denmark	25	The Netherlands	25.5	Ukraine	25
Dominican Republic	25	New Zealand	30	United Kingdom	28
Ecuador	25	Norway	28	United States	35/40[i]
Egypt	20	Oman	12	Uruguay	25
Fiji	31	Pakistan	35	Venezuela	34
Finland	26	Panama	30	Vietnam	25
France	33.33	Papua New Guinea	30	Zambia	35
Germany	29.51[c]	Peru	30		

Note:

A simple comparison of tax rates is not sufficient for assessing the relative tax burdens imposed by different governments. The method of computing the profits to which the tax rates will be applied (the tax base) should also be taken into account.

These rates do not reflect payroll taxes, social security taxes, net wealth taxes, turnover taxes, and other taxes not levied on income.

[a]*The sum of income tax and social contribution tax.*

[b]*Includes provincial income taxes.*

[c]*Includes local trade tax plus solidarity tax.*

[d]*The sum of income tax and regional tax rates.*

[e]*Includes corporate income tax and business, perfectural, and municipal taxes.*

[f]*Includes employment fund contribution and municipal business tax.*

[g]*Includes corporate income tax rate and effect of tax on dividends declared.*

[h]*Includes federal, cantonal, and municipal taxes.*

[i]*Federal tax rate is 35 percent State and local income tax rates range from less than 1 to 12 percent. State and local income taxes are deductible in determining federal income taxes, making the average effective tax rate 40 percent.*

Sources: "Tax Rates Around the World," www.worldwide-tax.com (May 31, 2009) and KPMG's Corporate and Indirect Tax Rate Survey 2008, www.kpmg.com/SiteCollectionDocuments/Corporate-and-Indirect-Tax-Rate-Survey-2008v2.pdf.

EXHIBIT 12-3	Value-Added Tax			
	Producer	**Wholesaler**	**Merchant**	**Consumer**
Cost	Assume 0	€12.00	€15.60	€21.60
Recoverable VAT	–	2.00	2.60	
Net cost	0	€10.00	€13.00	
Sales price before VAT	€10.00	13.00	18.00	
Value added	€10.00	€ 3.00	€ 5.00	
Value-added tax (20%)	2.00	0.60	1.00	
Sales price after VAT	€12.00	€15.60	21.60	
VAT paid	€ 2.00	€ 2.60	€ 3.60	
Recoverable VAT	0	2.00	2.60	
VAT due	€ 2.00	€ 0.60	€ 1.00	
VAT borne				€ 3.60

Tax Burdens

Differences in overall tax burdens are important in international business. Various statutory rates of income taxation are an important source of these differences, as can be seen in Exhibit 12-2. However, differences in tax rates tell only part of the story. Many other considerations may significantly affect the *effective tax burdens* for multinational enterprises. Differences in national definitions of taxable income are important.

Consider depreciation. In theory, a portion of the cost of an asset is said to expire as the asset is used up to produce revenue. In keeping with the matching principle, this expired cost is recognized as an expense and deducted from its related revenue. Where the asset is consumed equally in each reporting period, an equal portion of its cost is commonly expensed each period for external financial reporting purposes. In the United States, however, a distinction is generally made between depreciation for external reporting and depreciation for tax purposes. As an incentive to invest in capital assets, including commercial buildings, companies in the United States are allowed to use accelerated depreciation methods. In Germany, tax law specifies depreciation rates, and buildings are depreciated in straight-line fashion. Tax law also determines depreciation rates in France, with most assets depreciated on a straight-line basis. However, antipollution and energy-saving assets may be depreciated on an accelerated basis.

Another item that accounts for intercountry differences in effective tax burdens relates to the host country's social overhead. To attract foreign investments, less-industrialized countries often assess lower corporate income tax rates than their more industrialized counterparts. However, countries with low direct taxes need to fund government and other social services just like any other country. Therefore, lower direct corporate tax rates usually result in higher indirect taxes or in fewer and lower quality public services. Indirect taxes reduce purchasing power in the local market. Fewer and lower quality public services may impose a higher cost structure on multinational operations. Examples include poor transportation networks, inadequate postal services, ineffective telephone and telecommunications systems, and power shortages.

While more and more governments are reducing marginal corporate tax rates, many also are broadening corporate tax bases. In the real world, effective tax rates seldom equal nominal tax rates. Thus, it is improper to base intercountry comparisons on statutory tax rates alone. Furthermore, a low tax rate does not necessarily mean a low tax burden. Internationally, tax burdens should always be determined by examining *effective* tax rates.

Tax Administration Systems

National tax assessment systems also affect relative tax burdens. Several major systems are currently in use. For simplicity, we will only consider the classical and integrated systems.

Under the *classical system*, corporate income taxes on taxable income are levied at the corporate level and the shareholder level. Shareholders are taxed either when the corporate income is paid as a dividend or when they liquidate their investment. When a corporation is taxed on income measured before dividends are paid, and shareholders are then taxed on their dividends, the shareholders' dividend income is effectively taxed twice. To illustrate, assume that a parent corporation in Zonolia (fictitious), subject to a 33 percent corporate income tax, earns 100 zonos (Z) and distributes a 100 percent dividend to its sole shareholder, who is in the 30 percent tax bracket. Effective taxes paid on the corporate income are determined as follows:

Corporate income	Z100.00
– Income tax at 33%	33.00
= Net income (and dividend paid)	Z 67.00
Dividend income to shareholder	Z 67.00
– Personal income tax at 30%	20.10
= Net amount to shareholder	Z 46.90

Total tax paid on the Z100 of corporate income:

Corporate tax	Z33.00
Individual income tax	20.10
Total	Z53.10

Countries associated with this system include Belgium, Luxembourg, the Netherlands, and Sweden. The recent trend in most developed countries has been to move away from the double taxation of dividend income by adopting either an integrated or an imputation system.

Under an *integrated* system, corporate and shareholder taxes are integrated so as to reduce or eliminate the double taxation of corporate income. The *tax credit,* or *imputation,* system is a common variant of the integrated tax system. In this system, a tax is levied on corporate income, but part of the tax paid can be treated as a credit against personal income taxes when dividends are distributed to shareholders. This tax system is advocated by the European Union and is found in Australia,

Canada, Mexico, and many European countries, including France, Italy, and the United Kingdom.

To see how this tax system works, assume facts similar to that of our Zonolian parent company in the preceding illustration. Further assume that shareholders receive a tax credit equal to 25 percent of dividends received. Based on these assumptions, the total taxes paid is determined as follows:

Corporate income	Z100.00
− Income tax at 33%	33.00
= Net income (and dividend paid)	Z 67.00
Dividend income to shareholder	Z 67.00
+ Tax credit at 25%	16.75
= Grossed-up dividend	Z 83.75
Income tax liability at 30%	Z 25.12
− Tax credit	16.75
= Tax due from shareholder	Z 8.37

Total tax paid on the Z100 of corporate income:

Corporate tax	Z 33.00
Individual income tax	8.37
Total	Z 41.37

This example illustrates a partial imputation system in which double taxation is reduced but not eliminated. Full imputation eliminates double taxation.

The *split-rate* system is another variant of the integrated tax system, where a lower tax is levied on distributed earnings (i.e., dividends) than on retained earnings. Germany once had a split-rate system. Other ways to reduce double taxation are to exempt a percentage of dividends from personal taxation, as Germany does now, or to tax dividends at a lower rate than the personal rate, as in the United States.

Foreign Tax Incentives

Countries eager to accelerate their economic development are keenly aware of the benefits of international business. Many countries offer tax incentives to attract foreign investment. Incentives may include tax-free cash grants applied toward the cost of fixed assets of new industrial undertakings or relief from paying taxes for certain time periods (*tax holidays*). Other forms of temporary tax relief include reduced income tax rates, tax deferrals, and reduction or elimination of various indirect taxes. More-industrialized countries offer targeted incentives, such as Ireland's reduced corporate tax rate for manufacturing operations (10 percent) through the year 2010.[3]

---

[3] The Irish corporate tax rate is 12.5 percent. The 10 percent preferential tax rate for manufacturing companies will be eliminated after 2010.

Some countries, particularly those with few natural resources, offer permanent tax inducements. These countries include:

1. the Bahamas, Bermuda, and the Cayman Islands, which have no income taxes at all
2. Vanuatu, which has very low income tax rates
3. Hong Kong and Panama, which tax locally generated income but exempt income from foreign sources

Tax Havens and Harmful Tax Competition

For some time, the Organization for Economic Cooperation and Development (OECD) has been concerned about tax competition by certain *tax-haven* countries. The worldwide trend toward both lowering and converging corporate income tax rates is a direct result of tax competition. So is tax competition harmful? Certainly it is beneficial if it makes governments more efficient. On the other hand, it is harmful when it shifts tax revenues away from governments that need them to provide services on which businesses rely. The OECD's main concern has been about tax havens that allow businesses to avoid or evade another country's taxes. So-called *brass plate* subsidiaries have no real work or employment attached to them: They lack *substantial activities* and merely funnel financial transactions through the tax-haven country to avoid another country's taxes.[4]

The OECD lists four factors for identifying a tax haven:

1. No or low taxes on income,
2. Lack of effective exchange of information,
3. Lack of transparency, and
4. No substantial activities.

In 2000, the OECD identified over 40 countries as tax havens. These countries often advertized their no or low tax rates to lure foreign money and had a "don't ask, don't tell" policy regarding foreign income. They often stonewalled requests from other countries who were hunting tax evaders. The OECD applied pressure to so-called "uncooperative" tax havens: those that were unwilling to share information with tax authorities elsewhere and that applied or enforced tax laws unevenly or in secret. Uncooperative tax havens were pressured to adopt practices on the effective exchange of information and transparency. The pressure worked. By 2009, all uncooperative tax havens were removed from the original list.[5]

International Harmonization

Given the diversity of tax systems around the world, the global harmonization of tax policies would seem to be worthwhile. Multinational companies, burdened by the disparities of national taxes, are fueling the pressure for international tax reform. The

---

[4] For example, the U.S. Treasury Department estimates that it loses $100 billion a year in tax revenue from companies that ship their income offshore. It is estimated that tax havens have attracted $12 trillion in assets. See "Where Money Goes to Hide," *The Week* (May 8, 2009): 13.

[5] See OECD, "Overview of the OECD's Work on Countering International Tax Evasion" (June 17, 2009) and "Countering Offshore Tax Evasion (June 17, 2009), www.oecd.org.

European Union is expending much energy in this direction as it works to create a single market. The EU's introduction of a single currency, the euro, highlights the tax disparities among its members.[6]

TAXATION OF FOREIGN-SOURCE INCOME AND DOUBLE TAXATION

Every nation claims the right to tax income originating within its borders. National philosophies regarding the taxation of foreign-source earnings differ, however, and this is important from a tax-planning perspective. A few countries, such as France, Hong Kong, Panama, and Venezuela, adopt the *territorial* principle of taxation and exempt from taxation the income of resident corporations generated outside their borders. This reflects the idea that tax burdens of foreign affiliates should equal those of their local competitors. In this view, foreign affiliates of local companies are viewed as foreign companies that happen to be owned by local residents.

Most countries (e.g., Australia, Brazil, China, the Czech Republic, Germany, Japan, Mexico, the Netherlands, the United Kingdom, and the United States) adopt the *worldwide* principle and tax resident corporations and citizens on income regardless of national boundaries. The underlying idea here is that a foreign subsidiary of a local company is simply a local company that happens to operate abroad.

Foreign Tax Credit

Under the worldwide principle of taxation, the foreign earnings of a domestic company are subject to the full tax levies of its host and home countries. To avoid discouraging businesses from expanding abroad, and in keeping with the concept of foreign neutrality, a parent company's domicile (country of residence) can elect to treat foreign taxes paid as a credit against the parent's domestic tax liability or as a deduction from taxable income. Companies generally choose the credit, because it yields a one-for-one reduction of domestic taxes payable (limited to the amount of income taxes actually paid),[7] whereas a deduction is only worth the product of the foreign tax expense multiplied by the domestic marginal tax rate.

Foreign tax credits may be calculated as a straightforward credit against income taxes paid on branch or subsidiary earnings and any taxes withheld at the source, such as dividends, interest, and royalties remitted to a domestic investor. The tax credit can also be estimated when the amount of foreign income tax paid is not clearly evident (e.g., when a foreign subsidiary remits a fraction of its foreign-source earnings to its domestic parent). Here, reported dividends on the parent company's tax return would be grossed up to include the amount of the tax (deemed paid) plus any applicable foreign withholding taxes. It is as if the domestic parent received a dividend including the tax due the foreign government and then paid the tax.

---

[6] The EU focus is on harmonizing the corporate tax base rather than corporate tax rates. Under current proposals, companies would calculate one single, EU-wide income that would be divided among jurisdictions according to some rough measure of a firm's activities in each country. See "Harmony and Discord," *Economist* (May 5, 2007): 90–91.

[7] Indirect levies, such as foreign sales taxes, are generally not creditable.

The allowable foreign indirect tax credit (foreign income tax deemed paid) is determined as follows:

$$\frac{\text{Dividend payout (including any withholding tax)}}{\text{Earnings net of foreign income tax}} \times \text{Creditable foreign taxes}$$

To illustrate how foreign tax credits apply in a variety of situations, assume that a U.S. parent company receives royalties from Country A, foreign-branch earnings from Country B, and dividends from subsidiaries in Countries C and D. Withholding taxes on royalty and dividend payments are assumed to be 15 percent in Countries A, C, and D; income tax rates are assumed to be 30 percent in Country B and 40 percent in Country C. Country D assesses a 40 percent indirect sales tax as opposed to a direct tax on earnings within its jurisdiction.[8]

The key variables in this illustration, as shown in Exhibit 12-4, are the organizational form of the foreign activity (e.g., branch vs. subsidiary) and relative corporate income and withholding tax rates. In the first column, the royalty payment of $20.00 is subject to a 15 percent withholding tax in the host country (netting a $17.00 payment to the parent). For U.S. tax purposes, the net royalty is grossed up to include the withholding tax, which then forms the base for the U.S. domestic tax of 35 percent. The U.S. tax of $7.00 is offset by the credit for the foreign tax paid to yield a net U.S. tax liability of $4.00.

In the second column of Exhibit 12-4, the foreign branch earnings of the U.S. parent are grossed up to include foreign income taxes paid of $30.00. U.S. taxes payable on this amount of $35.00 are offset by a foreign tax credit of $30.00, to yield a net U.S. tax payable of $5.00. As with the royalty payment, the effect of the foreign tax credit is to limit the total tax on foreign-source income to the higher of the two countries' taxes. In this example, the U.S. tax rate of 35 percent was higher than the foreign tax rate of 30 percent, yielding a total tax on royalty and branch earnings of 35 percent.

Further scrutiny of Exhibit 12-4 is instructive. A comparison of columns 2 and 3 suggests the importance of organizational form on international taxes. A branch operation, viewed as an extension of the parent company, is subject to the full tax rate of the home country. In our example, the foreign branch pays a total tax of $35: $30 of foreign income taxes and $5 of U.S. taxes. Thus, the foreign branch bears the full burden of the U.S. income tax rate. However, it is spared any withholding taxes on earnings distributions to the parent because only a foreign subsidiary can distribute its earnings. On the other hand, a foreign operation organized as a subsidiary is taxed only on earnings that it remits to the parent company. It can defer taxes on retained income, and thus compete on an equal tax footing with local companies.

Columns 3 and 4 illustrate how a system of worldwide taxation places a subsidiary at a competitive disadvantage when it is located in a country that relies primarily on an indirect tax for revenue. Note that the subsidiary in Country D has a higher total tax burden because the tax credit only relieves direct taxes, not indirect taxes. Similarly, the benefits of tax incentives granted by host governments may also be nullified.

---

[8] Note that royalty income and branch/subsidiary earnings are grossed up (i.e., included in U.S. income) before deducting foreign taxes paid.

EXHIBIT 12-4   **U.S. Taxation of Foreign-Source Income**

	Royalties from Operation in Country A	Earnings from Branch in Country B	Dividend from Subsidiary in Country C	Dividend from Subsidiary in Country D
Branch/Subsidiary				
Before-tax earnings		100.00	100.00	60.00
Foreign income taxes (30%/40%)		30.00	40.00	-0-
After-tax earnings		70.00	60.00	60.00
Dividend paid (50% of after-tax earnings)			30.00	30.00
Other foreign income	20.00			
Foreign withholding taxes (15%)	3.00		4.50	4.50
Net payment to parent	17.00		25.50	25.50
U.S. income	20.00	100.00[a]	30.00	30.00
Dividend gross-up (30/60 × 40)	____	____	20.00	-0-
Taxable income	20.00	100.00	50.00	30.00
U.S. tax (35%)	7.00	35.00	17.50	10.50
Foreign tax credit				
Paid	(3.00)	(30.00)	(4.50)	(4.50)
Deemed paid (30/60 × 40)	____	____	(20.00)	-0-
Total	(3.00)	(30.00)	(24.50)	(4.50)
U.S. tax (net)	4.00	5.00	(7.00)[b]	6.00
Foreign taxes	3.00	30.00	24.50	40.00[c]
Total taxes of U.S. taxpayer	7.00	35.00	17.50[d]	46.00

[a]Grossed up to include foreign taxes actually paid.

[b]Excess foreign tax credits can be carried back one year or carried forward 10 years to offset U.S. tax on other foreign source (not U.S. source) income. If unavailable, total taxes = 24.50.

[c]40 percent indirect sales tax on 100.00.

[d]Excludes deferred tax on undistributed earnings of affiliate.

Limits to Tax Credits

Home countries can tax foreign-source income in many ways. A country may elect to tax income from each separate national source. At the other extreme, all foreign-source income from any foreign source may be combined and taxed once. Some countries tax foreign-source income on a source-by-source basis, with the tax credit for foreign-source income limited to the corresponding domestic tax applicable to that income. As illustrated in columns 2 and 3 of Exhibit 12-4, the maximum tax liability will always be the higher of the tax rates in the host or home country. Other countries allow parent companies to pool income from many country sources by income type (e.g., dividends vs. interest vs. royalties). Excess tax credits from countries with high tax rates (column 3 of Exhibit 12-4) can offset taxes on income received from low-tax-rate countries (column 2 of Exhibit 12-4).

To prevent foreign tax credits from offsetting taxes on domestic-source income, many countries impose an overall limit on the amount of foreign taxes creditable in any year. The United States, for instance, limits the tax credit to the proportion of the U.S. tax that equals the ratio of the taxpayer's foreign-source taxable income to its worldwide taxable income for the year. Assume that Alpha Company earned $2,000 of foreign-source income and $3,000 of U.S.-source taxable income. Its foreign tax credit would be the lesser of the foreign income taxes paid or the foreign tax credit limitation computed as follows:

$$\text{Foreign tax credit limit} = \frac{\text{Foreign source taxable income}}{\text{Worldwide taxable income}} \times \text{U.S. tax before credits}$$

$$= (\$2,000/\$5,000) \times (\$5,000 \times 35\%)$$

$$= \$700$$

Thus, only $700 would be allowed as a tax credit, even if foreign taxes paid exceeded $700. Excess foreign taxes paid can be carried back one year and forward 10 years (see footnote b in Exhibit 12-4).

A separate foreign tax credit limitation applies to U.S. taxes on the foreign-source taxable income of each of the following types of income (or *baskets*):

- Passive income (e.g., investment-type income, such as dividends, interest, royalties, and rents)
- General income (all other types)[9]

Foreign-source taxable income is foreign-source gross income less expenses, losses, and deductions allocable to the foreign-source income, plus a ratable share of expenses, losses, and deductions that cannot be allocated definitely to any item or class of gross income. The interpretation of this provision is reportedly one of the major areas of dispute between taxpayers and the IRS.[10]

Tax Treaties

Although foreign tax credits shield foreign-source income from double taxation (to some extent), tax treaties go further. Signatories to such treaties generally agree on how taxes and tax incentives will be imposed, honored, shared, or otherwise eliminated on business income earned in one taxing jurisdiction by citizens of another. Thus, most tax treaties between home and host countries provide that profits earned by a domestic enterprise in the host country shall be subject to its taxes only if the enterprise maintains a permanent establishment there. Tax treaties also affect withholding taxes on dividends, interest, and royalties paid by the enterprise of one country to foreign shareholders. They usually grant reciprocal reductions in withholding taxes on dividends and often entirely exempt royalties and interest from withholding.

---

[9] Before the American Jobs Creation Act of 2004, excess taxes paid could be carried back two years and forward five years. The act also reduced the number of income baskets from nine to two. Both changes were designed to improve tax breaks for multinational corporations.

[10] P. Bodner, "International Taxation," in *International Accounting and Finance Handbook*, ed. Frederick D. S. Choi, 3rd ed. (New York: John Wiley, 2003), p. 30.11.

Foreign Exchange Considerations

The Tax Reform Act of 1986 introduced formal rules regarding the taxation of foreign currency gains or losses in the United States. In keeping with SFAS No. 52 (described in Chapter 6), all tax determinations must be made in the taxpayer's functional currency. The functional currency is assumed to be the U.S. dollar unless the foreign operation is an autonomous unit, or *qualified business unit.* In general, tax rules are similar but not necessarily identical to generally accepted accounting principles described in Chapter 6. Following are examples of tax treatments.[11]

Transaction gains or losses in currencies other than the functional currency are generally accounted for under the two-transactions perspective. Under this approach, any exchange gain or loss recognized when the foreign currency transaction is settled is treated as ordinary income and accounted for separately from the underlying transaction. However, gains or losses on transactions qualifying as hedges of certain foreign currency transactions can be integrated with the underlying transaction. For example, a gain or loss incurred on a forward exchange contract designated as an effective hedge of a foreign currency loan would offset the transaction gain or loss on the underlying obligation.

Foreign exchange gains or losses are generally allocated between U.S. and foreign sources by reference to the residence of the taxpayer on whose books the foreign currency asset or liability is reflected. Thus, for a U.S. corporation, the source of the gain or loss would be the United States.

Taxable profits for foreign branches are initially based on their functional currencies. The functional currency then is converted to U.S. dollars using the weighted average exchange rate for the taxable period. Foreign income taxes paid are translated at the exchange rate in effect when the tax is paid and then added to foreign taxable income or grossed up. The foreign taxes paid are then claimed as a foreign tax credit for U.S. tax purposes.

For foreign subsidiaries, deemed distributions under Subpart F regulations (discussed in the next section) are translated using weighted average exchange rates for the foreign corporation's taxable year. Deemed-paid foreign taxes are translated into U.S. dollars using exchange rates in effect on the date the tax was paid.

TAX-PLANNING DIMENSIONS

In tax planning, multinational companies have a distinct advantage over purely domestic companies because they have more geographical flexibility in locating their production and distribution systems. This flexibility provides unique opportunities to exploit differences among national tax jurisdictions so as to lower the overall tax burden for the corporation. The shifting of revenues and expenses through intracompany ties also gives MNCs additional opportunities to minimize the global taxes paid. In response, national governments are constantly designing legislation to minimize arbitrage opportunities involving different national tax jurisdictions.

---

[11] Ibid., pp. 30.16–30.18.

We begin our examination of tax-planning issues with two caveats:

- Tax considerations should never control business strategy. The financial or operating strength of a business transaction must stand on its own.
- Constant changes in tax laws limit the benefits of long-term tax planning.

Organizational Considerations

In taxing foreign-source income, many taxing jurisdictions focus on the organizational form of a foreign operation. A branch is usually considered an extension of the parent company. Accordingly, its income is immediately consolidated with that of the parent (an option not available to a subsidiary) and fully taxed in the year earned whether remitted to the parent company or not. Earnings of a foreign subsidiary are not generally taxed until repatriated. Exceptions to this general rule are described in the next section.

If initial operations abroad are forecast to generate losses, it may be tax-advantageous to organize initially as a branch. Once foreign operations turn profitable, operating them as subsidiaries may be attractive. For one thing, the corporate overhead of the parent company cannot be allocated to a branch, because the branch is viewed as part of the parent. Moreover, if taxes on foreign profits are lower in the host country than in the parent country, profits of a subsidiary are not taxed by the parent country until repatriated (see columns 2 and 3 of Exhibit 12-4). If the subsidiary were organized in a tax-haven country that imposes no taxes at all, tax deferral would be even more attractive. National governments know this phenomenon, and many have taken steps to minimize corporate abuse of it. One example is the U.S. treatment of Subpart F income.

Controlled Foreign Corporations and Subpart F Income

Recall that in the United States, like many other countries adopting the worldwide principle of taxation, income of foreign subsidiaries is not taxable to the parent until it is repatriated as a dividend—the so-called deferral principle. Tax havens give multinationals an opportunity to avoid repatriation—and home-country taxes—by locating transactions and accumulating profits in "brass plate" subsidiaries. These transactions have no real work or employment attached to them. The income earned on these transactions is *passive* rather than *active*.

The United States closed this loophole with the Controlled Foreign Corporation (CFC) and Subpart F Income provisions.[12] A CFC is a corporation in which U.S. shareholders (U.S. corporations, citizens, or residents) directly or indirectly own more than 50 percent of its combined voting power or fair market value. Only shareholders holding more than a 10 percent voting interest are counted in determining the 50 percent requirement. Shareholders of a CFC are taxed on certain income of the CFC (referred to as *tainted* income) even before the income is distributed.

Subpart F income includes certain *related-party* sales and services income. For example, if a Bahamian subsidiary of a U.S. corporation "buys" inventory from its U.S. parent and sells the inventory to the European Union, the profits booked by the

---

[12] CFC legislation was first enacted in the United States in 1962. It has now been introduced in most industrialized countries as an anti–tax-haven measure.

Bahamian subsidiary are Subpart F income. On the other hand, if the Bahamian subsidiary sells the imported inventory in the Bahamas, income from the local sales is not Subpart F income. Subpart F income also includes passive income, such as dividends, interest, rents, and royalties; net gains on certain foreign exchange or commodities transactions; gains from the sale of certain investment property including securities; and certain insurance income.

Offshore Holding Companies

In some circumstances, a U.S.-based multinational parent company with operations in several foreign countries may find it advantageous to own its various foreign investments through a third-country holding company. The essential features of this structure are that the U.S. parent directly owns the shares of a holding company set up in one foreign juris-diction, and the holding company, in turn, owns the shares of one or more operating subsidiaries set up in other foreign jurisdictions. The tax-related advantages of this holding company organizational form could include:

1. Securing beneficial withholding tax rates on dividends, interest, royalties, and similar payments
2. Deferring U.S. tax on foreign earnings until they are repatriated to the U.S. parent company (namely by reinvesting such earnings overseas)
3. Deferring U.S. tax on gains from the sale of the shares of the foreign operating subsidiaries

Realizing these advantages depends in large part on proper planning under complex U.S. tax rules (such as the Subpart F and foreign tax credit rules) and avoiding anti-treaty shopping rules found in many tax treaties.

Financing Decisions

The manner in which foreign operations are financed can also be shaped by tax consid-erations. Other things equal, the tax deductibility of debt, which increases the after-tax returns on equity, increases the attractiveness of debt financing in high-tax countries. Where local-currency borrowing is constrained by local governments that mandate minimum levels of equity infusion by the foreign parent, parent-company borrowing to finance this capital infusion could achieve similar ends, provided the taxing jurisdiction of the parent allows the interest to be deductible.

In other instances, offshore financing subsidiaries domiciled in a low-tax or tax-haven country also could be used as a financing vehicle. At one time, U.S. companies wishing to borrow funds in the eurodollar market were constrained from doing so because the U.S. government imposed a withholding tax on interest paid to foreign lenders. To lower the cost of financing, they formed offshore financing subsidiaries in the Netherlands Antilles, a country that has no withholding tax on interest to nonresidents.

In general, an offshore financing subsidiary, located in a low- or no-tax country, will issue securities and then lend money to an operating subsidiary (or the parent) located in a country with higher taxes. This intracompany loan results in interest income for the (low-/no-tax) financing subsidiary and deductible interest expense for the (higher tax) operating subsidiary. The result is higher after-tax consolidated profits.

Pooling of Tax Credits

We mentioned earlier that some countries limit tax credits on a source-by-source basis. Pooling income from many sources allows excess credits generated from countries with high tax rates to offset taxes on income received from low-tax jurisdictions. Excess tax credits, for example, can be extended to taxes paid in connection with dividends distributed by second- and third-tier foreign corporations in a multinational network. The United States allows this treatment provided that the U.S. parent's indirect ownership in such corporations exceeds 5 percent. Forward planning in the use of such credits can produce worthwhile tax benefits. Assume, for example, that a U.S. parent owns 100 percent of the shares of Company X (a first-tier foreign corporation). Company X owns 100 percent of the voting stock of Company Y (a second-tier foreign corporation). During the period, Company Y pays a dividend of 100 to Company X. Company X, in turn, remits a dividend of 100 to the U.S. parent as follows:

	U.S.Parent	Overseas Company X (First-tier Foreign Subsidiary)	Overseas Company Y (Second-tier Foreign Subsidiary)
1. Taxable earnings	100	200	200
2. Foreign income tax (15%/40%)		30	80
3. After-tax earnings		170	120
4. Dividends		100	100
5. Foreign taxes deemed paid	57	67	
	(100/170 × 97)	(100/120 × 80)	
6. Total taxes (2.+ 5.)		97	

Company X will be deemed to have paid 67 of the foreign income taxes paid by Company Y. In turn, the U.S. parent company will receive an indirect credit against U.S. taxes payable of 57 based on its share of taxes actually paid and deemed to have been paid by Company X (30 + 67). (Refer to our earlier discussion of the calculation of foreign credits.) In this illustration, a dividend from Company Y to Company X increases the allowable U.S. foreign tax credit attendant upon a dividend from Company X to the U.S. parent when the income taxes in Company Y's country of domicile exceed those in Company X's, and conversely.

Cost Accounting Allocations

Internal cost allocations among group companies are yet another vehicle to shift profits from high-tax to low-tax countries. The most common of these are allocations of corporate overhead expenses to affiliates in high-tax countries. The allocation of such service expenses as human resources, technology, and research and development will maximize tax deductions for affiliates in high-tax countries.

Location and Transfer Pricing

The locations of production and distribution systems also offer tax advantages. Thus, final sales of goods or services can be channeled through affiliates located in jurisdictions that offer tax shelter or deferral. Alternatively, a manufacturer in a high-tax country can obtain components from affiliates located in low-tax countries to minimize corporate taxes for the group as a whole. A necessary element of such a strategy is the prices at which goods and services are transferred between group companies. Profits for the corporate system as a whole can be increased by setting high *transfer prices* on components shipped from subsidiaries in relatively low-tax countries, and low transfer prices on components shipped from subsidiaries in relatively high-tax countries.

Transfer pricing has attracted increasing worldwide attention. The significance of the issue is obvious when we recognize that transfer pricing (1) is conducted on a relatively larger scale internationally than domestically, (2) is affected by more variables than are found in a strictly domestic setting, (3) varies from company to company, industry to industry, and country to country, and (4) affects social, economic, and political relationships in multinational business entities and, sometimes, entire countries. International transfer pricing is the most important international tax issue facing MNCs today.[13]

The impact of intracompany transfer pricing on international tax burdens cannot be examined in a vacuum; transfer prices can distort other parts of a multinational company's planning and control system. Cross-country transactions expose the multinational company to a host of strategic concerns that range from environmental risk to global competitiveness. These concerns often transcend tax considerations.

Integrating International Tax Planning

International tax planning should be integrally woven into corporate activities. Advises one tax attorney, "A tax plan should never be simply tacked on as an afterthought or bolted awkwardly on the side of a business or transaction."[14] To achieve integration of international tax planning, he recommends the following steps.

1. Seek competent tax advice in every relevant jurisdiction.
2. Communicate all the facts to each tax adviser. Tax conclusions are often based on fine distinctions among facts.
3. Appoint a single tax adviser to coordinate and reconcile the advice from the various jurisdictions.
4. Be sure that the plan fits the business. Sophisticated cross-border tax planning cannot be bought off-the-shelf.
5. Put all of the tax analysis in writing.
6. Be careful with the documentation of transactions. The audit battle is often won or lost based on the documents.
7. Obtain high-quality legal advice for any tax position that falls into a gray area or might be considered aggressive.
8. Consider how you would feel if your tax planning appeared in the local newspaper. If what you are doing might embarrass the company, don't do it.

---

[13] Ernst & Young, *2005–2006 Global Transfer Pricing Surveys: Global Transfer Pricing Trends, Practices, and Analysis* (November 2005), p. 4 (www.ey.com).
[14] J. William Dantzler, Jr., as quoted in Fay Hansen, "Best Practices in Tax Planning," *Business Finance* (May 2004): 27.

Of these steps, 4 and 8 are the ones most frequently omitted, and the ones most likely to lead to trouble if they are not followed.[15]

INTERNATIONAL TRANSFER PRICING: COMPLICATING VARIABLES

The need for transfer pricing arises when goods or services are exchanged between organizational units of the same company. For example, it arises when one subsidiary of a corporation transfers inventory to another subsidiary or when the parent company charges a subsidiary for administrative and managerial services, royalties for intangibles rights, or interest on corporate-wide financing. The transfer price places a monetary value on intracompany exchanges that occur between operating units and is a substitute for a market price. It is generally recorded as revenue by one unit and a cost by the other.

Transfer pricing is of relatively recent origin. Transfer pricing in the United States developed along with the decentralization movement that influenced many American businesses during the first half of the 20th century. Once a company expands internationally, the transfer pricing problem quickly becomes more serious. It is estimated that 60 percent of all international trade consists of transfers between related business entities. Cross-country transactions also expose the multinational company to a host of environmental influences that both create and destroy opportunities to increase enterprise profits by transfer pricing. Such variables as taxes, tariffs, competition, inflation rates, currency values, restrictions on fund transfers, political risks, and the interests of joint-venture partners complicate transfer pricing decisions tremendously. On top of these issues, transfer pricing decisions generally involve many trade-offs, often unforeseen and unaccounted for.

Tax Considerations

Unless counteracted by law, corporate profits can be increased by setting transfer prices so as to move profits from subsidiaries domiciled in high-tax countries to subsidiaries domiciled in low-tax countries. As an example, Blu Jeans–Hong Kong, a wholly owned manufacturing subsidiary of Global Enterprises (USA), ships 500,000 pairs of designer blue jeans to a related U.S. sales affiliate, Blu Jeans–USA (also wholly owned by Global Enterprises), for $6 per pair. They cost Blu Jeans–Hong Kong $4.20 per pair to produce. Assuming that each garment wholesales for $12 in the United States, consolidated profits (after eliminating intercompany sales and costs) and taxes would total $1,309,000 and $591,000, respectively. This scenario is shown in Exhibit 12-5.

Given a U.S. corporate tax rate of 35 percent versus 16.5 percent in Hong Kong, an increase in the transfer price of blue jeans from $6 to $8 per pair would increase total after-tax income as shown in Exhibit 12-6.

In this example, raising the transfer price charged by the Hong Kong affiliate increases taxable income in Hong Kong and reduces taxable income for the U.S. affiliate by $1,000,000. Because the corporate tax rate is lower in Hong Kong than in the United States, corporate income taxes for the system as a whole decrease by $185,000, with a corresponding increase in consolidated after-tax earnings.

---

[15] Ibid.

EXHIBIT 12-5	Tax Effects of Transfer Pricing		
	Blu Jeans-HK	**Blu Jeans-USA**	**Global Enterprises**
Sales	$3,000,000[a]	$6,000,000	$6,000,000
Cost of sales	2,100,000	3,000,000[a]	2,100,000
Gross margin	$ 900,000	$3,000,000	$3,900,000
Operating expenses	500,000	1,500,000	2,000,000
Pretax income	$ 400,000	$1,500,000	$1,900,000
Income tax (16.5%/35%)[b]	66,000	525,000	591,000
Net income	$ 334,000	$ 975,000	$1,309,000

[a]Based on a transfer price of $6 per unit.
[b]Income tax rates: Hong Kong 16.5 percent, United States 35 percent.

EXHIBIT 12-6	Tax Effects of a Change in Transfer Prices		
	Blu Jeans–HK	**Blu Jeans–USA**	**Global Enterprises**
Sales	$4,000,000[a]	$6,000,000	$6,000,000
Cost of sales	2,100,000	4,000,000[a]	2,100,000
Gross margin	$1,900,000	$2,000,000	$3,900,000
Operating expenses	500,000	1,500,000	2,000,000
Pretax income	$1,400,000	$ 500,000	$1,900,000
Income tax (16.5%/35%)	231,000	175,000	406,000
Net income	$1,169,000	$ 325,000	$1,494,000

[a]Based on a transfer price of $8 per unit.

Unfortunately, such actions often create unanticipated problems. Governments often counteract such measures. In the United States, Section 482 of the Internal Revenue Code gives the Internal Revenue Service authority to prevent a shifting of income or deductions between related taxpayers to exploit differences in national tax rates. The purpose of Section 482 is to ensure that taxpayers clearly reflect income attributable to *controlled transactions* (transactions between related taxpayers) and prevent the avoidance of taxes as a result of these transactions. The IRS is empowered to adjust income, deductions, credits, allowances, taxable basis, or any other item affecting taxable income if true taxable income has not been reported.

Section 482 essentially requires that intracompany transfers be based on an *arm's-length price*. An arm's-length price is one that an unrelated party would receive for the same or similar item under identical or similar circumstances. Acceptable arm's-length pricing methods include (1) comparable uncontrolled pricing, (2) resale pricing, (3) cost-plus pricing, and (4) other pricing methods. Severe penalties are imposed on valuation misstatements in connection with Section 482 adjustments. Penalties may be up to 40 percent of the additional taxes that result from income adjustments.

An emerging consensus among governments views arm's-length pricing as the appropriate standard in calculating profits for tax purposes. However, countries vary in how they interpret and implement arm's-length pricing. As a result, it is a somewhat fluid concept internationally. Multinational corporations are often "caught in the middle" when tax authorities from different jurisdictions disagree on a transfer price, each trying to maintain its "fair share" of taxes collected from the multinational. The resulting controversy can be time-consuming and expensive to resolve. The rigor applied in monitoring the transfer pricing policies of multinational companies still varies worldwide. Nevertheless, tax authorities around the world are drafting new transfer pricing rules and stepping up enforcement efforts. In 1992, only Australia and the United States had documentation rules for multinationals' transfer pricing policies. Now, nearly 50 countries do. Audits are also being carried out with regularity, and a high percentage of completed audits are leading to transfer price adjustments. Whereas in the past many multinationals simply set transfer prices without further complications, now they have to justify them and document them, or run the risk of severe noncompliance penalties. Thus, transfer pricing has become a major compliance burden.

Transfer pricing schemes designed to minimize global taxes often distort the multinational control system. When each subsidiary is evaluated as a separate profit center, such pricing policies can result in misleading performance measures that generally lead to conflicts between subsidiary and enterprise goals. In our earlier example, Blu Jeans–USA would report a lower profit than its sister affiliate in Hong Kong, even though the management of the U.S. subsidiary may be far more productive and efficient than the management in Hong Kong.

Tariff Considerations

Tariffs on imported goods also affect the transfer pricing policies of multinational companies. For example, a company exporting goods to a subsidiary domiciled in a high-tariff country can reduce the tariff assessment by lowering the prices of merchandise sent there.

In addition to the trade-offs identified, the multinational company must consider additional costs and benefits, both external and internal. Externally, an MNC would have three taxing authorities to contend with: the customs officials of the importing country and the income tax administrators of the exporting and importing countries. A high tariff paid by the importer would result in a lower tax base for income taxes. Internally, the enterprise would have to evaluate the benefits of a lower (higher) income tax in the importing country against a higher (lower) import duty, as well as the potentially higher (lower) income tax paid by the company in the exporting country.

To illustrate, let us revisit our blue jeans example depicted in Exhibits 12-5 and 12-6. In our revised example (see Exhibit 12-7), assume that the United States imposes an ad valorem import duty of 10 percent. Under a low transfer pricing policy, lower import duties are paid ($300,000 vs. $400,000), but the import duty advantage of a low transfer price is offset by the increased income taxes that must be paid ($486,000 vs. $266,000). Considering both import duties and income taxes, Global Enterprises is still $120,000 better off under a high transfer pricing policy.

Competitive Factors

To facilitate the establishment of a foreign subsidiary abroad, a parent company could supply the subsidiary with inputs invoiced at very low prices. These price subsidies could be removed gradually as the foreign affiliate strengthens its position in the foreign

EXHIBIT 12-7	**Trade-Offs When Tariffs and Income Taxes are Considered**		
	Blu Jeans–HK	**Blu Jeans–USA**	**Global Enterprises**
Low Transfer Price			
Sales	$3,000,000	$6,000,000	$6,000,000
Cost of sales	2,100,000	3,000,000	2,100,000
Import duty at 10%	—	300,000	300,000
Gross margin	900,000	$2,700,000	$3,600,000
Operating expenses	500,000	1,500,000	2,000,000
Pretax income	400,000	1,200,000	1,600,000
Income tax (16.5%/35%)	66,000	420,000	486,000
Net income	$ 334,000	$ 780,000	$1,114,000
High Transfer Price			
Sales	$4,000,000	$6,000,000	$6,000,000
Cost of sales	2,100,000	4,000,000	2,100,000
Import duty at 10%	—	400,000	400,000
Gross margin	1,900,000	$1,600,000	$3,500,000
Operating expenses	500,000	1,500,000	2,000,000
Pretax income	1,400,000	100,000	1,500,000
Income tax (16.5%/35%)	231,000	35,000	266,000
Net income	$1,169,000	$ 65,000	$1,234,000

market. Similarly, lower transfer prices could be used to shield an existing operation from the effects of increased foreign competition in the local market or another market; in other words, profits earned in one country could subsidize the penetration of another market. Indirect competitive effects are also possible. To improve a foreign subsidiary's access to local capital markets, setting low transfer prices on its inputs and high transfer prices on its outputs could bolster its reported earnings and financial position. Sometimes, transfer prices could be used to weaken a subsidiary's competitors.

Such competitive considerations would have to be balanced against many offsetting disadvantages. Transfer prices may, for competitive reasons, invite antitrust actions by host governments or retaliatory actions by local competitors. Internally, pricing subsidies do little to instill a competitive mode of thinking in the minds of the managers whose companies gain from the subsidy. What begins as a temporary aid may easily become a permanent management crutch.

Environmental Risks

Whereas competitive considerations abroad might warrant charging low transfer prices to foreign subsidiaries, the risks of severe price inflation might call for the opposite. Inflation erodes the purchasing power of a firm's cash. High transfer prices on goods or services provided to a subsidiary facing high inflation can remove as much cash from the subsidiary as possible.

Balance-of-payment problems (often related to inflation) may prompt foreign governments to devalue their currencies, impose foreign exchange controls, and/or impose restrictions on the repatriation of profits from foreign-owned companies. Potential losses from exposures to currency devaluations may be avoided by shifting funds to the parent company (or related affiliates) through inflated transfer prices. With exchange controls (e.g., a government restricts the amount of foreign exchange available for importing a particular good), reduced transfer prices on the imported good would allow the affiliate affected by the controls to acquire more of the desired import. To circumvent repatriation restrictions, high transfer prices allow some cash to be returned to the parent company each time it sells a product or service to the foreign subsidiary.

Performance Evaluation Considerations

Transfer pricing policies are also affected by their impact on managerial behavior, and are often a major determinant of corporate performance. For example, if a foreign affiliate's mission is to furnish supplies for the rest of the corporate system, appropriate transfer prices enable corporate management to provide the affiliate with an earnings stream that can be used in performance comparisons. However, it is difficult for decentralized firms to set intracompany transfer prices that both (1) motivate managers to make decisions that maximize their unit's profits and are congruent with the goals of the company as whole, and (2) provide an equitable basis for judging the performance of managers and units of the firm. If subsidiaries are free to negotiate transfer prices, their managers may not be able to reconcile conflicts between what may be best for the subsidiary and what is best for the firm as a whole. However, the effect on subsidiary management may be even worse if corporate headquarters dictates transfer prices and sourcing alternatives that are seen as arbitrary or unreasonable. Moreover, the more decisions that are made by corporate headquarters, the less advantageous are decentralized profit centers, because local managers lose their incentive to act for the benefit of their local operations.

Resolving Trade-Offs

Management accountants can play a significant role in quantifying the trade-offs in transfer pricing strategy. The challenge is to keep a global perspective when mapping out the benefits and costs associated with a transfer pricing decision. The effects of the decision on the corporate system as a whole must come first.

Quantifying the numerous trade-offs is difficult because environmental influences must be considered as a group, not individually. Consider, for example, the difficulties in measuring the trade-offs surrounding transfer pricing policies for a subsidiary located in a country with high income taxes, high import tariffs, price controls, a thin capital market, chronic high inflation, foreign exchange controls, and an unstable government. As we have seen, a high transfer price on goods or services provided to the subsidiary would lower the subsidiary's income taxes and remove excess cash to the parent company. However, a high transfer price might also result in higher import duties, impair the subsidiary's competitive position (due to higher input prices), worsen the rate of inflation, raise the subsidiary's capital costs, and even cause retaliation by the host government to protect its balance-of-payments position. To further complicate matters, all of these variables are changing constantly. One thing is clear: Superficial calculations of the effects of transfer pricing policy on individual units within a multinational system are not acceptable.

TRANSFER PRICING METHODOLOGY

In a world of perfectly competitive markets, it would not be much of a problem to set prices for intracompany resource and service transfers. Transfer prices could be based either on incremental cost or on market prices. Neither system would necessarily conflict with the other. Unfortunately, there are seldom external competitive markets for products or services transferred between related entities. Environmental influences on transfer prices also raise questions of pricing methodology. How are transfer prices established? Are standard market prices generally better than those based on some measure of cost, or are negotiated prices the only feasible alternative? Can a single transfer pricing methodology serve all purposes equally well? The following sections shed some light on these questions.

Market vs. Cost vs. . . . ?

The use of market-oriented transfer prices offers several advantages. Market prices show the opportunity cost to the transferring entity of not selling on the external market, and their use will encourage the efficient use of the firm's scarce resources. Their use is also said to be consistent with a decentralized profit center orientation. Market prices help differentiate profitable from unprofitable operations, and are easier to defend to taxing authorities as arm's-length prices.

The advantages of market-based transfer prices must be weighed against several shortcomings. One is that using market prices does not give a firm much room to adjust prices for competitive or strategic purposes. A more fundamental problem is that there is often no intermediate market for the product or service in question. Multinationals engage in transactions that independent enterprises do not undertake, such as transferring a valuable, closely held technology to an affiliate. Transactional relationships among affiliates under common control often differ in important and fundamental ways from potentially comparable transactions among unrelated parties.

Cost-based transfer pricing systems overcome many of these limitations. Moreover, they are (1) simple to use, (2) based on readily available data, (3) easy to justify to tax authorities, and (4) easily routinized, thus helping to avoid internal frictions that often accompany more arbitrary systems.

Of course, cost-based transfer pricing systems are not flawless either. For example, the sale of goods or services at actual cost (or cost plus standard markup) may provide little incentive for sellers to control their costs. Production inefficiencies may simply be passed on to the buyer at inflated prices. Cost-based systems overemphasize historical costs, which ignore competitive demand-and-supply relationships, and do not allocate costs to particular products or services in a satisfactory manner. The problem of cost determination is compounded internationally because cost accounting concepts vary from country to country.

Arm's-Length Principle

The typical multinational is an integrated operation: Its subsidiaries are under common control and share common resources and goals. The need to declare taxable income in different countries means that multinationals must allocate revenues and expenses among subsidiaries and set transfer prices for intrafirm transactions.

Tax authorities around the world have developed complicated transfer-price and income allocation regulations as a part of their national income tax systems. Most are based on the *arm's-length principle*, which prices intrafirm transfers as if they took place between unrelated parties in competitive markets.[16] The OECD identifies several broad methods of ascertaining an arm's-length price. Resembling those specified by Section 482 of the U.S. Internal Revenue Code, they are (1) the comparable uncontrolled price method, (2) the comparable uncontrolled transaction method, (3) the resale price method, (4) the cost-plus method, (5) the comparable profit method, (6) the profit split method, and (7) other methods.

Comparable Uncontrolled Price Method

Under this approach, transfer prices are set by reference to prices used in comparable transactions between independent companies or between the corporation and an unrelated third party. It is appropriate when goods are sufficiently common that controlled sales are essentially comparable to sales on the open market. Commodity-type products ordinarily use this method for internal transactions.

Comparable Uncontrolled Transaction Method

This method applies to transfers of intangible assets. It identifies a benchmark royalty rate by referencing uncontrolled transactions in which the same or similar intangibles are transferred. Like the comparable uncontrolled price method, this method relies on market comparables.

Resale Price Method

This method calculates an arm's-length price by starting with the final selling price at which the item in question is sold to an uncontrolled third party. An appropriate margin to cover expenses and a normal profit is then deducted from this price to derive the intracompany transfer price. This method is typically used when the unit buying the item is a distributor or sales subsidiary.

To illustrate this pricing method, assume that a company wishes to price a product sold by one of its operating units to one of its foreign distribution units. Income statement accounts and other related facts for the distribution unit are as follows:

1. Net sales (by the distribution unit to third party) of 100,000 units at $300 per unit	$30,000,000
2. Other expenses (OE) of the distribution unit	1,200,000
3. OE as a percentage of net sales	4.0%
4. Freight and insurance to import (FI)	$1.50/unit
5. Packaging costs (PC)	$2.00/unit
6. Customs duties (CD)	5.0%
7. Net sales price (NSP) by the distribution unit	$300/unit

---

[16] Of course, the result is only hypothetical because the parties are related and the markets normally are not competitive. See L. Eden, M. T. Dacin, and W. P. Wan, "Standards Across Borders: Cross-border Diffusion of the Arm's-Length Standard in North America," *Accounting, Organizations and Society* (January 2001): 1–23.

The objective is to calculate a transfer price between the two units such that the distribution unit covers all costs and earns a normal profit. As we shall see, the resale price method is a *work backwards* approach. Assuming that the company requires a 5 percent additional margin to cover business risk and provide an appropriate profit, the total product margin would be computed as follows:

1. Other expenses	4.0%
2. Additional margin for risk and profit	5.0%
3. Total margin (TM)	9.0%

Here, the distribution unit must pay freight and insurance costs to import the product and customs duties in addition to the transfer price. (Thus, the distribution unit's cost to import differs from the transfer price.) Given the foregoing information, the transfer price (TP) per unit of product delivered to the distribution unit would be:

$$TP = \{[NSP \times (100\% - TM) - PC]/(100\% + CD)\} - FI$$
$$TP = \{[300 \times (100\% - 9\%) - \$2]/(100\% + 5\%)\} - \$1.50$$
$$TP = \$256.60$$

The foregoing calculation adjusts the net sales price for the total margin, packaging costs, freight and insurance costs, and customs duties to arrive at the transfer price. Specifically, the 1.05 factor adjusts the $271 cost-to-import price to a before-duties figure of $258.10. Other dutiable costs are subtracted from this figure to leave a transfer price of $256.60. The cost to import equals (1) the transfer price plus (2) freight and insurance, with duties applied to both. As a check on this result:

	Unit Cost
Transfer price	$256.60
+ Freight & Insurance	1.50
Subtotal	258.10
Duties (at 5%)	12.90
Cost to import	$271.00

To work backwards to the transfer price:

Net sales price	$300.00
Margin to cover expenses and normal profit (9%)	– 27.00
Packaging	– 2.00
Freight and insurance	– 1.50
Customs duties	– 12.90
Transfer price	$256.60

Cost-Plus Pricing Method

Cost-plus pricing is a *work forward* approach in which a markup is added to the transferring affiliate's cost in local currency. The markup typically includes (1) the imputed financing costs related to export inventories, receivables, and assets employed and

(2) a percentage of cost covering manufacturing, distribution, warehousing, internal shipping, and other costs related to export operations. An adjustment is often made to reflect any government subsidies that are designed to make manufacturing costs competitive in the international marketplace.

This pricing method is especially useful when semifinished goods are transferred between foreign affiliates, or where one entity is a subcontractor for another. A major measurement issue involves calculating the cost of the transferred item and ascertaining an appropriate markup.

To see how a transfer price is derived employing the cost-plus method, assume that a manufacturing unit in Portugal wishes to price an intracompany transfer based on the following information:

1. Total manufacturing cost per unit (1,000 units)	€ 200
2. Average net operating assets employed in manufacturing the item	€ 40,000
3. Average short-term interest rate in Portugal	8.0%
4. Financing cost as a percentage of total manufacturing cost [(8% × Euro 40,000)/Euro 200,000]	1.6%
5. Government subsidy based on final transfer price	6.0%
6. Credit terms to affiliates	90 days
7. Required profit and other expenses margin	8.0%

The cost-plus transfer price is that price which enables the transferring unit to earn a given percentage return above its production costs. That percentage return (the *plus* in cost-plus) is determined in the following manner:

1. Required margin before adjustments:		
Profit and other expenses	8.0%	
Financing cost	1.6%	9.60%
2. Government subsidy adjustment		6.00%
3. Adjusted margin with cash terms [(1.096/1.06) − 1]		3.39%
4. Adjusted margin with 90-day terms		5.46%[a]

[a] *This figure is equal to the adjusted margin-cash terms multiplied by 1 plus the short-term interest rate for 90 days, or {1 .0339 × [1 + (0.08 × 90/360)]} − 1. It allows the transferring unit to earn imputed interest for carrying a receivable for 90 days.*

This required margin of 5.46 percent, when multiplied by the transferred item's total manufacturing cost, yields the intracompany transfer price to be billed for that item. In this example, the transfer price is € 210.92, the result of (1.0546 × € 200). This transfer price causes the company to earn its required margin of 9.6 percent and an 8 percent (annualized compounded) return for carrying the affiliate's receivable for 90 days. As a check on this result:

Compounded return = {1.096 × [1 + (.08 × 90/360)]} − 1

$$= 11.79\%$$

Transfer price	=	€ 210.92
Cost		200.00
Margin		€ 10.92
Subsidy (6% × 210.92)		12.66
Total return		€ 23.58

Return as a % of cost = (€ 23.58)/(€ 200.00) = 11.79%

Comparable Profits Method

The comparable profits method supports the general notion that similarly situated tax-payers should earn similar returns over reasonable time periods.[17] Thus, intracompany profits on transactions between related parties should be comparable to profits on transactions between unrelated parties who engage in similar business activities under similar circumstances. *Return on capital employed* (ROCE) is a primary profit-level indicator. Under this approach, the operating income to average capital employed ratio of a benchmark entity is compared with the ROCE of the entity in question.

Application of this method will normally require adjustments for any differences between comparables. Factors requiring such adjustments include differing sales conditions, cost of capital differences, foreign exchange and other risks, and differences in accounting measurement practices.

Profit-Split Methods

Profit-split methods are used when product or market benchmarks are not available. Essentially they involve dividing profits generated in a related-party transaction between the affiliated companies in an arm's-length fashion. One variant of this approach, the *comparables profit-split method*, divides the profit generated by a related-party transaction using a percentage allocation of the combined profits of uncontrolled companies with similar types of transactions and activities.

A more sophisticated method, the *residual profit-split method*, employs a two-step approach. First, routine functions performed by affiliated entities—the parent and its subsidiary—are priced at each stage of the production process using relevant bench-marks. Any difference between total profits earned by the combined enterprise and those attributable to the routine functions is considered *residual profits*, essentially profits from nonroutine functions. This residual, which resembles a goodwill intangible, then is split on the basis of the relative value of each affiliated party's contribution to the intangible. This value can be determined using fair market value referents or the capitalized cost of developing the intangibles.

---

[17] The comparable profits method is similar to the transactional net margin method (TNMM) in the OECD guidelines. The key difference is that TNMM is applied on a transactional rather than a firm level. For more information on this and the profit-split method, see Victor H. Miesel, Harlow H. Higinbotham, and Chun W. Yi, "International Transfer Pricing: Practical Solutions for Intercompany Pricing: Part II," *International Tax Journal* (winter 2003): 1–40.

Other Pricing Methods

As existing pricing methodologies do not always reflect underlying circumstances, additional methodologies are allowed if they result in a more accurate measure of an arm's-length price. To quote the OECD:

> It has to be recognized that an arm's-length price will in many cases not be precisely ascertainable and that in such circumstances it will be necessary to seek a reasonable approximation to it. Frequently, it may be useful to take account of more than one method of reaching a satisfactory approximation to an arm's-length price in the light of the evidence available.[18]

Section 482 of the U.S. Internal Revenue Code specifies a *best methods rule* requiring the taxpayer to select the best transfer pricing method based on the facts and circumstances of the case. Argentina and Taiwan also have a best methods rule. Most countries with transfer pricing legislation prefer transaction-based methods (comparable uncontrolled price, comparable uncontrolled transaction, resale price, and cost-plus methods) to profit-based methods (comparable profit and profit-split methods). These countries include Belgium, Germany, Japan, the Netherlands, and the United Kingdom.[19] OECD guidelines specify that a *reasonable* method should be chosen, and also prefer transaction-based methods to profit-based methods.

It is not always possible to calculate a precise and accurate arm's-length price. Hence, documentation of any transfer price employed and its underlying rationale is important. This is true regardless of the tax jurisdiction and the transfer pricing methods it may prefer. An increasing number of countries now require companies to keep documentation substantiating the transfer pricing method(s) used for intracompany transactions. The following steps are helpful in justifying transfer prices:

- Analyze the risks assumed, functions performed by the affiliated companies, and the economic and legal determinants that affect pricing.
- Identify and analyze benchmark companies and transactions. Document reasons for any adjustments made.
- Compare the financial results of the comparable companies and the taxpayer.
- If comparable transactions are available, note their similarities and differences with the taxpayer's transactions.
- Document why the chosen pricing method is the most reasonable and why the other methods are not.
- Update the information before filing the tax return.[20]

---

[18] Organization for Economic Cooperation and Development, *Transfer Pricing and Multinational Enterprises* (Paris: OECD, 1979), p. 33.
[19] Deloitte, *Strategy Matrix for Global Transfer Pricing: Planning Methods, Documentation, Penalties and Other Issues* (2006), pp. 10–11 (www.deloitte.com).
[20] Alan Shapiro and Arnold McClellan, "New Transfer Pricing: New Rules Give Guidance on How to Avoid Penalties," *Deloitte Touche Tohmatsu International World Tax News* (March 1994): 2. For further information on transfer pricing documentation, see Cym H. Lowell, Mark R. Martin, and Michael J. Donahue, "Managing Transfer Pricing, Part I," *Journal of International Taxation* (July 2006): 44–58.

Advance Pricing Agreements

The acceptability of transfer prices to governments is a major concern. Aware that multinational enterprises use transfer prices to shift income, and worried about their economic and social consequences, governments are increasing their scrutiny of multinational operations. At the same time, the ambiguities and complexities of transfer pricing regulations make it likely that intracompany transactions will be the target of tax audits. Surveys of multinationals consistently show that they regard transfer pricing as their most important international tax issue and that facing a transfer pricing audit somewhere in the world is a near certainty.[21]

Advance pricing agreements (APAs) are a mechanism whereby a multinational and a taxing authority voluntarily negotiate an agreed transfer pricing methodology that is binding on both parties. These agreements reduce or eliminate the risk of a transfer pricing audit, saving time and money for both the multinational and the taxing authority. Multinationals are increasingly using APAs as a controversy-management tool. Introduced in the United States in 1991, APAs have been widely adopted by other countries.[22] The agreements are binding for a fixed period of time; for example, three years in the United States.

Exhibit 12-8 summarizes the transfer pricing requirements in the 10 countries discussed in Chapters 3 and 4.

EXHIBIT 12-8	Transfer Pricing Requirements in Selected Countries		
	Preference for Transfer Pricing Method	**Statutory Requirements for Transfer Pricing Documentation[a]**	**Availability of APA**
China	Best method	Yes	Yes
Czech Republic	Transaction-based	Yes	Yes
France	Transaction-based	No	Yes
Germany	Transaction-based	Yes	Yes
India	Best method	Yes	No
Japan	Transaction-based	No	Yes
Mexico	Transaction-based	Yes	Yes
Netherlands	No preference	Yes	Yes
United Kingdom	Transaction-based	Yes	Yes
United States	Best method	No	Yes

Sources: Compiled from Ernst & Young, *2005–2006 Global Transfer Pricing Surveys—Tax Authority Interviews: Perspectives, Interpretations, and Regulatory Changes* (2006), www.ey.com; Deloitte, *Strategy Matrix for Global Transfer Pricing* (2008), www.deloitte.com; Ernst & Young, *Transfer Pricing Global Reference Guide* (2008), www.ey.com.

[a]*Countries with no statutory requirements for maintaining transfer pricing documentation will require companies to produce documentation upon request, normally at the time of an audit. For example, taxpayers must produce such documentation within 30 days of the request in the United States and within 60 days in France. Given that a significant amount of documentation will need to be provided, companies are well advised to maintain the documentation in any event.*

---

[21] Ernst & Young, *Transfer Pricing 2003 Global Survey* (2003): 10–15 (www.ey.com) and PriceWaterhouseCoopers, *Transfer Pricing Perspectives: The Emerging Perfect Storm of Transfer Pricing Audits and Disputes* (2008), (www.pwc.com).
[22] APAs go by different names. For example, they are called advance pricing arrangements in the United Kingdom and preconfirmation systems in Japan. The U.S. APA program is the largest such program in the world.

TRANSFER PRICING PRACTICES

Multinational corporations obviously vary along many dimensions, such as size, industry, nationality, organizational structure, degree of international involvement, technology, products or services, and competitive conditions. Therefore, it is hardly surprising that a variety of transfer pricing methods are found in practice.[23] Most of the empirical evidence on transfer pricing practices is based on surveys. Because corporate pricing policies are often considered proprietary, such surveys should be interpreted cautiously. Given the dramatic effect of globalization on business operations since the 1990s, we are also cautious about whether early transfer pricing surveys are still valid today.[24]

What factors influence the choice of transfer pricing methods? Are transfer pricing effects considered in the planning process? One study from the 1990s asked financial executives of U.S. multinationals to identify the three most important objectives of international transfer pricing.[25] Managing the tax burden dominated the other objectives, but operational uses of transfer pricing, such as maintaining the company's competitive position, promoting equitable performance evaluation, and motivating employees, were also important. Managing inflation, managing foreign exchange risk, and mitigating restrictions on cash transfers were relatively unimportant.

Another study asked a similar question of managers of multinationals from 19 nations.[26] In their responses, operational issues had a slightly higher priority than tax issues. The study also found that the operational and tax effects of transfer pricing are most often considered only after the strategic decisions have been made. However, a subsequent survey indicated that transfer pricing now plays a more important role in the multinational planning process.[27] The multinational corporations surveyed indicate that significantly more of them consider tax issues earlier in the business planning cycle than they did five years earlier. Transfer pricing is increasingly perceived as less of a compliance issue and more of a planning issue that contributes value.

THE FUTURE

Technology and the global economy are challenging many of the principles on which international taxation is based. One of these principles is that every nation has the right to decide for itself how much tax to collect from the people and businesses within its

---

[23] Most multinationals use more than one method, depending on the circumstances.

[24] For example, one widely cited study [J. S. Arpan, "International Intracorporate Pricing: Non-American Systems and Views," *Journal of International Business Studies* (spring 1972): 1–18] found that U.S., French, British, and Japanese managers prefer cost-oriented transfer pricing methods, whereas Canadian, Italian, and Scandinavian managers prefer market-oriented methods; no particular preference was found for Belgian, Dutch, German, or Swiss managers. While we believe that nationality continues to influence the choice of transfer pricing methods, we question whether this particular conclusion is still valid.

[25] K. S. Cravens, "Examining the Role of Transfer Pricing as a Strategy of Multinational Firms," *International Business Review* 6, no. 2 (1997): 127–145.

[26] Ernst & Young, "1999 Global Transfer Pricing Survey," reprinted in R. Feinschrieber, *Transfer Pricing International: A Country-by-Country Comparison* (New York: John Wiley, 2000), pp. 35.1–35.49.

[27] Ernst & Young, *2005–2006 Global Transfer Pricing Surveys: Global Transfer Pricing Trends, Practices, and Analysis*, November 2005, p. 15 (www.ey.com). See also Ernst & Young, *Precision Under Pressure: Global Transfer Pricing Survey 2007–2008*, 2008 (www.ey.com).

borders. Tax laws evolved in a world where transactions took place in clearly identifiable locations, but this is increasingly less true. Electronic commerce over the Internet ignores borders and physical location. Commercial events now take place in cyberspace—on a server anywhere in the world.[28]

The ability to collect taxes depends on knowing who should pay, but increasingly sophisticated encryption techniques make it harder to identify taxpayers. Anonymous electronic money is a reality. The Internet also makes it easy for multinationals to shift their activities to low-tax countries that may be a long way from customers but as close as a mouse click to access. It is becoming more difficult to monitor and tax international transactions. Further, there is a growing unease among governments that they are losing their grip on companies that increasingly can and do move their employees, know-how, capital, headquarters—and taxable profits—overseas.

Governments around the world require transfer pricing methods based on the arm's-length principle. That is, a multinational's businesses in different countries are taxed as if they were independent firms operating at arm's-length from each other. The complex calculation of arm's-length prices is less relevant today for global companies because fewer of them operate this way. Many multinationals now have global brands, global research and development, and regional profit centers. It is difficult to say exactly where their profits are generated. Moreover, companies are increasingly service-oriented and rely on brand names, intellectual property, and intangibles that are hard to price.[29]

What do these developments imply for international taxation? Are national taxes compatible with a global economy? We already see greater cooperation and information sharing by tax authorities around the world. This trend will continue. At the same time, many experts foresee greater tax competition. The Internet makes it easier to take advantage of tax havens. Some observers advocate a *unitary tax* as an alternative to using transfer prices to determine taxable income. Under this approach, a multinational's global profit is allocated to individual countries based on a formula that reflects the company's relative economic presence in the country. Each country would then tax its piece of the profit at whatever rate it sees fit. Clearly, taxation in the future faces many changes and challenges.[30]

---

[28] The digitization of tangible products is an example. A compact disc bought at a record store is a tangible item purchased at a physical location. Taxing this transaction is fairly simple because it is easy to identify the source of income. If it is downloaded online, it is an intangible purchased in cyberspace. Who can tax this transaction, and how, is less clear.

[29] The 2006 transfer pricing settlement between the pharmaceutical company GlaxoSmithKline and the U.S. Internal Revenue Service involved such issues. The settlement was the largest tax dispute in the history of the IRS. GlaxoSmithKline agreed to pay the IRS $3.4 billion.

[30] See "The Mystery of the Vanishing Taxpayer: A Survey of Globalisation and Tax," *Economist* (January 29, 2000): 1–22; S. James, "The Future International Tax Environment," *International Tax Journal* (winter 1999): 1–9; N. Warren, "Internet Challenges to Tax System Design," in *The International Taxation System*, ed. A. Lymer and J. Hasseldine (Boston: Kluwer Academic Publishers, 2002), pp. 61–82; "A Taxing Battle," *Economist* (January 31, 2004): 71–72.

Discussion Questions

1. What is tax neutrality? Are taxes neutral with regard to business decisions? Is this good or bad?
2. What philosophies and types of taxes exist worldwide?
3. Consider the statement "National differences in statutory tax rates are the most obvious and yet least significant determinants of a company's effective tax burden." Do you agree? Explain.
4. Carried to its logical extreme, tax planning implies a conscientious policy of tax minimization. This mode of thinking raises an ethical question for international tax executives. Deliberate tax evasion is commonplace in many parts of the world. In Italy, for example, tax legislation is often honored only in the breach. Even when tax laws are enforced, actual tax settlements are usually subject to negotiation between the taxpayer and the tax collector. Should multinational corporations operating in such environments adopt a policy of "When in Rome do as the Romans do?" or should they adhere to the taxation norms of their domestic environments?
5. Compare and contrast the role of transfer pricing in national versus international operations.
6. Multinational transfer pricing causes serious concern for various corporate stakeholders. Identify potential concerns from the viewpoint of
   a. minority owners of a foreign affiliate,
   b. foreign taxing authorities,
   c. home-country taxing authorities,
   d. foreign-subsidiary managers, and
   e. headquarters managers.
7. The pricing of intracompany transfers is complicated by many economic, environmental, and organizational considerations. Identify six major considerations described in the chapter and briefly explain how they affect transfer pricing policy.
8. Identify the major bases for pricing intercompany transfers. Comment briefly on their relative merits. Which measurement method is best from the viewpoint of the multinational executive?
9. Explain the arm's-length price. Is the U.S. Internal Revenue Service alone in mandating such pricing of intracompany transfers? Would the concept of an arm's-length price resolve the measurement issue in pricing intracompany transfers?
10. What is an advance pricing agreement (APA)? What are the advantages and disadvantages of entering into an APA?

Exercises

1. A Chinese manufacturing subsidiary produces items sold in Australia. The items cost the equivalent of $7.00 to produce and are sold to customers for $9.50. A Cayman Islands subsidiary buys the items from the Chinese subsidiary for $7.00 and sells them to the Australian parent for $9.50.

   Required: Calculate the total amount of income taxes paid on these transactions. What are the implications for the company and the taxing authorities involved?

2. Kowloon Trading Company, a wholly owned subsidiary incorporated in Hong Kong, imports macadamia nuts from its parent company in Honolulu for export to various duty-free shops in the Far East. During the current fiscal year, the company imported $2,000,000 worth of nuts and retailed them for $6,000,000. Local income taxes are paid at the rate of 16.5 percent. Profits earned by the Hong Kong subsidiary are retained for future expansion.

   Required: Based on this information, calculate the U.S. parent company's U.S. tax liability under Subpart F provisions of the Internal Revenue Code.

3. A jewelry manufacturer domiciled in Amsterdam purchases gold from a precious metals dealer in Belgium for €2,400. The manufacturer

fabricates the raw material into an item of jewelry and wholesales it to a Dutch retailer for €4,000.

Required: Compute the value-added tax from the jewelry manufacturer's activities if the Dutch value-added tax rate is 17.5 percent.

4. Sweden has a classical system of taxation. Calculate the total taxes that would be paid by a company headquartered in Stockholm that earns 1,500,000 Swedish krona (SEK) and distributes 50 percent of its earnings as a dividend to its shareholders. Assume that the company's shareholders are in the 40 percent tax bracket and that the company's income tax rate is 28 percent.

5. Alubar, a U.S. multinational, receives royalties from Country A, foreign-branch earnings from Country B, and dividends equal to 50 percent of net income from subsidiaries in Countries C and D. There is a 10 percent withholding tax on the royalty from Country A and a 10 percent withholding tax on the dividend from Country C. Income tax rates are 20 percent in Country B and 40 percent in Country C. Country D assesses indirect taxes of 40 percent instead of direct taxes on income. Selected data are as follows:

	Country A	Country B	Country C	Country D
Royalty from Country A operations	$20			
Pretax income		$90	$90	$54
Income taxes (20%/40%)		18	36	-0-
Net income		$72	$54	$54

Required: Calculate the foreign and U.S. taxes paid on each foreign-source income.

6. Global Enterprises has a manufacturing affiliate in Country A that incurs costs of $600,000 for goods that it sells to its sales affiliate in Country B. The sales affiliate resells these goods to final consumers for $1,700,000. Both affiliates incur operating expenses of $100,000 each. Countries A and B levy a corporate income tax of 35 percent on taxable income in their jurisdictions.

Required: If Global Enterprises raises the aggregate transfer price such that shipments from its manufacturing to its sales affiliate increase from $1,000,000 to $1,200,000, what effect would this have on consolidated taxes?

7. Using the facts stated in Exercise 6, what would be the tax effects of the transfer pricing action if corporate income tax rates were 30 percent in Country A and 40 percent in Country B?

8. Drawing on the background facts in Exercises 6 and 7, assume that the manufacturing cost per unit, based on operations at full capacity of 10,000 units, is $60, and that the uncontrolled selling price of the unit in Country A is $120. Costs to transport the goods to the distribution affiliate in Country B are $16 per unit, and a reasonable profit margin on such cross-border sales is 20 percent of cost.

Now suppose that Country B levies a corporate income tax of 40 percent on taxable income (vs. 30 percent in Country A) and a tariff of 20 percent on the declared value of the imported goods. The minimum declared value legally allowed in Country B is $100 per unit with no upper limit. Import duties are deductible for income tax purposes in Country B.

Required:
a. Based on the foregoing information, formulate a transfer pricing strategy that would minimize Global Enterprise's overall tax burden.
b. What issues does your pricing decision raise?

9. Lumet Corporation, a manufacturer of cellular telephones, wishes to invoice a sales affiliate located in Fontainebleau for an order of 10,000 units. Wanting to minimize its exchange risk, it invoices all intracompany transactions in euros. Relevant facts on a per unit basis are as follows: net sales price, €450; other operating expenses, €63; freight and insurance, €1; packaging costs, €1.50. Customs duties are 5 percent, and Lumet Corporation wishes to earn a profit of 6 percent on the transaction.

Required: Determine the price at which Lumet would invoice its French affiliate for the cellular phones.

10. The partial income statement of the Lund Manufacturing Company, a Swedish-based concern producing pharmaceutical products, is presented below:

During the year, short-term interest rates in Sweden averaged 7 percent, while net operating assets averaged SEK 45,000,000.

The company is entitled to a government subsidy of 5 percent. Its required margin to provide a profit and cover other expenses is 8 percent. All affiliates receive credit terms of 60 days.

Required: Based on this information, at what price would the Lund Manufacturing Company invoice its distribution affiliate in neighboring Finland?

Sales	SEK 75,000,000
Cost of goods manufactured and sold:	
Finished goods, beginning inventory	-0-
Cost of goods manufactured: (100,000 units)	
Direct materials used	SEK 22,500,000
Direct labor	11,600,000
Overhead	6,000,000
Cost of goods available for sale	40,100,000
Finished goods, ending inventory	8,000,000
Cost of goods sold	32,100,000
Gross Margin	SEK 42,900,000

CASES

Case 12-1

The Shirts Off Their Backs

Do accountants share the blame for Third World poverty? A report by the U.K.-based Christian Aid says so.[31] It attacks accounting firms for helping to perpetuate poverty in the developing world through their aggressive marketing of tax-avoidance schemes: "The tax avoidance industry [including accounting firms] has a very negative impact on developing countries and their ability to raise taxation—which is . . . critical for their escape from poverty."[32]

According to the report, the debate over how poor countries fund their escape from poverty has up to this point focused mainly on calls for debt cancellation and increases in aid.[33] While these factors are important, they are only pieces in a larger and more complicated puzzle. Solving this puzzle involves looking not only at the money that flows into poor countries, but also at money they can't get their hands on and the money that leaks away.

Taxation is facing a crisis in poorer countries. In the rich world, government revenue from taxation between 1990 and 2000 averaged 30 percent of gross domestic product (GDP). In sub-Saharan Africa, the average over the same period was 17.9 percent, in Latin America it was 15.1 percent, and in south Asia it was 10.5 percent. The low tax yield in poorer regions of the world limits the amount of domestically generated resources that are available to governments for essential public services, such as healthcare and education.

To quote the report:

It is not by accident that poor countries have been unable to increase the amount of revenue they raise through taxation. There are three specific tax strategies that have hindered them:

1. *Tax competition* between countries means poorer nations have been forced to lower corporate tax rates, often dramatically, in order to attract foreign investment.
2. *Trade liberalization* has deprived poorer countries of taxes on imports. In some cases, these had yielded up to one-third of their tax revenue.
3. *Tolerance of tax havens* has helped wealthy individuals and multinational companies (as well as criminals, corrupt leaders and terrorists) move their wealth and profits offshore to avoid paying taxes.[34]

---

[31] Christian Aid, *The Shirts Off Their Backs: How Tax Policies Fleece the Poor* (September 2005), www.christianaid.org.uk.

[32] Andrew Pendleton, Christian Aid's senior policy officer, as quoted in Alice Nation, "Christian Aid Attacks Accountants over Tax Avoidance Schemes," *Accountancy* (October 2005): 11.

[33] Aid from the rich world is volatile and sometimes comes with strings attached.

[34] Christian Aid, *The Shirts Off Their Backs: How Tax Policies Fleece the Poor* (September 2005): 4 (www.christianaid.org.uk).

Tax havens affect developing countries in a number of ways:

- Secret bank accounts and offshore trusts encourage wealthy individuals and companies to escape paying taxes by providing a place for untaxed earnings and profits to be banked.
- Many multinational corporations launder profits earned in developing countries by importing goods at hugely inflated prices and exporting commodities at a fraction of their true value.[35] They do this through paper subsidiaries in tax havens, providing them with a significant tax advantage over their nationally based competitors and fleecing governments of tax revenue.
- Banking secrecy and trust services provided by globalized financial institutions operating offshore provide a secure cover for laundering the proceeds of political corruption, fraud, embezzlement, illicit arms trading, and the global drugs trade.[36]

Who is to blame for this crisis? The study points the finger at international institutions like the International Monetary Fund and the World Bank, multinational corporations, banks, and accountants.

Accountancy firms . . . are champions of 'tax planning' whereby, along with their clients they organize networks of offshore subsidiaries to avoid paying tax. The collapse of Enron provided a rare insight into precisely how this works. The U.S. Senate report into the Enron case shows how accountants Andersen facilitated Enron's massive tax avoidance. The company paid no tax at all between 1995 and 1999.[37] Tax planning by accountants made this possible and involved setting up a global network of 3,500 companies, more than 440 of which were in the Cayman Islands. The subsequent Sarbanes-Oxley legislation in the United States is intended to act as a deterrent, by making directors and shareholders more responsible for the consequences of such strategies. But it does little to lift the veil of secrecy surrounding tax havens.[38]

Required

1. Why should wealthy nations be concerned about seeing that poor ones collect their "fair share" of taxes?
2. Do you agree that accountants and accounting firms share the blame for perpetuating poverty in the developing world? Why or why not?
3. Is tax planning wrong?
4. Assume that you agree that new policies are needed to improve the ability of Third World countries to increase their tax yields. List policy recommendations that will achieve this result, and explain why you think these policies are needed.

---

[35] The report cites data that 45 to 50 percent of intracompany transfers are mispriced in Latin America and 60 percent are mispriced in Africa.

[36] Christian Aid, *The Shirts Off Their Backs: How Tax Policies Fleece the Poor* (September 2005): 11–12 (www.christianaid.org.uk).

[37] According to a 2004 U.S. Government Accountability Office report, 60 percent of U.S. corporations with at least $450 million in assets reported no federal tax liability for any of the years between 1996 and 2000.

[38] Christian Aid, *The Shirts Off Their Backs: How Tax Policies Fleece the Poor* (September 2005): 17 (www.christianaid.org.uk).

Case 12-2

Muscle Max: Your Very Own Personal Trainer

Muscle Max–Asia, a wholly owned affiliate of a French parent company, functions as a regional headquarters for operating activities in the Pacific Rim. It enjoys great autonomy from its French parent in conducting its primary line of business, the manufacture and sale of Muscle Max, a commercial-grade weight-lifting machine that can be used in athletic clubs or in the home. Muscle Max–Asia has manufacturing affiliates in Malaysia and Canton (China) and distribution outlets in Australia, Japan, New Zealand, South Korea, and Singapore. It plans to expand its operations to other Pacific Rim countries in the next several years.

Given the demand for weight-lifting equipment in Australia, the company's distribution affiliate there, Muscle Max–Australia, has been importing its equipment from both Canton and Malaysia, paying a customs duty of 5 percent. Competing suppliers of similar equipment have approached the Australian affiliate for orders. Prices quoted on such machinery have ranged between 650 to 750 Australian dollars (A$). Muscle Max–Australia, which currently retails the machine for A$1,349, recently complained to Muscle Max–Asia because of the differences in the prices it is being charged by its sister affiliates in Canton and Malaysia. Specifically, while the Malaysian affiliate charges a per unit price of A$675, the Canton supplier's price is 26 percent higher. Muscle Max–Asia explains that the transfer price, based on a cost-plus formula (production costs total A$540 per unit), reflects several considerations, including higher margins to compensate for credit risk, operating risk, and taxes. As for taxes, Muscle Max–Asia explains that the People's Republic of China provides fiscal incentives to enterprises that promote exports. Although normal corporate income tax rates are 33 percent, Cantonese tax authorities have agreed to a rate of 10 percent on all export-related earnings.

The manager of Muscle Max–Australia remains skeptical and believes that he is paying for the Cantonese manager's inefficiency. In his latest communication, he asks if he can consider alternative suppliers of weight-lifting equipment to preserve local market share.

Required

1. What issues does this case raise?
2. What courses of action would you recommend to resolve the issues you have identified?

INDEX

Note: The letters 'A', 'E', and 'n' denotes Appendix entries, Exhibits, and notes cited in the text.